Mastering Public Speaking

Second Edition

GEORGE L. GRICE

Radford University

JOHN F. SKINNER

San Antonio College

ALLYN AND BACON

BOSTON • LONDON • TORONTO • SYDNEY • TOKYO • SINGAPORE

Vice President, Humanities: Joseph Opiela
Series Editor: Carla Daves
Developmental Editor: Carol Alper, Virginia Feury-Gagnon
Editorial Assistant: Mary Visco
Cover Administrator: Linda Knowles
Composition and Prepress Buyer: Linda Cox
Manufacturing Buyer: Louise Richardson
Marketing Manager: Lisa Kimball
Editorial-Production Service: Helane Manditch-Prottas
Text Designer: Helane Manditch-Prottas
Photo Researcher: Helane Manditch-Prottas
Senior Layout Artist: Dayle Silverman

 Copyright © 1995, 1993 by Allyn & Bacon
A Simon & Schuster Company
Needham Heights, Massachusetts   02194

Library of Congress Cataloging-in-Publication Data

Grice, George L.
    Mastering public speaking / George L. Grice, John F. Skinner. — 2nd ed.
      p. cm.
    Includes bibliographical references and index.
    ISBN 0-13-120270-7
    1. Public speaking. I. Skinner, John F.   II. Title.
PN4121.G719 1994
808.5'1 — dc20   94-22768
                                                        CIP

This book is printed on recycled, acid-free paper

Printed in the United States of America.
10 9 8 7 6 5 4 3 2 1   99 98 97 96 95 94

To
Wrenn, Evelyn, Carol, and Leanne

To
Suzanne, Drew, and Devin;
Gertrude and Beverley;
Rick, Randy, G.W., and JFS;
Katy and Taylor

Contents

Preface

The word began as the *spoken* word. Long before anyone devised a way to record messages in writing, people told one another stories and taught each other lessons. Societies flourished and fell, battles were waged and won on the basis of the spoken word. Ancient storytellers preserved their culture's literature and history in their memories and translated them orally to eager audiences. Crowds could wander away from the unprepared, unskilled speaker, but the most competent, skilled storytellers received widespread attention and praise.

After the development of script and print, people continued to associate marks on the page with the human voice. Even today, linked as we are by radio, television, and computer networks, a speaker standing at the front of a hushed room makes a special claim on our attention and our imagination. As you develop and deliver speeches in this class — and in future years as you deliver reports, sell products, present and accept awards, or campaign for your candidates — you are a part of an oral tradition as ancient as the race. This book is about the contract that always exists between a speaker and an audience, and about the choices you make in your roles as speaker and listener.

We developed this book with two principles in mind. First, public speaking, like ancient storytelling, requires a level of competence that is teachable, skills that can be handed down from patient teacher to interested student. Yet this is more than a skills course. Although a working knowledge of skills is fundamental to your mastery of public speaking, the master speaker is principled as well as skilled. We want to instruct you in *how* to make wise choices as you choose topics, and then research, organize, practice, and deliver your speeches. Just as important, however, we also want to spur you at each point in the speech-making process to think about *why* you make the choices you do.

The second principle guiding us has been most economically stated by British journalist and author Gilbert K. Chesterton: "There are no uninteresting subjects, there are only uninterested people." This book is for those who believe, as we do, that the lessons we have to teach one another can enrich the lives of every listener. The student of art history can learn from the business major, just as the business student learns from the art historian. This course will give you the chance to investigate subjects that appeal to you. We challenge you to develop speech topics creatively and to listen to one another's speeches expecting to learn.

Public speaking is an important part of communication, and communication is not only part of your education, but is also the way you gain and apply your learning. A liberating and life-long education occurs only through communication, with ourselves and those around us. We wish you each the kind of education Steven C. Beering, President of Purdue University, described so eloquently in a speech inaugurating his university's School of Education:

> Education is dreaming, and thinking and asking questions. It is reading, writing, speaking, and listening. Education is exploring the unknown, discovering new ideas, communicating with the world about us. Education is finding yourself, recognizing human needs, and communicating that recognition to others. Education is learning to solve problems. It is acquiring useful knowledge and skills in order to improve the quality of life. Education is an understanding of the meaning of the past, and an inkling of the potential of the future. Education represents self-discipline, assumption of responsibility and the maintenance of flexibility, and most of all, an open mind. Education is unfinishable. It is an attitude and a way of life. It makes every day a new beginning.[1]

ACKNOWLEDGMENTS

We are, first and foremost, grateful to the many university, college, and community college educators whose enthusiasm contributed to the success of the first edition of this textbook. The second edition of *Mastering Public Speaking*, like the first, is the product of more than just two co-authors. Though we have tried to speak with one voice for the sake of our readers, the truth is that many voices resonate throughout this text — voices of our teachers, our colleagues, our editors, and our students. What we know, what we value, and thus what we write is shaped in part by their influence and insights. Wherever possible we have tried to acknowledge their contributions. For all their influence on this manuscript, we are thankful.

Significantly, our collaboration began at the urging of a former student, Pam Lancaster, now a district sales manager at Prentice Hall. We continue to be grateful to Prentice Hall for allowing us to make the first edition of *Mastering Public Speaking* the book we wanted it to be. Steve Dalphin, executive editor, deserves special thanks for his faith in the project, his patience, and his suggestions. We are indebted to Virginia Feury-Gagnon, our developmental editor on both the first and second editions, for venturing to the rim of the volcano yet again to fine tune our manuscript. We are also grateful to many authors and publishers for their permission to quote material in this book.

[1] Steven C. Beering, "The Liberally Educated Professional," *Vital Speeches of the Day* 15 April 1990: 400.

We want to thank Carla Daves and the entire editorial and production staffs at Allyn and Bacon for smoothing the transition during the restructuring of the Simon & Schuster Educational Group. Diane Kraut, thanks for securing permissions, and thank you, Leslie Brunetta, for your careful copyediting. We want to express our thanks to Dayle Silverman for her fortitude and skill in formatting pages. And Helane M. Prottas, you were the goddess of graphic design.

Three reference librarians read our revised research chapter closely: Ralph Domas of the San Antonio College Learning Resource Center, and Linda Farynk and Larry Pollard of Radford University's McConnell Library. Thanks for your expert advice and for your encouragement. In addition, Diane Gomez, computer graphics specialist at the San Antonio College Learning Resource Center, and Cynthia Cone gave us state-of-the-art advice on the preparation of computer graphics, while warning us how quickly new software develops in that vital field.

We have benefited immensely from the encouragement and advice of some former colleagues and our fellow faculty members at Radford University and San Antonio College: Maresa Brassil, Mary Crow, Merrill Jones, J. Drew McGukin, Larry Pollard, Janet Stahl, and Richard Worringham. We are especially grateful to Gwen Brown, Mike Cronin, Barbara Strain, Suzanne Skinner, Carolyn Delecour, Charles Falcon, and David Mrizek, who gave us their insights, suggestions, and encouragement. Rick Olsen, Ray Penn, and Gwen Brown, thanks for putting yourselves not only "on the line" but also on videotape to demonstrate the value of excellent speech criticism. Rick Olsen and Mike Cronin helped us refine the "Your First Speech" section in Chapter 1.

In addition, *Mastering Public Speaking* has been shaped and refined by the close readings and thoughtful suggestions of a number of reviewers: Pamela Cooper, Northwestern University; Elizabeth Bell, University of South Florida; David B. McLennan, Texas Christian University; Kimberly Batty Herbert, Eastern New Mexico University; Beth M. Waggenspack, Virginia Polytechnic Institute and State University; Carl R. Burgchardt, Colorado State University; Edward H. Sewell, Virginia Polytechnic Institute and State University; Barbara L. Baker, Central Missouri State University; Dayle C. Hardy-Short, Idaho State University; Doris Werkman, Portland State University; and Frances Swinny, professor emerita, Trinity University.

Finally, we are indebted to all our public speaking students who have crafted their messages, walked to the front of their classrooms, and informed, persuaded, entertained, and challenged us. Without their ideas and experiences, writing and revising this book would have been impossible, just as without tomorrow's students it would have been unnecessary.

Speech is civilization itself. The word, even the most contradictory word, preserves contact — it is silence which isolates.
~Thomas Mann

An Introduction to Public Speaking

Chapter 1

"The most important thing I learned in school was how to communicate.... You can have brilliant ideas, but if you can't get them across, your brains won't get you anywhere."

LEE IACOCCA

"All the great speakers were bad speakers at first."

RALPH WALDO EMERSON

■■ WHY STUDY PUBLIC SPEAKING?

*T*oday, beyond the relative security of the college or university classroom, nearly 7,000 speakers will stand in front of American audiences and deliver speeches.[1] And during those same twenty-four hours, people will make more than 30 *million* business presentations.[2] These speakers will express and elaborate their ideas, champion their causes, and promote their products or services. Those who are successful will make sales, enlist support, and educate and entertain their listeners. Many will also enhance their reputations as effective speakers. To achieve these goals, each will be using the skills, principles, and arts that are the subject of this textbook.

Consider, too, that somewhere on a college campus right now is the student who will one day deliver an inaugural address after being sworn in as president; the student who will appear on national television to accept the Heisman Trophy, the Tony Award for Best Actress, or the Academy Award for Best Director; and the student who will present breakthrough medical research findings to a national conference of doctors and medical technicians, or whose words will usher passage of important legislation.

You may be taking this course as an elective because you want to improve your public speaking skills in the relative security of a classroom. Chances are, however, that you are in this class because it is a requirement for graduation. If that's the case, you may rightfully be asking, "Why should I take a course in public speaking?" The answer, suggested in the preceding real-life examples, has three parts: Studying and practicing public speaking benefits you personally, professionally, and publicly.

Personal Benefits of Studying Public Speaking

This course can benefit you personally in three ways.

1. Studying public speaking helps you to succeed in college.
2. Studying public speaking increases your knowledge.
3. Studying public speaking helps build your confidence.

First, mastering public speaking can help you acquire skills important to your success in college. According to a recent Carnegie Foundation report,

> To succeed in college, undergraduates should be able to write and speak with clarity, and to read and listen with comprehension. Language and thought are inextricably connected, and as undergraduates develop their linguistic skills, they hone the quality of their thinking and become intellectually and socially empowered.[3]

Look at some of the chapter titles in this textbook. They include words such as *listening, analyzing, researching, organizing, wording,* and *delivering.* These are skills you will use in constructing and delivering your speeches. They are also *transferable* skills; they can help you throughout your academic studies, as well as in your chosen career.

Second, public speaking can help you become more knowledgeable. There is a saying that we learn:

10 percent of what we read,
20 percent of what we hear,
30 percent of what we see, and
70 percent of what we speak.[4]

Consider for a moment two different ways of studying lecture notes for an exam. One method is to read and reread your notes silently. An alternative is more active and makes you a sender of messages. You stand in your room, put your lecture notes on your dresser, and deliver the lecture out loud, pretending you are the instructor explaining the material to the class. Which method do you think promotes better understanding and retention of the course material? You will not be surprised to learn that it's the second method.

Speaking is an active process. You discover ideas, shape them into a message, and deliver that message using your voice and body. The act of speaking is a crucial test of your thinking skills. As author E.M. Forster observed, "How do I know what I think until I've seen what I've said?" The process of developing and delivering an idea clarifies it and helps make it uniquely your own. In this course, you will learn a lot about the topics on which you choose to speak. By learning how to construct an effective public speech, you will also become a better listener to others' speeches, oral reports, and lectures, and this will further increase your learning.

A third personal benefit of this course is that it can help build your confidence and self-esteem. We devote Chapter 3 to discussing the most common fear of adult Americans: the fear of speaking to a group of people. In this course, you will learn how to turn this apprehension into confidence. You will do so by reading this textbook, by listening to your instructor, and, most important, by doing. The confidence and poise you gain as you begin to master public speaking will help you when you give that oral report on "Gender Roles in the Plays of Shakespeare" in your British literature class, when you address your school board urging them to expand the district's arts education program, or when you are asked to say a few words upon receiving the Outstanding Community Service award for your involvement in the neighborhood watch program. As the Emerson quotation suggests, great speaking requires practice, but your efforts will bring you these three rewards.

Professional Benefits of Studying Public Speaking

Studying communication, and specifically public speaking, is important to you not only personally but also professionally. In fact, numerous studies document a strong relationship between communication competence and career success. Effective speaking skills enhance your chances of first securing employment and then advancing in your career. John Hafer and C.C. Hoth surveyed thirty-seven companies, asking them to rate the characteristics they considered most important when hiring an employee. Out of twenty-six total characteristics, oral communication skills ranked first.[5]

More recently, three speech and business professors collected 428 responses from personnel managers in business organizations to determine the "factors most important in helping graduating college students obtain employment." Oral communication skills ranked first and listening second.[6] The researchers concluded:

> From the results of this study, it appears that the skills most valued in the contemporary job-entry market are communication skills. The skills of oral communication (both interpersonal and public), listening, written communication, and the trait of enthusiasm are seen as the most important. It would appear to follow that university officials wishing to be of the greatest help to their graduates in finding employment would make sure that basic competencies in oral and written communication are developed. Courses in listening, interpersonal, and public communication would form the basis of meeting the oral communication competencies.[7]

This course will instruct you in two of those vital skills: public speaking and listening.

Once you are hired, your speaking skills continue to work for you, becoming your ticket to career success and advancement. Researchers Roger Mosvick and Robert Nelson found that managers and technical professionals spend approximately twice as much time speaking and listening as they do reading and writing.[8] A survey of 500 executives found that speaking skills "rated second only to job knowledge as important factors in a businessperson's success." That same study also showed that effective communication helped improve company productivity and understanding among employees.[9]

Although you will likely spend only a small portion of your communication at work giving presentations and speeches, your ability to stand in front of a group of people and present your ideas is important to your career success. One survey of sixty-six companies found that 76 percent of executives gave oral reports.[10] Another survey found that while on-the-job public speaking accounted for only 6 percent of managers' and technical professionals' time, it nevertheless ranked as more important to job performance than did time spent reading mail and other documents, dictating letters and writing reports, and talking on the phone.[11] Oral communication and public speaking clearly play a critical role in your professional life.

Public Benefits of Studying Public Speaking

Finally, public speaking can help you play your role as a member of society. As Thomas Mann noted in the quotation preceding this chapter, it is communication that connects us with each other. Public speaking is an important part of creating a society of informed and active citizens.

A democratic society is shaped, in part, by the eloquence of its leaders:

Franklin Delano Roosevelt, who rallied a nation during the Great Depression by declaring, "The only thing we have to fear is fear itself";

John F. Kennedy, who urged citizen involvement, exhorting us to "Ask not what your country can do for you; ask what you can do for your country";

Martin Luther King, Jr., who challenged us to dream of a day when people will be judged not "by the color of their skin but by the content of their character";

Ronald Reagan, who spoke the words that helped us "mourn the loss of seven brave Americans" aboard the space shuttle Challenger.

But a democratic society is also shaped by the quiet eloquence of everyday citizens:

the police officer who informs residents of a crime-plagued area how to set up a neighborhood watch program;

the social worker who addresses the city council and secures funding for a safe house for abused and runaway children;

the elementary school teacher who speaks to civic clubs, generating their support for a meals-on-wheels program for elderly citizens confined to their homes;

the minister who consoles a grieving congregation after the fatal crash of a bus bringing their children home from summer camp.

In each of these instances, the speaker used the power of the spoken word to address a need and solicit an appropriate audience response.

While we recognize effective speaking when we meet the person who always says "just the right thing" or who says things in funny and colorful ways, few of us have been trained to speak well. To appreciate the power of communication you must understand just what it is. That requires a look at some definitions of communication and at some of its essential components.

▄▄▄ DEFINITIONS OF COMMUNICATION

The word *communicate* comes from the Latin verb *communicare,* meaning "to make common to many, share, impart, divide."[12] This concept of sharing is important in understanding communication and is implicit in our definition of the term. Simply stated, when you communicate you share, or make common, your knowledge and ideas with someone else.

You can understand communication best when you view it as both a *process* and a *product.* Some scholars believe that communication is basically a process. For example, Thomas Scheidel provides a process perspective when he defines communication as "the transmission and reception of symbolic cues."[13] Other scholars see communication as an outcome or a product and define it simply as shared meaning. We believe both of these perspectives offer insights into the concept of communication. **Communication,** then, *is the sharing of meaning by sending and receiving symbolic cues.*

You can understand how meaning is shared by studying Figure 1.1, Charles Ogden and I.A. Richards's triangle of meaning.[14] This figure illustrates the three elements necessary when someone communicates; those elements are interpreter, symbol, and referent. The word interpreter refers to both the sender and the receiver of a message. The **interpreter** is simply the person who is communicating, with words or other symbols.

The second element of this model, the **symbol,** is anything to which people attach or assign a meaning. Symbols can be pictures, drawings, or objects. We know, for example, that a sign in an airport showing a fork, a spoon, a glass, and an arrow means that we can find a restaurant or a snack bar in the direction the arrow points. The police officer's uniform and squad car are symbols of the authority of the police. The most famil-

communication: the process of sharing meaning by sending and receiving symbolic cues.

interpreter: any person using symbols to send or receive messages.
symbol: anything to which people attach meaning.

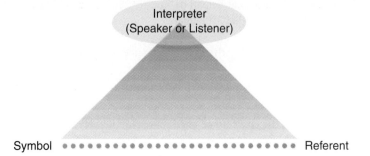

Figure1.1 *The triangle of meaning*

Symbol ● Referent

iar symbols, however, are words in a particular language. Many words refer to particular objects, places, and people: *chair, Long Beach, California,* and *Eudora Welty,* for example. Some words refer to concepts, such as *freedom of expression, existentialism,* and *fair play.*

referent: the object or idea each interpreter attaches to a symbol.

The third and final element of the triangle of meaning is the **referent,** the object or idea for which the symbol stands. Both the sender and the receiver of a message have a referent for the symbols used. This referent depends upon each individual's knowledge and experience. People cannot exchange referents in the way they can exchange objects. For example, someone can hand you a paper clip, and that paper clip is the same in your hand as it is in your friend's. Your friends, however, cannot transfer their ideas or information to you. All they can do is to code their ideas into symbols and hope that as you decode them, the ideas you receive will be similar to the ones they intended. In short, as senders we select a symbol based on our referent. That symbol, in turn, triggers the receiver's referent. To check your understanding of how interpreters, symbols, and referents interact, consider an incident one of us experienced.

> A father casually asked his son one evening, "How's your homework coming?" The boy, a seventh grader taking his first computer class, said, "I have to summarize some articles on computers. I've got three, and I need four." The father, planning to go to a book store later that night, said, "OK, I'll buy you a new computer magazine." However, the next morning when his father showed him the magazine with the article on computers, the boy asked, "Where are the others? I told you I need four."

The interpreters in this case, the boy and his father, obviously had a communication problem centering around the symbols, "I've got three, and I need four." The son's referent, the idea he had in mind, was, "I've got three articles, and I need four more." The father's referent, however, was, "He's got three of the four articles he needs."

As this example demonstrates, communication is successful only when the interpreters involved attach similar referents to the message being communicated. The *New Yorker* cartoon illustrates the consequences of speaker and listener having different referents. You can, no doubt, think of similar experiences you have had when people misinterpreted what you said because they attached a different referent to your words. The most important thing to remember about the triangle of meaning and the process of communication is this: *Words and other symbols have no inherent meaning. People have meaning; words do not.* The word takes on the meaning that the interpreter attaches to it.

What does the triangle of meaning have to do with public speaking? As you will discover throughout this book, this model applies to public speaking just as it does to all

Drawing by Shanahan: © 1989 The *New Yorker Magazine,* Inc.

other forms of communication. If speakers and listeners always used specific symbols, interpreted them objectively, and attached similar referents to them, we would experience few if any communication problems arising from the content of the message. As a result, your work in a public speaking class could be limited to improving your organization and polishing your style of delivery. Yet many of our communication problems can be traced directly to difficulties in the relationships between interpreters, the symbols they use, and the referents behind those symbols.

As a public speaker, you must try to ensure that the message your audience hears matches as closely as possible the message you intended. You do that by paying particular attention to your content, organization, and delivery, major subjects of this book. To understand the complexity of public speaking, you need to realize how it relates to other levels of communication.

LEVELS OF COMMUNICATION

Communication can occur on five different levels:

1. intrapersonal
2. interpersonal
3. group
4. public
5. mass communication

Each of these levels is distinguished by the number of people involved, the formality of the situation, and the opportunities for feedback. One of these levels, public communication, is the subject of this book and the focus of the course you are now taking. Yet public speaking incorporates elements of the other four levels of communication, and a brief look at each of them will help you better understand public speaking.

Intrapersonal Communication

intrapersonal communication: cognition or thought; communicating with oneself.

Simply stated, **intrapersonal communication** is communication with yourself. The prefix *intra-* means "within." Intrapersonal communication serves many functions, and we all practice it every waking moment. If you woke up late this morning, for example, and panicked because you overslept for a class, you were communicating intrapersonally. If you sit in class worrying about a problem, or reminding yourself to do something later in the day, or daydreaming about someone or something, you are communicating intrapersonally. If in the middle of a public speech you tell yourself, "This is really going well," or "I can't believe I just said that," you are also communicating intrapersonally.

As these examples demonstrate, much intrapersonal communication is geared toward a specific, conscious purpose: evaluating how we are doing in a particular situation, solving a problem, relieving stress, or planning for the near or distant future. Though we all have probably uttered something aloud to ourselves at times of stress, joy, puzzlement, or discouragement, intrapersonal communication is typically silent. We sit quietly as we reflect on a speaker explaining the difference between whole life and term life insurance. We are attentive as we hear another speaker explain the necessary preparations for a first sky dive. These examples show the connection between public speaking and intrapersonal communication. Both as public speakers and as audience members for others' speeches, we communicate intrapersonally a great deal. Key features of intrapersonal communication to keep in mind are that it is a continuous process of self-feedback and that it involves only one person.

Interpersonal Communication

interpersonal communication: communication between individuals in pairs; also called dyadic communication.

As soon as our communication involves ourselves and one other person, it moves to a second level, that of interpersonal communication. Interpersonal communication occurs between people, usually two of them. **Interpersonal communication** is sometimes called dyadic communication; *dyad* is Latin for "pair." Conversations between friends, colleagues, or acquaintances are a common form of interpersonal communication. Yet even strangers communicate interpersonally: A police officer questioning a witness to a crime, a company interviewer meeting a job applicant, and a new student talking to a teacher are all communicating interpersonally.

Whenever two communicators are face to face or speaking over the telephone, the opportunity for verbal interaction always exists. Consider, for example, your last conversation with your best friend, and how easily and naturally you interacted. In fact, if someone had secretly tape-recorded that conversation and typed a transcript of it for you to read, you would probably be surprised by the number of incomplete sentences you and your friend spoke. Ideas that do not appear to make much sense in writing were likely quite clear in conversation. Your best friend is someone who is really on your wave-

*The extensive practice you have
had observing and evaluating the
feedback of others in face-to-face
communication is excellent
preparation for interacting with
your public speaking audience.*
(SOURCE: © Ron Sherman/
Stock, Boston)

length, often knows how you are going to finish a sentence, and either finishes it for you
or nods agreement and switches to another idea.

In some interpersonal situations, of course, the verbal interaction is less frequent
and more self-conscious. We do not interrupt the interviewer sizing us up for a job or
the police officer who has just pulled us over for a traffic violation as easily as we do a
close friend. Yet the opportunity for verbal interaction exists in even those relatively stressful situations, and is always a characteristic of spoken interpersonal communication.

Group Communication

As we add to the number of people involved, the next level is **group communication.**
Although we discuss group interaction more thoroughly in Chapter 18, we will present
some important points about it here. Group communication generally takes place with
three or more people interacting and influencing each other in pursuit of a common goal.
Although researchers place varying limits on the size of a group, everyone recognizes
that a sense of cohesion or group identity is essential to any definition of this level of
communication.

Seven students who get together and spend half the night reviewing material and
quizzing one another for an upcoming exam are obviously engaged in group communication. A restaurant's owners and managers meeting to revise the menu are similarly
involved in a process of group communication. When you present your speeches in class,
you will not be engaged in group communication. However, if your presentation on a
particularly interesting topic generates questions and discussion, your public speaking
class might qualify as an example of group communication.

The important thing to remember about group communication is that the people
involved must have a sense of group identity. A group of fourteen people, for example,
is not just seven dyads or pairs of people. They must believe and accept that they belong

**group communi-
cation:**   three or more
people interacting and
influencing one another
for a reason and with a
sense that they belong
together.

together for some reason, whether they face a common problem, share similar interests, or simply work in the same division of a company.

Group communication may be informal, with all group members free to discuss issues as they wish, or formal, operating under the rules of parliamentary procedure. As long as members are relatively free to contribute to the discussion, what occurs is clearly group communication. However, once someone stands up and begins to present a report or make a speech, the communication shifts to the fourth level, public communication.

Public Communication

public communication: one person communicating face to face with an audience.

Public communication, the subject of this course, occurs when one person speaks face to face with an audience. That audience may be as small as your public speaking class or as large as the masses of people who fill stadiums and other public areas to hear certain speakers. As the size of the audience grows, the flow of communication becomes increasingly one-directional, from speaker to audience. When the audience is large, individual members have less opportunity for verbal interaction with the speaker.

For example, your public speaking class is probably small enough that you feel free to have your instructor answer any questions you have during class. In a lecture class of several hundred students, however, you might feel more pressure to keep silent, even if you had a legitimate question. If you were part of an audience of several thousand people, not only would you feel pressure to keep quiet during a speech, but even if you did voice a question the speaker probably could not hear it.

The key characteristics of public communication, therefore, are a more one-directional flow of information and a more formal feeling than the other types of communication we have discussed so far. Whether the audience is as small as a class of twenty, or as large as a convention assembly of 2,000, or a congregation of 200,000 standing outside the Vatican to hear an Easter message from the Pope, public communication always involves one person communicating to an audience that is physically present.

Mass Communication

mass communication: one person or group communicating to a large audience through some print or electronic medium.

But what happens if we sit in front of our television sets and see videotape clips from that Easter service at the Vatican or a telecast of an Academy Awards ceremony? In such a situation we have entered the fifth and final level of communication, **mass communication.** Once the audience becomes so large that it cannot be gathered in one place, some type of print or electronic medium — newspaper, magazine, radio, or television, among others — must be placed between speaker or writer and the intended audience. The physical isolation of speaker and audience severely limits the possibilities for spontaneous interaction between them. In fact, an important characteristic of mass communication is that audience feedback is *always* delayed. Assume, for example, that a magazine or newspaper article inspires or angers you enough that you write a letter to the editor. Your response will be slowed by the necessities of composing the letter and mailing it. Then, before your response can be shared with the magazine or newspaper readership, someone must review it, decide to publish it, have it typeset and printed, and distribute it to readers. You have the opportunity to send feedback, but it is delayed.

*Millions of people watched Vice-
President Al Gore and Ross Perot
debate the North American Free
Trade Agreement on the popular*
Larry King Live.
(SOURCE: © AP/Wide World
Photos)

A second characteristic we should consider about mass communication is that the
method of message transmission can become very important. Advertising agencies,
political consultants, and the people who use them know very well that the *way* a message is sent can be as important as the *content* of that message, something public speakers should also remember. Advertisements for products, services, and political candidates
reach different sizes and types of audiences via radio, television, billboards, magazines,
or newspapers. We devote a portion of Chapter 17 to the special challenges of speaking before a video camera because future technology will surely expand the importance
of mass media in getting messages across to the public.

You will master public speaking skills more quickly and easily if you remain aware
of the connections between public communication and the four other levels of communication. In this class, you may use interpersonal and group communication to determine your speech topics and how you approach them. You may interview an expert on
a topic you are considering for a speech. Through informal conversations with your classmates, you will form a clearer picture of your audience by discovering their interests,
attitudes, and values. You may offer others feedback on their speeches and receive their
comments regarding your speech. If you have the opportunity to videotape one or more
of your speeches, you will gain experience with one of the important electronic media
of mass communication, even if your speech is not broadcast publicly. Certainly, you will
consult print or electronic media resources as you research your speech. And, all the time
you are delivering your public speeches, you will be giving yourself intrapersonal feedback about the job you are doing and the positive responses we hope you are receiving.

COMPONENTS OF COMMUNICATION

Now that you have an understanding of the different levels of communication, we will
look at the various components common to any type of communication and, specifical-

ly, to public speaking. Remember, the better you understand how communication works in general, the better you will be able to make communication work for you in specific speaking situations. A brief look at the elements in two communication models will allow us to develop a more accurate view of this complex phenomenon. Just as important, these models will let us see where some common communication problems arise.

Linear Model of Communication

encoding: the process of selecting symbols to carry a message.

The earliest models devised by scholars show three basic elements of communication: a speaker sending a message to a listener (see Figure 1.2). The *speaker* may also be called the sender, the source, or the encoder. **Encoding** is the process of putting ideas into symbols, and we encode so much and so well that we are aware of the process only when we find ourselves "at a loss for words" while either speaking or writing. The ideas of the *message* originate with the speaker, who determines the form that the message will take. Unless the communication is intrapersonal, the message is sent to a *listener* or receiver. This person then begins **decoding** the message, attaching meanings to the words, gestures, and voice inflections that are received.

decoding: the process of attaching meanings to symbols received.

Those three elements are important to communication. So what was wrong with the early, linear models of communication? First, they assumed that a person is either a sender or a receiver of messages. The truth is that we perform both of these roles simultaneously. The early one-directional model of communication shown in Figure 1.2 does not account for this.

The second weakness of this simple model is its suggestion that communication involves only one message. Yet remember our earlier discussion of the triangle of meaning. The truth is that there are as many messages as there are communicators involved. The message the speaker intends is never identical to the one received. As long as they are similar, communication will usually be effective.

Interactive Model of Communication

Once communication scholars began to see the limitations of this early linear, three-element model, they began to add other components. Today, the most widely accepted model of communication has seven elements. To the three elements already mentioned — speaker, message, and listener — we add channel, feedback, environment, and noise. Figure 1.3 illustrates this more complete model of communication.

channel or **medium:** the way a message is sent.

Channel. The first element we need to add is the **channel** or **medium,** which refers to the way the message is sent. In public speaking, the medium is vibrations in the air between speaker and listener, set in motion by the speaker's voice. The message could also be written in any language, put into some code known to both speaker and listen-

Fig. 1.2 *Linear model of communication. Simple, early models of communication depicted a speaker sending a message to a listener.*

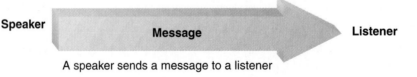

A speaker sends a message to a listener

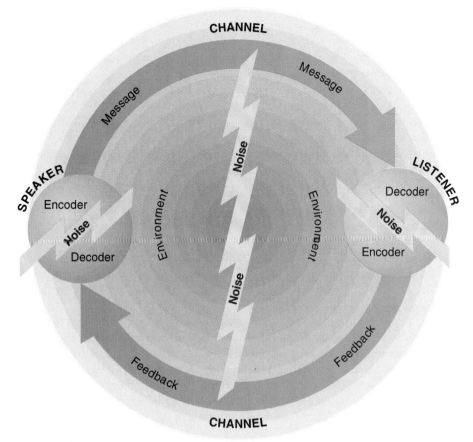

Fig. 1.3 *Interactive model of communication. A speaker encodes a message, sending it through a channel to a listener, who decodes it. The listener provides feedback, sending it through a channel to a speaker. This interaction takes place in an environment with varying levels of internal and external noise.*

er, tape-recorded or videotaped, put into sign language, translated into Braille, or even sent by smoke signal, among other methods. As you realize, voice and words are not our only media for communication. In fact, communication scholar Albert Mehrabian has estimated that when cues conflict, nonverbal cues are more important than verbal cues in communicating our feelings or attitudes to others. He summarized his research in the following equation:

Total feeling = 7% verbal feeling + 38% vocal feeling + 55% facial feeling[15]

Mehrabian's formula means that any time you communicate with someone, the majority of the feeling behind your message is carried by visual elements such as facial expression, eye contact, gestures, and movement. More than one-third of your message is carried paralinguistically, that is, by vocal elements such as rate, volume, voice quality, and changes in pitch level. Your actual words carry less than 10 percent of the message about how you feel. As a public speaker, you must learn to manipulate and control all three of these channels: visual, vocal, and verbal. As you can see, public speaking, like every other level of communication, is more complicated than just saying the right words.

Feedback.   A second element added to that preliminary model of communication is **feedback.** Feedback includes all messages, verbal and nonverbal, sent by listeners to

feedback: verbal and nonverbal responses between communicators about the clarity or acceptability of messages.

speakers. If you tell a joke, your listeners will tell you through vocal (laughter), verbal, and visual feedback whether they understood the joke and how they evaluated it. If you are paying attention, you will know who liked it, who didn't, who hasn't understood it, and who was offended by it. "If you are paying attention" is the particularly important clause, for, in order to be effective, feedback must be received.

Because public speaking is an audience-centered activity, you as speaker must be sensitive to feedback from your audience. Some feedback is deliberate and conscious; some is unintentional and unconscious. But your audience will always provide you with feedback of some kind. If you are paying attention to it, you will know when they appreciate your humor, understand the point you are making, disagree with the position you advocate, or are momentarily confused by something you have said.

environment: the physical setting and the occasion for communication.

Environment.   The third element we need to add to make a more accurate model of communication is the **environment.** Two factors shape a communication environment: (1) the occasion during which communication occurs, and (2) the physical setting or site where communication occurs. The occasion refers to the reasons why people have assembled. Circumstances may be serious or festive, planned or spontaneous. Occasions for communication may be as relaxed and informal as a party with friends, as rule-bound as a college debate, or as formal and traditional as a commencement address at a graduation ceremony.

The physical setting for your classroom speeches is probably apparent to you. You know the size of the room and the number of people in the audience. You know whether the seating arrangement is fixed or changeable. You know whether a lectern, a chalkboard, or a projection screen are available. You know, or will soon discover, potential problems with the room: The table at the front of the room is wobbly; the air seems stuffy about halfway through each class meeting; one of the fluorescent lights flickers. Each of these distracting elements is a form of noise, a fourth element for which any accurate model of communication must account.

noise: anything that distracts from effective communication.
physical noise: distractions originating in the communication environment.

Noise.   **Noise** is anything that interferes with communication, and some form of noise is always present. We will discuss three different forms. First, much noise is **physical;** that is, it occurs in the physical environment in which people are communicating. When we think of noise, we usually think of physical noise: the sounds of traffic, the loud whoosh of an air conditioner or a heater, the voices of people talking and laughing as they pass by your classroom. Some physical noise may not involve a sound at all, however. If your classroom is so cold that you shiver or so hot that you fan yourself, then its temperature is a form of noise. If the lighting in the room is poor, then that form of noise will certainly affect the communication occurring there. If your classroom is near a construction site and the heavy, acrid smell of creosote is nauseating you, then that odor is a form of noise. Anything in the immediate environment that interferes with communication is physical noise.

physiological noise: distractions originating in the bodies of communicators.
psychological noise: distractions originating in the thoughts of communicators.

A second type of noise is **physiological:** A bad cold that affects your hearing and speech, a headache, or an empty, growling stomach are examples. Each of these bodily conditions can shift your focus from communicating with others to thinking about how uncomfortable you feel, a form of intrapersonal communication.

A third and final type of noise is **psychological.** This type of noise refers to mental rather than bodily distractions. Anxiety, worry, daydreaming, and even joy over some recent event can distract you from the message at hand. Each of these forms of noise — physical, physiological, and psychological — can occur independently or in combination, and as we have said, some form of noise is always present. Music lovers continually search for better audio equipment — a compact disc player, for example — to reduce the noise involved in playing recorded music. As a speaker, you must make similar efforts to minimize the effects of noise in public communication: by varying your rate, volume, and pitch, for example, or through lively physical delivery that combats noise and rivets the audience's attention to your message.

▰▰ YOUR FIRST SPEECH

Each time that you speak in public, you are, in effect, entering a contract with your listeners. Terms of this contract require that your listeners listen expecting to learn, that they listen without prejudging you or your ideas, but that they ultimately evaluate the messages you present to them. As a speaker, you assume responsibility for being well prepared, for having something interesting or useful to say, and for speaking in the best interests of your listeners. Those requirements can seem like a very tall order, especially if you are an inexperienced speaker preparing to give your first speech.

In addition, this class will undoubtedly require you to give your first speech before you have read much of this textbook. What is absolutely necessary to know, then, in order to be able to deliver that first speech successfully?

"Success" in your first speech will likely be measured differently than in your speeches later in the semester or quarter. If you are a first-time public speaker, success may mean being able to get up in front of the class, speak for at least the minimum time limit, and have a decently organized speech on an appropriate topic. If you have had previous experience speaking in public, you should set your sights higher. For you, success may include having a well-organized and interesting message, smooth delivery, and a confident attitude. No matter what your level of experience, you will benefit from recognizing two concerns that you share with everyone else in your class.

First, most of your classmates are probably as apprehensive as you are about the first speech. Almost everyone worries about questions such as, "Will I be able to get through my speech? Will I remember what I wanted to say? Will I be able to make my listeners understand what I want to say? Will I sound OK and look as though I know what I'm doing?" Your nervousness is natural, typical, and healthy. In fact, your nervousness is a good sign that you have reasonably high expectations of yourself and that you care about doing well.

Do not approach the first speech expecting perfection of yourself or of others. You already may be apprehensive about the prospect of standing at the front of the room and speaking for the first time. Why compound your nervousness by holding unrealistic expectations about your performance? Keep a positive, realistic attitude about how you will do.

Second, you should know that public speaking is a teachable skill, much like math, reading, and writing. So, yes, you can *learn* to speak well. We share responsibility for part of that learning with your instructor. You are also responsible for much of your learning through your own effort and initiative. If you skipped the preface to this book, we urge you to take the few minutes necessary to turn back and read it. Written primarily for you, not just for your instructor, the preface condenses our philosophy about this course and about education in general.

Preparing your first speech will be easier if you also keep in mind two principles of public speaking. First, the more effectively that you prepare, the better the speech you will deliver and the more confident you will feel. Only then can you recognize what you already do competently and begin to identify skills you want to improve. In addition, your confidence will grow with each speaking experience throughout this course and later in your life.

The second principle is that every public speech is a blend of *content, organization,* and *delivery.* Each of these aspects affects the others. For example, choosing a topic you already know well or have researched thoroughly should easily translate into animated, confident delivery. Elements of speech delivery such as pause and movement can emphasize your speech's organization. Moreover, as you will soon learn, we believe that any speech on any topic should be well organized. The more you know about the principles of speech content, organization, and delivery, then, the better your first speech will be. The following seven guidelines will help you toward that goal.

Understand the Assignment

For your first speech assignment, your instructor may prescribe a specific purpose or leave that choice to you. Often your first speech assignment is to introduce yourself or a classmate, and, so, is informative rather than persuasive. The speech may be graded or ungraded; if graded, it may count less than or as much as speeches you will deliver later. Whether your instructor is trying an innovative assignment or using one that has been tested and proven, he or she is your first and final authority for the specific details of the assignment.

A primary, vital requirement for preparing any speech is to know exactly what you are to do. You must clearly understand the assignment your instructor has given you. The following questions can help you identify your goals for the speech.

- What am I supposed to do in this speech: inform, persuade, or entertain?
- What are my minimum and maximum time limits for the speech?
- Are there special requirements for the delivery of the speech? If so, what are they?

Develop Your Speech Content

As you select a speech topic, you need to decide the number of main ideas you will cover. To determine what those ideas will be, think about what you would want to hear if you were in the audience. If your instructor assigns you a topic, the specific things you say and the order in which you say them will be uniquely your own. If you are asked to choose your topic, you have even greater creative latitude, of course. In either of these cases, you need to keep your audience in mind. The topic you select or the way you approach an assigned topic should be guided by what you think your listeners will find most interesting or useful.

If your assignment is to introduce yourself, begin by jotting down as many aspects of your life as you can. Audit your history, assess your current circumstances, and project your future goals. Among others, topics that apply to your life and the lives of all your listeners include:

accomplishments	people who have been significant influences
career plans	unusual life events
educational backgrounds	personal values
skills or aptitudes	prized possessions
hobbies	pet peeves
special interests	aspirations

In addition, you may have a particularly interesting work history or may have traveled to unusual places. You could decide to limit your speech to one of the preceding areas or to combine several that you think your listeners will find most interesting.

If the ideas you disclose are truly unusual, your speech will be memorable. But don't be intimidated or worried if your experiences seem fairly tame and ordinary. Some of your listeners will be relieved to find that they have backgrounds similar to yours. Whether ordinary or extraordinary, your background and your classmates' will provide the basis for conversation before class, for classroom discussion, and for audience analysis as you prepare for future speeches.

If you are asked to select the subject for your first speech, brainstorm for topics that are of interest to you and those that you think would benefit or be of interest to your audience. Your speaking occasion, the time of year that you speak, and upcoming or recent holidays can also suggest topic ideas. In addition, consider subjects that you discover as you conduct research. Don't settle for the first topic that comes to mind, however. If you generate a number of possible topics and spend some time reflecting on them, the subject you finally choose will probably be more satisfying for you and more interesting to your listeners. To make sure that you have a clear grasp of your speech topic, answer questions such as these:

- What is my speech topic, and why have I chosen it?
- Who are the people in my audience?
- What do I want my listeners to know or remember when I'm finished speaking?

The best way to answer that last question is to ask, "What aspects of my topic interest me and are likely to interest my audience?" Select only a few points to discuss. A time limit of two to four minutes, for example, may seem endless to you right now. It's not; it goes by very quickly. As you develop your speech content, check to be sure that everything you say is relevant to your purpose and to those few main points you want your listeners to remember. Limiting your number of main ideas should give you enough time to develop them with adequate supporting materials — definitions, stories, statistics, comparisons, and contrasts — that are interesting and relevant to your listeners. Once you have done this preliminary work, you are ready to assess your speech content by asking questions such as:

- Have I selected a few key points that I can develop in the time allowed?
- Do I use a variety of specific supporting materials, such as examples and stories, to develop my key points?
- Will my supporting materials be clear and interesting to my classroom audience?

- Do I acknowledge sources for anything I quote or paraphrase from other speakers or writers?
- Is everything that I say relevant to my topic?

Once you begin to generate the main ideas of your topic and then to limit yourself to the ones you think the audience will find most interesting, you have begun to organize your content.

Organize Your Speech

Organizing a speech is similar to writing an essay. Every essay must have an introductory paragraph, a body, and a concluding paragraph. A speech has the same three divisions: an introduction, a body, and a conclusion. To determine whether your ideas are clearly organized and easy to follow, you must consider the organization of each of those three parts of your speech.

Organize Your Speech Introduction.   Though usually brief, your speech introduction serves four vital functions. First, it focuses the audience's attention on you and your message. You want to command the audience's attention with your first words. How can you do this? Question your audience, amuse them, arouse their curiosity about your subject, or stimulate their imaginations.

Second, your introduction should clarify your topic or your purpose in speaking. If your listeners are confused about your exact topic, you limit their ability to listen actively. To minimize any chances of this, state your purpose clearly in a well-worded sentence.

A third function of your introduction is to establish the significance of your topic, explain your interest in it, or reveal any special qualifications you have for speaking on your topic. Finally, your introduction should highlight or preview the aspects of your subject that you will discuss in the body. Well-planned and well-delivered opening remarks will make the audience want to listen and will prepare them for what comes next. To check the integrity of your speech introduction, answer the following questions:

- Does my speech have an introduction?
  What is my attention-getter?
  What is my statement of purpose?
  What rationale do I provide for speaking about this topic?
  What are the points I will cover in my speech?

Organize the Body of Your Speech.   The body of your speech is its longest, most substantial section. Though it follows your introduction, you should prepare the body of your speech first. Here you introduce your key ideas and support, or explain, each one of them. You should develop only a few main ideas, probably between two and five, in any speech that you give. Why? You can more easily develop two to five ideas within your time limit. Your audience will also more easily grasp and remember a few well-developed ideas. Restricting your main points to a few is particularly important in a first speech, since it may be the shortest presentation you make during the semester or quarter.

Your organizational goal in the body of your speech should be to structure your main points so clearly that they are not just distinct but unmistakable to your listeners. To help you do so, we recommend a four-step sequence — the **"4 *S*'s"** — for organizing each of your main ideas. First, *signpost* each main idea. Typical signposts are numbers ("first" or "one") and words such as *initially* or *finally*. Second, *state* the idea clearly. Third, the step that will take you the most time, *support*, or explain, the idea. Finally, *summarize* the idea before moving to your next one. Those four steps will help you highlight and develop each of your main ideas in a logical, orderly way. The following questions and outline form should help you determine whether the body of your speech is well organized.

- Do I have the body of my speech organized clearly?
  I. What is my first main idea?
     A. What will I say about it?
     B. How will I summarize it?
  II. What is my second main idea?
     A. What will I say about it?
     B. How will I summarize it?
  III. What is my third main idea?
     A. What will I say about it?
     B. How will I summarize it? and so forth.

Organize Your Speech Conclusion. Your speech conclusion is a brief final step with two main functions. The first step, the summary, is a final review of the main points you have covered. Summarizing may be as simple as listing the key ideas you discussed in the body of the speech. Your summary may require more elaboration than a simple listing, but you should not introduce and develop any new ideas in the conclusion. When you summarize, you bring your speech to a logical close.

The last step of your conclusion should provide your speech with a strong sense of closure. To do this, end on a positive, forceful note. You can use many of the same techniques here that you used to get the audience's attention at the very beginning of the speech: question the audience, amuse them, stimulate their imaginations, and so forth. Your final remarks should be carefully thought out and extremely well worded. Ask and answer these three questions to test your speech conclusion:

- Does my speech have a conclusion?
  How have I summarized my main ideas?
  What will my closing statement be?

If you answer each of the questions we've posed so far, you should have an interesting, well-developed speech that is easy to follow. Both your content and your organization are in good shape. Up to this point, you have spent most of your time thinking about the speech and jotting down ideas. Now you have to word those ideas and practice getting them across to your audience through your vocal and physical delivery.

Word Your Speech

Unless your instructor requests that you do so, avoid writing out your first speech word for word. Even though having the text of your speech in front of you may make you feel more secure, our experience has been that students who deliver speeches from manuscripts early in the semester or quarter often suffer two consequences. One is that what they say tends to sound like writing rather than speech. Our speaking differs from our writing in several significant ways. We speak in shorter sentences marked by a simpler vocabulary than those we write. We also use more first- and second-person plural pronouns ("we" and "you") when we speak. Finally, we use more repetition and more colloquial language than we usually employ in writing.

A second problem you may encounter if you deliver your speech from manuscript is a lack of eye contact. Effective speakers make eye contact with their listeners. If you are reading, you can't do this. Therefore, if you have a choice, speak from just a few notes, rather than from a prepared manuscript. If you are required to compose and submit a manuscript of your speech, make sure that it sounds like something you would say, not just write.

The language of your speech should be correct, clear, and vivid. To illustrate this, assume that you have been assigned a practice speech of self-introduction early in the course. Assume, too, that you have decided to make your travels one of your main points. "I've traveled quite a bit" is a vague, general statement. Without supporting materials, the statement is also superficial. But suppose you said, instead:

> I've traveled quite a bit. I had lived in five states before I was in middle school, for example. When I was seven, my father worked in the booming oil business and my family even got a chance to live in South America for more than a year. My brother and I went to an American school in the tiny village of Anaco, Venezuela; we were students 99 and 100 in a school that taught grades one through eight. Instruction in Spanish started in the first grade, and by the time we returned to the States, I was bilingual. I have vivid memories of picking mangoes and papayas off the trees, swimming outdoors on Christmas day, and having my youngest brother born in Venezuela.

The second statement is a great deal clearer and more vivid than the first. It begins with the general comment, but then amplifies it with a more detailed story. The language is personal, conversational, and crisp. Notice how vivid language enhances the content of your speech. The following questions should help you test the language of your own speech:

- Does my speech sound conversational?
- Is the language of my speech correct?
- Will the language of my speech be clear to my listeners?
- Will the language of my speech be vivid for my listeners?

Practice Your Speech

Mental rehearsal is no substitute for oral and physical practice. Merely thinking about what you plan to say will never adequately ready you to deliver a prepared speech in class. As we said toward the beginning of this chapter, speechmaking is an active process. You gain a heightened knowledge of what you plan to say, as well as increased confidence in your abilities, just by practicing your speech out loud. Before you can do that, however, you must create the notes you will use to practice and deliver the speech.

Prepare Your Notes. Make certain that your speaking notes are in the form of key words or phrases, rather than complete sentences. Remember, you want your listeners to remember your main *ideas,* not necessarily your exact wording. Your goal in preparing your notes should be the same: You should need only a word or phrase to remind you of the order of your ideas. As you elaborate those points, your specific wording can change slightly each time you practice your speech. Make sure that your notes are easy to read. If your speaking notes are on notecards, be certain to number the cards and have them in the correct order before each practice session.

Practice Productively. Most of your practice will probably be done in seclusion. Practice any way that will help you, being sure to stand as you rehearse. Visualize your audience and gesture to them as you hope to when giving the speech. You may even want to record and listen to your speech on audiotape or videotape, if you have access to that equipment. Give yourself the opportunity to stop for intensive practice of rough spots in your speech. Just make sure that you also practice the speech from beginning to end without stopping.

As valuable as solitary practice is, you should also try your speech out on at least a few listeners, if at all possible. Enlist roommates and friends to listen to your speech and help you time it. The presence of listeners should make it easier to practice the way that you approach your speaking position before you speak and the way you will leave it after finishing. Your rehearsal audience can tell you if there are parts of your speech that are so complex that they are hard to grasp. They may also be able to suggest clearer, more colorful, or more powerful ways of wording certain statements you make. A practice audience can point out strengths of your delivery, as well as help you eliminate distractions that draw their attention away from your message. Most importantly, serious practice in front of others should focus your attention on the important interaction involved in delivering a speech to an audience. The following questions make up a checklist for your speech practice:

- Have I practiced my speech as I intend to deliver it in class?
- Have I made my speaking notes concise and easy to use and read?
- Have I recorded my speech and made changes after listening to or viewing it?
- How many times have others listened to my speech, and what suggestions have they offered for improving it?
- Have I timed my speech? Is the average time within my overall time limit?
- What adjustments can I make in my speech if it is too long or too short?

Deliver Your Speech

The biggest differences between speaking and writing become apparent as you say your speech aloud. Your "delivery system" for something you write includes the typeface you choose, punctuation marks, organization into paragraphs, and even the paper on which you print or type your text. As you deliver the words of your speech to an audience, however, you must provide all of that information with your voice and body.

Your speech delivery is made up of your language, your voice, and your body. Remember that speaking in public should feel natural to you and seem natural to your audience. You want to be conversational and to talk with your listeners, not at them. Use a presentational style with which you are comfortable but which also meets the requirements of your audience, your topic, and your speaking occasion.

Effective vocal delivery is energetic, easily heard, and understandable. Your voice should also show that you are thinking about what you are saying as you deliver your speech. With practice, your voice can communicate humor, seriousness, sarcasm, anger, and a range of other possible emotions behind your words. Check your vocal delivery by answering the following questions:

- Do I change the pitch of my voice enough to create a lively vocal delivery?
- Do I speak with enough volume to be heard easily?
- Do I vary my rate of speaking to match my audience's comprehension of what I am saying?

The message your listeners see should match the one they hear. Effective physical delivery is direct and immediate; effective speakers demonstrate their involvement in their topics and in their speaking situations by interacting with their audiences. You must make eye contact with listeners in all parts of your audience. Your facial expression should signal that you are thinking moment to moment about what you are saying. Physical delivery is not limited to your face, however. Gestures with your arms and hands and selective movement from place to place can emphasize what you say and mark important transitions in your speech.

If you are concentrating on your message and your audience's nonverbal feedback, your physical delivery will likely seem most natural. To gauge your directness, immediacy, and involvement, answer the following questions about your physical delivery:

- Do I look at members of my audience most of the time I am speaking? Do I look at listeners in all parts of the room?
- Do my gestures add emphasis to appropriate parts of the speech? Do my gestures look and feel natural and spontaneous?
- Do my facial expressions show that I am thinking about what I am saying, rather than about how I look or sound?
- Are my clothing and other elements of my appearance appropriate to my topic, my audience, and the speaking occasion?
- If I include place-to-place movement, does it serve a purpose?

Your goal should be delivery that looks and sounds effortless. Yet, ironically, that will require significant practice and attention to the vocal and physical elements of your delivery.

Evaluate Your Speech

Don't forget your speech as soon as you deliver your final words and return to your seat. While the experience is fresh in your memory, evaluate what you said, your organization, and how you delivered your speech. What sorts of feedback did you get from your listeners? What did you do well? What aspects of your speech can you target for improvement? In short, how did you respond to the challenge of preparing and delivering a speech? To evaluate the kind of speaker you are now, and the kind of speaker you can become, answer the following questions:

- What did I do well?
- What areas can I target for improvement in this class?
- What specific efforts do I need to make in order to improve my next speech?

▉ THE PUBLIC SPEAKER AS CRITICAL THINKER

We began this chapter by discussing benefits you gain from studying and practicing public speaking. One of those benefits is developing the critical thinking skills that are so important to your college and career success.

Drawing from the works of Stuart Rankin and Carolyn Hughes, Robert Marzano and his colleagues have identified eight categories of critical thinking skills. As a public speaker you will exercise all of these as you develop and deliver your speech.

Critical Thinking Skills

1. Focusing
2. Information Gathering
3. Remembering
4. Organizing
5. Analyzing
6. Generating
7. Integrating
8. Evaluating[16]

You *focus* when you select your topic, narrow it to key points, and set goals for your speech. You *gather information* to develop your speech content. From your research, you determine your key ideas and how you will support them. You *remember* as you call up information stored in your memory that may be relevant to your topic. You also exercise these skills when you practice with a set of speaking notes, relying on key words to trigger your ideas and explanations.

You *organize* as you outline your key ideas and develop the introduction, body, and conclusion of your speech in a logical way. Throughout the speech-making process, you must *analyze*. You interpret your audience's needs and values; you identify key points from the research you've collected; and you select supporting materials that contribute to sound reasoning.

You use *generating* skills when you brainstorm a list of possible speech topics, when you draw conclusions from your evidence, and when you predict the effects of what you propose. You *integrate* when you synthesize your ideas and supporting material to reinforce your specific purpose, and when you summarize your speech for your listeners. Finally, you *evaluate* when you assess the validity of what you say and your effectiveness in saying it.

Consider the way one student applied these eight skills in developing a particular speech. Wanda's first assignment in her public speaking class was to prepare and deliver a speech about someone she admired. She immediately began *generating* a list of names: her mother, who held down two jobs to help raise five children; a high school teacher who inspired Wanda to go to college; Coretta Scott King, First Lady of the Civil Rights Movement; and Thurgood Marshall, the first African American to serve on the U.S. Supreme Court. Wanda was a high school student when Marshall died in 1992, and she recalled how his commitment to justice for all was one of the reasons she decided to become a prelaw major. So Wanda decided to *focus* her speech on Marshall.

She devised a research plan and began to *gather information*. *Remembering* the moving tributes following Marshall's death, Wanda located some of these articles and also found several books about him.

She *analyzed* her audience, the occasion, and the information she had collected, and began to focus her speech further. Wanda decided that a biography of Marshall's life was far too encompassing for a three- to five-minute speech. She also chose not to discuss his more controversial decisions on abortion and capital punishment. Rather, she *organized* her key ideas and *integrated* her supporting materials around two central images: closed doors and open doors.

First, she would describe some of the doors closed to African Americans during much of Marshall's life: equal education, housing, public transportation, and voting. She would recount that Marshall, the great-grandson of a slave, was denied admission to the University of Maryland Law School.

Second, she would tell how Marshall fought to open these doors by expanding access to housing, public transportation, and voting. And she would, of course, note that it was Marshall who successfully argued the *Brown v. Board of Education of Topeka* case (1954) which declared racial segregation in public schools unconstitutional. She would conclude her story by observing that it was Marshall who litigated the admission of the first African American to graduate from the University of Maryland. Wanda *evaluated* each of these examples as she prepared her speech to ensure that her ideas were well supported.

As she constructed her speaking notes, Wanda used only a brief outline to help her *remember* her ideas. And after delivering her speech, she *evaluated* her speaking strengths and weaknesses to help her improve her next speech.

You will have ample opportunity to exercise your critical thinking as you study the remainder of this textbook and put its principles into action. Your first speech establishes a point of reference from which to increase your confidence and polish your speaking skills. If you ask and answer each of the questions we have posed about the nature of the speaking assignment, your speech content, organization, wording, practice, delivery, and self-evaluation, you will begin to put your critical thinking skills to the test. You will have done a thorough, conscientious job of preparing for your first speech, and we wish you success that matches your efforts.

SUMMARY

Public speaking offers personal, professional, and public benefits for the individual. On a personal level, public speaking teaches you skills you can use in other courses of study. It is also an active form of learning and can increase your retention of information. Finally, gaining public speaking skills and experience will build your confidence and self-esteem. On a professional level, public speaking is an important form of communication, and excellent communication skills increase your chances of getting the job you want and advancing in it. On a public level, public speaking binds people into groups and propels social movements and social change.

We may view *communication* as either a process or a product, but the most accurate definition of the term probably includes both perspectives. Effective communication is the sharing of meaning by sending and receiving symbolic cues.

Public communication, the focus of this textbook, is one of five levels of communication. *Intrapersonal communication* refers to the communication we do with ourselves individually. *Interpersonal*, or *dyadic*, *communication* is that carried out between pairs of people. *Group communication* involves three or more people communicating for some purpose, and with a clear sense that they belong together. *Public communication* occurs when one person speaks face to face with an audience, either large or small. *Mass communication* involves one person communicating to a large audience through some print or electronic medium. These five levels of communication are differentiated by the numbers of people involved, the direction of communication flow, and the opportunities for audience feedback.

Terms to be used throughout this book include seven components of communication. The *speaker* or sender is the person originating the *message*, the ideas communicated. The *channel* or *medium* of communication is the way the message is sent. Public speaking involves verbal, vocal, and visual channels. The *listener* is the person receiving and interpreting the message. *Feedback* refers to all verbal and nonverbal responses from listener to speaker, either intentional or unintentional. The *environment* includes the speaking occasion and the setting where communication occurs. Finally, *noise* is the name given to anything that interferes with communication. Noise can be physical (environmental), physiological (bodily), or psychological (mental).

Preparing your first speech will be easier if you realize that your nervousness is normal and that you can learn to be an effective speaker. To do so, however, you must know what to prepare and you must expend the necessary effort. The more effectively you work on the content, organization, wording, practice, delivery, and evaluation of your first speaking assignment, the better your first speech will be.

The process of developing and delivering a public speech requires you to sharpen and use eight categories of critical thinking skills. You use *focusing* skills as you select your speech topic and narrow it to key points. You use *information gathering* skills as you conduct research, identify your key ideas, and decide how you will support them. You use *remembering* skills as you tap personal knowledge and experience relevant to your topic and as you practice speaking only from key words and phrases. You use *organizing* skills as you outline your key ideas and develop your speech introduction, body, and conclusion in a logical way.

Throughout the speech making process, you use *analyzing* skills as you study your audience, your research, your main points, your supporting materials, and the ideas or arguments you develop. As you brainstorm for topic ideas, draw conclusions from your evidence, and predict the effect of what you propose, you are using *generating* skills. You use *integrating* skills as you arrange your supporting material to reinforce your specific purpose and as you summarize your main points for your listeners. Finally, you use *evaluating* skills as you assess the validity of what you say and you effectiveness in saying it.

1. Using the interactive model of communication as a guide (Figure 1.3), analyze a lecture given by an instructor in one of your classes. Focus specifically on the listeners and feedback. Was the instructor attentive to the verbal and nonverbal behaviors of the students? If your answer is no, what could the instructor have done to make the communication event more of a two-way experience? If your answer is yes, give examples to illustrate the instructor's attentiveness to student feedback.

2. Find an article in a magazine or journal discussing speech communication in business and professional environments. Write a one-page summary and attach it to the article. Be prepared to discuss the article in class.

3. Analyze the physical noise present in your classroom. As a listener, how does this affect your reception of your instructor's message? As a speaker, how might you minimize the effect of this noise? If you were redesigning the classroom, what changes would you make to lessen this type of noise?

4. On a sheet of paper make two lists: "My Communication Strengths" and "My Communication Weaknesses." In the first list, indicate those strengths you think will help you in this public speaking course. In the second list, note those weaknesses you would most like to improve in this course. Keep the lists and refer to them at the conclusion of this course. What changes would you make to the lists at that time?

*N*OTES

1. Robert Johnson, "For One Reagan, You Can Get Many Mikki Williamses," *Wall Street Journal* 30 January 1992: A1.

2. "Critical Link Between Presentation Skills, Upward Mobility," *Supervision* October 1991: 24.

3. Ernest L. Boyer, *College: The Undergraduate Experience in America* (New York: Harper, 1987) 73.

4. Cited in Judy Self, "The Picture of Writing to Learn," *Plain Talk: About Learning and Writing Across the Curriculum* ed. Judy Self (Richmond: Virginia Dept. of Education, Spring 1987) 13.

5. John C. Hafer and C.C. Hoth, "Selection Characteristics: Your Priorities and How Students Perceive Them," *Personnel Administrator* March 1983: 26.

6. Dan B. Curtis, Jerry L. Winsor, and Ronald D. Stephens, "National Preferences in Business and Communication Education," *Communication Education* 38 (January 1989): 11.

7. Curtis 13.

8. Roger K. Mosvick and Robert B. Nelson, *We've Got to Start Meeting Like This!* (Glenview, IL: Scott, 1987) 225.

9. This survey was conducted by Communispond, Inc., and is reported in "Executives Say Training Helps Them Speak Better," *Training: The Magazine of Human Resources Development* October 1981: 20-21, 75.

10. James Wyllie, "Oral Communications: Survey and Suggestions," *ABCA [American Business Communication Association] Bulletin* June 1980: 15.

11. Mosvick 224.

12. *The Oxford English Dictionary* 2nd ed. (Oxford: Clarendon, 1989) 577.

13. Thomas M. Scheidel, *Persuasive Speaking* (Glenview, IL: Scott, 1967) 2.

14. C.K. Ogden and I.A. Richards, *The Meaning of Meaning* 9th ed. (New York: Harcourt, Brace, 1953) 10-12. Chapter 1, "Thoughts, Words and

Things" (pp. 1-23), explains in detail the relationships between symbols, referents, and interpreters.

15. Albert Mehrabian, *Silent Messages: Implicit Communication of Emotions and Attitudes* 2nd ed. (Belmont, CA: Wadsworth, 1981) 77.

16. Adapted from Robert J. Marzano, Ronald S. Brandt, Carolyn Sue Hughes, Beau Fly Jones, Barbara Z. Presseisen, Stuart C. Rankin, and Charles Suhor, *Dimensions of Thinking: A Framework for Curriculum and Instruction* (Alexandria, VA: Association for Supervision and Curriculum Development, 1988) 66. The authors elaborate these eight skills in Chapter 5.

Knowledge is not a loose-leaf notebook of facts. Above all, it is a responsibility for the integrity of what we are, primarily of what we are as ethical creatures.
~Jacob Bronowski

The Ethics of Public Speaking

Chapter 2

peech making is an artistic process. A good speech is not developed by routine or formula. It needs the spark of creativity to live. The accomplished artist will tell you, however, that although inventiveness is an essential component in the creation process, it alone cannot produce excellence. Excellence results from combining that spark of creativity with a good deal of hard work. How does that process happen?

The successful author begins with a blank sheet of paper. The successful director begins with an empty stage. In order to achieve a finished product — a book or a play — both must go through several complicated steps. For example, in order to stage a play, directors must study the literary form, understand its dynamics, research the script, generate ideas, focus and organize those ideas, and then translate them into performance. In so doing, they give the finished product their individual signatures. Writers follow a similar process to complete a project.

As a public speaker, you are both author *and* director, and you seek to fill two voids: a blank sheet of paper and an empty space before an audience. As an artist, you will use your creativity as well as your skills of research and organization to transform your ideas into a living speech. At the end of this process, you will be able to stand in front of an audience and impart information and ideas in a meaningful and memorable way.

Before you can exercise your artistry with language, your persistence as a researcher, or your organizational skills, you must first make the decision to speak and you must have an audience. Your goal in mastering public speaking is not to develop skills as ends in themselves but to serve the various audiences that you may face throughout your life. *Effective public speakers understand and respect their audiences.* They demonstrate this respect by entering into and honoring an unwritten contract with their listeners. In this chapter we focus on issues concerning that contract between speaker and audience: ethical speaking and listening, and plagiarism. Since each speech you make will reveal aspects of your personality and your values, you should study and consider these issues before even planning your first speech.

■ DEFINITION OF ETHICS

It is virtually impossible to read a newspaper or listen to a newscast today without encountering the topic of ethics. We hear of politicians selling out to special interest groups, stockbrokers engaged in insider trading, laboratories charging Medicare millions of dollars for blood tests doctors never ordered, contractors taking shortcuts in construction projects, musicians accepting awards for music they did not record, and college officials illegally recruiting student athletes. We read stories of people who agonized over the decision to allow, and in some cases even to help, a terminally ill loved one to die. We watch news clips of rallies and demonstrations by constituents accusing their elected officials of abusing the public trust. Society is so concerned with unethical behavior that many professions even include the term *ethics* as a component: We have all heard of medical ethics, business ethics, bioethics, journalistic ethics, environmental ethics, and so forth.

When we talk about **ethics,** we are referring to the standards we use to determine right from wrong, or good from bad, in thought and behavior. Our sense of ethics guides the choices we make in all aspects of our professional and private lives. You should not be surprised that your academic studies include a discussion of ethics. You are, after all,

ethics: standards used to discriminate between right and wrong, good and bad, in thought and action.

educating yourself to function in a world where you will make ethical decisions daily. You may be surprised to learn, however, that colleges throughout the United States offer more than 11,000 courses in ethics.[1] In Chapter 1, we established the importance of speech communication in our lives. We will now examine why it is important for you to ensure that you communicate ethically.

■■■ PRINCIPLES OF ETHICS

In discussing communication ethics, Donald Smith notes that "speaking skill is frequently studied as an ethically neutral instrument...." He compares communication skills to the skill of shooting a rifle. It is not wrong to practice your marksmanship shooting skeet; ethical concerns arise, however, when your target is another human being. "From this point of view," Smith writes, "speaking skill per se is neither good nor bad. The skill can be used by good persons or bad persons. It can be put to the service of good purposes [or] bad purposes...."[2] In this course you will learn fundamental communication skills that will empower you as both a speaker and a listener, just as the act of picking up a gun empowers an individual. How you exercise these skills will involve ethical choices and responsibilities.

Two principles frame our discussion of ethics. *First, we contend that all parties in the communication process have ethical responsibilities.* Assume, for example, that one of your instructors had been denied promotion or a requested leave of absence, or had some other reason for holding a grudge against your college administrators. Assume as well that this instructor, without revealing his or her true motives, used class time to provoke and anger you about inadequate parking or poor food quality in the student center at your school, then led you across campus to take the school president hostage, barricade yourselves in the administration building, and tear up the place.

All parties in the communication process — speakers and listeners — have ethical responsibilities. (Source: © AP/Wide World Photos)

Anyone who knew the facts of this case would agree that the instructor acted unethically; it is wrong to manipulate people by keeping your true motives hidden from them. Yet we contend that any students who let themselves be exploited by participating in such a violent and destructive episode would also share ethical responsibility for what happened. College students, no matter what their age, know that their actions have consequences. As this outlandish example demonstrates, all parties involved in communication share ethical obligations.

In spite of this, public speaking textbooks often discuss ethics only from a speaker's perspective, presenting ethical standards as a list of dos and don'ts for the sender of the message. Certainly, a speaker has ethical responsibilities, but a speaker-centered approach to ethics is incomplete. Communication, as we suggest throughout this textbook, is an activity shared by both the speaker and listener. As such, both parties have ethical responsibilities. For that reason, we will discuss the ethics of speaking and listening.

Second, we contend that ethical speakers and listeners possess attitudes and standards that pervade their character and guide their actions before, during, and after their speaking and listening. In other words, ethical speakers and listeners do more than just abstain from unethical behaviors. Ethics is as much a frame of mind as it is a pattern of behavior. Ethics is not something you apply to one speech; it is a working philosophy you apply to your daily life and bring to all speaking situations. Consider the actions of the speaker in the following incident that one of us witnessed in a classroom.

> Lisa presented a persuasive speech on the need for recycling paper, plastic, and aluminum products. To illustrate the many types of recyclables and how over-packaged many grocery products are, she used as an effective visual aid a paper grocery bag filled with empty cans, paper products, and a variety of plastic bottles and containers. After listening to her well-researched, well-delivered speech, with its impassioned final appeal for us to help save the planet by recycling, the class watched in amazement as she put the empty containers back in the bag, walked to the corner of the room, and dropped the bag in the trash can! After a few seconds, someone finally asked the question that had to be asked: "You mean you're not going to take those home to recycle them?" "Nah," said Lisa. "I'm tired of lugging them around. I've done my job."

As Dana Carvey's Church Lady might have said of Lisa's behavior, "How conve-e-enient!" You may or may not believe that people have an ethical responsibility to recycle. But regardless of your views on that issue, you likely question the ethics of someone who insists, in effect, "Do as I say, not as I do." Lisa's actions made the entire class question the sincerity with which she spoke. Ethical standards cannot be turned on and off at an individual's convenience.

▄▄▄ ETHICAL SPEAKING

"A speech is a solemn responsibility. The man who makes a bad thirty-minute speech to 200 people wastes only a half hour of his own time. But he wastes 100 hours of the audience's time — more than four days — which should be a hanging offense."

JENKIN LLOYD JONES

The first and perhaps the most basic obligation of speakers is that they have something meaningful to say to their listeners. Speakers and listeners participate in a transactional relationship; both should benefit from their participation. As the Jones quotation suggests, listeners give speakers their time; speakers should provide something interesting or useful in return.

You may often speak for personal benefit, and this is not necessarily unethical. You may, for instance, speak to a group, urging them to support you for president of the student body. There is nothing wrong with pursuing such personal goals, but ethical speakers do not try to fulfill personal needs at the expense of their listeners. As one popular book on business ethics states, "There is no right way to do a wrong thing."[3] Speakers whose objective is to persuade, for example, should do so with the goal of benefiting both the audience and themselves. Even informative speakers have an ethical obligation to benefit their audiences. Here's an example of how this can work in your public speaking class.

> Assigned to give an informative speech demonstrating a process or procedure, plant lover Evelyn decided to show how to plant a seed in a pot. Her instructor, who had asked students to write down their topic choices, was privately worried that this subject was something everyone already knew about. Evelyn was, after all, speaking to college students who presumably could read the planting instructions on the back of a seed packet. The instructor did not want to discourage Evelyn, but wanted the class to benefit from her speech.
>
> Without saying, "You cannot speak on this topic," the instructor shared her concerns with Evelyn. She found out that Evelyn had several other plant-related topics in mind. Evelyn agreed that a more unusual topic would be more interesting to the class and more challenging for her to deliver. On the day she was assigned to speak, Evelyn presented an interesting speech demonstrating how to propagate tropical plants by "air layering" them. Evelyn got a chance to demonstrate her green thumb and her classmates learned something most had never heard of before.

Notice how Evelyn finally paid attention to her audience. At her teacher's suggestion, she rejected the simple, familiar topic that would probably not have taught her audience anything.

Having something meaningful to say leads to the second ethical consideration for speakers: deciding whether or not to speak. Silence is certainly an option, and probably one that is too infrequently exercised. There are times, though, when you need to convey information or when you feel strongly about an issue or an injustice. *Ethical speakers voice their opinions and champion causes.* Our nation's history has been shaped by the voices of Thomas Jefferson, Patrick Henry, Frederick Douglass, Susan B. Anthony, Martin Luther King, Jr., William F. Buckley, Jr., Cesar Chavez, and other advocates. That shaping continues today in the voices of Coretta Scott King, Henry Cisneros, Jesse Jackson, Bill Clinton, Jack Kemp, Marian Wright Edelman, and Elie Wiesel, among many others.

You may not have the impact of those famous speakers, but you do have an opportunity to better the communities of which you are a part. This class provides you with an opportunity to share information your classmates can use to help them get more from their college experience, or to help them function better in their careers and personal lives. You also have a chance to educate others about problems you feel need to be confronted. We remember one student who showed special sensitivity in addressing a topic she opposed on ethical grounds.

Pam, a sophomore public relations major, had been an animal welfare advocate for a long time, but she knew from class discussions and conversations before class that a number of her classmates hunted for sport or for food. She realized that if she turned her ten-minute persuasive speech into a general sermon against killing animals she would only make a number of her classmates feel defensive. She wanted to speak on some aspect of animal welfare but knew she had to narrow and focus the topic.

As a volunteer worker for several animal protection agencies, Pam had become aware of the problems associated with the use of steel leg-hold traps. Inside city limits, they posed a threat to pets, children, and adults who did not know where they had been set. She also opposed their use in the wilderness because, she said, they inflict pain and suffering and kill nontarget animals. Pam delivered a well-documented speech to persuade her listeners that the use of these traps should be outlawed. Her carefully worded thesis was not that killing animals is wrong, but that use of this particular trap is cruel and inhumane. She even discussed two other types of traps as humane alternatives. The class listened intently to Pam, and toward the end of the speech she was gratified to see that many of her classmates, hunters included, were nodding in apparent agreement with her.

Much of your speaking in this class and later in life may not be on significant social or political issues. Yet this class provides you with the training ground to hone your skills as speaker and listener. Use these skills as you move from involvement in class and campus issues to improvement of your community.

Third, ethical speakers pay attention to the values implied in their topic choices. Selecting a topic is one of the first ethical choices you will make as a speaker. Unless you are assigned a topic, you can choose from a wide range of subjects. In a real sense, you give your topic credibility simply by selecting it. As an ethical speaker, your choice should reflect what you think is important for your audience.

In the courses we teach, many student speeches have expanded our knowledge or moved us to act on significant issues. But consider this list of informative speech topics:

How to get a fake I.D.
How to "walk" (avoid paying) a restaurant check
How to get a faculty parking permit
How to beat police radar
How to get out of a speeding ticket

We have heard speeches on each of these topics. Even though they were informative rather than persuasive speeches, each of these how-to topics implies that its action is acceptable. We do not know why students chose these topics, but we suggest that all of those speakers disregarded their listeners, failed to consider the values they were promoting, and presented unethical speeches.

Fourth, ethical speakers present their listeners with ideas that are logically developed and support-ed. Listeners have a right to know not only the speaker's ideas but also the material supporting those claims. Ethical speakers are well informed, and should thus test their ideas for validity and support. They should not knowingly use false information or faulty reasoning. We witnessed a student presenting incomplete or out-of-date material:

Janet presented an informative speech on the detection and treatment of breast cancer. Her discussion of the disease's detection seemed thorough, but when she got to her second point, she said that the only treatments were radical mastectomy, partial mastectomy, radiation therapy, and chemotherapy. She failed to mention lumpectomy, a popular surgical measure often combined with radiation or chemotherapy. Her bibliography revealed that her research stopped with sources published in the early 1980s, explaining the gap in her speech content.

Janet did not necessarily act unethically; she was simply uninformed and ended up being embarrassed. But what if Janet had known of the lumpectomy procedure and had just not wanted to do further research to find out about it? Then we would question her ethics.

In this case, certain listeners did not notice the factual errors and the lapses in content while others did. Not getting caught in a factual or logical error does not free the speaker of ethical responsibility to present complete, factual information. If you speak on a current topic, you need to use the most recent information you can find and to try to be as well informed as possible.

Fifth, ethical speakers make their intentions clear to the audience. In other words, they do not intentionally manipulate the audience. Allan Cohen and David Bradford define manipulation as "actions to achieve influence that would be rendered less effective if the target knew your actual intentions."[4]

We are familiar with one company whose sales strategy certainly matches that definition of manipulation. This company relies on door-to-door salespersons, especially college students, and instructs new employees to make a list of friends who might be interested in purchasing the product. The employees are told to contact these friends and tell them the good news about their new job. The company also coaches employees to say that part of the job involves making presentations to potential customers and to ask if they could practice giving their presentation to the friend in order to get some helpful feedback. In addition, because the company wants to encourage its workers to succeed, employees offer each volunteer "critic" a gift. However, the company also tells each salesperson confidentially that the presentations are actually a test to see if they can sell the product, and that they should take advantage of these sales opportunities.

We consider this strategy manipulative and unethical. The salespersons make the appointments under false pretenses. The company exploits its employees' friendships; the employees in turn exploit their friends' willingness to be helpful. These helpful critics might not participate if they knew their friends' real intent. A public speaker may try to inform, convince, persuade, direct, or even anger an audience. Ethical speakers, however, do not deceive their listeners. They are up-front about their intentions, and those intentions include benefiting the audience.

Sixth, ethical speakers concern themselves with the consequences of their speaking. Mary Cunningham observed, "Words are sacred things. They are also like hand grenades: Handled casually, they tend to go off."[5] Ethical speakers have a respect for the power of language and the process of communication.

It is difficult to track, let alone to predict, the impact of any one message. Statements you make are interpreted by your immediate audience and may be communicated by those listeners to others. Individuals may form opinions and behave differently because of what you say or what you fail to say. Incorrect information and misinterpretations may have unintended, and potentially harmful, consequences. If you provide an audience with inaccurate information, you may contaminate the quality of their subsequent decisions. If you persuade someone to act in a particular way, you are, in part, responsible for the impact of the person's new action. With that principle in mind, consider the following experience a friend of ours had.

> A colleague has had a long and distinguished career teaching communication. She returned to her office visibly upset after a class one day. When questioned, she said she had just had a student announce in his speech introduction that his purpose was to teach the class how to make a lethal poison using ingredients people either already had in their homes or could easily buy. "Moreover," she said, "to stress the significance of the topic, he assured us that this substance would kill any living animal, certainly even the heaviest human being."
>
> Upon hearing this, her colleagues' reactions were, "That's frightening. What did you do?" She said, "I sat there thinking of the rash of teenage suicides, even copycat suicides, we've been hearing about lately, and all the other meanness in the world. I wrestled with my conscience for about a minute and a half, and then, for the first time since I started teaching, I interrupted a speaker, told him I didn't think we needed to hear this information, and asked him to be seated."

Placed in that teacher's position, what would you have done? Such an obvious clash between a speaker's freedom of expression and the ethical standards of listeners leads us to consider the standards of ethical listening.

KEY POINTS	1. Say something meaningful.
Responsibilities of an Ethical Speaker	2. Speak up about issues you consider important.
	3. Choose topics that promote positive ethical values.
	4. Use truthful, accurate supporting materials and valid reasoning.
	5. Let the audience know your true motives for speaking.
	6. Consider the consequences of your words and actions.

ETHICAL LISTENING

"A mind that is stretched to a new idea never returns to its original dimension."
OLIVER WENDELL HOLMES

The ethics of listening involves four basic principles. *First, ethical listeners seek out speakers who expand their knowledge, increase their understanding, introduce them to new ideas, and challenge their beliefs.* These listeners reject the philosophy, "My mind's made up, so don't confuse me with the facts." A controversial speaker visiting your campus can expand your knowledge or intensify your feelings about a subject, whether you agree or disagree with the

Effective speakers connect with their listeners and speak about issues that are important to them. (SOURCE: © Mark Ludak/Impact Visuals)

speaker's viewpoint. Even in situations in which students are a captive audience for other students' speeches, such as this class, ethical listening should be the standard.

Second, ethical listeners listen openly without prejudging speakers or their ideas. This may be difficult. Listening without bias requires that we temporarily suspend impressions we have formed from the other person's past actions. But the rewards of doing so can be great, as in this example.

Linda's first speech in class completely confused her classmates. She seemed nervous and unsure of herself and what she was going to say, and the point of her speech really eluded everyone. Class discussion after the speech focused primarily on Linda's delivery, and some of the distracting mannerisms she exhibited and needed to control. When she went to the front of the room to begin her next speech weeks later, no one was really expecting to be impressed. But they were.

Linda's second speech dealt with the problem of homelessness. Her opening sentence told the class that three years before she had been living on the street for a time. She had their attention from that point on. In addition to citing recent newspaper and magazine articles, Linda had conducted a great deal of original research. She had interviewed the directors of local shelters and a number of the homeless people who took refuge there, and she quoted these individuals. Her speech was well organized and well delivered. It was both educational and inspiring.

When discussing the speech later, classmates kept referring to her first speech and noting the remarkable improvements Linda had made. One person was blunt, but apparently summed up the feelings of a number of listeners that day: "Linda, I wasn't expecting much from you because your first speech was so unclear to me, but today you had a topic that you obviously care about and you made us understand and care about it, too. I can't get over the difference between those two speeches!"

When listening to your classmates, you should assume that you may learn something important from each speaker, and therefore listen intently. Information and ideas are best shared in such an atmosphere of mutual respect.

Listening eagerly and openly does not imply a permanent suspension of evaluation, however. *A third standard is that ethical listeners evaluate the messages presented to them.* A listener who accepts a premise without evaluating its foundation is like someone who buys a used car without looking under the hood. The warning "let the buyer beware" is good advice not only for consumers of products but also for consumers of messages. As a listener, you should critically evaluate the ideas of the speaker. Is each idea logically constructed? Is each supported with evidence that is relevant, sufficient, and authoritative?

Ethical speakers and listeners read and listen critically. To see how some students listen more critically than others, consider the example of the following persuasive speaker.

> Sharon presented a speech arguing that all of the problems high school students face today — drug use, gang violence, teenage pregnancy, lack of discipline in class, academic failure — resulted from the Supreme Court decision that ended prayer in school. She had two primary supporting materials: quotations from a local religious leader and a comparison of school conditions in the 1950s with conditions in the 1990s.
>
> Sharon argued her case with a great deal of conviction. As she spoke, many listeners indicated agreement with her by nodding their heads and looking concerned. But after her speech, several students asked, "Sharon, aren't there other differences between schools in the '50s and the '90s? There are more students today, and more peer pressure. Drugs that were not even known in the '50s are readily available today. Could it be that teachers in the '50s expected more of students than they do today?" Finally one student said, "I personally agree with you. I think prayer or at least a moment of silence for voluntary prayer might encourage students to be more reverent or thoughtful. But you haven't proved to me that all of these problems you mentioned are a direct result of lack of school prayer. There's a logical flaw in your speech."

Whether offered a product, an idea, or a proposed course of action, ethical listeners evaluate critically.

Fourth, ethical listeners concern themselves with the consequences of their listening. As the following example illustrates, listeners who assimilate only part of a public speaker's message because they fail to listen actively are responsible for the distorted message that results.

> Hank listened to his classmate Jeff deliver a speech about problems with their college's registration procedures. As Jeff spoke, Hank remembered problems he had encountered: long lines, inconvenient registration times, filled classes. At one point Hank heard Jeff talking about experimental phone registration the school was offering next semester to students with last names beginning from A to L. At the next class meeting, Hank said to Jeff, "I called the registrar's office yesterday to register by phone. They asked for my last name. When I said it was Thompson, they told me phone registration this semester was only for students with last names beginning from A to L." "I told you that in my speech," Jeff said. "Weren't you listening?"

Hank may have been embarrassed, but he did not suffer greatly as a result of not listening carefully to Jeff. In other cases, however, the consequences of not listening are more serious. When you fail to listen to someone's directions and are late for an interview, you miss an employment opportunity. In both of these examples, the listener, not the speaker, bears responsibility for the breakdown in communication.

At other times, listener and speaker may share responsibility for unethical behavior. For example, audience members who become victims of "scams" because they did not listen critically share with the speaker responsibility for their behavior. Voters who tolerate exaggerated, vague, and inconsistent campaign statements from those who ask to represent them similarly become part of the problem and not the solution.

KEY POINTS

Responsibilities of an Ethical Listener

1. Seek exposure to well-informed speakers.
2. Listen openly, without prejudging the speaker or the speaker's ideas.
3. Evaluate the logic and credibility of the speaker's ideas.
4. Beware of the consequences of not listening carefully.

Most of us begin learning ethical principles as children: "It's wrong to lie." "It's wrong to deceive others." "It's wrong to blame others for what we say and do." In the past, views of communication ethics implied a dotted line across the front of a classroom, with ethics being solely the speaker's responsibility. In contrast, we view ethics as a shared responsibility of the speaker and each listener. An absence of ethical motives among speakers and listeners devalues the currency of communication. One aspect of ethics, however, does begin as the speaker's responsibility: plagiarism. We feel that the topic of plagiarism deserves special attention.

■ PLAGIARISM

"You must renounce imagination forever if you hope to succeed in plagiarism. Forgery is intention, not invention."   **HORACE WALPOLE**

"Your manuscript is both good and original; but the part that is good is not original, and the part that is original is not good."   **SAMUEL JOHNSON**

The word *plagiarize* comes from a Latin word meaning "to kidnap," so in a sense, a plagiarist is a kidnapper of the ideas and words of another. A modern definition of **plagiarism** is "literary — or artistic or musical — theft. It is the false assumption of authorship: the wrongful act of taking the product of another person's mind, and presenting it as one's own."[6]

plagiarism: the unattributed use of another's ideas, words, or pattern of organization.

When you write a paper and submit it to a teacher, you are in effect publishing that work. If, in that paper, you copy something from another source and pass it off as your own work, you are plagiarizing. This act is such a serious offense that in most colleges and universities it is grounds for failing the course, or even for dismissal from the school. Yet recent history has shown us numerous examples of politicians, educators, and other public figures caught plagiarizing materials, either consciously or unconsciously. An offense serious enough to derail a candidate's campaign for office, to force the resignation of a corporate officer, or to end a student's academic career certainly deserves the attention of students in a public speaking class.

Of course, some spoken language is repeated from person to person with no real thought given to the question of copyright or ownership. Facts or ideas considered common knowledge ("Water freezes at zero degrees Celsius," or "Ronald Reagan served two terms as our fortieth president") do not have to be attributed to a source. Jokes are another example of speech that does not have to be footnoted orally. You may tell your listeners where you heard the joke, but people do not typically concern themselves with copyright law where jokes, tall tales, or popular sayings are concerned. The facts and the wording of a public speech are quite another matter, though. For one thing, most speeches are more formal than joking or conversation. Second, the audience for a public speech assumes that the ideas expressed and the words used are the speaker's unless they are told otherwise.

Just as you publish the paper you write and submit to your teacher, when you deliver a speech in this class or on any other occasion you are also "publishing" your material. Even without putting your words in print or placing a copyright notice on them, you hold the copyright on your ideas expressed in your own words. The current copyright law is interpreted to say, "Even if a speech has merely been delivered orally and not [formally] published, it is subject to copyright protection and may not be used without written permission."[7] Plagiarism of well-known speeches or speakers is both unethical and foolish, as the following example shows.

> Some years ago one of us judged a high school speech tournament event that called upon contestants to speak to entertain. Even though the contest rules stipulated that the speech must be the student's original work, one student copied virtually his entire speech word for word from a George Carlin concert recording. Of course, that blatant plagiarism, noted by several judges, led to the student's prompt disqualification from the competition.

As we have said, repeating a joke a friend tells you is one thing; memorizing and reciting a comedy routine by George Carlin, Rita Rudner, Marsha Warfield, or Robin Williams is quite another. Repeating distinctive, well-known material as though it were your own may be the most foolish type of plagiarism. No less serious, however, is plagiarizing from obscure sources. If you deliver a speech someone else has researched, organized, and worded, you are presenting another's work as your own. You are plagiarizing.

Plagiarism applies to more than simply the copying of another's words, however. You may also plagiarize another's ideas and organization of material. For example, if you presented a speech organized around the five stages of dying (denial, anger, bargaining, depression, and acceptance) and did not give credit to Elisabeth Kübler-Ross, you would be guilty of plagiarism. On the other hand, if your speech analyzed the political, economic, and social implications of a pending piece of legislation, you would probably not be guilty of plagiarism. Kübler-Ross developed, explained, and published her framework or model in her book *On Death and Dying*, whereas the second example relies on a commonly accepted pattern of analyzing public policy initiatives. As you can see, the line between legitimate appropriation of material and plagiarism is sometimes unclear. As a speaker, you must always be on guard to credit the source of your ideas and their structure.

As another example of potential plagiarism, suppose a speaker, after reading *Game Plans: Sports Strategies for Business*, selected as his or her specific purpose to explain business management using sports as models. Using three chapter titles from that book, the speaker could word the major ideas of the speech as follows:

I. Filling Out the Lineup Card (Baseball)
II. Preparing the Game Plan (Football)
III. Managing the Flow (Basketball)[8]

Such a speaker would be guilty of plagiarism if he or she did not attribute the ideas to Robert W. Keidel, the author of *Game Plans: Sports Strategies for Business*. Keidel not only supported these ideas, he created them. To avoid plagiarism, the speaker could change the wording of his or her specific purpose: to explain to the audience Robert Keidel's use of sports models for business management. In this way, the speaker clearly attributes the ideas in the speech to Keidel.

As we mentioned earlier, plagiarism may be intentional or unintentional. *Intentional plagiarism* occurs when speakers or writers knowingly represent another person's words, ideas, or organization as their own. *Unintentional plagiarism* is "the careless paraphrasing and citing of source material such that improper or misleading credit is given."[9] Intentional plagiarism is considered the more severe offense. Unintentional plagiarism may be committed due to ignorance, but the effect is still the same: You are taking credit for the work of another.

Unintentional plagiarism sometimes occurs because of a common misconception that by simply changing a few words of another's writing you have paraphrased the statement and need not cite it. Michael O'Neill refers to this "hybrid of half textual source, half original writing" as a "paraplage."[10] Note the differences and similarities in the original and adapted passages of the following statement by Paul Sheehan.

Statement by Paul Sheehan

The U.S. airline industry has endured a period of historic upheaval. Like much history, it has not been pretty. In 1978 the United States had twenty large airlines. Today the names of many of those companies read like a roll call of the dead: Pan American, Eastern, Western, Braniff, National, Frontier, Allegheny, Hughes Airwest, North Central, Ozark, Piedmont, Southern, and Texas International. As these airlines died or were taken over, another dozen companies were born, but they, too, have nearly all gone. Of the nine large survivors, TWA and America West are operating under bankruptcy protection, Continental has just emerged from bankruptcy for the second time since deregulation, and Northwest is in extreme structural distress.[11]

Speaker's Paraplagiage of Paul Sheehan

The history of the American airline industry since it was deregulated in 1978 hasn't been pretty. Of the twenty large U.S. carriers that existed in 1978, only nine remain. The names of companies that have disappeared or have been taken over in less than twenty years include Pan American, Eastern, Braniff, National, Frontier, Piedmont, and Texas International. TWA and America West are currently operating under bankruptcy protection. Continental has just emerged from its second bankruptcy since deregulation, and Northwest is in extreme distress.

Speaker's Appropriate Citation of Paul Sheehan

The history of the American airline industry since deregulation in 1978 hasn't been pretty. That's the assessment of Paul Sheehan, U.S. correspondent for an Australian magazine group, who studied the airline industry during a fellowship at Harvard University. In an article in the August 1993 *Atlantic Monthly,* he notes that the twenty large carriers operating at the time of deregulation have now shrunk to nine. And of those, TWA and America West are operating under bankruptcy protection, and Northwest is experiencing distress.

Notice that the appropriate citation above not only tells the listener who Paul Sheehan is, but also explains exactly where his words appeared in print. With that information, any listener wanting to read the entire article could go to a library and find it quickly.

To avoid plagiarizing, let these five simple rules guide you.

1. *Establish a clear and consistent method of notetaking when you research.* As you review your notes, you should be able to discern which words, ideas, examples, and organizational structures belong to which authors.

2. *Record complete source citations on each sheet of notes or write this information on each photocopied article.*

3. *Clearly indicate in your speech any words, ideas, examples, or organizational structures that are not your own.* If you cite a source early in your speech and then use another idea from that author later, you must again give that author credit. You need not, however, repeat the complete citation. The statement "he notes" in the appropriate citation of Sheehan signals the listener that the speaker is again quoting or paraphrasing his words.

4. *When you paraphrase ideas, credit their originator.* Remember that another's statements are characterized by both content and structure. When paraphrasing, you should use not only your words but also your own language style and thought structure.

5. *When in doubt, cite the source.* At times, you will be unsure whether you need to acknowledge a source. It is always wise to err on the side of caution.

We have discussed some reasons *not* to hide the true authorship of words and ideas. There are also at least two reasons why speakers *should* mention their sources. The first reason may seem self-serving, but it is nevertheless true that speakers who cite their sources increase their credibility or believability with the audience. When you quote from a book, an article, or an interview and name the author or speaker of those words, you show the audience that you have researched the topic and that you know what you are talking about. Second, and far more important, acknowledging your sources is the right thing to do. It is honest. Good ideas and memorably worded thoughts are rare enough that the original writer or speaker deserves credit.

> **KEY POINTS**
>
> **Guidelines to Avoid Plagiarism**
>
> 1. Take clear and consistent notes while researching.
> 2. Record complete source citations for notes or photocopied pages.
> 3. Indicate any quoted material as you deliver the speech.
> 4. Credit the source of any ideas or structures you paraphrase.
> 5. Cite the source when in doubt.

SUMMARY

Ethics and plagiarism are topics of concern to students and teachers of public speaking. *Ethics* refers to fundamental questions of right and wrong in thought and behavior. We offer some positive observations on ethics from the viewpoints of both speaker and listener. Ethics is not a standard for acceptable practice that we turn on before speaking and off after the speech is over; it is a value system pervading our lives. We believe that everyone involved in public communication should be guided by the following ethical considerations.

First, ethical speakers have something meaningful to say. Their messages interest and benefit the audience. Second, ethical speakers are willing to voice their opinions on issues that concern them. They make the decision to speak out, even when remaining silent would be easier. Third, ethical speakers care about the values reflected in their topic choices. Fourth, ethical speakers develop and support the ideas of their speeches accurately and logically. Fifth, ethical speakers make their intentions clear to their audiences and avoid conscious manipulation. Finally, ethical speakers care about the consequences their speaking may have for listeners.

Listening should be guided by four ethical principles. First, ethical listeners welcome challenges to their beliefs just as they embrace learning. Second, ethical listening means listening openly, without prejudging the speaker's ideas. Third, ethical listeners evaluate the speaker's ideas before acting upon them. Finally, ethical listeners care about and accept responsibility for the consequences of their listening.

Both speakers and listeners need to be aware of the issue of *plagiarism,* the unattributed use of another's ideas, words, or organization. Plagiarism may be either intentional or unintentional. To avoid plagiarizing sources, speakers should (1) establish a clear and consistent method of notetaking; (2) record a complete source citation on each page of notes or each photocopied article; (3) clearly indicate in the speech any words, ideas, or organizational techniques not their own; (4) orally cite sources for paraphrased, as well as quoted, materials; and (5) when in doubt, acknowledge the source. Careful source citation not only increases a speaker's credibility with the audience but is also ethically right.

EXERCISES

1. Select two individuals prominent on the international, national, state, or local scene whom you consider ethical speakers. What characteristics do they possess that make them ethical? Select two people you consider unethical. What ethical standards do you think they abuse?

2. Answer each of the following questions and be prepared to defend your position.
   a. Should a speech instructor have the right to censor topics students select for their speeches?
   b. Should students have the right to use profanity and obscenity in their speeches in this class?
   c. Should the Ku Klux Klan be allowed to hold a rally on your campus?
   d. Should public prayers be a part of opening ceremonies at athletic contests at publicly supported schools?
   e. Should lawyers defend clients they know are guilty?

3. In the news, find a company that has been accused of some ethical wrongdoing. Follow the story as it is reported for a week, and then discuss the ethics of the company's statements and actions.

4. Read the statement about George Smathers on page 222 of Chapter 11. Discuss the ethics of Smathers and his listeners.

5. Find an article on any subject written by an expert. Summarize the article in one or two paragraphs. Use appropriate source citation, paraphrasing, and quotations to avoid plagiarism.

6. Politicians often do not write the speeches they deliver, instead relying on the words of speechwriters. Lyndon Johnson used a record twenty-four writers for his State of the Union address in 1964.[12] Journalist Ari Posner laments this tradition, observing, "If college or high school students relied on ghosts the way most public figures do, they'd be expelled on charges of plagiarism."[13] Be prepared to defend your answers to the following questions: Is the practice of ghostwriting in politics unethical? What are the advantages and disadvantages of politicians relying on speechwriters? Should students be permitted to use ghostwriters for their classroom speeches?

NOTES

1. James A. Jaksa and Michael S. Pritchard, *Communication Ethics* (Belmont, CA: Wadsworth, 1988) xi.

2. Donald K. Smith, *Man Speaking: A Rhetoric of Public Speech* (New York: Dodd, 1969) 228.

3. Kenneth Blanchard and Norman Vincent Peale, *The Power of Ethical Management* (New York: Fawcett-Ballantine, 1988) 9.

4. Allan R. Cohen and David L. Bradford, *Influence without Authority* (New York: Wiley, 1990) ix.

5. Mary Cunningham, "What Price 'Good Copy'?" *Newsweek* 29 November 1982: 15.

6. Alexander Lindey, *Plagiarism and Originality* (New York: Harper, 1952) 2.

7. *Prentice Hall Author's Guide* (Englewood Cliffs, NJ: Prentice, 1978) 9.

Speaking Confidently

Chapter 3

■ PERVASIVENESS OF SPEAKER NERVOUSNESS

"According to most studies, people's number one fear is public speaking. Number two is death. Death is number two. Does that seem right? This means to the average person, if you have to go to a funeral, you're better off in the casket than doing the eulogy."

JERRY SEINFELD[1]

S einfeld may be playing a bit fast and loose with his facts and his logic, but the point of his humor is sound: Apprehension about speaking in public is widespread, even among people with a great deal of public speaking experience. Carol Burnett, another accomplished comedian and actor, has appeared in her own television series, in movies, and as host of various televised award shows. Nevertheless, she has said, "The idea of making a speech does more than make me a nervous wreck; it terrifies me…. I'd rather scrub floors — without knee pads."[2]

Burnett would probably be able to scrub those floors quickly with help from a number of men and women who would make the same choice she did. Meryl Streep, one of America's most versatile actors, has said, "It's odd: I have this career that spans continents, but the pathetic thing is that I can't get up in front of people and speak. I get really, really nervous."[3] Lee Iacocca, former chief executive officer of the Chrysler Corporation, confesses that "to this day I still get a little nervous before giving a speech."[4] And the list of performers and public figures who have disclosed their nervousness about public speaking includes former president Ronald Reagan, NBC weatherperson Willard Scott, singer Barbra Streisand, actor Tom Selleck, and quarterback Joe Montana.

These examples demonstrate that if you are nervous about public speaking and experience what we sometimes call "platform panic," you are in good company. In fact, the first edition of *The Book of Lists* reported a survey that asked 3,000 Americans, "What are you the most afraid of?" "Speaking before a group" came in first, ahead of heights, insects, financial problems, deep water, sickness, and, yes, even death.[5] Psychiatrists John Greist, James Jefferson, and Isaac Marks contend that public speaking anxiety is "probably the most common social phobia."[6] Today, when so many people are apprehensive about even striking up a conversation with a stranger, is it any wonder that the fear of public speaking is so widespread?

Our experience and research confirm the prevalence of this common fear among college students. When asked to list their communication weaknesses, a clear majority of our students rank speaking before a group of people as their primary fear. James McCroskey has studied the anxieties of public speaking extensively. McCroskey's Personal Report of Public Speaking Anxiety assesses the fear college students have about giving public speeches. His data, collected from several thousand students, confirm that public speaking generates greater apprehension than other forms of communication and that this fear spans several levels:

high anxiety	40%
moderately high anxiety	30%
moderate anxiety	20%
moderately low anxiety	5%
low anxiety	5%

Note that nearly three-fourths of college students fall into the moderately high to high anxiety range! This means that even the person who always has the quick response, who can make others in the class laugh, and who always looks together may be just as worried as you are right now about getting up in front of this class to give a speech. McCroskey and co-author Virginia Richmond conclude: "What this suggests, then, is that it is 'normal' to experience a fairly high degree of anxiety about public speaking. Most people do. If you are highly anxious about public speaking, then you are 'normal.'"[7]

What is this platform panic and how does it affect us? Chemically and physiologically, we all experience stage fright in the same way. Adrenaline is suddenly pumped into the bloodstream. Respiration increases dramatically. So do heart rate and "galvanic skin response" — the amount of perspiration on the surface of the skin. All these things occur so that oxygen-rich blood can be quickly channeled to the large muscle groups. You may have heard stories of a 135-pound person who lifts the front of a car to help rescue someone pinned under it. Such incidents happen because the body is suddenly mobilized to do what must be done.

Yet the body can be similarly mobilized in stressful situations that are not life threatening. Musicians waiting for the start of the opening selection, athletes for the game to begin, actors for the curtain to go up, and speakers for their call to the podium often feel their bodies marshalling all their resources either to perform to capacity or to get away from the threatening situation. This phenomenon is called, appropriately, the "fight or flight" syndrome.

Although our bodies' chemical and physiological responses to stress are identical, the outward signs of this anxiety vary from person to person. As the time approaches for your first speech in this class, you may experience any of several symptoms to varying degrees. Our students tell us that their symptoms include blushing or redness, accelerated heart rate, perspiring, dry mouth, shaking, churning stomach, increased rate of speech, forgetfulness and broken speech, and nervous mannerisms such as playing with jewelry, tapping fingers, and clutching the lectern.

As we indicated earlier, it is important to realize that these symptoms are typical, not atypical, of a public speaker. If you experience any of these symptoms, you have plenty of company.

CONTROLLING SPEAKER NERVOUSNESS

Before discussing what your goal should be regarding speaker nervousness, it is important to note what it should not be. Do *not* make your goal to eliminate nervousness. Such

Reprinted by permission of
UFS, Inc.

FRANCIE

a goal is counterproductive for at least two reasons. First, as we have noted, nervousness is natural. Attempting to eliminate it is therefore unrealistic and probably undesirable. Speakers having far more experience in front of the public have failed to do so — remember Burnett, Streep, and Iacocca. In fact, the more you concentrate on your nervousness, the more nervous you may become. As someone has said, "You never get rid of the butterflies in your stomach, but you can teach them to fly in formation."

A second reason why you should not try to eliminate nervousness is that some nervousness can actually benefit a speaker. Nervousness is energy. Use that energy to enliven your delivery and to give your ideas impact. Instead of nervously tapping your fingers on the lectern, for example, you can gesture. Rather than shifting your body weight from foot to foot, incorporate motivated movement into your speech.

Your goal, then, is not to eliminate nervousness but to control and channel it. The coping strategies we suggest in the next section and in Chapter 12 will enable you to control the symptoms of nervousness and to channel that energy into dynamic, effective vocal and physical delivery.

▀▀▀ COPING STRATEGIES

One popular, nonacademic book on public speaking suggests this "quick-fix" for reducing stage fright:

> Take an orange crate to a busy downtown street where you're not known, get up on the crate and, using all your lung power, proceed to exhort the passersby with the speech you're preparing. I'm serious. This works because you can't continue feeling the really paralyzing fear of stage fright over and over — your nervous system rebels against going through all that turmoil for no reason.[8]

Before you panic further, note that we do *not* suggest that you try this. In fact, we disagree with this exercise as well as its rationale. If you are nervous about speaking in front of your classmates, wouldn't you be even more nervous shouting to strangers on a street corner? You might even risk arrest and still not reduce your nervousness.

We advocate a far less dramatic approach to ease your nervousness. We offer eleven suggestions to help you become a more confident communicator. If you consider each suggestion seriously, you will control your nervousness and learn to channel it into a dynamic and effective public speaking style.

KEY POINTS	1. Know how you react to stress. 6. Believe in your topic.
Guidelines to Control Speaker Nervousness	2. Know your strengths and weaknesses. 7. View speech making positively.
	3. Know speech principles. 8. Project control.
	4. Know your audience. 9. Test your message.
	5. Know your speech. 10. Practice. 11. Learn from experience.

We have already noted that nervousness affects different people in different ways. Perhaps you feel that your hands or knees shake uncontrollably as you speak in public. The people sitting next to you may not ever experience those symptoms of nervousness, but they may have difficulty breathing comfortably and feel that their voices are shaky or quivery. Whatever your individual responses to stress, don't wait until you are delivering a public speech to discover them.

Knowing your reactions to stressful situations helps you in two ways. First, this knowledge lets you predict and cope with these physical conditions. Your dry mouth or sweaty palms will not surprise you; instead, you will recognize them as signs that your body is performing well under pressure. Second, since you are anticipating these physical conditions, you will be better able to mask them from the audience. How do you do this? Try these techniques.

If you know that your hands shake when you are nervous, don't hold a sheet of paper during the speech; the shaking paper will only amplify the movement of your hands and will telegraph this sign of nervousness to your audience. If your voice is likely to be thin and quivery as you begin speaking, take several deep, slow breaths before you begin to speak. If you get tense before speaking, try some muscle relaxation techniques: Tense your hands, arms, and shoulders, and then slowly relax them. If you get flustered before speaking, make sure you arrive on time or even a little early — never late. If looking at an audience intimidates you, talk to audience members before class, and when you speak, look for friendly faces in the audience.

Know Your Strengths and Weaknesses

Surgeons spend many hours learning how to use the equipment they need to perform operations. Each surgeon knows just what each instrument is capable of doing and can use it to maximum effectiveness. As a public speaker, your instruments are your voice, body, mind, and personality. You will use all these instruments together to create and communicate messages.

To know yourself, you must honestly appraise both your strengths and your weaknesses. Use your strengths to communicate your message with force and impact. If you are a lively and enthusiastic person, channel that energy to reinforce your speech physically and enliven your listeners. If you have a talent for creating memorable phrases, allow that creativity to help your listeners attend to and remember your ideas. Just as you can tap your strengths in these ways, you can minimize or avoid your weaknesses if you know them. If you are not effective in delivering humor, you probably should not begin your speech with a joke. To do so would risk failure at this critical point in the speech, and that would make you even more nervous.

The more you understand your strengths and weaknesses, the better you will be able to craft your speech to your abilities. The more confident you are that you can accomplish what you set out to do, the less nervous you will be. One note of caution, however: Don't be too critical of yourself and construct a "safe" speech because you have exaggerated your weaknesses. Instead, expand your abilities by incorporating new strategies into your speech making. Only through thoughtful, measured risk taking will you develop as a public speaker.

Confident speakers are physically involved in the delivery of their messages. Like this speaker, their facial expression is animated, their eye contact with the audience is direct, and their gestures appear natural and enthusiastic.
(SOURCE: © Michael Grecco/ Stock, Boston)

Know Speech Principles

If you are confident that you have constructed an effective speech, you will be more confident as you step to the lectern. This textbook and your instructor will assist you in learning speech principles. What are the four steps of an effective speech introduction? How should you construct the body of your speech, and how should you develop each key idea? What strategies help you conclude your speech? How can you use your voice and body to communicate your ideas dynamically? What strategies help you word ideas correctly, clearly, and vividly? We address all these questions, and many others, in this book. As you begin to answer these questions and apply what you learn, you will feel more confident about the content, organization, and delivery of your ideas.

Know Your Audience

A confident speaker must believe that the content of a speech will interest or satisfy a need of the audience. If your listeners are bored with your topic, you will sense it, and that will make you more nervous. If the audience is interested in the content of your speech, they will be attentive. They will provide you with nonverbal cues affirming that they are benefiting from, and even enjoying, your speech. The more they focus on what you say, the less attention they will pay to the specifics of your delivery.

At the same time, keep in mind the adage that it always looks worse from the inside. Because you feel nervous, you focus on your anxiety, exaggerate it, and become more nervous. Remember, though, your audience cannot see your internal state! Many times our students have lamented their nervousness after concluding a speech, only to learn that classmates envied them for being so calm and free from stage fright. The authors of a study of ninety-five speakers found that "untrained audiences are not very good at detecting the self-perceived anxiety of beginning speakers."[9] Even if you feel extremely nervous, then, your audience probably does not realize it. Knowing this should make you more secure and lessen your nervousness.

One of our students, Susan, wrote the following in her self-evaluation of her first graded classroom speech:

> Too fast, too rushed. I forgot 1/2 of it. Yuck! Yuck! Yuck! I used to think I was a good public speaker. People ask me to speak — I'm not going to do it ever again. I was so nervous my insides were on fire. I got up to give my speech, and I felt like I went "mind blank." I looked out at my audience, and I just knew they could feel my fear as I gripped the lectern and my mouth went dry.

The truth is that Susan experienced her speech in a radically different way than her instructor and classmates did. In fact, here are a few of her peers' comments about her speech:

"Wow! You seemed really relaxed! Your speech was organized, informative, and interesting."
"I really saw no weakness in the speech."
"Definitely the best speech given so far."
"She seemed to know what she was talking about."

When the instructor gave Susan her classmates' written comments, he asked her to write how she felt as she read them. Here is some of what Susan wrote:

> Dr. Grice. Excuse me, Dr. Grice. You've given me the wrong feedback sheets. These just can't be mine. This person, they all say, seemed relaxed, well organized, interesting, and informative. These just can't be mine. If only I could get with this person, maybe she could help me with my upcoming speech.... Are you sure, Dr. Grice, that these [critiques] are mine?

Susan concluded her reaction paper, "Wow! What you said is definitely true. It does look worse from the inside."

If Susan had not received feedback from her audience, she would probably have retained her high level of fear of public speaking, perhaps even avoiding future opportunities to share her ideas with others. By offering honest evaluation, her classmates let her see her speech from "the other side," lessened some of her anxieties, and motivated her to continue to improve her public speaking skills.

In addition, remember our earlier statement about the pervasiveness of nervousness. Your fellow classmates are also apprehensive about speaking to a group of people. Like you, they respect the person who makes public speaking look effortless. View your listeners as supportive individuals who want only the best for you. They know it's their turn next!

Know Your Speech

Knowing your strengths and weaknesses, speech principles, and your audience gains you little, however, if you do not know your speech. This textbook will acquaint you with strategies that will enable you to remember the ideas and supporting material of your speech. If you don't know what you want to say, you won't say it. If you think you will forget, you probably will. The more confident you are, the less nervous you will be.

Keep in mind that we certainly do not believe you need to memorize the entire speech. Yet, if you are well prepared, you should have memorized the outline of major points for your speech and the order in which they are to be presented. If you forget your notes, or drop them on the way to the lectern and cannot get them back into proper order, you should still be able to deliver the speech. (Take a minute to number your note cards, of course, and you have one less worry.)

Believe in Your Topic

If you are giving an informative speech, you must believe that what you say will benefit your listeners — that hearing your speech will improve them in some way. If you are giving a persuasive speech, be committed to the belief you attempt to instill or the action you attempt to initiate in your audience. Convincing your audience that they should listen to your speech is easier if you believe that the topic is important. The more you believe in your topic, the more earnestly you will want to inform or convince your listeners. In short, if you doubt the importance of the topic, you will feel and seem tentative.

View Speech Making Positively

Poet Howard Nemerov has said about perception, "What we know is never the object, but only our knowledge."[10] In other words, we do not experience the world directly, but only through the various labels we have attached to things and experiences. More and more we are discovering and investigating the mind's ability to affect behavior. Doctors have learned, for example, that patients' attitudes about their illnesses significantly affect their speeds of recuperation or their chances for recovery. Athletes have demonstrated improved performance after visualizing themselves competing successfully, and a study of 430 college speech students revealed lowered speech anxiety among those who visualized themselves delivering an effective presentation.[11]

If you view public speaking as a tedious chore, your audience will sense it from your vocal and physical delivery and perhaps even from your choice of speech topic. On the other hand, if you look upon public speaking as an opportunity, your positive attitude will help you control your nervousness. The following examples illustrate how you can replace negative thoughts with positive ones.

Replace the negative thought …
"When I get up to speak, my mind will probably go blank and I'll have nothing to say."

… with a positive thought
"I've rehearsed my speech and I have a good set of speaking notes. If I momentarily forget a point, I'll just look at my notecards and then continue."

Replace the negative thought …
"My audience will probably be bored with my speech."

"I found the topic of how 3-D films are made interesting, and my audience probably will too."

Thinking positively can help turn anxiety into anticipation. Genuine enthusiasm about the chance to speak in public will guide your choice of topic and will reveal itself to the audience through your lively delivery. Seek out opportunities to test and develop your communication skills. Volunteer for oral reports in classes; speak out at organizational meetings; offer to introduce a guest speaker at your club's banquet. This positive attitude, coupled with practice and experience, will help make you less apprehensive and more confident.

Project Control

Most people would probably agree that our attitudes help determine our behavior. Yet ample evidence suggests that our behavior also helps determine our attitudes. Daryl Bem's theory of self-perception states that if you perceive yourself acting one way, you will assume you feel that way.[12] Thus, if you want to feel confident, act confidently.

You convey your nervousness in a variety of ways: You shift your body weight from foot to foot, you play with your ring, you tap your fingers on the lectern, or you jingle the change in your pocket. Bem would argue, and we agree, that before you can change your perception that you are nervous, you must eliminate your nervous behaviors. In other words, project control. Stand erect, gesture emphatically, look directly at your audience, and speak forcefully. These are characteristics of the confident speaker. If you assume these behaviors, you should develop a feeling of confidence.

Test Your Message

Advertisers know the importance of message testing. Before they print an ad or air a commercial, they test the message to gauge public reaction. As a speaker, you can test your message by practicing your speech in front of friends. Can they restate your main points after listening to you? Do they find your supporting material believable? Is your vocal delivery lively and varied? Does your physical delivery detract from or reinforce your message? Answers to these questions will guide your subsequent practice sessions. The more confident you are that your message will achieve the desired effect on your audience, the less nervous you will be.

Practice

In discussing the previous coping strategies, we have implied the importance of practice. Practicing your speech is so important, however, that it deserves a separate category. Jack Valenti, former presidential speechwriter and now president of the Motion Picture Association of America, correctly observes, "The most effective antidote to stage fright and other calamities of speech making is total, slavish, monkish preparation."[13]

Your approach to your practice sessions will vary, depending on how your presentation develops. Sometimes you may practice specific sections of your speech that give you difficulty. But you should also practice your speech several times from start to finish without stopping. Too often when students mess up in practice, they stop and begin again. This is not a luxury you have when you address an audience, so as you practice, practice recovering from mistakes. Knowing that you can make it through your speech despite blunders in practice should make you more confident.

We also recommend that you occasionally practice your speech in an environment laden with distractions. Students who practice only in the silence of an empty classroom may not be prepared for distractions that arise when they actually deliver their speeches — for example, a student coming into the classroom during the speech, a lawnmower passing by the window, two students talking in the back of the room, or a classmate inadvertently pushing books off a desk. These distractions, especially those stemming from rudeness, should not occur; in reality, though, they sometimes do. Practicing with the television on in the background or in your room with noise in the hallway forces you to concentrate on what you are saying and not on what you are hearing. You develop poise as a speaker only through practice.

Learn from Experience

You've heard the expression, "Experience is the best teacher." Well, there's some truth in that folk wisdom. After your speech, assess your performance. What did you try that worked? What didn't work? How did you react when you walked to the front of the room,

Effective public speakers are not born, but learn from experience and develop their own distinctive speaking styles.
(SOURCE: © AP/Wide World Photos)

turned, and looked at the audience looking at you? Did you remember what you planned to say? Did you have trouble finding your place in your notes? How nervous did you feel? Did you get more or less nervous as the speech progressed? Your instructor will give you feedback to help you answer some of those questions; others you will need to answer for yourself, since you alone know the true answers. This is difficult for most of us to do. Especially if you think you made mistakes, your reaction may be to put the whole episode out of your mind. Resist this temptation. You can learn a great deal from reviewing your performance.

On the other hand, don't be too critical as you evaluate your performance. You will do some things well, and this should build your confidence. Other aspects of your speech you can improve, and you should work on these. Suppose, however, that you do encounter a serious problem: You completely lose your place, your mind goes blank, and so you bury your head in your notes and race to the end of your speech. Rather than trying to forget this, use it as a learning experience. Ask yourself why you forgot. Did you try to memorize your speech instead of speaking from a set of notes? Were your notes disorganized, or did they contain too little or too much information? Did you focus too much on your instructor and not enough on the entire audience? Once you face the problem and determine its cause, you will be better able to plan so that it does not occur again.

We have devoted this entire chapter to speaker nervousness because we know that it is a real worry for most people. We have suggested some techniques to help manage and channel your platform panic into a lively, enthusiastic speech. If you stop to think about public speaking for a moment, though, you will realize that the worst thing that could happen to you is that you might embarrass yourself. Stop and ask yourself, "Have I ever embarrassed myself before?" Unless you never leave your house, the answer to that question will be yes. You may have even embarrassed yourself so badly that you thought, "I'll never be able to face them again" or "I'll never live this down." But you do. The sun rises the next day. None of us is perfect, and it is unreasonable to expect perfection of ourselves or the people around us. So the best advice of all may be, "Keep public speaking in perspective." Your audience is made up of colleagues. They are pulling for you. Use this friendly atmosphere as a training ground to become a more effective speaker.

SUMMARY

The topic of this chapter is the widespread and normal phenomenon of speaker nervousness or stage fright. Caused by the body's preparation to perform to capacity, stage fright is a condition the speaker should try not to eliminate, but rather to control. We offer eleven suggestions for controlling nervousness: (1) Know how you react to stress. (2) Know your strengths and weaknesses. (3) Know basic speech principles. (4) Know your audience, so that you realize they are not expecting you to be perfect. (5) Without memorizing your speech, know what you plan to say in it. (6) Believe in your topic. (7) Have a positive attitude about speech making. (8) Project control. (9) Test your message prior to delivering it in class. (10) Practice as much as possible in a variety of situations. (11) Learn from your experience and keep public speaking in its proper perspective. Only by reflecting on your performance and on criticisms others give you can you develop as a speaker and deliver your next speech with less anxiety.

EXERCISES

1. Divide a sheet of paper into two columns. In Column A, list nervous symptoms you experience when speaking to a group of people. In Column B, list ways you can control each symptom. For example:

Column A	*Column B*
Play with ring on my finger, turning it while speaking	Remove ring before speaking
	Keep hands apart by gesturing more often

2. Again, divide a sheet of paper in two columns. In Column A, list ten of your strengths. In Column B, state how those strengths can benefit you in your public speaking. For example:

Column A	*Column B*
Like to read a lot	Have lots of ideas for possible speech topics
	Can put this skill to good use when I start researching my speech

3. Interview someone who occasionally gives public speeches asking how he or she handles speaker nervousness. Based on your interview, compile a list of suggestions for controlling nervousness. How does that list compare with the one in this chapter?

NOTES

1. Jerry Seinfeld, *SeinLanguage* (New York: Bantam, 1993) 120.

2. "Ask Them Yourself," in *Family Weekly* 28 January 1979: 2.

3. Wendy Wasserstein, "Streeping Beauty: A Rare Interview with Cinema's First Lady," *Interview* December 1988: 90.

4. Lee Iacocca with William Novak, *Iacocca: An Autobiography* (New York: Bantam, 1984) 16.

5. David Wallechinsky, Irving Wallace, and Amy

Wallace, *The Book of Lists* (New York: Morrow, 1977) 469-70.

6. John H. Greist, James W. Jefferson, and Isaac M. Marks, *Anxiety and its Treatment* (New York: Warner, 1986) 33.

7. Virginia P. Richmond and James C. McCroskey, *Communication: Apprehension, Avoidance, and Effectiveness*, 2nd ed. (Scottsdale, AZ: Gorsuch, 1989) 41-42.

8. Ed McMahon, *The Art of Public Speaking* (New York: Ballantine, 1986) 4.

9. Ralph B. Behnke, Chris R. Sawyer, and Paul E. King, "The Communication of Public Speaking Anxiety," *Communication Education* 36 (1987): 140.

10. Howard Nemerov, *Figures of Thought: Speculations on the Meaning of Poetry and Other Essays* (Boston: Godine, 1978) 19.

11. Joe Ayres and Theodore S. Hopf, "Visualization: A Means of Reducing Speech Anxiety," *Communication Education* 34 (1985): 321.

12. Daryl J. Bem, *Beliefs, Attitudes, and Human Affairs* (Belmont, CA: Brooks/Cole, 1970) 57.

13. Jack Valenti, *Speak Up with Confidence* (New York: Morrow, 1982) 19.

. . . [L]istening requires something more than remaining mute while looking attentive — namely, it requires the ability to attend imaginatively to another's language. Actually, in listening we speak the other's words.
~Leslie H. Farber

Listening

Chapter 4

*N*o wonder Dagwood is confused! Poor listening is the most common cause of message distortion, and when communication is serial, or composed of a chain of transactions between people, the cumulative message distortion can be severe. You probably remember playing the game of "telephone" when you were a child. Someone whispered a phrase or sentence to another person, who whispered it to the next one, and so on. The last person to receive the message then said it aloud. Usually, the final message bore little resemblance to what the first person whispered, and the group laughed at the outcome.

Unfortunately, examples of poor listening exist in areas of life where the results are often far from humorous. In fact, researchers estimate that U.S. businesses lose billions of dollars each year simply because of ineffective listening:

> Because of poor listening, letters have to be retyped; appointments have to be rescheduled; shipments have to be reshipped; individuals and organizations are unable to understand and respond to customers' and clients' real needs; employees feel ignored, disgruntled, and ultimately alienated from management; ideas are distorted by as much as 80 percent as they travel through communication channels; unnecessary conflicts disrupt operations and decrease production; and entire organizations are manipulated by propaganda techniques.[1]

Of course, ineffective listening is not confined to commercial settings. You can probably think of several examples of problems, or at least embarrassing situations, caused by your own ineffective listening. You went to the wrong building to begin registering for classes, or you went to the right place at the wrong time. You asked a question the teacher had just answered. You didn't realize that the biology exam covered your lab notes as well as the lecture material, or that a complete sentence outline of your informative speech on the causes and cures of snoring was due a week before you were scheduled to speak. You arrived at a party dressed in jeans and a flannel shirt only to find everyone else dressed formally.

Each day, you send and receive both oral and written messages. Of the four roles you perform — speaker, listener, writer, and reader — you spend more time listening than doing any of the other actions. College students, for example, spend approximately 53 percent of their communication time listening.[2] You listen to your parents, teachers, and friends; to television, radio, and movies; and to many other sounds around you. Yet, despite listening's monopoly on your time, you probably know less about this activity than about other forms of communication. While you have taken several courses teaching you to read and write, you have probably never taken a course in listening. In short, you have received the least training in what you do the most!

It will probably not surprise you, then, to learn that most of us are inefficient listeners. In fact, immediately after listening to your classmates' speeches, chances are high that you will remember, at most, only 50 percent of what you heard, and two days later only 25 percent. This doesn't surprise listening expert Robert Montgomery, who summarizes the sad plight of listening:

> Listening is the most neglected and the least understood of the communication arts. It has become the weakest link in today's communications system. Poor

Reprinted with special permission of King Features Syndicate

listening is a result of bad habits that develop because we haven't been trained to listen.

But there is good news, as Montgomery adds: "Fortunately, it is a skill that can be learned."[3] In this chapter we focus on the process, problems, and potential of listening in order to give you the tools to improve your listening skills.

◼ LISTENING VS. HEARING

Has the following ever happened to you? You are watching *The Late Show with David Letterman,* listening to a new Anita Baker tape, or doing economics homework when one of your parents walks by and tells you to put out the trash. Fifteen minutes later, that person walks back to find you still preoccupied with television, music, or homework, and the trash still setting by the door. Your parent asks, "Didn't you hear me?" Well, of course you did. You *heard* the direction to put out the trash just as you heard Letterman joking with Paul Shaffer, Anita Baker harmonizing, the dog barking at a passing car, and the air conditioner clicking on in the hall. You heard all of these things, but you might not have been *listening* to any of them.

What is the difference between **listening** and **hearing?** Listening differs from hearing in at least four important ways.

listening: the intermittent, learned, and active process of giving attention to aural stimuli.

hearing: the continuous, natural, and passive process of receiving aural stimuli.

Listening Is Intermittent.   Listening is not a continuous activity, but occurs only from time to time when we choose to focus and respond to stimuli around us. Hearing, on the other hand, is a continuous function for a person having normal hearing ability.

Listening Is a Learned Skill.   Listening must be taught and learned. Unless you were born with a hearing loss, however, hearing is a natural capacity for which you need no training. We hear sounds before we are born; fetuses grow accustomed to certain voices, noises, and music. For this reason, pediatricians advise new parents not to tiptoe or whisper around the infant they have just brought home from the hospital. The child is already used to a lot of noise and must grow accustomed to the rest of it. Throughout our lives, we hear sounds even as we sleep.

Listening Is Active.   Hearing means simply receiving an aural stimulus. The act of hearing is passive; it requires no work. Anytime the tiny bones of the inner ear are set in vibration, we are hearing something, and the activity requires no expenditure of energy. We can limit hearing only by trying to reduce or eliminate the sources of sound in the environment or by covering our ears.

Listening, in contrast, is active. It requires you to concentrate, interpret, and respond — in short, to be involved. You can hear the sound of a fire engine as you sit at your desk working on your psychology paper. You listen to the sound of the fire engine if you concentrate on its sound, identify it as a fire engine rather than an ambulance, wonder if it is coming in your direction, and then turn back to your work as you hear the sound fade away.

Listening Implies Using the Message Received.   Audiences assemble for many reasons. We choose to listen to gain new information; to learn new uses for existing information; to discover arguments for beliefs or actions; to assess those arguments; to laugh and be entertained; to provide emotional support for a speaker; to celebrate a person, place, object, or idea; and to be inspired.

We are attracted to novel ideas and information just because we may have some future use for that data. There are literally thousands of topics you could listen to; for example, characteristics of gangsta rap, converting to electronic currency, the history of blue jeans, adapting Japanese management style to American businesses, the ethics of criminal entrapment, preparing lemon-grass chicken, fantasy league football and baseball, the history of the National Cathedral, and the life of Arthur Ashe. Some of these topics might induce you to listen carefully. Others might not interest you, so you choose not to listen. The perceived usefulness of the topic helps determine how actively you will listen to a speaker. Listening implies a choice; you must choose to participate in the process of listening.

THE PROCESS OF LISTENING

In Chapter 1, we introduced the listener as one component of communication. Indeed, the listener is vital to successful communication; without at least one listener, communication cannot occur beyond the intrapersonal level. Remember that any time two people communicate, two messages are involved: the one that the sender intends and the one that the listener actually receives. As we discussed in Chapter 1, these messages will never be identical because people operate from different frames of reference and with different perceptions. As you examine the six steps in the process of listening shown in Figure 4.1, you will better understand this concept.

Receive

The first step in listening is to *receive* sounds. In face-to-face communication, we receive sound waves set in motion through the air by the speaker; on the telephone, those same sound waves are transmitted electronically. In both cases, the first step in listening to the speaker is receiving the sounds, the auditory stimuli. In other words, hearing is the first step in effective listening.

You may have heard people say, "I can't hear without my glasses." What they usually mean is that they hear better when they can clearly see the person speaking. Normally, we validate one sense by checking it against others. Thus, even if you recognize the voice of a classmate behind you asking a question, you are likely to turn around and look to make sure. At other times, we may use our senses of taste, smell, or touch to confirm or contradict the auditory message we have received.

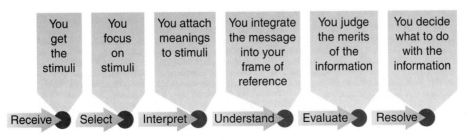

Figure 4.1 *The process of listening*

Some people unintentionally filter or leave out part of the stimulus. People with a hearing loss, for example, unintentionally filter parts of the messages around them. Whenever we filter, parts of the messages available to us will be lost.

Select

"Millions of items of the outward order are present to my senses which never properly enter into my experience. Why? Because they have no interest for me. My experience is what I agree to attend to."[4]
WILLIAM JAMES

Individuals *select* different stimuli from those competing for their attention, a phenomenon sometimes called selective perception. When the police gather reports from various witnesses to a traffic accident, they often find conflicting information. Each bystander's report will be shaped by where the person was standing or sitting, what the person was focusing on at the moment of impact, how the person was feeling, and a host of other factors. Each witness had a selective perception of the event.

In public speaking situations, the audience reacts in a similar way. One person in the audience may focus primarily on what speakers are saying, another on their tones of voice or their gestures, still another on what they are wearing, or even the distracting hum of the heating system. If you are intrigued by the speaker's accent, you have selected to focus on that element of speech delivery, and you will probably hear a slightly different speech than the person sitting next to you. You may even be distracted by internal noise, such as worrying about an upcoming chemistry exam or trying to resolve a conflict with your roommate. As William James said over 100 years ago, our view of the world is truly shaped by what we decide to heed.

Interpret

Not only do individuals choose differently among stimuli competing for their attention, they also *interpret* those stimuli differently. Interpreting is the process of decoding the message. When you interpret, you attach meanings to the cluster of verbal and non-verbal symbols the speaker provides — words, tone of voice, and facial expression, for example. At this stage, the listener is paying careful attention to those verbal and non-verbal symbols and their meanings. When a speaker introduced her speech on euthanasia, one listener heard "youth in Asia." Only after correcting this misinterpretation was the listener prepared to understand the speaker's message. As we noted in our discussion of the triangle of meaning in Chapter 1, the speaker's frame of reference must be similar to the listener's if communication is to be clear and effective.

Understand

Once you have decoded, or attached meanings to, a speaker's symbols, you begin fitting the message into your framework of existing knowledge and beliefs. To *understand* a speaker, you must consider both a message's content and its context. Is the speaker attempting to inform or persuade you? Is the speaker serious or joking? In short, what is the speaker trying to do?

It is easier to judge the context of communication when you listen to friends rather than to strangers. When you communicate with your friends, you can tell whether they are joking, upset, or teasing by their facial expressions or tones of voice, but you cannot always tell with strangers. You know your friends well and are more familiar with their cues. Communication from friends provides you cues to understand the context of the message. As you learn more about speakers, then, you enable yourself to understand their messages more accurately.

Evaluate

Before acting upon the message you have decoded and understood, you *evaluate* it. Evaluating is the process of judging both the reliability of the speaker and the quality and consistency of the speaker's information. If the speaker is someone you know, you reflect on the history of that person's interactions with you. Has the person ever tried to deceive you? Or does the speaker have a track record of honest, open communication with you? If the speaker is a stranger, you often gauge the person's credibility based on the non-verbal cues of communication. Is the speaker making eye contact with you? Does he or she speak fluently, without unnecessary pauses or filler words? Do the speaker's gestures and other body language seem relaxed and spontaneous? In short, does the person seem well prepared, confident, and sincere? If your answer to any of these questions is no, you may wonder whether the speaker has ulterior motives for speaking to you. As you evaluate the speaker's message, you decide whether you believe the data presented, and whether you agree or disagree with the position the speaker advocates.

Resolve

The final step in listening, resolving, involves deciding what to do with the information we have received. As listeners, we can *resolve* to accept the information, reject it, take action on it, decide to investigate further, or just try to remember the information so that we can resolve it later.

Obviously, we do not consciously go through and dwell upon each of these six steps each time we listen to someone. As the significance of the message increases for us, however, we become more involved in the process of listening — a point each speaker should remember.

▬ OBSTACLES TO EFFECTIVE LISTENING

Speakers and audience members should recognize some of the reasons why effective listening is so difficult. Learning to listen better is easier if you know what you're up against. For this reason, you need to identify the major obstacles to effective listening. We list and discuss five barriers to listening in this section.

Individuals must adapt their speaking and listening behaviors to cope with distractions in the communication environment.
(SOURCE: © Paul Chesley/ Tony Stone Images)

Physical Distractions

physical distractions: listening disturbances that originate in the physical environment and are perceived by the listener's senses.

Have you ever told someone that he or she was being so loud that you couldn't hear yourself think? If so, you were commenting on one obstacle to effective listening: physical distraction. **Physical distractions** are interferences coming to you through any of your senses, and they may take many forms: glare from a sunny window, chill from an air conditioner vent, or the smell of formaldehyde in your anatomy and physiology lab. We've even heard that to reduce physical distractions to its patrons, one New York restaurant has this sign at its entrance: "No cigars or Giorgio perfume in the main dining room." Like a diner whose enjoyment of a meal is spoiled by cigar smoke, you may have trouble focusing on the message of a speech on toxic waste if you concentrate on the speaker's outlandish clothing, on a PE class playing a vigorous game of touch football outside, or on the overpowering smell of after shave on the person near you.

Physiological Distractions

physiological distractions: listening disturbances that originate in a listener's illness, fatigue, or unusual bodily stress.

Physiological distractions have to do with the body. Any illness or unusual physiological condition is a potential distraction to effective listening. A bout of flu, a painful earache, or a sleepless night all place obvious and familiar limitations on our willingness and ability to listen.

Psychological Distractions

psychological distractions: listening disturbances that originate in the listener's attitudes, preoccupations, or worries.

Your attitudes also affect your listening behavior. **Psychological distractions,** such as a negative attitude toward the speaker, the topic, or your reason for attending a speech, can all affect how you listen. If you are antagonistic toward the speaker or the point of view the speaker is advocating, you may resist or mentally debate the statements you hear. If you are coerced to be in the audience, you may also be more critical and less open-minded about what is being said. In short, if you are concentrating on thoughts unrelated to what the speaker is saying, you will receive less of the intended message.

Factual Distractions

College students, who should be among the most adept listeners in our society, find that they are often hampered by **factual distractions,** such as listening disturbances caused by the flood of facts presented to them in lectures. You may be tempted to treat each fact as a potential test question. But this way of listening can pose problems for you. For example, have you ever taken copious notes in your Western civilization class only to find when you reread them that, although you have lots of facts, you missed the key ideas? Students and other victims of factual distractions sometimes listen for details, but miss the general point that the speaker is making.

factual distractions: listening disturbances caused by attempts to re-call minute details of what is being communicated.

Semantic Distractions

Semantic distractions are those caused by confusion over the meanings of words. Listeners may be confused by a word they have never before seen or heard, one they have seen in print but have never heard spoken, or a word the speaker is mispronouncing. If a student gave a speech about her native country, Eritrea, without showing that word on a visual aid, the typical American listener would probably begin wondering, "How do I spell that?" "Have I ever seen that word on a map before?" "Is this a new name for an established country?" "Is the speaker pronouncing correctly a word I've always heard mispronounced?" These thoughts divert you from the serious business of listening to a speech filled with new and interesting information. In Chapter 11, "Wording Your Speech," we will discuss some ways speakers can minimize misunderstandings about the meanings of words.

semantic distractions: listening disturbances caused by confusion over the meanings of words.

■ PROMOTING BETTER LISTENING

Once you understand the obstacles to effective listening, you can develop a plan of action to improve your listening behavior and that of your audience. A major theme of this book, as you no doubt are now aware, is that each party in the communication process has a responsibility to promote effective communication. Promoting better listening should be a goal of both the sender and the receiver of the message. How can you encour-age better listening?

As a speaker, you can use many of the suggestions in the following chapters to help your audience hear and retain your message. You enhance the audience's retention, for example, when you select your ideas carefully, organize your ideas clearly, support your ideas convincingly, word your ideas vividly, and deliver your ideas forcefully.

As a listener, you must also work hard to understand and remember the speaker's message. So far in this chapter we have examined the process of listening and have discussed the obstacles to effective listening. The following nine suggestions will help you become a more effective listener. As you master these suggestions, you will find yourself understanding and remembering more of what you hear.

<table>
<tr><td colspan="3">

KEY POINTS

Guidelines to Promote Better Listening
</td>
<td>

1. Desire to listen.
2. Focus on the message.
3. Listen for main ideas.
4. Understand the speaker's point of view.
</td>
<td>

5. Withhold judgment.
6. Reinforce the message.
7. Provide feedback.
8. Listen with the body.
9. Listen critically.
</td></tr>
</table>

Desire to Listen

Your attitude will determine, in part, your listening effectiveness. In this class you have the opportunity to learn a great deal of information from your classmates' speeches. Some topics will interest you; others, no doubt, will not. Good listeners, however, begin with the assumption that each speech can potentially benefit them. You may not find a speech on how financial institutions determine a person's credit rating of great interest right now. Nevertheless, the first time you apply for a loan you may be happy that you paid attention and prepared for your visit to the bank.

Some speeches you hear in this class will be excellently prepared and delivered; others will not. Again, good listeners can learn something from any speech, even if it is poorly prepared and awkwardly delivered. For example, you can determine what the speaker could have done to improve the poorly developed speech. This experience enables you to apply speech principles you have learned and to improve your own speaking.

In your class you may also have the opportunity to offer helpful suggestions to your colleagues who present speeches. You will want to listen carefully so that you can help them improve. If you have a genuine desire to listen to a speaker, you will understand and remember more.

Speakers can promote better listening by demonstrating early in their speeches how the information will benefit their listeners. Let your audience know quickly just why it is in their interest to listen carefully to your speech. We believe this step is so important that we discuss it in Chapter 9, "Organizing Your Speech," as one of the four steps of an effective speech introduction.

Focus On the Message

Your first responsibility as a listener is to listen attentively to the speaker's message. Yet, a speaker's message competes with other, often quite powerful, stimuli for your attention. One of us once conducted a seminar entitled "First Impressions — Lasting Impressions" in a large room adjacent to a hallway that was being painted. The smell of the paint became a powerful distraction for both speaker and audience. During the presentation, one of the audience members opened a door allowing outside air to freshen the room. In addition, the speaker moved from behind the lectern and enlivened his delivery by changing his speaking tone and using more varied gestures. In this situation, both the speaker and the audience worked together to focus more on the message and less on the distracting smell.

Often speakers themselves create distractions. They may play with change or keys in their pockets, dress inappropriately, sway nervously from side to side, use offensive language, or say "um" throughout their speeches. These quirks can be very distracting. We have had students, for example, who actually counted the number of "ums" in a speech. After a classmate's speech, they would write in their critiques, "You said 'um' thirty-one times in your speech." While this may have provided the speaker with some valuable feedback, we suspect these listeners learned little else from the speaker's message. You may not be able to ignore distractions completely as you listen, but you can try to minimize them.

As we discussed earlier, messages may be both verbal and nonverbal. For this reason, listeners should listen with their eyes as well as their ears. We have all heard someone begin a statement, "I'm not saying this to be critical, but. . ." That preface often reveals more about the speaker's intent than about the words that follow; usually, the person *is* being critical. When we perceive a discrepancy between a person's verbal and nonverbal messages, we tend to believe the nonverbal message, and this response may be justified. People are better at disguising their emotions with their words than with their bodies. You can often read body and voice cues to evaluate both what speakers think is important and their degree of commitment to what they are saying.

Speakers, of course, can help listeners focus on the message by eliminating distracting mannerisms and by incorporating nonverbal behaviors that reinforce rather than contradict their ideas. For example, appropriate gestures can make a speech easier to remember by describing objects, providing directions, and illustrating dimensions.

Listen for Main Ideas

You are familiar with the cliché that sometimes you can't see the forest for the trees; well, that saying applies to listening. A person who listens for facts often misses the main point of the message. While it is important to attend to the supporting material of a speech, you should be able to relate it to the major point being developed. As in the simple game of tic tac toe, in which the evolving strategy is most important, "Listening for just the facts is like paying attention to only one O or one X without seeing the relationship or pattern that is emerging. You'll get beaten every time."[5]

When listening to a speech, pay close attention to the speaker's organization of the material. The structure of a speech provides a framework for both speaker and listeners to organize the supporting points and materials of the speech. Speakers who clearly enumerate their key ideas and repeat them at several points in their speeches give their audience a better opportunity to be attentive listeners than do disorganized speakers. We discuss organizational techniques in Chapter 9.

Understand the Speaker's Point of View

As we discussed in Chapter 1, each of us has different referents for the words we hear or speak because we have different life experiences. These life experiences affect how we view our world.

Speaking in favor of agricultural programs that would preserve the family farm, our student Cathy tried to involve her audience in her speech by tapping their memories. She asked her classmates to think of the houses they grew up in and the memories created there.

> Think of Thanksgiving and Christmas gatherings. Think of slumber parties and birthday celebrations. Of how you changed your room as you moved from child to teenager to young adult. Think of your feelings as you left home to come to college, and of your feelings when you return to those comfortable confines.

After the speech several students said they were moved by Cathy's eloquence and passion. She had tapped memories important to them. Others in the audience, however, said they were unable to relate to the topic in the way the speaker intended. Several had grown up in more than one house. Some were in military families and had moved often. Still others said they had lived in rented townhomes or apartments. And a few commented that their childhood memories were not fond ones. Both speakers and listeners need to remember that different experiences shape and limit our understanding of another's message.

When speakers and listeners come from different cultures, the chances for misunderstanding increase. Differences in language, education, and customs challenge listeners to work especially hard at understanding the speaker's message and intent. These differences are often evident in today's multicultural classroom. Some foreign students, for example, come from educational environments that are more structured and formal than the typical American college classroom. They may interpret a speaker's casual dress and use of humor as an indication that the speaker is not serious about the speech. On the other hand, some American students may perceive the more formal presentations of some of their foreign counterparts as stiff and indicating a lack of interest in the topic. Understanding each other's frame of reference minimizes this distortion.

Speakers should do two things to clarify their points of view in speeches. First, explain early in the speech if you have some particular reason for selecting your topic, or some special qualifications to speak on the subject. If you choose to speak on radio formats because you work at your campus radio station or because you are a radio-television-film major, tell the audience a little about your background. If you are a registered gemologist and decide to speak on the subject of emeralds, be sure to tell the audience about your qualifications. Second, try to relate your subject to your listeners' frames of reference. Your use of technical jargon or complex explanations may limit their ability to listen effectively. Use examples and language your audience will understand.

Withhold Judgment

You have probably listened to some political debates and heard discussions of them afterwards. You and a friend may even have discussed the pros and cons of each candidate and differed over who won. What was important and memorable to you may have been quite different from what your friend found impressive. You may even have wondered if you had been watching the same debate.

In a sense, you and your friend did watch two different debates. Two people with contrasting perspectives receive two different messages while watching one communication event. You filtered what you heard through your set of beliefs and values. You began judging the candidates and the debate before it ever took place. This is quite common. Many of us have a problem withholding judgment. We hear something and immediately label it as right or wrong, good or bad. The problem is that once we do that, we cease to listen objectively to the rest of the message.

It is difficult for you to withhold judgment, of course, when you listen to a speech advocating a position you strongly oppose. The following list includes topics student speakers sometimes discuss: legalization of drugs, capital punishment, mandatory drug testing, abortion, flag burning, euthanasia, gun control, and hiring quotas. We suspect you have some fairly strong opinions on most of these issues. You may even find it difficult to listen to a speech opposing your view without silently debating the speaker. Yet, as you mentally challenge these arguments, you miss much of what the speaker is saying. If you can suspend evaluation until after speakers have presented and supported their arguments, you will be a better listener.

Reinforce the Message

Most Americans speak at rates between 125 and 190 words per minute. Those numbers may seem high to you, but consider the average speaking rates of the following people. You might think that Ronald Reagan, our oldest president when he began his first term, would have slowed his rate of speaking. In fact, he averages 170 words per minute.[6] Former president Jimmy Carter, often described as a plodding speaker, averages 160 words per minute. Bill Clinton averages 120 words per minute. Gene Shalit, the *Today* show's cantankerous movie critic, speaks very fast but very clearly. He rarely strays from an average rate of 190 words per minute. If you communicate simple ideas at a rate between 120 and 140 words per minute, your listeners may think you ill, reluctant, or uncertain.[7] Why? As listeners, we can process 400 to 500 words per minute. This means that, depending on the situation, we may be able to listen at a rate four times faster than a particular person speaks! As a result, we can get bored and move our attention back and forth between what the speaker is saying and some extraneous message, perhaps a personal problem that concerns us. Sometimes, the unrelated thought takes over and psychological noise, which we discussed earlier, drowns out the speaker's message. To be a better listener, you must make better use of this extra time.

You can fill some of this time and better focus on the message by mentally repeating, paraphrasing, and summarizing what the speaker is saying. You use *repetition* when you state exactly what the speaker has said. Consider, for example, a speaker who argues that a tuition increase is necessary to preserve educational excellence at your college or university. The first reason she offers is this: "A tuition increase will enable us to expand our library." If, after the speaker makes this claim, you mentally repeat her argument, you are using repetition to help you remember the speaker's message.

Using *paraphrase* is a second way of helping yourself remember the message. By putting the speaker's ideas into your own words, you become actively involved in message transmission. Suppose the same speaker offers this statement to justify one benefit of a tuition increase:

A tuition increase would generate funds that could be used to enhance our library facilities and resources. In the chancellor's budget proposal, one-third of the tuition increase would go directly to the library. The chancellor estimates that this would enable us to increase our library holdings of books, periodicals, and audiovisual resources by 10 percent. Also, projected construction would create at least twelve new study rooms.

Obviously, it would be difficult to restate the speaker's explanation word for word. Yet you could paraphrase and summarize her message this way:

A tuition hike would increase our library holdings by 10 percent and expand the number of study rooms by twelve.

You use *summary* when you condense what a speaker says. The above paraphrase includes summary as it leaves out some of the specific information the speaker presented. As a speaker concludes his or her message, you should recollect the key points of the speech. Your summary might be, for example: "A tuition increase will help us expand the library, increase the number of faculty, and renovate some of the older dormitories." By getting you actively involved in the communication process, repetition, paraphrase, and summary increase your chances of understanding and remembering the message.

Provide Feedback

A listener can enhance the communication process by providing feedback to the speaker. Although there is greater opportunity for *verbal* feedback in interpersonal and group environments, it is nevertheless also possible in public speaking contexts. The effective speaker will especially read the *nonverbal* cues of the audience to assist in the presentation of the speech. If you understand and accept the point of the speaker and nod in agreement, the speaker can move to the next idea. If you appear perplexed, that signal should prompt the speaker to explain the idea more fully before moving to the next point.

Listen with the Body

We listen with more than our ears. In a sense, we listen with our entire bodies. If, as your instructor lectures, you lean back, stretch your legs, cross your arms, and glance at a fellow classmate, you detract from your listening effectiveness. Part of listening is simply being physically ready to listen.

You can ready yourself for listening if you sit erect, lean slightly forward, and place both feet flat on the floor. As you listen, look at the speaker. As important as the message you hear is the message you see. Remember, you want to detect any nonverbal messages that intensify or contradict the speaker's verbal message.

Listen Critically

Even though listeners should understand a speaker's point of view and withhold judgment, they should nevertheless test the merits of what they hear. If you accept ideas and

Listeners' nonverbal feedback helps speakers adapt their messages and delivery to specific audiences. (SOURCE: © Mark Ludak, Impact Visuals)

information without questioning them, you are in part responsible for the consequences. If the speaker advocating a tuition increase quotes from the chancellor's budget proposal before it has even been submitted, you have every right to be skeptical. "Will the final budget actually earmark one-third of the tuition increase for library use? Will the board of regents accept the chancellor's proposal? Or is this all speculation?" Decisions based on incorrect or incomplete data are seldom prudent and sometimes disastrous.

Critical listeners examine what they hear by asking several questions: Is the speech factually correct? Are sources clearly identified, and are they unbiased and credible? Does the speaker draw logical conclusions from the data presented? Has the speaker overlooked or omitted important information? Speakers help listeners answer those questions by presenting credible information, identifying their sources, and using valid reasoning.

John Marshall, Chief Justice of the United States from 1801 to 1835, once stated, "To listen well is as powerful a means of communication and influence as to talk well." If you use these nine suggestions you will become a better listener.

SUMMARY

Poor listening costs American businesses billions of dollars yearly. The personal costs of poor listening include lost opportunities, embarrassment, financial losses, and, probably most important, lost time. We spend more time listening than we do involved in any other communication activity. Yet, ironically, we receive less instruction in listening than we do in reading, writing, or speaking. Luckily, we can teach and learn effective listening.

Listening differs from *hearing* in four ways. First, we listen only from time to time throughout the day, while hearing is continuous. Second, listening is a learned behavior, while hearing is a natural capacity for most people. Third, listening is active, hearing passive. Finally, listening implies doing something with the message received.

The complex act of listening contains six steps or phases. First, the listener *receives* sound stimuli from various senders or sources. Second, the listener *selects* particular parts of the total stimulus field for attention. Third, the listener *interprets* or decodes the message, attaching meanings to the various symbols received. The fourth step, *understanding*, involves matching the speaker's message with the listener's frame of reference. In the fifth step, the listener *evaluates* the reliability of the speaker and the speaker's message. Finally, after the reflection involved in the previous steps, the listener *resolves*, or decides what to do with, the information received.

Physical distractions from any part of the environment are one type of obstacle to effective listening. *Physiological distractions,* a second category, arise from conditions in the listener's body. A third obstacle is formed by *psychological distractions,* such as worry or preconceived attitudes toward the speaker or the message. *Factual distractions* are caused by our tendency to listen for small supporting details, even when we miss the main point the speaker is trying to make. Fifth and finally, listeners may be victims of *semantic distractions*, or confusion over the meanings of words.

Both speakers and listeners can contribute to effective listening in nine ways. First, listeners should develop a genuine desire to listen. Speakers promote this openness to listening by expressing a sincere desire to communicate. Second, listeners should focus on the speaker's message rather than on distracting elements of delivery. Speakers assist listening when they minimize or eliminate distracting behaviors and employ forceful delivery to underscore their messages. Third, listeners should listen for the speaker's main ideas. Speakers make this task much easier by careful speech organization. Fourth, listeners should try to understand the speaker's point of view. Speakers ought to reveal their credentials and explain their reasons for speaking on a particular topic. Fifth, listeners should withhold judgment about the speaker and the message until after hearing and considering both. Sixth, listeners should reinforce the speaker's message by using repetition, paraphrase, and summary. Seventh, effective listeners should provide the speaker with feedback. Speakers should adapt to those responses. Eighth, listeners should be ready to listen with the whole body. Finally, though we have urged you to listen objectively to avoid prejudging speakers and their ideas, effective listening is ultimately critical listening. Gauging the credibility of the speaker's information is easier if the speaker has presented logically supported ideas and has cited credible sources.

EXERCISES

1. On a sheet of paper, list your listening strengths and weaknesses. Beside each weakness, indicate specific strategies that could minimize or eliminate the problem.
2. Listen to a speech or lecture, paying particular attention to the five types of distractions discussed in this chapter. Give examples of distractions you encountered. What could you or the speaker have done to minimize these interferences? Discuss these options.

NOTES

1. Meada Gibbs, Pernell Hewing, Jack E. Hulbert, David Ramsey, and Arthur Smith, "How to Teach Effective Listening Skills in a Basic Business Communication Class," *The Bulletin of the Association for Business Communication* 48.2 (1985): 30.

2. Larry Barker, Renee Edwards, Connie Gaines, Karen Gladney, and Frances Holley, "An Investigation of Proportional Time Spent in Various Communication Activities by College Students," *Journal of Applied Communications Research* 8 (1980): 101-9.

3. Robert L. Montgomery, *Listening Made Easy* (New York: AMACOM, 1981) n.p.

4. William James, *The Principles of Psychology*, vol. 2 (Cambridge: Harvard UP, 1981), 380. (This is a reprint of the original 1890 Henry Holt edition.)

5. Michael Cronin, Rick Olsen, and Jan Stahl, *Mission Possible: Listening Skills for Better Communication*, computer software, Oral Communication Program, Radford University, Radford, VA, 1992.

6. Lyle V. Mayer, *Fundamentals of Voice and Diction*, 8th ed. (Dubuque, IA: Brown, 1988) 178.

7. Lyle V. Mayer, *Fundamentals of Voice and Diction*, 10th ed. (Dubuque, IA: Brown, 1994) 229.

e have all heard stories so amazing that they seem to take on the qualities of legends. One well-known example is that of Abraham Lincoln and the "Gettysburg Address." As the story goes, Lincoln was such a fine man and such a great thinker that he wrote his now-famous speech on some scraps of paper while on the train to Gettysburg, Pennsylvania.[1] Repeated for many, many years, the story seemed plausible because the speech is only 272 words long. Like many other stories that seem too good to be true, however, this one is false. Today, we have a better picture of how Lincoln composed the "Gettysburg Address" and why it is as brief as it is.

Lincoln was asked to speak at a ceremony dedicating a memorial cemetery for soldiers who had died in the Civil War battle at Gettysburg. He was not to be the main speaker on this occasion, however: Edward Everett, the most famous orator of his day, had top billing. Everett spoke for an hour and fifty-seven minutes to an audience estimated at between 15,000 and 50,000 people seated and standing outdoors.[2] Afterward, Lincoln rose and, holding two pieces of paper, spoke ten sentences in less than three minutes.[3] Why were Lincoln's remarks so brief?

The answer is that Lincoln had done some excellent analysis of the audience and the speaking occasion. He knew, first, of Everett's reputation for making very long speeches. Lincoln undoubtedly knew that if he also delivered a long speech, he would lose either much of his audience's attention or even their presence. Remember, the speech was to be given outdoors, with audience members free to leave whenever they chose!

Second, Lincoln knew, as did his audience, that he was not the featured speaker on this occasion and was, therefore, not expected to make a major address. He had been asked only two weeks ahead of time to make "a few appropriate remarks." Everett, on the other hand, was invited six weeks earlier, and the date for the dedication had actually been changed to fit his schedule. Even though he was president, Lincoln was losing popular support by 1863 and knew that a long speech would seem an inappropriate challenge to the importance of Everett's.

The third and final reason for the length of Lincoln's "Gettysburg Address" was that he had been anticipating for some time an occasion for an important speech on the same theme. The words of the speech began to take shape in his mind long before he wrote them on paper. For example, Lincoln began his speech at Gettysburg by saying, "Four score and seven years ago our fathers brought forth on this continent a new nation, conceived in liberty and dedicated to the proposition that all men are created equal." Yet Thomas Scheidel points out that, in informal remarks four months before delivering the "Gettysburg Address," Lincoln had said:

> How long ago is it? — eighty-odd years since, on the Fourth of July for the first time in the history of the world a nation by its representatives, assembled and declared as a self-evident truth, that "all men are created equal."... Gentlemen, this is a glorious theme, and the occasion for a speech; but I am not prepared to make one worthy of the occasion.[4]

Making speeches "worthy of the occasion" requires meticulous audience analysis today, just as it did in Lincoln's time. Lincoln's careful audience analysis helped him decide the topic, length, and scope of his remarks at Gettysburg. Smart speakers today must also conduct careful listener analysis.

Every speech in a college public speaking class such as this may be considered a speech of introduction. That is, each speech introduces new facets of your personality and builds on your relationship with the audience. As you and your classmates select the topics for your speeches, keep in mind that the most effective speeches will be those on subjects in which you are genuinely interested. Each topic that you consider interesting or valuable enough to speak on says something about you as a person. Even if your instructor assigns the topics, your approach to the subject will be unique and will reveal aspects of your personal values and your personality. Yet the phrase "public speaking" always implies the presence of an audience. Public speaking is an audience-centered, not speaker-centered, activity. To be a successful speaker you must learn to be an audience-centered speaker. How can you accomplish this?

An audience-centered speaker must develop three important approaches:

1. Recognize your place as part of the audience.
2. Respect your listeners.
3. Recognize and act on audience feedback.

First, you must recognize your own place as part of the speech audience. This means that the topics you are genuinely interested in hearing about probably reflect the interests of some other people in the classroom. You must also be ready to admit that you are only one part of the total audience, a fact that should make you want to learn as much as possible about the other parts.

Second, as an audience-centered speaker, you will respect your listeners, as we mentioned in discussing ethics in Chapter 2. Respect and care for the audience means wanting to improve them by providing interesting or useful information. Respect also means recognizing and appreciating their values. In addition, consideration for the audience means trusting the opinions and advice of individual audience members. If you honor the worth of your listeners, you will value their questions and suggestions about your speech. This, in turn, leads to a third and final aspect of audience-centeredness: recog-

Reprinted by permission of UFS, Inc.

nizing and acting on the feedback from your audience, whether that feedback is verbal or nonverbal.

How can you as a speaker better relate to your audience? You may consider the ways in which you as an individual are part of various audiences. To what magazines do you subscribe, for example? What newspaper do you read? What television shows do you make it a point to watch? What are your favorite clubs and restaurants? What station is your car radio tuned to right now? Your answers to these questions place you in several different audiences.

Television is a particularly interesting place to study various audiences. Notice, for example, what your public broadcasting station programs the next time it holds pledge week. Carlos Santana's *Sacred Fire Live in Mexico?* Linda Ronstadt's *Canciones de mi Padre?* A superb production of African-American playwright Lorraine Hansberry's *A Raisin in the Sun?* Award-winning documentaries? Concerts by musicians your parents like and remember? Classic films featuring Bette Davis, Cary Grant, or Humphrey Bogart? In each case, the PBS affiliate is trying to attract different segments of an audience it believes will benefit from public broadcasting, including people who may seldom watch PBS. In the same way, speakers attuned to their audience members will try to discover and cultivate interests their listeners already have as well as to challenge them with new, useful topics.

We believe audience analysis is a process that shapes and molds the preparation, delivery, and evaluation of any well-thought-out public speech. In other words, audience analysis occurs before, during, and after the act of speaking. Let's consider more closely how this process works.

■■■■ AUDIENCE ANALYSIS *BEFORE* THE SPEECH

You will spend more time analyzing your audience before you speak than during or after your speech. Your speech may last only five or ten minutes, for example. Yet if you care about doing well, your audience analysis before the speech will take more than five or ten minutes.

Your public speaking class is a special type of audience and provides you with unique challenges and opportunities. At the beginning of the semester or quarter, you may know few if any of your classmates. As with any general, unfamiliar audience you are preparing to address, you initially analyze your classroom audience by active sleuthing as well as by using your own common sense. As you prepare your first speech, you could ask around about people's knowledge of or interest in a particular subject area. This is a good way to gauge your listeners' interest when you still do not know them well.

On the other hand, this class provides you the rare opportunity to "live" with your audience for the duration of the course. From the comments they make in and outside of class, from the questions they ask other student speakers or your instructor, and from their nonverbal feedback while listening to classroom speeches, you will gradually assemble an increasingly accurate portrait of this group of people. They will disclose, or you will deduce, information about their beliefs, values, interests, likes, and dislikes. Your audience analysis will be a semester- or quarter-long process, and by the time you deliver your final speech in the class, your audience analysis should be both easier and more accurate than it was at the beginning of the term.

Your first step as a speaker is to discover and evaluate as many specific characteristics of your audience as possible. **Demographics** is the term for those characteristics. Discovering the specifics about your audience will help you answer the question, "Who is my target audience?"

demographics: characteristics of the audience, such as age, gender, ethnicity, education, religion, economic status, and group membership.

Demographic analysis helps you tailor a message to a specific audience. You will never know everything about your listeners, and so you will make generalizations from the information you do know. One note of caution is in order, however: Be careful not to turn these generalizations into stereotypes about audience members. This will undermine your speech-making efforts. For example, we have observed speakers who assumed that audiences of similar demographic makeup inherently have similar interests. They selected topics they thought would fit those groups. Sometimes the audience accepted the speech favorably; other audiences perceived some speeches as patronizing or even insulting.

Some topics may be appropriate to only one type of audience; most subjects, however, can have broader appeal. A speech on the Seneca Falls Declaration of Sentiments is not just a women's topic — it could be informative to both men and women. A speech on gender bias in language can also have wide appeal. The solvency of the social security system may be of immediate concern to someone approaching retirement, but with some creative thinking you can make it interesting to anyone who is a taxpayer or who plans to retire some day. The economic plight of the American farmer should interest not only the agriculture major but also anyone who eats.

The function of education is to introduce us to new ideas and information. As a speaker, you defeat that goal when you stereotype an audience and choose only topics you think they will find familiar and comfortable. As a listener, you similarly undermine the goal of education when you tune out speeches on topics you do not find immediately interesting.

Successful speakers avoid stereotyping their audiences, but view them as collections of individual listeners.
(SOURCE: © 1993, Comstock, Inc.)

audience segmenta-
tion: the strategy of targeting a speech primarily
toward one portion of the
total audience.

Sometimes speakers choose to speak to only one segment of a larger audience, a strategy called **audience segmentation** or audience selection. For example, if you know that some of your listeners love to travel but are on tight budgets, you could inform them about the option of becoming airline couriers. An informative speech on the dangers of heatstroke and heat exhaustion might be appropriate for athletes in your audience. If you know there are cigarette smokers in your class, they are an obvious target for a persuasive speech on the hazards of smoking. But smokers are common targets lately, so part of your audience analysis needs to consider their prior exposure to your message and their willingness to listen objectively.

In each of these cases, your target audience is a subgroup of the audience as a whole; you direct your speech to them, hoping that others will also be interested or find your information useful. Notice, though, that even this strategy requires careful audience analysis. You must be sure that your target audience does exist, and that it is sufficient in size to justify giving them your primary focus. Generally, the more you know about your audience, the more secure you will be and the better speech you will deliver.

Seven of the most common characteristics you will want to analyze about your potential audience are age, gender, ethnicity, education, religion, economic status, and group membership. You will not always be able to learn this much information about your audience. Keep in mind, however, that the more you know, the better prepared you will be to present a successful speech.

Age.

"Communicating with college students is always somewhat of a challenge. It is not that I have too much difficulty understanding your changing expressions and attitudes. It is that I forget what you never saw." **TERRY SANFORD, FORMER U.S. SENATOR**[5]

One of the most obvious concerns you have as you research your audience is their age. You may need to find out not only what the average age of your audience is, but also what the age range will be. Your public speaking class may include first-year college students, people returning to college to change careers, and others pursuing interests after retirement. People who are eighteen to twenty years old today relate to the stock market crash of 1929, World War II, and the assassination of John F. Kennedy only as important topics of history. While that means that they may be eager to learn more about those topics, it also means they may not understand most casual references to these. If you compare the long gasoline lines of 1973 to food rationing during World War II, an audience of eighteen-year-olds won't remember either of those events. Ask a college classroom audience today, "Do you remember where you were on July 20, 1969, when Neil Armstrong stepped onto the moon's surface?" and only some of your listeners will have an answer. Many in your audience were not yet born. To make a clear speech on one of the preceding topics, a speaker must use supporting materials that are familiar to the audience, and age is one of the most obvious influences on the audience's frame of reference.

Gender. The next factor you need to consider in your audience analysis is gender. It is obviously easier to determine gender than age. Some students run into difficulties with stereotyping when they take gender into consideration for speech making, however. For example, we remember college men who would deliver speeches with purposes such as "to inform you girls about the rules of football so that you don't drive your boyfriends crazy by asking silly questions when you watch a game with them." Most women today would listen to such a speech only under protest.

Yet even today what seems to be consideration for the gender of audience members sometimes turns out to be disguised sexism. We remember a speech informing women how to change a flat tire. While a speaker with genuine safety concerns might be able to deliver such a speech effectively, this particular speaker patronized the women in his audience by repeatedly talking down to them: "Take off your pretty little high heels and put on the pair of running shoes I told you to put in the trunk." "Cover up your fancy little dress with that work shirt I told you to carry in the trunk." Women in the class bristled at the speaker's suggestion that they didn't know enough to change a tire.

Women can be equally guilty of sex role stereotyping. Helen, a student of ours, selected microwave technology as her speech topic. When discussing the advantages of microwave ovens, she said that "the guys" in the audience should seriously consider purchasing a microwave oven because it makes cooking easier. She was surprised at some of the responses her audience made after her speech. Some males were offended that the speaker in effect labeled men cooking klutzes. One man said he was a gourmet cook. Some females objected to Helen's assumption that they liked to cook or that they were good cooks. "Just because I'm female, does that mean I am supposed to enjoy cooking?" Helen could have avoided these reactions had she not stereotyped her audience according to gender. She could have phrased her statement, "Anyone who wants to make cooking easier and faster should seriously consider purchasing a microwave oven."

As these examples show, speakers make a mistake if they stereotype listeners according to their gender. You would be wise to *disregard* the advice found in one college public speaking text published in the mid-1960s:

> Generally, women are more interested than men in subjects related to the feminine gender, such as women's clothing, cosmetics, housework, the rearing of children, the local ladies' aid society, home decoration, etc. On the other hand, men show strong masculine interests in rough competitive sports like football. More than women, men tend to enjoy technical and scientific subjects, particularly those related to mechanics, electronics, and engineering. Since more men than women serve as chief breadwinners for their families, they are more apt to be interested in matters pertaining to occupations and professions — but remember the possible exceptions.[6]

Today, those "possible exceptions" are ordinary and routine. As society continues to remove barriers based on gender, gender-specific topics will become fewer. Audience-centered speakers need to remember that.

Ethnicity. Today the college classroom, like most other segments of American life, is increasingly multicultural. Our differences simultaneously strengthen and threaten to divide us. The truth of the "melting pot" image of America is that no group melted completely, but neither did any resist melting to some degree. Australian Robert Hughes offers an alternative view of the United States' many cultures: "Reading America is like scanning a mosaic. If you look only at the big picture, you do not see its parts — the distinct glass tiles, each a different color. If you concentrate only on the tiles, you cannot see the picture."[7]

Ethnicity means the classification of a subgroup of people who have a common cultural heritage with shared customs, characteristics, language, history, and so on. Members of an ethnic group may share a collective heritage and exhibit strong ethnic pride;

speakers appropriately tap these common experiences and feelings as they construct their speeches for audiences having similar ethnic backgrounds. For example, John Jacob, president of the National Urban League, spoke to an audience of African Americans and observed: "Too often, we approach racial issues in a conceptual vacuum. We take a historical view. We forget that while most Americans' forebears came to this nation seeking freedom and opportunity, ours came in chains and were enslaved and oppressed."[8] Jacob's statement was entirely appropriate for his audience, yet he would not have said the words "our forebears" were he speaking, for example, to listeners of diverse ethnic backgrounds.

As with the issue of gender, speakers should avoid ethnic stereotypes. Never assume that because individuals share the same ethnicity they also share similar experiences and attitudes. If you have a working-class Irish Catholic ancestry, do not assume that others having Irish surnames are working-class or Catholic. Two people of the same ethnicity may have diverse attitudes, interests, and experiences because of differences in their ages, education, income levels, and religion.

Education.   The educational level of your audience affects not only what subjects you can choose, but also how you approach those particular subjects.

> John, a computer and information sciences major and a math whiz, wanted to deliver an informative speech on the binary number system. His initial outlines for the speech focused on binary theory and Boolean algebra, abstract topics that fascinated him. He planned to discuss the concept of binary existence and to demonstrate some complicated mathematical operations. Yet he knew from conversations he had overheard that more than a few classmates were struggling with their math classes. As a result, he refocused his speech, demonstrating simple conversions from decimal to binary numbers and emphasizing the application of such math in computer programming and CD technology. Audience questions after his speech showed that John met his goals without intimidating or talking down to his audience.

Like John's audience, the college students in your class have a variety of educational backgrounds. Some may have attended private schools, had home schooling, or earned graduate equivalency degrees after interruptions in their high school educations. Others may have lived and studied overseas. Smart speakers will find out as much as they can about the levels and types of education their listeners have.

Remember, also, that education can be informal as well as formal. Just as a high school diploma is unfortunately no guarantee of a solid educational background, listeners who have not completed high school or college are not necessarily uneducated. They may in fact have a wealth of "book" knowledge obtained through personal reading and study, as well as specialized practical knowledge and training.

If you have the opportunity, find out not only what your audience knows about a potential speech topic, but also whether audience members have experience relevant to that topic. The speaker in the following example put such knowledge to good use:

> Matt, a movie buff, decided to speak on how to audition for a movie. He went to the library, prepared a research bibliography, and began collecting information. The week before he was to give his speech, he learned that Sarah, a classmate

and drama major, had auditioned for a role in a movie that was shot in town last summer. Matt decided to talk with Sarah about the experience. Although she was not cast in the part, Sarah talked excitedly about her auditioning experience. This information helped Matt fill in some of the gaps in his research. In addition, mentioning Sarah's experience in his speech connected the topic to the audience and made it seem more immediate.

Religion.   Your college public speaking class may contain members of various Protestant denominations, Catholics, Jews, Muslims, Hindus, Buddhists, and members of other religious groups, as well as agnostics and atheists. Native American classmates may have religious beliefs with which you are not familiar. Students from other countries may also practice religions you do not know about, or they may practice familiar religions in a different way. Even among people who belong to the same denomination, religion will be very important to some and relatively unimportant to others. You have formulated your religious beliefs, whatever they are, over a period of time and you may feel defensive about those beliefs when they are challenged.

Stereotyping people on the basis of what you know of their religious views is as potentially inaccurate and harmful as making generalizations based on other demographic characteristics. Do all Catholics oppose birth control and the ordination of women as priests? Do all Jews observe Hanukkah and Yom Kippur, or observe them in the same way? Do all Protestants interpret scripture in the same manner? Clearly, the answer is no, and this should remind you of the limitations of simply finding out the religious denominations represented in your audience. If your audience's religious views are truly important to a topic you are considering, you will need to find out more about the beliefs behind the denominational labels they prefer.

Economic Status.   Economic status is another key factor affecting audience attitudes and behaviors. If a family earns barely enough to subsist, they will probably be more concerned with filling basic life needs than with social or status needs. For that reason, they may readily relate to a speaker who advocates expanded health care benefits and automatic cost-of-living adjustments. They may be more receptive to a progressive income tax than to a flat-rate sales tax on products and services. Analyses of survey data and voting behavior suggest that, generally, the higher the income of a family, the more conservative its political attitudes. Even though many students in your class may not yet have significant incomes, their political attitudes are often similar to those of their parents. Just don't assume that all families who have substantial wealth hold conservative views.

Judging the range of incomes of your classmates' families may be difficult. Certainly, it would be impolite to ask. However, you can probably locate or construct several general profiles of the typical students at your college, as the following speaker did.

For her first informative speech, Julie decided to discuss demographics of students at her college. Her primary sources were student profiles based on registration surveys released by the administration. This proved to be a subject her classmates enjoyed because it was about them and their friends. Some of the information Julie presented was surprising but seemed reasonable; other items were so funny that they seemed to be mistaken. Julie's research provided her information to analyze her own classroom audience. In addition, it helped her classmates in their audience analysis for future speeches.

If you speak on significant national concerns, consult public opinion surveys on those issues. Such polls categorize responses according to several demographic characteristics, and one of them is often income.

Overall, be realistic, be fair, and be sensitive when choosing topics dealing with economic issues. We remember one student who was offended when a speaker said that students shouldn't go home for spring break but should travel with friends to different parts of the United States to expand their historical and cultural knowledge. The offended student argued that some students simply did not have that option. They needed to work in order to remain in college. Speeches that urge college students to consider investing in the stock market or in real estate usually ignore one important fact: Most college students do not have money to spend for these purposes. On the other hand, we have observed student speakers generate lively audience interest on topics such as how to select an excellent yet inexpensive wine, summer employment opportunities at national parks and historic sites, and how to negotiate the price of a new or used car. Although money may be of greater concern to some people than to others, few people want to spend money needlessly.

Group Membership.   Today we join groups in order to spend time with others who enjoy our hobbies and pastimes, to learn more about subjects that can help us, or to further our political and social goals. Many of these groups are voluntary, such as the IBM computer users club, the art guild, the karate club, Amnesty International, the Young Democrats, the Young Republicans, honor societies, and social fraternities or sororities. We may also belong to some groups — labor unions and professional associations, for example — because we are required to in order to get or keep jobs or special licenses.

Political parties are also important groups. Knowing your listeners' political affiliations can be particularly helpful as you prepare persuasive speeches. How you develop your persuasive appeal, as well as the supporting material you select, will reflect assumptions you have made about your audience. You can make an educated assumption, for example, that an audience composed mainly of Republicans will accept statements from Republican sources more readily than from Democratic ones. We usually identify with a political party because of its positions on significant issues, and it shouldn't be too hard for you to locate positions associated with key political parties. Both major parties prepare position papers on key issues. Newspapers, magazines, and electronic media gather polling data. Publications such as the *Gallup Poll Monthly* may provide useful information as well.

You can also presume that audience members who belong to the Sierra Club, Greenpeace, the Nature Conservancy, or the Audubon Society have environmental concerns. Members of People for the Ethical Treatment of Animals, the World Wildlife Federation, and the Animal Liberation Front share a concern for animal welfare. Yet some of those groups have diverse goals and different methods of achieving them. If you are speaking to an organization — local, regional, or national — your audience analysis will require you to research the nature of that group as thoroughly as you can.

Analyze Audience Needs

Demographic analysis is not an end in itself; you waste your time if you do not move beyond discovering the characteristics of your audience. Some of the previous demographic items may be irrelevant to the topic you choose for a classroom speech; others may be vital. Your task is to discover the significant items and then explore them more completely. Once you have considered the age, gender, ethnicity, educational background, religion, economic status, and group affiliations of your listeners, you will be in a better position to determine what they need or what motivates them. One particular model, Maslow's hierarchy, will get you thinking about audience needs in an organized way.

Maslow's Hierarchy Defined.   The sociologist and psychologist Abraham Maslow (1908-1970) is best remembered for a model of human needs commonly referred to as **Maslow's hierarchy.**[9] Hierarchy means an arrangement of items according to their importance, power, or dominance. Maslow's thesis was that all human needs can be grouped into five categories, based on the order in which they must be filled.[10] These categories, represented in Figure 5.1, are (1) physiological needs, (2) safety needs, (3) belongingness and love needs, (4) esteem needs, and (5) self-actualization needs. As a public speaker, you should be aware of the needs dominating any particular audience you address. To do that you must consider the five categories of needs in more detail.

The *physiological,* or *physical, needs* refer to basic human requirements for water, food, and sleep. These needs are the most basic and are ordinarily satisfied before any of the others. As Maslow and others have observed, hungry people don't play; in other words, we can occupy ourselves with trivial matters only as long as we have the luxury of taking our food, drink, and rest for granted. Maslow included sex among the physiological needs because, while people can live without sexual contact, sex is necessary for the survival of the species.

After those physiological needs have been largely met, new categories of needs begin to emerge to concern us: the *safety needs.* This category includes everything that contributes to the "safe, orderly, predictable, lawful, organized world" upon which we depend.[11] Having safe roofs over our heads and reliable transportation obviously con-

Maslow's hierarchy: a model of five basic human needs — physical, safety, social, esteem, and self-actualization — in an ordered arrangement.

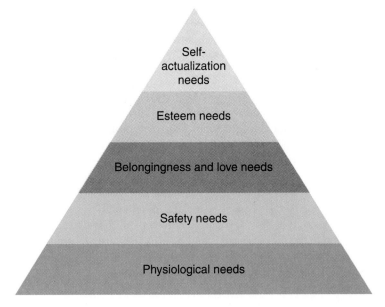

Figure 5.1 *Maslow's hierarchy of needs*

tribute to the predictable routines of our lives. These and any other items necessary to keep us from physical or mental harm make up the safety needs.

Once we feel relatively secure about a predictable, orderly world, we begin to look to the people around us — friends, spouses, children, parents — and our relationships with them. The third category of Maslow's needs, the *belongingness and love needs*, provides us with a sense of community, of fitting in. According to Maslow, the precise group we choose does not matter. Members may be colleagues at work, a group of people we see socially, friends at church, our family members, or even members of an antisocial gang. What matters is that we all need to feel that we belong to a group of some sort, and that we give affection to and receive affection from those people. Every human needs human contact.

From the people with whom we associate, each of us forms a picture of our worth or value. With his fourth category of needs, the *esteem needs*, Maslow reminds us that we all need reasonably high self-evaluation. We all need a pat on the back from time to time. The people around us often satisfy this need: the boss who gives us a promotion, a compliment, or a bonus of some kind; or the teacher who rewards our work with high grades or praise for our effort and improvement. Some of the time, of course, we master things on our own, such as speaking a foreign language, learning a computer program, or playing a musical instrument, and these achievements give us feelings of competence. But such feelings are confirmed and validated when other people recognize and appreciate them in us.

Once we have achieved reasonably high self-evaluation in the endeavors that are important to us, we are motivated by the fifth and highest level of Maslow's categories of needs. *Self-actualization,* or self-fulfillment, means becoming what you were destined to become. The athlete must compete; the novelist must write; the pianist must play music; the mechanic must fix things. When Marlon Brando said in the movie *On the Waterfront,* "I could have been somebody, I could have been a contender," he was revealing a self-actualization need of Terry Malloy, the dockworker character he was portraying.

Many people live their lives without reaching their self-actualization goals. In fact, reaching the goal may be less important than trying. Self-actualization needs are the "carrot" we hold ahead of ourselves to keep us working toward a goal. A good way to identify your own self-actualization needs is to imagine that you have reached the end of your life and you are reflecting, "I wish that I had…." The ways you complete that sentence will reveal the range of your own self-actualization needs.

The Importance of Maslow's Hierarchy.   But what does this mean for you in your public speaking class? How does Maslow's hierarchy apply to your classroom audience? We can show you several ways to make the hierarchy work for you.

First, the people sitting around you in class probably already have most of their physiological and safety needs satisfied. If not, they would be working at a job, or a second job, in order to provide these life necessities for themselves and their families. This does not mean that you cannot appeal to them on the physiological or safety needs levels. You could certainly adapt a speech to your audience by targeting those concerns. If you alert listeners to the harms of passive smoking, dangerous food additives, or potentially deadly drug interactions, for example, you move them to focus on basic issues of survival. In fact, no matter how prosperous and healthy they are, everyone in class would likely be interested in a topic showing them how to save money or demonstrating the health hazards of certain products or practices.

Second, if your classmates are typical college undergraduates, they are probably interested in being well liked and in fitting in. In other words, Maslow's third category, social needs, are extremely important at this point in their lives. If many or most of the people in your class are in their first year of college, their self-esteem may depend partly upon whether they succeed or fail in college, and speeches on scholastic success may easily hold their attention.

Finally, although many college students are unsure of the careers they will undertake upon graduation, most people have formed or are forming self-actualization needs by the time they are in their teens or twenties. Older students may be reassessing and reformulating their self-actualization needs. Those goals are changeable and will adapt as the individual discovers new talents, interests, and abilities. For that reason, a college-age audience is likely quite receptive to speeches showing how various topics can provide personal rewards or self-fulfillment.

It is critical for you to understand, however, that you cannot easily categorize your listeners with a specific set of needs. In fact, as Maslow admits, all of us probably have unmet needs at each of the five levels. We move from one level to another more frequently than we suspect. *Your challenge as a speaker is to identify and emphasize audience needs that are relevant to your topic.*

For example, if you feel secure in your surroundings, you may take your safety needs for granted. However, if you read in your school newspaper reports of several nighttime assaults on campus, your concern for your own and others' safety will increase. This concern for personal safety may not be on your mind as you walk to your classes during the day, but it may surface as you walk back to the dorm or to your car in the evening. If you choose to address this issue in a persuasive speech, you would want to stress this need for safety, bringing it to the front of your audience's awareness. Once the situation is evident to your listeners, you can point out ways to satisfy that need. You might advocate better campus lighting, more security patrols, or personal escort services. Successful speakers identify the unmet needs of their listeners and respond appropriately in an informative, persuasive, or entertaining speech.

Using Maslow's hierarchy can also help the speaker facing an unfamiliar audience outside the college classroom. Even though you may initially know little about such an audience, your goal will be to find out as much as possible about them before the speech. Knowing what motivates them, what they need or want to hear, is an excellent starting point in your audience analysis. It will also help you avoid unfortunate, unnecessary situations such as speaking on the joys of skydiving to a group of people barely able to provide food and clothing for themselves.

Analyze Audience Psychology

Four important components of audience psychology are values, beliefs, attitudes, and behaviors. These elements, depicted as a pyramid in Figure 5.2, help us understand how our listeners think, feel, and behave. If you look at Figure 5.2, you will see that, typically, our behavior is shaped by our attitudes, which are based on our beliefs, which are validated by our values. In order to understand better the interaction among these elements, we will look at each level of the pyramid, beginning with values and moving upward.

Values. We value something because we deem it to be desirable, or to have some inherent goodness. A **value** expresses a judgment of what is desirable and undesirable, right and wrong, or good and evil. Values are usually stated in the form of a word or phrase.

value: judgment of what is right or wrong, desirable or undesirable, usually expressed as words or phrases.

For example, most of us probably share the values of equality, freedom, honesty, fairness, justice, good health, and family. These values compose the principles or standards we use to judge and develop our beliefs, attitudes, and behaviors.

If we value honesty, for example, we are probably offended when we learn that a political leader has lied to us. If we value equality and fairness, we will no doubt oppose employment practices that discriminate on the basis of gender, ethnicity, religion, or age. While our actions may not always be consistent with our values, those standards nevertheless guide what we believe and how we act. When we act contrary to our values, we may experience conflict or even guilt. That perceived inconsistency will often motivate us either to change our behavior to match our beliefs and values, or to change our beliefs by rationalizing our behavior.

belief: statement that people accept as true.

Beliefs. A **belief** is something you accept as true, and it is usually stated as a declarative sentence. We probably do not think about many of our beliefs because they are seldom challenged: Brushing your teeth regularly reduces your chances of getting cavities; observing speed limits saves lives; sexual abuse is psychologically harmful to children; illiteracy in the United States undermines economic productivity; and so on.

Other beliefs are more controversial, and we often find ourselves defending them. Each of the statements below is debatable.

- Placement of toxic landfills discriminates against poor and ethnic minority populations.
- Colleges place too much emphasis on athletics.
- The benefits of surveillance technology in the workplace outweigh its harms.
- The English language is gender-biased.
- IQ tests are culturally biased.
- Organ transplant policies discriminate against the poor and powerless.

There are, no doubt, statements on this list with which you agree and disagree. Those you accept as true are part of your beliefs.

attitudes: statements expressing an individual's approval or disapproval, likes or dislikes.

Attitudes. **Attitudes** are expressions of approval or disapproval. They are our likes and dislikes. A statement of an attitude makes a judgment about the desirability of an individual, object, idea, or action. Examples of statements of attitude include the following: I endorse Bob Estrada for SGA president; I favor a decrease in defense spending; I support capping enrollment at our college; I like broccoli; I prefer classical music to jazz; I favor a pass-fail grading system for our school.

Attitudes usually evolve from our values and beliefs. Several values and beliefs may interact to complicate our decision making. When two values or two beliefs collide, the stronger one will generally predominate and determine attitudes. You may value both the right to privacy and the right to good health. If a speaker convinces you that a proposed government action will diminish the right to privacy, you may oppose the action. If another speaker demonstrates that the plan is necessary to gather information to contain the spread of a deadly disease, you may support the proposal. A single belief, then, in and of itself, is not a reliable predictor of a person's attitude. Again, when values collide, the stronger value usually takes precedence.

behavior: an individual's observable action.

Behaviors. A **behavior** is an overt action; in other words, it is how we act. Unlike values, beliefs, and attitudes, which are all psychological principles, behaviors are observable. You may feel that giving blood is important (attitude) because an adequate blood

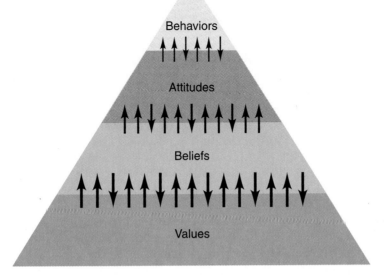

Figure 5.2 *Levels of influence*

supply is necessary to save lives (belief) and because you respect human life (value). Your behavior as you participate in a blood drive and donate blood is a logical and observable extension of your outlook.

Gather Information About Your Audience

If you understand the foregoing components of psychology, you begin to understand the audience you intend to inform, persuade, or entertain. Your knowledge of those principles will help you as you work to analyze your audience, and will help you develop their psychological profile. How do you obtain information about your audience's values, beliefs, attitudes, and behaviors? You have two options, both requiring some work.

The first is to use your powers of observation and deduction. You can make educated guesses about people's values, beliefs, and attitudes by observing their behaviors. For example, what are your classmates talking about before and after class? What subjects have they chosen for classroom speeches? How do they respond to various speeches they hear? What do you guess their age range to be? How do they dress? What books do they carry with them to class? The answers to these and many other questions help you infer a psychological profile of your audience. The longer you are around your classmates, the less this profile will be based on stereotypes and the more accurate it will become.

The second way to gather information about your audience's values, beliefs, attitudes, and behaviors is to conduct interviews or administer questionnaires. Interviews and questionnaires may be informal or, if you have the time and resources, formal. You could interview classmates informally during conversation before or after class. Questionnaires administered during class may be as simple as asking for a show of hands to answer a question ("How many of you have access to a personal computer?") or as formal as asking classmates to answer a written questionnaire you have photocopied and distributed. It's true that audience interviews and questionnaires are somewhat artificial;

you don't often have the luxury of using them for presentations outside your college class-room. Still, if you are invited or required to address a group of strangers, you would be wise to ask your contact person lots of questions about the audience you will be facing.

Analyze Specific Speaking Situations

voluntary audience:
a group of people who have assembled of their own free will to listen to a speaker.

captive audience: a group of people who are compelled or feel compelled to assemble to listen to a speaker.

audience disposition:
listeners' feelings of like, dislike, or neutrality toward a speaker, the speaker's topic, or the occasion for a speech.

Types of Audiences.   In terms of their reasons for attending a speech, audiences fall into two categories: voluntary and captive. A **voluntary audience** has assembled of its own free will. Most adults who attend a worship service or a political rally are there voluntarily. Similarly, you may be taking this class as an elective, just because you believe it will benefit you. The **captive audience,** in contrast, feels required to be present. Chances are that you have been part of a captive audience at many school assemblies during your education. You may even be taking this class to fulfill a requirement. You may attend a speech by someone visiting your campus because you are required to do so for this or some other course. Your reasons for attending a speech, a presentation, or a class may have a significant effect on your disposition as you listen.

Audience Disposition.   **Audience disposition** describes how listeners are inclined to react to a speaker and his or her ideas. Listeners may have any of three general attitudes toward speakers or their ideas: *favorable, unfavorable,* or *neutral.* Each of these categories, however, looks deceptively simple. Listeners can be slightly, moderately, or strongly favorable or unfavorable toward your topic, and you should try to determine this level of intensity. A listener who only slightly opposes your position that home schooling is a desirable method of instruction will probably be easier to persuade than one who strongly opposes it.

If you sense that some of your listeners are neutral toward your topic, you should try to uncover the reasons for their neutrality. Some may be *uninterested* in your topic, and you will want to convince these listeners of its importance. Other listeners may be *uninformed* about your topic, and your strategy here should be to introduce your listeners to the data they need to understand and believe your ideas. Still other listeners may simply be *undecided* about your topic. They may be both interested and informed, aware of the pros and cons of your position. They may not have decided, however, which position they support. Your strategy in this instance should be to bolster your arguments and point out weaknesses in the opposition's case. As you can see, evaluating your audience's disposition is a complex activity. The more you know about your listeners, the easier this process becomes.

Listeners can be favorable, unfavorable, or neutral not only to speakers and their topics, but also to the reason for assembling to hear a speech. We are often tempted to view voluntary audiences as friendly and captive ones as hostile, and those situations certainly do occur. A person may go listen to a public lecture at a museum because of interest in the subject or out of respect for the speaker's reputation. On the other hand, members of captive audiences may be so antagonistic about having to be present that they listen to any speaker through a filter of hostility. The connection between the audience's reasons for attending and their attitudes toward the speaker is not this simple and predictable, however.

An audience that has assembled freely may well be unfavorable to the speaker or the speaker's organization. As examples, consider the people who attend a political

How would you describe the person who owns this van? What do you think are some of this person's values, beliefs, attitudes, and behaviors?
(SOURCE: © Comstock, Inc., Sven Martson)

speech to protest or to heckle the speaker. Alternatively, a captive audience, instead of being hostile because they feel coerced into attending, may actually look forward to a speech. Audience dynamics get even more complicated when a voluntary, favorable audience is forced to listen to other speakers before the person they came to hear. Members of a captive audience initially unsympathetic to the speaker may find themselves becoming friendly as a result of the speaker's interesting message or engaging style of delivery.

Because attendance is a requirement of most college courses, you face a captive audience when you stand before your classmates. That shouldn't frighten you, though; as we've said, a captive audience is not necessarily unfavorable toward the speaker or the speaking occasion. As a matter of fact, your colleagues in this class will be especially friendly because they share some of your concerns and apprehensions. However, the situation does pose an added challenge for you and makes your audience analysis especially important. You have a responsibility to choose novel, interesting topics for informative speeches, to choose significant topics for persuasive speeches, and to be thoroughly prepared for any speech you give. Listeners may develop an unfavorable impression of you if they perceive that you are taking your speech too lightly or exploiting the occasion to preach

audience profile: a descriptive sketch of listeners' characteristics, values, beliefs, attitudes, and/or actions.

your own political or religious views. Remember that public speaking is an audience-centered activity; keep your listeners' needs and concerns in mind as you construct your message.

When you use the techniques discussed in this chapter, you will be able to construct an **audience profile.** As you do this, however, be aware of the following points. First, your understanding of your audience will never be complete. It is simply impossible (and probably illegal!) to discover everything about your listeners. Sometimes you have to make educated guesses based on incomplete data. Second, remember our earlier point that much of the information you gather may be of little or no help in preparing your speech. How important is it, for example, to know your listeners' religious affiliations if you are informing them about the benefits of interactive video instruction? On the other hand, if you are discussing the issue of prayer in school, your listeners' religious beliefs may be extremely important.

Finally, keep in mind that your audience is not a uniform mass, but a collection of individual listeners having different experiences, values, beliefs, attitudes, behaviors, and personalities. While opinions may overlap, do not think of your audience as having one opinion toward your topic. Rarely will you be able to say, "This audience opposes converting the intramural athletic field to a multi-story parking facility." More likely, your audience analysis statement will show that your audience has a variety of opinions about your topic. If you need more precise information, you may want to construct a questionnaire, distribute it to your classmates, and then collect, compile, and interpret the results, as Trevor did.

Trevor favored an amendment to the U.S. Constitution mandating a balanced budget. To help him construct his speech, he prepared and distributed to his class the questionnaire shown in Figure 5.3.

Trevor discovered that a significant majority of his classmates believed that the federal budget deficit was a serious problem and that current budget reduction efforts were ineffective. Nearly three-fourths of the class favored an amendment mandating a balanced budget, although slightly fewer than half thought such an amendment would solve the problem. Approximately half the class thought an amendment would hurt social programs, and a clear majority felt taxes would increase and defense programs would suffer. The class was almost equally divided among Democrats, Republicans, and independents. A majority viewed themselves as moderate, with conservative running a close second, and liberal a distant third. A few students shared additional comments, such as: "boring topic," "probably important, but what can we do?" and "who cares?" Trevor reviewed the results of his survey and wrote the following analysis of his audience:

"The challenge doesn't seem to be getting the audience to support my position that the U.S. Constitution should be amended to require a balanced budget. Most already agree. The difficulty may be, first, getting them interested in the topic and, second, getting them to think that they can have an impact on the solution."

In his speech, Trevor tried to increase audience involvement in the topic by showing how the deficit affected the pocketbooks of each of his listeners. He attempted to defuse the arguments that a balanced budget would necessarily result in a cutback of needed social programs and hurt U.S. national security. He supported his arguments with a balance of opinions from Democrats and Republicans, mainly those with moderate views. Trevor's hard work paid off. He

Audience Questionnaire

Please take a few minutes to complete the following survey to help me in preparing my persuasive speech. Do not put your name on this survey. Thanks!

Using the scale below, please circle the number that best indicates your agreement/disagreement with each of the statements in Questions 1-7.

7 = strongly agree   3 = slightly disagree
6 = moderately agree   2 = moderately disagree
5 = slightly agree   1 = strongly disagree
4 = neutral/neither agree nor disagree

1. The federal budget deficit is a serious problem.

| 1 | 2 | 3 | 4 | 5 | 6 | 7 |
| strongly disagree | | | neutral | | | strongly agree |

2. Current efforts to reduce the federal budget deficit are ineffective.

| 1 | 2 | 3 | 4 | 5 | 6 | 7 |
| strongly disagree | | | neutral | | | strongly agree |

3. A constitutional amendment mandating a balanced budget would solve the federal budget deficit.

| 1 | 2 | 3 | 4 | 5 | 6 | 7 |
| strongly disagree | | | neutral | | | strongly agree |

4. A constitutional amendment mandating a balanced budget would result in increased taxes.

| 1 | 2 | 3 | 4 | 5 | 6 | 7 |
| strongly disagree | | | neutral | | | strongly agree |

5. A constitutional amendment mandating a balanced federal budget would end up hurting social programs.

| 1 | 2 | 3 | 4 | 5 | 6 | 7 |
| strongly disagree | | | neutral | | | strongly agree |

6. A constitutional amendment mandating a balanced federal budget would end up hurting defense programs.

| 1 | 2 | 3 | 4 | 5 | 6 | 7 |
| strongly disagree | | | neutral | | | strongly agree |

7. I favor a constitutional amendment mandating a balanced federal budget.

| 1 | 2 | 3 | 4 | 5 | 6 | 7 |
| strongly disagree | | | neutral | | | strongly agree |

Place an "X" by the word that best describes you.

1. I have the following political affiliation:
____ Democrat
____ Republican
____ Independent
____ other (please specify) _____

2. Politically, I consider myself to be:
____ liberal
____ moderate
____ conservative
____ other (please specify) _____

Please share any additional comments you would like about the federal budget deficit on the back of this sheet.

Figure 5.3 *Audience questionnaire. Trevor used information he gathered from this audience questionnaire to help him construct his speech advocating a balanced budget amendment to the U.S. Constitution.*

delivered a speech that was adapted to his specific audience, and the audience responded favorably.

You may not always have the opportunity to get as much detailed information as Trevor did before you prepare your speech. The more specific and accurate your audience analysis, however, the better you can develop your ideas and accomplish your specific purpose. You need to use the demographic and psychological information you have gathered about your listeners to develop your audience profile.

Size of the Audience.　In Chapter 1, we stated that the greater the number of people involved in speech communication, the less chance there is for verbal interaction between the speaker and individual listeners. In speaking before a small group, a speaker may be frequently interrupted with questions. The situation may be so informal that the speaker sits in a chair or on the edge of a table during the presentation. A speaker in such a situation may use jargon and colloquial language, prepared visual aids (as well as those devised on the spot with transparencies and chalkboards), and a relaxed, conversational style of delivery.

As the audience grows larger, however, the speaker will have to use greater volume and larger gestures. The language of the speech may become more formal, especially if the speaker knows that the speech will be published or videotaped. As the distance between the speaker and the last row of audience members increases, the speaker's volume must increase, gestures and facial expression must be exaggerated slightly, and visual aids must be projected in order to be seen. Unless the audience is encouraged to ask questions after the speech, they will likely remain silent. As you can see, the size of your audience affects both the type of speech you deliver and your manner of presentation.

Occasion.　The occasion, the reason for the speaking event, is a critical factor in determining what type of audience you will be facing. You need to ask yourself (and maybe even some members of the group), "Why is this audience gathering? What special circumstances bring them together?" A class, an annual convention, a banquet, a party, a competition, a reunion, and a regular meeting of an organization are all examples of occasions. Occasions can be formal or informal, serious or fun, planned or spontaneous, closed to the public or open to all.

In addition to a simple description of the occasion, you as a speaker may need to know about the history of the occasion or about the recent history of the group you will address. Say, for example, that the officers of an organization have invited you to speak to their entire organization. If there has been recent conflict between the members and the officers, the majority of your audience may look upon you and your speech skeptically. To understand any occasion, you must know both the purpose and the circumstances of the gathering.

Physical Environment.　In Chapters 1 and 2, we discussed the forms of noise that speakers and listeners must battle. Every physical environment or setting contains unique obstacles to communication. The size of the room itself may impede communication. You may be speaking as some audience members finish a meal. You may be speaking to a large audience through an inadequate or defective public address system. You may compete with a variety of physical noise: the sounds of another meeting next door, a room that is too warm, interruptions from caterers bringing in carts of ice water. Just as it makes good sense to practice a speech in the classroom where you will speak, you should always try to find out something about the physical location where you will be speaking to a group.

Time.   If you had your choice, would you rather take a college class at 9:00 a.m. or 1:00 p.m.? If you're typical, you'll choose the 9:00 a.m. class, even though you might not consider yourself a morning person. Both students and faculty seem to agree that classes at 1:00 p.m. are particularly difficult to attend and to teach because everyone's energy seems low.

The time at which you deliver your speech is an obvious part of your analysis of the speaking occasion. An address given at 4:00 p.m. on Friday will almost surely find an audience more fatigued and restless than will one given Tuesday at 9:30 a.m. If you are scheduled to speak first in a class that meets at 8:00 a.m., you may face an audience half asleep, so you may need to boost your own energy to enliven them.

Your speech's placement in a program may also affect how your audience receives it. If you follow several other speakers, you may need to work harder at getting and keeping the attention of your listeners. In short, if your listeners are not at their best, plan on working extra hard to enliven your delivery. Think about your class and when you will present your speech. The time factor may not cause you to change your topic, but it may affect how you deliver your speech.

■ AUDIENCE ANALYSIS *DURING* THE SPEECH

If your audience analysis before the speech has been careful and thorough, you will approach any speaking situation — both in this class and outside it — with a fairly complete and accurate picture of your audience. Your analysis to this point will have guided your selection of a topic and the specific ways that you have developed that topic and plan to deliver the speech. Yet even the most scrupulous, conscientious audience analysis will not guarantee that your speech will be compelling and effective. Whether you speak from notes, from a manuscript, from memory, or on the spur of the moment, your audience analysis must continue during the delivery of your speech if you are to make that vital connection with your listeners. Communication scholars suggest that, as a speaker, you must be aware of three things about your listeners as you speak.

First, you must be aware of the audience's *attention* or interest. Do their eye contact, posture, and other body language indicate to you that they are concentrating on you and your message? Are there physical distractions in the speech setting that are competing with you for the audience's attention? Do you seem to have the audience's attention throughout some parts of the speech, only to lose it during other parts? If you are concentrating on your message and on your listeners, rather than on how you sound and look, you will know the answers to these questions about the audience's attention.

If you detect a lapse of audience attention during your speech, how can you solve this problem? Recovering your listeners' attention may be as simple as changing some aspect of your delivery: speaking more loudly or softly, for example, or moving away from the lectern for part of the speech so that you are closer to the audience. Any change in your established pattern of delivery will likely rekindle audience attention and interest. In addition, changing your usual style of delivery may be essential to overcome the distractions of a stuffy room, a noisy heater, or the coughs and other audience noise that occur whenever people assemble.

A second characteristic of your audience that you must try to assess is their *understanding* or comprehension of your message. If you have ever produced a false and hollow sounding laugh when you didn't really understand the joke that was just told, you know how difficult it is to fake comprehension. No matter how hard most of us try to cover up a lack of understanding, something about our voices or our bodies signals to others that we didn't really get it.

Of course, your audience may not try to hide their incomprehension. Members may deliberately tell you with puzzled expressions and other nonverbals that they are confused. The worst thing a speaker can do under either circumstance is to continue as if there were no problems. Clarifying something for the audience may be as simple as repeating or rephrasing the problem statement. If a particular word seems to be the source of confusion, defining the word or writing it on the board may solve the problem.

The third and final component of audience analysis during the speech is your listeners' *evaluation* of you and your message. Sensitive speakers attuned to their audiences are able to gauge the reactions of those listeners. Do members of the audience seem to agree with what you are saying? Do they approve of the suggestions you are making? Answers to these questions are particularly important when you are seeking to persuade your audience.

Sometimes the answer to such questions will be no. You may be delivering bad news or taking what you know will be an unpopular stand on an issue. Having the audience disagree with the content of your message doesn't necessarily mean that your speech has been a failure. Simply knowing that many listeners agree or disagree with you at the end of a persuasive speech shows that you are an audience-centered speaker, and that's an accomplishment in itself.

■■■ AUDIENCE ANALYSIS *AFTER* THE SPEECH

Too often speakers assume that the speech-making process concludes as you utter your final statement and walk to your seat. Your influence on audience members can continue for some time, however. We encourage you to add one additional step: *post-speech analysis*. Part of this step should be self-reflection as you analyze your performance. Did you accomplish what you hoped you would? What do you sense were the strongest aspects of your speech? What were the weakest? How would you rate the content, organization, and delivery of the speech? What can you do to improve these aspects of your next speech?

Your answers to these questions provide a very subjective evaluation of your speech efforts. You may be much more critical than your listeners were because only you know how you planned to deliver the speech. For that reason, you should also consider your audience's assessment of your speech content, organization, and delivery.

In this class, that information may come from oral or written critiques from your peers, or from comments some of them give you after class. If you have given a good speech on an interesting topic, one of the pleasant rewards in a college classroom is that audience members may have questions to ask you. The tone and content of those questions will tell you a great deal about how the audience received your message. You will also receive helpful suggestions from your instructor. If you expect to improve as a public speaker, pay attention to the feedback given you by all your listeners and act upon the comments that are particularly relevant.

SUMMARY

The best speeches are those that seem exactly right for the audience to whom they are delivered. They focus on interesting topics, use colorful but familiar language and supporting materials, are delivered with enthusiasm, and are the right length for the topic and the occasion. Such an accomplishment requires careful audience analysis before, during, and after delivery of the speech.

Before the speech, a speaker should consider audience demographics, audience needs, and audience psychology. *Demographics* refers to characteristics of the audience, including age, gender, ethnicity, education, religion, economic status, and group membership. Information you gather about these characteristics can help you select a topic and then develop and support it for a particular group of listeners. Realize, however, that simply stereotyping listeners in terms of one or more of these characteristics may not only be incorrect, but may also cause a speaker to offend the audience.

Maslow's hierarchy of needs is a useful tool for analyzing audience motivation. That model ranks five human needs in terms of their predominance. The *physiological needs,* the most basic, include our needs for food, water, and rest. The *safety needs* include everything that contributes to a predictable, orderly existence — secure housing, reliable transportation, and freedom from civil unrest or war, for example. Once these needs are largely met, we begin to concentrate on our community of friends and associates and the ways that they ful-

fill our *love and belongingness needs.* Feeling that we fit in, that we give and receive affection from a group of people, contributes to our *esteem needs.* This fourth level is important, Maslow says, because we all need a pat on the back from time to time. The highest level of needs, the *self-actualization needs,* refers to our desire to fulfill our potential as human beings.

Four key components of audience psychology are values, beliefs, attitudes, and behaviors. *Values,* such as freedom and honesty, are expressions of worth or rightness. Our values are the basis for the development of beliefs and attitudes. *Beliefs* are statements we accept as true. They may be either provable or open to debate. *Attitudes* express our approval or disapproval of individuals, objects, ideas, or actions. Several values or beliefs may interact to form our attitudes. When these values or beliefs conflict, the stronger one usually predominates. A fourth element is *behavior,* an overt action that may *reflect* our values, beliefs, and attitudes.

Gathering information about your audience's values, beliefs, and attitudes can be formal or informal. You can simply observe their behaviors and infer the thoughts behind them. Or you may have the need and the opportunity to question the audience, orally or in writing, by administering questionnaires and surveys to gauge their feelings.

A final part of audience analysis before the speech focuses on the specific speaking situation. Will you be facing a *captive* or a *voluntary audience?* Are they likely to be favorable, unfavorable, or neutral to you and your topic? What is the nature of the speaking occasion? Where will the speech take place? What time is it to be delivered? Considering the answers to these questions is the final step in audience analysis before the speech.

During a speech, the speaker should pay attention to listeners' interest or *attention,* their *comprehension* or understanding of the message, and their *evaluation* of the speech. Speakers can influence each of these elements. Lively, sincere delivery helps generate audience interest in the topic. A speaker can help ensure the audience's com-

prehension of the message by defining unusual terms, slowing down the delivery of technical materials, and using repetition.

Finally, after delivering the speech, a speaker should continue to analyze the audience for signals about their evaluation of the message. What comments do audience members make about the speech, orally or in writing? What questions do they ask? What suggestions does the class instructor offer? Any student who is serious about improving as a public speaker must be aware of and act upon audience feedback after the speech is over.

*E*XERCISES

1. Select a speech from *Vital Speeches* or some other published source. Read the speech to discern how the speaker adapted, or failed to adapt, the message to the specific audience. Mark examples of audience adaptation strategies, writing in the margins of a copy of the speech the specific appeal or strategy used. Indicate where the speaker could better have adapted to the audience.

2. Using the speech you selected in the above exercise, discuss how the speaker would need to adapt the purpose, content, organization, and language if he or she were speaking to your class.

3. Based on your analysis of students in this class, predict their opinions on the following questions.
   a. Should women be excluded from combat roles in the U.S. military?
   b. Generally, is a private college education superior to a public college education?
   c. Should the U.S. Constitution be amended to require a balanced budget?
   d. Should women have the right to have an abortion?
   e. Do social fraternities and sororities do more harm than good?
   After you have made your predictions, poll the class to determine their responses to the above questions. Were your predictions fairly accurate? Were you surprised at some of the answers? What factors caused you to predict as you did?

4. Choose a specific brand-name product advertised in several magazines. Analyze how the product is promoted in each publication. Are there differences in the ads' headlines, body copy, and visuals? If so, what do these distinctions reveal about how the advertisers viewed their audiences? If the ads are identical, suggest ways that the product appeal could be tailored to each audience.

5. Each issue of *Congressional Digest* poses a specific policy question; for example, "Should Congress fund completion of the space station?" Each issue presents several speeches, affirming and negating the question. Select a copy of *Congressional Digest* and read

the speeches included. Discuss the differences between the pro and the con sides in terms of the values supporting each side's arguments.

6. To give you some experience in analyzing off-campus audiences, select one of the following groups, find out what you can about it, and report back to the class.
   a. Knights of Columbus
   b. Optimist Club
   c. B'nai B'rith
   d. Veterans of Foreign Wars
   e. League of Women Voters
   f. NAACP
   g. Rotary Club

Notes

1. Mary Raymond Shipman Andrews, *The Perfect Tribute* (New York: Scribner's, 1906) 1-9.

2. Carl Sandburg, *Abraham Lincoln: The Prairie Years and the War Years* (New York: Harcourt, 1954) 443-44.

3. Newspaper reporters the next day began to reflect widely different public views of the president's surprisingly brief speech. The *Chicago Times* referred to "the silly, flat, and dish-watery utterances" of Lincoln; the *Harrisburg* [Pennsylvania] *Patriot and Union* simply reported, "We pass over the silly remarks of the President…" (Sandburg 445). Other newspapers, however, made entirely positive evaluations of Lincoln's speech. The *Chicago Tribune* predicted, "The dedicatory remarks of President Lincoln will live among the annals of man" (Sandburg 445). The *Philadelphia Evening Bulletin* noted that thousands who would not wade through Everett's elaborate oration would read Lincoln's brief remarks, "and not many will do it without a moistening of the eye and a swelling of the heart" (Sandburg 446). The *Providence Journal* reminded its readers of the adage that the hardest thing in the world is to make a good five-minute speech, and said, "We know not where to look for a more admirable speech than the brief one which the President made at the close of Mr. Everett's oration" (Sandburg 446).

4. Thomas M. Scheidel, *Persuasive Speaking* (Glenview, IL: Scott, 1967) 97. For a fuller account, see Mark E. Neely, *The Last Best Hope of Earth: Abraham Lincoln and the Promise of America* (Cambridge: Harvard UP, 1993) 154-55. Neely notes that Lincoln made these remarks to acknowledge a serenade celebrating recent Union victories at Gettysburg and Vicksburg.

5. Terry Sanford, quoted in "Commencement Remarks: Learning to Care and Share," *Representative American Speeches 1988-1989,* ed. Owen Peterson (New York: Wilson, 1989) 154.

6. Win Kelley, *The Art of Public Address* (Dubuque, IA: Brown, 1965) 25.

7. Robert Hughes, *Culture of Complaint: The Fraying of America* (New York: Oxford UP, 1993) 14.

8. John Jacob, "Racism and Race Relations: To Grow Beyond our Racial Animosities," *Vital Speeches of the Day* 15 January 1990: 214.

9. Abraham H. Maslow, *Motivation and Personality,* 2nd ed. (New York: Random, 1970) 35-47.

10. Maslow 38.

11. Maslow 41.

. . . [T]here is no such thing as a boring subject.... [W]hether it's the plastics industry or the mating habits of a certain insect, you will always find there are people out there who have devoted their entire lives to the subject.... Well, if it can fascinate one person, then you can extract a kind of enthusiasm from that person and transfer it to others out there.
—Ted Koppel

Selecting Your Speech Topic

Generating Ideas
Self-Generated Topics
Audience-Generated Topics
Occasion-Generated Topics
Research-Generated Topics

Selecting Your Topic

Focusing Your Topic

Determining Your General Purpose

Speeches to Inform
Speeches to Persuade
Speeches to Entertain

Formulating Your Specific Purpose

Wording Your Thesis Statement

Developing Your Speech Title

Chapter 6

*F*irst, the bad news: "A recent study of today's college students concludes that they 'seem to have no confidence or willingness to extend their knowledge.'" Thomas Kopp of Miami University in Oxford, Ohio, the author of the study, notes that college students are "bored by almost everything," and as a result "they are also boring people. Today's college students, more than any other generation, he says, … are dogmatic and uncreative, motivated more by desire for good grades than [by] excitement for learning."[1]

The good news is that we don't accept this as a blanket statement about college students in the 1990s any more than you do. The best news of all, of course, is that this public speaking class provides you the perfect opportunity to prove such studies wrong. In most of your college courses you learn from reading textbooks, listening to your instructors, and participating in class discussions. Occasionally, you research topics raised in the class and present your conclusions, usually in the form of a research paper. Too rarely do you communicate your ideas orally to the class or listen to the researched, documented opinions of your classmates.

In this class, too, you will read the textbook, listen to your instructor, and participate in class discussions. You will also have the opportunity to investigate issues that concern you and present your ideas to your classmates and your instructor. You are studying some fundamental speech principles, and you will demonstrate your mastery of them when you prepare and deliver interesting, well-researched speeches on topics of your choice.

Selecting a topic for a speech is more complex than you may think. Students often fail to choose a topic wisely because they adopt counterproductive strategies. For example, some students select too quickly. They pick up a magazine, find an interesting article, and decide to use its subject as their topic. Much later, they discover that the topic is really inappropriate for the audience or the occasion, or they find no more information on the topic. If they keep the hastily chosen topic and approach the assignment halfheartedly, the quality of the speech suffers. If they change topics, they lose valuable speech preparation time. Either option presents a no-win situation.

Eric had three weeks to prepare his informative speech, and he wanted to select a topic that would excite him, his audience, and his instructor. Because he enjoyed watching the street performers near campus, he thought this would make an excellent speech topic. He went to the library, looked at a couple of indexes, but couldn't find anything listed under the topic of street performers. So he changed topics. In the library reading room, Eric found and skimmed through several magazines. He came across an article in *Discover* magazine on 3-D music. "Everybody's interested in music," Eric said to himself, so he photocopied the article and stuffed it in a notebook.

A couple of days later, he took out a pencil, a notepad, and the article. As he began reading, however, he encountered words such as *psychoacoustics, transponder, binaural imaging,* and *Convolvotron.* Eric realized that the topic as presented in the article was too technical for his audience (and for him!), and he began thinking of other interests he had that he could turn into a speech topic. Eric enjoyed airbrush artwork, but worried that others might find the topic boring. In his psychology class, he was studying dream interpretation, but Eric reasoned that others might have taken the course and would already know much of his information. There had recently been an earthquake in an adjacent state, and he thought this might be a timely topic. But because it had been in the news, he was afraid that someone else would choose the same topic. As the day of his speech quickly approached, Eric was still selecting and rejecting speech topics.

Students like Eric spend far too much time searching for the perfect topic. They jump from one idea to another because none seems quite right. As you can see, this select-and-reject syndrome wastes valuable time that could be devoted to researching and developing a topic. As the speaking date nears, the student usually panics and selects any topic, develops it hastily in the limited time that remains, and never feels really comfortable with the topic. Unfortunately, this lack of preparation and commitment usually shows up in the speech presentation. At some point in the selection process, you must pick your best topic and commit yourself to developing it. Each of Eric's topics, for example, *could* have been both interesting and informative if he had committed his time to it.

The example of Eric should help you see that you cannot treat choosing your speech topic too lightly. Determining your speech topic, then, is an important part of speech making that should not be slighted. If you select a topic of interest to you and your audience for which you can find authoritative supporting material, you greatly enhance your chances of a successful speaking experience. You will also probably find it easier to construct your speech.

Right about now you may be asking yourself, "How am I ever going to pick the right topic?" Choosing your topic involves several steps. You should (1) generate a list of ideas for possible topics, (2) select a topic, (3) focus the topic, (4) determine your general purpose, (5) formulate your specific purpose, and (6) word your thesis statement. Depending on the specific speaking situation, you may also want or be asked to develop a speech title.

◼ GENERATING IDEAS

"You can't have good ideas if you don't have a lot of ideas." **LINUS PAULING**

The first step in the process of selecting a speech topic is **brainstorming.** With this technique, you list all the ideas that come to your mind, without evaluating or censoring any of them. Too often, a speaker spends insufficient time generating a list of potential topics. Yet, as Dr. Pauling suggests, in order to select a good topic you must generate many topics. Author John Steinbeck compared ideas to rabbits, saying, "You get a couple and learn how to handle them, and pretty soon you have a dozen." As a rule, the larger your list of possible topics, the better the topic you will finally select. Remember, do not evaluate or criticize your list as you brainstorm. What may seem silly to you at first can turn out to be an unusual speech subject with a lot of potential to interest your audience.

For example, a Chicago Cubs fan, puzzling over the team's failure to win a National League pennant in nearly half a century, might be interested in the question, "Why can't the Cubs win?" Some sports analysts have noted that, without stadium lights until 1988, the Cubs played all home games during the day and most of their road games at night. This time differential, worsened by traveling across time zones for away games, may have affected team performance, according to these experts. Interesting theory, isn't it? If you began researching this topic, you might come across the term *chronobiology,* "the effect of time on living systems."[2] You could also learn about the consequences of jet lag on the performance of athletes, businesspeople, politicians, and others who travel.

brainstorming: non-critical free association to generate as many ideas as possible in a short time.

Thinking about your own interests, hobbies, and experiences is one way to brainstorm for possible speech topics.
(SOURCE: © Frank Siteman)

What began as a narrow topic (why the Cubs haven't won the National League pennant since 1945) has become a topic with broader appeal. Brainstorming, then, is an important first step, and you should jot down all the topics you think of and postpone evaluating them until later.

You can turn brainstorming into productive work toward your speech by asking and then answering these four questions:

1. What topics interest *you?*
2. What topics interest your *listeners?*
3. What topics develop from the *occasion?*
4. What topics develop from your *research?*

Your answers will help you devise a list of many topics from which you can then select the most appropriate.

Self-Generated Topics

self-generated topics: speech subjects based on the speaker's interests, experiences, and knowledge.

Self-generated topics come from you — your memory, your notes, your interests, your experiences, and your personal files. Take out a sheet of paper and jot down your hobbies, your favorite courses, books you have read, your pet peeves, names of people who intrigue you, and issues and events that excite you. What are your likes and dislikes? On what topics do you consider yourself knowledgeable? Review your list, writing beside each item possible speech topics. If you enjoy listening to music, perhaps a speech on the history of jazz would be informative. If you are irritated by people who are late, you could inform your audience about why people procrastinate, or about how to set and meet goals. Are you uncomfortable in enclosed places? A speech on claustrophobia might interest you and your audience. If you are nearing graduation and have been reading books on how to land your first job, a speech on how to construct a résumé or dos and don'ts for the employment interview may be fitting.

Self-generated topics may also include subjects you *need* to know. If, for example, you expect to travel soon and will be making your own arrangements for the first time, you may find yourself riding in taxis, staying in hotels, and dining in some good restaurants. But are you familiar with tipping etiquette for cab drivers, baggage carriers, and waiters? Researching and delivering a speech on tipping will not only serve your needs but can be an interesting and informative topic for your listeners.

Consider the following topics generated by our students, using just their personal interests and knowledge:

Aquariums, salt water	Marshall, Thurgood
Black history in textbooks	Men's movement
Calligraphy	Music software
Cancer, heredity as a risk factor	Parachuting, importance to military
Colleges of the future	Photograph restoration
Drying flowers	Racism in America
Fashion illustration	Rappelling
Hazing	Robotics
Indian silver jewelry of the Southwest	Sleep disorders
	Spelunking
Jet-skiing	

Use what you know as a starting point in your topic selection process. Don't worry that you don't know enough about each topic at this stage to construct a speech. Research will help you later in focusing, developing, and supporting your topic. *What is important is that you have a list of possible topics that interest you.* Because these topics come from *your* knowledge, experience, and interests, your commitment to them is usually strong. Your interest and knowledge will motivate you in preparing your speech. In addition, your enthusiasm for your topic will enliven and enhance your speech delivery.

As you can see, self-generated topics can provide you with interesting ideas. However, they can also pose some difficulties for a speaker. One potential pitfall of self-generated topics is the use of overly technical language and jargon. If your topic is technical, be especially attentive to the language you choose to convey your meaning. The speaker in the following example forgot that advice.

Caryn, a pre-med student with a double major in biology and chemistry, found an interesting article that explained how some animals survive winter by freezing and then thawing in the spring.[3] She chose this as an informative speech topic and did further research. She reasoned correctly that many of her classmates wouldn't know of this phenomenon or how it occurs.

Yet most of her listeners knew they were in trouble when Caryn said in her introduction: "Today I want to explain how some animals such as the wood frog, the gray tree frog, painted turtles, and gallfly larvae use so-called antifreeze proteins, ice-nucleating proteins, trehalose, proline, and cryoprotectants to maintain the integrity of cells while their extracellular fluid freezes."

The audience never recovered. The remainder of her speech contained words and phrases such as *colligative cryoprotectants, polyhydroxyl alcohols, cytoplasm,* and *recrystallization.*

Caryn's problem was not with her topic; indeed, it's a fascinating subject. With simplified language and clear visual aids, she could have made that topic accessible to her listeners and drawn them into the speech. But the technical vocabulary and jargon that she found understandable only confused and alienated most of her classmates who were not pre-med majors. Remember that your speech on any technical topic will lose its intended impact if you fail to define key terms clearly for listeners less knowledgeable about the subject. You will create semantic distractions, one of those major obstacles to listening that we discussed in Chapter 4.

A second potential problem with self-generated topics is the speaker's lack of objectivity about the subject. If you become too involved with a topic, you cannot always develop it objectively. Researching your subject is a process of discovery. When you begin with rigid preconceptions, you may disregard important information that doesn't match your preconceived ideas. Take the example of Ken and his proposed speech topic on the legal drinking age.

When the time came to develop and deliver a persuasive speech for his public speaking class, Ken decided to try to persuade his classmates, most of them first-year students, that the legal drinking age should be lowered from twenty-one to eighteen. He was committed to this point of view. He had been mentally rehearsing his arguments since his eighteenth birthday: "If I'm old enough to register with Selective Service and defend my country, I'm old enough to drink if I care to." "If I'm old enough to marry without my parents' consent, I should be able to buy and consume any beverage I want."

Yet two days before his speech was due, Ken asked his speech teacher for an extension. The reason, he explained, was that all of the published sources he had researched *supported* the increased legal drinking age. "Some of the sources even had graphs showing decreases in traffic fatalities among eighteen- to twenty-one-year-olds or reductions in juvenile crimes since the drinking age was raised," he complained. Ken's instructor prodded him, "If all the evidence says that the new law is a benefit in these ways, have you considered changing your view?" Ken's answer was no. He remained sure that, given more time, he could find the evidence that supported his position.

Ken's predicament is typical of people who form rigid expectations of what their research will reveal. If, after doing some research, he still supported lowering the drinking age, Ken probably should have abandoned the traffic safety and juvenile crime issues altogether. Instead, he could have pursued those philosophical arguments he believed strongly. His primary argument could have centered on the theme that society sends mixed messages by treating eighteen-year-olds as mature and responsible in many areas of life and irresponsible in others. Make sure you don't follow Ken's example. Gather some good supporting data before you commit yourself to a specific focus for your topic.

Finally, lack of objectivity about a self-generated topic can take a second form: excessive devotion to the speech topic. You may choose as a topic an interest or hobby that has been a passion of yours for years. You are enthusiastic about the topic, you already have a wealth of information on it, and doing further research will seem a pleasure rather than a chore. What could possibly go wrong?

"The audience will love this topic," you think. Be careful. Your audience may not share your enthusiasm for aardvarks or restoring Studebaker cars. Your interest in a topic is just one criterion in the selection process. For most speech topics, you must also work to generate audience interest. We are not suggesting that you avoid self-generated topics of great interest to you. Just do not assume that your audience already has the same level of interest. They may not initially share your enthusiasm for aardvarks (or Bob Marley or the history of fireworks or optical illusions), but if you *work* at it, you can *make* them interested. Be prepared to work hard to do so.

In addition, be prepared to listen openly to others' speeches. Remember that ethical listeners do not prejudge either a speaker or that speaker's ideas. We started this chapter with a reference to the Kopp study because, although we do not agree with his blanket characterization of college students, we do encounter a number of students who seem skeptical of any information that won't help them make the car payment. Granted, some topics seem so narrow or so offbeat that you can imagine thinking, "Who cares about aardvarks?" But can't you also imagine a *terrific* speech on aardvarks by a speaker who was genuinely interested in them and who had lots of vivid supporting material? Much of the value of education is that it makes you a better (smarter, happier, more well-rounded) person. Some information is intrinsically rewarding and just plain fun to know. Don't dismiss information presented in a speech (or anywhere else) just because it won't make you more money, save you time, or whiten your teeth.

Audience-Generated Topics

Pursuing **audience-generated topics** is a second way of triggering speech subjects. What topics are of interest or importance to your listeners? If you are asked to speak to a group, you are often asked because of your expertise in a particular area. Topic selection, in this case, may be predetermined.

On other occasions, such as in this class, you are not provided with topics or topic areas. How can you find out what interests your classmates? There are three ways to do this. *First, ask them.* In this class, ask some of your classmates in casual conversation about topics they would like to hear discussed. If allowed the opportunity, you could also use a formal questionnaire to seek topic suggestions from the entire class. When you speak outside class to an organization, ask the person who contacted you about issues of probable interest to the group.

Second, listen and read. What do your classmates discuss before and after class? Articles in your campus or local paper, or letters to the editor, may suggest issues of concern. *Finally, use the audience analysis strategies* detailed in Chapter 5 to generate topics. Consider your listeners' needs. If your class is composed primarily of students just entering college, a speech on the history of your school would be interesting, informative, and appropriate. If your class is composed primarily of seniors, a speech on establishing a good credit history may be timely.

You may even find that most members of your audience seem to feel one way about a controversial topic, while you take the opposite view. You may choose to use this situation to develop and deliver a persuasive speech aimed at winning support for your side of the issue.

audience-generated topics: speech subjects geared to the interests and needs of a speaker's listeners.

The following topics were generated by our students using an audience-centered approach:

Barter systems	Pre-Columbian artifacts
Car-jackings	Prescription drugs, price
Cellular phones	comparisons
Clothing, symbolism of	Reupholstering furniture
Coca-Cola, history of	Self-defense for women
Country and western line dancing	Small businesses, how to start
Cruise vacations	Step aerobics
Ethereal music	Stress management
Goal setting	Superwoman syndrome
Horror movies, appeal of	Test anxiety, how to control
Interviews, dressing for	Tipping, guidelines for
Mnemonic (memory) devices	Used cars, how to buy
Palmistry (palm reading)	

Occasion-Generated Topics

occasion-generated topics: speech subjects derived from particular circumstances, seasons, holidays, or life events.

Occasion-generated topics constitute a third source of speech subjects. When and where a speech is given may guide you in selecting a topic. For example, a speech on setting goals may benefit your classmates more at the beginning of the semester or quarter, whereas a speech on stress management may be particularly relevant preceding midterm or final examinations. A speech advocating the use of airbags may be especially effective if you deliver it just before your classmates head home for semester or spring break. A speech on the dangers of overexposure to the sun will have more impact if it is given in the spring or the summer rather than in the fall.

If you are scheduled to speak near a particular holiday, a speech on the history or importance of that holiday may be appropriate. If you have a speech scheduled on or near Victoria Day, for instance, you can take the opportunity to introduce your classmates to a part of Canadian history. To find examples of other holidays, look at your calendar, or examine different calendars at a book store. Specialty calendars or almanacs list unusual but interesting holidays, birthdates of notable and notorious people, or anniversaries of important historical events. For example, we opened *The World Almanac Fact-A-Day Calendar* to July 7, and found the following birthdays listed:

Marc Chagall, artist (1887)
George Cukor, film director (1899)
Gustav Mahler, composer (1860)
Satchel Paige, baseball player (1906)
Ringo Starr, musician (1940)

This page of the calendar also told us that Satchel Paige was forty-two years old when his pitching helped the Cleveland Indians win the American League pennant in 1948, and that July 7 is the anniversary of the day in 1981 when President Ronald Reagan nominated Sandra Day O'Connor to be the first female Supreme Court justice. And if none

Special occasions you may know about, such as this festival in Merida, can provide excellent speech topics.
(Source: © Frank Siteman)

of those names or events appealed to you or aroused your curiosity, you would be holding 364 other pages of possible occasion-generated speech topics!

We truly are a people who love to celebrate occasions, whether they are established national holidays or quirky, lesser-known ones. Many of these occasions can suggest possible speech topics. A speech detailing cable television's impact on the viewing habits of the American family would seem appropriately timed during National Cable Month. Banned Book Month may be the ideal occasion for a speech on censorship. Consider some of the possible speech topics suggested by the following: Women's History Month, National Cigar Lovers Day, American Beer Week, International Left-Handers Day, National Pasta Week, Straw Hat Day, National Relaxation Day, American Chocolate Week, National Singles Week, and Mailbox Improvement Week. There are even months to celebrate ice cream, baked beans, and the hot dog.

Our students generated the following topics as they focused on different occasions for speeches:

Bat mitzvah (female equivalent of bar mitzvah)
Black Monday
Black Music Month
Dia de los Muertos
Festival of the Lanterns
Fireworks, designing displays
Flag Day
Guy Fawkes Day
Home childbirth
Hurricanes
Juneteenth
Mardi Gras
Oktoberfest in Germany
Parades, history of
Punxsutawney Phil (Groundhog Day)
Ramadan
Rodeos, history of
Roshashana
Running of the Bulls in Pamplona, Spain
Shrove Tuesday
Telethons, success of
Wedding traditions, origins of
Whooping crane migration
Wildflowers, excursions to view

Note that an occasion-generated topic can often lead you to other interesting topic possibilities. Thinking about a current labor strike may spark your interest in the history of labor unions. From there you could decide to focus your informative speech on child labor. Drought conditions in your area may lead you to consider the subjects of cloud seeding or desalting sea water. The occasion of Memorial Day may get you thinking about The Wall, the Vietnam Veterans Memorial in Washington, D.C. You may then decide to focus on the competition for the design of the monument; on Maya Lin, whose design won that competition; or on the aesthetics of the wall and the stirring effect it has on visitors.

Research-Generated Topics

research-generated topics: speech subjects discovered by investigating a variety of sources.

Research-generated topics, a fourth strategy for sparking speech ideas, require you to explore a variety of sources. First, you could consult indexes, such as the *Readers' Guide to Periodical Literature* or any of the other indexes we list in Chapter 7. Look at the listing of subjects and jot down those that interest you. A second research strategy is to browse through some magazines or journals in the current periodical section of your library or at a local newsstand. Just remember that this exploration is the first step in selecting a speech topic. Don't leap at the first interesting topic you find, as Eric did in the earlier example. A third strategy for generating topics is to peruse book titles at a good bookstore, noting those that interest you. Bookstores are convenient places to discover speech topics because the books are grouped by general subject area and are arranged to catch your eye. By using these three research tools — indexes, magazines and journals, and books — you can not only discover a speech topic but may also locate your first source of information.

Consider the following topics. You might not have thought of these on your own, but they all have the potential to be excellent topics and they all came from resources our students found.

Adams, Ansel	Home schooling
Amish life	Hot air balloons
Animals, communication with humans	Hubble space telescope
Artwork, airbrush	Indian folklore
Behavior modification	Insomnia, treatment of
Cartography	Jet lag
Color's effects on moods	Landscape design
Computer crime	Language acquisition, theories of
Computer-generated music	Malcolm X
Cryonics	Marley, Bob
Curanderismo (Mexican folk healing)	Medicinal herbs
Disney, Walt	Movies, how they are rated
Fingerprints, features of	Nightmares
Forensic hypnosis	Nuclear medicine, future of
Genetic engineering	Numbers, history of
High-definition television	Obsessive-compulsive disorder
	O'Keeffe, Georgia

Origami (Japanese paper art)
Paranormal phenomena
Political cartoons, history of
Pyramids, Aztec
Roller coasters
Sexual orientation, determinants of

Sleep apnea
Stonehenge
Subliminal messages
Tomb sculptures
Yoga techniques

It is important that you use all four of these strategies to generate possible speech topics. If you end your topic generation process too quickly, you limit your options. A substantive list of self-, audience-, occasion-, and research-generated topics gives you maximum flexibility in selecting a topic.

Once you have selected your topic area, we suggest that you use a technique called **visual brainstorming** to investigate the range of possibilities within that topic. Take out a sheet of paper and write your topic in the center. Now, think of how you might divide and narrow that topic. It may help you to think of some generic categories such as "causes," "types," and "solutions" that are appropriate to numerous topics. As you think of subtopics, draw a line from the center in any direction and write the narrower topic.

As your thinking suggests additional topics, you will probably be surprised at the web of potential speech topics you have created just from your brainstorming. Figure 6.1 illustrates the end product of a visual brainstorming exercise on the topic of "advertising." Certainly, you can add to this list, but in just a few minutes we were able to provide several options for focusing the subject of advertising. Some of these, such as comparing how television ads depicted families in the 1960s with how they are depicted now, are excellent topics that would probably not have come to mind without this brainstorming exercise.

You can incorporate library research into your discovery and focusing process. For example, if you are interested in advertising awards and conducted some research on that topic, you would discover that awards for outstanding television ads include the CLIOs and LIONs. If you are considering the topic of phobias, consult indexes to see how they divide this topic. In just a few minutes, we generated a list of topic areas that included the following:

visual brainstorming: informal written outline achieved by free associating around a key word or idea.

Phobias (sources of fear)
Acrophobia (fear of high places)
Aerophobia (fear of flying)
Agoraphobia (fear of open spaces)
Ailurophobia (fear of cats)
Akousticophobia (fear of sounds)
Aquaphobia (fear of water)
Claustrophobia (fear of closed spaces)
Cynophobia (fear of dogs)
Entomophobia (fear of insects)
Gymnophobia (fear of nudity)
Hypnophobia (fear of sleep)

Logophobia (fear of words)
Mikrophobia (fear of germs)
Misophobia (fear of dirt, contamination)
Nyctophobia (fear of dark)
Ophiophobia (fear of snakes)
Phobophobia (fear of fears)
Phonophobia (fear of speaking aloud)
Pyrophobia (fear of fire)
Thanatophobia (fear of death)
Xenophobia (fear of strangers)
Zoophobia (fear of animals)

Phobia predisposition
  Biological processes
  Learning processes
Prevalence
  By age
  By sex
  By culture
Treatment
  Psychotherapy
  Exposure therapy
  Drug therapy

Systematic desensitization
Diagnosis
Panic-prone personality
Panic attacks
Fear
Anxiety
Symptoms
  Dizziness
  Rapid heart rate
  Breathing difficulties

Some of these topics may be too narrow, but most would make excellent speech topics.

Figure 6.1 *Visual brainstorming can reveal possible topic areas or clusters of subtopics for speeches.*

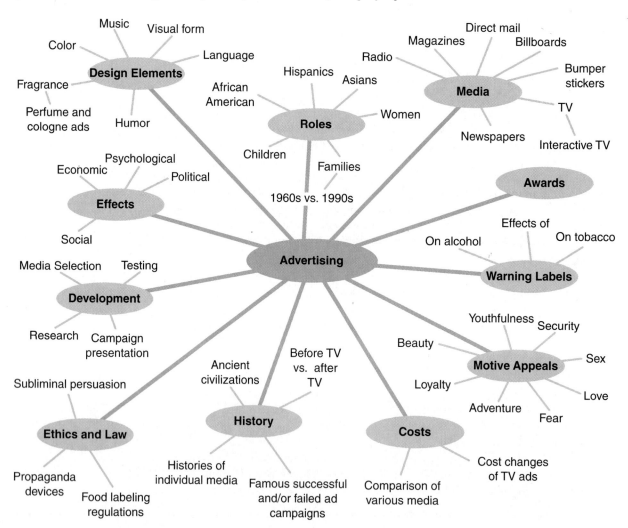

Once you have generated a list of possible speech topics, you must then select the best one. Determining what is best is an individual choice; neither a classmate, a friend, nor your instructor can make that choice. However, you can apply some criteria to each of your options to help you make a wise selection.

Four questions should guide your choice of topics. First, *"Am I interested or likely to become interested in the topic?"* The more enthusiastic you are about a topic, the greater the time and attention you will give to researching, constructing, and practicing your speech. When you enjoy learning, you learn better. As a result, speakers motivated by their topics are almost always more productive than those bored with their topics.

Second, ask, *"Is the topic of interest or importance to my audience?"* This question helps you avoid choosing a topic that you love but that your audience will never care about. Speech making is easier when your listeners are potentially interested in what you have to say. When your audience is more attentive and receptive, you can relax and make your delivery livelier. Sometimes, topics seem to be of little initial interest to audience members but may, nevertheless, be important to their personal or career success. As long as you can demonstrate the importance and relevance of the topic to them, you will motivate your audience to listen.

A third question you should answer in selecting your speech topic is, *"Am I likely to find sufficient authoritative supporting material in the time allotted for researching and developing the speech?"* Rarely do students select topics so narrow that they cannot find sufficient accessible information. You may, however, select a topic so recent that your library has not yet received adequate information. Often, because of your research deadline, you cannot obtain information on your topic through the mail. Occasionally, students contact us just before their speeches are scheduled and tell us that they are unable to complete their speeches because information they ordered has not arrived. That's usually a sign that the student's research started too late or progressed too slowly. In researching your speech, remember the adage that if something can go wrong, it will. Build some flexibility into your schedule so that you can adapt to any crisis that may arise.

Finally, consider the question, *"Do I understand the topic enough to undertake and interpret my research?"* A speaker arguing the merits of a tax increase must have an understanding of economics in order to assess research data. When you inform the audience about music therapy, you need some understanding of psychological treatment techniques and procedures. A speaker may misinterpret the reasons that violent crime in the United States is higher than in Japan if he or she does not understand Japanese culture. You do not need to know much about your topic as you begin your research, but you must know enough to be able to make sense of the data you discover.

---

1. Does this topic interest me or have the potential to do so?
2. Is this topic interesting or important to my listeners?
3. Am I likely to find sufficient supporting materials on this topic?
4. Do I know enough about this topic to start researching it and to interpret what I discover?

KEY POINTS

Questions to Guide Topic Selection

▉ FOCUSING YOUR TOPIC

Once you have selected your topic, you must focus it. Even though we have heard students speak on topics that were too narrow, this is rare. More commonly, students fail to narrow their topics sufficiently, leaving too little time to develop their ideas. The result is a speech that is more surface than substance.

When you decide on a topic area, use visual brainstorming to determine some of its divisions, or subtopics. The subject of "loneliness," for example, could focus on any of the following topics: the causes of loneliness, the relationship between loneliness and depression, loneliness and the elderly, loneliness as a cause of teenage suicide, characteristics of the lonely person, the differences between being alone and being lonely, or strategies for coping with loneliness. You could never discuss all of these topics meaningfully in a short speech. Narrowing the scope of your inquiry gives direction to your research and allows you sufficient time to support the ideas you will present to your audience.

Visual brainstorming is an excellent way of focusing your topic. A second way is through research. The more you read about your topic, the more you will likely discover its many aspects. Some may be too narrow for a complete speech, but others may be suitable for an entire speech or may be combined to form a speech.

For a five- to seven-minute informative speech assignment, Rob developed three main points in the body of his speech on baseball:

  I. The history of baseball
  II. How the game is played
  III. The uniform and equipment used

As you might guess, Rob found himself rushing through the speech, and he still did not finish it within the time limit. You probably noticed that each of his main points is too broad. Rob's problem was that he needed to focus his topic further.

One possibility for Rob was to concentrate on the history of baseball and maybe focus on a specific era that interested him. For example, he could have surprised and enlightened his listeners by discussing baseball during the Civil War. Or he could have focused on the all-black leagues operating from the 1920s until the integration of baseball during the 1950s. Rob could have used the popular movie *A League of Their Own* as backdrop and spoken about the All-American Girl's Baseball League formed during World War II when many professional baseball players were being drafted. Each of these topics would probably have interested and informed Rob's listeners, regardless of their fondness for baseball. Notice, too, that each of these narrower topics also places baseball in a sociological context. Rob's speech on the history of baseball could have thus become a lesson in a particular period of American history, having appeal even for listeners not especially interested in baseball.

▉ DETERMINING YOUR GENERAL PURPOSE

Broadly speaking, a speech may have one of three purposes: to inform, to persuade, or to entertain. The general purpose of your speech defines your relationship with the audience. You play the role of mentor when you provide information. You are an advocate when you seek to change beliefs, attitudes, values, or behaviors through a persuasive speech. Your speech to entertain is meant to amuse your audience. As the entertainer, you set a mood to relax your audience using your delivery style, tone, and content.

You may find it difficult at times to distinguish these purposes. Since information may affect both what we believe and how we act, the distinction between informative speaking and persuasive speaking is sometimes particularly blurred. A speech meant to entertain is frequently persuasive because it may make a serious point through the use of humor. Despite the overlap between these general purposes, you must be secure about your primary purpose any time you speak in public. A closer look at the objectives and intended outcomes of each general purpose will help you distinguish them.

Speeches to Inform

A **speech to inform** has as its objective to impart knowledge to an audience. You convey this information in an objective and unbiased manner. Your goal is not to alter the listeners' attitudes or behaviors but to facilitate their understanding of your subject and their ability to retain this new information. We discuss the speech to inform in greater detail in Chapter 14. A speech on any of the following topics could be informative:

> Artificial intelligence
> Cloning
> Hispanic film industry
> History of science fiction movies
> The middle child syndrome
> Muralist movement in Mexican art
> Right and left hemispheres of the brain
> Shopping addiction

speech to inform: a speech designed to convey new and/or useful information in a balanced, objective way.

Speeches to Persuade

A **speech to persuade** seeks to influence either beliefs or actions. The former, sometimes called a **speech to convince,** focuses on audience beliefs and attitudes. A speech designed to persuade audience members to embrace a belief stops short of advocating specific action. A speaker may argue, for example, that polygraph testing is unreliable without suggesting a plan of action. Another speaker may try to convince listeners that women have been neglected in medical research without offering a plan to solve the problem.

A speech designed to persuade to action, or a **speech to actuate,** attempts to change not only the listeners' beliefs and attitudes, but also their behavior. A speech to actuate could move the audience to boycott a controversial art exhibit, to contribute money to a charity, to enroll in a specific course, or to urge their elected officials to increase funding for women's health research. In each of these cases, the speaker's first goal would be to intensify or alter the audience's beliefs, and then to show how easy and beneficial taking action could be. We discuss the speech to persuade in Chapters 15 and 16.

speech to persuade: a speech designed to influence listeners' beliefs and/or actions.

speech to convince: a persuasive speech designed to influence audience beliefs and attitudes rather than behaviors.

speech to actuate: a persuasive speech designed to influence audience behaviors.

Speeches to Entertain

A third general purpose of speech is to entertain. A speech to entertain differs from speaking to entertain. *Speaking to entertain* is a general phrase covering several types of speaking. It includes humorous monologues, stand-up comedy routines, and storytelling, for example. When you tell your friends jokes or recount a humorous anecdote, you are trying to entertain them. You are probably not trying to develop a key point in an organized, methodical way.

A **speech to entertain** is more formal than simply speaking to entertain because it is more highly organized and its development is more detailed. Speeches to entertain are often delivered on occasions when people are in a festive mood, such as after a banquet or as part of an awards ceremony. For that reason, we discuss the speech to entertain in more detail in Chapter 17, "Speaking on Special Occasions." Remember that all speeches, including those to entertain, should develop a central thought through an organized presentation of supporting material and ideas. Though the ideas in a speech to entertain will be illustrated and highlighted by humor, a mere collection of jokes does not qualify as a speech. We agree with the communication scholars who contend that a speech to entertain is actually either a speech to inform or a speech to persuade, usually the latter.

speech to entertain: a speech designed to make a point through the creative, organized use of humorous supporting materials.

general purpose: the broad goal of a speech, such as to inform, to persuade, or to entertain.

specific purpose: a statement of the general purpose of the speech, the speaker's intended audience, and the limited goal or outcome.

■ FORMULATING YOUR SPECIFIC PURPOSE

When you are asked to state the **general purpose** of your speech, you will respond with two words from among the following: *to inform, to persuade* (or *to convince* or *to actuate),* or *to entertain.* When asked to state your specific purpose, however, you will need to be more descriptive. A **specific purpose** statement has three parts.

KEY POINTS **To Develop Your Specific Purpose Statement**	**1.** State your general purpose. **2.** Name your intended audience. **3.** State the goal of your speech.

First, you begin with the general purpose of the speech, stated as an infinitive; for example, "to convince." Second, you name the individuals to whom the speech is addressed. This is usually phrased simply as "the audience" or "my listeners." Third, you state what you want your speech to accomplish. What should the audience know, what should they believe, or what should they do as a result of your speech? You may want to establish the belief that alcoholism is hereditary. In this example, then, the complete specific purpose statement would be: To convince the audience that alcoholism is hereditary. A speech advocating compulsory national service for all U.S. citizens may have this as its specific purpose: to persuade the audience to write Congress urging the passage of a compulsory national service program. Other examples of specific purpose statements are:

- To inform the audience on how to communicate constructive criticism.
- To convince the audience that laughter is medically therapeutic.
- To convince the audience that aspartame is harmful.
- To convince the audience that "men only" social clubs inherently discriminate against businesswomen.
- To move the audience to draft and sign a living will.
- To move the audience to spend their spring break building a house for Habitat for Humanity.

■ WORDING YOUR THESIS STATEMENT

A **thesis statement** presents the central idea of the speech. It is a one-sentence synopsis of your speech. Although we discuss it in this chapter, a thesis statement, like the specific purpose, is usually constructed after you have finished your initial research and as you decide on your key ideas. The thesis statement of the persuasive speech on compulsory national service, mentioned earlier, could be this: "Compulsory national service would benefit the nation by promoting the national spirit, promoting the national defense, and promoting the national welfare." This statement is the central idea of the speech, a proposition the speaker will support with evidence and argument.

thesis statement: a one-sentence synopsis of a speaker's message.

Notice that the process of topic selection has, up to this point, enabled you to focus your subject on something specific and manageable. You have a handle on your subject and, as you begin to develop your key ideas, you will be able to determine whether you can support your thesis statement. In organizing the body of the speech, you may realize that your ideas are not balanced or that two of your main points should be collapsed into one. As you research your speech, you may discover additional ideas that are more important than some you had planned to present. That was the experience of our student who spoke on compulsory national service.

Stuart was developing a persuasive speech advocating a system of compulsory national service (CNS). As he began his research, he planned to focus only on the national security that compulsory military service would provide. He imagined that his thesis statement would be, "Compulsory national service would benefit the nation by ensuring its military readiness." Yet his research quickly revealed many other benefits of CNS.

Some programs of compulsory national service that have been proposed include a domestic volunteer service that would address issues other than military readiness. For example, Stuart learned that such a program could help conservation and recycling efforts. By training doctors' assistants, CNS could also extend quality health care into rural areas. CNS could serve millions of elderly people who need only light assistance in order to be able to live independently in their own homes.

By the time he had completed his research, Stuart had broadened the focus of his speech and felt he had developed a much stronger case for instituting a CNS program. When he delivered his speech, he presented three main arguments:

I. CNS would promote the national spirit.
II. CNS would promote the national defense.
III. CNS would promote the national welfare.

Stuart made certain to revise his thesis statement to reflect his new organization. (Remember, you will also need to modify your thesis statement any time you revise the content and structure of your speech.)

The following examples illustrate how you can narrow a topic's focus from a general area to the speech's thesis statement.

Topic Area: Gender
Topic: Pre-selecting a baby's gender
General Purpose: To inform
Specific Purpose: To inform the audience of issues involved in gender selection.
Thesis Statement: Before deciding on pre-selection, parents should consider the medical, social, and ethical issues involved in gender selection.

Topic Area: Surgery
Topic: Elective cosmetic surgery
General Purpose: To persuade
Specific Purpose: To persuade the audience of the harms of elective cosmetic surgery.
Thesis Statement: Elective cosmetic surgery leaves physical scars, psychological scars, and financial scars.

▆▆▆ DEVELOPING YOUR SPEECH TITLE

Some speeches do not require titles. Many public speaking instructors, for example, do not require titles for speeches delivered in class. In most formal public speaking situations, however, the audience knows the speaker and topic beforehand. The title is often included in a printed program or mentioned by the person introducing the speaker. Therefore, whenever you have the opportunity, you should title all your speeches, including your classroom speeches.

A well-crafted title accomplishes three purposes. First, it generates audience interest in your speech. A speech title disclosed to the audience should arouse interest, secure attention, and make people want to listen. By appealing to the needs and interests of your audience, a title can encourage active listening.

Interesting titles may also enhance your image as a communicator and make the audience want to listen to you specifically. When you speak to an audience that does not know you, your title may generate the audience's first impression of you. Creative titles engender more interest than general, technical, or overused ones. A speech about the All-American Girl's Baseball League, for example, could be titled "A History of the All-American Girl's Baseball League" or "A Diamond is a Girl's Best Friend." Which title do you you think is more interesting? Which title would interest you more in hearing a speech on tedium in the workplace: "Job Burnout" or "Making Your Work Relaxing and Rewarding"?

A second purpose of a title is to make your message more memorable. While there is an up side to creativity, you should avoid the temptation of selecting a title simply for the sake of creativity. If, in the process, you sacrifice clarity, you may actually divert audience attention from your central thesis. Remember, when you encapsulate the point of your speech in the title, you prepare the audience to listen for its development or to use it as a reference point when they explain to others what you discussed.

If you study print advertisements, you will see that they usually use this strategy successfully. The headline usually contains a selling promise designed to capture the attention of those likely to buy the product or service. Speech titles such as "Converting Anger to Action" or "Making Your Anger Work for You" are clear and direct. A person who frequently experiences anger can expect to learn how that negative emotion can become a positive option. These titles identify the audience (those who experience anger) and include a promise (anger can work for you). A speech describing the healing nature of the grieving process, for example, could be titled simply "Good Grief!" The title is short, attention-getting, and easy to remember, and it highlights the concept that grief can be good.

We found the following titles of student speeches printed in *Winning Orations*, an annual publication of the Interstate Oratorical Association.[4] You probably have an idea of what each speech is about even though you have not heard or read it.

Gossip: It's Worth Talking About
Charities' Telesolicitation: Fundraising or Fraud?
National Parks: A Scenery of Destruction and Degradation
Budget Motels: Cheaper Costs, Higher Risks
Term Limits: A Solution Worse than the Problem

If you accomplish the objectives of securing your listeners' interest and enhancing the memorability of your key ideas before you utter your first word, you have gone a long way toward ensuring the success of your speech.

A third and final benefit of a good speech title is primarily for you, the speaker. When you give your speech a title, you are forced to state your point clearly and concisely. If you have difficulty constructing a title that encapsulates your key ideas, your speech probably lacks a clear central thought, or you have strayed from your intended thesis. It is better to discover this before you speak so you have time to make proper adjustments.

There is no one best way to develop a title for a speech, but consider these three options. First, if your speech contains a key phrase or sentence that is used repeatedly, that statement may be your title. Martin Luther King, Jr., used the repeated theme *I have a dream* for the title of his "I Have a Dream" speech. (See Appendix C for a reprint.) A speech arguing the harm of plastic surgery performed just to make a person feel more beautiful could be titled, "Making Stars, Leaving Scars." The title contrasts the search for physical beauty with the scars it may leave behind. The use of rhyme also makes the title easy to remember.

A second strategy for developing a good speech title is to promise your audience something beneficial in the title. A speech on the benefits of exercise could be titled "Living Longer, Feeling Better." Titles that begin with "How to" follow this strategy, and are particularly appropriate when you know the audience is interested in acquiring a skill you can teach them. "How You Can Pass This Course Without Spending Any More Time Studying" may not be the most creative title for a speech, but we bet you and your classmates would listen with rapt attention to it!

Finally, a third strategy is to word your title as a question. A speech investigating laughter therapy could be titled "Is Laughter Really the Best Medicine?" Asking the question signals to the audience what they will know by the end of the speech. Keep in mind that your listeners will expect to be able to answer the question by the end of your speech. We remember one speech professor who titled a speech convention paper on the effects of humor "Can Humor Increase Persuasion, or Is It All a Joke?" The title used humor because the paper was *about* humor, and the fact that we still remember the title attests to its effectiveness.

SUMMARY

By selecting topics for their speeches, students in public speaking classes determine the majority of what they will hear during the course. Six steps can simplify the important process of choosing an appropriate speech topic.

First, brainstorm a list of potential topics focused around your own interests, the needs and interests of your audience, and the occasion for your speech. Your research adds a fourth category of possible topics. Having a large list of subjects gives you the freedom and flexibility to make an appropriate selection.

The second step is to select your topic. Making this decision is easier if you ask yourself four questions while reviewing your topic list: "Am I already interested or likely to become interested in this topic as I develop the speech?" "Is the topic already interesting or important to my audience, or can I interest them in it?" "Am I likely to find adequate, quality supporting materials on this topic in the time I have?" And "Do I know enough about the topic to start researching it and to interpret what I discover?"

The third step is to focus or narrow the subject you've selected. Two ways to accomplish this are *visual brainstorming* and initial research on the topic. Focusing the topic is important in guiding your research and helping you stay within the time limit for the speech.

The fourth step is to determine your *general purpose:* to inform, to persuade, or to entertain. The general purpose may be predetermined, as in most classroom speech assignments, or left to the judgment of the speaker. Whether you are determining the purpose or just reminding yourself of it, having that goal clearly in mind will keep you on target as you research and organize the speech.

The fifth step of selecting a topic is to formulate your *specific purpose.* That statement should specify three things: the general purpose in infinitive form ("to inform," for example), the intended audience, and what you want your listeners to know, believe, or do as a result of your speech.

The sixth step, wording your *thesis statement,* means distilling the message of the speech into one sentence. This step must come last, since it depends upon your initial research and tentative organization of the speech. With the thesis statement in mind, a speaker is ready to conduct in-depth research and to proceed with the development of the speech.

A possible final step, not always required, is to title the speech. Creative, provocative titles achieve three goals. First, they intrigue the audience and make them want to listen to you. Second, they make your message more memorable. Third, they help speakers check to see that the speech has a central focus or thesis.

EXERCISES

1. On a sheet of paper, list eight self-generated, eight audience-generated, eight occasion-generated, and fifteen research-generated topics. Place an *I* by the topics you would develop as informative speeches, and a *P* by those that are persuasive. Place an asterisk (*) by five informative topics and five persuasive topics you think would make the best speeches. Bring your list to class. Meeting in small groups, share your list with your classmates, having them decide the five best topics in each category. Now review your list and decide the topics on which you would like to speak.

2. Choose a topic area and use the technique of visual brainstorming to generate a list of specific topics. Continue diagramming as long as it is productive. Now look at your list and select those that you think are probably the best topics for a speech in this class.

3. Using the topic areas listed below, narrow each subject and write a specific purpose statement for an informative speech and a persuasive speech on each topic.
   a. Fast food   **b.** Funerals   **c.** Illiteracy   **d.** Stress   **e.** UFOs

4. Select and read a speech in Appendix C. Determine its general purpose. Word its specific purpose and thesis statement.

5. Construct at least two titles for a speech on each of the specific purposes listed below. Word the title so that it attracts audience interest or captures the central idea of the speech.
   a. To inform the audience on how to interpret their dreams.
   b. To inform the audience on how the stock market works.
   c. To inform the audience on the history of Valentine's Day.
   d. To inform the audience on the problems of being a single parent.
   e. To persuade the audience of the benefits (or the hazards) of nuclear energy.
   f. To persuade the audience that professional boxing should be outlawed.
   g. To persuade the audience to get involved in campus government.
   h. To persuade the audience that IQ tests are culturally biased.

NOTES

1. Hunter S. Thompson, *Generation of Swine: Tales of Shame and Degradation in the '80s* (New York: Vintage, 1989) 209.

2. Patrick Murphy, "Chronobiology: For Athletes It's a Matter of Time," *The Physician and Sportsmedicine* September 1984: 160. Murphy discusses the Cubs and chronobiology in his article on pages 160-62, 164.

3. Kenneth B. Storey and Janet M. Storey, "Frozen and Alive," *Scientific American* December 1990: 92-97.

4. These titles come from *Winning Orations 1991* and *Winning Orations 1992* (Mankato, MN: Interstate Oratorical Association, 1991, 1992).

If we would have knowledge, we must get a world of new questions.

       Susanne K. Langer

Researching Your Topic

Chapter 7

"Knowledge is of two kinds. We know a subject ourselves, or we know where we can find information upon it."

SAMUEL JOHNSON

T his year approximately 50,000 books will be published in the United States.[1] Add to this the information provided by millions of pages printed in newspapers, magazines, and other periodicals; volumes of public and private agencies' reports, hearings, and pamphlets; and hours of news and opinions broadcast through television and radio. These print and electronic media have given us access to an explosion of knowledge and opinion. As a result, public speakers face the challenge of selecting from this wide range of data the information most appropriate for their speeches.

In Chapter 6, we discussed how to select a topic. In this chapter we consider the second step — how to research a topic. **Research** is the gathering of evidence and arguments you will need to understand, develop, and explain your subject. Remember that research is not one step of the speech construction process. Research should occur throughout that process. For example, we have already seen in Chapter 6 how research can help you select your topic. Once you have chosen your topic for certain, additional research helps you focus it and determine your specific purpose. As you move to the next step and begin to construct the body of your speech, you may need to develop some of your ideas further with additional research. Your research continues even as you consult dictionaries, thesauruses, and books of quotations to help you word the ideas of your speech before you deliver it in class.

research: the process of gathering evidence and arguments to understand, develop, and explain a speech topic.

"Who is the fairest one of all, and state your sources!"

Drawing by Ed Fisher; © 1984 *The New Yorker Magazine*, Inc.

Students often wonder how much research to conduct for a classroom speech. Obviously, there is no one answer to this question. Research your topic until you have enough authoritative evidence for you to make an informative or a persuasive statement to your listeners. As the *New Yorker* cartoon suggests, you need to back up your ideas with credible sources. Your instructor may specify a minimum number of sources you are to cite during your speech. Does that mean your research is finished when you have reached that magic number? The answer is, not necessarily. Sometimes the information you have collected may be insufficient to support your intended central idea, or may even contradict it. In these cases you must continue research to gain additional information. You may find that you have to shift your focus or change your topic altogether. Research can also lead you to discover new aspects of your subject that you had not considered. These new aspects may be more interesting and worthwhile than your original topic. The excellent public speaker, then, does not view research as a phase preceding the construction of the speech, but as an evolving process. We research so that excellent evidence supports excellent ideas that can, in turn, be excellently organized and delivered.

Occasionally, if you are lucky, you may stumble onto one or two sources of great help as you craft your speech. But most of the time you will work hard on your research to ensure that you collect the information pertinent to your topic. Your research strategy will depend on your particular topic and the available research facilities. However, we provide you with the following general five-step sequence to assist you in generating excellent ideas and supporting material, regardless of the topic of your speech.

1. Assess your personal knowledge of the topic.
2. Develop your research plan.
3. Collect your information.
4. Record your information.
5. Evaluate your information.

Let us look more closely at each of these steps.

ASSESS PERSONAL KNOWLEDGE

Samuel Johnson correctly noted that personal knowledge is the starting point of research. The first question you should ask and answer is, "What do I know that will help me develop my topic?" When you begin your research, do not make the mistake of confining yourself only to library holdings. Your personal memory has been shaped by what you have read, heard, observed, and experienced. Use that knowledge as a starting point for researching your topic.

The concept of mastering public speaking we sketched in the preface to this book requires a public speaker to have an ongoing commitment to public communication. Establishing a personal information base is important for any speaker who wants to be informed and credible. You already have a great deal of personal knowledge. Don't be afraid to tap this resource as you select and develop your speech topic. For example, a student who worked as a plainclothes security guard for a major department store drew from personal experience in his speech on detecting and apprehending shoplifters. A student who assisted her father in administering polygraph tests chose as her speech topic the use and misuse of lie detectors. A person whose hobby was playing the bagpipes informed his audience about the history of this musical instrument. A vegetarian decided to persuade others to consider her diet. These speakers used their personal knowledge and experiences as starting points for their research. Each developed and delivered an interesting speech.

Throughout your life, you will occasionally, perhaps often, be called upon to share your expertise and opinions with others in public speeches. Therefore, you should consider developing a personal filing system of information you can retrieve for those occasions. We have found three kinds of files helpful in constructing our speeches: a clipping file, a quotation file, and a speech file.

clipping file: a collection of newspaper or magazine articles a speaker finds interesting or important.

A **clipping file** includes informative articles cut or copied from newspapers and magazines on topics of interest to you. This type of file gives you a head start in selecting a topic and researching your speech. When you read a provocative passage in a book or an interesting magazine article, photocopy it, record the complete source citation on the photocopy, and file it in a labeled folder. When you are asked to speak to a group, consult your clipping file for possible topics appropriate to the occasion and audience.

quotation file: a collection of passages a speaker finds memorable or important, together with the source citation for each passage.

A second useful file is a **quotation file.** Many good books of quotations are available in the reference section of your library or local bookstore. They can assist you in wording and explaining your speech. (See a partial list on pages 140-141.) You may also find it helpful to generate your own collection of quotations. When you read or hear a memorable statement, copy it and the name of the speaker or writer onto a 3-inch-by-5-inch notecard, putting the card in a filebox. As your collection grows, you can divide the quotations into categories. When preparing your speech, consult your file for statements that illustrate or highlight your ideas.

Quotations can also serve as excellent attention-getting or concluding statements. For example, Jodi began her speech with the statement: "'Memory,' it has been said, 'is the power to gather roses in winter.'" She used that quotation to underpin her thesis that the tragedy of Alzheimer's disease is that, by destroying memory, it eliminates one's past. We have also heard several students urge their listeners to action by quoting Edmund Burke: "The only thing necessary for the triumph of evil is for good men to do nothing."

speech file: a personal collection of materials about the research, preparation, and delivery of speeches completed or initiated.

A third file, the **speech file,** contains a folder for each speech you have given or have started to prepare. After you present a speech to one audience, a listener may ask you to speak on the same topic to another group. Therefore, save and file your speaking notes or manuscript. This file should also include your research notes. You may want to refocus your topic to adapt to the new audience, but you will still have saved valuable research and preparation time if you can review your original research notes and articles. It is important to remember, however, that every student speaker should research and develop his or her own speech. One speaker's files should never be used by another speaker to construct a speech.

Winston Churchill was once asked how long he had prepared for one of his speeches. He replied, "For forty years." In discussing this incident, Robert Jeffrey and Owen Peterson observe, "In a sense, a speaker spends his or her entire life preparing for a speech. Everything we have learned and experienced, as well as the attitudes we have developed, shapes and influences our speech."[2] Your knowledge and personal files give you a head start in selecting and developing your topic.

Someone once posed this question: "If you don't know where you're going, how will you know when you get there?" Experienced explorers focus on a destination while equipping themselves with detailed plans of action and appropriate tools to reach the target. Similarly, speakers should develop research plans and marshal the tools necessary to achieve their targets — well-presented speeches. Your research plan begins as you answer several questions:

1. What information do I need?
2. Where am I most likely to find it?
3. How can I obtain this information?
4. How will time constraints affect my research options?

Your research plan depends, in large part, on your topic and specific purpose. As we mentioned earlier, many speech topics require library research. Topics such as the electronic encyclopedia, mathematical illiteracy, environmental racism, or the history of graffiti would rely heavily on library resources. Other speech topics rely on personal interviews for most of their information. If, for example, your purpose is to inform your classmates of your school's new registration procedures, your library may be of little assistance. More helpful would be an interview with your college's registrar. A speech explaining new breakthroughs in cancer research could benefit from collecting information from the American Cancer Society. In short, different topics demand different research strategies. A good research plan accounts for these differences. Keep a running list of what you need and where you can obtain it.

Not only should you prepare a list of what you need and where you can obtain it, but you should also prepare a timetable for constructing your speech. If you are going to speak two weeks from now, you still have time to go to the library and work. You may even have time to set up an interview with an expert, conduct it, and transcribe key quotations. However, two weeks is not enough time to write for information and be assured of its arrival in time to integrate it into your speech.

Although you should explore all appropriate options, most of your research will probably take place in your college or community library. One of the most helpful sources of information to assist you in creating your research plan is also one of the least often used: the library staff, particularly those members who work in the reference department. A good reference librarian can: (1) acquaint you with the services and holdings of the library, (2) guide you to particular sources of information helpful for your research, and (3) instruct you in the use of library equipment.

Although all libraries have much in common, each is organized to serve its specific constituency. No college library can subscribe to all periodicals and newspapers, for example. Don't waste your time copying index citations for periodicals that are not in your library. Your reference librarian can guide you to the library's areas of strength, thus making your research more efficient.

In many ways you learn to use a library just as you learn to drive a car. A good driver receives instruction on driving principles and the workings of an automobile before soloing. The driver's goal is not to remain dependent on the instructor but to become proficient so that he or she can venture out alone. Similarly, the effective researcher receives valuable instruction on research principles and the workings of the library from an experienced research librarian. Together they work to develop a research plan. If pursued aggressively, that research plan can yield excellent supporting materials for a public speech.

■ COLLECT YOUR INFORMATION

Once you have developed a research plan, begin to collect the information you need to understand and develop your topic. Students who complain, "I can't find any information on my topic," usually do not know where to look. For most topics, your library probably has more information than you can locate and read in the time allotted for your research. If you have developed a good research strategy, you will make efficient use of the following resources in generating the information you need to prepare your speech.

In this chapter we cannot list all, or even most, of the resources available to you. We discuss magazines and journals, newspapers, government documents, books, reference works, and some alternative research sources. These resources will provide most of the background information you will need. For the serious researcher we also recommend Lois Horowitz's book *Knowing Where to Look: The Ultimate Guide to Research,* an excellent introduction to where and how to find information.[3]

Magazines and Journals

Articles in magazines and journals are probably the most common source of information for student speeches. With more than 70,000 magazines from which to choose, however, how do you keep from being overwhelmed with information?[4] Using an index will help you filter useful from extraneous information. Hundreds of excellent indexes of peri-

A library reference section can unlock a wealth of information in indexes, encyclopedias, and almanacs.
(SOURCE: © Brian Smith, Stock, Boston)

odicals exist, and many standard indexes are now available in compact disk or magnetic tape versions. These indexes can guide you as you focus your search even more.

The most commonly used index for researching magazines is the *Readers' Guide to Periodical Literature*, now more than ninety years old. With entries indexed by author and subject, and published every other week, this resource is especially useful because it references more than 250 English-language periodicals, including those most frequently found in libraries. You will find the subject index particularly useful, as it specifies articles pertaining to your subject area written during a designated time period. Look at the sample entries and their explanation in Figure 7.1.

Another useful index is the *Public Affairs Information Service (PAIS) Bulletin*, which indexes articles from periodicals as well as selected books, government publications,

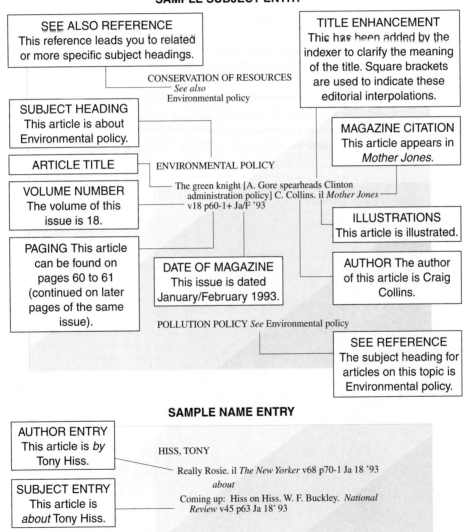

SAMPLE SUBJECT ENTRY

SEE ALSO REFERENCE
This reference leads you to related or more specific subject headings.

TITLE ENHANCEMENT
This has been added by the indexer to clarify the meaning of the title. Square brackets are used to indicate these editorial interpolations.

CONSERVATION OF RESOURCES
See also
Environmental policy

SUBJECT HEADING
This article is about Environmental policy.

MAGAZINE CITATION
This article appears in *Mother Jones*.

ARTICLE TITLE

ENVIRONMENTAL POLICY

VOLUME NUMBER
The volume of this issue is 18.

The green knight [A. Gore spearheads Clinton administration policy] C. Collins. il *Mother Jones* v18 p60-1+ Ja/F '93

ILLUSTRATIONS
This article is illustrated.

PAGING This article can be found on pages 60 to 61 (continued on later pages of the same issue).

DATE OF MAGAZINE
This issue is dated January/February 1993.

AUTHOR The author of this article is Craig Collins.

POLLUTION POLICY *See* Environmental policy

SEE REFERENCE
The subject heading for articles on this topic is Environmental policy.

SAMPLE NAME ENTRY

AUTHOR ENTRY
This article is *by* Tony Hiss.

HISS, TONY

Really Rosie. il *The New Yorker* v68 p70-1 Ja 18 '93
about
Coming up: Hiss on Hiss. W. F. Buckley. *National Review* v45 p63 Ja 18' 93

SUBJECT ENTRY
This article is *about* Tony Hiss.

Source: Readers' Guide to Periodical Literature, February 1994. Used with permission.

Figure 7.1 *Readers' Guide to Periodical Literature*

tion of newspapers from throughout the U.S. You can access the full text of many news-papers from some online services. At some libraries, you can even download text to your own computer disk. The citation in Figure 7.2, taken from the *National Newspaper Index* under the topic "Appalachian region," illustrates the type of information typically included in a newspaper index.

Other indexes will guide you to newspapers targeted at specific ethnic, professional, and geographical audiences. The *Black Newspapers Index*, for example, references newspapers oriented to African-American audiences and often contains stories not found in more mainstream newspapers. The *Wall Street Journal Index* is a source of information on business and economic topics. Your library may also subscribe to the indexes and newspapers of major city papers.

If your city's newspaper is not indexed, it may still be in your library on microfilm. Without an index, however, its usefulness is limited, unless you know the actual or approximate date of the article you want.

Another excellent guide to newspapers is *NewsBank*. Articles on political, economic, social, scientific, legal, health, and international issues are selected, organized, and recorded on microfiche. The *NewsBank Index*, available on computer as well as in hard copy, puts at your fingertips articles from over 450 newspapers and regional business publications it references. Included in the front of the bound volumes of the index is an easy to understand, step-by-step guide to locating articles in *NewsBank*.

Government Documents

The most prolific publisher of information in the United States is the federal government. Much of our bureaucracy is devoted to collecting, cataloguing, and disseminating information. The U.S. government generates a wealth of information on a wide range of topics from its many congressional, executive, and judicial agencies.

Accessing government documents may initially seem intimidating to you, but learning how to locate this information is well worth your investment of time and effort. Two publications can help you find information in government documents: the *CIS/Index* and the *Monthly Catalog of U.S. Government Publications*. The Congressional Information Service publishes the *CIS/Index* and *CIS Abstracts* to help you select from the more than 800,000 pages of information produced by Congress each year.

In book form, the *CIS/Index* is superior to the *Monthly Catalog* because it is more specific and easier to use. The *CIS* is, however, limited to congressional publications. The *Monthly Catalog* references documents from all branches of government, and is also available in a CD-ROM version known as *Marcive GPO CAT/PAC*. For access to federal statistical publications, you can consult the *American Statistics Index*, published by the Congressional Information Service.

Books

Books, of course, are excellent sources of information. Because they are longer than magazine and newspaper articles, books allow authors to discuss topics in greater depth and often provide an index to key ideas and a bibliography of sources consulted. Recognize, however, that if your speech topic requires the most up-to-date data you can find, information in magazines may be more current and accessible than what you can find in books. Despite this limitation, books can be an integral part of your research plan.

Your library probably uses one of several cataloging systems. Three of the most common are the computer catalog, the card catalog, and the microfilm catalog. Many libraries have installed computer catalogs, although some libraries still use the other two for parts of their collections. The *computer catalog* (Figure 7.3) permits you to access subject, title, and author listings without having to move from one station to another. The computer catalog usually provides better cross-referencing of related topics than does the card catalog. An additional feature is the "status" column, which indicates whether the book is on the library shelves, checked out, or on order. Many computer catalogs also have printers attached, allowing you to print entries for items you want to find on the library shelves.

The *card catalog*, familiar to most of us since we first began to use libraries, consists of index cards filed alphabetically according to subject, title, and author. Figure 7.4 shows examples of these three types of cards for a particular book.

Entries in a *microfilm catalog* (Figure 7.5) are usually more concise than card catalog references, but they are still indexed according to subject, title, and author. One major

Figure 7.3 *Computer catalog*

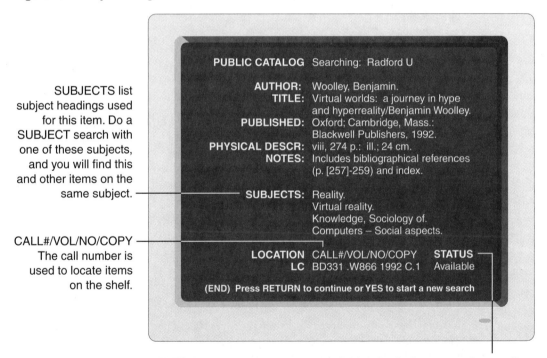

SUBJECTS list subject headings used for this item. Do a SUBJECT search with one of these subjects, and you will find this and other items on the same subject.

CALL#/VOL/NO/COPY The call number is used to locate items on the shelf.

STATUS tells whether a book is available, checked out, on order, etc. If a book is checked out, the due date will appear under STATUS.

Source: Updated and adapted from *LS/2000 Online Catalog Instruction Tutorial* (Radford, VA: McConnell Library, Radford University, 1990) 4. This computer catalog is produced by Ameritech Information Services. Used with permission.

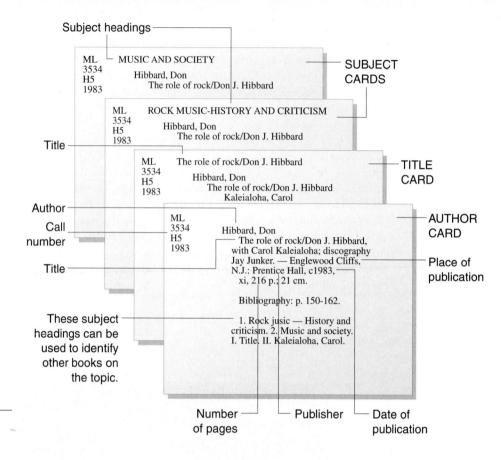

Subject headings

MUSIC AND SOCIETY

ML
3534
H5
1983
    Hibbard, Don
      The role of rock/Don J. Hibbard

SUBJECT CARDS

ROCK MUSIC-HISTORY AND CRITICISM

ML
3534
H5
1983
    Hibbard, Don
      The role of rock/Don J. Hibbard

Title

The role of rock/Don J. Hibbard

ML
3534
H5
1983
    Hibbard, Don
      The role of rock/Don J. Hibbard
      Kaleialoha, Carol

TITLE CARD

Author
Call number
Title

ML
3534
H5
1983

Hibbard, Don
  The role of rock/Don J. Hibbard,
with Carol Kaleialoha; discography
Jay Junker. — Englewood Cliffs,
N.J.: Prentice Hall, c1983,
xi, 216 p.; 21 cm.

Bibliography: p. 150-162.

1. Rock jusic — History and
criticism. 2. Music and society.
I. Title. II. Kaleialoha, Carol.

AUTHOR CARD

Place of publication

These subject headings can be used to identify other books on the topic.

Number of pages   Publisher   Date of publication

Figure 7.4 *Card catalog*

disadvantage of the microfilm catalog is that it is more difficult to update than the computer or card catalogs. If you were using a microfilm catalog to research the history of restaurants, you could locate books on that topic using any of the indexes.

Reference Works

"There are times when I think that the ideal library is composed solely of reference books. They are like understanding friends — always ready to meet your mood, always ready to change the subject when you have had enough of this or that." **J. DONALD ADAMS**

Perhaps the heart of any library is its reference section. These resources, usually available for use only in the library, include many types of collections to aid you in your research. A few that you will find helpful are dictionaries, encyclopedias, almanacs, yearbooks, and books of quotations.

Dictionaries. Dictionaries help you clarify the meanings of words and their spellings and pronunciations. There are many good general dictionaries, and you undoubtedly use these regularly. A number of more specialized dictionaries covering a wide range of topic areas are also available. A list of a few of these follows.

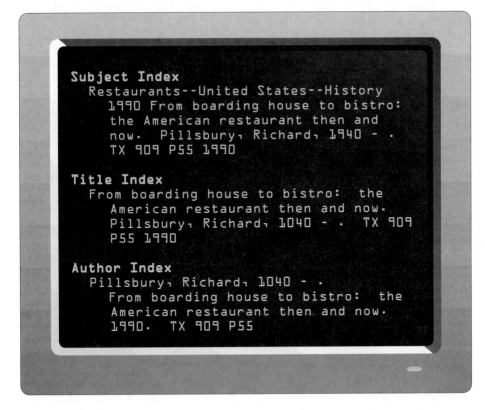

Figure 7.5 *A microfilm catalog*

The Dictionary of Advertising
A Dictionary of Bad Manners
Dictionary of Business and Economics
A Dictionary of Color
A Dictionary of Dates

A Dictionary of Slang and Unconventional English
A Dictionary of Statistical Terms
A Feminist Dictionary

Even a quick glance through that list should tell you that some of these dictionaries would be good places to begin your search for a speech topic.

Encyclopedias.   You have, no doubt, used general encyclopedias, such as *Encyclopedia Americana, Encyclopædia Britannica,* and *World Book,* to prepare reports and papers in elementary and high school. These multivolume sets of books organize information on many branches of knowledge. However, did you know that numerous encyclopedias, such as the following, focus on specific bodies of knowledge?

Encyclopedia of American Humorists
Encyclopedia of American Shipwrecks
Encyclopedia of Black America

Encyclopedia of Jazz
Encyclopedia of Medical History
The Encyclopedia of Sports Talk

Examining some of these volumes can both generate topics for future speeches and give you background information about your current topic.

Almanacs.   "Almanacs and Bibles were the first books to come to the United States," writes Lois Horowitz:

At a time when there were few newspapers, the settlers used almanacs for a melange of valuable information and entertainment. Almanacs predicted the weather for the coming year; gave advice on crops and planting; listed home remedies, multiplication tables, interest charts, and even stagecoach schedules. They also included inspirational verse and stories.[5]

Almanacs have changed over the years — certainly, they no longer publish stagecoach schedules — but their character remains the same. Almanacs contain a wide range of specific and statistical information about topics including education, politics, sports, entertainment, and significant events of a particular year. Almanacs are excellent sources when you need specific facts and background information. What is the exact wording of Amendment II of the United States Constitution? Who is the head of state of Zambia? In what year did Mother Teresa win the Nobel Peace Prize? How many hazardous waste sites operate in the state of New Jersey? A good almanac answers these questions and many others. If you selected the history of manned space flights as your speech topic, an almanac would be a ready reference for the dates, duration, and description of those flights.

General almanacs include the *World Almanac and Book of Facts, Information Please Almanac, The Universal Almanac*, and the *New York Public Library Desk Reference*. Specialized almanacs cover a wide range of subjects, as illustrated by these examples: *Almanac for Computers, Almanac for American Politics, Almanac of Higher Education*, and *Almanac of World Crime*.

Yearbooks. Yearbooks are usually published annually and include information pertinent to that year or the previous year. Encyclopedia publishers, for example, often offer yearbooks as supplements to their main set of books. Yearbooks enable researchers to update information on a particular topic. *Facts on File Yearbook,* for example, digests and catalogs world news originally published in the weekly publication, *Facts on File.* The diversity of topics covered in yearbooks is illustrated by the following titles: *Yearbook of Agriculture, Yearbook of Higher Education, Yearbook of Emergency Medicine, Yearbook of School Law,* and the *World Yearbook of Robotics Research and Development.*

Books of Quotations. Captivating quotations, both serious and funny, can enliven the language of your speech. As we noted earlier, they are particularly appropriate in speech introductions and conclusions. Quoting another person also adds authority to your comments and, thus, can strengthen the development of your ideas. Fortunately, many excellent books of quotations are available in bookstores and libraries. Some of our favorites follow.

> *Bartlett's Familiar Quotations*
> *A Dictionary of Economic Quotations*
> *The Dictionary of War Quotations*
> *Famous Last Words*
> *Famous Phrases from History*
> *The International Thesaurus of Quotations*
> *My Soul Looks Back, 'Less I Forget: A Collection of Quotations by People of Color*
> *The New International Dictionary of Quotations*
> *The New Quotable Woman: The Definitive Treasury of Notable Words by Women from Eve to the Present*
> *Oxford Dictionary of Quotations*

Books of quotations are organized alphabetically by author or subject. Almost all of them have indexes, allowing you to find a quotation by a specific person or about a specific subject.

Interviews

Although the library will, undoubtedly, be the place where you do most of your research, you can find a wealth of information outside your library, and some of it is not confined to the written word. Depending on your topic, an interview may be the best source of firsthand information. The personal interview can aid you in four ways. First, if published sources are inaccessible, the personal interview may be your only option. The topic you have chosen may be so recent that sufficient information is not yet in print or, if it is, it has not arrived in your library. Your topic may also be so localized as to receive little or no coverage by area media.

Suppose, for example, that your college announces that it will adopt a telephone registration procedure next year. You decide that this will make a timely topic for your informative speech to your classmates. You could make an appointment with the college registrar to learn more about the new procedure. If you learn that other colleges have tried a system similar to the one proposed at your school, you could call officials at those institutions and solicit additional information. Using both telephone and face-to-face interviews, you could generate much of the supporting material you need for your speech, information that would probably not be available at your library.

Interviews with experts can yield excellent original research for your speech.
(Source: © Peter Menzel/Stock, Boston)

A second advantage of the personal interview is that it permits you to adapt your topic to your specific audience. Take, for example, the topic of recycling. Your audience would probably be interested in data estimating the amount of resources and landfill space the United States could save annually from recycling. If you interview the director of your school's physical plant to find out how much trash custodians collect and dispose of each day, you give your speech a personal touch. You could take your speech one step further by figuring out how much your college could contribute to resource conservation. What you have done is show your audience how this topic, recycling, affects them directly. You will grab their attention.

Third, personal interviews provide opportunities for you to secure expert evaluation of your research and suggestions for further research. The experts you interview may challenge some of your assumptions or data. If this happens, encourage such feedback and do not get defensive. Knowing all the angles can only help you give a more thoughtful speech. Near the end of your interview, ask your interviewee to suggest additional sources that will help you better research and understand your topic.

Finally, personal interviews can enhance your image as a speaker. In addition to gathering information in the library, you took the time to conduct an interview. Listeners are usually impressed that you went beyond library research in preparing your message for them. Think of the speech topic we just discussed on recycling. Your classmates will probably see your extra effort as confirmation of your commitment to the topic and the speechmaking process.

KEY POINTS		
Preparing for the Interview	**1.** Determine whom you want to interview.	**3.** Schedule the interview.
	2. Decide the format for the interview.	**4.** Research the person to be interviewed.
		5. Prepare a list of questions.

Prepare for the Interview.

Two days before her speech was due, Marie began thinking of a topic. She remembered reading in the campus newspaper that the school of business at her college was seeking accreditation. Since a majority of students in her public speaking class were business majors, she decided to inform them on the benefits of receiving accreditation and the steps in the accreditation process. She called her accounting professor and arranged for an appointment the next afternoon.

Arriving ten minutes late, she apologized and then explained the reason for the interview. She took out a tape recorder, but Professor Saunders said that he'd rather not be recorded. Since she hadn't prepared a list of questions, Marie began the interview by saying, "Just tell me anything you can about this accreditation thing and how it will benefit the university." Saunders said that he was not involved in the process and didn't think he could be too helpful. He added that he thought accreditation would help the university recruit better students and faculty. After the interview, a disappointed Marie went to the library, found an encyclopedia, photocopied an article on reptiles indigenous to Florida, and went back to the dorm to prepare her speech for the next day's class.

What went wrong during this phase of Marie's speech preparation? Her original topic — accreditation — was a good one; it was timely and relevant to her audience. The personal interview was an appropriate research strategy. Unfortunately, Marie's plan of action was poorly conceived, planned, and executed. Once you decide to conduct a personal interview, you must take several steps in preparation. First, determine whom you want to interview. Your interviewee should be someone who is both knowledgeable on the topic and willing to speak with you. Marie did not bother to find out if her accounting professor was the most knowledgeable person on her topic before she set up the interview.

Second, decide on the format for the interview. Will you conduct it face to face, by phone, or by letter? A face-to-face interview will probably give you the most information. People tend to open up more when they interact verbally and nonverbally. As a face-to-face interviewer, you can both listen to what the interviewee says and observe the nonverbal messages. An interview over the phone is another possibility when you cannot travel to the expert. A third option, conducting an interview through written correspondence, has both advantages and disadvantages. It is time-consuming because you must prepare a set of questions, mail or deliver it to the interviewee, and wait for a response. It has the added disadvantage of not allowing for immediate follow-up questions. If something needs clarification, you must submit another question. The written interview, however, often results in more thoughtful and better worded responses than face-to-face or telephone interviews.

The third preparation step is to schedule the interview. When requesting an interview, identify yourself and the topic on which you seek information. Let the person know how you intend to use that information, the amount of time needed for the interview, and any special recording procedures you plan to use. Some people may object to being quoted or to having their comments recorded. If this is the case, it is best to find that out ahead of time rather than at the interview, as Marie did. You will likely discover that most people you seek to interview are flattered that you selected them as experts and are therefore happy to cooperate.

Fourth, research the person to be interviewed before you show up at his or her doorstep. Obviously, your selection of the interviewee suggests that you already know something about him or her. In addition, read any articles the interviewee has published on your topic before the interview. This enables you to conduct the interview efficiently. You won't ask questions that the person has already answered in print, and your prior reading may prompt some specific questions on points you would like clarified. Also, your research will show that you are prepared. The interviewee will take you and the interview seriously. Marie did not do this.

Fifth, prepare a list of questions. Always have more questions than you think you will be able to ask, just in case you are mistaken. Mark those that are most important to your research and make sure you ask them first. You may want to have some closed and some open questions, as Joel did when he interviewed a professor of recreation for his speech on how American adults spend their leisure time. *Closed questions* are those that can be answered with a "yes," a "no," or a short answer. For example, Joel asked, "Do American adults have more time for leisure activities today than they did a generation ago?" and "How may hours per week does the typical adult spend watching TV?" The first question can be answered by a "yes" or a "no"; the second, with a specific figure.

Open questions invite longer answers, and can produce a great deal of information.

Joel asked the open question: "How do American adults typically spend their leisure time?" When you ask open questions, sit back and prepare to listen for a while! The less time you have for the interview, the fewer open questions you should ask. Open questions can sometimes result in rambling, unnecessary information. At other times, the interviewee's rambling will trigger questions you would not have thought of otherwise. Joel was surprised to learn that American adults spend approximately two hours a week in adult education, a venture he had not included on his initial list of adult leisure activities. When you and the interviewee have plenty of time, and particularly if you are tape recording the interview, open questions can provide the richest information.

Conduct the Interview.　The personal interview is an excellent opportunity to practice your interpersonal communication skills. Specifically, you should follow these guidelines. First, introduce yourself when you arrive, thank the person for giving you time, and restate the purpose of the interview.

Second, conduct the interview in a professional manner. If you interview the president of the local savings and loan, don't show up in cut-off jeans, sandals, and your favorite flannel shirt. Make sure you arrive appropriately dressed, ready and able to set up and handle any recording equipment with a minimum of distractions. Try to relax the interviewee, establish a professional atmosphere, pose questions that are clear and direct, listen actively, take notes efficiently, and follow up when necessary. You should control the interview without appearing to be pushy or abrupt.

Third, thank the person again for the interview when you have finished.

Follow up on the Interview.　After the interview, review your notes or listen to your tape recording. Do this as soon as possible after the interview, when your memory is still fresh. If you are unclear about something that was said, do not use that information in your speech. You could call your subject to clarify the point if you think it will be important to the audience's understanding of the topic.

As a matter of courtesy, you should write to the people you interviewed, thanking them for the time and help they gave you. You may even want to send them a copy of your finished speech if it is in manuscript form.

Writing and Calling for Information

Some years ago, one of us taught a student, Lindahl, who wanted to develop an informative speech on the savant syndrome. This was long before Dustin Hoffman's portrayal of Raymond in the film *Rain Man* made many people aware of the special talents and disabilities of savants. Lindahl had seen a *60 Minutes* segment on the syndrome, but could not find recent written sources in the local libraries she visited. Her best source, she said, was an article from a three-year-old issue of *Time*. Others might have abandoned their research and switched topics, but Lindahl followed a hunch that paid off for her.

The *Time* article quoted several university professors and medical doctors who were engaged in ongoing research on the savant syndrome. Lindahl got their office telephone numbers through directory assistance. She called these experts to see if they could recommend new sources she had been unable to locate. Lindahl found that the people she called were all flattered by her attention and complimented her perseverance as a researcher. One psychologist mailed her a photocopy of a book chapter she had written on the savant syndrome; a medical doctor mailed Lindahl a packet of journal articles, including the galleys of an article of his that was about to be published; a psychology professor mailed her a tape of savants who had incredible musical talents playing piano concertos they had heard for the first time only moments before. In short, Lindahl received a gold mine of new, expert research as a result of her few long-distance calls.

Lindahl was lucky that she began her research more than a month before her speech was due. To take advantage of pamphlets and brochures available through the mail, you will need to plan ahead as well. But thousands of organizations, such as the American Cancer Society and the United Way, publish their own informational literature. Political parties and lobbying groups prepare position papers on issues that affect them. Corporations distribute annual reports to their stockholders and will share these with people who request them. You can write to any of these organizations. Some have toll-free phone numbers; for others you would have to pay long-distance charges. Unfortunately, no index comprehensively catalogs the information available from such groups, so you must take the initiative in tracking down what you need. One source that can be helpful is the *Encyclopedia of Associations.* This publication is divided into three volumes: National Organizations of the U.S.; International Organizations; and Regional, State, and Local Organizations. Each volume lists names, addresses, telephone numbers, and descriptions of organizations. The information is also available on computers at some libraries. Remember, this research source will not help you if you have five days left before your deadline. But if time permits and research warrants, writing or calling these organizations to request information can add relevant primary research to your speech.

Electronic Media

News, information, and opinion come to us not only through print media but also through the electronic media. In fact, most of us get our news from television. When we think of research, however, we generally focus on magazines, newspapers, books, and other print resources. Information in print is more accessible to the researcher and is usually indexed. Nevertheless, you should not ignore broadcast information as a research option.

For example, you can find some excellent speech topics among the investigative reports presented on television and radio. Many programs provide transcripts for purchase. This information is usually given at a program's conclusion. For a nominal cost, you can obtain transcripts of many programs, such as *60 Minutes, Nightline, 20/20, This Week with David Brinkley, Firing Line, Face the Nation, Meet the Press, Washington Week in Review,* and the *MacNeil/Lehrer NewsHour.*

Your library and video rental stores may have copies of special televised broadcasts such as the PBS documentary series *Eyes on the Prize* on the civil rights struggle or Bill Moyers' *A Walk Through the 20th Century.* Through videotapes, you can research topics such as military battles, McCarthyism, and space exploration, to name just a few. Informational tapes can take you on tours of museums such as the Louvre or the British Museum, and distant places such as Australia and Italy. Instructional tapes can teach you how to garden, refinish furniture, and make a sales presentation. As videotape becomes an increasingly valuable and accessible source of information, speakers should consider exploring it. You may even find a trip to your video store or the video section of your library an important part of your brainstorming strategy.

■ RECORD INFORMATION

Once you have located information, you must determine what to record and how to record it.

What to Record

When in doubt, record more rather than less. Certainly, it is possible to copy too much information. If you find everything potentially important, your topic probably needs better focus. Without some focus, you run the risk of becoming so bogged down in research that you leave little time for organizing and practicing your speech.

On the other hand, if you are too selective, you may be inefficient. As you research your speech, you may shift your topic focus and, hence, the supporting material you previously thought was irrelevant becomes important. Discarding unnecessary information is easier than trying to remember a source, retracing your steps, hoping that the information is still on the library shelves, and then recording that information.

How to Record Information

Traditional advice to researchers is to record each piece of information on a separate notecard, along with the source citation, as you find it. With this strategy, you can organize your speech visually and experiment with different structures. The disadvantage of this method of recording information is that it consumes a great deal of library time that might be better devoted to searching for other sources. In addition, much of what you record on notecards may not be used in your speech at all.

Another, more common method is to photocopy material at the library and read it later. Sometimes the simplest and most thorough way to record research information is to photocopy pages from books, documents, reference works, or even entire articles. Later, at your leisure and in more comfortable surroundings, you can review, evaluate, and select from the photocopied materials. However, be aware that photocopies may lull you into a false sense of accomplishment. What you have copied may later turn out to be of little or no use. How can you avoid this problem? Read your material before or very shortly after photocopying it. Do not wait until the night before your speech to read the pile of information you have been collecting on the role of women pilots in World War II.

Also, remember to note your sources on the copied pages. If you follow these simple directions, photocopying has two additional advantages over using notecards. First, you may not know what you want to use from an article at the time you first find it. If the focus of your speech changes, a different part of the article may become important. Indeed, sometimes your research forces you to refocus the speech topic. Second, if you are quoting from or paraphrasing one specific part of an article, you may need to check later to make sure that you are not quoting the author out of context. Having a photocopy of the book chapter, the journal article, or the encyclopedia entry lets you check the context and the accuracy of your quotation.

It is important to record full citations of sources you have consulted in your research in a bibliography at the end of your speech. Your **bibliography** is simply a list of works

bibliography: an orderly list of works consulted or cited during the preparation and delivery of a speech.

Gersham, Michael. *Diamonds: The Evolution of the Ballpark.* Boston: Houghton, 1993.

Gersham, Michael. *Diamonds: The Evolution of the Ballpark.* Boston: Houghton Mifflin, 1993.

Gersham, M. (1993). *Diamonds: The evolution of the ballpark.* Boston: Houghton Mifflin.

Book with One Author

Lichtenstein, Grace, and Laura Dankner. *Musical Gumbo: The Music of New Orleans.* New York: Norton, 1993.

Lichtenstein, Grace, and Laura Dankner. *Musical Gumbo: The Music of New Orleans.* New York: Norton, 1993.

Lichtenstein, G., & Dankner, L. (1993). *Musical gumbo: The Music of New Orleans.* New York: Norton.

Book with Two or More Authors

Meyer, Michael. "The 'On-Line' War Heats Up." *Newsweek* 28 March 1994: 38-9.

Meyer, Michael. "The 'On-Line' War Heats Up." *Newsweek,* 28 March 1994, 38-9.

Meyer, M. (1994, March 28). The 'on-line' war heats up. *Newsweek, 123,* 38-9.

Article in Weekly Magazine

Watson, Bruce. "In the Heydey of Men's Hats, Fashion Began at the Top." *Smithsonian* March 1994: 73-82.

Watson, Bruce. "In the Heydey of Men's Hats, Fashion Began at the Top." *Smithsonian,* March 1994, 73-82.

Watson, B. (1994, March). In the heydey of men's hats, fashion began at the top. *Smithsonian, 25,* 73-82.

Article in Monthly or Bi-monthly

Kolata, Gina. "3 Companies in Landmark Accord on Lawsuits over Breast Implants." *New York Times* 24 March 1994, natl. ed.: A1, 11.

Kolata, Gina. "3 Companies in Landmark Accord on Lawsuits over Breast Implants." *New York Times,* 24 March 1994, natl. ed., sec A, pp. 1, 11.

Kolata, G. (1994, March 24). 3 companies in landmark accord on lawsuits over breast implants. *The New York Times,* pp. A1, A11.

Newspaper Article

United States. Cong. House. Subcommittee on Technology, Environment and Aviation of the Committee on Science, Space, and Technology. *National Initiatives in Green Technologies.* 103rd Cong., 1st sess. Washington: GPO, 1993.

U.S. Cong. House. Subcommittee on Technology, Environment and Aviation of the Committee on Science, Space, and Technology. *National Initiatives in Green Technologies.* 103rd Cong., 1st sess. Washington, DC: GPO, 1993.

U.S. House of Representatives, Subcommittee on Technology, Environment and Aviation of the Committee on Science, Space, and Technology. (1993). *National initiatives in green technologies.* Washington, DC: U.S. Government Printing Office.

Government Document

MLA Form
Turabian Form
APA Form

Figure 7.6 Comparison of popular bibliography forms

you have consulted in developing your speech. Most writer's handbooks will recommend a particular bibliographic form. Some of the popular forms include those presented in the *Publication Manual of the American Psychological Association*, Kate Turabian's *A Manual for Writers of Term Papers, Theses, and Dissertations*, and the *Modern Language Association Handbook for Writers of Research Papers*. Be sure to check with your instructor, who may have a preference for one of these or some other bibliographic form.

Copies of the three style manuals we just listed are probably in your library's reference section. Figure 7.6 compares the bibliographic forms each presents. Whether you want to cite a segment of National Public Radio's *All Things Considered*, a stop-smoking videotape, or lecture notes you took in an anthropology class last week, the most recent editions of these reference books can likely give you a pattern to follow.

■ EVALUATE INFORMATION

As you prepare your speech, you must make choices. Your goal is to support your ideas with the most compelling evidence and arguments you can find. The adage "Knowledge is power" certainly applies to speech making; the more you know about your topic, the greater your flexibility in determining its content and, subsequently, its impact. This concept of choice may make your task more complex, but it will also produce a more effective speech.

There is a limit, however, to the time you can spend researching. An important part of effective research is knowing when to stop accumulating materials and when to start using them. In his book *Finding Facts Fast*, Alden Todd provides the following guideline for research projects:

> If the last 10 percent of your planned research time has brought excellent results, you are doubtless on a productive new track and should extend the project. But if the last 25 percent of your scheduled time has brought greatly diminished results, this fact is a signal to wind up your research.[6]

Although Todd's 10/25 formula may not be wholly applicable to your researching a speech for this class, it does highlight an important issue: At some point you must stop researching and start structuring your speech.

In the next chapter, "Supporting Your Speech," we discuss the purposes and types of supporting material. Understanding these topics will help you evaluate your research and select the best information to support the ideas of your speech.

SUMMARY

Research is the process of gathering information and evidence to understand, develop, and explain your topic. Learning to research is fundamental to mastering public speaking. Even if you are not required to use outside sources for a particular speech, knowing your subject thoroughly greatly reduces your speech anxiety. Of course, knowing your subject probably demands knowing how to use the best library in your area. An agenda for thorough research of a subject involves five steps.

First, assess your knowledge of the subject and begin to organize that knowledge. Chances are good that you chose the topic because you were interested in it or already knew something about it. Keeping a *clipping file* and a *quotations file* on subjects that interest you gives you a head start in your research. As you prepare the speech and after you deliver it, keep your research notes and speaking notes or manuscript in a *speech file*.

Second, develop a research plan for your topic. What information do you need? Where can you find it? How can you get it in the time you have? Your topic may lead you to interview people or collect printed information from businesses and organizations. Sooner or later, however, you will probably need to learn to use a local library efficiently. Reference librarians can teach you the strengths and limitations of the library you select.

The third step in research is to collect information from a variety of sources. Potential sources include magazines and journals, newspapers, government documents, books, and reference works, including dictionaries, encyclopedias, almanacs, yearbooks, and books of quotations. Sources outside the library include interviews and electronic media resources such as radio, television, and videotape. Interviews allow you to collect authoritative, unpublished information on your subject, but they require special planning and preparation. You must select the best interviewee, decide on the format, schedule the interview, research the interviewee you have selected, and prepare a list of questions. After conducting the interview in a competent, professional manner and promptly recording the information you have gathered from it, you should send a note of thanks to the person you interviewed.

The fourth step in research is to record the information you consider important and useful. You may choose to take notes on notecards or to photocopy your information. In either case, be sure to record the source of the information — author, title, and publication information — using a current *bibliography* form.

The fifth and final step in research is to evaluate the material you are collecting. The quality and quantity of the information you collect will not only help you focus and organize the subject, but should also signal you when you have exhausted your research efforts.

EXERCISES

1. Locate and look at a recent issue of each of the following magazines: *Mother Jones, National Review, New Republic, Newsweek,* the *Progressive, Time,* and *U.S. News & World Report.* Based on their content, rank the seven magazines from most liberal to most conservative. Which would you classify as liberal, which as conservative, and which as middle of the road? What information helped you decide your rankings? Were similar topics treated in different ways in these publications?
2. Using any magazine or journal index listed in this chapter, construct a bibliography of at least seven sources for an upcoming speech. Locate at least three of these articles.

3. Using a newspaper or *NewsBank Index,* construct a bibliography of at least five sources for an upcoming speech. Locate at least three of these articles.

4. Using the *CIS/Index* and *CIS Abstract* or the *Monthly Catalog,* locate a congressional document on a topic that would be appropriate for a speech in this class.

5. Using the resources in parentheses, answer the following questions.
   a. What is the derivation of the word *deadline?* (dictionary)
   b. The Speaker of the U.S. House of Representatives comes from what district and state? (almanac)
   c. In what year was Henrik Ibsen's play *A Doll's House* published? (encyclopedia)
   d. What are the chief crops of Cameroon? (almanac)
   e. On what date did the Alexander Hamilton-Aaron Burr duel occur? Who won? (encyclopedia)
   f. What color is the flag of Libya? (almanac)
   g. Who was the last U.S. major league baseball player to bat over .400 for the year? What was the year, and what was his batting average? (almanac)
   h. What is the elevation of Mount Rainier? (encyclopedia)
   i. What is the preferred pronunciation of the word *data?* In how many other ways can it be correctly pronounced? (dictionary)
   j. Who received the Oscar for Best Actor in 1942? In what movie did he star? (almanac)
   k. What is the meaning of the Greek words from which *dinosaur* is derived? (encyclopedia)
   l. How and for whom was the word *boycott* coined? (dictionary)

6. Using books of quotations, such as those listed in this chapter, prepare a list of at least two quotations on each of the following topics.
   a. The Art of Conversation
   b. The Importance of Teachers
   c. Overcoming Failure
   d. The Dangers of Apathy
   e. Turning Problems into Opportunities
   Bring your list to class and be prepared to discuss how you could use some of the quotations in a speech. Which would contribute to good introductions or conclusions? Which could be used to illustrate an idea in the body of the speech?

7. Consult the *Encyclopedia of Associations* and locate at least three organizations you think may have information pertaining to ideas you are considering for upcoming speeches. Write letters requesting relevant information.

8. Select an expert to interview for an upcoming speech. Using suggestions in this chapter, arrange, prepare for, and conduct an interview, and follow up on it.

NOTES

1. Chandler B. Grannis, "Book Title Output and Average Prices: 1991 Preliminary Figures," *The Bowker Annual 1992,* ed. Catherine Barr, 37th ed. (New Providence, NJ: Reed Reference, 1992) 502.

2. Robert C. Jeffrey and Owen Peterson, *Speech: A Text with Adapted Readings,* 2nd ed. (New York: Harper, 1983) 169.

3. Lois Horowitz, *Knowing Where to Look: The*

Ultimate Guide to Research (Cincinnati: Writer's Digest, 1988).

4. Bill Katz and Linda Sternberg Katz, *Magazines for Libraries,* 7th ed. (New Providence, NJ: Bowker, 1992) ix.

5. Horowitz 115.

6. Alden Todd, *Finding Facts Fast,* 2nd ed. (Berkeley: Ten Speed, 1979) 14.

Supporting materials make:
    the general specific…
    the abstract concrete…
      the impersonal personal…
      the obscure clear…
    the routine surprising…
    the irrelevant relevant…
      the typical atypical…
      the dull vivid…
    the complicated understandable…
    the questionable credible…
      the ordinary extraordinary.

*J*ust as mountain climbers use spikes to secure themselves to points on the face of a cliff, you can use the supporting materials in your speech to provide specific points of reference for your audience. Effective supporting materials help you anchor your ideas in the minds of your listeners.

Toward the end of Chapter 1, we recommended a formula for structuring each major idea in your speech. This pattern, called the **"4 S's,"** consists of *signposting, stating, supporting,* and *summarizing* each of your key ideas. In the next chapter, "Organizing Your Speech," we will explain this pattern in detail and show examples of how to use it. However, this chapter concerns the third of these **4 S's:** *supporting* your major ideas. In supporting an idea you apply the results of your research and original thinking about your speech topic in the form of examples, comparisons, and statistics, among other methods. In this chapter, you will learn more about the purposes of supporting materials. We will also discuss and show you examples of seven types of supporting materials you can use to communicate your ideas clearly, memorably, and authoritatively.

PURPOSES OF SUPPORTING MATERIALS

Supporting materials in a speech serve a variety of purposes. They help give your ideas clarity, vividness, and credibility.

Clarity

When the space shuttle *Challenger* exploded within minutes of its liftoff on January 28, 1986, the world recognized that a tragedy had occurred. President Ronald Reagan referred to it as a disaster in his eulogy for the crew members three days later. Yet NASA called the explosion an "anomaly." During the investigation into the cause of the explosion, Arnold Aldrich, manager of the National Space Transportation Systems Program at Houston's Johnson Space Center, said, in part:

> The normal process during the countdown is that the countdown proceeds, assuming we are in a go posture, and at various points during the countdown we tag up on the operational loops and face to face in the firing room to ascertain the

facts that project elements that are monitoring the data and that are understanding the situation as we proceed are still in the go condition.[1]

Is it any wonder that it took NASA a while to discover the likely cause of the explosion?

As a speaker, your first goal is to communicate clearly. *Clarity* refers to the exactness of a message. The clarity of any message you send results partly from your language, as we discuss in Chapter 11, "Wording Your Speech." In addition, the supporting material you choose will help make your message clear. As you develop your speech, ask yourself the question, "Does my supporting material really explain, amplify, or illustrate the point I am trying to make?" If it does not, disregard it and continue your search for relevant material. Clear supporting materials help listeners better understand your ideas.

Vividness

Which of the following makes a stronger impression on you?

Mike Wallace takes people into his confidence and disarms them,

or

Mike is interviewing this bad-ass accountant, and there are … forty million people watching this broadcast. And only Mike would say to a guy whom he interviews, "Just between you and me.…" Now this guy forgets; he thinks it is just between him and Mike. Mike has a way of doing that.[2]

Effective speakers use supporting materials that help their listeners understand, remember, and believe their messages.
(SOURCE: © Frank Siteman)

The first comment is something Don Hewitt, executive producer of CBS's *60 Minutes,* might have said about Mike Wallace. The second is what Hewitt actually did use to explain why Wallace is such a successful interviewer for the show. Which statement do you think is more vivid?

Most people would choose the second sentence as the more vivid and memorable. Why? The first remark is general; the second, specific. In a speech on Mike Wallace's interviewing techniques, the first statement could be one of your main ideas. The second is something you could say to support that main idea because it is both clearer and more vivid.

In this chapter, we use several excerpts from speeches to illustrate various types of supporting materials. Once you finish reading the chapter, you will no doubt remember some of the examples and forget others. Those you remember will be ones you found particularly vivid. *Vivid* supporting materials are striking, graphic, intense, and memorable. A major purpose of supporting materials, then, is to help your audience remember the key points in your speech. You will accomplish this best by using vivid forms of support chosen with your unique audience in mind.

Credibility

credibility: the believablity or dependability of speakers and their sources.

You gasp as you see the headline "Scientists Discover Microbial Life on Mars." Would it make a difference whether you saw this on the cover of *Scientific American* or the *National Enquirer?* Of course it would. "Microbial life" is nothing to the folks who write for the tabloids; they've shown photographic evidence of human faces carved into the Martian landscape! On the other hand, a scientific article reviewed and selected for publication by a panel of experts is significantly more believable than an article from any tabloid weekly. **Credibility** refers to the dependability or believability of a speaker or that speaker's sources.

Many ideas in the speeches you prepare will require simple supporting materials: short definitions, brief examples, or quick comparisons, for example. In other instances, you may present complex or controversial ideas that require several types of supporting materials. A speech with all of its ideas and support taken from a single source is too limited. Using several sources to corroborate your ideas and facts can be a valuable and per-

In the middle of pitching his no-hitter, Jim Abbott surely did not think about the press conferences, newspaper interviews, or talk show appearances that would soon follow.
(SOURCE: © AP/Wide World Photos)

suasive tool. Your main points will be more credible if you present evidence that these ideas are shared by several experts.

You establish clarity by explaining your idea so that listeners *understand* it. You establish vividness by presenting your idea so that listeners will *remember* it. Finally, you establish credibility by presenting the idea so that listeners *believe* it. If the supporting materials in your speech get the audience to understand, remember, and believe what you say, you have done a good job selecting your materials.

You know that you want to present clear, vivid, and believable supporting materials. But how do you make sure people understand, remember, and believe your message? You have a wide range to choose from as you organize your supporting materials. Below we discuss the most common types of supporting materials and show you how they can work effectively in your speech.

TYPES OF SUPPORTING MATERIALS

To help you achieve clarity, vividness, and credibility in your speaking, consider seven types of supporting material available to you: examples, definition, narration, comparison, contrast, statistics, and testimony. Keep in mind that there is no one best type of support for your ideas. Select what is most appropriate to your topic, your audience, and yourself.

actua
true insta
illustration.

example: a sample or illustration of a category of people, places, objects, actions, experiences, or conditions.

An **example** is a specific illustration of a category of people, places, objects, actions, experiences, or conditions. In other words, examples are specimens or representations of a general group. The sound of the word itself gives perhaps the easiest definition to remember, however: An *example* is a *sample* of something. Measles, mumps, and chicken pox are examples of common childhood illnesses. New York, Los Angeles, and Miami are examples of the largest cities in the United States. *E.T. — The Extra-Terrestrial, The Color Purple,* and *Schindler's List* are examples of Steven Spielberg movies. Soccer, football, and baseball are examples of popular team sports.

Brief Examples. In your speech you can use either brief examples, such as those noted above, or extended ones. Brief examples are short, specific instances of the general category you are discussing. They may be used individually, but are often grouped together. Notice how Jocelyn combined a number of brief examples early in her speech on the attractions of New York City:

> Your walking tour of midtown Manhattan could take you to places as diverse as St. Patrick's Cathedral, Rockefeller Center, the Gotham Book Mart, and the Museum of Modern Art. Try not to gawk as you look at some of the most famous architecture in the world — the Chrysler Building, the Empire State Building, and Grand Central Station. Tired of pounding the pavement? Slip into a chair in the Algonquin Hotel's dim lobby, soak up the literary history, ring the bell on your table, and order something to drink. Hungry? You've got the world's table to choose from — everything from four-star restaurants to little holes in the wall serving the best ethnic dishes: Chinese, Vietnamese, Indian, Mexican, Thai.

Extended Examples. Extended examples are lengthier and more elaborate than brief examples. They allow you to create more detailed pictures of a person, place, object, experience, or condition. Later in her speech, Jocelyn developed an extended example of one of her favorite New York City attractions:

> Beginning with my second visit to New York, one of my first stops has usually been the Museum of Modern Art. If you're like me, you'll need to give yourself at least a couple of hours here, because for a small admission price you're going to get a chance to see up close art that you've only seen before as photographs in books. Upstairs on my last visit, I saw works such as Pablo Picasso's *Guernica* and Roy Lichtenstein's huge pop art paintings of comic strip panels. My favorite Lichtenstein was one called *Oh, Jeff, I Love You Too, But....* On a wall with a number of other paintings was a canvas so small that I almost missed it. I'm glad I didn't. It was Salvador Dali's famous surrealist work, *The Persistence of Memory,* with its melting clock and watch faces. Then over in a corner is a special room that holds only one painting. As you walk in, you see an expanse of gray carpet and several upholstered benches. One wall is glass, two others are white and bare, but the fourth one holds the three panels of Claude Monet's massive painting, *Waterlilies.*

Notice how vividly this extended example suggests a scene and recreates an experience. But whether your examples are brief or extended, they can be of two further types: actual and hypothetical.

example: a ... nce or

Actual Examples. An **actual example** is real or true. Each of the examples we used above is an actual example. Steven Spielberg did direct the three films listed. Soccer, football, and baseball are familiar, established team sports. The Chrysler Building and the Empire State Building are famous New York landmarks.

Les McCraw, president of the Fluor Corporation, delivered a speech at Clemson University using a series of actual examples to illustrate the point and title of his speech: "Nothing Much Happens Without a Dream." One example focused on a baseball player named Jim Abbott:

> Jim Abbott had a dream. It takes a special kind of person to make a dream come true against all odds. Jim is the 21-year-old rookie pitcher for the California Angels. He's a left-handed pitcher. He throws left-handed because he was born without a right hand. His parents raised this remarkable man by never treating him too remarkably.
>
> "When I was growing up," he says, "I always pictured myself as a baseball player but I can't remember how many hands I had in my dreams. I just went out and did things." And he certainly has "done things." He earned the 1987 Sullivan Award as America's best amateur athlete, won the gold medal [in] baseball in the Seoul Olympics, was drafted number 1 by the Angels, and is pitching in the big leagues today.[3]

Abbott, who pitched a no-hitter as a member of the New York Yankees during the 1993 baseball season, is an actual person with an amazing story.

Hypothetical Examples.   A **hypothetical example,** on the other hand, is imaginary or fictitious. A speaker often signals hypothetical examples with phrases such as, "Suppose that," "Imagine yourself," or "What if." Hypothetical examples clarify and vivify the point you are making, but they do not prove the point.

Notice how the following introduction mentions actual products but places them in a hypothetical situation. The speaker chose this method knowing that not all listeners would have all the products listed. The speaker then generalizes from these examples to support the claim that we live in an electronic world.

> We wake up in the morning to soothing music coming from our AM/FM digital clock radio equipped with a gentle wake-up feature. We stumble downstairs, enticed by the aroma of coffee brewed by a preset coffee maker with 24-hour digital clock timer and automatic shut-off function. We zap on our 27-inch color TV with on-screen display of current time and channel and with 139-channel cable-capable tuner. As we sit in our six-way action recliner, we use our 26-function wireless remote to perform the ritual of the morning channel check. Finding nothing that captures our interest, we decide instead to watch the videotape of last week's family reunion recorded with our 12X power zoom, fully automatic camcorder with self-timer, electronic viewfinder, and "flying erase head for 'rainbow'-free edits." Oh dear! What would our grandparents think? Certainly, we live in an electronic world!

Definition

A **definition** tells us the meaning of a word, a phrase, or a concept. Definitions are essential if your audience is unfamiliar with the vocabulary you use or if there are multiple definitions of a particular term. You want to clarify terms early in your speech so you do not confuse your listeners and lose their attention. In a speech on computer hacking, for example, you should define terms such as *hacker, cracker, virus,* and *worm.* We have found at least three different definitions of *hacker,* ranging from favorable to unfavorable. Even

hypothetical example: an imaginary or fictitious instance or illustration.

definition: an explanation of the meaning of a word, phrase, or concept.

if your listeners are familiar with computer terminology, you need to clarify your use of the word.

Definitions can take several forms. Four of the most common are: definition by synonym, definition by etymology, definition by example, and definition by operation. Choose the form most appropriate to your audience and to the term you want to clarify, and your audience will remember it.

definition by synonym: substituting a word having similar meaning for the word being defined.

Definition by Synonym.   The first type of definition is **definition by synonym.** Synonyms are words that have similar meanings. You have probably used a thesaurus when writing a term paper or report. A thesaurus is simply a dictionary of synonyms. Consider these pairs of words:

mendacity and *dishonesty*　　　*pariah* and *outcast*
plethora and *excess*　　　　　　*anathema* and *curse*
mitigate and *lessen*　　　　　　*surreptitious* and *secret*

Each word is coupled with one of its synonyms. The first word of each pair is probably not a part of your listeners' working vocabulary. As a speaker, you would want to use the second word in each pair; those words are more familiar and thus more vivid. The second word of each pair communicates more clearly. If you suffer from "thesaurus-itis," a disease causing you always to choose a fancy word over a simple, more appropriate one, you will be more likely to confuse your listeners. As the joke goes, never use a big word when a diminutive one will do.

A student in one of our introductory public speaking classes used definition by synonym in his speech on the ritual of bullfighting. After introducing each Spanish term, he provided its English translation. Notice how unobtrusively he defines terms in the following excerpt describing the parade to the bullfighting ring: "The *matadores* enter the ring as the band strikes up a *paso doble,* or two-step. Each matador is followed by a *guardia,* or a team of helpers...." By using two languages, the speaker gave his speech a Spanish flavor, yet his English-speaking audience understood his description clearly.

definition by etymology: explaining the origin of the word being defined.

Definition by Etymology.   A second type of definition is **definition by etymology.** Etymology is the study of word origins. You may find that describing how a word has developed clarifies its meaning. For example, the word *decimate* means "to destroy a large portion of," as in, "The hailstorm decimated the soybean crop." You may not know that *decimate* comes from the Latin word for *ten* or *tenth.* The word *decim* was a common military term used by the ancient Romans. If soldiers mutinied against their generals, the entire group was punished. The troops were lined up and every tenth soldier was killed, whether guilty or innocent. This arbitrary punishment made others think twice before trying similar action against their leaders. Not only a word's origin but also the history of a word's use can be fascinating.

Most of the time we use definitions to make an unfamiliar term familiar. However, you can also use definition by etymology to highlight the unusual nature of a familiar term. The following etymological definition of the word *debate* is from John Ciardi's *A Browser's Dictionary.* Notice how Ciardi captures both the meaning and the flavor of the word as he traces its historical evolution:

debate: Now signifies a formal presentation of arguments and counterarguments within parliamentary guidelines and time limits. As the formal rules of debate are lost, the discussion descends to wrangling. [Yet wrangling is the root sense. <L.

de-, down (also functions as an intensive); *battere,* to beat (BATTERY, ABATE). This root sense is nicely expressed by the colorful It. word *battibecco,* hot argument; lit. "a beating of beaks" (as if two birds are fencing).][4]

That image of birds fighting with their beaks certainly enlivens this definition. The reference section of your library will have a number of dictionaries of word origins and histories of word usage. We enjoy browsing in them, and in Chapter 16, "The Structure of Persuasion," we use definition by etymology to explain the red herring and bandwagon fallacies of reasoning (see pages 352, 354).

Definition by Example. As we mentioned earlier, an example is a specific instance or illustration of a larger group or classification. **Definition by example** uses a specific instance to clarify a general category or concept. Cactus Pryor, a popular radio personality in Austin, Texas, chose definition by example to explain what he meant when he used the word *Bubba:*

> Bubba is a good ol' boy. Bubba likes the NRA and Bubba dips snuff and Bubba likes Ollie North and Bubba likes to fish and hunt and eat barbecue and talk about women and frequently is found in Texas politics. Dallas is full of Bubbas, but they dress better. Bubbas are hard to not like because they're friendly. They hate Yankees. Bubba wears cowboy clothes.[5]

Pryor's definition not only clarifies the word *Bubba,* it also makes the concept more vivid.

You need not confine your definitions by example to language, however. Often audible and visual examples can be your quickest and most vivid ways to define a term or concept.

Audible examples are those you let your audience hear. Speeches on types of music, voice patterns, or speech dialects could define key terms by audible examples. For example, if you were using the word *scat* in a speech on jazz, you could offer a dictionary definition of the term: "jazz singing with nonsense syllables."[6] But wouldn't a taped example of Ella Fitzgerald, Al Jarreau, or Bobby McFerrin singing scat be more memorable to your audience? Other terms appropriate for audible definitions include the following:

bird calls	nasality and denasality
Boston Brahmin dialect	sonata form
conjunto music	stuttering and cluttering
counterpoint	vocalese
glottal fry	yodeling
industrial music	

Visual examples define a term by letting the audience see a form of it. Speeches on styles of architecture or painting could benefit from visual definition, as could any of the following terms:

Abstract Expressionism	Cubism
Art Deco	double exposure
caricature	Fauvism
complementary colors	optical illusion
concrete poetry	photorealism

**definition by opera-
tion:** explaining how
the object or concept
being defined works, what
it does, or what it was
designed to do.

Definition by Operation. Sometimes the quickest and liveliest way to define a term is to explain how it is used. **Definition by operation** clarifies a word or phrase by explaining how an object or concept works, what it does, or what it was designed to do. The terms *wok, radar detector, fax machine, food processor,* and *laser scalpel* are but a few of the physical objects best defined by explaining their operation.

You can also define concepts, actions, or processes by operation. To define magnetic resonance imaging, you would have to explain how that technology operates. Notice how the following person defines virtual reality by explaining how musicians and composers of the near future will use it:

> You're ready to enter an alternate reality. You slip on a pair of headphones, a helmet with a tiny video screen for each eye, and a special glove. Three-dimensional, generated images are projected onto your eye screens. Video "hands" match the movements of your own limbs. Sound seems to be coming from all around, not just inside your head, as you'd normally expect with 'phones.
>
> There's a mixing console floating before you. The music is coming from an apparent distance of a couple yards, but when a channel is "soloed," that sound moves to a point inches from your ear, while the rest of the mix stays put. By grabbing the edge of the board and pulling, you get as many input channels as you need, stretching away to infinity.[7]

Definition by operation is often livelier and more complete than most dictionary definitions. And, as the example above illustrates, it is especially useful in the case of new technologies whose dictionary definitions have yet to be written.

Narration

narration: the process
of describing an action or
series of occurrences;
storytelling.

personal narrative: a
story told from the point
of view of a participant in
the action and using the
pronouns *I* or *we*.

Narration is storytelling, the process of describing an action or a series of occurrences. If you come to school on Monday and tell a friend about something you did during the weekend, you are narrating those events.

Personal Narrative. As a participant in the events, you will probably speak in first person at least part of the time, using the pronouns *I* or *we*. Such a story is called a **personal narrative.** We have suggested that you draw upon your own experiences as you select and develop a speech topic, and personal narratives can be rich and interesting supporting materials.

Sultana, a student whose husband is Muslim and who had herself converted to the Muslim religion, used a personal narrative effectively. She told the story of her first experience with the celebration of Ramadan, a period of daylight fasting during the ninth month of the Muslim year:

> My first Ramadan I was a bit nervous. I had just become a Muslim, and I thought, "There is no way I can go from sunup to sunset without food. It's not even logical." I like to eat, as some of you may have noticed. And I thought, "There's no way that I can do this." Also, I was a student at the time, and it was finals. I honestly believe that you can't function if you don't eat. I mean, how can you think and pass a final? But I was determined at least to begin Ramadan; it goes for thirty days. So I set out and the first few days were a bit difficult. You can get hungry; there's no denying that. Your stomach growls out loud in class. But after

about three days, the body adjusts. You don't really need as much food as most of us consume. You can live a long time on that stored up fat we have and survive quite well. But the experience provides a lot of self-confidence, because if you can spend thirty days fasting, you can do just about anything.

Her classmates laughed along with Sultana as she poked fun at students' eating habits during the stress of final exams, as well as at her own tendency to be finishing a snack as her speech class started. In addition to creating interest in the topic, Sultana's story reinforced her credibility to speak on the topic of Ramadan. We tend to believe the accounts of people who have experienced events firsthand. That is an important reason for using personal narratives.

Third-Person Narrative. Narratives, of course, need not be personal but may relate a series of incidents in the lives of others. When you speak from the point of view of a witness and use the pronouns *he, she,* or *they,* you are telling a **third-person narrative.** In the following example, notice how the speaker, a teacher speaking on the subject of education, uses narration to illustrate her point that each child deserves special attention.

> I'd like to tell you the story of two children — two educationally handicapped children.
>
> The parents of the first child were not considered successful. His father was unemployed, with no formal schooling. His mother was a teacher — and there was probably tension in the family because of this mismatch. This child, born in Port Huron, Michigan, was estimated to have an IQ of 81. He was withdrawn from school after months — and was considered backward by school officials. Physically, the child enrolled two years late due to scarlet fever and respiratory infections. And he was going deaf. His emotional health was poor — stubborn, aloof, showing very little emotion. He liked mechanics. He liked to play with fire and burned down his father's barn. He showed some manual dexterity, but used very poor grammar. But he did want to be a scientist or a railroad mechanic.
>
> The second child showed not much more promise. This child was born of an alcoholic father who worked as an itinerant — a mother who stayed at home. As a child she was sickly, bedridden, and often hospitalized. She was considered erratic and withdrawn. She would bite her nails, and had numerous phobias. She wore a back brace from a spinal defect and would constantly seek attention. She was a daydreamer with no vocational goals, although she expressed a desire to help the elderly and the poor.
>
> Who were these children? The boy from Port Huron became one of the world's greatest inventors — Thomas A. Edison. And the awkward and sickly young girl became a champion of the oppressed — Eleanor Roosevelt.[8]

third-person narrative: a story told from the point of view of a witness and using the pronouns *he, she,* or *they.*

Comparison and Contrast

Comparison is the process of depicting one item — person, place, object, or concept — by pointing out its similarities to another, more familiar item. **Contrast** links two items by showing their differences. We use comparison and contrast to clarify that less familiar term or concept by relating it to a more common one. Your listeners must be familiar with one of the items involved in your comparison or contrast in order for either strategy to serve its purpose and have impact.

comparison: the process of associating two items by pointing out their similarities.

contrast: the process of distinguishing two items by pointing out their differences.

literal comparison or contrast: associations or distinctions between two items that share actual similarities or differences.

Literal Comparison and Contrast.   Just as examples can be actual or hypothetical, comparisons and contrasts can be literal or figurative. A **literal comparison** associates items that share actual similarities. Notice the interesting literal comparison in this quotation from the book *Tribes*, by sociologists Desmond Morris and Peter Marsh. A student, Marcia, used it to support her speech on youth gangs and their dress codes:

> Where a single species of birds inhabits, say, a small island, its members tend to have very dull plumage, lacking in pattern and color. As the number of species or sub-species in any one area increases, so too does the number of species-specific markings in the feathers and beaks. The most extravagant patterns and colors of plumage occur when the variety of avian life in a given area is greatest and the need for identification becomes highly important. Youth groups are, in this sense, very much like species of birds — although, of course, their decoration is of cultural rather than genetic origin.[9]

In a persuasive speech on the dangers of overexposure to the sun, another student, Patricia, also made effective use of a **literal contrast:**

> Sunblocks are either chemical or physical. Oils, lotions, and creams that claim a certain SPF factor all contain chemical blocks. On the other hand, zinc oxide, the white or colored clay-looking material you see some people wearing, usually on their noses, is a physical sunblock.

figurative comparison or contrast: associations or distinctions between two items that do not share actual similarities.

Figurative Comparison and Contrast.   When you draw a **figurative comparison or contrast,** you associate two items that do not necessarily share any actual similarities. The purpose of figurative comparisons is to surprise the listener into seeing or considering one person, place, object, or concept in a new way.

Effective figurative comparisons must contain an element of surprise, as well as a spark of recognition. In a speech of self-introduction in which students were to explain some of the events occurring the year they were born, one student, Carolyn, mentioned the low prices advertised for girdles in a 1946 newspaper she had consulted. She then said, "For those of you women who have never had the pleasure of putting on and wearing a girdle, let me tell you that getting into a girdle was the aerobic dancing of 1946." The figurative comparison evokes a vivid and funny image.

One student, describing the density of a neutron star, quoted from *Sky & Telescope* magazine that "your bathroom sink could hold the Great Lakes if the water were compressed to the density of a neutron star."

Another student introduced his informative speech on karate with the following contrast:

> What images come to your mind when I say the word *karate?* Chuck Norris or Bruce Lee jumping across the movie screen? A flash of fists and feet as dozens of bad guys fall? That's the popular conception of karate. Though it is an excellent form of self-defense, the actual practice of karate is quite different from those images created by the movies.

You can use comparison and contrast together in your speech. If you clarify a term by showing how it is similar to something the audience knows, you can often make the term even clearer by showing how it is different from something the audience also knows.

Statistics are collections of data. Broadly speaking, any number used as supporting material is a statistic. Used appropriately, statistics, too, can make your ideas clear and vivid, increase your credibility, and prove your point.

statistics: data collected in the form of numbers.

We place a great deal of trust in statistics that we feel have been accurately gathered and interpreted. Think of how much trust politicians as well as the general public put in preference polls gathered before elections. Statistics can predict certain events in our daily lives, such as price increases or decreases on certain goods and services. When you use statistics in your speech, you can demonstrate trends or compare a situation today with one in the past.

However, you must be careful about how you use statistics in your speech. Used inappropriately, statistics may baffle or even bore your audience. The following four suggestions should guide you in presenting statistical material.

Do Not Rely Exclusively on Statistics. If statistics are your only form of supporting material, your audience will likely feel bombarded by numbers. Remember, your listening audience has only one chance to hear and assimilate your statistics. As a speaker, then, use statistics judiciously and in combination with other forms of support. A few key statistics combined with examples can be quite powerful. Too many statistics will confuse your audience.

Notice in the following speech excerpt how Professor Louis Rader successfully joins statistics with comparison to argue that American industry must commit itself to increasing product quality:

> Many of our CEOs felt that 99 percent good was good enough. If this figure (99 percent good) were converted into our daily non-industrial life, what would it mean? More than 30,000 newborn babies would be accidentally dropped by doctors and nurses each year. There would be 200,000 wrong drug prescriptions each year. Electricity would be off for fifteen minutes each day. Ninety-nine percent good means 10,000 bad out of 1 million.[10]

Round off Statistics. A statistic of 74.6 percent has less impact and is more difficult for your audience to remember than "nearly three-fourths." No one in your audience will remember the statistic of $1,497,568.42; many, however, may be able to remember "a million and a half dollars." Rounding off statistics for your listeners is neither deceptive nor unethical. Instead, it reflects your concern for helping your audience understand and retain key statistical information.

Use Units of Measure that are Familiar to Your Audience. In a speech on the breakup of the Soviet Union, telling your audience that the average monthly salary of a Soviet worker in 1990 was 257 rubles would mean little to them. They would also need to know that the official ruble exchange rate at that time was fifty-six cents.[11] Telling your audience that the average monthly salary of a Soviet worker in 1990 was equivalent to $143.92, or nearly $150 in U.S. currency, would be much more vivid. Use familiar units of measure or translate unfamiliar units into familiar ones.

Use Visual Aids to Represent or Clarify Relationships among Statistics. Suppose you wanted to use the following paragraph in a speech about baseball players:

Since professional baseball began, in 1876, California has produced 1,282 major leaguers and Pennsylvania has produced 1,260. These states are followed by New York (943), Illinois (859), Ohio (858), and Texas (541).[12]

If you're a baseball fan, you probably find these facts interesting. But remember, even the most avid fans in your audience would probably not remember all these numbers. Your listeners would be more likely to remember the information if you presented the facts both orally and visually. In this case you could construct a chart ranking the states, with the number of players each produced beside the state's name.

Testimony

Examples, definition, narration, comparison, contrast, and statistics are discrete types of supporting materials. Each is a different strategy for validating the ideas of a speech. Speakers sometimes generate these types of support themselves. Other times, they glean them from their research, citing their sources but justifying the point in their own words. Still other times, speakers find the words and structure of the original source so compelling that they quote directly or paraphrase the source. This latter strategy is known as **testimony**. Testimony, sometimes called quotation, is another method of presenting types of supporting material. When you quote or paraphrase the words and ideas of others, you use testimony. Look at the two examples below of a speaker making the same basic statement:

testimony: quotations or paraphrases of an authoritative source to clarify or prove a point.

> A second characteristic of American families today is that they have two incomes. The days of Ricky and Lucy Ricardo, Ward and June Cleaver, and Archie and Edith Bunker are over. In fact, nearly two-thirds of couples with children are supported by incomes from the husband and wife, many of whom work full-time.

Suppose a speaker, instead, phrased and supported the idea like this:

> A second characteristic of American families today is that they have two incomes. The days of Ricky and Lucy Ricardo, Ward and June Cleaver, and Archie and Edith Bunker are over, at least according to Eugene Fram, a research professor at Rochester Institute of Technology, and Joel Axelrod, president of an international marketing research organization. They write in the October 1990 issue of *American Demographics,* "In 1988, almost two-thirds of married couples with children — 16 million families — had two incomes. In 8 million of these families, both husband and wife worked full-time, year-round."[13]

As you can see, the key idea in each of the examples is the same: The typical American family has two incomes. Both examples rely on statistics to support the key idea. However, by quoting a source in the second example, the speaker has added an additional element of support. The expert testimony increases the credibility of the idea. In this example, testimony or quotation has not changed the *type* of support; it has merely enhanced its *believability.*

Testimony sometimes draws its effectiveness from the content of the quotation, as in the example above. Other times, testimony relies largely on the reputation of the person making the statement. Nancy used examples and statistics to warn her listeners of widespread faulty credit reports that could affect their ability to get a job or to buy a car or house. She also added testimony to heighten the impact and credibility of her argument:

167

Supporting Your Speech

> Stephen Gardener, Texas Assistant Attorney General, declared in the May 27, 1991, issue of *The Wall Street Journal,* "The whole credit system is frighteningly out of control. Not only are your financial matters virtually an open book, but it's an open book with a couple of pages missing, some lines crossed out, and some pieces in backwards!"[14]

Notice how in all these examples the speakers used the words and ideas of others to enhance the credibility of their ideas. Expert testimony, however, is not limited to the statements of other people. As a speaker, you use *personal testimony* when you support your ideas with your own experiences and observations. Many students select a speech topic because they have some special knowledge or experience with the subject. One of our students, for example, gave a speech comparing retail prices at large supermarkets to those at convenience stores. He was careful to explain his credentials and establish his expertise in the subject. Not only did he wear his store apron and manager's name tag, but he also said early in his introduction, "As a former receiving control manager, I was in charge of purchasing products for the store, so I have some knowledge of how wholesale prices are translated into the retail prices you and I pay." The speaker enhanced his credibility both verbally and nonverbally.

TESTS OF SUPPORTING MATERIALS

Speakers should choose supporting materials carefully and ethically. The positions you develop in your speech will be only as strong as the evidence supporting them. Seven guidelines will help you evaluate the validity and strength of your supporting materials. These suggestions will also aid your evaluation of evidence you hear others present in their speeches.

KEY POINTS
Tests of Supporting Materials

1. Is the evidence quoted in context?
2. Is the source of the evidence an expert?
3. Is the source of the evidence unbiased?
4. Is the evidence relevant to the point being made?
5. Is the evidence specific?
6. Is the evidence sufficient to prove the point?
7. Is the evidence timely?

Is the Evidence Quoted in Context?   Evidence is quoted *in context* if it accurately reflects the source's statement of the topic. Evidence is quoted *out of context* if it distorts the source's position on the topic.

For example, suppose Joyce was preparing a speech on the topic of hate crimes on campus. She has read in the campus paper the following statement by the president of her college:

We've been fortunate that our campus has been relatively free of bias-motivated crimes. In fact, last year, only two such incidents were reported — the lowest figure in the past five years. Yet, no matter how small the number is, any hate crime constitutes a serious problem on this campus. We will not be satisfied until our campus is completely free from all bias-motivated intimidation.

Now, suppose Joyce used the following statement to support her position that hate crimes are prevalent on campus:

We need to be concerned about a widespread and growing problem on our campus: the prevalence of hate crimes. Just this past week, for example, our president argued that hate crimes constitute, and I quote, "a serious problem on this campus."

The president did say those words, but Joyce did not also mention the president's position that hate crimes on campus are few and decreasing. By omitting this fact, she has distorted the president's message. Joyce has presented the evidence out of context. The evidence you cite in your speech should accurately represent each source's position on the topic.

Is the Source of the Evidence an Expert?   An expert is a person qualified to speak on a particular topic. We trust the opinions and observations of others based on their position, education, training, or experience. The chairperson of a committee that has just completed a study on the effects of a community-based sentencing program is knowledgeable about the facts concerning that issue. A person completing graduate study on the effects of a local Head Start program on literacy has also developed an area of expertise. As a speaker, select the most qualified sources to support your position.

For a persuasive speech condemning the growth of tabloid news, which source would you find more credible: a cub reporter or a Pulitzer Prize-winning journalist? In an informative speech comparing the philosophies of various environmental action groups, would you be more impressed by testimony from a local member of a small environmental organization or from a nationally acclaimed environmental expert? If you delivered a speech advocating the licensing of law clerks to draft wills and conduct other routine legal business, would you rather quote a first-year lawyer or a senior law partner of a major legal corporation? Of course it would depend on the specific individuals and what they said, but you would probably place more trust in the latter, more experienced person in each of these examples.

Our student who compared the pricing policies of large supermarkets and convenience stores was careful to establish his own credibility both verbally and nonverbally. When you as a speaker fail to present your qualifications, or the qualifications of those you quote, you give listeners little reason to believe you.

Is the Source of the Evidence Unbiased?   When Markdown Marty of Marty's Used Cars tells you he has the best deals in town, do you accept that claim without questioning it? Probably not. Marty may be an expert on used cars, but he's understandably biased. When individuals have a vested interest in a product, service, or issue, they are often less objective about it.

You expect representatives of political parties, special-interest groups, business corporations, labor unions, and so forth to make statements advancing their interests. It will probably not surprise you, for example, that the supermarket receiving control manager we quoted earlier concluded his speech by stating that it is more economical to shop at large supermarkets than at convenience stores. When you include testimony and quotations in your speeches, try to rely on objective experts who do not have a vested interest in sustaining the position they voice.

Is the Evidence Relevant to the Point Being Made?   Evidence should relate to the speaker's claim. Sounds pretty obvious, doesn't it? However, both speakers and listeners often fail to apply this guideline in evaluating evidence. A speaker who contends that amateur boxing is dangerous but presents only evidence of injuries to professional boxers has clearly violated the relevance criterion. But many times irrelevant evidence is more difficult to detect.

Ryan's speech called for increased funding of medical trauma centers. Throughout his speech, he cited the need for the specialized care provided in these facilities. Yet, when he estimated the demand for this care, he used statistics of emergency room use. But trauma centers are not the same as emergency rooms. Therefore, Ryan's evidence was irrelevant to his argument. As you construct your speech, identify your key points and make certain your evidence relates specifically to them.

Is the Evidence Specific?   Which of the following statements is more informative?

The new convention center will increase tourism a lot.
The new convention center will increase tourism by 40 percent.

What does "a lot" mean in the first statement? Twenty percent? Fifty percent? Eighty percent? We don't know. The second statement is more precise. Because it is more specific, we are better able to assess the impact of the new convention center. Words such as *lots, many, numerous,* and *very* are vague. When possible, replace them with more specific words or phrases.

In her speech "Debunking the Vitamin Myth," Dana discussed the problem of misuse of vitamins. She stated:

> An article entitled "The Real Power of Vitamins" in the April 6, 1992, issue of *Time* magazine suggests that misuse of and misconceptions about vitamins can be harmful and even deadly. In fact, the vitamin problem plagues many Americans.

If Dana had stopped there, her audience might have asked: "Is the problem really that harmful? How many people have actually died because of it? How many is 'many Americans'?" But Dana wisely continued:

> According to the October 23, 1991, issue of the *New York Times,* on any given day 80 percent of the American population will consume a vitamin, 37 percent will overindulge, and 19 percent will reach toxic levels. They go on to report that 1,752 people lost their lives in 1991 due to the overconsumption of vitamins. Clearly, this subject warrants further examination.[15]

Dana's specific evidence better informed her listeners and made her point: The problem of vitamin misuse is serious.

Is the Evidence Sufficient to Prove the Point?   In her speech on rap music, Lea played excerpts from two rap songs, one of which she characterized as antiwoman and the other as antipolice. She encouraged her listeners to boycott rap music because "it demeans women and law enforcement officers." Lea did not apply this sixth guideline to her evidence. Two examples do not justify a blanket indictment of rap music.

When considering the guideline of sufficiency, ask yourself, "Is there enough evidence to prove the point?" One unpleasant experience at Fred's Cafe is insufficient to conclude that it's a bad bistro. Two examples of individuals who chose welfare over a job are insufficient to conclude that this attitude is widespread among all welfare recipients. Three examples of college athletes graduating without acquiring basic writing skills are insufficient to prove that athletes are failing to get a good education. One example

Type of Support	Use
Example	Provides instances or samples of people, places, objects, actions, conditions, or experiences.
Actual example	Provides clarification and proof.
Hypothetical example	Provides clarification, but does not alone provide proof.
Definition	Clarifies an unfamiliar word or phrase.
Definition by synonym	Substitutes a familiar word for the one defined.
Definition by etymology	Explains the origin of the word defined.
Definition by example	Provides an illustration or sample of the word defined.
Audible example	Lets listeners hear sample of the term defined.
Visual example	Lets listeners see sample of the term defined.
Definition by operation	Explains use, function, or purpose of the object or concept defined.
Narration	Describes action or event.
Personal narrative	Describes action from participant's point of view; uses *I* and *we*.
Third-person narrative	Describes action from witness's point of view; uses *he, she,* and *they*.
Comparison	Clarifies term by showing its similarity to a more familiar term.
Literal comparison	Associates items having actual similarities.
Figurative comparison	Associates items not having actual similarities.
Contrast	Clarifies term by showing its difference from a more familiar term.
Literal contrast	Distinguishes items having actual differences.
Figurative contrast	Distinguishes items not having actual differences.
Statistics	Clarify or prove a point with numbers.
Testimony	Clarifies or proves a point using the speaker's words or those of an expert.

Figure 8.1 *Supporting materials: types and uses.*

may illustrate a claim, but it will rarely prove it. Make certain you have sufficient evidence to support your points.

Is the Evidence Timely?   If you were preparing a travel budget for a trip overseas, which would you find more helpful: an airline ticket pricing schedule you had from last year or one your roommate picked up at the airport this week? Of course, you would want to rely on your roommate's more recent information. The timeliness of information is especially important if you are speaking about constantly changing issues, conditions, or events. What you read today may already be dated by the time you give your speech.

Some speech topics, however, are timeless. If you speak about the gods of Mount Olympus, no one would question your use of Thomas Bulfinch's books about mythology, even though they were published in the mid-1800s. Both Edith Hamilton's *Mythology*, published in 1940, and Robert Graves's *Greek Gods and Heroes,* published in 1960, would also add credibility to your speech. As scholars of mythology, Bulfinch, Hamilton, and Graves earned reputations that time is not likely to diminish. Similarly, if you deliver a speech on the ancient Olympic Games, your most authoritative sources may be history textbooks. If, however, your topic concerns current drug-testing procedures in Olympic competition, it would be vital for you to use the most recent sources of the best quality you can find. The date of your evidence must be appropriate to your specific argument.

Figure 8.1 summarizes the uses of the types of supporting materials we have discussed.

SUMMARY

We use supporting materials in a speech to achieve three purposes: *clarity, vividness,* and *credibility.* Clarity helps the audience understand your ideas. Vividness assists them in remembering your ideas. Credible supporting materials make your ideas believable.

Types of material you can use to support the main ideas of your speech include examples, definition, narration, comparison, contrast, statistics, and testimony. *Examples* are samples or illustrations of a category. Those categories may be people, places, objects, actions, experiences, or conditions. Examples may be *brief* or *extended,* and actual or hypothetical. *Actual examples* are real or factual. *Hypothetical examples* are imaginary or fictitious. Both types of examples make a general or abstract term more specific and vivid for the audience.

Definitions are explanations of an unfamiliar term or of a word having several possible meanings. We can define terms by synonym, by etymology, by example, or by operation. *Definition by synonym* offers a word or phrase that is the rough equivalent of the word being defined. *Definition by etymology* shows the origin of the word being defined. *Definition by example* gives an illustration or sample of the word in question. *Definition by operation* explains how something works or what it was designed to do. Definitions are crucial if you are using words you suspect your audience will not know, or if you want them to adopt one particular meaning for a term.

Narration is storytelling. Narratives may be personal or third-person. *Personal narratives* originate from the speaker's experience; they use the first-person pronouns *I* or *we*. *Third-person narratives* are stories about other people, and they are delivered using either people's names or the third-person pronouns *she*, *he*, or *they*.

Comparisons associate two or more items to show the similarities between or among them. Comparisons can be either literal or figurative. A *literal comparison* links two items that share actual similarities. A *figurative comparison* associates items that do not share any actual similarities.

Contrasts function like comparisons except that their purpose is to distinguish or show differences between two or more items.

Statistics are data collected in the form of numbers. Used properly, statistics can bolster a speaker's credibility and lend vivid support to the ideas of the speech. To ensure your proper use of statistics, you should follow four guidelines. First, don't rely exclusively on statistics, but combine them with other supporting materials. Second, round off statistics to help your listeners remember them. Third, either use units of measure familiar to your audience or translate your statistics into familiar units. Fourth, use visual aids to clarify the relationships among various statistics.

The final form of support is testimony. You use *testimony* when you cite, quote, or paraphrase authoritative sources. The authorities you cite may employ examples, definitions, narration, comparison, contrast, or statistics. To help ensure that your supporting materials are credible, you should ask seven questions of each piece of evidence you consider using. Is the evidence quoted in context? Is the source of the evidence an expert? Is the source of the evidence unbiased? Is the evidence relevant to the point you are making? Is the evidence specific? Is the evidence sufficient to prove your point? And is the evidence timely?

*E*XERCISES

1. Select a key idea of a speech you are preparing for this class. Try developing it using three different types of supporting materials. What are the advantages and disadvantages of each? Is the idea best developed by combining two or three of these methods?
2. Locate a speech in *Vital Speeches of the Day* or some other publication. Read it and identify the types of supporting materials we have presented in this chapter. Discuss the materials used most effectively and account for their effectiveness. Discuss those used least effectively and suggest ways the speaker could improve them.
3. Read a newspaper, keeping in mind the types of supporting materials presented in this chapter. Select the best and worst example you find for each type of support. Justify your choices.
4. Read the five statements below, indicating those with which you agree and disagree. Discuss the type(s) of supporting materials you would likely use to support your positions.
   a. Soccer is a more popular sport than football.
   b. The fear of giving a speech can be reduced.
   c. Art is more important than science.

d. Life in the country is more fun than life in the city.

e. This state is an excellent place to visit.

5. Think of someone who is known to you but unknown to your classmates. Describe this person (personality traits, physical features, attitudes, etc.) by comparing and contrasting him or her with people in your class.

6. Discuss a method of definition you could use for each of the following terms:

a. Modem

b. Aphorism

c. Contralto

d. Palpable

e. Chlorophyll

f. Eardrum

g. Autocad drafting

h. Pandemic

i. Contour map

NOTES

1. William Lutz, *Doublespeak: How Government, Business, Advertisers, and Others Use Language to Deceive You* (New York: HarperCollins, 1990) 223.

2. Jack Huber and Dean Higgins, "Mike Wallace," in *Interviewing the World's Top Interviewers: The Inside Story of Journalism's Most Momentous Revelations* (New York: S.P.I. — Shapolsky, 1993) 37.

3. Les McCraw, "Nothing Much Happens Without a Dream," *Vital Speeches of the Day* 15 January 1990: 217.

4. John Ciardi, *A Browser's Dictionary* (New York: Harper & Row, 1980) 206-07.

5. Cactus Pryor, in Elizabeth A. Moize, "Austin: Deep in the Heart of Texas," *National Geographic* June 1990: 63.

6. *Webster's Ninth New Collegiate Dictionary* (Springfield, MA: Merriam Webster, 1990) 1049.

7. David Trubitt, "Into New Worlds: Virtual Reality and the Electronic Musician," *Electronic Musician* July 1990: 31.

8. Cynthia Ann Broad, "I Touch the Future: I Teach," *Vital Speeches of the Day* 15 April 1990: 410.

9. Desmond Morris and Peter Marsh, *Tribes* (Salt Lake City: Gibbs Smith, 1988) 68.

10. Louis T. Rader, "Outstanding Engineering Achievements of the Past," *Vital Speeches of the Day* 1 July 1990: 566.

11. Jo An Tooley, "Database," *U. S. News and World Report* 12 November 1990: 12.

12. Nancy Ten Kate, "Batter Up," *American Demographics* October 1990: 16.

13. Eugene H. Fram and Joel Axelrod, "The Distressed Shopper," *American Demographics* October 1990: 44.

14. Nancy Letourneau, "Faulty Credit Reports," *Winning Orations, 1992* (Mankato, MN: Interstate Oratorical Association, 1992) 43.

15. Dana M. Perino, "Debunking the Vitamin Myth," *Winning Orations, 1992* (Mankato, MN: Interstate Oratorical Association, 1992) 15.

If you want me to talk for ten minutes, I'll come next week. If you want me to talk for an hour, I'll come tonight.
—Woodrow Wilson

Organizing Your Speech

Chapter 9

he seventeenth-century mathematician and philosopher Blaise Pascal once wrote to a friend, "I have made this letter longer than usual, because I lack the time to make it short."[1] Have you ever furiously written several pages to answer an essay question on an exam only to discover that the answer requires just one brief paragraph? Or perhaps you have given a driver long-winded directions for getting to a particular location, then remembered a shortcut. If you have had experiences similar to these, Pascal's comment probably makes a great deal of sense to you. It takes time to organize your thoughts to write a coherent letter, give a succinct answer to an essay, or give clear directions. Spending the time to organize, however, simplifies the task in the end. Getting organized will also simplify your speech preparation and make your speech more vivid and memorable for your listeners. This chapter is your blueprint for organizing the various parts of your speech.

THE PROCESS OF ORGANIZATION

By the time you enter college, you have already had a good deal of experience with written communication. On the receiving end, you have read numerous essays, short stories, and novels. As a sender, you have written essays, reports, and term papers. You have learned that a good essay or term paper has a clear beginning, middle, and end. When you write an essay, you seek to interest the reader and introduce the topic in the opening. The middle develops your ideas through examples, comparison, contrast, statistics, and other forms of supporting material. The end ties the ideas together and provides closure. If you have learned to do these things well in your writing, you have a head start in speech making. Even if this is your first experience with constructing a speech, you have already mastered some basic organizational skills. If you think you are not good at writing essays and reports, do not despair. The steps we describe in this chapter will help you develop a well-organized speech.

A coherent speech is similar to a written essay because it also has a beginning, middle, and end — what we call the introduction, body, and conclusion. Orally, you seek to achieve goals similar to those you set when writing. Many speech textbooks and instructors summarize the overall strategy of a speech as follows: *"Tell us what you are going to tell us. Tell us. Then, tell us what you told us."* Use this organizational perspective in every speech.

Though the organization of speech and writing is similar, these two channels of communication also have significant differences. When you write, for example, you can highlight ideas by using subheads, paragraph indentations, capitalization, boldface type, punctuation, and italics. Note how we use all of these cues in this text to organize our ideas for you. An audience listening to a speech, however, cannot rely on these cues. As a speaker, you must supply these missing elements with a clear organizational pattern and effective delivery.

Another difference between writing and speaking is the audience's control over the flow of information. As a reader, you can pause, reread a sentence, think about it, take a break, and come back to your reading when you feel fresher. As a listener, you do not have the freedom to do any of these things. A listener is at the mercy of the speaker. Therefore, the speaker must make the task of listening easier. How does the speaker highlight key ideas and help the audience remember them during and after the speech?

A speaker supplies the missing elements with a clear organizational pattern and effective delivery. Good organization maximizes a speaker's information and arranges ideas so that an audience will remember them. In Chapter 12, we suggest techniques of delivery to help you reinforce the ideas of your speech. This chapter focuses on structure — how to organize the supporting materials you have assembled through your research.

A well-organized, well-delivered speech can have as great an impact on your listeners as a well-written essay has on readers. We will teach you how to organize first the body of your speech, and then the introduction and the conclusion. You may find this an unusual order in which to organize the parts of a speech. Be assured that by the end of this chapter you will see the logic of this sequence.

ORGANIZING THE BODY OF THE SPEECH

Although you deliver it after the introduction, organize the body of your speech first, for in order to "tell us what you are going to tell us," you must first determine what to tell us. In constructing the body of a speech, your best strategy is to divide the speech into key ideas and then to develop each idea.

Divide the Speech into Key Ideas

In the body of the speech, you develop your key ideas according to a specific organizational pattern. Public speakers employ a wide variety of organizational structures. We will discuss six patterns most commonly used: topical, chronological, spatial, causal, pro-con, and gimmick division. These patterns are appropriate for either informative or persuasive speeches. In Chapter 16, we discuss four additional patterns suitable for persuasive speeches only: refutational strategy, problem-solution, need-plan, and the motivated sequence.

Keep in mind as you consider these patterns that no one of them is best. In order to achieve the best results, you must select the structure that best achieves the purpose of your speech. In other words, fit the organization to your topic rather than your topic to the organization. Study these patterns of organization carefully and you should have no difficulty in finding one that works for any topic you speak on in this class.

---

1. Topical division	**4.** Causal division
2. Chronological division	**5.** Pro-Con division
3. Spatial division	**6.** Gimmick division

KEY POINTS

Patterns for Dividing Your Speech into Key Ideas

Topical Division.   The **topical division** is the most common organizational pattern for public speeches. This strategy creates subtopics, categories which constitute the larger topic. For example, a speech on graffiti is divided topically if it focuses on graffiti as artistic expression, as political expression, and as vandalism. A speech on the categories of clowns is arranged topically if the speaker's main points cover the whiteface clown, the auguste clown, and the character or "tramp" clown.

topical division: organizes a speech according to aspects, or subtopics, of the subject.

Here are more examples of topical division.

Specific Purpose: To inform the audience of some potential uses of virtual reality.
Key Ideas: **I.** In business
II. In education
III. In medicine
IV. In entertainment

Specific Purpose: To inform the audience of the American Indian tribal colleges.
Key Ideas: **I.** History of the tribal colleges
II. Examples of American Indian colleges
III. Successes of the tribal colleges

Specific Purpose: To persuade the audience of the importance of personal dress.
Key Ideas: **I.** Clothing's effects on image
A. The image you have of yourself
B. The image others have of you
II. Clothing's effects on behavior
A. How you behave
B. How others behave when with you

As these examples suggest, topical organization is particularly appropriate as a method of narrowing broad topics, and that may explain its popularity and widespread use. In addition to helping you stay within your time limits, the topical pattern is also attractive because it lets you select subtopics to match your own interests and the interests and needs of your audience.

chronological division: organizes a speech according to a time sequence.

Chronological Division.   The **chronological division** pattern follows a time sequence. Topics that begin with phrases such as "the steps to" or "the history of" are especially appropriate to this organization. Examples of such topics might include the history of your university, the development of computers, the stages of intoxication, the process of silk screening, steps to getting your first job, or how a product is marketed.

The following ideas are developed chronologically.

Specific Purpose: To inform the audience of Elisabeth Kübler-Ross's five stages of dying.
Key Ideas: **I.** Denial
II. Anger
III. Bargaining
IV. Depression
V. Acceptance

Specific Purpose: To inform the audience of the steps to a succesful job interview.
Key Ideas: **I.** Prepare thoroughly.
II. Arrive promptly.
III. Enter confidently.
IV. Communicate effectively.
V. Follow up immediately.

Chronological organization works best if you are explaining procedures or processes. A simple and familiar example of chronological organization is a recipe. Any well-written recipe is organized in a time sequence: First, make sure that you have these ingredients; second, preheat the oven; and so forth.

Although the key ideas of a speech should follow a single method of division, you can use another pattern as you develop one of the key ideas. For example, a speech on ventriloquism could be divided topically to include (1) the history of ventriloquism, (2) the types of ventriloquism, and (3) the psychology of ventriloquism. Developing the first idea, however, is best accomplished by a chronological format: The speaker could discuss the history of ventriloquism beginning in Ancient Greece and then show its development in the Middle Ages, the Renaissance, and in modern times.

Spatial Division.   You use **spatial division** when your main points are organized according to their physical proximity or geography. This pattern is appropriate for a speech discussing the parts of an object or a place. For example, a speech on Jules Verne's Coal City, a mythical city fifteen hundred feet beneath the earth's surface, could contain four divisions: the entrance tunnel, the New Aberfoyle caverns, Lake Malcolm, and St. Giles Chapel.

spatial division: organizes a speech according to the geography or physical structure of the subject.

Other examples of spatial division are:

Specific Purpose: To inform the audience about the design of Shakespeare's Globe Theatre.
Key Ideas: **I.** The stage
        II. The galleries
        III. The "yard"

Specific Purpose: To inform the audience of the parts of the U.S. National Holocaust Memorial Museum.
Key Ideas: **I.** Four classrooms, two auditoriums, and two galleries for temporary exhibits occupy the lower level.
        II. The permanent exhibit occupies four floors of the main building.
        III. The library and archives of the U.S. Holocaust Research Institute occupy the top floor.

Causal Division.   You would choose a **causal division** pattern when you want to trace a condition or action from its causes to its effects, or from effects back to causes. Medical topics, in which a speaker discusses the symptoms and causes of a disease, can be easily organized using this method of division. Informative speeches on topics such as hurricanes, lightning, earthquakes, and other natural phenomena may also use this pattern. The following speech outline illustrates the causal pattern.

causal division: organizes a speech from cause to effect, or from effect to cause.

Specific Purpose: To inform the audience about the effects and causes of sports-victory riots.
Key Ideas: **I.** Effects
        A. Death and injuries
        B. Vandalism
        C. Law enforcement costs
      II. Causes
        A. The competitive nature of sports
        B. Mob psychology
        C. Unfavorable economic conditions
        D. Inadequate police presence

Because the causal pattern may be used any time a speaker attributes causes for a particular condition, it is suitable for persuasive as well as informative speeches. A speaker could attempt to prove that certain prescription drugs are, in part, responsible for violent behavior among those who use them; that the availability of handguns fosters needless death; that televising executions would lead to a call for an end to capital punishment; or that new antibiotic-resistant bacteria are increasing infections once thought under control. The causal pattern would work well for speeches on any of these topics.

pro-con division: organizes a speech according to arguments for and against some policy, position, or action.

Pro-Con Division. The **pro-con division** presents both sides of an issue. You explain the arguments for a position and the arguments against. Because it is balanced in perspective, this pattern is more appropriate for an informative speech than a persuasive one. After discussing each side of an issue, however, you may choose to defend the stronger position. In this case, your division becomes *pro-con-assessment*, and this pattern is more appropriate for a speech to persuade than a speech to inform.

An advantage of the pro-con pattern is that it sets an issue in its broader context and provides balance and objectivity. A disadvantage, however, is the time required to do this. You need plenty of time to discuss both sides of an issue in sufficient detail. Therefore, you will probably want to use this strategy only in one of your longer speeches for this class. If you do not devote sufficient time to each idea, a pro-con or pro-con-assessment development may seem simplistic or superficial to your audience.

The following outlines demonstrate pro-con analyses of two controversial issues.

Specific Purpose: To inform the audience of the arguments for and against an increase in the minimum wage.

Key Ideas:
 I. Increasing the minimum wage would be beneficial.
  A. The number of poor would decrease.
  B. The number of people on welfare would decrease.
  C. The concept of social justice would be affirmed.
 II. Increasing the minimum wage would be harmful.
  A. Unemployment would increase.
  B. Inflation would increase.
  C. Business bankruptcies would increase.

Specific Purpose: To inform the audience of the pros and cons of limiting campaign contributions by political action committees (PACs).

Key Ideas:
 I. Limitations on PAC money are desirable.
  A. PAC money undermines the concept of equal representation.
  B. PAC money undermines the concept of local representation.
  C. PAC money promotes public cynicism.
 II. Limitations on PAC money are undesirable.
  A. Limitations would decrease political participation.
  B. Limitations would strengthen the advantage of the incumbent.
  C. Limitations would violate the right of free expression.

gimmick division: organizes a speech according to a special memory device, such as alliteration, rhyme, or initial letters that spell a word.

Gimmick Division. A final organizational strategy you can consider for a speech to inform is **gimmick division,** or what some authors call the formula pattern. The most common use of this strategy develops and words the key ideas in such a way that the first letter of each key idea forms a word. As a student, you have been using gimmicks for years to help you retain information you need to know. In elementary school, you may have learned to spell *geography* by memorizing the sentence, **"G**eorge **E**liot's **o**ld **g**rand-mother **r**ode **a p**ig **h**ome **y**esterday." In a science class, you may have memorized the order of colors in the visible spectrum by remembering the name Roy G. Biv: **r**ed-**o**range-**y**ellow-**g**reen-**b**lue-**i**ndigo-**v**iolet.

Gimmicks work so well as memory devices that even advertisers and public service groups occasionally use them. If you can recall what the "four ***C*'s**" of diamond grading refer to, you probably memorized that information according to a gimmick. The four ***C*'s** stand for **c**ut, **c**olor, **c**larity, and **c**arat weight. Some health advisers tell us to remember **rice** in the event that we suffer a sprain: **r**est, **i**ce, **c**ompression, and **e**levation. We have heard students use both of these gimmicks to organize informative speeches on these topics.

If you were giving a speech explaining how to improve listening, you could use the gimmick developed by Robert Montgomery (giving him credit in your speech, of course).[2] Montgomery suggests six guidelines for better listening:

L — Look at the other person.
A — Ask questions.
D — Don't interrupt.
D — Don't change the subject.
E — Express emotions with control.
R — Responsively listen.

No doubt, the word *ladder* would help you remember your major points as you prepared and delivered such a speech. More important, though, the gimmick would help your listeners retain what you had said.

At times, the gimmick pattern of organizing a speech may seem corny or trivial to you. If you feel that way about this pattern, you probably should avoid it, as your speech delivery may seem self-conscious. When used well and with confidence, however, the gimmick helps your audience remember not only what points you have covered, but also the order in which you have covered them. That is a major accomplishment! In the next section of this chapter, we use a gimmick as we introduce you to our **"4 *S*'s"** of developing the ideas of the speech. See if it helps you remember these important points.

Develop the Key Ideas

Assume that your speech is divided into the key ideas, that you have selected the most appropriate pattern to organize them, and that you have decided their order in the speech. Now you need to develop each major point. Obviously, the number of major points you can develop in a speech depends on the time you have been allocated to speak, the complexity of the topic, and the audience's level of education and knowledge of the subject. There is no fixed rule, but most speech instructors recommend that you develop at least two but not more than five main points. Many speakers find that a three-point structure works best.

Regardless of the number of points you select, your responsibility is to explain and support each one sufficiently. The organizational strategy we suggest is one we call the **"4 *S*'s."** Your listeners will better comprehend and remember your speech if you *signpost, state, support,* and *summarize* each idea.

KEY POINTS

The "4 S" Strategy of Developing Key Ideas

1. Signpost the idea.
2. State the idea.
3. Support the idea.
4. Summarize the idea.

signpost: numbers *(one)* or words *(initially, second, or finally)* that signal the listener of the speaker's place in the speech.

Signpost the Idea.   Just as a highway signpost tells travelers where they are in their journey, so a signpost in a speech tells the audience where they are in the speaker's message. A **signpost** is a word such as *initially, first, second,* and *finally.* Signposts enable listeners to follow your organizational pattern and, hence, increase the likelihood that they will remember your key ideas.

State the Idea.   Each major idea needs to be worded precisely and with impact. Typically, a speaker will phrase each major idea either as a declarative sentence or as a question.

If you choose to word your main ideas as declarative sentences, you can usually accomplish the first two **S's,** signposting and stating your idea, in one sentence. Suppose the specific purpose of your speech is to persuade the audience to oppose mandatory drug testing in the workplace. If you say, "The first reason mandatory drug testing is harmful is that it is cost-prohibitive," you are signposting — "first" — and stating your idea — "mandatory drug testing is cost-prohibitive."

An alternative to introducing your key idea as a declarative sentence is to ask a question. For example, the specific purpose of Elly's speech was "to persuade the audience that the U.S. should continue to fund the space station *Freedom.*" She organized her supporting materials to answer three questions: (1) What will we gain scientifically? (2) What will we gain technologically? (3) What will we gain economically? She introduced each of these ideas with a signpost, for example: "A third question we must answer to determine the merits of the space station is: What do we have to gain economically?" She was then ready to answer that question using various types of supporting materials.

Support the Idea.   This third **S** is the meat of the **4 S's.** Once you have signposted and stated the idea, you must support it. A variety of types of supporting materials is at your disposal, limited only by the amount of research you have done and by time limits on your speech. Some of those types of supporting materials, discussed in detail in Chapter 8, are examples, definitions, comparisons, and statistics.

How would you support your statement that mandatory drug testing is cost-prohibitive? Your strongest form of support will likely be statistics — statistics on the average cost of a single drug screening test, estimates of the number of people currently employed in the United States, and projections of the total cost of testing the entire American workforce for drug use. The figures will be high and will serve as persuasive support for your claim.

Elly used a combination of statistics, examples, and testimony as she demonstrated the economic benefits of the space station. She presented evidence claiming that the project employed 20,000 people in 37 states directly, and that the project generated another 55,000 jobs indirectly. She provided examples of communities that would be economically devastated if the program were canceled. And she quoted Vice President Al Gore, who claimed that, in light of defense cutbacks, we need the space station to "help stabilize our nation's industrial base."

Effective gestures help speakers emphasize the organization of their remarks for listeners. (SOURCE: © Charles Gupton/ Stock, Boston)

Summarize the Idea.   A summary at the end of each major division helps wrap up the discussion and refocus attention on the key idea. These periodic summaries may be as brief as one sentence. To continue with our drug testing example, you could summarize your first subpoint by saying, "Clearly, then, the enormous costs of mandatory drug testing would make it an unreasonable burden on the economy." Such a statement reinforces your point by repeating it — "the cost of drug testing would be too high" — and also provides a note of closure, suggesting that you have said all you plan to about the economics of mandatory drug testing. Now you are ready to introduce your second point, that drug testing results in lost work time — again by signposting, stating, supporting, and summarizing.

If you introduced your idea as a question, your summary should provide the answer. Remember, your point is lost if the audience remembers only your question; they must remember your answer. Elly summarized her point this way: "So the answer to our third question is clear and convincing. What do we have to gain economically from continued funding of the space station? A brighter economic future for American workers, American communities, and the American economy."

Another example of the **4 *S*** strategy is included in Figure 9.1. Notice how the speaker signposts, states, supports, and summarizes her argument that the school year should be extended for American elementary and high school students.

We believe that use of the **4 *S*'s** is fundamental to effective organization within the body of any speech. As you begin to master and apply this four-step strategy, it may seem to be a cookie-cutter approach to public speaking. It *is* exactly that. The **4 *S*'s** are to speech organization what the required movements are to gymnastics — basics that you must learn before you are able to develop your own style or flair. As you master the **4 *S*'s** and gain confidence in public speaking, clear organization will become almost a reflex reaction performed without conscious effort. As your ability to organize ideas clearly becomes second nature to you, you will find that the structure of your thinking, writing, and speaking have greatly improved.

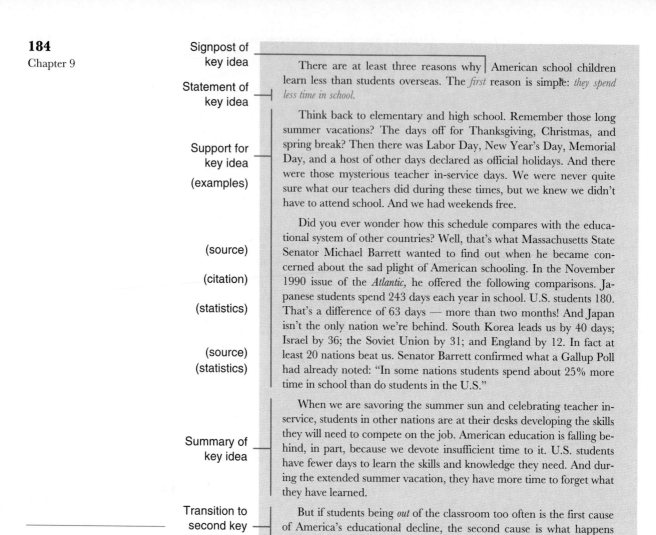

Signpost of key idea

Statement of key idea

Support for key idea (examples)

(source)

(citation)

(statistics)

(source)
(statistics)

Summary of key idea

Transition to second key idea

Figure. 9.1 *The **4 S** strategy of developing key ideas*

There are at least three reasons why | American school children learn less than students overseas. The *first* reason is simple: *they spend less time in school.*

Think back to elementary and high school. Remember those long summer vacations? The days off for Thanksgiving, Christmas, and spring break? Then there was Labor Day, New Year's Day, Memorial Day, and a host of other days declared as official holidays. And there were those mysterious teacher in-service days. We were never quite sure what our teachers did during these times, but we knew we didn't have to attend school. And we had weekends free.

Did you ever wonder how this schedule compares with the educational system of other countries? Well, that's what Massachusetts State Senator Michael Barrett wanted to find out when he became concerned about the sad plight of American schooling. In the November 1990 issue of the *Atlantic,* he offered the following comparisons. Japanese students spend 243 days each year in school. U.S. students 180. That's a difference of 63 days — more than two months! And Japan isn't the only nation we're behind. South Korea leads us by 40 days; Israel by 36; the Soviet Union by 31; and England by 12. In fact at least 20 nations beat us. Senator Barrett confirmed what a Gallup Poll had already noted: "In some nations students spend about 25% more time in school than do students in the U.S."

When we are savoring the summer sun and celebrating teacher in-service, students in other nations are at their desks developing the skills they will need to compete on the job. American education is falling behind, in part, because we devote insufficient time to it. U.S. students have fewer days to learn the skills and knowledge they need. And during the extended summer vacation, they have more time to forget what they have learned.

But if students being *out* of the classroom too often is the first cause of America's educational decline, the second cause is what happens when they are *in* the classroom.

Connect the Key Ideas

A speech is composed of key ideas, and you have just seen how to develop each one according to the **4 S's** approach. Those key ideas form the building blocks of your speech. In order for your speech to hang together, however, you must connect those ideas, just as a mason joins bricks and stones with mortar. A speaker moves from one idea to the next — puts mortar between the units — with the aid of a transition. A **transition** is a statement connecting one thought to another. Without transitions, the ideas of a speech are introduced abruptly. As a result, the speech lacks a smooth flow of ideas and sounds choppy.

A transition not only connects two ideas, but also indicates the nature of the connection between the ideas. Transitions are usually indicated by *markers,* words or phras-

transition: a statement that connects parts of the speech and indicates the nature of their connection.

es near the beginning of a sentence that indicate how that sentence relates to the previous one.[3] Transitions can indicate four basic types of connections: complementary, causal, contrasting, and chronological.

A **complementary transition** adds one idea to another, thus reinforcing the major point of the speech. Typical transitional markers for complementary transitions include:

complementary transition: adds one idea to another.

also	likewise
and	next
in addition	not only
just as important	

Each of the following transitions uses the complementary approach to reinforce the speaker's thesis.

> Not only does PAC money undermine the concept of equal representation, it also undermines the concept of local representation.
>
> It is clear, then, that clothing affects your image. Just as important is a second effect of personal dress: Clothing affects your behavior.
>
> Vocal cues, however, are not the only source of information that may help you determine if someone is lying. You may also look for body cues.

A **causal transition** emphasizes a cause-and-effect relation between two ideas. Words and phrases that mark a causal relationship include:

causal transition: establishes a cause-effect relation between two ideas.

as a result	consequently
because	therefore

In his speech, Victor documented problems resulting from excessive noise. As he shifted his focus from cause to effect, he used the following transition:

> We can see, then, that we live, work, and play in a noisy world. An unfortunate result of this clamor and cacophony is illustrated in my second point: Excessive noise harms interpersonal interaction.

A **contrasting transition** shows how two ideas differ. These transitions often use markers such as:

contrasting transition: shows how two ideas differ.

although	nevertheless
but	on the contrary
in contrast	on the other hand
in spite of	

Patricia used a contrasting transition in her speech on theories of alcoholism:

> Although some researchers argue that alcoholism is caused by biological factors, others reject this theory, arguing instead that the cause is cultural.

A **chronological transition** shows the time relationships between ideas, and uses words or phrases such as:

chronological transition: shows how one idea precedes or follows another in time.

after	at last	later
afterward	at the same time	while
as soon as	before	

Will informed his classmates on the SQ3R system of studying and remembering written material. He organized his five main points around five key words: survey, question, read, recite, and review. His transitions emphasized the natural sequence of these stages, as in:

> After surveying, or overviewing, what you are about to read, you are ready for the second stage of the SQ3R system: to question.

A second example of a chronological transition is:

> If thorough preparation is the first step in a successful job interview, the second step is to arrive on time.

A good transition serves as a bridge, reminding listeners of the idea just presented and preparing them for the one to come. It smooths the rough edges of the speech and enhances the cohesiveness of your ideas. The preceding lists of key words signal different types of transitions. However, you must do more than simply insert a word or phrase between two ideas. If you find yourself using a single word such as *now, next,* or *OK* to introduce your ideas, you need to work on your transitions. Avoid using weak and pedestrian phrases as transitions, such as, "Moving on to my next point," or, "The next thing I would like to discuss." Instead, work on composing smooth, functional transition statements as one of our students did in the following example.

In her persuasive speech, Bonnie advocated voluntary school uniforms for students in kindergarten through high school. She previewed her ideas in her introduction by stating that pilot programs demonstrate that "voluntary uniforms would help create a safer school environment, enhance academic achievement, and promote a positive social climate." In the body of her speech, Bonnie explained and supported each of these points, connecting them by using smooth transitions. Bonnie used the following excellent transition as she moved from her first to her second idea:

> Every student has a right to learn in a safe environment, and school uniforms help eliminate one cause of school violence. But schools should do more than ensure safety, they should promote learning. A second benefit of school uniforms is that they enhance academic achievement.

As Bonnie moved from her second to her third idea, she said:

> In addition to creating a safer environment and enhancing academic achievement, voluntary school uniforms promote a positive social environment.

■ ORGANIZING THE INTRODUCTION OF THE SPEECH

After you work on the body of your speech, you are ready to turn your attention to the introduction and conclusion. An introduction should be constructed to achieve four objectives: (1) get the attention of your audience, (2) state your topic, (3) establish the importance of your topic, and (4) preview the key ideas of your speech. Study these objectives and the ways to accomplish them and you will get your speech off to a clear and interesting start.

	KEY POINTS
1. Get the attention of your audience.	
2. State your topic.	**Steps of a Speech**
3. Establish the importance of your topic.	**Introduction**
4. Preview the key ideas of your speech.	

Get the Attention of Your Audience

Your first objective as a speaker is to secure the audience's attention. If you are fortunate enough to have a reputation as a powerful, captivating speaker, you may already have the attention of your listeners before you utter your first word. Most of us, however, have not yet achieved this reputation. Consequently, it is important to get the audience quickly involved in your speech. The strategy you select will depend on your personality, your purpose, your topic, your audience, and the occasion. We offer you seven possible techniques for getting the audience's attention.

	KEY POINTS
1. Question your audience.	**5.** Amuse your audience.
2. Arouse curiosity.	**6.** Energize your audience.
3. Stimulate imagination.	**7.** Acknowledge and compliment
4. Promise something beneficial.	your audience.

Strategies for Getting Your Audience's Attention

Question Your Audience. A speaker can get an audience involved with the speech through the use of questions. Questions can be either rhetorical or direct. A **rhetorical question** stimulates thought but is not intended to elicit an overt response. For example, consider the following opening questions:

> **rhetorical question:** a question designed to stimulate thought without demanding an overt response.

- How did you spend last weekend? Watching television? Going to a movie? Sleeping late?
- If you learned that your best friend had AIDS, how would you respond?
- Do you remember when you first suspected that there really wasn't a Santa Claus?

A speaker who asks any of the above questions does not expect an overt audience response. In fact, it would probably disrupt the rhythm of the presentation if someone answered orally. A question is rhetorical if it is designed to get the audience thinking about the topic.

A **direct question** seeks a public response. Audience members may be asked to respond vocally or physically. For example, the following questions could all be answered by a show of hands:

> **direct question:** a question that asks for an overt response from listeners.

- How many of you drove to school today? How many wore your seat belts?
- Last week the Student Government Association sponsored a blood drive. Who in this class donated blood?

Like the rhetorical question, a direct question gets the audience thinking about your topic. But the direct question has the additional advantage of getting your listeners physically involved in your speech and, consequently, making them more alert. This strategy may be especially appropriate if your class meets at 8:00 a.m. and you are the first speaker, or if you have an evening class and are the last speaker, or if you give your speech during midterm week when your classmates are especially tired.

Sometimes a direct question may invite an oral response. In his speech advocating the use of seat belts, Gene discovered by a show of hands that only a few of his classmates buckled up regularly. He then asked the rest of the class why they did not. One classmate complained of wrinkled clothes; another said the seat belt was uncomfortable; others said it was too confining. Gene continued, incorporating these excuses into his speech and refuting them.

When you ask a direct question and you want oral responses, you need to pause, look at your listeners, and give them sufficient time to respond. If you want your direct question answered by a show of hands, raise your hand as you end the question. In this way you indicate nonverbally how you want the question answered. If you seek and get oral responses, however, make sure that you neither lose control nor turn your public speech into a group discussion. Practice this technique as you rehearse in front of friends before making it part of your speech.

A few final cautions about using a question to get the audience's attention. First, avoid asking embarrassing questions of your listeners. "How many of you are on scholastic probation?" "Has anyone in here ever spent a night in jail?" "How many of you come from families earning less than $20,000 a year?" Common sense should tell you that most people would be reluctant to answer direct questions such as these. Second, make sure that you don't answer your opening question nonverbally before asking it. We remember one student who lined up a number of different tennis racquets — wood, aluminum, and aluminum and graphite — on the chalk tray under the blackboard. He then turned to the audience and asked, "What would you guess is the fastest-growing sport in the United States?" By asking a silly question in a sincere manner, he got a laugh he did not expect and surely did not want. That student's experience leads us to a final caution: Don't use a question without first considering its usefulness to your speech. Many questions are creative and intriguing. Remember, asking a valid question that listeners answer either openly or to themselves gets them immediately involved and thinking about your speech topic. Just don't rely on a question because you haven't developed or found a more creative attention-getter.

Arouse Your Audience's Curiosity. A lively way to engage the minds of your listeners is the technique of suspense. Get them wondering what is to come. Consider the following introduction our student Dan used in 1993:

> There is a guitarist on today's rock scene who is amazing listeners with his playing. Other players are praising him and shaking their heads in awe at his virtuosity. He sold more records than the Spin Doctors last year, and he's well on his way to becoming one of the most popular and influential guitarists of the '90s. His name is Jimi Hendrix, and he's been dead for twenty-three years.

The first three sentences of Dan's introduction got his audience's attention by making them guess the person he was describing. Eric Clapton? Joe Satriani? The opening statements create ambiguity or uncertainty and make you want to hear more. His fourth sentence resolves that ambiguity.

You can also arouse curiosity by what you do as well as what you say. One student began his speech by placing a small paper sack on the table at the front of the room and saying, "What I have in this sack is imported, costs about five dollars, and is alive." With the audience expecting to see some sort of animal, he then took a bottle of wine from the bag, explaining that its yeast cultures were alive and that his purpose was to inform the audience on how to select good, inexpensive wines.

Another student speaking on sign language began her speech in silence, signing the question, "Can you understand what I am saying?" She paused and then said, "I said, 'Can you understand what I am saying?',", signing as she spoke. She tapped her audience's feelings by arguing that they, undoubtedly, felt the same way a deaf person may feel in a hearing world.

Stimulate Your Audience's Imagination. Another way to engage the minds of your listeners is to stimulate their imaginations. To do this, you must know what referents they share, and this requires some good audience analysis on your part. Notice in the following example how Patricia introduces her topic by relating a personal experience with which many in the audience could probably identify:

> I can remember as a child the excitement of swinging high on the swings, walking on the teeter totter to balance it, and playing squeeze the lemon on the slide at recess. I can also remember breaking my nose because I was standing too close to the teeter totter, falling off the slide to lay unconscious for half an hour, and spraining my neck after falling off the monkey bars. All of these incidents left me a little bruised and feeling stupid for being such a klutz, but nothing a trip to the hospital couldn't fix. Unfortunately, not all children are as lucky as I was.[4]

Noting that 200,000 children suffer injuries caused by playground equipment each year, Patricia then discussed the reasons and remedies for the problem.

Jonathan used imagery to stimulate the audience's imagination and create interest in his topic:

> Imagine yourself viewing the most beautiful landscape on Earth. Surrounded by trees, you look ahead and see a deep blue lake shining. In it, the reflection of beautiful, white-capped mountains, with only the chattering of the squirrels and the music of the birds to keep you company. You feel you could sit back and stay forever. Then — darkness, and credits start to roll.
>
> What you have been watching, according to *Audubon* of February, 1990, is a movie promoting our nation's parks. But if current trends continue, this movie is all that will be left of the beauty our national parks have to offer.[5]

Jonathan then attempted to persuade his audience that the degradation of our national parks is a serious problem that demands our attention. Notice the strong appeals to our senses of sight and hearing in this example. In Chapter 11, we discuss the use of language to create these and other sensory impressions in your audience.

Promise Your Audience Something Beneficial.   We listen more carefully to messages that are in our self-interest. In Chapter 5, we recommended that you consider your listeners' needs using Maslow's hierarchy: physical needs, safety needs, love and belongingness needs, self-esteem needs, and self-actualization needs. If you can promise your audience something that meets one or more of these needs, you secure their attention very quickly. Beginning your speech, for example, with the statement, "Every person in this room can be a millionaire by age thirty!" immediately secures the attention of your listeners — at least those under the age of thirty! Less dramatic though still effective examples are ones in which a speaker promises that her information can save audience members hundreds of dollars in income tax next April, or in which a speaker says, "The information I will give you in the next ten minutes will help you buy an excellent used car with complete confidence." Saving money, the promise of all three of these attention-getters, is directly related to the interests of every audience member.

Amuse Your Audience.   The use of humor can be one of a speaker's most effective attention-getting strategies. Getting the audience to laugh with you makes them alert and relaxed. You can use humor to emphasize key ideas in your speech, to show a favorable self-image, or to defuse audience hostility. However, any humor you use should be tasteful and relevant to your topic or the speaking occasion. As a speaker, you must be able to make a smooth and logical transition between your humorous opening and the topic of your speech. Telling a joke or a funny story and then switching abruptly to a serious topic trivializes the topic and may offend your listeners. Imagine the effect if, as in the cartoon on page 191, Lincoln had actually started the "Gettysburg Address" with, "A guy walks into a bar...."

Carl Wayne Hensley, professor of speech communication at Bethel College, used humor to introduce his speech on effective communication:

A speaker's effective use of humor relaxes the audience, gets listeners physically involved, and builds speaker-listener rapport.
(SOURCE: © Charles Gupton/ Stock, Boston)

A woman went to an attorney and said, "I want to divorce my husband." Lawyer: "Do you have any grounds." Woman: "About 10 acres." Lawyer: "Do you have a grudge?" Woman: "No, just a carport." Lawyer: "Does your husband beat you up?" Woman: "No, I get up about an hour before he does every morning." Lawyer: "Why do you want a divorce?" Woman: "We just can't seem to communicate."

This woman's problem is not unique. Many husbands and wives, many parents and children, many managers and employees, many professionals and clients can't seem to communicate.[6]

Clyde Prestowitz, Jr., president of the Economic Strategy Institute, used humor to introduce the key points of his speech on economic policy:

Some of the major problems underlying the U.S. economy are well illustrated by a recent story about the hiker in California who ate a condor, a protected species of bird. It seems that the hiker was apprehended and taken before a judge, who sentenced him to life at hard labor. Before leaving the courtroom, however, the defendant asked the judge to listen to his side of the story because he felt there were exonerating circumstances. The hiker explained that he had been lost in the wilderness and had been hiking for three days and three nights without food or water, and just by chance had spotted this bird sitting on a rock, had thrown a rock at it, killed it and ate it, and then walked for three more days and three more nights before getting to civilization. Said the hiker, "If I hadn't eaten that bird, I wouldn't be alive to be here today." The judge responded by saying that those certainly were unusual circumstances and in view of the fact that the hiker's life had been in danger he, the judge, would suspend the sentence. The defendant thanked him and began to leave the courtroom, but as he

THE FAR SIDE   By GARY LARSON

did the judge asked, "Oh, by the way, what did that condor taste like?" The hiker paused for a moment and then responded, "Well, it was kind of between a bald eagle and a spotted owl."

The point is, you see, that the judge was operating on the basis of a false premise. He was assuming that he and the hiker adhered to similar premises and views about protected species. In the same way, the United States has been operating on a basis of three false premises for most of the past forty-five years with regard to its economic policies.[7]

Notice how the speaker in each of these examples used humor to provide a smooth transition to the main topic of the speech.

Similarly, Stacey encouraged her classmates to study a foreign language, introducing her classroom speech with the following attention-getting riddle:

What do you call someone who is fluent in many languages? A polylingual. What do you call someone who is fluent in two languages? A bilingual. What do you call someone who is fluent in only one language? An American!

This is a joke commonly told among the Japanese. Behind the apparent humor of this joke are some embarrassing truths.

Stacey combined humor and rhetorical questions to get her listeners' attention. She then discussed those "embarrassing truths" and the price we pay for speaking only one language.

Energize Your Audience. Sometimes, speakers can command attention simply by their "presence." John F. Kennedy, Winston Churchill, and Martin Luther King, Jr., for example, brought to their audiences an expectation that excited listeners. While not everyone can achieve this charisma, most speakers can work to enhance their dynamism. A positive attitude, appropriate dress, a confident walk to the platform, direct eye contact, a friendly smile, erect posture, a strong voice, and forceful gestures give an introduction as much impact as any of the above strategies. Conversely, the absence of these elements can destroy the effect of even the best worded opening statement. The advantages of an "energized" presence, however, extend far beyond a speech introduction. In Chapter 12, we give you specific suggestions for achieving a dynamic delivery throughout your speech.

Acknowledge and Compliment Your Audience. At some point in your life, you will probably be called upon to deliver a formal, public speech to an assembled group. Perhaps you will be the keynote speaker for a convention, or maybe you will accept an award from a civic group. The group inviting you to speak may even be paying you, anything from a small honorarium to a substantial fee. Such an occasion usually requires that you begin by acknowledging the audience and key dignitaries.

Notice how David Dinkins, then mayor of New York City, included his audience in the introduction of a speech he gave at the University of California at Berkeley:

I am deeply grateful to former Chancellor Ira Heyman and his successor, Chancellor Chang-Lin Tien, for inviting me to address the distinguished students, faculty, staff, and alumni at this great center of learning, the University of California at Berkeley, a symbol of freedom for universities throughout the world.

To step onto these historic grounds today is to fulfill an American pilgrimage. The most basic human impulse is to communicate; the Free Speech movement rescued the life of the mind of our country, and neither America nor the academy has been the same since.

It was at Berkeley that the academy emerged as America's searing conscience; it was from Berkeley that students spread throughout the Deep South to aid the Negro struggle for civil rights; and it was again at Berkeley that the first Asian-American was appointed to lead a major American university. Congratulations, Dr. Tien.[8]

In this class, your classmates make up your audience. You have interacted with them and, by now, probably know them pretty well. To begin your speech formally by acknowledging and complimenting them would seem stiff and insincere. You should not have to compliment fellow classmates; in fact, if you have prepared well, they should be thanking you for providing excellent information. For your assigned speeches, therefore, you should probably choose one of the other attention-getting strategies.

State Your Topic

Once you have the attention of your audience, state the topic or purpose of your speech directly and succinctly. For an informative speech, your statement of purpose should always take the form of a simple declarative sentence. "Today, I will show you how you can improve your study skills" clearly informs the audience of your topic.

This second step in a speech introduction is vitally important, even though the actual statement of purpose will take only a few seconds for you to say. Consider the following beginning section of a speech introduction:

How many of you have had a cholesterol count taken in the last year? Do you know what your numbers are and what they mean? It seems like we have all recently become much more aware of good cholesterol and bad, high-density lipoproteins and low-density ones, the dangers of high-fat diets and how difficult they can be to avoid in these fast-food, nuke-it-till-it's-hot times. People who never really considered exercising are spending a lot of money to join health clubs and work out. They know that a high cholesterol count can mean you are in danger of developing arteriosclerosis and finding yourself a candidate for surgery. Even if you don't have a heart attack, you may be hospitalized for one of several new procedures to clean out arteries clogged with plaque.

Now answer the following question: This speaker's purpose was to:

(a) discuss the interpretation of cholesterol tests.
(b) explain sources of cholesterol in popular foods.
(c) encourage exercise as a key to reducing serum cholesterol.
(d) explain new non-surgical procedures for opening clogged arteries.
(e) I can't tell what the speaker's purpose was.

Unfortunately, in this case, the correct answer is e. What went wrong? The speaker started off well enough by using two legitimate questions — the first direct, the second rhetorical — as an attention-getter. But then things got out of control; for almost a minute of speaking time, the speaker lapsed into a series of generalizations without ever stating the purpose of the speech. This excerpt represents a minute of wasted time! In a five- to seven-minute speech, that minute represents one-fifth to one-seventh of total speaking time. The speaker has confused the audience with vague statements and has lost their confidence. The real shame is that any of the four purposes listed above could be the goal of a good speech. Prepare properly and you will know your purpose. Then, state that purpose clearly as the second step of your introduction.

Establish the Importance of Your Topic

This third step in organizing the introduction to your speech should convince the listeners that the topic is important to them. You want to motivate them to listen further. A speaker addressing a women's group on rape prevention could include the statement, "One out of three women will at some point in her life be confronted by a rapist. That's one-third of all the women in this room! Because we cannot be sure that we will not be a victim, we must learn how to defend ourselves against rape." If you speak before an audience that includes men, you can easily invite their involvement in the topic. Show them how the potential rape victim may be a girlfriend, wife, sister, daughter, or mother.

Preview Your Key Ideas

preview: a statement that orients the audience by revealing how the speaker has organized the body of a speech.

The fourth step in organizing your introduction is the **preview** step, by which you "tell us what you're going to tell us." The preview step, working like a map, shows a final destination and reveals how the speaker intends to get there. As a result, the audience can travel more easily through the body of the speech. A person discussing the political, economic, and medical implications of national health insurance should inform the audience of these three divisions. A speaker addressing the issue of urban decay could preview her speech by saying, "In order to better understand the scope of this problem, we must look at four measurable conditions: the unemployment rate, housing starts, the poverty level, and the crime rate." That preview lists the four topics to be covered in the body of the speech and prepares the audience to listen more intelligently.

Preview statements are usually from one to three sentences in length. Rarely do they need to be longer. Each of the following examples is appropriately brief and specific in preparing the audience for the key ideas and the organizational pattern of the speech.

Assuming that you have the necessary materials, the three steps to constructing a piece of stained glass are first, selecting or creating a design; second, cutting the glass; and third, assembling and fixing the individual pieces.

An enhanced self-concept benefits us in at least three ways. Specifically, it improves our social interaction, our academic achievement, and our chances for career success.

In selecting a personal computer that's right for you, you need to be guided by three criteria. Utility: Does it meet your needs? Economy: Does it fit your budget? And quality: Will it last?

A person suffering from narcolepsy, then, experiences unexpected attacks of deep sleep. This little-known sleep disorder is better understood if we know its symptoms, its causes, and its treatment.

The first of these examples uses a chronological, step-by-step organization, while the remaining three employ a topical pattern. Having accomplished this final step of the introduction, these four speakers would be well prepared to begin the bodies of their speeches by signposting, stating, supporting, and summarizing their key points one by one.

How does the introduction sound when you put all four steps together? Our student, Rose, showed us that she certainly knows how to develop a complete and effective introduction:

> According to an old Indian saying, every person dies three times. The first time is the moment your life ends. The second is when your body is lowered into the ground. The third is when there is no one around to remember you. I'm going to talk to you today about death, or rather the celebration of death. This is a special celebration that comes from a Mexican tradition called *Dia de los Muertos,* or Day of the Dead. Now it may seem strange and morbid to speak of celebration and death in the same breath, but in the Mexican culture, death is embraced and worshipped just as much as life is. After I give you a little background on *Dia de los Muertos,* I'll explain the different ways this holiday is celebrated and show you some of the traditional objects used in the celebration.

Kevin, a student interested in screenwriting, selected an occasion-generated topic. He delivered the following introduction to his speech on the afternoon before that year's Academy Awards ceremony:

> Oliver Stone rewrote a Vietnam War novel into the successful screenplay *Platoon,* which won an Academy Award, much critical acclaim, and big money. Since Academy Awards are being handed out tonight, I'd like to take this opportunity to teach you some of the basics of writing a screenplay. According to *Successful Scriptwriting* by Kerry Cox and Jurgen Wolff, writing a screenplay is essentially the same as writing a story. Both need three basic elements: a beginning, a middle, and an end, or to use the language of scriptwriters, an introduction, a conflict, and a resolution.

Follow the four steps we have outlined for a speech introduction, and your audience should be attentive, know the purpose of your speech, be motivated to listen, and know the major ideas you will discuss. The only remaining part of the speech is the conclusion. Although it is often briefer than the introduction, your conclusion is vitally important to achieving your desired response. The conclusion is the last section your listeners hear and see, and must be well planned and carefully organized.

ORGANIZING THE CONCLUSION OF THE SPEECH

The last division of a public speech is the conclusion. In concluding a speech, you should summarize the key ideas and provide closure.

Summarize

summary: a statement or statements reviewing the major ideas of a speech.

In the **summary** you "tell us what you told us." Of all the steps in the process of organization, this should be the easiest to construct. You have already organized the body of the speech and, from it, constructed a preview statement. The summary parallels your preview. If your speech develops three key ideas, you reiterate them. If your speech is on self-concept enhancement, for example, you may simply say, "A good self-concept, therefore, benefits us in three ways. It enhances our social interaction, our academic achievement, and our career success." A speech on dying might be summarized: "Denial. Anger. Bargaining. Depression. Acceptance. These are the five stages of dying as described by Kübler-Ross."

Remember Stacey's attention-getter to her speech encouraging her classmates to study a foreign language? In the speech she discussed three harms from the nation's failure to promote bilingualism: "First, we lose economically.... Second, we lose scholastically.... Third, we lose culturally." Notice how Stacey reiterates and reinforces these points in the summary step of her conclusion:

> Clearly, these three points show us that by being monolingual we lose *economically, scholastically,* and *culturally.* Becoming proficient in another language and its culture may help us reduce our deficit and increase our competitiveness in world trade by recognizing possible problems in marketing campaigns. We will gain intellectually by increasing our vocabulary and expanding our minds. We will gain culturally by breaking barriers and possibly eliminating misunderstandings that occur as a result of being unfamiliar with another language, its people, and its culture.

The summary step gives the listener one last chance to hear and remember the main points of your presentation. Thus, the summary step reinforces the ideas of the speech and brings it to a logical conclusion.

Provide Closure

While a final summary of your key ideas is important, ending a speech on the summary step is unsatisfying. Such a strategy is what we call, to borrow from Porky Pig, the "b'dee, b'dee, b'dee, that's all folks" conclusion. You should not have to tell your listeners that the speech is finished. Your wording, as well as your delivery, should make this clear.

If your summary concludes your speech *logically*, your final statement ends the speech *psychologically*. An effective final statement ties the speech together and provides a strong note of finality or closure. The audience should know that you are about to finish, and they should have the feeling that you have said exactly as much as you need to say. Without resorting to saying, "In conclusion," or, "To conclude," you should mark the end of your speech by slowing your rate, maintaining direct eye contact with your listeners, and pausing briefly before and after your final sentence.

An example from literature may clarify what we mean by a psychological conclusion. Remember for a moment Catherine and Heathcliff, the main characters in Emily Brontë's *Wuthering Heights*. Though they roamed the moors together in their youth and later fell in love, circumstances kept them apart during the rest of their lives. The book ends after both have died. Novelist and short story writer Katherine Anne Porter once wrote: "One of the most perfect and marvelous endings in literature — it raises my hair now — is the little boy at the end of *Wuthering Heights*, crying that he's afraid to go across the moor because there's a man and woman walking there."[9] The final step of your speech conclusion does not have to be dramatic, but it should seem as satisfying as Brontë's final pages.

Sometimes a speaker employs what is called a **circular conclusion,** in which the final statement echoes or refers to the attention-getting step of the introduction. Bonnie used a circular conclusion in her speech advocating voluntary school uniforms. Notice how she refers in her conclusion to the examples she presented in her attention-getter.

circular conclusion: a conclusion that repeats or refers to material used in the attention-getting step of the introduction.

Attention-getting step:

In Los Angeles, a little girl dressing for school puts on her favorite red sweater. Her choice of color results in her being attacked and hit on the head with a rock. The reason: Red is the color worn by one gang, and a member of a rival gang retaliated upon seeing red.

Calvin Wash enjoys football and shows his loyalty to his favorite team by wearing a Cincinnati Bengals' jacket. Calvin was shot when he tried to escape from a man who demanded his jacket.

An 18-year-old was shot and killed by someone who wanted his Triple F.A.T. Goose parka and his $70 Nike shoes.

There's an old saying: "Clothes make the person." One thing clothes should not do, however, is make the person a target.

Conclusion:

Currently, Virginia's House of Delegates is considering a bill that would require public schools to implement a voluntary school uniform program. I encourage you to call or write your representative and voice your support of this bill. In addition, if your local school does not already have such a program, contact the school board and urge them to implement one. Remember to tell them that voluntary school programs will help create a safer school environment, enhance academic achievement, and promote a positive social climate.

When a little girl is trying to decide what to wear to school, she shouldn't be faced with a life-or-death decision. When a boy puts on his jacket and shoes, he shouldn't be preparing for combat. A voluntary school uniform is one way of helping schools become what they should be: a place where children can learn and grow.

Our student Steve also used a circular conclusion. He began his informative speech by saying: "It is one of the most dreaded, incurable diseases facing humankind today.

Everyone in this room knows someone who has it. The disease is diabetes mellitus." In his conclusion, he summarized the main points he had covered and then ended the speech this way:

> At the beginning of this presentation I said that each of you knows someone who has diabetes. The reason I could say that without hesitation is that for the past 10 years I have been an insulin-dependent diabetic taking three shots a day. The good news is that I'm able to lead almost as normal a life as each one of you. The *best* news is that each day we come closer to finding a cure!

Your final statement does not have to allude to your attention-getting step. Any of the specific techniques we discussed for gaining audience attention can help bring your speech to a strong, clear, psychologically satisfying conclusion. You can ask a question, even the same one you began with or a variation of it. Or you can answer the question you initially asked. Once you arouse your audience's curiosity in your speech, you must satisfy it in order to provide closure. You could stimulate their imaginations through vivid imagery, or promise them that the information you have provided can bring them benefits. You could conclude with a joke or humorous story relevant to your topic. Through lively delivery you could energize the audience to act on the information you have provided them. In a speech presented on more formal occasions than a classroom assignment, you may end by complimenting and thanking the audience.

Both steps of the conclusion are important. The summary step reinforces the ideas of the speech, while the final statement reinforces the impact of the speech. Consider the following conclusion of a student's speech opposing capital punishment: "Those in favor of capital punishment should reexamine the issues of dignity, deterrence, and death. We must be motivated by reason rather than retribution if we want our country to be known for 'executing justice, not people.'" The student restated her main divisions and ended with impact through her use of language, voice, and gestures.

Remember Kevin's speech on screenplays (p. 195)? He concluded his speech this way:

> All screenplays carry three basic elements: an introduction, which establishes the storyline and the characters; conflict, which pits the main character against obstacles in the quest of some goal; and a conclusion, which resolves the conflict and reflects on the theme of the work. Let's face it, if *Porky's, Friday the 13th,* and *Attack of the Killer Tomatoes* made it to the big screen, most ideas can make it, if you just have the elements of a good screenplay.

A diagram of the individual elements in a well-organized speech would contain the following:

1. Attention-getting step
2. Statement of topic
3. Emphasis on importance of topic
4. Preview step
5. Body of speech
6. Summary step
7. Closure

This is the correct order of steps in the delivered speech. In your preparation, however, you will follow the sequence we discussed in this chapter. As we mentioned earlier, you

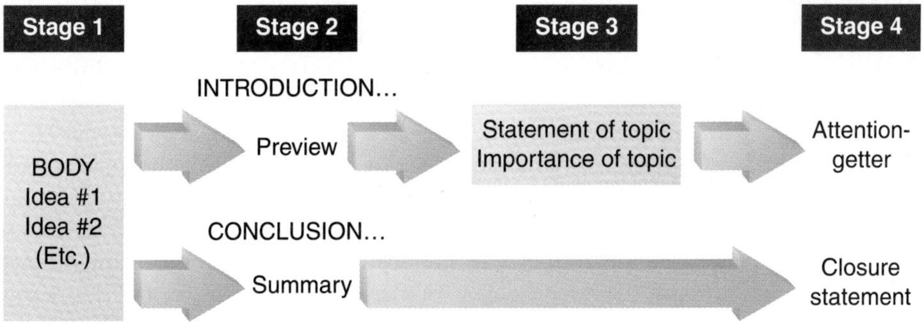

| Stage 1 | Stage 2 | Stage 3 | Stage 4 |

INTRODUCTION...

BODY
Idea #1
Idea #2
(Etc.)

Preview → Statement of topic / Importance of topic → Attention-getter

CONCLUSION...

Summary → Closure statement

Figure. 9.2 *Stages in organizing a speech*

should prepare the body of your speech first. Some instructors recommend that you develop your introduction next and your conclusion last. Others suggest that you prepare your introduction last. Remember, there is no one correct way of constructing a speech. Select the method that works best for you.

We suggest an alternative strategy (see Figure 9.2), which is divided into four stages. In Stage 1, you construct the body of your speech, determining the key ideas and developing them using the **4 S's.** After completing this stage, you then work outward.

Rather than going just to the introduction or just to the conclusion, you work on both simultaneously, focusing on elements that have similar purposes. With your key ideas determined, you can easily word your preview and summary statements. These two steps are similar because they highlight a speech's key ideas. As you complete Stage 2, you have fulfilled the overall organizational strategy we mentioned at the beginning of this chapter: You are ready to "tell us what you're going to tell us," "tell us," and "tell us what you told us."

In Stage 3, you decide how you will state your topic and explain its importance to your audience. This should not be difficult. You have already thought through these steps when you selected your topic. Your choice of words and supporting materials should lead naturally to your preview statement, which you have already worded. In the final stage of your preparation, you devise your attention-getting and closure statements, two crucial steps at the furthest extremes from the speech body. Developing the attention-getter and the final statement at the same time should increase the total unity of the speech, and this is particularly important if you are using a circular conclusion.

Speakers who begin preparing speeches by starting with the introduction often end up trying to fit the rest of their speech to the introduction. Speakers who write their introduction, body, and conclusion separately often produce three parts rather than a unified whole. The outward method of development we suggest helps you avoid these pitfalls and enables you to present your ideas clearly, cohesively, and convincingly.

*S*UMMARY

Being sure of your speech organization gives you confidence as a speaker; communicating your information in a well-organized manner makes it much easier for the audience to remember what you have said. The chief goal of speech organization is to assist your listeners in understanding and retaining your information.

The three parts of a speech are the *introduction, body,* and *conclusion.* You should organize the body first because it is the most substantial part of the speech, and because its content determines the content of the introduction and the conclusion. Depending upon your purpose in speaking, you may select any of six organizational patterns for the body of the speech. *Topical division* narrows a broad topic by limiting it to certain subtopics chosen by the speaker. *Chronological division* organizes a historical topic or a speech explaining a process into a time sequence. *Spatial division* lets the geography or physical structure of a place or thing organize the speech for you. *Causal division* allows a speaker to explore a condition or action from its causes to its effects, or from effects back to causes. *Pro-con division* presents the arguments for and against some policy, position, or action, and with the addition of a final assessment step becomes a persuasive speech pattern. The final organizational pattern, the *gimmick division,* uses a memory device such as the letters of a word to organize key points in the speech and help the audience recall them.

After choosing a general organizational pattern and establishing your main points, you are ready to organize the presentation of each major idea in the body of your speech. To do this, we recommend a memory device we call the **4 S's:** *signpost* the idea, *state* the idea, *support* the idea, and *summarize* the idea. Apply these four steps to each major idea in the speech.

Each of the main points you develop needs to be connected to the others by *transitions.* Effective transitions indicate the nature of the relation between the ideas: *complementary, causal, contrasting,* or *chronological.*

The introduction and conclusion are brief parts of the speech, but they must be well organized and practiced since they are, respectively, your first and last chances to create a favorable impression for yourself or your topic. The introduction should accomplish four steps, in this order: (1) Get the attention of your audience, (2) state your topic or purpose, (3) stress the importance or relevance of your topic, and (4) preview the key ideas you will be developing in the body of the speech. To get your audience's attention, you can question your listeners, arouse their curiosity, stimulate their imaginations, promise them something beneficial, amuse them, energize them, or acknowledge and compliment them. An effective conclusion must do two things: (1) summarize, or bring your speech to a logical conclusion, and (2) provide closure, or bring the speech to a satisfying psychological conclusion.

Rather than organizing the introduction, body, and conclusion of your speech separately, we recommend that you organize the body first and then work outward from that center. Once you have determined the main ideas of the body, you can easily construct your *preview* statement for the introduction and your *summary* statement for the conclusion. Next, amplify your introduction by stating your purpose clearly and emphasizing the significance of your topic. Finally, work on your attention-getter and your closure statement simultaneously to help ensure that your speech holds together as a satisfying, cohesive unit.

If you follow the suggestions in this chapter, your speech should be well organized. That clear organization will, in turn, make your information easier for the audience to remember, and that's a major goal of public speaking.

1. Prepare three introductions for the same body of content. Discuss the advantages and disadvantages of each. Select the one you think is best and explain why.
2. Using the **4 *S*'s,** prepare and deliver one major point in the body of a speech. You should document and cite your source(s) in the support step.
3. Prepare three conclusions for the same body of content. Discuss the advantages and disadvantages of each. Select the one you think is best and explain why.
4. Select an organizational pattern you think would be appropriate for speeches with the specific purposes listed below. Could the specific purpose be achieved using other patterns? Are there some patterns that would clearly be inappropriate?
   a. To inform the audience about relaxation techniques.
   b. To inform the audience about the history of Groundhog Day.
   c. To inform the audience about the advantages and disadvantages of raising money for charitable causes by telethons.
   d. To inform the audience about marriage rituals in various cultures.
   e. To persuade the audience that illiteracy is seriously harming national productivity.
   f. To persuade the audience that the health benefits from one exercise program are greater than those from another.
5. Select one topic and show how it could be developed using three different organizational patterns. Which do you think would make the best speech? Why?

*N*OTES

1. Robert Half, "Memomania," *American Way* 1 November 1987: 21.

2. Robert L. Montgomery, *Listening Made Easy* (New York: AMACOM, 1981) 65-78.

3. Glenn Leggett, C. David Mead, Melinda Kramer, and Richard S. Beal, *Prentice Hall Handbook for Writers,* 11th ed. (Englewood Cliffs, NJ: Prentice, 1991) 417-18. We have drawn on examples these authors use in their excellent section on connecting language.

4. Patricia A. Cirucci, "Grounds for Disaster," *Winning Orations, 1991* (Mankato, MN: Interstate Oratorical Association, 1991) 102.

5. Jonathan J. Esslinger, "National Parks: A Scenery of Destruction and Degradation," *Winning Orations, 1992* (Mankato, MN: Interstate Oratorical Association, 1992) 133.

6. Carl Wayne Hensley, "What You Share Is What You Get: Tips for Effective Communication," *Vital Speeches of the Day* 1 December 1992: 115.

7. Clyde Prestowitz, Jr., "In Search of Survival: Why Haven't We Done Anything?" *Vital Speeches of the Day* 1 September 1992: 698.

8. David N. Dinkins, "In Praise of Cities," *Representative American Speeches 1990-1991* (New York: Wilson, 1991) 133.

9. Katherine Anne Porter, "The Art of Fiction XXIX," *The Paris Review* 29 (Winter-Spring 1963): 102.

Order and simplification are the first steps toward the mastery of a subject.
    ~Thomas Mann

Outlining Your Speech

Functions of Outlining

Principles of Outlining

Stages of Outlining
The Working Outline
The Formal Outline
The Speaking Outline

*C*hapter *10*

ow long would it take you to memorize and be able to repeat the following twenty-six letters: *c-p-s-y-n-i-r-t-y-m-v-i-e-m-r-t-o-i-p-o-e-m-o-m-e-m?* A typical learner would need a good deal of practice to remember more than the first four to seven letters you just read.[1] Would it help you if the letters were rearranged as follows: *y-m-c-o-i-t-p-s-i-p-t-y-m-m-v-e-n-e-o-i-r-r-m-e-o-m?* Unless you have an eidetic or photographic memory, such a shuffling of letters is likely no help at all. But what if the letters were scrambled again: *m-y-t-o-p-i-c-i-s-p-t-y-m-m-v-e-n-e-o-i-r-r-m-e-o-m?* Those first nine letters are now recognizable as the English words *my, topic,* and *is,* and you can easily repeat them in correct sequence. Those three words would be even more obvious if we eliminated the dashes and used a familiar pattern of grouping and spacing: *my topic is.* If the last seventeen letters were also reorganized as *m-e-m-o-r-y-i-m-p-r-o-v-e-m-e-n-t,* or *memory improvement,* you could master the entire sequence of twenty-six letters in correct order, orally or in writing, without much effort.

Notice that we did not add or delete any letters. We merely reorganized them until they formed a pattern that is easy to recognize and repeat. When you outline, you perform essentially the same task. You organize and reorganize material into a pattern easy to recognize and remember. As you prepare your speech, you will find that outlining is an indispensable element of speech organization.

In Chapter 9, we discussed the importance of organization to the delivered speech and suggested some ways of achieving a well-organized presentation. Outlining your speech is the preliminary written work necessary to foster clear organization of your oral message. In this chapter, you will learn why outlines are important to your speech, examine some different types of outlines, and finally, study how to write an excellent outline.

▬ FUNCTIONS OF OUTLINING

A well-prepared outline serves five important functions for a speaker:

1. It tests the scope of the speaker's content.
2. It tests the logical relations among parts of the speech.
3. It tests the relevance of supporting ideas.
4. It checks the balance or proportion of the speech.
5. It serves as notes during the delivery of the speech.

The first purpose of outlining is to test the scope of the speaker's content. Have you narrowed the topic sufficiently to cover your key ideas in some depth? Or are you trying to cover too much material, so that you will merely skim the surface of the subject, repeating things your audience already knows? In Chapter 9, we stated that a speaker should ordinarily have no more than two to five main points in a speech. Outlining allows you to use paper and pen to organize your main ideas, and then add, delete, regroup, shuffle, condense, or expand these ideas so you approach your topic in a manageable way. In other words, outlining is a process of setting goals for the speech.

Second, outlining allows speakers to test the logical relations among the various parts of the speech. Does one idea in the outline lead to the next in a meaningful way? Do the arguments or subtopics under each of your main points really develop that point? In order to answer these questions, you must understand the concepts of coordination and subordination. **Coordinate ideas** are those of equal value or importance in the

coordinate ideas:
ideas that have equal value in a speech.

overall pattern of the speech. The following hypothetical example illustrates the relation between coordinate and subordinate ideas.

Suppose you find in the library Wilson Bryan Key's books *Subliminal Seduction, Media Sexploitation,* and *The Clam Plate Orgy,* works claiming to show evidence of subliminal messages in print advertisements. Intrigued, you do further research on the topic of subliminal messages. You learn that audio subliminal messages have increased sales and reduced shoplifting in stores where they have been played under background music. If you delivered an informative speech on subliminal messages, you might arrange your speech topically and focus on those two areas:

I. Visual subliminals
II. Audio subliminals

These two topics are coordinate because they are of equal value. You may have more information on one of them than on the other, and consequently spend more time in the speech discussing that topic, but neither is a subtopic of the other. Under that first main topic, you would list **subordinate ideas,** subtopics that support it. Two subordinate points for visual subliminals could be:

I. Visual subliminals
  A. Subliminals in print advertising
  B. Subliminals in movies

Notice that A and B above are not only subordinate to the main idea, visual subliminals, but are also coordinate with one another since they seem to be equally important. Subordinate ideas for the second main point, audio subliminals, could include:

II. Audio subliminals
  A. Subliminals to increase sales
  B. Subliminals to reduce theft

Your outline is not yet complete, but you can begin to ask yourself the following questions at this point: Are my main ideas different enough to qualify as separate points? Do those subordinate points really support the main ideas? At this stage, the answers to both of those questions seem to be yes. In this way, the visual form of the outline helps you test the logical connections between parts of your speech. You continue this process to further refine and add to the outline.

Third, an outline helps the speaker test the relevance of supporting ideas. To understand how this works, assume that you had written the following portion of an outline for a speech on roller coasters:

I. Famous roller coasters
  A. Coney Island's "Cyclone"
  B. Montreal's "Le Monstre"
  C. Busch Gardens' "Kumba"
  D. New design technology

Notice that the fourth subpoint, "new design technology," is out of place because it is irrelevant to the main point. How do you solve this problem? Careful study of this portion of the outline should signal you to make "new design technology" a separate main point if you can gather adequate supporting material on it; if you can't, eliminate it.

subordinate ideas:
ideas that support more general or more important points in a speech.

A fourth function outlining serves for the speaker is to check the balance or proportion of the speech. If you look back to the outline on subliminal messages we used earlier, you will notice that two subpoints support each of the main ideas. As a result, the division of the speech looks balanced, even though a speaker could actually spend more time on one of those main ideas than on the other. The speech would still be balanced if one main point contained three subpoints and the other included two. Yet if the main point of "visual subliminals" contained five subpoints and "audio subliminals" had only two, the outline may not be balanced. This lack of balance in the outline will be reflected in the speech.

How can you fix an imbalance in your speech? In the speech on subliminal messages, the speaker might focus only on visual subliminals rather than have the second topic seem undeveloped or tacked on hastily. As you can see, your outline tests the balance of your speech and can even lead you to alter your specific purpose.

Fifth, and finally, a special type of abbreviated outline can serve as notes for the speaker during the actual delivery of the speech. This outline, called a speaking outline and discussed later in this chapter, has only one rule: It must be brief. If you have prepared adequately for your speech, you should need only key words and phrases to remind you of each point you want to discuss. Moreover, having your notes in outline form rather than arranged randomly on notecards or sheets of paper will constantly remind you of the importance of clear organization as you are delivering the speech.

complete sentence outline: an outline in which all numbers and letters introduce complete sentences.

key word or phrase outline: an outline in which all numbers and letters introduce words or groups of words.

■ PRINCIPLES OF OUTLINING

Correct outlines take one of two possible forms: **the complete sentence outline** and the **key word or phrase outline.** In a complete sentence outline, each and every item is a sentence; each item in a key word or phrase outline is a word or group of words. These two forms of outlines should be kept consistent and distinct. Combine them only in the speaker's outline from which you deliver your speech. So far in this chapter, we have used only phrase outlines. More word or phrase outlines and an example of a complete sentence outline will follow.

KEY POINTS

Principles of Outlining

1. Each number or letter in the outline should represent only one idea.
2. Coordinate and subordinate points in the outline should be represented by a consistent system of numbers and letters.
3. If any point has subpoints under it, there must be at least two subpoints.
4. Each symbol in a sentence outline should introduce a complete sentence. Each symbol in a word or phrase outline should introduce a word or phrase.
5. Coordinate points throughout the outline should have parallel grammatical construction.

As you construct your outline, you will work more efficiently and produce a clearer outline if you follow a few rules, or principles. First, each number or letter in the outline should represent only one idea. Remember that a chief goal of outlining is to achieve a clear visual representation of the connections between parts of the speech. This is possible only if you separate the ideas. For example, suppose a speaker preparing a speech on color blindness has worded a key idea as "causes of and tests for color blindness." The phrase contains two distinct ideas, each requiring separate discussion and development. Instead, the speaker should divide the statement into two coordinate points: "causes of color blindness" and "tests for color blindness."

Second, coordinate and subordinate points in the outline should be represented by a consistent system of numbers and letters. Main ideas are typically represented by Roman numerals: I, II, III, and so forth. Don't worry about brushing up on those higher Roman numerals because you will not have more than five or so main points! Label subpoints under the main points with capital letters: A, B, C, and so forth. Beneath those, identify your supporting points with Arabic numerals: 1, 2, 3, and so on. Identify ideas subordinate to those with lowercase letters: a, b, c, and so on. Using this notation system, the labeling and indentation of a typical outline may appear as follows:

I. Main point
   A. Subpoint
      1. Sub-subpoint
      2. Sub-subpoint
      3. Sub-subpoint
   B. Subpoint
      1. Sub-subpoint
      2. Sub-subpoint
         a. Sub-sub-subpoint
         b. Sub-sub-subpoint
II. Main point
   A. Subpoint
   B. Subpoint
      1. Sub-subpoint
      2. Sub-subpoint
   C. Subpoint

A third principle is that if any point has subpoints under it, there must be at least two subpoints. A basic law of physics is that you cannot divide something into only one part. If you have an A, you must also have a B. (You may, of course, also have subpoints C, D, and E.) If you have a 1, you must also have at least a 2.

Fourth, each symbol in a sentence outline should introduce a complete sentence. Each symbol in a word or phrase outline should introduce a word or phrase. In other words, keep the form of the outline consistent. Sentences and phrases should be mixed only in your speaking outline.

Finally, coordinate points throughout the outline should have parallel grammatical construction. For example, a key phrase outline of a speech on how to write a résumé begins with a first main point labeled "Things to include." The second point should be "Things to omit," rather than "Leaving out unnecessary information." The first point is worded as a noun phrase and, therefore, you must follow it with another noun phrase

("Things to omit") rather than a predicate phrase ("Leaving out unnecessary information"). This does not mean that you must choose noun phrases over verb phrases, but rather that all points match grammatically. In this next example, all coordinate points have parallel grammatical construction.

> I. Including essential information
>   A. Address
>   B. Career objective
>   C. Educational background
>   D. Employment history
>   E. References
> II. Omitting unnecessary information
>   A. Marital status
>   B. Religious denomination
>   C. Political affiliation

As you can see, coordinate main points I and II are verb phrases, while the coordinate subpoints are all nouns or noun phrases.

STAGES OF OUTLINING

Do you have difficulty generating or discovering the main points for a speech topic you have chosen? Don't worry, you are not alone. Many people are intimidated by the prospect of selecting and organizing ideas, particularly for a first speech. We especially worry if an organization plan doesn't come to us quickly. When we get a plan, we worry

Visual aids can help outline speakers comments and clarify speech structure in even the noisiest communication environments.
(SOURCE: © Jim West/Impact Visuals)

that it is not the right organizational pattern to use. You can avoid these self-defeating lines of thinking if you keep in mind four guidelines to organizing and outlining.

First, organization is not something that comes to you, but rather it is something that you must go after. Structuring a speech requires you to invest time and thought, investments whose dividends may not be apparent until you deliver the speech. Second, there is no one right way of organizing all speeches on a particular topic. True, some topics logically lend themselves to certain patterns of organization. As you learned in Chapter 9, speeches about processes often almost organize themselves according to a chronological pattern. Speeches about people may be arranged chronologically or topically. Persuasive speeches on social issues are perhaps most logically organized according to a problem-solution format, discussed in Chapter 16. Yet different speakers may use different structures. You have to determine what works best for you, your topic, and your audience.

Third, the early stages of organizing and outlining a speech are filled with uncertainty. You may find yourself asking these questions: Do I have enough main points, too many, or too few? Can I find adequate information to support all of those main points? Am I overlooking other main points the audience would be interested in hearing me discuss? Rather than feeling pressured by such questions, look on the early stages of outlining as a period of flexibility. Remember that the early, informal versions of your working outline are all provisional — temporary and open to change. Don't be afraid to experiment a little. Fourth, and finally, identifying the main points in a speech is also easier than many people imagine. In the remainder of this chapter we will guide you through the process of outlining, from those first tentative ideas a speaker puts on paper to the final outline used as speaking notes.

The Working Outline

The first step in preparing an outline is to construct what we like to call a **working outline,** a list of aspects of your chosen topic. Such a list may result from research you have already conducted, or it may simply be a result of some productive brainstorming. Once you have spent significant time researching the subject, you will notice topics that are repeated in different sources on the subject. If, for example, you had selected Grave's disease as the topic for an informative speech and had conducted adequate research, your list of possible aspects of the topic would include:

working outline: an informal, initial outline recording a speaker's process of narrowing, focusing, and balancing a topic.

Cause	Diagnosis	Prevention
Symptoms	Treatment	

Notice that these same topics could be applied to any disease, physical illness, or mental condition.

You can also generate topic areas through brainstorming and visual brainstorming, techniques we discussed in Chapter 6 (see pages 107-16). Not only can brainstorming help you generate topics, it can also help you explore areas of the topic you finally select.[2] Your creative brainstorming might even reveal interesting areas of your topic that have not been adequately treated in the existing research. This discovery provides you an opportunity to conduct original research or experimentation.

As you can see, at this stage the term *outline* is very loose; the list of key ideas you are developing does not have any numbers or letters attached to it. That's fine, since these notes are for your benefit alone. This working outline is not so much a finished product as it is a record of the process you go through in thinking about a speech topic.

For a fuller demonstration of this first step in outline preparation, assume that you had read an interesting article on the perfume industry and were considering perfumes as a topic for an informative speech. Using the visual brainstorming technique discussed in Chapter 6, you might generate the related topics shown in Figure 10.1.

Your working outline would therefore begin with just the following main points:

History of perfumes	Uses of perfumes
Production of perfumes	Selection of perfumes
Levels of strength	Ingredients of perfumes

After some preliminary research on perfumes, you could expand your working outline with the following subpoints:

History of perfumes
  In religion
  In myth
  In commerce
  In literature
  In medicine
Production of perfumes
  Research
  Development
  Advertising
  Retailing
Ingredients
  Solvents
  Fixatives
  Essential oils
    Sources
    Methods of extraction

Levels of Strength
  Perfume
  Eau de toilette
  Cologne
  Aftershave
Uses
  In cosmetics
  In household cleaners
  In production of plastics and
    rubber
  In tanning of leather
Selection
  According to wearer's personality
  According to season
Care of perfumes
  Protection from light
  Protection from heat

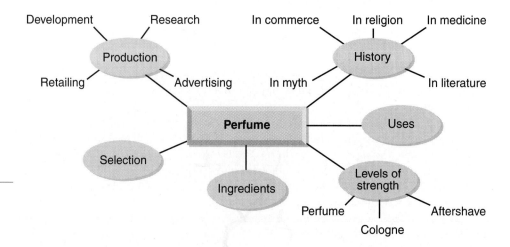

Figure 10.1 *Visual brainstorming on the subject "Perfume"*

Obviously, this is too much material for a typical short classroom speech. How do you decide what to include and what to eliminate? First, consider your interests, those of your audience, and the quantity of research materials you have found on each of these topics.

This is how John focused the topic of perfume from his working outline:

The history of perfumes is really interesting. When I decided on this topic, I did so partly because it was such an unusual subject and one that's interesting without being too serious. What I found out about the history of perfumes and their uses today in lots of industries showed me that the topic is more important than I thought at first. But I don't think I want to concentrate on either of those aspects of the topic. Maybe I can refer to "history" and "uses" in the introduction to emphasize the significance of the topic, though.

The care of fragrances is too brief to be the main point of the speech. Most sources mentioned that topic, but they just said "perfumes are volatile chemicals that break down easily. Keep them away from heat and light." I learned a lot in my research about the different categories or levels of strength of perfumes. I now know the difference between a perfume, a cologne, and an aftershave, but that's really a simple point and not enough to base the whole speech on. I think the class would be interested in knowing how the cologne or aftershave you select may reveal aspects of your personality, but most of what I found in two articles was geared toward women, and there are almost as many men as women in our class.

I've decided to speak on the ingredients of perfumes because three of the sources I've looked at had sections on this subject and it's something the audience won't know. What interested me most in my research were the sources of these different ingredients and how they are collected. While technology is important to the perfume industry today, some of the techniques being used are the same ones that were practiced by alchemists thousands of years ago!

This speaker has narrowed the working outline above to one section:

Ingredients
   Solvents
   Fixatives
   Essential oils
      Sources
      Methods of extraction

After some more detailed research in this topic area, John devised another working outline:

   I. Three categories of ingredients
     A. Aromatics or "essential oils"
       1. From flowers
       2. From spices, seeds, woods
       3. From synthetic aldehydes
       4. Methods of collecting
          a. Distillation
          b. Solvent extraction
          c. Enfleurage

              d. Expression, or "cold pressing"
      B. Fixatives or stabilizers
          1. Purpose
          2. Sources
              a. Natural sources from animals
                  (1) Civet from civet cat
                  (2) Castoreum from beavers
                  (3) Musk from musk deer
                  (4) Ambergris from sperm whale
              b. Synthesis of musk and ambergris
      C. Solvents, the "pushers" and "fillers" of perfumes

This version still has problems, but that's OK. Remember, the real function of the working outline is to test the waters of your topic and reveal any problems in your approach. The most obvious problem with this working outline is that it has only one main point, one Roman numeral. As we discussed earlier, you cannot divide something into only one part. John will have to correct that problem in subsequent versions of the outline. He also felt that the speech ended on a weak note with the relatively simple point of "solvents."

With some shifting, John easily developed a stronger outline. He had enough interesting information about the four methods of collecting essential oils to qualify them as a main point. Therefore, he decided to begin the first main point on the categories of ingredients with the subpoint solvents, follow with the more interesting points of fixatives and essential oils, and then develop the four methods of collecting as a separate main point. John's revised working outline was as follows.

    I. Three categories of ingredients
        A. Solvents, the "pushers" and "fillers" of perfumes
        B. Fixatives or stabilizers
            1. Purpose
            2. Sources
                a. Natural sources from animals
                    (1) Civet from civet cat
                    (2) Castoreum from beavers
                    (3) Musk from musk deer
                    (4) Ambergris from sperm whale
                b. Synthesis of musk and ambergris
        C. Aromatics or "essential oils"
            1. From flowers
            2. From spices, seeds, woods
            3. From synthetic aldehydes
   II. Methods of collecting essential oils
        A. Distillation
        B. Solvent extraction
        C. Enfleurage
        D. Expression, or "cold pressing"

This second version of the working outline develops two main points and seems more balanced than the first version. It also begins with a subpoint the speaker thinks will be quick and simple to explain. From there, the outline develops more unusual and complicated ideas.

"The problem now," John noted, "is that I don't think I can cover all of this material in the four- to six-minute time limit for the speech. I'd be racing through it and I doubt that audience members could remember even the main points." Even though he had interesting material on the second point, John decided to develop only the first point in order to meet his time limit. As a result, Roman numeral I became his specific purpose: to inform the audience of the three ingredients in perfumes. Points A, B, and C became the three main ideas of his speech and, as you will see, John renumbered them I, II, and III.

You may think that as a speaker prepares a speech, the outline will become longer and more complex. To a certain point this is true. As you flesh out your ideas over a period of time, your outline does grow more detailed. What evolves is finally called your formal outline. Once you have decided for certain on the number of main points you can cover in the allowed time, what those points are, and how you will support them, you then select words and phrases from the formal outline to make up your much briefer speaking outline.

The Formal Outline

Your **formal outline** is a complete sentence outline reflecting the full content and organization of your speech. In its final form, it is the finished product of your research and planning for your speech. A stranger, picking up your formal outline, should be able to read how you have organized and supported all your main points. If you keep that goal in mind, you should have no trouble deciding what needs to be included.

Your instructor may require you to include any or all of the following items at the beginning of your formal outline: your speech title, a statement of your specific purpose, and your thesis statement, appropriately labeled. The actual outline should follow the accepted pattern of symbols and indentation, with each item in the outline making up a complete sentence. Your instructor may ask you to label the superstructure of the speech — introduction, body, and conclusion — by inserting these words at the appropriate places in the outline but without Roman numerals or other symbols attached to them. Finally, the formal outline should be followed by a bibliography listing the sources you have used in the development of the speech.

Now let's see how John developed his formal outline for his speech on perfumes. The final version of John's formal outline, with a complete introduction and conclusion, looked like this:

formal outline: a complete sentence outline written in sufficient detail that a person other than the speaker could understand it.

Speech title: Making Sense of Scents
Specific purpose: To inform the audience of the three ingredients in perfumes.
Thesis statement: All fragrances contain solvents, fixatives, and aromatics, obtained from a variety of natural and synthetic sources.

Introduction
Napoleon wouldn't go into battle without them. Egyptian priests used to rub them on statues of gods and goddesses each morning. Doctors used to put them in leather "snouts" over the noses of the sick. Cultured women used to carry them in lock-

ets or in the hollow heads of canes. Today, Americans spend one and a half billion dollars a year on them. "Them," in each of these cases, refers to perfumes. Perfumes have been the prize for which battles were fought, have affected trade routes, and have had a place in every advanced culture on earth. Today, even if you don't buy perfumes, colognes, or aftershaves, you're a perfume consumer almost every time you buy soap, a household cleaner, a cosmetic, or a piece of leather or plastic. Knowing what actually goes into perfumes is not only interesting information, but also helps explain the variety of perfumes available and their typically high costs. Every ingredient in a perfume, cologne, or aftershave falls into one of three categories: solvents, fixatives, and aromatics or essential oils.

Body of speech

I. Solvents are the "fillers" and "pushers" of perfumes.
    A. Pure, sterile water is the biggest component of perfumes.
    B. Purified ethyl alcohol is the other solvent.
II. Fixatives are the stabilizers in fragrances.
    A. Fixatives stabilize the rates of evaporation of the various aromatics used.
    B. Without fixatives, fragrances would change suddenly and dramatically.
    C. Fixative sources may be natural or synthetic.
       1. Natural fixatives come from animals.
          a. Civet comes from the small East African civet cat.
            (1) Civet is collected from both male and female cats.
            (2) Civet can be removed from captive cats twice a week without harming the animals.
          b. Castoreum is collected from two abdominal sacs of Russian and Canadian beavers.
          c. Musk comes from the tiny musk deer of western China.
            (1) The male deer has a sac to secrete musk as a sexual signal.
            (2) Hunters remove the sacs from slaughtered deer.
          d. Ambergris comes from the sperm whale.
            (1) Whales produce the substance to lubricate their digestive tracts against the bones of the cuttlefish, their primary food.
            (2) Ambergris has an extremely sweet smell and great fixative properties.
       2. Both musk and ambergris are now commonly synthesized.
          a. Perfume manufacturers have voluntarily agreed not to purchase ambergris to protect the sperm whale population.
          b. Synthesized musk and ambergris are much less costly than their natural counterparts.
III. Aromatics or "essential oils" are the primary scents.
    A. Most aromatics come from flowers.
       1. Rose, jasmine, and iris are typical floral scents.
       2. Perfumes may be based on a single flower or a combination.
    B. Some aromatics come from spices, seeds, or woods.
       1. Rosemary, mint, and cloves are typical spices used.
       2. Almond, apricot, and sesame seeds are typical seeds used.
       3. Sandalwood, pine, and cedar are typical woods used.
    C. Some of the brightest aromatics today are the synthetic aldehydes.
       1. Like formaldehyde, these aromatics are strong.
       2. Though immediately detectable, they don't last long.

Conclusion

The perfume, cologne, or aftershave you're wearing now or saving for a special occasion probably began one morning as workers gathered flowers, spices, or wood bark before dawn. After a costly and time-consuming collection process, the essential oils were shipped to laboratories where chemists began their combination with fixatives and solvents. Knowing these ingredients may help you explain why you pass over some fragrances, but for others you're willing to pay your part of that one and a half billion dollars we Americans spend on fragrance each year.

Bibliography

Boyer, Pamela. "Selecting a Perfect Scent." *Prevention* February 1989: 88+.

Green, Annette. "Perfume." *The Encyclopedia Americana: International Edition.* 1986 ed.

Lamotte, Michael. "Bottled Up." *Esquire* May 1989: 162-65.

Morris, Edwin T. *Fragrance: The Story of Perfume from Cleopatra to Chanel.* New York: Scribner's, 1984

Oliver, Joan D. "Making Sense of Scent." *Health* November 1989: 57+.

"Perfume." *Encyclopædia Britannica.* 1971 ed.

Weber, Bruce. "Nose Job." *New York Times Magazine* 5 Feb. 1989: 78.

The Speaking Outline

The **speaking outline,** the one you actually use to deliver your speech, is a pared-down version of your full formal outline. You construct the formal outline for an interested reader having no necessary prior knowledge of your topic. However, you write the speaking outline for yourself as a unique speaker. As we mentioned earlier, the only rule for the speaking outline is that it be brief.

Why is the speaking outline briefer than the formal outline? Chances are that your instructor will want most or all of your speeches delivered from notes rather than from a written manuscript. Your brief speaking outline, made up of essential words and phrases, meets the requirements of the assignment while also serving as your speaking notes. But more important, if you spoke from a complete sentence outline, you might be tempted to read the speech, sacrificing eye contact and other vital interaction with your audience. Alternatively, you might try to memorize the formal outline, another dangerous tactic since you then face the prospect of forgetting part of the speech. If, instead, you speak using the outline having just key words and phrases to jog your memory, your delivery will seem more natural and conversational, and you will find yourself freer to interact with your audience.

Though the speaking outline leaves out a lot of what the formal outline includes, it also contains some important items not found in the formal outline. For example, you can include directions to yourself about the delivery of the speech. A speaker with a tendency to speak too softly may write reminders in the margins, such as "volume" or "Speak up!" You can note in your outline when you want to pause, to slow down, or to show visual aids. Some speakers find it particularly helpful to make these delivery notes in a color of ink different from the rest of the outline.

Second, most speaking outlines include any supporting material you plan to use. Quotations and definitions should be written out in complete sentences, even though the rest of the outline is in words and phrases. When you quote others, you must be exact. Examples, illustrations, and statistics may be noted in only a few words or numbers. In a speech

speaking outline: a brief outline for the speaker's use alone and containing source citations and delivery prompts.

on the United States' billionaires, for example, if you plan to describe how Sam Walton made his fortune as founder of Wal-Mart Stores, you could write simply "Sam Walton" in your notes. If your explanation includes specific dates or statistics, you may include those. In addition, you should insert any sources you will cite.

For the speech on perfumes, John condensed his formal outline and then added the following notations for the actual delivery of the speech:

Introduction
   Napoleon
     Egyptian priests
       Doctors
         Cultured women
     $1 1/2 billion *(Encyc. Americana '86)*
  Solvents — fixatives — Aromatics
    I. *Solvents*
     A. Water
     B. Ethyl alcohol

PAUSE
(Solvents .... canvas/fixatives ... acrylic)

   II. *Fixatives* — stabilizers
     A. High molecular weight — evaporate slowly
     B. Sources (Edwin Morris, *Fragrance)*
       1. Natural
         a. Civet cat
         b. Castoreum — Russian/Canadian beaver
         c. Musk — deer, western China
         d. Ambergris — sperm whale
       2. Musk & ambergris synthesized
         a. Protects species
         b. Saves money

PAUSE
(Fixatives stabilize aromatics.)

  III. *Aromatics or essential oils* — primary scents
     A. Flowers *(Encyc. Brit.)*
       1. Rose ...
       2. Single scent/blend
     B. Spices, seeds, woods
       1. Rosemary ...
       2. Almond ...
       3. Sandalwood ...
     C. Synthetic aldehydes (Morris, *Fragrance)*
       1. Strong but pleasant
       2. Don't last long
       3. Usually balanced with other aromatics

PAUSE BEFORE CONCLUSION

Conclusion
   Solvents, fixatives, aromatics
   $1.5 billion / year

Someone who knows nothing about the topic of perfumes might not be able to make much sense of John's speaking notes. That's OK. Your speaking notes are not meant to be read and understood by others. As long as your notes make sense to you, you're fine. For example, you are probably puzzled by John's note, "Solvents ... canvas/fixatives ... acrylic." For John, though, those four words triggered the following transitional statement: "If solvents are the canvas the perfumer paints on, fixatives are the acrylic or oil holding the paints together." Similarly, "Fixatives stabilize aromatics" prompted John to say, "Fixatives give perfumes stability, but the ingredients they stabilize, the most distinctive elements of a perfume, are the aromatics." If you practice your introduction, conclusion, and transitions as carefully as John did, you should need only a few words to remind you of what you planned to say in those important sections of your speech.

SUMMARY

Outlining serves five main purposes for a speaker preparing a speech. First, it allows the speaker to check the scope of the topic. Is the topic too broad? Are you trying to cover too much or too little? Second, the outline permits a speaker to test the logical relations between main points and subpoints. Are the points related and yet distinctive enough to qualify as separate ideas? Third, outlining provides a check of the relevance of subpoints. Supporting ideas should all be related to the main idea under which they are listed. Fourth, a speaker can use an outline to gauge the balance of the speech. Does it look as though you will be spending too much time on one of your points and too little on others? Should you eliminate the points that have little support and reorganize those with a great deal of support? Finally, an outline can function as speaking notes, jogging the speaker's memory with key words in correct order.

Outlines can take one of two possible forms: the *complete sentence outline* or the *key word or phrase outline*. In the first of these outlines, each item introduced by a number or letter is a complete sentence. The key word or phrase outline avoids complete sentences. The two forms of outlines should generally not be combined.

Effective outlining is greatly simplified if the speaker keeps in mind these traditional principles or rules. First, each symbol — number or letter — in the outline should represent only one idea. Second, coordination and subordination should be represented by a consistent system of letters and numbers properly indented. Third, any point divided into subpoints must have at least two subpoints. Fourth, complete sentences and key words should be mixed only in the speaking outline. Finally, coordinate points throughout the outline should have simple, parallel grammatical construction.

The first phase of outlining is a *work-*

ing outline, an informal list of different aspects of the selected speech topic. From there, the speaker should develop a complete sentence outline, or *formal outline,* that is clear and thorough enough to communicate the essence of the speech to any reader. Having checked the scope of the topic, and the logical connections, relevance, and balance of the subpoints, the speaker can then select key words and phrases for a *speaking outline.* That outline may also include transitions, quotations, and source citations, as well as personal directions or prompts for the delivery of the speech.

A speaking outline provides a visual test of the organization of a speech. While effective outlining does not guarantee clear organization in the delivered speech, chances are good that any well-organized speech has been carefully outlined at some stage in its development.

*E*XERCISES

1. Select one of the speeches in Appendix C and prepare a key word or phrase outline of the speech. Identify three ways the outline reveals whether the speech was well organized, whether the ideas are balanced, and whether each point directly relates to the specific purpose of the speech.

2. Using the outline you constructed above, reword it as a complete sentence outline. When is it better to develop a key word or phrase outline? When is a complete sentence outline preferred?

3. Listen to a speech in person or on radio, television, or videotape, and outline its main and supporting ideas. Review the outline. Did the speaker try to cover too many points? Are the main points and subpoints relevant, balanced, and logically sequenced? Based on the outline, what suggestions could you give the speaker to improve the speech?

4. Select one of the following topics: superstitions, hiccups, mandatory retirement, or amusement parks. Without doing any research, brainstorm ideas you could include in a speech. Prepare a key word or phrase outline developing coordinate and subordinate ideas.

5. Using the entries below, construct an outline of three major points on the topic of "plastics." The major headings are included in the entries.

clarity	types
silicon plastics	containers
piping	vinyl plastics
uses	amino plastics
strength	resistance
polyurethane plastics	cellulose plastics
toys	properties
kitchenware	auto body parts

Words, as symbols of ideas and ideals, have the power to make people fall in love or out of love, to be faithful or unfaithful to their vows and pledges.... They can produce tears or laughter, success or disaster. They can bring luster or brightness to the face of a child or send him to bed sobbing and sorrowful....

Words can change the face of a city, build churches, schools, playgrounds, boys' clubs, scout groups, civic forums, civic clubs, Little Theatres, Civic Music organizations, garden clubs, and better governments....

The force of words is great, good, glorious, or terrifying.[3]

In this chapter you will learn five functions language serves for us. We will also discuss four principles of language use and offer suggestions for achieving them. The study of language is important because the more you know about language, the greater control you will have as you communicate in public.

It is hard to stretch a small vocabulary to make it do all the things that intelligent people require of words. It's like trying to plan a series of menus from the limited resources of a poverty-stricken war-torn country compared to planning such a series in a prosperous, stable country. Words are one of our chief means of adjusting to all the situations of life. The better control we have over words, the more successful our adjustment is likely to be.[4]

■ FUNCTIONS OF LANGUAGE

Language fulfills at least five functions for those who use it.[5]

	KEY POINTS
1. Language communicates ideas. **2.** Language sends messages about the people using it. **3.** Language strengthens social bonds between groups of people. **4.** Language can be an instrument of play. **5.** Language checks and controls our use of language.	**Functions of Language**

Communicate Ideas

Our language can communicate an infinite number of ideas because it has a structure of separate words. Unlike the sounds most animals make to signal danger, for example, our language allows us to specify the type of threat, the immediacy of the danger, and any number of other characteristics of the situation.[6] However, we must remember that the speaker's language is effective only if it communicates to the listeners. As we mentioned in Chapter 1 in discussing the "triangle of meaning," as long as the speaker and the listener attach similar referents to the words they use, the two can communicate indefinitely.

Like coins, words get their value from the community at large, which must agree on what they represent. The word *dog* may mean a furry creature with four legs and a wagging tail, for instance, but *hippopotamus* or *ziglot* would serve just as well, as long as both speaker and listener agreed on its meaning.[7]

Send Messages About User

Our vocabulary reveals aspects of our educational background, our age, and even what area of the country we call home. Consider the two following statements about Natalie: "Regardless of the occasion, Natalie is noticed by all who attend." "Wherever she goes, Natalie stands out like a blackeyed pea in a plate full of grits." You probably formed contrasting images of the two speakers based solely on the words they used.

In addition, language expresses the feelings or emotions of the speaker. The words we select communicate how we feel about both our listeners and the subject under discussion. Which of these terms suggests the strongest emotion, for example?

     fire   blaze   inferno

Inferno obviously suggests a stronger emotional response from the speaker than either of the other terms. Consider another example:

     crisis   dilemma   problem

In this case, *crisis* suggests a more powerful feeling than do the other terms. Language can carry considerable emotional impact, and the words you select carry messages — sometimes obvious, sometimes subtle — about your background and the nature and strength of your emotions.

Strengthen Social Bonds

Precisely because it communicates ideas and emotions between people, language serves a social function. For example, we often use language to identify ourselves as part of a particular group. Think of the slang expressions you used around friends when you were younger to signal that you were a member of a certain group and in the know. A ten-year-old child comes home from school one day and suddenly begins calling everything "radical." The next week everything is "radical, dude." The following week he bewilders everyone over the age of ten by calling things "dudical." We have had to guess at that spelling because, of course, *dudical* is not yet in any dictionary. Is it a contraction of "radical, dude"? We may never know, because after using it for a week or so the child never repeated the word. The boy's social group apparently dropped the term and moved on to some more interesting expression.

Other forms of language also serve a social function. A group of kindergarten students reciting the alphabet or counting from one to twenty strengthen their group identity and celebrate the group's accomplishment. Adults repeating a pledge, oath, or prayer experience similar group feelings. Or consider the words we use to greet one another. The exchange, "Hi, how are you?" and, "Fine, how are you doing?" may be a hollow, automatic social ritual. Nevertheless, such rituals acknowledge the social bond that exists even between strangers.

On December 7, 1993, between her Nobel lecture and her acceptance speech, Toni Morrison became the first African-American woman and only the eighth American to receive the Nobel Prize for Literature. The Nobel Committee of the Swedish Academy noted, "She delves into the language itself," addressing us with "the luster of poetry."
(SOURCE: AP/Wide World Photos)

Serve as Instrument of Play

Our language not only works, it also entertains. For example, movie history buffs tell the story of the famed gossip columnist of the 1950s, Hedda Hopper. As part of her research on him, Hopper sent Cary Grant the following telegram: "How old Cary Grant?" Grant responded by telegram: "Old Cary Grant fine. How old Hedda Hopper?"

We use language not only for such verbal dueling, but also for the pleasure of its sounds. Many linguists believe we all vocalize as children partly because it just feels and sounds good. Luckily, we do not entirely lose that capacity for play as we mature. The "Ob-la-di, ob-la-da" refrain in the Beatles song of the same name and the forced rhymes in a lot of rap music are but two examples of language used for the sheer fun of its sounds.

Check Language Use

When in doubt, we as speakers will sometimes check with our listeners to see whether they are decoding a message similar to the one we intended: "Do you understand?" "Get it?" As listeners during interpersonal communication, we may even interrupt a speaker to signal our misunderstanding: "Wait a minute. I don't follow you."

These five functions of language should be obvious to you by this point in your public speaking class. The fact that most of your classmates understood the speeches you have given so far testifies to the power of language to carry a speaker's ideas. Yet your listeners have learned more about you than the ideas you communicated. From your language during your speeches and while commenting on others' speeches, they have learned about your likes and dislikes. They may have even made accurate guesses about aspects of your background. During the semester or quarter, the language you used in your speeches and in class discussion has also established and strengthened the social bonds between you and your classmates. Anytime speakers used humor or showed any verbal virtuosity, they invited you to play with language. Whenever you used an interjection such as "Get this" or "This is important," or whenever you questioned a speaker after a speech, you used language to check and measure your understanding.

Language has many registers, from chatty and confidential to simple and direct, complex and technical, lofty and formal. You speak differently to different people, depending upon the environment, the subject under discussion, and your relationship with your listeners. Though public speaking is generally more formal than casual conversation, the precise level of language you use will depend on what you want your speech to accomplish.

Before we briefly discuss language from a speaker's point of view, consider the ways you respond to language as a reader. Do you read a recipe or a textbook the same way that you read a favorite novel or short story? Do you read a plot summary of *King Lear* the same way that you read Shakespeare's play? The answer to both questions is almost surely no. When you read a textbook for a class, you focus on what you get out of it: the main ideas, how they are developed, and how you can use this information. In addition, as a student, you are most likely imagining possible test questions you may be asked about this material. To that extent, you value textbook language that is clear, simple, and direct.

In the case of a favorite novel, however, you pay a great deal more attention to its language. As a result, you read imaginative literature more slowly than you do textbooks, newspapers, or instructions for using a new VCR. You may even reread a passage you particularly like, or read it aloud to someone. As you savor the language of a fictional work, your focus is not so much on what you get out of it, but rather on what you and the author together create from the language of the text.[8]

We not only read and respond to language in these two ways, we also speak in two different ways. At times, we want our language to be "transparent," almost to disappear. In these instances, we focus on getting our meaning across to our listeners quickly and clearly. If you were reporting a fire, a gas leak, or some other emergency to a group of people and advising them to vacate their building, you would try to communicate that information directly, simply, and quickly, without causing panic. You would not waste time mentally editing and practicing the message to make it more clever or more memorable. In giving instructions or issuing a warning, you would never want to use language your audience did not know. Because your goal in these circumstances is getting your message across to a listener, you would use language with clear denotations. **Denotation** is the dictionary definition of a word.

On other occasions, you speak to get a message across, but also to convey it in an especially vivid way. At such times, you pay particular attention to the way you encode

denotation: the literal meaning or dictionary definition of a word or phrase.

the message, choosing words as carefully as you might select a birthday gift for an important friend. When your purpose is to signal your feelings about a subject, to strengthen the social bonds between you and your listeners, or to engage them in verbal play, you will likely use language having strong connotations. **Connotation** is the emotional association that a particular word has for an individual listener. The word *fire* may have pleasant connotations for you if you spent some time around a campfire recently. The same word will have negative connotations for someone whose home was burned down.

Your choice of language depends on the purpose of your speech. Usually, you will use a combination of denotative and connotative language registers. Whether the wording of your speech is straightforward or evocative, direct or highly embroidered, however, you must use language carefully. The following section offers guidelines for using language correctly, clearly, vividly, and appropriately.

connotation: the emotional associations that a word or phrase may evoke in individual listeners.

■ PRINCIPLES OF EFFECTIVE LANGUAGE USE

"Language is the armory of the human mind, and at once contains the trophies of its past and the weapons of its future conquests." **SAMUEL TAYLOR COLERIDGE**

Words are sometimes compared to tools and weapons, and, in a sense, you draw from that arsenal every time you speak. The words you choose help determine your success in informing, persuading, and entertaining your audience. Four principles should guide your use of language and make you a more effective speaker.

KEY POINTS
Principles of Effective Language Use

1. Use language correctly.
2. Use language clearly.
3. Use language vividly.
4. Use language appropriately.

Use Language Correctly

"Socrates was a famous Greek teacher who went around giving people advice. They killed him. Socrates died from an overdose of wedlock. After his death, his career suffered a dramatic decline." From a student paper[9]

"If the people don't want to come out to the park, nobody's going to stop 'em." Yogi Berra

"And you don't need to draw me any diaphragms neither!" Archie Bunker[10]

"Sisters Reunited after 18 Years in Checkout Line at Supermarket" Newspaper headline[11]

Whether it be a Yogiism, an Archieism, or some other kind of "ism," language abuse is all around us. We see our language assaulted in letters, term papers, newspapers, and magazines. We hear it abused on radio, on television, and in conversations with our friends.

As a speaker, your first requirement is to use language correctly, and you achieve this goal in two ways. First, select the right word for the thought you wish to convey. Socrates died of an overdose of *hemlock*, not *wedlock*. The correct word for Archie's referent is *diagram*, not *diaphragm*. After you select the correct words, phrase them correctly. We doubt that the sisters mentioned earlier had to wait in the supermarket checkout line for eighteen years, even if there were lots of double coupon days!

When you use language incorrectly in your speech, you run the risk of sending unintended messages, as well as of undermining your credibility and the causes you support. Poorly worded ideas are sometimes evaluated as poor ideas, although this may not be the case. For example, in a speech on how to dress and groom for an interview, a student of ours recently advised, "Men should not wear long hair to a business interview. Long hair has a real astigmatism attached to it." The speaker's advice may be sound, but he has worded it incorrectly; the student meant that long hair has a *stigma* attached to it. Another student, concerned about the increase of sexually transmitted diseases, encouraged her students to commit to "long-term monotonous relationships." She should have used the word *monogamous*.

If you hear examples of incorrect language in your class, they will likely be more subtle than the examples given above. Nevertheless, it is important for speakers to rid their speeches of all unnecessary intrusions. Speakers perceived to care about how they state their ideas are also perceived to care about what they say.

The following examples illustrate some common language errors we have heard in student speeches:

1. The first criteria for selecting a good wine is to experience its bouquet. (The speaker should use the singular noun *criterion*.)

2. If our school is to remain financially solvent, we must choose between three options: (1) increasing tuition, (2) laying off faculty and staff employees, or (3) forgoing the planned construction of a new athletic complex. *(Among is the correct word when more than two options are included.)*

3. Because she failed to wear her seat belt, she was hurt bad: a broken leg, fractured ribs, and a mild concussion. (She was hurt *badly*.)

4. Because they conduct most of their missions at night, a drug trafficker often alludes our understaffed border patrol. *(They is plural, so the speaker should use drug traffickers. Also, the correct word is elude, not allude.)*

5. He don't realize that his poor credit history as a college student will continue to follow him after graduation. (The verb should be the singular *doesn't*.)

6. Members of our legislature voted theirselves a pay raise at the same time they voted down an increase in the state's education budget. *(Theirselves is not a word. The correct word is themselves.)*

Some of these transgressions may seem less severe to you than others. Remember, though, that your language is an important part of the delivery of your speech. Your language, like your physical and vocal delivery, should be free of all distractions. Errors in subject/verb agreement, misplaced modifiers, and incorrect word choice immediately attract the attention of everyone who recognizes these errors. You won't upset anyone if your language is grammatically correct, but even small errors run the risk of monopolizing some people's attention. In turn, they stop listening carefully to *what* you say because they are paying attention to *how* you speak.

You can speak correctly if you follow a few simple guidelines. First, make a note of grammatical mistakes you hear yourself and other people make in casual conversation. Attentive listening is a first step to improving your use of language. Second, when you are unsure of a word's meaning, consult a dictionary. Third, if you have a question about proper grammar, refer to a handbook for writers. Fourth, when practicing your speech, record it and play it back, listening for mistakes you may not have noticed as you were practicing. Fifth, practice your speech in front of friends and ask them to point out mistakes. These strategies will help you detect and correct errors. Not only will your speaking improve, but you may also save yourself some embarrassment. As Mark Twain noted, "The difference between the right word and the almost right word is the difference between lightning and the lightning bug."

Use Language Clearly

How would you respond if a friend said to you, "Let's work on our project for a while after dinner. Could you bring a quire with you?" You would probably ask several questions because your friend failed to communicate clearly. What specifically is "our project"? How long is "for a while"? What time is "after dinner"? Where will this meeting take place? Your friend would have communicated the first part of the message more clearly if she had said, "Let's meet in my room from 6:00 to 7:00 this evening to work on our group report for Psychology 100." You might also ask, "Did you say something about a choir?" After being corrected, you would probably ask, "OK, what's a *q-u-i-r-e?*" Though it is specific, the word *quire* is not common and may be confusing unless you know that it means twenty-four sheets of paper.

Language use must not only be correct, it must also be clear. In order to achieve clarity, a speaker should use language that is specific and familiar. If you sacrifice either criterion, your language may confuse your listeners.

Use Specific Language.   In Chapter 1, we mentioned that many of our communication problems spring from the fact that there are always two messages involved whenever two people are communicating. There is, first, the message that the speaker intends. In addition, there is the message that the listener infers or interprets. If you tell your instructor that you missed an assignment deadline because you were "having some problems," you leave yourself open to a wide range of possible interpretations. Do you have health problems, family troubles, or stress from a personal relationship? You could be having trouble juggling a work schedule with your study time, or having car problems. You could be grieving over the loss of a loved one, or struggling with one particularly difficult course. These and other interpretations are possible because *problem* is an abstract term.

To clarify your ideas, use the lowest level of abstraction possible. Words are not *either* abstract or concrete, but take on these qualities in relation to other words. Look at the following lists of terms, for example.

theatre

Western theatre

twentieth-century Western theatre

documentary theatre

plays of Michael Hastings

The Silence of Lee Harvey Oswald

class
college class
college communication class
Speech 210: Fundamentals of Public Communication
Speech 210 at Ball State University
Speech 210 with Prof. Buckrop at Ball State University

The terms at the top of these lists are more abstract than those at the bottom. As we add those limiting, descriptive words, or *qualifiers*, the referent becomes increasingly specific. The lower the level of abstraction used, the more clearly the listener will understand the speaker.

Suppose you were giving a speech on how citizens can protect their homes from burglaries, and you made the following statement:

> Crime is rampant in our city. Burglary alone has gone way up in the past year or so. So you can see that having the right kind of lock on your door is essential to your safety.

What is wrong with this statement? The language is vague. What does "rampant" mean? How much of an increase is "way up" — 15 percent, 50 percent, 400 percent? Is "the past year or so" one year, two years, or more? What is "the right kind of lock"? As a speaker you should help your audience by making these ideas more concrete. After some research, you might rephrase your argument like this:

> Last week I spoke with Captain James Winton, head of our City Police Department's Records Division. He told me that crime in our city has increased by 54 percent in the last year, and the number of burglaries has doubled. We can help deter crime by making our homes burglar-proof, and one way of doing this is to make sure that all doors have solid locks. I brought one such lock with me: It's a double-keyed deadbolt lock.

Notice the improvement in the second paragraph. Your message is clearer, and with that clarity you would gain added credibility as a speaker.

Use Familiar Language.

"The chief virtue that language can have is clearness, and nothing detracts from it so much as the use of unfamiliar words."

HIPPOCRATES

Anyone who has purchased a video cassette recorder has suffered through the complicated instructions that usually accompanied these machines. According to Karen Schriver, English professor at Carnegie Mellon University, those awkward, unclear instructions are usually written by entry-level engineers who are much more concerned with the capabilities of the equipment's features than is the poor consumer who will be using the VCR. Mitsubishi Electronics America recently recruited Schriver to help rewrite their VCR user manuals. A sample of her changes follows:

> *Before:* "This VCR employs direct function switching where any playback mode may be directly entered from any other playback mode (normal playback, still

frame, speed search, etc.) simply by pressing the appropriate buttons."
After: "When you use a feature (like Play or Rewind), you can go directly to another feature (like Speed Search) without first pressing Stop."[12]

Both sentences are specific, but the second communicates the message in a language style more familiar to nonengineers.

Your language may be specific but still not be clear. If listeners are not familiar with your words, communication is impaired. The statement "The Sultan of Swat was famous for his batboy shots" is specific but probably unclear to most listeners. Some may know that the Sultan of Swat is a nickname for baseball great Babe Ruth. Probably only the most avid baseball enthusiast, however, knows that the term *batboy shot* refers to a home run hit so powerfully that the batter knows instantly that it is out of the park and has time to hand the bat to the batboy (no batgirls in Babe Ruth's time) before rounding the bases.

Occasionally we hear speeches in which students try to impress us with their vocabularies. We suspect they drafted their remarks with a pen in one hand and a thesaurus in the other. Phrases such as "a plethora of regulations," "this obviates the need for," "the apotheosis of deceit," and "the anathema of censorship" detract from rather than enhance the speaker's message. "We must ever be mindful to eschew verbosity and deprecate tautology" is good advice and fun to say. But if you are trying to communicate with another person, it's probably better simply to say, "Avoid wordiness."

The use of jargon can also undermine clarity. **Jargon** is the special language of a particular activity, business, or group of people. Computer experts, for example, talk about "RAM" and "ROM," bytes and bits, shells and crashes — abbreviations and words having specialized meanings when applied to computers. Real estate agents will say that a particular house has a good "drive up," meaning that it makes a good first impression. Stockbrokers and their clients discuss "bear markets," "selling short," and "buying on the margin." Say you tell your audience that Orlando, Florida, will have the first high-speed train using maglev technology in the U.S. You will probably also need to tell your listeners that *maglev* is short for "magnetic levitation," and then explain what that means.

jargon: the special language used by people in a particular activity, business, or group.

If you are certain that the people you are addressing know such terms, jargon presents no problem. In fact, it is usually quite specific and can save a lot of time. Jargon can even increase your credibility by indicating that you are familiar with the subject matter. If you have any doubts about whether your listeners know the jargon, however, either avoid such terms or define each one the first time you use it.

Use Language Vividly

In addition to selecting language that is correct and clear, speakers should choose language that is colorful and picturesque. Vivid language engages the audience and makes the task of listening easier. Read the following critiques of the speeches of our twenty-ninth president, Warren Harding:

1. Warren Harding was not an effective public speaker. His speeches often were confusing and uninspired. He did not make his points well.

2. "His speeches left the impression of an army of pompous phrases moving over the landscape in search of an idea; sometimes these meandering words would actually capture a straggling thought and bear it triumphantly a prisoner in their midst, until it died of servitude and overwork." William G. McAdoo, Democratic party leader[13]

3. "He writes the worst English that I have ever encountered. It reminds me of a string of wet sponges; it reminds me of tattered washing on the line; it reminds me of stale bean soup, of college yells, of dogs barking idiotically through endless nights. It is so bad that a sort of grandeur creeps into it. It drags itself out of the dark abysm (I was about to write abscess!) of pish and crawls insanely up to the topmost pinnacle of posh. It is rumble and bumble. It is flap and doodle. It is balder and dash." H.L. Mencken[14]

Which of these three statements did you most enjoy reading? Which characterization of Harding's speaking did you find the most colorful? Which paragraph contains the most vivid images? Which would you most like to read again? While we don't know your answers to these questions, we're fairly certain that you did *not* select the first statement. Why?

The language of the first critique communicates an idea as simply and economically as possible without calling attention to itself. To use a term we introduced earlier in this chapter, its language is transparent. It is also drab and colorless, and displays little creativity. The language style of the first example is not nearly as lively and its images are not as vivid as the other two. The language of the second and third statements is opaque; it calls attention to its sounds, textures, and rhythms. Vivid language helps listeners remember both your message and you.

cliché: a once-colorful figure of speech that has lost impact from overuse.

One of the fiercest enemies of vivid language is the **cliché,** a once-colorful expression that has lost most of its impact through overuse. Many clichés involve comparisons. For example, complete the following phrases:

Cute as a _____ .
Dead as a_____ .
Between a rock and a _____.
Burning the midnight _____.
Colder than a _____.

Did you have any trouble completing the expressions above? Probably not. In fact, button, doornail, hard place, oil, and mackerel most likely popped into your mind without much thought. Each of these sayings is a cliché, an overworked expression that doesn't require (or stimulate) much thinking. Clichés are bland, and hackneyed. Avoid them!

Perhaps the speech genre most susceptible to clichés is the commencement speech. Robert Leestamper remembers receiving this advice as he prepared his commencement address for Richmond College of London: "Commencement speeches are easy. Just do what any good advertising man does. Take several clichés, quotes and brief passages that worked in the past, rearrange them and offer them to the public as a wonderful new creation." Borrowing from Churchill, Jefferson, Kennedy, Kipling, Lincoln, Shakespeare, and others, Leestamper created this parody:

> Members of the graduating class, lend me your ears: These are the times that try men's souls, but tell me not in mournful words that life is but an empty dream, for when in the course of human events it becomes necessary to strive, to seek, to find, and not to yield, then we must summon up remembrance of things past, recalling that our forefathers brought forth new nations, and asked not what they

could do for them, but said instead "we have nothing to fear, but fear itself." In this our time, ask not for whom the bell tolls, for ours is not to reason why, ours is but to hang together or we will all hang separately! I want to make one thing perfectly clear: The world will little note nor long remember what I say here, but generations yet unborn will hold this truth to be self-evident: To thine own self be true, for no man is an island. Fear not the slings and arrows of outrageous fortune, but keep your head when all about you are losing theirs and blaming it on you — and then, like a bridge over troubled waters, from sea to shining sea, a brighter day will dawn and bring your finest hour, and never before will so many have owed so much to so few.[15]

How do you suppose an audience would react if he had really delivered this speech?

Now that you have seen some of the effects of dull wording, what techniques can you use to make your language more vivid? The answer to this question may be limited only by your imagination. We offer three strategies for your consideration: (1) use active language, (2) appeal to your listeners' senses, and (3) use figures and structures of speech. Following these suggestions will give you a good start on making your speeches more colorful and, thus, more memorable.

Use Active Language.   Which of the following statements is more forceful?

> It was decided by the Student Government Association that the election would be delayed for one week.

> The Student Government Association decided to delay the election for one week.

The second one, right? The first sentence uses passive voice; the second active. Active voice is always more direct because it identifies the agent producing the action and places it first in the sentence. In addition, active voice is more economical than passive voice; the second sentence is shorter than the first by five words.

Active language, however, involves more than active voice. Active language is language that works. It has energy, vitality, and drive. It is not bogged down by filler phrases such as "you know," "like," and "stuff like that." Rather than being cliché-ridden, it may convert the commonplace into the unexpected. Notice how two student speakers used familiar phrases in unexpected ways as they concluded their speeches.

> Cherie spoke of injuries, even deaths, children suffer from playing baseball. After detailing some ways the game could be made safer, she concluded, "[C]hildren may be dying to play baseball, but they should never die because of it."[16]

Reprinted by permission of UFS, Inc.

Joni claimed there was gender bias in medical research and called for greater attention to women's health issues. She gave an interesting twist to a familiar saying in her final statement: "The old cliché no longer holds true. What's good for the gander is no longer good for the goose."[17]

Coining a word or phrase is another way of making your language work for you. When the Chicago Bulls won their third consecutive NBA championship in 1993, merchandisers began to cash in on all the "three-peat" caps and T-shirts they had ready. The word's novelty makes it much more memorable than *repeat*. Basketball coach Pat Riley had shrewdly trademarked the term during the 1988-89 season when his Los Angeles Lakers tried unsuccessfully for their third consecutive championship.[18] A well-turned phrase also actively engages the minds of your listeners as they hear the interplay of words and ideas. Indian nationalist leader Mohandas Gandhi, for example, urged his listeners to "live simply so others might simply live."

Appeal to Your Listeners' Senses. Another way you can achieve impact with language is by appealing to your listeners' senses. The obvious and familiar senses are sight, hearing, touch, taste, and smell. To these we can add the sense of motion or movement and the sense of muscular tension. Colorful language can create vivid images that appeal

Describing a ride on Coney Island's Cyclone calls for language that creates vivid sensory impressions in listeners.
(Source: AP/Wide World Photos)

to each of these various senses. Those sharp images in turn heighten audience involvement in the speech, inviting listeners to participate with their feelings and thereby increasing their retention of what you have said.

Assume that you are a roller coaster enthusiast and have decided to deliver an informative speech on roller coasters. Such a topic certainly begs for language to create or recreate the various sensations of a coaster ride for your audience. But what if you are not confident about your ability to appeal to your audience's various senses in your speech? You can always do some research on this topic and use the words of others, as long as you accurately attribute your quotations. We easily found four recent magazine articles on roller coasters. Let's look at examples from two particularly vivid articles written to tap all the senses of a reader. Notice how the examples vivify the topic by using the eight sensory images we list below.

A **visual image** recreates the sight of a person, place, or thing. Speakers can use visual images to set the scene for future action or further explanation. The following passage recreates the sight of walking up to and boarding the famous roller coaster at Coney Island:

> The Cyclone differs from other roller coasters in being (a) a work of art and (b) old, and not only old but old-looking, decrepit, rusting in its metal parts and peeling in its more numerous wooden parts, filthy throughout and jammed into a wire (Cyclone!) fence abutting cracked sidewalks of the Third World sinkhole that Coney Island is, intoxicatingly.[19]

Visual images can even be used to speculate what an imagined person, place, or thing might look like.

An **auditory image** suggests the sound of something by appealing to our sense of hearing. You may be familiar with the term *onomatopoeia* for a word that evokes specific sounds, as in *buzz, crack,* or *snarl.* Notice the use of that device in this description of the first part of the ride:

> Yes, it may be anguishing initially … Terrifying, even, the first time or two the train is hauled upward with groans and creaks and with you in it. At the top then — where there is sudden strange quiet but for the fluttering of two tattered flags....[20]

A **tactile image** recreates the feel of something. Tactile images spark the audience's memories of textures, shapes, and temperatures, as in this example:

> I should mention that a heavy, cushioned restraining bar locks down snugly into your lap and is very reassuring, although, like everything upholstered in the cars, it may be cracked or slashed and leaking tufts of stuffing from under swatches of gray gaffer's tape. One thing consistently disquieting is how, under stress, a car's wooden sides may *give* a bit.[21]

A special type of tactile image, called a **thermal image** creates impressions of heat or cold or any temperature in between those extremes. Notice the vivid thermal image toward the end of this description:

> One time the vibration, with the wheels shrieking and the cars threatening to explode with strain, made me think, "This is *no fun at all!*" It was an awful

---

Margin notes:

visual image: language that causes listeners to remember or imagine the way a thing looks.

auditory image: language that causes listeners to remember or imagine the way a thing sounds.

tactile image: language that causes listeners to remember or imagine the way a thing feels.

thermal image: language that causes listeners to remember or imagine the temperature of a thing.

moment, with a sickening sense of betrayal and icy-fingered doubt: Was my love malign?[22]

gustatory image: language that causes listeners to remember or imagine the way something tastes.

A **gustatory image** vividly reminds the audience of how something tastes, for example:

> Nothing matches the faint metallic taste of fear you experience as the clanking stops and you feel the train set free to begin falling from the top of that first hill.

kinetic image: language that causes listeners to remember or imagine a sensation of motion.

A **kinetic image** creates feelings of motion or movement, as in this example from the middle of the ride:

> This time the drop was a mere 18 degrees, but stretched out over a long, curving length of track, to make the torture of acceleration more exquisite. At nearly 65 mph, the train shot into a tunnel and spun 540 degrees around a banked helix, slowed down only by the screaming of one rider, who felt like a bug being sucked down a bathtub drain.[23]

kinesthetic image: language that causes listeners to remember or imagine states of muscular tension or relaxation.

A **kinesthetic image** appeals to the audience's sense of muscular tension or relaxation:

> A sharp, wincing intake of breath (expletive deleted) and the feeling of innards popping up like a parachute in my rib cage. My hair flew back, and my eyes peeled wide and filled with tears, a product of the 60-mph wind and also of self-pity. My teeth clenched and my knuckles locked bone-white around the lap bar.[24]

olfactory image: language that causes listeners to remember or imagine the way something smells.

An **olfactory image** appeals to our sense of smell by recreating pleasant or unpleasant aromas. Fragrances have a strong capacity to evoke our memories of people, places, and objects. Even an unpleasant smell may have pleasant associations, as at the end of a coaster ride:

> The payoff is intimacy in the sweet diminuendo, the jiggling and chuckling smart little bumps and dandling dips that bring us to a quick, pillowy deceleration in the shed, smelling of dirty machine oil, where we began and will begin again.[25]

synesthesia: the combination of sensory appeals in a single image.

Synesthesia is the combination of sensory appeals in a single image. If you speak of a "stoney silence," that phrase evokes auditory, tactile, and possibly thermal sensations. Notice how the following two sentences combine vivid kinetic, kinesthetic, and even auditory images:

> [Riding a coaster is] like driving your car with your head out the window at 70 miles per hour. But to get the full effect, you have to drive it off a cliff.[26]

Notice how many of these examples of sensory impressions are not only evocative but also funny and fun to say. Active language and appeals to the senses are not your only techniques for enlivening your speech language, however. Public speaking gives you an opportunity to devise some of the figures of speech and special language structures you may have studied before in English classes.

Use Figures and Structures of Speech. Important ideas are easier to remember if they are memorably worded, so don't be afraid of sounding flowery. You can use many figures and structures of speech to enliven your language. Some of the most common are alliteration, parallelism, repetition, antithesis, personification, simile, and metaphor.

Alliteration is the repetition of beginning sounds in adjacent or nearby words. A speaker who asks us "to dream, to dare, and to do" uses alliteration. The sounds of words give your speech impact. A student speaking on the topic of child abuse described the victims as "badly bruised and beaten." Not only did these words themselves convey a severe problem, but the repetition of the stern, forceful *b* sound vocally accentuated the violence of the act.

alliteration: the repetition of beginning sounds in words that are adjacent or near one another.

In his "I Have a Dream" speech (see Appendix C), Martin Luther King, Jr., used alliteration to describe his dream of a nation where people "will not be judged by the color of their skin but by the content of their character." Elie Wiesel used alliteration in his speech (also in Appendix C) when he spoke of "faith in the future," "complacency if not complicity," and "hunger and humiliation."

Speaking on the subject of educational reform, Vincent Ryan Ruggiero, professor of humanities at State University of New York at Delhi, complained of "mindstuffing," a current practice in education "which renders students passive and transforms the 3 Rs into Receiving, Recalling, and Regurgitating information."[27]

Speakers use **parallelism** when they express two or more ideas in similar language structure. When they restate words, phrases, or sentences, they use **repetition.** Parallelism and repetition work in concert to emphasize an idea or a call for action. President Ronald Reagan's moving tribute to the shuttle crew killed in the *Challenger* disaster effectively connected ideas by using parallelism. Near the beginning of the speech, Reagan used repetition to introduce the goal of his speech: "The best we can do is remember our seven astronauts, our *Challenger* seven, remember them as they lived...." Reagan then combined repetition and parallel structure as he issued a final roll call of the ill-fated crew:

parallelism: the expression of ideas using similar grammatical structures.
repetition: restating words, phrases, or sentences for emphasis.

> We remember Dick Scobee, the commander who spoke the last words we heard from the space shuttle *Challenger.* He served as a fighter pilot in Vietnam earning many medals for bravery and later as a test pilot of advanced aircraft before joining the space program. Danger was a familiar companion to Commander Scobee.
> We remember Michael Smith, who earned enough medals as a combat pilot to cover his chest, including the Navy Distinguished Flying Cross, three Air Medals, and the Vietnamese Cross of Gallantry with Silver Star in gratitude from a nation he fought to keep free.
> We remember Judith Resnick, known as J.R. to her friends, always smiling, always eager to make a contribution, finding beauty in the music she played on her piano in her off-hours.

The list continued, "We remember Ellison Onizuka," "We remember Ronald McNair," "We remember Gregory Jarvis," "We remember Christa McAuliffe," each repetition of "we remember" like the forlorn tolling of a bell.[28]

Another excellent example of the use of parallel construction is Martin Luther King, Jr.'s, "I Have a Dream" speech. King repeats the phrase "one hundred years later" to dramatize the "shameful condition" of inequality. He prefaces his hopes for the future with the phrase "I have a dream." And near the end of his speech he uses parallelism and repetition to create a dramatic climax:

> So *let freedom ring* from the prodigious hilltops of New Hampshire. *Let freedom ring* from the mighty mountains of New York. *Let freedom ring* from the heighten-

ing Alleghenies of Pennsylvania! *Let freedom ring* from the snowcapped Rockies of Colorado!

But not only that. *Let freedom ring* from Stone Mountain of Georgia! *Let freedom ring* from Lookout Mountain of Tennessee! *Let freedom ring* from every hill and molehill of Mississippi. From every mountainside, *let freedom ring*.

And when this happens … we will be able to join hands and sing, in the words of the old Negro spiritual, *"Free at last! Free at last!* Thank God almighty, we are *free at last!"*

antithesis: the use of parallel construction to contrast ideas.

Antithesis uses parallel construction to contrast ideas. You can probably quote from memory John Kennedy's statement: "Ask not what your country can do for you, ask what you can do for your country." The fact that it is so memorable attests to its power. Mario Cuomo used antithesis in his keynote address to the 1984 Democratic National Convention:

We must get the American public to look past the glitter, beyond the showmanship — to reality, to the hard substance of things. And we will do that not so much with speeches that sound good as with speeches that are good and sound. Not so much with speeches that bring people to their feet as with speeches that bring people to their senses.[29]

personification: a figure of speech that attributes human qualities to a concept or inanimate object.

Personification gives human qualities to objects, ideas, or organizations. One speech teacher used personification as the organizing concept of her speech titled "The Anatomy of an Association." In her address, she argued that an association's muscle is its unity, its brains are the knowledge it generates, its lifeblood is its ability to renew its membership, and its heart is its people.[30]

Virginia Postrel, editor of *Reason* magazine, began her speech on the environmental movement using personification this way:

On Earth Day, Henry Allen of the *Washington Post* published a pointed and amusing article. In it he suggested that we've created a new image of Mother Nature:

"A sort of combination of Joan Crawford in *Mildred Pierce* and Mrs. Portnoy in *Portnoy's Complaint,* a disappointed, long-suffering martyr who makes us wish, at least for her sake, that we'd never been born.

"She weeps. She threatens. She nags.…

"She's a kvetch who makes us feel guilty for eating Big Macs, dumping paint thinner down the cellar sink, driving to work instead of riding the bus, and riding the bus instead of riding a bicycle. Then she makes us feel even guiltier for not feeling guilty enough.

"'Go ahead, use that deodorant, don't even think about me, God knows I'll be gone soon enough, I won't be here to see you get skin cancer when the ozone hole lets in the ultraviolet rays.…'"[31]

simile: a comparison of two things using the words *as* or *like*.

metaphor: an implied comparison of two things without the use of *as* or *like*.

Simile and **metaphor** are comparisons of two seemingly dissimilar things. In simile, the comparison is explicitly stated, using words such as *like* and *as;* for example: "Trying to pin the Senator down on the issue is like trying to nail a poached egg to a tree."

In metaphor, the comparison is not explicitly stated but is implied. *Like* and *as* are omitted. Sportscasters who called quarterback Joe Montana's passes "heat seeking missiles" were using metaphor. Peter Schjeldahl, author of the article on Coney Island's Cyclone, uses metaphor when he compares that roller coaster to a poem:

The coaster is basically an ornate means of falling and a poem about physics in parts or stanzas, with jokes. The special quality of the Cyclone is how different, how *articulated,* all the components of its poem are, the whole of which lasts a minute and thirty-some seconds — exactly the right length, composed of distinct and perfect moments. By my fifth ride, my heart was leaping at the onset of each segment as at the approach of a dear old friend, and melting with instantaneous nostalgia for each at its finish.[32]

Notice that near the end of the description, Schjeldahl introduces personification, and the roller coaster begins to take on human characteristics.

Extraordinary circumstances sometimes require extraordinary responses. One such event was triggered by the death of President John F. Kennedy. Kennedy's successor, Lyndon Johnson, chose to respond to the nation's sorrow and uncertainty in a televised address to Congress and the American people. His purposes were four: (1) to honor the memory of the assassinated president, (2) to assure the citizenry that their government continued to function, (3) to unite the American people, and (4) to point the nation to the challenges ahead. Notice in the following excerpt how Johnson used several of the techniques mentioned above to help him accomplish his objectives:

We meet in grief, but let us also meet in renewed dedication and renewed vigor. Let us meet in action, in tolerance, and in mutual understanding. John Kennedy's death commands what his life conveyed — that America must move forward. The time has come for Americans of all races and creeds and political beliefs to understand and to respect one another. So let us put an end to the teaching and the preaching of hate and evil and violence. Let us turn away from the fanatics of the far left and the far right, from the apostles of bitterness and bigotry, from the defiant of law, and those who pour venom into our Nation's bloodstream.[33]

Alliteration, parallelism, repetition, antithesis, personification, simile, and metaphor enable speakers to create vivid language and images. One note of caution, however: always remember that your objective as a speaker is not to impress your listeners with your ability to create vivid language. Vivid language is not an end in itself but rather a means of achieving the larger objectives of the speech. As language expert William Safire notes, "A good speech is not a collection of crisp one-liners, workable metaphors, and effective rhetorical devices; a good speech truly reflects the thoughts and emotions of the speaker...."[34]

Use Language Appropriately

As we have discussed through out this book, appropriateness has several dimensions. Your language should be appropriate to you, your topic, your audience, and the occasion. Sometimes it may seem impossible to achieve all four of these goals. We have heard speakers criticized for poor grammar or incorrect pronunciation respond, "But that's the way I talk." They apparently believe it's more important for language to reflect their speaking style than for it to be correct. Some listeners may neither detect nor be offended by your incorrect language use, but others will. They are the ones who should concern you. The safest rule for you to follow is this: Correct language never offends and incorrect language is never appropriate.

If your language is correct, clear, and vivid, you have a good start on achieving appropriateness. However, spoken language that is in good form should possess two other characteristics: oral style and nonsexist language.

Use Oral Style.   In order to speak appropriately, you must recognize that your oral style differs from your written style. Unless your instructor asks you to deliver some speeches from a manuscript, we believe that you will be better off if you think of "developing" speeches rather than "writing" them. We can give you two good reasons for avoiding writing your speeches. First, you will likely try to memorize what you have written, and the fear of forgetting part of the speech will add to your nervousness and make your delivery seem stiff and wooden.

tone: the relation established by language and grammar between speakers and their listeners.

The second and more important reason for not writing out a speech is that the act of writing itself often affects the tone of the communication. **Tone** is the relationship established by language and grammar between a writer or speaker and that person's readers or listeners. Many of us think of writing as something formal and correct. In fact, many of us are intimidated by writing specifically because we think it must be formal and correct. For that reason, we tend not to write the way that we speak.

Our oral style differs from our written style in at least four important ways. First, in speaking we tend to use shorter sentences than we write. Speakers who write out their speeches often find themselves gasping for air when they try to deliver a long sentence in one breath.

Second, when we communicate orally, we tend to use more contractions, colloquial expressions, and slang. Our speaking vocabulary is smaller than our writing vocabulary, so we tend to speak a simpler language than we write. Speakers who write out their speeches often draw from their larger written vocabularies. As a result, their presentational style seems formal and often creates a barrier between them and their listeners.

Third, oral style makes greater use of personal pronouns and references than written style does. Speakers must acknowledge the presence of their listeners, and one way of doing this is by including them in the speech. Saying "We must rid our speech of sexist language" is more powerful than saying "People must rid their speech of sexist language." Using the pronouns *I, we,* and *you* makes your speech more immediate and enhances your rapport with your listeners. You may even want to mention specific audience members by name: "Last week John told us how to construct a power résumé. I'm going to tell you what to do once your résumé gets you a job interview. In preparing for an employment interview, there are three steps you should keep in mind." Notice how the name of the student, coupled with several personal pronouns, brings the speaker and audience together and sets up the possibility for lively interaction.

A fourth difference between oral and written style is the frequency of repetition. Oral style uses more repetition. As we discussed in Chapter 4, "Listening," readers can slow down and reread the material in front of them. They control the pace. Listeners do not have that luxury. Speakers must take special care to reinforce their messages, and one way of accomplishing this is by using repetition.

sexist language: language that excludes one gender, creates special categories for one gender, or assigns roles based solely on gender.

nonsexist language: language that treats both genders fairly and avoids stereotyping either one.

Use Nonsexist Language.   Language is sexist if it "promotes and maintains attitudes that stereotype people according to gender. It [**sexist language**] assumes that the male is the norm — the significant gender. **Nonsexist language** treats all people equally and either does not refer to a person's sex at all when it is irrelevant or refers to men and women in symmetrical ways when their gender is relevant."[35]

Notice the gender identification in each of the following two statements:

> One of the most important qualities a company executive must possess is effective communication. In fact, the higher he advances in the company, the more important it is that he be able to speak clearly and convincingly.

> A secretary is no longer only a receptionist and a typist. Today she performs the role of information manager for the office.

Both of these examples are sexist because they imply that executives are male and secretaries female. Nonsexist language allows for the fact that either gender can assume the roles of executive or secretary.

You can eliminate sexist language in these statements if you replace each "he" and "she" with "he or she." This remedy, however, can be wordy and intrusive at times, especially when a sentence includes several third-person singular pronouns. You can solve this problem by using the plural form if it is appropriate. Note how the statements change when they are reworded with this approach:

> One of the most important qualities company presidents must possess is effective communication. In fact, the higher they advance in their companies, the more important it is that they be able to speak clearly and convincingly.

> Secretaries are no longer only receptionists and typists. Today they perform the role of information manager for the office.

A more serious form of sexism occurs when language creates special categories for one gender, with no corresponding parallel category for the other gender. *Man* and *wife,* for example, are not parallel terms. *Man* and *woman* or *husband* and *wife* are parallel. Other examples of nonparallel language are *nurse* and *male nurse, chairman* and *chairperson,* and *Wildcats* and *Lady Wildcats.* We remember hearing about one high school whose mascot was the hen. Its football and boys' basketball teams were the Hens. Yet the school called its girls' basketball team the Lady Hens, a redundancy at best and sexist at worst! One university named its official host student group the Statesmen and First Ladies, changing the name only after several individuals complained that it assigned men and women to inherently unequal positions. A colleague tells us that when she worked at a television station, she was called a weather girl, even though a male employee of the same age was referred to as a weather man.

Speakers exhibit fairness when they express their ideas and examples in language that treats all members of the audience equally and fairly. If you have difficulty selecting a gender-free term for one that may be considered sexist, consult a dictionary such as *The Bias-Free Word Finder: A Dictionary of Nondiscriminatory Language,* by Rosalie Maggio.

No matter which of the world's roughly 5,000 languages you speak, the words you choose telegraph messages about your background, your involvement with your topic, and your relationship with your listeners.[36] Like the unique voice and body you use to deliver your speeches, your language is an extremely important part of your delivery. If you are conscientious, you must know when to speak simply and directly, and when to embellish your language with sensory images, figures of speech, and unusual structural devices. In short, you don't have to be a poet to agree with poet Robert Frost, "All the fun's in how you say a thing."[37]

SUMMARY

Language is a distinctly human instrument, no less important than any other tool we have developed for building and creating. Although other animals produce sounds and noises, the human language alone is articulated into words, and alone is capable of expressing an infinite variety of thoughts.

Language serves five functions. First, it communicates ideas between speaker and listener. Second, language sends messages, either intentional or unintentional, about the person who uses it. Your choice of language may reveal your age, your background, and your attitudes about the subjects you discuss. Third, language establishes and strengthens social bonds between groups of people. Fourth, language is an instrument of play since it is the arena for joking and battles of wits. Fifth, we use language to monitor and check our use of language.

As a speaker you use different language on different occasions, depending on the environment, the topic, and your relationship with your listeners. Four principles should guide your use of language: (1) Use language correctly, (2) use language clearly, (3) use language vividly, and (4) use language appropriately.

As a speaker, your first obligation is to use language *correctly*. Select the right word for the thought you wish to convey, and then phrase the thought correctly. Incorrect language may communicate unintended messages as well as undermine a speaker's credibility. Five guidelines will help you detect and correct language errors. First, listen to the language you and others use and focus on how it can be improved. Second, consult a dictionary when you are unsure of the meaning of a word. Third, refer to a writing handbook when you have a question about proper grammar. Fourth, use a tape recorder to help you detect incorrect language use. Fifth, practice your speech in front of friends and ask them to point out your mistakes.

A second principle of language use is to use language *clearly*. You achieve clarity when you use specific and familiar language. The more concrete your language, the more closely your referents will match those of your listeners. In addition to being specific, language must also be familiar. Listeners must know the meanings of the words you use. One type of language that may undermine clarity is *jargon*, a special language of a particular activity, business, or group of people. If you doubt that your listeners know the jargon, either avoid such terms or else define each one the first time you use it.

A third guideline is to use language *vividly*. Colorful language makes the task of listening easier and the message more memorable. Three strategies for making your language more vivid are to use active language, appeal to your listeners' senses, and use figures and structures of speech. Active language avoids *clichés* and filler phrases, using instead active voice, coined words, and well-turned phrases.

A speaker can use any of eight types of sensory images to appeal to listeners' senses. *Visual images* appeal to the sense of sight. *Auditory images* suggest sounds. *Tactile images* recreate the feel of an object. *Thermal images* suggest temperatures. *Gustatory images* appeal to the sense of taste. *Kinetic images* suggest movement or motion. *Kinesthetic images* recreate states of muscular tension or relaxation. *Olfactory images* appeal to the sense of smell. *Synesthesia* is the combination of two or more sensory appeals in a single image.

A third way to achieve vividness is to

use figures and structures of speech. *Alliteration* is the repetition of beginning sounds. *Parallelism* expresses two or more ideas in similar language structure. *Repetition* is the restatement of words, phrases, or sentences. Like parallelism, *antithesis* uses parallel construction, but it does so to contrast ideas. *Personification* attributes human qualities to objects, ideas, or organizations. *Simile* and *metaphor* are comparisons of two dissimilar things. In simile the comparison is explicit, using words such as *like* and *as*. These words are omitted in metaphors because the comparison is implied.

A final criterion for effective language is to use language *appropriately*. You should select language that is appropriate to you, your topic, your audience, and the occasion.

Two additional dimensions of appropriateness are oral style and nonsexist language. *Oral style* differs from written style in at least four important ways. First, in speaking we tend to use shorter sentences. Second, when we communicate orally we use more contractions, colloquial expressions, and slang. Third, oral style makes greater use of personal pronouns and references. Fourth, we use more repetition when we speak than when we write.

Nonsexist language treats both genders symmetrically and fairly. It does not create special categories or assign roles based solely on gender. Speakers who have difficulty selecting gender-free language should consult a dictionary of nonsexist terms.

EXERCISES

1. Select a one- or two-paragraph passage from a book or magazine. Using the guidelines listed in this chapter, rewrite the passage for a speech, incorporating elements of oral style.
2. Decide on nonsexist words that could be substituted for each of the following examples:
   a. Policeman
   b. Enlisted men
   c. Fatherland
   d. Tomboy
   e. Clothes make the man.
   f. Man's best friend
   g. All men are created equal.
   h. Brotherly love
3. Listen to an album, cassette tape, or compact disc of your favorite vocal recording artist or group. Try to identify at least one example of each of the following language devices in song lyrics:
   a. Alliteration
   b. Metaphor
   c. Simile
   d. Personification
   e. Visual image
   f. Tactile image
   g. Olfactory image
   h. Gustatory image
   i. Auditory image
   j. Kinesthetic image
   k. Kinetic image
4. Select a speech from *Vital Speeches of the Day* or another published source. Identify examples of as many types of the language devices listed in Exercise 3 as possible.

NOTES

1. "Anything Goes," *Time* 17 April 1950: 28.

2. "Accentuate the Negative," *Harper's* November 1990: 17-18.

3. E.C. Nance, "The Power and the Glory of the Word: Civilization Is Where It Is Today by the Force of Words," *Vital Speeches of the Day* 1 April 1957: 382.

4. Bergen Evans, "The Power of Words," in *Language Awareness*, 5th ed., eds. Paul Eschholz, Alfred Rosa, and Virginia Clark (New York: St. Martin's, 1990) 34.

5. This discussion of functions of language is based on Roman Jakobson, "Closing Statement: Linguistics and Poetics," in *Style in Language*, ed. Thomas A. Sebeok (Cambridge, MA: MIT P, 1964) 350-74.

6. Charles L. Barber, *The Story of Speech and Language* (New York: Crowell, 1965) 9-10.

7. William F. Allman, "The Mother Tongue," *U.S. News & World Report* 5 November 1990: 62.

8. This discussion of two different ways of responding to language is based on Louise M. Rosenblatt, *The Reader, The Text, The Poem: The Transactional Theory of the Literary Work* (Carbondale: Southern Illinois UP, 1978), particularly Chapter 3, "Efferent and Aesthetic Reading."

9. Richard Lederer, *Anguished English: An Anthology of Accidental Assaults Upon Our Language* (Charleston, SC: Wyrick, 1987) 8.

10. Alfred Rosa and Paul Eschholz, "Bunkerisms: Archie's Suppository Remarks in 'All in the Family,'" *Language Awareness*, 3rd ed., eds. Paul Eschholz, Alfreda Rosa, and Virginia Clark (New York: St. Martin's, 1982) 125.

11. Gloria Cooper, ed., *Red Tape Holds Up New Bridge, and More Flubs from the Nation's Press* (New York: Perigee, 1987) n. pag.

12. Jeffrey Bair, "'Techno-dolts' Face Obstacle of Electronic Manuals," *San Antonio Light* 14 October 1990: Classified 44.

13. Miriam Ringo, *Nobody Said It Better!* (Chicago: Rand, 1980) 201.

14. Ringo 201.

15. Robert E. Leestamper, "Run Richmond Graduates, Run! Today's Challenges," *Vital Speeches of the Day* 15 December 1989: 156.

16. Cherie Spurling, "Batter Up — Batter Down," *Winning Orations, 1992* (Mankato, MN: Interstate Oratorical Association, 1992) 12.

17. Joni Oakley, "Inequality in Medicine," *Winning Orations, 1992* (Mankato, MN: Interstate Oratorical Association, 1992) 22.

18. Richard O'Brien, "Scorecard," *Sports Illustrated* 21 June 1993: 14.

19. Peter Schjeldahl, "Cyclone! Rising to the Fall," *Harper's* June 1988: 70.

20. Schjeldahl 68.

21. Schjeldahl 70.

22. Schjeldahl 70.

23. Richard Conniff, "Coasters Used to be Scary, Now They're Downright Weird," *Smithsonian* August 1989: 85.

24. Conniff 84.

25. Schjeldahl 70.

26. Conniff 84. Conniff is quoting coaster enthusiast Paul Ruben.

27. Vincent Ryan Ruggiero, "The Role of Business in Educational Reform: Pessimism and Popular Culture," *Vital Speeches of the Day* 15 February 1989: 287.

28. Ronald Reagan, Remarks at the Johnson Space Center in Houston, TX, January 31, 1986, *Weekly Compilation of Presidential Documents* 3 February 1986: 118.

29. Mario Cuomo, Keynote Address, Democratic National Convention, *Vital Speeches of the Day* 15 August 1984: 647.

30. Maridell Fryar, "The Anatomy of an Association," address, First General Sess., Texas Speech Communication Association Convention, Dallas, 30 September 1983.

31. Virginia I. Postrel, "The Environmental Movement: A Skeptical View," *Vital Speeches of the Day* 15 September 1990: 729.

32. Schjeldahl 68.

33. Lyndon B. Johnson, Address Before a Joint Session of the Congress, November 27, 1963, *Public Papers of the President: Lyndon B. Johnson 1963-64,* vol. 1 (Washington: G.P.O., 1965) 10.

34. William Safire, "On Language: Marking Bush's Inaugural," *New York Times Magazine* 5 February 1989: 12.

35. Rosalie Maggio, *The Nonsexist Word Finder: A Dictionary of Gender-Free Usage* (Boston: Beacon, 1991) 7.

36. Allman 60.

37. Qtd. in George Plimpton, ed., *The Writer's Chapbook: A Compendium of Fact, Opinion, Wit, and Advice from the 20th Century's Preeminent Writers* (New York: Viking, 1989) 176.

On the night of September 22, 1993, President Bill Clinton delivered one of the most important speeches of his political life to members of the House and Senate, Supreme Court justices, members of his cabinet, and a prime time television audience. That speech, introducing his vision of national health care reform, was the culmination of thousands of hours of research, meetings, and deliberation by the president's health care task force and hundreds of other people.

As he waited for the sustained applause to fade, Clinton looked into the TelePrompTer and saw the text of an economic address he had made to Congress and the nation eight months earlier! An aide operating the computer had accidentally merged the text of Clinton's current speech with that of the February speech, still in the system.[1] For the seven minutes that it took to load the correct manuscript and program the TelePrompTer to catch up with the president, Clinton spoke using only the written text in front of him. Clinton would tell ABC's Ted Koppel during a national forum the next night, "I thought to myself, 'That was a pretty good speech, but not good enough to give twice.'" The fact that Clinton could speak fluently and calmly under that unexpected stress is a testament to his significant delivery skills.

If grace under pressure is a part of Clinton's speech delivery, so, too, is his Arkansas drawl. He is not alone in having a distinctive voice. Barbara Jordan, former U.S. Representative from Texas, and poet Maya Angelou, who read at Clinton's inauguration, are two women whose deep voices and patterns of clear, careful articulation and enunciation make them immediately recognizable to many people. Two ministers, Jesse Jackson and the late Martin Luther King, Jr., are also known and remembered for their impassioned voices. In 1984, Jackson delivered one of the most dramatic political speeches in recent memory. Many Democrats that year feared that Jackson would lend only lukewarm support to the party's presidential and vice-presidential candidates, Walter Mondale and Geraldine Ferraro. In part of its coverage of Jackson's address to the 1984 Democratic National Convention, *Newsweek* spotlighted Jackson's distinctive speech delivery:

> The moment of highest drama came early, when Jackson met the fears head-on. Suddenly, Jackson's voice grew quiet — and with it, the vast, packed hall. "If in my low moments, in word, deed, or attitude, through some error of temper, taste, or tone, I have caused anyone discomfort, created pain, or revived someone's fears, that was not my truest self," he said. "If there were occasions when my grape turned into a raisin and my joy bell lost its resonance, please forgive me.... I am not a perfect servant. I am a public servant doing my best against the odds. As I develop and serve, be patient. God is not finished with me yet." All apprehension evaporated. And by the time Jackson's voice rose again to its perfect preacher's pitch, almost the entire rainbow congregation was on its feet, ... many weeping with exhilarated pride.[2]

Most of us do not have the extensive public speaking experience that Bill Clinton and Maya Angelou have or voices as impassioned as Jesse Jackson's. But each of us has a unique voice, body, and way of wording ideas. The manner in which you present your speech — through your voice, body, and language together — forms your style of delivery. In other words, *what* you say is your speech content, and *how* you say it is your **delivery.** If you and a classmate presented a speech with the same words arranged in the same order (something we don't recommend!), your listeners would still receive two different

delivery: the way a speaker presents a speech, through voice qualities, bodily actions, and language.

messages. This is because your delivery not only shapes your image as a speaker, but also changes your message in subtle ways. Your presentational style can amplify or undermine your intended message. Your speech delivery is bound to be either an asset or a liability, for as author Hermann Hesse observed, "Everything becomes a little different as soon as it is spoken out loud."

Speech delivery is so important that one of the criticisms of televised presidential debates is that they turn into "beauty contests," emphasizing looks and poise and minimizing the importance of what the candidates say. Strong delivery can no doubt mask weak content for some listeners. More important, though, effective delivery can bolster important, well-organized ideas, and poor delivery can diminish the impact of those same ideas.

As Paul Lorain suggests, your delivery gives color and fragrance to your words. To help you understand how that invigoration occurs, we discuss the qualities and various elements of effective delivery in this chapter. Before we examine the individual physical and vocal elements that constitute delivery, let's consider some rules that apply to all nonverbal communication.

PRINCIPLES OF NONVERBAL COMMUNICATION

Your nonverbal behavior communicates a great deal of information concerning your feelings about what you say. Recall Albert Mehrabian's formula from Chapter 1 (see page 13). In particular, four principles of nonverbal communication help account for the importance of speech delivery. These principles provide a framework we will use later to evaluate the specific elements of vocal and physical delivery.

1. *Part of our nonverbal communication is conscious and deliberate, while another part is unconscious and unintentional.* You do certain things deliberately to make other people feel comfortable around you or attracted to you. You dress in colors and fabrics that flatter you or make you feel comfortable. You cut your hair in a style that is fashionable, traditional, or uniquely flattering. When speaking or listening to others, you look them directly in the eyes. You smile when they tell you good news and show concern when they share a problem.

On the other hand, you may have habits of which you are unaware. You fold your arms, assuming a closed and defensive body position, or jingle your keys when nervous. You tap your fingers on the lectern when anxious or look down at the floor when embarrassed. You can control only those things you know about. Therefore, the first step toward improving your speech delivery is to identify and isolate any distracting nonverbal behaviors you exhibit.

In this chapter, we discuss the following nonverbal elements of speech delivery: rate, pause, volume, pitch, inflection, voice quality, articulation, pronunciation, appearance, posture, facial expression, eye contact, movement, and gestures. Of these elements, only one — vocal quality — is difficult to change or control. The others are much easier to modify. But how can you learn whether you have annoying and distracting habits? Feedback from your instructor and your classmates can show you areas in which you need to improve. If you have access to a cassette recorder, you can listen to your voice as you practice your speech, and a video camera will enable you to observe and assess your physical delivery. Keep in mind that discovering and improving your delivery weaknesses is not a quick, one-shot event, but continues with each successive speech you deliver in class.

2. *Few if any nonverbal signals have universal meaning.* Standing at a bakery in Paris, France, you can't resist the aroma of long, golden loaves of bread hot from the oven. Unable to speak French, you get the clerk's attention, point to the loaves, and hold up two fingers, as in a V for victory. The clerk nods, hands you three loaves, and charges you for all three. Why? The French count from the thumb, whether it is extended or not. The same thing would happen if you used an identical gesture to order another two drinks in a German tavern. The French and German people simply apply different rules to their counting gestures than we do.

Just as the meanings of gestures and movements can change from one culture to the next, nonverbal delivery that is appropriate and effective in one speaking situation may be inappropriate and ineffective in another. Smiling and lively gesturing are appropriate if you are informing your audience on the history of clowning. On the other hand, your body should show more tension and your face more concern if you were persuading others of the devastating effects of unnecessary surgery. Though this chapter focuses on improving delivery of your classroom speeches, you can adapt many of our suggestions to your delivery in other speaking situations.

3. *When a speaker's verbal and nonverbal channels send conflicting messages, we tend to trust the nonverbal message.* A used car sales representative rushes you into signing a purchase agreement while saying, "Man, this is the best deal on the lot. You are so lucky!" A supervisor at work tells you privately that she is impressed with your work, but then doesn't allow you to speak at staff meetings. A person keeps saying, "I love you," but never does anything to show consideration for you. Would you doubt the sincerity of these people? If you are typical, you certainly would.

We have each been interpreting and responding to other people's nonverbal communication for so long that we lose sight of its significance. But we are reminded of the importance of nonverbal communication when someone breaks a nonverbal rule. One of those rules demands that a person's words and actions match. Suppose Doris walks reluctantly to the front of the classroom, clutches the lectern, stands motionless, frowns, and says, "I'm absolutely delighted to be speaking to you today." Do you believe her? No. Why? Doris's speech began not with her first words, but with the multiple nonverbal messages that signaled her reluctance to speak. Nonverbal messages should complement and reinforce verbal ones. When they do not, as in Doris's case, actions speak louder than words. In such instances, we tend to trust the nonverbal message to help us answer the question, "What's really going on here?" As a result of this, one final principle of nonverbal communication becomes extremely important.

4. *The message you intend may be overridden by other messages people attach to your nonverbal communication.* You stare out the window while delivering your speech because you feel too nervous to make eye contact with your listeners. The audience, however, assumes that you are bored and not really interested in speaking to them. Because we cannot read one another's minds, your audience's perception that you are disinterested is the more important one in this case, even though it may be far from the truth. Eliminate distracting behaviors that mask your good intentions if you care about presenting the best speech you can.

In this chapter, we also discuss several guidelines to help you improve your vocal and physical delivery. We present four methods of delivery and show you how to give a successful speech, whether it is delivered impromptu, from memory, from manuscript, or extemporaneously. But first let's make sure we understand the qualities of effective delivery.

QUALITIES OF EFFECTIVE DELIVERY

As you begin to think about the way you deliver a speech, keep in mind three characteristics of effective delivery. First, effective delivery helps the listeners as well as the speaker. If you are well prepared for a particular speech, you have probably spent a good deal of time formulating and rehearsing it. You know what you want to say, but your audience does not. Your audience has only one chance to receive your message. Just as clear organization makes your ideas easier to remember, effective delivery can underscore your key points, sell your ideas, or communicate your concern for the topic.

Second, understand that the best delivery looks and feels natural, comfortable, and spontaneous. Former tennis great Helen Wills Moody once said, "If you see a tennis player who looks as if he is working very hard, then that means he isn't very good."[3] The same thing could be said of a speaker's delivery. No one should notice how hard you are working to deliver your speech effectively. Some occasions and audiences require you to be more formal than others, of course. Speaking to a large audience through a stationary microphone, for example, will naturally restrict your movement. For a presentation in this class, on the other hand, you may find yourself moving, gesturing, and using visual aids extensively. You want to orchestrate all these elements so that your presentation looks and feels relaxed and natural, not strained or awkward. You achieve spontaneous delivery such as this only through practice.

Third, and finally, delivery is best when the audience is not aware of it at all. Your goal should be delivery that reinforces your ideas and is free of distractions. When the audience begins to notice how you twist your ring, to count the number of times you say "um," or to categorize the types of grammatical mistakes you make, your delivery is momentarily distracting them from what you are saying. Your delivery has now become a liability rather than an asset. If you eliminate distractions from your delivery and use the elements of delivery to reinforce your purpose in speaking, you help your audience pay attention.

		KEY POINTS
1. Effective delivery helps everyone — the listener as well as the speaker. **2.** The best delivery looks and	feels natural, comfortable, and spontaneous. **3.** Delivery is best when the audience is not aware of it.	**Characteristics of Effective Delivery**

How can you help ensure effective delivery? Concentrate on your ideas and how the audience is receiving them, rather than on how you look or sound. If you are really interacting with your listeners, you will pay attention to their interest in your speech, their understanding of your message, and their acceptance or rejection of what you are saying. If you notice listeners checking their watches, reading papers, whispering to friends, or snoozing, they are probably bored. At this point you can enliven your delivery with movement and changes in your volume. Such relatively simple changes in your delivery may revive their interest.

But what if you notice looks of confusion on your audience's faces? You want to make certain your listeners understand the point you are making. Slow down your rate of delivery and use descriptive gestures to reinforce your ideas. If you observe frowns or heads shaking from side to side, you've encountered a hostile audience! There are ways to help break down the resistance of even an antagonistic group. Look directly at such listeners, establish a conversational tone, incorporate friendly facial expressions, and use your body to demonstrate involvement with your topic. These helpful tips take practice. Start with the basics. Once you have mastered the essentials of speech delivery, you will be flexible and able to adapt to various audiences. Your delivery will complement your message, not detract from it.

Any prescription for effective delivery will include three basic elements: the *voice,* or vocal delivery; the *body,* or physical delivery; and *language.* In Chapter 11, we discussed how your language contributes to your delivery style. In this chapter we focus on vocal and physical delivery. Vocal delivery includes rate, pause, volume, pitch, inflection, voice quality, articulation, and pronunciation. The elements of physical delivery are appearance, posture, facial expression, eye contact, movement, and gestures. Let's consider, first, how vocal delivery can enhance your speech.

ELEMENTS OF VOCAL DELIVERY

KEY POINTS		
Elements of Vocal Delivery	**1.** Rate and pause	**4.** Voice quality
	2. Volume	**5.** Articulation and pronunciation
	3. Pitch and inflection	

Rate and Pause

You have probably heard the warning, "Look out for him; he's a fast talker," or words to that effect. Such a statement implies that someone who talks fast may be trying to put something over on us. At the other end of the spectrum, we often grow impatient with people who talk much slower than we do, even labeling them uncertain, dull, or dense. Though these stereotypes may be inaccurate, we have already noted that the impressions people form based on our nonverbal communication can become more important than anything we intend to communicate.

rate: the speed at which a speech is delivered.

Your **rate** or speed of speaking can communicate something, intentionally or unintentionally, about your motives in speaking, your disposition, or your involvement with the topic. Your goal in a speech, therefore, should be to avoid extremely fast or slow delivery; you should instead use a variety of rates. Your various rates should, in turn, reinforce your purpose in speaking and make you seem conversational.

In Chapter 4, "Listening," you learned that the typical American speaker talks at a rate between 125 and 190 words per minute. To test your own rate of speaking, read the following paragraphs once silently. Then read them aloud at a rate that seems natural and conversational, using pauses to mark transitions from one idea to the next. Imagine yourself presenting this information to someone who has not read it. Ignore the slash marks and make a note of the word you have reached after one minute:

> Grassroots democracy depends on small groups of people meeting to talk about topics they consider important. Voluntary membership in such groups isn't easy today. People seem to connect with others mainly through television, radio, magazines, and newspapers. In reaction to the isolation many people feel, salons — groups of people meeting for directed discussion — are springing up at a rate not seen in recent history.
>
> *Salon* comes from the French word for "drawing room," and a meeting place is necessary for almost all salons. Gossip is an important ingredient in the recipe for a successful salon, but it's only secondary. The / salon must be focused on an exchange of ideas. A salon must also meet on a regular basis, on established days and at established times, whether it's once a week, every two weeks, or only once a month. The salon may have a core group that attends each meeting, but // it's also important to have new guests from time to time.
>
> The development of the electronic salon is a recent phenomenon. People with access to computers hooked up to modems can become a part of a lively network known as the WELL (Whole Earth 'Lectronic Link), for example. Electronic salons /// lack the spark of face-to-face interaction, though in the world of ideas, this may even be an advantage. Jon Carroll, one WELL fanatic, notes that the medium "favors people who are articulate in print" and that "it provides an absolutely level playing field in terms of physical appearance."[4]

How fast did you read? The first slash mark (/) indicates 100 words, and you probably passed that mark easily. The double slash (//) indicates 150 words, the triple slash 200, and the final word of the third paragraph is number 250. You probably did not finish the final paragraph if you were truly pausing and reading conversationally. Chances are that your final word falls somewhere between the single and triple slash marks, or between 100 and 200 words per minute.

This exercise cannot accurately measure your normal speaking rate, and is not intended to do so. You may, after all, speak faster or slower than you read aloud. But you now have some idea of how easy it is to speak more than 100 words a minute. To get an idea of how slow a rate of 100 words per minute actually is, try taking exactly one minute to read up to the first slash mark. You probably feel that you are plodding along sluggishly.

Although we can process information at rates faster than people speak, our comprehension depends on the type of material we are hearing. You should slow down, for example, when presenting detailed, highly complex information, particularly to a group that knows little about your subject. Our student René did just that in his informative speech, detailing the history of political and religious conflict in the Middle East. Not only did he speak slower than he had in other speeches, but he also used a clearly labeled map of the area and a timeline showing the splintering of groups into smaller factions. His reduced rate of delivery and his repetition of information in visual form showed his concern for his audience's comprehension. This can work both ways, however. In other situations, speaking slightly faster than the rate of normal conversation may actually increase your persuasiveness by carrying the message that you know exactly what you want to say.

Pauses or silences are an important element in your rate of delivery. You pause to allow the audience time to reflect upon something you have just said or to heighten suspense about something you are going to say. Pauses also mark important transitions in your speech, helping you and your audience shift gears. World-renowned violinist Isaac Stern was once asked why some violinists were considered gifted and others merely proficient or competent when they all played the correct notes in the proper order. "The important thing is not the notes. It's the intervals between the notes," he responded.

Let's take a sentence from Jesse Jackson's speech quoted earlier in this chapter. Try reading it without any internal punctuation or pauses.

> If in my low moments in word deed or attitude through some error of temper taste or tone I have caused anyone discomfort created pain or revived someone's fears that was not my truest self.

The sentence makes sense only if you insert pauses. The statement takes on power when you make those pauses meaningful! Speakers reading from a written text sometimes mark their manuscripts to help them pause appropriately. Now try reading Jackson's sentence, pausing a beat when you see one slash (/) and pausing a bit longer when you encounter two (//).

> If in my low moments, / in word, / deed, / or attitude, // through some error of temper, / taste, / or tone, // I have caused anyone discomfort, / created pain, / or revived someone's fears, // that was not my truest self.

Did you notice how much more impact the statement had when you included pauses? You may even disagree with our placement of pauses and their lengths. You might say the sentence differently, and that's fine. Public speaking is, after all, a creative and individual process. Remember, though, that to be effective in a speech, pauses must be used intentionally and selectively. If your speech is filled with too many awkwardly placed pauses, or too many vocalized pauses, such as "um" and "uh," you will seem hesitant or unprepared and your credibility will erode quickly.

Volume

Your audience must be able to hear you before they can listen to your ideas. **Volume** is simply how loudly or softly you speak. A person who speaks too loudly in a classroom speech may be considered boisterous or obnoxious. In contrast, we often label the inaudible speaker unsure, timid, "wimpy." The truth could be that you speak too loudly because of a hearing loss and you are not aware that your volume is uncomfortable to your listeners. The frustratingly quiet speaker may have grown up in a household with six other children and parents who were constantly yelling, "Quiet!" But your audience will not know about your history. What they will know is that you are shouting or whispering your speech and they will judge you by that behavior. Remember that hearing is the first step in listening. If you frustrate your audience or divert their attention with inappropriate volume, your chances of getting them to listen carefully to your message are slim.

Make sure you adapt your volume to the size of the room where you speak. In your classroom, you can probably use a volume just slightly louder than your usual conversational level. When you speak before a large group, a microphone may be helpful or even essential. If possible, practice beforehand so that the sound of your amplified voice does not startle you. You may even be called upon to speak before a large audience without a microphone. This is not as difficult as it sounds. In fact, your voice will carry well if you support your breath from your diaphragm. To test your breathing, place your hand on your abdomen while repeating the sentence "Those old boats don't float" louder and louder. If you are breathing from the diaphragm, you should feel your abdominal muscles tightening. Without that support, you are probably trying to increase your volume from your throat, a mistake that could strain your voice.

At times, you may have to conquer not only a large space but also external noise, such as the chattering of people in a hallway, the roar of nearby traffic, or the whoosh of the air conditioning system. That may require hard work. If you can, use a microphone in such a situation, speak at normal volume, and let the public address system do the work for you. If a microphone is unnecessary, don't use it; in a small room, a microphone distances you from the audience. We discuss the use of two different types of microphones in more detail in Chapter 17 (see pages 389-390).

Pitch and Inflection

Pitch is a musical term, and when we talk about vocal pitch we are referring to the highness or lowness of vocal tones, similar to the notes on a musical staff. Every speaker has an optimal pitch range, or key. This is the range in which you are most comfortable speaking, and chances are good that in this range your voice is also pleasant to hear. People who speak in unusually high or low voices are rare, and in these cases work with speech therapists helps them to achieve a flexible, useful pitch range.

pitch: the highness or lowness of a speaker's voice.

Speakers who are unusually nervous sometimes raise their pitch. Other speakers think that if they lower their pitch, they will seem more authoritative. (If you have seen the *Mary Tyler Moore Show,* you will recognize this as the Ted Baxter factor.) In truth, speakers who do not use their normal pitch usually sound artificial.

The following practice technique may help you retain or recapture a natural, conversational tone in your delivery. Begin some of your practice sessions seated. Imagine a good friend sitting across from you, and pretend that she asks you what your speech is about. Answer her question by summarizing and paraphrasing your speech: "Mary, I'm going to talk about the advantages of mandatory school uniforms in elementary and middle schools. I've divided my speech into three main arguments. School uniforms will enhance student self-esteem; they will reduce discipline problems; and they will save parents money." Listen closely to the tone of your voice as you speak. You are having a conversation with a friend. You're not tense; you feel comfortable.

Now, keeping this natural, conversational tone in mind, stand up, walk to the lectern, and begin your speech. Your words will change, but the tone of your speech should be comfortable and conversational, as it was before. In a sense, you are merely having a conversation with a larger audience. We have found this technique helpful for students whose vocal delivery sounds artificial or mechanical. Not only do they find their natural pitch range, but they also incorporate more meaningful pauses.

A problem more typical than an unusually high- or low-pitched voice is vocal delivery that lacks adequate **inflection,** or changes in pitch. Someone who speaks without changing pitch delivers sentences in a flat, uniform pitch pattern that becomes monot-

inflection: patterns of change in a person's pitch level while speaking.

onous. Indeed, the word *monotone* means "one tone," and you may have had instructors whose monotonous droning invited you to doze. People whose voices sound monotonous are usually actually using three tones: one in the middle, one slightly higher, and one lower. That's still too little vocal variety, however. Your inflection is an essential tool for conveying meaning accurately. A simple four-word sentence such as "She is my friend" can be given four distinct meanings by raising the pitch and volume of one word at a time:

> "**She** is my friend." (Not the young woman standing with her.)
> "She **is** my friend." (Don't try to tell me she isn't!)
> "She is **my** friend." (Not yours.)
> "She is my **friend.**" (There's nothing more to our relationship than that.)

Did you ever make a comment jokingly only to have people take you seriously? Chances are that you did not adequately signal with your inflection that it was a joke. In public speaking, women can generally make wider use of their pitch ranges than men can without sounding affected or unnatural. For this reason, men often find that they need to vary other vocal and physical elements of delivery — volume, rate, and gestures, for example — to compensate for a limited pitch range.

Voice Quality

voice quality or **timbre:** the unique characteristics that distinguish one person's voice from others.

Voice quality or **timbre,** the least flexible of the vocal elements discussed here, is the characteristic that distinguishes your voice from other voices. You may have called a friend on the phone and had difficulty telling him from his father, or her from her mother or sisters. Most of the time, however, even through the telephone, an instrument causing a lot of distortion, you recognize the voices of friends easily. In general, our individual voices are easily recognized as distinct. In fact, you may have heard that police investigators often use voice prints to identify and distinguish individual voices on tape recordings.

Sometimes the clarity and resonance of your voice can be temporarily affected by colds, by allergies, or by strain after you spend hours screaming support for a favorite team. That temporary change should not cause alarm. However, if many people describe your voice as strident, harsh, nasal, breathy, or hoarse over a long period of time, you may want to consult a speech therapist.

Articulation and Pronunciation

articulation: the mechanical process of forming the sounds necessary to communicate in a particular language.

The final elements of vocal delivery we will discuss are articulation and pronunciation. **Articulation** is the mechanical process of forming the sounds necessary to communicate in a particular language. Most articulation errors are made from habit. You tell your parents that you're going to the "libary," for example. Even though you know how to spell the word and would say it correctly if pressed to do so, you have fallen into a habit of misarticulating it. Sometimes our articulation errors are reinforced by people around us who make the same mistakes. Sometimes illness or fatigue affect our articulation temporarily.

Articulation errors take four principal forms: deletion, addition, substitution, and transposition. One of these, represented by the example of "libary," is the *deletion* or leaving out of sounds. Saying "goverment" for "government" is another example of a deletion error. If you have heard someone say "athalete" for "athlete," you've heard an example of an articulation error caused by the *addition* of a sound. Examples of errors caused by the *substitution* of one sound for another are "kin" for "can" and "git" for "get." The final type of articulation error is one of *transposition*, or the reversal of two sounds that are close together. This error is the vocal equivalent of transposing two letters in a typed word. Saying "lectren" for "lectern" or "hunderd" for "hundred" are examples of transposition errors.

Articulation errors made as a result of habit may be so ingrained that you can no longer identify your mistakes. Your speech instructor, your friends, and your classmates can help you significantly by pointing out articulation problems. You may need to listen to tape recordings of your speeches to locate problems and then practice the problem words or sounds to correct your articulation.

Pronunciation, in contrast to articulation, is simply a matter of knowing how the letters of a word sound and where the stress falls when that word is spoken. We all have two vocabularies: a speaking vocabulary and a reading vocabulary. Your speaking vocabulary — the group of words you use in day-to-day conversation — is much smaller than your reading vocabulary. To test this, think of the times you have been reading something and encountered a word you have never spoken or even heard spoken: "Her *vitriolic* parting words stung him," for example. You may have seen the word before in print. Even though you may have never looked up its pronunciation or meaning in a dictionary, you probably feel that you know more or less what it means in the context of the sentence. Such a word is part of your reading vocabulary.

Most of us make errors in pronunciation primarily when we try to move a word from our reading vocabulary to our speaking vocabulary without consulting the dictionary. In a public speech, the resulting pronunciation error can be a minor distraction or a major disaster, depending upon how far off your mispronunciation is and how many times you make the error. For example, a few years ago one of our students delivered a persuasive speech against *apartheid* in South Africa, mispronouncing that important word more than fifty times during the presentation! (Both "a PART hite" and "a PART hayt" are acceptable pronunciations; "A par theed" is not.) The real misfortune is that this mispronunciation was what almost all listeners remembered most vividly about the speech. Although the speaker presented a well-researched speech on a topic that obviously concerned him, the audience was left thinking, "If he is so concerned about it, why didn't he learn to pronounce the word correctly?" If you have any doubt about the pronunciation of a word you plan to use in a speech, look it up in a current dictionary and then practice the correct pronunciation out loud before the speech. Apply this rule to every word you select, including those in quotations. If you follow this simple rule, you will avoid embarrassing errors of pronunciation.

Pronunciation of proper nouns, the names of specific people, places, and things, can also pose difficulties. Suppose that for your speech on mountain climbing you want to quote from a fine book entitled *Flow: The Psychology of Optimal Experience.*[5] You copy an excellent passage about the psychology of dangerous sports onto a notecard. Then you turn to the title page to find the author's name: Mihaly Csikszentmihalyi! Don't tear up the notecard.

Obviously, proper nouns should be pronounced the way that the people who have the name (or who live in the place, or who named the thing) pronounce them. The large

pronunciation: how the sounds of a word are to be said and which parts are to be stressed.

city on the Texas Gulf Coast is pronounced "HEW stun"; the street in New York City spelled the same way is pronounced "HOW stun." The surname Koch can be pronounced "Kotch" (as in former New York mayor Ed Koch) or "Koke" (as in poet Kenneth Koch). But many people with the last name Koch pronounce it "Cook." When you see the name Schroeder, you may think of the *Peanuts* character and mentally pronounce the word with a long *o* sound. Yet the late William Schroeder, world's first artificial heart recipient, pronounced his family's name as though the *oe* were a long *a*.

If you refer to people who are well known and are or were mentioned frequently on radio and television, as in the Ed Koch and William Schroeder examples, make sure that your pronunciation corresponds to common usage. If you quote or refer to a person who is unfamiliar to your audience — as Csikszentmihalyi may well be — your listeners will not know that you have mispronounced the name unless you appear to stumble uncertainly over it. You could be lucky enough to read an article that tells how the person pronounces his or her name; *Psychology Today* says Csikszentmihalyi is pronounced Chick-sent-me-HIGH.[6] The only other way to confirm your pronunciation of a name like "Csikszentmihalyi" would be to locate the person, place a long-distance call, and ask. No one expects you to do that. Instead, decide on a reasonable pronunciation, practice it, and deliver it with confidence in your speech. For names of places, consult the *Pronouncing Gazetteer* or list of geographical names found at the back of many dictionaries.

Once you have mastered these elements of vocal delivery, your speech will be free of articulation errors and mispronounced words. Your unique voice quality will be pleasant to hear. Your voice will be well modulated, with enough inflection to communicate your ideas clearly. You will speak loudly enough that all your listeners can hear you easily. You will adapt your rate to the content of your message, and you will pause to punctuate key ideas and major transitions. In short, your sound will be coming through loud and clear. Now let's consider the picture your listeners will see by examining the aspects of physical delivery.

ELEMENTS OF PHYSICAL DELIVERY

KEY POINTS		
Elements of Physical Delivery	**1.** Appearance **2.** Posture **3.** Facial expression	**4.** Eye contact **5.** Movement **6.** Gestures

Appearance

appearance: a speaker's physical features, including dress and grooming.

As we mentioned earlier in this text, we all form quick impressions of people we meet based on subtle nonverbal signals. **Appearance,** in particular our grooming and the way we dress, is an important nonverbal signal that helps people judge us. Why is appearance so important? You may ask, "What about the inner me? Does it really come down to 'it's not who you are but what you wear?'" Of course, that is not the case. But you would be foolish to underestimate the power of first impressions and the initial reactions people have to your appearance.

Studies demonstrate that people we consider attractive can persuade us much more easily than can those we find unattractive. In addition, high-status clothing carries more authority than does low-status clothing. For example, studies show we are more likely to jaywalk behind a person dressed in a dark blue suit, a crisp white shirt, and a dark tie, and carrying an expensive black-leather briefcase, than we would behind a person dressed in rags or even in jeans. We will also take orders more easily from that well-dressed person than we would from someone poorly dressed. These studies reinforce the adage that "clothes make the person," a saying any public speaker would do well to remember.

Since John T. Molloy's first book, *Dress for Success*, came out in 1975, we have all been getting plenty of advice about the best colors, fabrics, and styles of clothing for the business office. Dressing for success has become big business. Today, "image consultants" across the country teach men and women how to dress for increased productivity and influence. Some of this may seem unrealistic or inappropriate for you as a public speaker. But some common sense tips will help you choose clothing that eliminates problems and adds impact to your speech.

The safest advice we can offer the public speaker on appearance is to avoid extremes in dress and grooming. Use clothes to reinforce your purpose in speaking, not to draw too much attention to themselves. Every moment that the audience spends admiring your European-cut navy blue suit or wondering why you wore the torn Stone Temple Pilots T-shirt when you're not talking about rock music is a moment they are distracted from your message.

Here are some "Dress for Address" guidelines for you to follow. In selecting your attire, take into consideration the occasion, audience, topic, and speaker.

1. Consider the Occasion. The formality or informality of your clothing is dictated in part by the speaking occasion. A student delivering a valedictory would dress differently from one delivering an impromptu campaign speech in the school cafeteria. A speech in your classroom permits you more informality than would a business presentation to a board of directors, a sermon to a congregation, or an acceptance speech at an awards ceremony.

2. Consider Your Audience. Some of your listeners dress more casually than others. In any audience, there is a range of attire. As a rule, we suggest that you dress at the top of that range. For speeches outside the classroom, traditional, tasteful, and subdued clothing is your wisest choice. Your aim is to appear as nicely dressed as the best dressed in your audience. In other words, when in doubt, dress "up" a little. An audience is more easily insulted if you appear to treat the speaking occasion too casually than if you treat it too formally. Remember, your listeners will make judgments based on your appearance before you even open your mouth.

3. Consider Your Topic. Your topic may also affect your choice of clothes. While the public speech is not a costumed performance, clothing can underscore or undermine the impact you want your speech to have. A hot pink dress or lime green shirt would be appropriate for a speech on the festival of Mardi Gras, but not for one on the high cost of funerals. On the other hand, you would look foolish presenting a speech on step aerobics if you demonstrated exercises dressed in a business suit.

4. Consider Your Image. Finally, the image you want to create as a speaker should shape your selection of clothing. Darker colors, for example, convey authority. Lighter colors establish a friendlier image. A student perceived as the class clown could dress more formally on the day of his or her speech to help dispel this image.

Clothing not only influences our perceptions of others, it also shapes our self-perception. Just think of your own experiences. You probably have certain clothes that give you a sense of confidence or make you feel especially assertive or powerful. You feel differently about yourself when you wear them. Dressing "up" conveys your seriousness of purpose to your listeners. It also establishes this same positive attitude in your own mind.

As a practical matter, we suggest that you decide what you will wear before the day of your speech and that you practice, at least once, in those clothes. You will discover that this benefits you in three ways. First, you reduce by one the number of decisions you must make on the day of your speech. Second, you will be more comfortable as you deliver your speech. If you wear a suit coat and are not used to doing so, you will have practiced gesturing with it on. You will have decided if it is best buttoned or unbuttoned. Third, practicing in what you actually plan to wear alerts you to problems and enables you to correct them. Make sure that what you plan to wear is clean and pressed. You may also discover, for example, that a favorite bracelet creates a distracting sound as it taps on the lectern when you move your arm. One of our students complained that she was distracted during her presentation because every time she moved her arms to gesture her coat made a rustling sound. She could have eliminated this distraction had she

Clothing can send powerful messages about a speaker's attitudes toward the topic, the occasion, and the audience. What topics do you think would be appropriate and inappropriate for this student dressed these three ways? (SOURCE: © Drew Skinner)

practiced in that suit coat before the day of her speech. Whatever the problems, it's best to encounter and fix them before the speech. You can then concentrate fully on the speech itself.

Posture

A public speaker should look comfortable, confident, and prepared to speak. You have the appropriate attire. Your next concern is your **posture,** the position or bearing of your body. In posture, the two extremes to avoid are rigidity and sloppiness. Don't hang on to or drape yourself across the lectern, if you are using one. Keep your weight balanced on both legs and avoid shifting your weight back and forth in a nervous swaying pattern. Equally distracting is standing on one leg and shuffling or tapping the other foot. You may not realize that you do those things. Other people will have to point them out to you. Remember that before your delivery can reinforce your message, it must be free of annoying mannerisms

posture: the position or bearing of a speaker's body while delivering a speech.

Facial Expression

Researchers estimate that the human face is capable of 250,000 — a quarter of a million — different facial expressions.[7] That's a vast amount of communication potential! Yet, ironically, many people giving a speech for the first time put on a blank mask, reducing their **facial expression** to one neutral look. We have often seen our students do this, and we know why it occurs. Inexperienced speakers are understandably nervous and may be more concerned with the way they look and sound than they are with the ideas they are trying to communicate.

facial expression: the tension and movement of various parts of a speaker's face.

To articulate clearly you must open your mouth freely; as you speak, your face must move. However, your facial expression must match what you are saying. The speaker who smiles and blushes self-consciously through a speech on date rape will simply not be taken seriously by the audience, and may offend many listeners. If you detail the plight of earthquake victims, make sure your face reflects your concern. If you tell a joke and your listeners can't stop chuckling, you certainly should break into a smile rather than a frown. In other words, your face should register the thoughts and feelings that motivate your words.

The way to use facial expression appropriately to bolster your message is really simple: Concentrate as much as possible on the ideas you present and the way your audience receives and responds to them. Try not to be overly conscious of how you look and sound. This takes practice, but your classroom speeches provide a good forum for such rehearsal. You will learn to interact with the audience, maintain eye contact, and respond with them to your own message. Chances are that, if you do those things, your facial expression will be varied and appropriate and will reinforce your spoken words.

Eye Contact

We've all heard the challenge, "Look me in the eye and say that." We use direct eye contact as one gauge of a person's truthfulness. **Eye contact** can also carry many other

eye contact: gaze behavior in which a speaker looks at listeners' eyes.

messages: confidence, concern, sincerity, interest, and enthusiasm. Lack of eye contact, on the other hand, may signal deceit, disinterest, or insecurity.

Try this simple experiment. The next time you talk to a good friend, look at a spot on that person's hair rather than look him or her in the eyes. What will happen? Chances are good that your friend will either ask you, "What's the deal?" or use one of those nervous, self-directed, preening gestures we all have to make sure that there's nothing wrong with our hair. Your friend may even do both, because the speaker who avoids eye contact with us, or who looks beyond us, will frustrate or anger us or at least make us very self-conscious.

Your face is the most important source of nonverbal cues as you deliver your speech, and your eyes carry more information than any other facial feature. As you speak, you will probably look occasionally at your notes or manuscript. You may even glance away from the audience briefly as you try to put your thoughts into words. Yet you must keep coming back to the eyes of your listeners to check their understanding, interest, and evaluation of your message.

As a public speaker, your goal is to make eye contact with as much of the audience as much of the time as possible. The way to do that is to make sure that you take in your entire audience, from front to back and from left to right. Include all those boundaries in the scope of your eye contact, and make contact especially with those individuals who seem to be listening carefully and responding positively to your message. Whether you actually make eye contact with each member of the audience is immaterial. You must, however, create that impression. Again, this takes practice before you feel comfortable.

Movement

movement: a speaker's motion from place to place during speech delivery.

Effective **movement** benefits you the speaker, your audience, and your speech. First, place-to-place movement can actually help you relax. Moving to a visual aid, for example, can help you energize and loosen up physically. From the audience's perspective, move-

Speakers must adapt their volume to the size and location of their audiences.
(SOURCE: © Fred Chase/Impact Visuals)

ment adds visual variety to your speech, and appropriate movement can arouse or rekindle the listeners' interest. Most important, though, physical movement serves your speech by guiding the audience's attention. Through movement, you can underscore key ideas, mark major transitions, or intensify an appeal for belief or action.

Remember that your speech starts the moment you enter the presence of your audience. Your behavior, including your movement, sends signals about your attitudes toward the audience and your speech topic. When your time to speak arrives, approach your speaking position confidently, knowing that you have something important to say. Addressing a large audience through a microphone mounted on the lectern will naturally restrict your movement. If the lectern is there as a matter of convenience, and particularly if you are speaking to a relatively small audience, don't automatically box yourself into one position behind the lectern. Remember that even the smallest lectern puts a physical barrier between you and your audience. Moving to the side or the front of it reduces both the physical and the psychological distance between you and your listeners, and may be especially helpful whenever you conclude your speech with a persuasive appeal.

Make certain that your movement is selective and that it serves a purpose. Avoid random pacing. Movement to mark a transition should occur at the beginning or the end of a sentence, not in the middle. Finally, bring the speech to a satisfying psychological conclusion and pause for a second or two before gathering your materials and moving toward your seat in the audience.

Gestures

Gestures are important adjuncts to our verbal messages; at times, they can even replace words altogether. As a public speaker, you can use gestures to draw a picture of an object, to indicate the size of objects or the relationships between them, to re-create some bodily motion, to emphasize or underscore key ideas, to point to things such as visual aids, or to trace the flow of your ideas. If you don't normally gesture in conversation, force yourself to include some gestures as you practice your speech. At first you may feel self-conscious about gesturing. Keep practicing. Gestures that are natural and spontaneous are well worth whatever time you spend practicing them. Not only do they reinforce your ideas and make you seem more confident and dynamic, but gestures, like movement, can help you relax.

gestures: movements of a speaker's hands and arms while delivering a speech.

To be effective, then, gestures must be coordinated with your words, and must appear natural and spontaneous. In addition, any gesture should be large enough for the audience to see it clearly. The speaker who gestures below the waist, or whose gestures are barely visible over the top of a lectern, may appear timid, unsure, or nervous. Speakers who gesture too much — who talk with their hands — may also be perceived as nervous, flighty, or excitable. The two extremes to avoid, therefore, are the absence of gestures (hands clenched in a death-grip on the sides of the lectern) and excessive gestures (gestures emphasizing everything, with the result that nothing stands out). Remember, if your audience is waiting for you to gesture or counting your many gestures, they are distracted from your message.

The following two generalizations from research on gestures are particularly helpful for the public speaker. First, people who are confident, relaxed, and have high status tend to expand into the space around them and use gestures that are wider than those of other people. Speakers who wish to emphasize their authority, or to seem more authoritative, can therefore help do so by increasing the width of their gestures. Second, a wide, palm-up gesture with both hands creates an openness that is entirely appropriate when a speaker is appealing for a certain belief or urging the audience to some action. A palm-down gesture with one or both hands carries more force and authority, and can be used to command an audience into action or to exhort them to a certain belief. Stand up and deliver the following statement, gesturing with both hands palms-up: "We need to communicate our message to the university administration: It's time to get serious about adequate funding of our library. Give us the resources we deserve!" Now repeat those sentences gesturing with both hands palms-down. Did you feel a subtle difference in tone and intensity?

As a speaker, adapt the size of your gestures to the size of your audience. On stage before a crowd of several thousand, your gestures should be more expansive than when you stand at the front of a small classroom. In a cavernous auditorium, you must adjust your gestures, as well as your facial expression and eye contact, so that they will be clear to those in the back rows.

These, then, are the tools of vocal and physical speech delivery, from rate of speaking to hand gestures. Your goal throughout this class and in your future public speaking experience will be to eliminate any distracting elements and then work toward delivery that is conversational, forceful, and as formal or informal as your audience and subject require. Once you have marshaled these aspects of vocal and physical delivery to work for you, you can then use them in any of four ways of delivering a speech.

■ METHODS OF DELIVERY

The four basic ways you can deliver your public speech are (1) impromptu, or without advanced preparation; (2) from memory; (3) from a manuscript; or (4) extemporaneously, or from notes. The impromptu and the memorized methods have very limited applications, particularly for an important speech, but they deserve at least brief attention.

Speaking Impromptu

impromptu speaking: speaking without advanced preparation.

We engage in **impromptu speaking** whenever a teacher, a colleague, or a boss calls on us to express an opinion on some issue, or whenever someone unexpectedly asks us to "say a few words" to a group. We deal with those special occasions and offer specific guidelines for impromptu speaking in Chapter 17 (see pages 383-385). In those informal situations, other people do not necessarily expect us to be forceful or well organized, and we are probably more or less comfortable speaking without any preparation. Yet the more important the speech is, the more inappropriate the impromptu method of delivery. In short, impromptu speaking is excellent practice for anyone, but no conscientious person will risk a grade, an important proposal, or professional advancement on an unprepared speech.

Speaking from Memory

speaking from memory: delivering a speech that is recalled word-for-word from a written text.

Speaking from memory is similarly appropriate only on rare occasions. We speak from memory when we prepare a written text and then memorize it word for word. At

its best, the memorized speech allows a smooth, almost effortless-looking delivery, since the speaker has neither notes nor a manuscript and can concentrate on interacting with the audience. For most of us, however, memorizing takes a long time. Our concentration on the memory work we've done and our fear of forgetting part of the speech can also make us sound mechanical or programmed when reciting. For these reasons, the memorized method of delivery is usually appropriate only for brief speeches, such as when introducing another speaker, or presenting or accepting an award, for example.

Speaking from Manuscript

Speaking from manuscript, or delivering a speech from a complete text prepared in advance, not only ensures that the speaker will not be at a loss for words, but is also essential in some situations. An address that will be quoted or later published in its entirety is typically delivered from a manuscript. Major foreign policy speeches or State of the Union addresses by U.S. presidents are always delivered from manuscript, because the premium is not just on being understood but on not being misunderstood. Speeches of tribute and commencement addresses are often also scripted. Any speaking situation calling for precise, well-worded communication is appropriate for manuscript delivery.

    Having every word of your speech scripted should boost your confidence, but it does not ensure your effective delivery. When you write the manuscript, you must take care to write in an oral style. In other words, the manuscript must sound like something you would say in conversation. The text of your speech thus requires a good deal of time to prepare, edit, revise, and type for final delivery. In addition, if you do not also take time to practice delivering the manuscript in a fluent, conversational manner and with appropriate emphasis, well-placed pauses, and adequate eye contact, you are preparing to fail as an effective speaker.

speaking from manuscript: delivering a speech from a text written word for word and practiced in advance.

**speaking extempor-
aneously:** delivering a
speech from notes or from
a memorized outline.

Speaking Extemporaneously

The final method of delivery, and by far the most popular, is **speaking extemporaneously,** or from notes. Assuming that you have researched and organized your materials carefully, and that you have adequately practiced the speech, speaking from notes
offers several advantages over other methods of delivery. You don't have to worry about
one particular way of wording your ideas, because you have not scripted the speech. Neither do you have to worry that you will forget something you have memorized. With your
notes before you, you are free to interact with the audience in a natural, conversational
manner. If something you say confuses the audience, you can repeat it, explain it using
other words, or think of a better example to clarify it. Your language may not be as forceful or colorful as with a carefully prepared manuscript or a memorized speech, but
speaking from notes helps ensure that you will be natural and spontaneous.

New York governor Mario Cuomo, skilled in various methods of delivery, reveals
that he speaks extemporaneously whenever possible because of its advantages:

> Spontaneity is one. Audience contact is another. Because you're not tied to a text,
> your eyes scan the audience and you can detect signs of agreement that
> encourage you to elaborate effective points. Or you see impatient fidgeting, the
> sidelong glances of disapproval, and occasionally, the sure sign of abject failure
> — eyes closed, chin on chest, a customer not only declaring "no sale," but

*Speakers must listen effectively
when they field and answer
questions from audience members.*
(SOURCE: © Fred Chase/Impact
Visuals)

making it clear he or she is no longer shopping. Alerted, the speaker can then change pace, improvise, move on to a more interesting proposition. It's easier to engage the audience when you have both eyes in direct contact with the people you're addressing, both arms drawing pictures in the air, adding punctuation, fighting off the glaze.

It's more fun, too. It has an adventurous quality that one misses when the assignment is just to read a prepared text.[8]

When speaking either from a manuscript or from notes, you need to keep several practical points in mind:

1. Practice with the notes or manuscript you will actually use in delivering the speech. You need to know where things are on the page so that you have to glance down only briefly.

2. Number the pages of your manuscript or your notecards so that you can check their order just before you speak.

3. Determine when you should and when you should not look at your notes. Looking at your notes when you quote an authority or present statistics is acceptable. In fact, it may even convey to your audience your concern for exactness in supporting your ideas. However, do not look down while previewing, stating, or summarizing your key ideas. If you cannot remember your key points, what hope is there for the audience? Also, avoid looking down when you use personal pronouns such as *I, we,* and *you,* or when you address members of the audience by name. A break in your eye contact at those points suddenly distances you from the audience, and creates the impression that the speech is coming from a script rather than from you.

4. Slide the pages of your manuscript or notes rather than turning them. As a rule, if you use a lectern, do not let the audience see your notes after you place them in front of you. The less the audience is aware of your notes, the more direct and personal your communication with them will be.

5. Devote extra practice time to your conclusion. The last thing you say can make a deep impression, but not if you rush through it or deliver it while gathering up your notes and walking back to your seat. Your goal at this critical point in the speech is the same as your goal for all of your delivery: to eliminate distractions and to reinforce your message through your body, voice, and language.

The most satisfactory way of delivering your classroom speeches combines all four of the methods we have discussed. We have advised you not to look at your notes during the preview of your introduction or the summary step of your conclusion. We stressed the importance of the introduction and conclusion in Chapter 9. To demonstrate that you are well prepared and to ensure contact with your audience, you may even want to have your introduction and conclusion memorized. That won't be difficult since they are brief sections. You may decide or be assigned to deliver the body of your speech extemporaneously, looking at your notes occasionally. Just don't look at your notes while you are stating or summarizing each main point. If you quote sources at different points in your speech, you are, in effect, briefly using a manuscript. Finally, as an audience-centered speaker, you should be flexible enough to improvise a bit. You speak impromptu whenever you repeat an idea or think of a better example to increase your clarity or your persuasiveness. If you are well prepared, this combination of delivery methods should look natural to your audience and feel comfortable to you.

One standard in the American work ethic has been the traditional saying, "If it's worth doing, it's worth doing well." That's wise counsel for the public speaker. Your gestures, rate of delivery, and grammar may seem trivial until they begin to interfere with your communication, undermine your credibility, and dilute your persuasiveness. Delivery is a vital part of your public speech, and effective delivery is an asset worth cultivating.

SUMMARY

Speech *delivery* is composed of a speaker's voice qualities, bodily actions, and language. This chapter focused on vocal and physical delivery, aspects of a speech presentation that are subject to four principles of nonverbal communication. First, part of our nonverbal communication is intentional, while another part is unconscious and unintentional. Second, few if any nonverbal signals have universal meaning. Third, when a speaker's verbal and nonverbal channels send conflicting messages, we tend to trust the nonverbal message. These three principles contribute to a fourth: The message you intend may be overridden by other messages people attach to your nonverbal communication.

The nonverbal elements of delivery include everything about your speech that could not be captured and recorded in a manuscript of the speech. *Vocal delivery* is comprised of your rate, use of pauses, volume, pitch and inflection, voice quality, articulation, and pronunciation. Your appearance, posture, facial expression, eye contact, movement, and gestures make up the elements of your *physical delivery*. With each of these elements, your goal as a speaker should be to eliminate distractions and to work for variety so that you look and sound natural. Once you are aware of unconscious mannerisms you may have and of the characteristics of effective delivery that you should have, you can make significant improvements in the way you deliver a speech.

You exercise a good deal of control over most of these physical and vocal elements of delivery. With the confidence that comes from practice, you should be able to adapt your delivery to different speaking situations and audience sizes. Though this chapter examined several different elements of delivery, speech delivery is best when none of those elements makes an impression on the audience. Instead, delivery should reinforce the clear, forceful communication of your ideas.

With a repertoire of effective vocal and physical skills at your command, you can then select one of four methods of delivery: *impromptu speaking*, or speaking without advanced preparation; *speaking from memory; speaking from manuscript;* and *speaking extemporaneously*, or from notes. While each of those types of delivery is appropriate under certain public speaking circumstances, impromptu speaking and speaking from memory should almost certainly be avoided for prepared, graded classroom speeches. Speeches from a manuscript and, particularly, from notes, have far fewer limitations and more applications than the other two methods of delivery. Those who can speak clearly and emphatically from a few notes after the necessary period of practice have gone a long way toward ensuring success, not only in the public speaking classroom but also in any future public speaking situations.

EXERCISES

1. Select a short passage from a novel, short story, speech, or other prose selection and photocopy it. Study the meaning and emotion of the excerpt. After marking the copied text, read the passage aloud, emphasizing key words and phrases and using pauses to enhance the message's impact.
2. Record your speech on audiotape and listen to it. Analyze your use of rate, pauses, volume, pitch, inflection, articulation, and pronunciation. What can you do to ensure that your delivery is lively and reinforces the message of the speech?
3. Record your speech on videotape. Watch and listen to it. Analyze your physical delivery, focusing on those aspects discussed in this chapter. What are your strengths? What are your weaknesses? What can you do to improve the physical delivery of your message?
4. Attend a speech and analyze the speaker's vocal and physical delivery. Was the message delivered effectively? What nonverbal elements enhanced and what detracted from the speech? What suggestions could you give the speaker to improve the delivery of the speech?

NOTES

1. "Tale of the TelePrompTer," *Newsweek* 4 October 1993: 4.

2. Sylvester Monroe, "Let the Joy Bells Ring," *Newsweek* 30 July 1984: 22.

3. Laurence J. Peter, *Peter's Quotations: Ideas for Our Time* (New York: Bantam, 1979) 476.

4. Information in these paragraphs is based on two articles: Stephanie Mills, "Salons and Beyond: Changing the World One Evening at a Time," *Utne Reader* March/April 1991: 68-77, and John Berendt, "The Salon," *Esquire* November 1990: 48. Jon Carroll is quoted on page 75 of the Mills article.

5. Mihaly Csikszentmihalyi, *Flow: The Psychology of Optimal Experience* (New York: Harper-Perennial, 1990).

6. Mihaly Csikszentmihalyi, "How to Shape Our Selves," *Psychology Today* January/February 1994: 38.

7. Ray L. Birdwhistell, *Kinesics and Context: Essays on Body Motion Communication* (Philadelphia: U of Philadelphia P, 1970) 8.

8. Mario Cuomo, "Introduction," *More than Words: The Speeches of Mario Cuomo* (New York: St. Martin's, 1993) xiv-xv.

Remember: It is 10 times harder to command the ear than to catch the eye.
— Duncan Maxwell Anderson

Using Visual Aids

Chapter *13*

A *three-year-old boy with bangs and short pants saluting at his father's funeral …*
An anguished woman kneeling over the body of a student shot by the National Guard …
Two helmeted figures saluting an American flag staked into a desolate, gray landscape …
A space shuttle exploding in a cloudless azure sky …
A tiny, battered girl being lifted from a well …
A young man standing motionless in a street in front of four tanks …
People dancing and spraying champagne all night from atop a wall …
Sheet-metal buildings erupting in flames on a windswept Texas prairie …
People boating past rooftops of houses and barns …

If you form a vivid mental image at the description of any of these events, you prove the haunting power of pictures.[1] We have all grown up in a visually oriented society. Even our language reflects the power of the visual message. Consider these familiar sayings:

"A picture is worth a thousand words."
"Don't believe anything you hear and only half of what you see."
"Missouri — the Show Me State."
"I wouldn't have believed it if I hadn't seen it with my own eyes."

Today, television and film are our primary entertainment media. Most Americans get the majority of their news from television. Even our newspapers are filled with pictures, black and white or color. When the news is bad, we expect to see pictures or videotape of the airplane wreckage, the flooding, or the aftermath of the earthquake. When the news is good, we expect to see pictures of the winning team, the successful space mission, or the heroic rescue. We are, indeed, people for whom "seeing is believing."

Because pictures are such an important part of life, delivering a public speech without considering using visual aids is a little like playing tennis with your racquet hand tied behind your back. As a speaker, you need not rely only on words to communicate your ideas precisely and powerfully. You can add force and impact to your message by incorporating a visual dimension as well.

◼◼ THE IMPORTANCE OF USING VISUAL AIDS

A well-designed, appropriate visual aid can add significantly to the effectiveness of the speech and the speaker. Visual aids serve three important functions. First, they add clarity to a speaker's message. Second, they reinforce the impact of the message. Third, they can increase the dynamism of a speaker's delivery. Consider these three functions as you determine whether to include visual aids in a particular speech.

Increases Message Clarity

First, visual aids give your speech greater clarity. They can specify the demographic breakdown of voters in the past presidential election, for example, or illustrate how a hologram is constructed, or explain the steps in the new university registration procedure. Detailed statistical information is more clearly conveyed in a simplified line graph than through a recitation of data. Speeches that use a spatial organizational pattern in particular often benefit from visual reinforcement.

Reinforces Message Impact

Second, visual aids give your speech greater impact. Seeing may encourage believing; certainly, it aids remembering. Consider the following data from the business world:

> A study conducted by the University of Minnesota in 1986 showed that when computer-generated overhead transparencies or slides were used to present an idea, the presenter was perceived to be 43 percent more persuasive than in meetings with unaided presentations. The study also concluded that the use of visuals could reduce the length of a typical meeting by 28 percent.[2]

Studies draw different conclusions as to the degree of impact visual aids give to a speech. They all conclude, however, that a well-constructed visual aid helps listeners remember more of your speech for a longer period of time. Because they both hear and see the message, listeners are more fully involved in the speech. This greater sensory involvement with the message lessens the opportunity for outside distractions and increases retention.

Increases Speaker Dynamism

Third, visual aids make you seem more dynamic. In Chapter 12, we discussed the importance of gestures as part of your delivery. Most speakers, unfortunately, have difficulty incorporating meaningful gestures into their delivery. They remain behind a lectern, their hands resting on, or clutching, their notes. Consequently, they may appear uninvolved, perhaps even bored, with their speech. Using visual aids forces you to move, to point, to become physically involved with your speech. Your gestures become motivated and meaningful. You burn off some of your nervous energy and, consequently, you appear more dynamic and forceful.

Before you can use visual aids to clarify and enliven your speech, ask yourself, "Will visual aids make my presentation more effective?" This question is important because any visual aid, no matter how well designed and planned, involves some distractions for both speaker and audience. It may require setup time, for example. When you uncover the aid for audience view and cover it later, you create a visual break in the speech. In addition, visual aids remove part of a listener's focus from the speaker. In short, *use visual aids only if they are necessary to the speech,* and be prepared for possible distractions. Now that you understand both how visual aids can enhance your presentation and some of the problems they potentially present, let's examine the various types of visual aids you can use in a speech.

Once you have decided to use visual aids, you need to determine the type most appropriate to your presentation. Visual aids come in many forms, but they can generally be divided into four classifications: objects, graphics, projections, and handouts.

Objects

objects: actual items or three-dimensional models of items used during the delivery of a speech.

Objects may be either actual, such as a 35-millimeter camera, or scaled, such as an architect's model of the new campus library. Other three-dimensional visual aids are, for instance, a scuba diver's oxygen tank and breathing regulator, a deck of tarot cards, a replica of the Statue of Liberty, or a new model of computer hardware. Our student James presented an informative speech on product packaging design. Among other objects he used were several Pepsi cans of a design used in 1990. In a matter of seconds he showed how the lines on the cans clearly spelled out the word *sex* when two cans were stacked and aligned in a certain way.

Also included under the category of objects are any people you use to help demonstrate a procedure, such as cardiopulmonary resuscitation or the Heimlich maneuver. Objects used effectively give your speech immediacy and carry a great deal of impact.

Three-dimensional models that are helpful in learning environments like an anatomy and physiology lab can also be useful visual aids for the public speaker.
(SOURCE: © Charles Gupton/ Stock, Boston)

The term **graphics** includes a variety of two-dimensional visual aids used to clarify or illustrate a point being made orally. Five types of graphics to consider are pictures, diagrams, graphs, charts, and maps.

Pictures can make a speaker's oral presentation more concrete and vivid. It is difficult to imagine how a speech on the artistic styles of Georgia O'Keeffe or Edward Hopper could be effective without pictures or prints of some of their paintings. A speaker trying to persuade the audience that subliminal messages are common in advertising would be both vague and unconvincing unless he or she presented actual examples.

Speakers can also use pictures to dramatize a point, as with photographs showing the extent of tornado damage in a particular area. A speaker who advocates legislation mandating seat belt use could display two pictures of badly mangled automobiles. The impact of the message would be clear and forceful as the speaker observes, "The driver of the car in the first picture was not wearing his seat belt and died. The driver in the second picture was wearing hers and walked away."

When you use pictures, make sure that you select them with size and clarity in mind. A small snapshot of the Palace of Versailles or a picture from an encyclopedia held up for audience view detracts from, rather than reinforces, the speaker's purpose. Pictures used as visual aids often must be enlarged. Luckily, color laser copiers found at many copy shops today make enlarged copies of pictures quickly and inexpensively. You can also check the library for books with large pictures. The picture you want to show may even be available as an inexpensive poster from a local museum gift shop or a bookstore. For very large audiences, you may need to project pictures for easy viewing. Here again, you may be able to borrow slides from your school's art department library or to purchase them from a museum gift shop.

Diagrams are graphics, typically drawn on posterboard, showing the parts of an object or organization, or the steps in a process. Posterboard is ideal for diagrams used in classroom speeches because its large size makes it easy for audience members to see. It is also thick and rigid enough to make handling it easy. A diagram could show the features of a new aircraft design, the organizational structure of the U.S. judicial system, or the steps in the lost wax method of casting jewelry. The best diagrams achieve their impact by simplifying and exaggerating key points. For example, no diagram of manageable size could illustrate all the parts of a six-cylinder engine clearly enough for the audience to see easily. A carefully constructed diagram could isolate and label key parts of that engine design, however.

Steven's speech on Poplar Forest, Thomas Jefferson's getaway home, sought both to capture the uniqueness of Jefferson's architectural style and to re-create life in those postpresidential years. Steven used two visual aids: a picture (Figure 13.1) and a diagram (Figure 13.2). He based his diagram on one he found in a brochure picked up when he toured Poplar Forest. Steven knew he did not have time to discuss each of the ten areas identified. In his speech he cited the brochure as a source, mentioned each area in passing, but focused on four key areas: (1) the west bedroom, (2) the dining room, (3) the east bedroom, and (4) the parlor. In preparing his visual aid, he labeled each area and then covered the words with slips of white paper. He used the diagram to guide the audience through the house, removing the slips of paper so that the audience could identify each location as he discussed it. When he had concluded his speech, the audience had a better understanding of the house's layout.

graphics: two-dimensional visual aids, including pictures, diagrams, graphs, charts, and maps, used during the delivery of a speech.

pictures: photographs, paintings and drawings, or prints used to make a point more vivid or convincing.

diagrams: graphics, usually drawn on posterboard, showing the parts of an object or organization, or the steps in a process.

Figure 13.1 *Picture: Poplar Forest, home of Thomas Jefferson*

line graph: a diagram used to depict changes among variables over time.

Graphs are visual aids that illustrate some condition or progress, and graphs take several familiar forms. A **line graph** is useful in depicting changes over time. A speaker might convincingly use a line graph to illustrate the rising cost of a college education over the past twenty years. Some line graphs trace two or more variables — income and expenditures, for example — in contrasting colors.

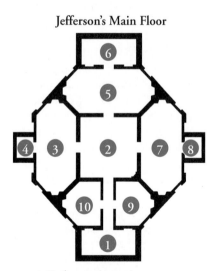

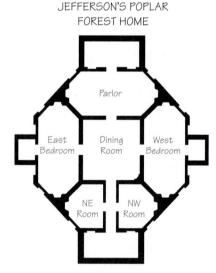

1 *North portico (entrance)*
2 *Dining room*
3 *East bedroom*
4 *Site of original stairway; east stairs*
5 *Parlor*
6 *South portico*
7 *West bedroom*
8 *Site of original stairway: west stairs*
9 *Northwest room*
10 *Northeast room*

Visual Aid Adapted from Brochure Diagram

Figure 13.2 *Diagram: Floor plan of Jefferson's Poplar Forest home*

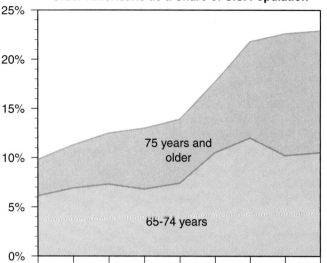

Older Americans as a Share of U.S. Population

75 years and older

65-74 years

Source: U.S. Bureau of Census, 1992

Figure 13.3 *Line graph*

Genna used a line graph (Figure 13.3) in her informative speech on the aging of America. In a Department of Labor publication, she found a table that listed by decade the percentage of the U.S. population falling into two age groups: 65 to 74 years, and 75 years and older. She constructed a chart using this information and practiced her speech in front of her roommates. However, they found the chart cluttered and confusing, and Genna agreed. She decided that a line graph would more clearly and vividly make her point that the U.S. population was aging and would continue to do so.

A **bar graph** is useful in comparing quantities or amounts. We can measure the economic health of an institution, a company, or a nation, for example, by learning whether it is "in the red" or "in the black." A bar graph contrasting deficits and profits, showing their relative size, provides us a clear, visual indication of economic health, particularly when income is represented in black and deficits in red.

A third type of graph, the **pie graph,** is helpful when you want to show relative proportions of the various parts of a whole. If you are analyzing the federal budget, for example, a pie graph could illustrate the percentage of the budget allocated for defense. Pie graphs can show proportions of how people spend their time in a typical day, the causes of cancer deaths, how the average grocery dollar is spent, and the composition of your university according to the majors chosen by the student population. When using a pie graph, emphasize the pertinent "slice" of the pie graph with a contrasting color.

Combining types of visual aids may be the clearest way to convey statistical information in a speech. For example, Damon became interested in the diversity of Hispanic Americans and their countries of origin from information he read in his sociology textbook. He decided to inform his public speaking class about the topic. In an *American Demographics* article he researched, Damon found U.S. census data that discussed 12 countries of origin for Hispanics. To make this information clearer and more vivid, he used two visual aids: a pie graph and a bar graph. He reasoned that a pie graph cut into

bar graph: a diagram used to show quantitative comparisons among variables.

pie graph: a diagram used to show the relative proportions of a whole.

charts: graphics, usually drawn on posterboard, used to condense a large amount of information, to list the steps in a process, or to introduce new terms.

12 pieces would look cluttered and might confuse his listeners. So he constructed his pie graph to show the three primary counties of origin and an "other" category (Figure 13.4). He then used a bar graph (Figure 13.5) to show those nine other countries and the number of Hispanic Americans in each group.

Similar to diagrams and graphs, **charts** condense a large amount of information into a small space. For visibility and ease of handling, charts are also usually drawn on posterboard when used as visual aids for a small audience. Speakers introducing an audience to new terms will sometimes list those words on a chart. This strategy is particularly effective if the words can be uncovered one at a time in the order they are discussed. Using charts, you could list the top ten states in per capita lottery ticket sales, or rank professional sports according to players' average salaries. Charts are particularly appropriate for medical and other technical topics. A speaker detailing the solution phase of a problem-solution speech could list steps advocated on a chart and introduce them in the order they are discussed.

As a speaker, you can either prepare charts in advance or draw them during the speech. For example, charts could show how regular investment in an Individual Retirement Account can lead to financial security in later life, and those calculations could be done ahead of time or during the course of the presentation. If you plan to draw one or more charts during your speech, rehearse the drawing. Make sure that you can continue to speak as you draw, so that your speech is not marred by long gaps of silence. If a chart is so complex that you cannot draw it as you speak, prepare it in advance. You can use a flip-chart, a large sketch pad bound at the top, to accommodate a series of charts. Available at most art supply stores, flip-charts have a sturdy backing that will stand up straight on an easel. They allow you to flip each visual aid back after using it. If you need to show one chart briefly, speak for a while, and then show another chart, simply leave a blank page between charts that need to be separated.

A volunteer for the American Red Cross, Carla was interested in learning more about private support of charitable organizations. In an issue of the *Chronicle of Philanthropy,* she found a list of the top 50 U.S. charities in terms of donations. Carla decided that a visual aid would help her audience remember these charities. To simplify her presentation, she made two important decisions as she constructed her chart (Figure 13.6). She short-

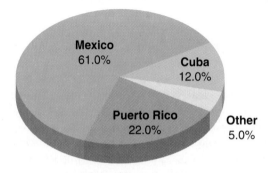

Figure 13.4 *Pie graph*   Source: 1990 U.S. Census

**Other Countries of Origin
U.S. Hispanic Population**

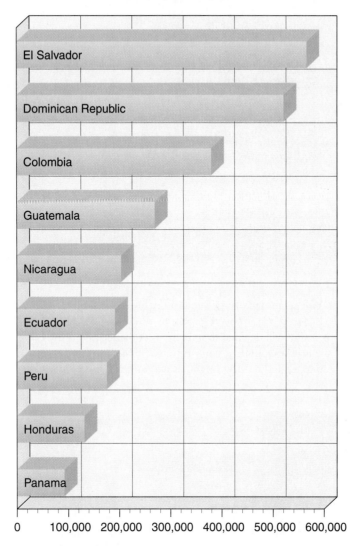

Source: 1990 U.S. Census

Figure 13.5 *Bar graph*

ened her list to the top ten charities, and she rounded dollar figures such as $726,297,274 to the nearest million.

Maps, the final type of graphic visual aid, lend themselves especially well to speeches discussing or referring to unfamiliar geographic areas. Speakers informing an audience on the islands of Hawaii, the Battle of Gettysburg, or threats to the Alaskan wildlife refuge would do well to include maps to illustrate their ideas. Although commercial maps are professionally prepared and look good, they may be either too small or too detailed for a speaker's purpose. If you cannot isolate and project a section of the map for a larger audience, you will probably want to prepare a simplified, large-scale map of the territory in question.

maps: graphics representing real or imaginary geographic areas.

The Top 10 U.S. Charities (1992)	
Organization	**Donations (in millions)**
1. Salvation Army	$726
2. Catholic Charities USA	$411
3. United Jewish Appeal (National)	$407
4. Second Harvest	$407
5. American Red Cross	$395
6. American Cancer Society	$355
7. YMCA of the USA	$317
8. American Heart Association	$235
9. YWCA of the USA	$218
10. Boy Scouts of America	$211

Figure 13.6   *Chart*

Will generated his speech topic by brainstorming about his favorite childhood movie, *The Wizard of Oz*. In his research, he discovered that L. Frank Baum wrote fourteen Oz books, and Will decided to inform his audience about the Land of Oz. He found a map of Oz and surrounding countries in *The Dictionary of Imaginary Places.*[3] Will photocopied the map, edited out the surrounding countries, and enlarged the map of Oz so that his

Speakers often use maps when referring to specific, unfamiliar geographic areas.
(SOURCE: © Stephen Agricola/ Stock, Boston)

Figure 13.7 *Map: The Land of Oz*

audience could see it as he described this mythical nation (see Figure 13.7). Will's audience will probably find *The Wizard of Oz* more enjoyable the next time they watch it.

Computer-Generated Graphics

Computer technology has revolutionized the production and display of visual aids, perhaps even more than it has transformed library research. Today, if you have access to a computer and any of the wide spectrum of graphics software, you can produce high-quality, professional-looking visual aids. Some of this software will produce items such as pie graphs that are more accurate than you could produce freehand. All you need to do is program the percentages and the identifying labels that you want represented. With a color laser copier, you can tint the sections of the graph different colors, or produce a line graph that shows two variables in contrasting colors.

Some graphics software will let you create on the computer screen any image you can draw. Larger copy shops or a campus computer lab may be able to scan an image of your choice that you can then preserve on diskette. Some software will allow you to import such images and then manipulate them: You can simplify a graph or diagram, for example, or isolate and enlarge one section of a map or photograph. Digital cameras allow you to take photographs, display them immediately on a Video Graphics Adaptor (VGA) computer screen, then enlarge sections of them, adjust their color, or even superimpose images to your satisfaction. Multimedia software lets you create slide programs and animation that you can then display on one or more computer monitors, depending on the size of your audience.

Rapid innovations in the field of computer graphics are exciting. But be sure that any visual aids you produce this way enhance your message, rather than just showcase what the software can do. Avoid the temptation to overload or complicate your computer-generated visual by using all the bells and whistles of the program you utilize. The same qualities that we've discussed for freehand visual aids — clarity, simplicity, and contrast — should be evident in any computer graphic you use.

The computer-generated image or text that you print on a laser printer or color laser printer will probably be the size of a sheet of typing paper. That size would be appropriate for handouts given to each audience member, but would be too small to display to an audience during your speech. What are your other options? You can enlarge that image up to 150 percent on most color laser copiers at print shops. If the image is still too small for easy audience viewing, most print shops can create transparencies quickly and inexpensively. Or if you know from the outset that you want to create images to project, special slide programs are available in some graphics software packages.

Projections

projections: a manner of presenting visual aids by casting their images onto a screen or other background.

Projections refer not so much to a type of visual aid as to a manner of presentation. Any of the graphics mentioned earlier — pictures, diagrams, graphs, charts, or maps — can be projected. This is especially appropriate when your audience is too large to see the visual aid easily and clearly. In such a case, you may want to use projections, such as slides, transparencies, or opaque projections. For convenience, we can group projections into two categories: *still projections* (slides, filmstrips, opaque projections, and transparencies) and *moving projections* (films and videotapes).

Still and moving projections can be critical to business and other public presentations. They may not, however, always serve the purpose of the public speaker and, particularly, the student of this class. Two notes of caution are in order. First, filmstrips, films, and videotapes are lengthy, and their organization is predetermined. It is important that you, not a visual aid, organize and present the ideas of your speech. Second, as a beginning public speaker, you need to control and be the primary focus of the public speaking event. When you stand at the back of the room, with lights dimmed, and narrate a slide show, you get little experience in speaking before an audience. For this reason, your instructor may not allow you to give a slide show, although you may be able to present a few relevant slides. Visual aids must always support, not become, your speech.

slides: small mounted transparencies projected one at a time.

Still Projections. **Slides** are small mounted transparencies projected one at a time, and most of us associate slides with photographs or pictures. Yet any of the graphics we discussed earlier can be photographed and developed into slides. Whereas maps, charts, graphs, and diagrams may be cumbersome and subject to wear, slides of those graphic visual aids are easily transported and easily reproduced. However, you should be aware of two disadvantages. One, slides require projection equipment that is frequently noisy and intrusive. The second disadvantage is that slides must be projected in darkness to be easily visible, and this, of course, takes the focus away from you, the speaker.

filmstrips: a series of pictures, diagrams, or any other graphic projected one at a time from a roll of plastic.

Filmstrips are familiar to most of us from as far back as our elementary schooling, but that does not mean that they are necessarily simplistic. Filmstrips can be used to instruct a group in parliamentary procedure or on how to conduct a business meeting, for example. Not only are a wide variety of filmstrips available commercially, but certain companies will also design and manufacture filmstrips to meet the needs of speakers in specific businesses or professions. You will probably find filmstrips a more useful visual aid in your career than in your classroom speeches.

The **opaque projection** is an image projected directly from a sheet of paper. Any of the graphic visual aids discussed earlier can be projected in this manner. Opaque projections offer the advantage of enlarging and projecting visual aids without the work or expense of preparing transparencies. Two disadvantages of this type of visual aid are that the opaque projector is not as widely available as the slide projector and that it is noisier to operate. In fact, its noise may rule out its use for extended periods of time in a small classroom.

Transparencies are clear or tinted sheets of plastic with words or images drawn or printed on them. Shown with an overhead projector, the transparency may be either prepared in advance or drawn with a felt-tip marker during the presentation. Many computer graphics programs can generate professional-looking transparencies. Overhead transparencies allow you to work through a problem, for example, without turning your back to the audience, thus helping you maintain audience involvement and interaction. If you plan to use transparencies in your very first speech, prepare them beforehand. You will be nervous enough without having to worry about drawing your visual aid as you speak.

Each of these types of still projections can visually enhance a presentation. They help ensure that the images are big enough for even the largest audiences to see clearly. All require special projection equipment, however. You may need to reserve that equipment through the audio-visual department of your school library. Your instructor may have some basic equipment in the department. Check all of this in advance and practice with the equipment so that you know how to operate it and how to minimize any noise it makes. On the day of your speech, you will need to be extremely well organized and punctual since projection equipment requires time for setup and focusing and is subject to mechanical failure. Your diligence can pay off handsomely, however. If you are sure that the visual aid is important enough to project, its contribution to your speech will probably outweigh these potential disadvantages and reward your extra effort.

Moving Projections.   Moving projections include **films** and **videotapes,** and they are appropriate whenever action will enhance a visual presentation. Moreover, with the widespread popularity of video cassette recording equipment, this particular type of visual aid is becoming easier and cheaper to use. The choice between films and videotapes is dictated both by the projection equipment available to you and by the size of the audience. Images are clearer and can be projected larger from film than from videotape, making film a wise choice for presentations to large groups. Videotapes are entirely appropriate for presentations to small audiences or before larger groups that have multiple viewing monitors. Again, use only short clips from videotapes to illustrate the ideas of your speech. Do not let the visual aid monopolize your presentation.

Videotapes have one obvious advantage over films: They do not require you to darken the room for projection. Though both the film and the videotape carry with them possible distractions, their potential impact is undeniable. We will remember for many years a persuasive presentation one of our students, George, gave on the problem of teenage inhalant abuse, or paint sniffing. After establishing the problem with statistics and testimony from experts, George pressed the play button on the remote control. Suddenly his

opaque projection: image cast directly from a sheet of paper by use of an opaque projector.

transparencies: sheets of clear or tinted plastic with images drawn or printed on them and projected using an overhead projector.

films and **videotapes:** moving projections used to enhance a speaker's point.

handout: any graphic visual aid distributed to individual audience members.

audience was seeing videotaped excerpts from news features about the problem: young people on downtown streets and under bridges, unable to answer quickly when the reporter asked, "What's your name?" Such flesh-and-blood examples of the effects of the problem are difficult to dismiss. Many speeches on social problems are significantly more compelling if the audience not only hears about but also sees graphic evidence of the problem.

Handouts

A final method of visually presenting material is the **handout.** Copies of any graphic visual aid — pictures, diagrams, graphs, charts, or maps — may be handed out to individual audience members.

Handouts are appropriately used under two conditions: (1) when the information cannot be effectively displayed or projected, or (2) when the audience needs to study or refer to the information after the speech. Gwen, a student presenting a speech on "The Power Résumé," used a handout to great benefit. She distributed a sample power résumé and referred to it at key intervals in her speech: "If you look at line fifteen, you will see...." She had numbered the lines of the résumé in the margin so that the audience could find the references without fumbling. Not only could the audience refer to the résumé as Gwen discussed its key features, but many also probably saved it to use later as they prepared to enter the career world upon graduation. Gwen's speech and her visual aid made a convincing argument for the importance of the power résumé.

In a similar way, if you try to persuade your audience to contribute time and money to local charities, you will more likely achieve your goal if you distribute a handout with the name, address, telephone number, and brief description of each charity.

Audio Aids

audio aids: cassette tapes, compact discs, or records used to clarify or prove a point by letting listeners hear an example.

Audio aids include records, tapes, and compact discs, and certainly there is an audio dimension of films and videotapes. Certain speech topics lend themselves to audio reinforcement of the message. A speech on Janis Joplin, for example, would be more vivid and informative if the audience could see and hear a videotaped clip of one of her performances. Lindahl, a student whose research we mentioned in Chapter 7, began her speech on the savant syndrome by playing half a minute of a taped piano performance of Chopin's Polonaise no. 6 in A-Flat Major. Her first words were, "The person who was playing that music is considered handicapped, but he heard this piece of music for the first time only minutes before sitting down to play it." The audiotape was a compelling example of one form of the savant syndrome. A speech comparing the jazz styles of Branford Marsalis and Hugh Masakela could hardly be effective without letting listeners hear examples from each of those artists. A speech comparing and contrasting the protest music of World War I with that of the Vietnam War would certainly be more powerful with audio examples.

Audio aids need not be confined to music topics, however. An audience listening to a speech on Winston Churchill could benefit from hearing his quiet eloquence as he addressed Great Britain's House of Commons and declared, "I have nothing to offer but blood, toil, tears, and sweat." A speaker analyzing the persuasive appeals of radio and television advertisements could play pertinent examples. Dan, a criminal justice major and intern with the police department, began his speech by playing an audiotape recorded in a police squad car. The officers were deciding whether they should stop a motorist suspected of driving while intoxicated (DWI). The audience heard the law enforcement officials describe what they saw that alerted them to a possible DWI and heard them discuss criteria for stopping the motorist. As the siren sounded, Dan stopped the tape. He used the audio aid to introduce his topic on the criteria for making a DWI arrest.

We have discussed the importance and major types of visual aids. Remember, though, that even the most brilliant visual aid cannot salvage a poorly planned, poorly delivered speech. Visuals can aid, but they cannot resuscitate a weak speech. On the other hand, even the most carefully designed and professionally executed visual aid can be spoiled by clumsy handling during a presentation. The effect of public speaking is cumulative, with each element contributing toward one final effect. If you use visual aids in a presentation, you cannot afford to use them poorly. The following section offers some practical guidelines on how to prepare and use visual aids in your public speech.

▬ STRATEGIES FOR USING VISUAL AIDS

Before the Speech
1. Determine the information to be presented visually.
2. Select the type of visual aid best suited to your resources and speech.
3. Ensure easy viewing by all audience members.
4. Make sure that the visual aid communicates the information clearly.
5. Construct a visual aid that is professional in appearance.
6. Practice using your visual aid.
7. Arrange for safe transportation of your visual aids.
8. Carry back-up supplies with you.
9. Properly position the visual aid.

During the Speech
1. Reveal the visual aid only when you are ready for it.
2. Talk to your audience — not to the visual aid.
3. Refer to the visual aid.
4. Keep your visual aid in view until the audience understands your point.
5. Conceal the visual aid after you have made your point.
6. Use handouts with caution.

KEY POINTS

Strategies for Using Visual Aids

Before the Speech

Determine the Information to be Presented Visually.   Sections of a presentation that are complex or detailed may be particularly appropriate for visualization. Be careful, however, not to use too many visual aids. The premium in a speech is on the spoken word. Multimedia presentations can be exciting; they may also be extremely difficult to coordinate. Handling too many charts and posters quickly becomes cumbersome and distracting.

Select the Type of Visual Aid Best Suited to Your Resources and Speech. The visual aid you select will be influenced by the information you need to present, the amount of preparation time you have, your technical expertise at producing the visual aid, and the cost involved. In the business and professional world, professionally produced visual aids can be costly, but they are worth the investment. As a student, you may find the cost too high. If preparing quality visual aids to illustrate your speech will take more time, money, or expertise than you have, you are probably better off without them. A visual aid that calls attention to its poor production is a handicap, no matter how important the information it contains.

Ensure Easy Viewing by All Audience Members. A speaker addressing an audience of 500 would not want to use a videotaped presentation displayed on a single television monitor. A bar graph on posterboard should be visible to more than just the first four rows of the audience. If possible, practice with your visual aids in the room where you will speak. Position the visual aid and then sit in the seat of your farthest possible audience member. (In an auditorium, make it the back row; people will not move forward unless forced to.) If you can read your visual aid from that distance, it is sufficient in size. If you cannot, you must either enlarge the visual aid or eliminate it.

Make Sure That the Visual Aid Communicates the Information Clearly. Simplicity should be your guiding principle in constructing your visual aid. Michael Talman, a graphics design consultant, compares a graphic in a presentation to "going by a highway billboard at 55 miles per hour. Its effectiveness can be judged by how quickly the viewer sees and understands its message."[4] Too much information may clutter or confuse. For example, speakers sometimes construct posters in technicolor to make them lively and interesting. But, remember that the purpose of visual aids is to inform, not to impress, the audience. You may use red to indicate a budget deficit, but, as a rule, black or dark blue on white is the most visually distinct color combination for graphics.

Construct a Visual Aid That is Professional in Appearance. In the business and professional world, a hand-lettered poster, no matter how neatly done, is inappropriate. Professionals understand the importance of a good impression. How can you as a student on a limited budget make a professional-looking graphic without spending a fortune? A simple solution is to use inexpensive, commercially prepared "press-on" letters. Many print shops have word processors and printers with many different-sized fonts for your use for about $10 an hour. You can then enlarge your graphics on a copy machine. If you have access to a computer and are familiar with a computer graphics program that meets your needs, by all means use it. If you can't use a computer and doubt your freehand skills, hiring an art student to draw and letter a visual aid you have designed is another alternative.

If you throw together a chart or graph the night before your speech, that is exactly what it will look like. Your hastily prepared work will undermine an image of careful and thorough preparation.

Practice Using Your Visual Aid. A conscientious speaker will spend hours preparing a speech; visual aids are a part of that presentation. Just as you rehearse the words of your speech, you should rehearse referring to your visual aid, uncovering and covering charts, advancing slides, and writing on overhead transparencies. In short, if you plan to use visual aids, learn how *before* your speech; no audience will be impressed by how much you learn during the course of your presentation.

Arrange for Safe Transportation of Your Visual Aids.   Visual aids worth using are worth transporting safely. Posterboards should be protected from moisture and bending. Cover your visual aid with plastic to protect it from a freak rainstorm or that flying Frisbee you encounter just before speech class. Do not roll up paper or posterboard charts, carrying them to different classes or leaving them in a car trunk throughout the day, and then expect them to lay flat when you speak. You will have a cylinder, not an effective visual aid.

Carry Back-up Supplies with You.   An exciting and informative presentation can be ruined when a projector bulb blows as you are preparing to speak. Make an inventory of equipment you may need, such as extension cords, bulbs, and batteries, and then take them with you.

Properly Position the Visual Aid.   Arrive at the place where you will give your speech *before* the audience arrives. Position your visual aid in the most desirable location. Make sure that the maximum number of people will see it and that nothing obstructs the audience's view. If you are not the first speaker, have your visual aid and equipment conveniently located so that you can set up quickly and with little disruption.

During the Speech

Reveal the Visual Aid Only When You Are Ready for It.   A visual aid is designed to attract attention and convey information. If it is visible at the beginning of the speech, the audience may focus on it rather than on what you are saying. Your visual aid should be seen only when you are ready to discuss the point it illustrates.

With an aid on posterboard, cover it with a blank posterboard or turn the blank side to the audience. At the appropriate time, expose the visual aid. If you are using projections, have someone cued to turn the lights off and the projector on at the appropriate time.

Occasionally, a speaker will stop speaking, uncover a visual aid, and then continue. This is where rehearsal can really help you. You want to avoid creating unnecessary breaks in the flow of your speech. With practice you will be able to keep talking as you uncover your visual aid.

Talk to Your Audience — Not to the Visual Aid.   Remember, eye contact is a speaker's most important nonverbal tool. Sustained visual interaction with your audience keeps their attention on you and allows you to monitor their feedback regarding your speech. Turning your back to your listeners undermines your impact. For this reason, use prepared graphics rather than a blackboard.

Refer to the Visual Aid.   Speakers sometimes stand at the lectern using their notes or reading their manuscript, relatively far from their visual aid. This creates two lines of vision and can confuse your audience. It may also give the impression that you must rely on your notes since you do not fully understand what the visual aid conveys.

Other speakers carry their notes with them as they move to the visual aid, referring to them as they point out key concepts. This is cumbersome, and again reinforces the image of a speaker unsure of what he or she wants to say.

A well-constructed visual aid should be used as a set of notes. The key ideas represented on the aid should trigger the explanation you will provide. You should not need to refer to anything else as you discuss the point your visual aid illustrates. When you practice using your visual aid, use your aid as your notes.

If you use a pointer to refer to the visual aid, have it easily accessible, use it only when pointing to the visual aid, and set it down immediately after you are finished with it. Too many speakers pick up a pen to use when referring to their visual aid and end up playing with the pen during the rest of the speech.

Finally, point to your visual aid with the hand closer to it. This keeps your body open and makes communication physically more direct with your audience.

Keep Your Visual Aid in View Until the Audience Understands Your Point.
Remember that you are more familiar with your speech than is your audience. Too often, a speaker hurries through an explanation and covers the visual aid before the audience fully comprehends its significance or the point being made. Just as you should not reveal your visual aid too soon, do not cover it up too quickly. You will have invested time and effort in preparing the visual aid. Give your audience the time necessary to digest the information it conveys. As you discuss and describe the visual aid, check your audience response. Many will likely signal their understanding of the visual aid by nodding their heads or changing their posture.

Conceal the Visual Aid After You Have Made Your Point.   Once you proceed to the next section of your speech, you do not want the audience to continue thinking about the visual aid. If the aid is an object or posterboard, cover it. If you are using projections, turn off the projector and turn on the room lights.

Use Handouts with Caution.   Of all the forms of visual aids, the handout may be the most troublesome. If you distribute handouts before your remarks, the audience is already ahead of you. Passing out information during a presentation can be distracting, especially if you stop talking as you do so. Disseminating material after the presentation eliminates distractions but does not allow the listener to refer to the printed information as you are explaining it. In general, then, use handouts in a public speech only if that is the best way to clarify and give impact to your ideas.

You will encounter some speaking situations, such as the business presentation, that not only benefit from but may also demand handout material. Those audiences are often decision-making groups. During an especially technical presentation, they may need to take notes. Afterward, they may need to study the information presented. Handouts provide a record of the presenter's remarks and supplementary information the speaker did not have time to explain.

Visual aids — objects, graphics, projections, and handouts — can make your speech more effective. By seeing as well as hearing your message, the audience becomes more involved with your speech and more responsive to your appeals.

SUMMARY

We live in a visually oriented world, expecting not only to hear about events around the globe, but also to see color pictures and videotapes of those events. Various studies show that visual aids complement the spoken word by increasing audience involvement with a speech and aiding listeners' retention of the information presented. Visual aids can contribute to the clarity and impact of a speaker's message and, when handled well, can make a speaker's delivery seem more dynamic.

The four categories of visual aids discussed in this chapter are objects, graphics, projections, and handouts. *Objects* are three-dimensional and may be either actual items or models of large or small items. *Graphics* refers to a large group of two-dimensional visual aids, including pictures, diagrams, graphs (line, bar, or pie graphs), charts, and maps. If you have access to a computer and any of the wide range of graphics programs, you can produce computer-generated graphics. *Projections* may be either still or moving. Still projections include slides, filmstrips, opaque projections, and transparencies. Any type of graphic may be shown by a still projection. Moving projections include films and videotapes. *Handouts* of any type of graphic may be given to audience members when no other method of presentation is possible. In addition to these strictly visual supports, a speaker may choose *audio aids* such as records, tapes, and compact discs of music, spoken words, and other sounds.

To use visual aids for maximum impact, a speaker needs to prepare them carefully using the following steps as guidelines: (1) Determine the amount of information to be presented visually; (2) select the type of visual aid best suited to the speaker's resources and speech topic; (3) ensure easy viewing by all audience members; (4) ensure that the visual aid communicates its information clearly; (5) construct a visual aid that appears carefully or professionally done; (6) practice using the visual aid; (7) arrange for safe transportation of the visual aid; (8) carry back-up supplies in case of equipment failure; and (9) properly position the visual aid before beginning the speech.

During the actual delivery of the speech, the speaker using visual aids needs to remember the following: (1) Reveal the visual aid only when ready to use it; (2) talk to the audience, not to the visual aid; (3) refer to the visual aid; (4) keep the visual aid in view until the audience understands the point it makes; (5) conceal the visual aid after making your point with it; and (6) use handouts with caution.

Visual aids can greatly enhance many speeches, and some speeches would be difficult to deliver without appropriate audio or visual aids. Effective use of those visual aids, however, requires careful planning and practice to integrate them into your speech delivery without distraction.

*E*XERCISES

1. Select a graph, diagram, or chart that you find in a magazine article. Describe how you would adapt it as a visual aid for a speech.
2. Sketch a visual aid you could construct for one of the speeches in Appendix C. Describe how the aid would make the message of the speech clearer and more memorable.
3. Describe at least two different types of visual aids you could use for a speech having the following specific purposes:
   a. To inform the audience about techniques of handwriting analysis.
   b. To inform the audience about origami, the Japanese art of paper folding.
   c. To inform the audience about the process of photograph restoration.
   d. To persuade the audience that more money should be spent on AIDS research.

e. To persuade the audience that the government should invest more money in the U.S. space program.

f. To persuade the audience that [name of building on campus] should be razed and replaced with another facility.

4. Go to the library and consult a book on graphic design or read a chapter on the topic in an advertising textbook. What suggestions concerning layout and illustration are appropriate for a speaker's visual aids? What suggestions seem unsuited to the medium?

NOTES

1. We adapted this chapter opening from four images described in an effective Nikon advertisement we saw for the first time in *American Photo* March/April 1991: 19.

2. Michael Antonoff, "Meetings Take Off with Graphics," *Personal Computing* July 1990: 62.

3. Alberto Manguel and Gianni Guadalupi, *The Dictionary of Imaginary Places*, expanded ed. (San Diego: Harvest-Harcourt, 1987) 287.

4. Michael Talman, *Understanding Presentation Graphics* (San Francisco: SYBEX, 1992) 270.

We are drowning in information and starving for knowledge.
—John Naisbitt

Speaking to Inform

Chapter 14

*P*eople respond to information today in a contradictory way. On one hand, study after study reveals that young people seem to know little about the world around them. A few years ago, a test of nearly 8,000 high school juniors representing all sections of the country and all subgroups revealed that, on average, students got only half the history and literature questions correct. As the authors reporting this study point out, if we think of this as a national report card in history and literature, eleventh graders in the United States fail both these crucial subjects.[1] Even more troubling is the number of adults who are functionally illiterate. In 1993, the most comprehensive test of adult literacy conducted so far suggested, "Nearly half of the nation's 191 million adults … cannot do such tasks as fill out a bank-deposit slip, compute the cost of carpeting a room, or translate information from a table to a graph."[2]

The problem is compounded because, just as we learn to appreciate the value of knowing as much as possible, we are bombarded with too much information. The average adult American now reads 100 newspapers, thirty-six magazines, and 3,000 forms and notices in one year. This same person listens to 730 hours of radio, watches 2,463 hours of television, and talks on the phone for almost 61 hours.[3] Did you know that more information has been published during the past thirty years than during the previous 5,000?[4] According to William Banach, executive director of the Institute for Future Studies, "Information is doubling every 2 1/2 years — every 900 days! By the time today's kindergartner moves through the grades to graduation, the body of knowledge will quadruple!"[5] Is it any wonder that some people suffer stress from trying to keep abreast of this avalanche of information?

As a college student, you suffer greater information overload than most other people. Not only are you bombarded by the same media aimed at every other citizen, but you also spend much of your time receiving, interpreting, evaluating, and committing to memory information presented in books, articles, handouts, lectures, and discussion. With this extensive experience as receivers of information, why are most students intimidated by the prospect of sending information in informative speeches?

Informative speaking poses three challenges to you as a speaker. First, you must be able to select an appropriate informative topic. You don't want to repeat information that your audience already knows. Yet you may worry that a topic you find personally interesting might seem irrelevant to your listeners. Once you select a topic, you face a second challenge: research. Finally, to determine what supporting material is most suitable for your audience and relevant to your purpose, you must organize your information in the most fitting manner. These three tasks form the essence of informative speaking, the subject of this chapter.

CHARACTERISTICS OF A SPEECH TO INFORM

Dr. Jones, your geology professor, enters the classroom, takes out a folder of notes, puts up the first of a series of slides, and begins to lecture on the differences between active and inactive volcanoes. At the morning staff meeting, Dr. Mendez explains how the hospital would implement its new policy to secure the confidentiality of patient records. Scott, a classmate in your business communication class, spends half the period summarizing his outside reading on factors that shape a company's corporate culture. The lecture, briefing, and oral report these people deliver are three of the forms informative speeches can take. We discuss the oral report in Chapter 17, "Speaking on Special Occasions"; in this chapter we focus on the **speech to inform.**

At the most fundamental level, we seek knowledge for three reasons: We want to *know*, *understand*, and *use* information. The goals of any informative speaker, in turn, are to impart knowledge, enhance understanding, or permit application. Suppose you decided to prepare an informative speech on the general subject of advertising. You could select as your specific purpose to inform the audience about advertising in ancient times. Your listeners probably know little about this topic and you can readily assume that your speech would add to their knowledge. Alternately, you could have this as your specific purpose: to inform my audience on how effective advertising succeeds. Using examples your audience already knows, you could deepen their understanding of advertising strategies and principles. A third specific purpose could be to inform your listeners about how they can prepare effective, low-cost advertisements when they want to promote a charity fundraising project or a garage sale. In this instance you would help the audience apply basic advertising principles.

Speakers inform us, then, when they provide us with new information, when they help us understand better some information we already possess, or when they enable us to apply information. You must make sure, when you prepare an informative speech, that you do not slip into giving a persuasive speech. How can you avoid this problem? After all, a persuasive speech also conveys information. In fact, the best persuasive speeches usually include supporting material that is both expository and compelling.

You must be able to distinguish between informative and persuasive speeches. Some topics, of course, are easy to classify. A speaker urging audience members to sign and carry an organ donor card is clearly trying to persuade; the speaker is attempting to intensify beliefs and either change or reinforce behavior. On the other hand, a speech charting the recent increases in organ transplant procedures is a speech to inform. A speech on the history of computers is informative, while a speech advocating an IBM clone as the best computer buy for the college student is persuasive. A speech describing different forms of alcohol addiction is informative, whereas a speech advocating the Alcoholics Anonymous program to overcome addiction would be persuasive.

Many speakers, both beginning and experienced, at times have trouble distinguishing between informing and persuading. The reason is that speakers sometimes begin preparing a speech with the intention to inform, only to discover that somewhere during the speech construction process their objective has become persuasion. In other instances, speakers deliver what they intended to be an informative speech only to find that their listeners received it as a persuasive message. How can this happen? Let's look at the experience of one speaker, Sarah.

> Sarah designed a speech with the specific purpose of informing the audience of the arguments for and against allowing women to serve in military combat. In her speech, she took care to represent each side's arguments accurately and objectively. After her speech, however, Sarah discovered that some listeners previously undecided on the issue found the pro arguments more persuasive and now supported permitting women to serve in combat roles. But Sarah also learned that others in the audience became more convinced that women should be excluded from such roles. Did Sarah's speech persuade? Apparently for some audience members the answer is yes; they changed their attitudes because of this speech. Yet Sarah's objective was to inform, not to persuade.

speech to inform: a speech to impart knowledge, enhance understanding, or facilitate application of information.

In determining the general purpose of your speech, remember that both speakers and listeners are active participants in the communication process. As we discussed earlier in this text, listeners will interpret what they hear and integrate it into their frames of reference. Your objectivity as a speaker will not stop the listener from hearing with subjectivity. As a speaker, though, you determine the motive for and manner of your presentation. Your goal in your informative speech is not to advocate specific beliefs, attitudes, and behaviors on controversial issues. Your objective is to assist your hearers as they come to know, understand, or apply an idea or issue. As you word the specific purpose of your speech, you should be able to determine whether your general purpose is to persuade or to inform.

TYPES OF INFORMATIVE SPEECHES

Experts identify several ways of classifying informative speeches. We have chosen a topical pattern that we think will work well for you. This approach is based on the types of topics you can choose for your speech. As you read about these topic categories, keep two guidelines in mind. First, approach each category of topics with the broadest possible perspective. Second, recognize that the categories overlap; the boundaries between them are not distinct. Whether you consider the Great Pyramid of Cheops an object or a place, for example, is much less important than the fact that it is a fascinating informative speech topic. The purpose of our categories is to stimulate, not to limit, your topic selection and development. If you can concentrate on these matters, you will avoid the dangers of persuading your audience rather than informing them. As you begin brainstorming, consider information you could provide your listeners regarding people, objects, places, events, processes, concepts, conditions, and issues. In the following sections, we discuss these eight major topic areas for informative speeches and the patterns of organization appropriate for each.

KEY POINTS		
Subject Categories for Informative Speeches	**1.** Speeches about people **2.** Speeches about objects **3.** Speeches about places **4.** Speeches about events	**5.** Speeches about processes **6.** Speeches about concepts **7.** Speeches about conditions **8.** Speeches about issues

Speeches About People

Activities and accomplishments of other people fascinate us. We gravitate toward books, magazine articles, television programs, films, and even supermarket tabloids that reveal the lives of celebrities. We are interested in the lives of the rich and the famous. We are also interested in the lives of the poor and the not-so-famous. People, then, are an abundant resource of topics for your informative speech. Choosing to inform about a person lets you be as historical or as contemporary as you wish. A speech about a person allows you the opportunity to expand your knowledge in a field that interests you while sharing those interests with your listeners. If you are majoring in computer and information sciences, you could speak on Steve Jobs or Steve Wozniak, founders of Apple Computer, as contemporary leaders, or Thomas J. Watson, founder of IBM, as a historical figure. If you are studying art, speeches on Claude Monet or Mary Cassatt are just two of hundreds of options available to you. If you are an avid photographer, an informative speech assignment gives you the opportunity to discover and communicate something about the life and accomplishments of Ansel Adams, Diane Arbus, Alfred Stieglitz, or Annie Leibovitz, for instance.

Of course, you don't need to confine your topic to individuals associated with your major or areas of interest. You could interest and inform audiences by discussing the lives and contributions of people such as:

Cesar Chavez	Sally Hemings	Jackie Robinson
e.e. cummings	Jimi Hendrix	Eleanor Roosevelt
Clarence Darrow	Alfred Kinsey	Andy Warhol
Walt Disney	Gary Larson	Eudora Welty
D.W. Griffith	Margaret Mead	Frank Lloyd Wright

Perhaps your class meets in a building bearing the name of a person with whom you are not familiar. A speech telling your class about this person could be enlightening and memorable. Our student Margaret began her first informative speech of the semester as follows:

> If you're like me, the first semester you registered here on campus and got a printout of your course schedule, you had to ask someone what LH stands for. Or you looked it up on a campus map: Laughton Hall. We've been meeting here in LH203 for three weeks, and some of us have had other classes in this building before. But did you ever wonder who this Laughton person is — or was? Well, John H. Laughton not only bequeathed the money to build this classroom building when he died, but was also a graduate of the school, the founder of Laughton Electronics, and a former mayor of the city.

You may choose to discuss not one person but a group of people, such as the Marx Brothers, FDR's brain trust, the Four Horsemen of Notre Dame, or the rock group Aerosmith. You could even compare and contrast two or more individuals to highlight their philosophies and contributions. The following pairs of noted figures could generate lively exposition:

Rachel Carson and Ralph Nader
Hillary Rodham Clinton and Barbara Bush
The Dalai Lama and Pope John Paul II
J. Edgar Hoover and Elliott Ness
Mao Tse-tung and Joseph Stalin
Thurgood Marshall and Clarence Thomas
Edward R. Murrow and Joseph McCarthy
Malcolm X and Martin Luther King, Jr.

In considering an informative speech about a person, you must decide not only what is important but also what the audience will remember. Too often, students organize speeches about people so that the speeches resemble biographical listings in an encyclopedia. The speech amounts to a seemingly limitless compendium of dates. This is a mistake. Even the most attentive listener will remember few of the details in such a speech.

If you selected the life of Thomas Jefferson as your speech topic, for example, you would need to narrow and focus that subject. Listeners would probably not remember that Jefferson was born on April 13, 1743, according to the modern calendar and April 2 according to the old calendar; that he entered the College of William and Mary in 1760; that he was admitted to the Virginia bar in 1767; and that he married Martha Wayles Skelton on January 1, 1772. On the other hand, an audience probably would remember that Jefferson died on the fiftieth anniversary of the Declaration of Independence, July 4, 1826.

Speeches about people are often organized either chronologically or topically. One chronological pattern for a speech about Jefferson could be:

I. Jefferson's Early Life
II. Jefferson's Middle Years
III. Jefferson's Last Years

You could organize your speech topically based on the epitaph Jefferson wrote for his tombstone:

I. Author of the Declaration of Independence
II. Author of the Statute of Virginia for Religious Freedom
III. Father of the University of Virginia

If you wanted to focus on the three major roles Jefferson assumed in different stages of his life, you could develop your speech topically and chronologically, as in the following example:

I. Jefferson as Revolutionary
II. Jefferson as President
III. Jefferson as Elder Statesman

Speeches About Objects

A second resource of informative topics is objects. Speeches about objects focus on what is concrete rather than on what is abstract. Again, consider objects from the broadest perspective possible so that you can generate a maximum number of topic ideas. Topics for this type of speech could include the following:

the Acropolis	Fabergé eggs
coffee	the Great Pyramid of Cheops
crocodiles	the Great Wall of China
electric cars	smart roads
endangered species	volcanoes

Speeches about objects can use any of several organizational patterns. A speech on the Cathedral of Notre Dame or the Statue of Liberty could be organized spatially. A speech tracing the development of cyclones and anticyclones evolves chronologically. A speech on condors discussing (1) the Andean condor and (2) the California condor is organized topically. A speaker discussing the origins, types, and uses of pasta also uses a topical divi-

Speeches about processes explain how something works, functions, or is accomplished.
(SOURCE: © Jim Pickerell)

sion. If the speech focused only on the history of pasta, however, it may best be structured chronologically.

Speeches About Places

One of the favorite pastimes for many of us is the summer vacation. Families pack their suitcases and, maps in hand, take to the road in search of historical, cultural, and recreational sites. Returning with souvenirs, pictures, postcards, and informational literature, we are able to relive our vacation.

Places are an easily tapped resource for informative speech topics. These speeches introduce listeners to new locales or expand their knowledge of familiar places. Topics may include real places, such as historic sites, emerging nations, national parks, famous prisons, and planets. Topics may also include fictitious places, such as the islands of Scylla and Charybdis, the Island of the Lord of the Flies, and the Sea of Frozen Words. Speeches about places challenge speakers to select words that create vivid images.

To organize your speech about places you would typically use one of three organizational patterns: spatial, chronological, or topical. A speech about the Nile, the world's longest river, is organized spatially if it discusses the upper, middle, and lower Nile. A presentation about your college could trace its development chronologically. A speech on Poplar Forest, Thomas Jefferson's getaway home, could use a topical pattern discussing Jefferson's architectural style.

Suppose you selected as your informative speech topic Ellis Island, the site of the chief U.S. immigration center from 1892 to 1954. You could choose any of the following patterns of development.

> ***Pattern:*** Spatial
> ***Specific Purpose:*** To inform the audience about Ellis Island's Main Building.
> ***Key Ideas:***   **I.** The Registry Room
>   **II.** The Baggage Room
>   **III.** The Oral History Studio

Pattern: Chronological
Specific Purpose: To inform the audience of the history of Ellis Island.
Key Ideas: **I.** Years of Immigration, 1892-1954
               II. Years of Dormancy, 1954-84
               III. Years of Remembrance, 1984-present

Pattern: Topical
Specific Purpose: To inform the audience of the history of Ellis Island.
Key Ideas: **I.** The Process of Immigration
               II. The Place of Immigration
               III. The People Who Immigrated

Notice that each of these outlines is organized according to a distinct pattern. The key ideas in the first outline are organized spatially. Although the specific purposes of the second and third speeches are identical, the former is organized chronologically and the latter topically.

If you choose to speak about a place, be aware of a couple of common pitfalls. First, avoid making your speech sound like a travelogue. The speaking occasion is not an opportunity to show a captive audience slides you took during your last vacation ("And here are my cousins Lois and Louie. If you look closely, you can see part of Berkeley Plantation, the site of the first Thanksgiving and the birthplace of William Henry Harrison and Benjamin Harrison."). Your speech should identify and develop ideas that contribute to the general education of your listeners.

A second pitfall to avoid is inappropriate visuals. We have too often seen speakers illustrate their ideas visually by holding up postcards or books and magazines containing pictures of places. This strategy is a mistake. These pictures are too small to be seen. As we advised in the previous chapter, use visual aids that are large enough to be viewed by all audience members. On other occasions, students speaking about places have distributed photographs or postcards to be passed among audience members during the speech. Although listeners could see the visual aids clearly as they held them, they often became preoccupied with the pictures and missed much of what the speaker was saying at the time. Remember, your visual aids should not distract your audience from the main attraction: you, speaking to inform.

Speeches About Events

Events are important or interesting occurrences. Speeches about events focus on these occurrences, personal or historical, and seek to convey knowledge so that an audience can better understand them. Examples of topics for this type of speech include:

the Chautauqua movement	the sinking of the *Titanic*
D-Day	the *War of the Worlds* broadcast
the explosion of the zeppelin *Hindenburg*	the Woodstock festivals
the Scottsboro case	

For a speech assignment that does not require you to conduct research, you could speak about an event in your life you consider important, funny, or instructive. Exam-

Broadcast journalists speak to inform when they report news to the public.
(SOURCE: © Steve Fenn, 1993, Capital Cities/ ABC, Inc.

ples of such topics could include "the day I registered for my first semester in college," "the day my first child was born," or "my most embarrassing moment."

Speeches about events typically use a chronological or topical pattern. For example, if your topic is the daring Great Train Robbery that took place in Britain in 1963, you could organize your speech chronologically, describing what happened before, during, and after those famous fifteen minutes. If your specific purpose is to inform the audience about aerial sports, you could use a topical pattern and discuss (1) gliding, (2) ballooning, and (3) skydiving.

A speaker wanting to inform the audience about the Scopes "Monkey" Trial could use any of the following developmental patterns:

Pattern: Topical
Specific Purpose: To inform the audience of the theological dispute of the trial.
Key Ideas: **I.** The literal interpretation of the Scriptures
              II. The figurative interpretation of the Scriptures

Pattern: Topical
Specific Purpose: To inform the audience of the key players of the drama.
Key Ideas: **I.** John T. Scopes, the defendant
              II. Clarence Darrow, the defense attorney
             III. William Jennings Bryan, the prosecutor

Pattern: Chronological
Specific Purpose: To inform the audience of the background and outcome of the controversy.
Key Ideas: **I.** The law
              II. The challenge
             III. The verdict

The first two speeches are organized topically; the third is structured chronologically. Notice how each organizational strategy neatly matches the specific purpose of the speech.

Speeches About Processes

A process is a series of steps producing an outcome. Your informative speech about a process could explain how something works, functions, or is accomplished. Our students have given informative speeches on such how-to topics as how to read a food packaging label, detect plagiarism, write an effective term paper, administer first aid for burns, suit up and enter a "clean room," and tie-dye T-shirts. Informative topics, such as how batik materials are made, how Doppler radar works, and how to make children "waterproof" (a speech on the process of teaching water safety) are all process speeches. Speeches on critical path analysis, the Nielsen ratings, nuclear medicine, and cryptography (encoding and decoding messages in a code known only to those who understand) are also potentially good informative topics about processes.

Because a process is by definition a time-ordered sequence, speeches about processes commonly use chronological organization. They are not, however, confined to this pattern. As we have argued earlier, the best organization is the one that achieves the purpose of the speech. A student presenting a speech on colorization of black-and-white movies might choose a chronological pattern if the specific purpose is to explain how the process works. A pro-con division detailing the arguments for and against colorization would also be informative if the speaker discussed both sides in an unbiased manner.

Suppose you select cartooning as a topic area for a speech to inform. You would choose the organizational pattern best suited to your specific purpose. Let's look at some examples illustrating how you can narrow your topic on cartooning and what organizational patterns fit each topic.

> *Pattern:* Topical
> *Specific Purpose:* To inform my audience on cartooning.
> *Key Ideas:* **I.** Definition of cartoons
> **II.** Purposes of cartoons
> **III.** Types of cartoons

> *Pattern:* Chronological
> *Specific Purpose:* To inform my audience on the process of creating a comic strip.
> *Key Ideas:* **I.** Designing a comic strip
> **II.** Drawing a comic strip
> **III.** Producing a comic strip

> *Pattern:* Spatial
> *Specific Purpose:* To inform my audience on how to draw a cartoon character.
> *Key Ideas:* **I.** Drawing the head
> **II.** Drawing the upper body
> **III.** Drawing the lower body

Notice that each of the speeches outlined above is progressively narrowed. Each organizational pattern is also suitable for the specific purpose, whether the pattern is topical, chronological, or spatial.

Speeches about concepts, or ideas, focus on what is abstract rather than on what is concrete. Whereas a speech about an object such as the Statue of Liberty may focus on the history or physical attributes of the statue itself, a speech about an idea may focus on the concept of liberty. Other topics suitable for informative speeches about concepts include eco-tourism, concrete poetry, nihilism, traumatic obsessions, the Doppler effect, nirvana, and religious dualism.

Speeches about concepts challenge you to make specific something that is abstract. These speeches typically rely on definitions and examples to support their explanations. Appropriate organizational patterns vary. A speech on Norse mythology could use a topical division of materials and focus on key figures.

Drew, a student of ours, entertained all his listeners with a speech on onomastics, or the study of names. Notice how his introduction personalizes his speech and quickly involves his listeners. You can also see from his preview statement that he, too, used a topical organization for this speech about a concept:

> These are some actual names reported by John Train in his books *Remarkable Names of Real People* and *Even More Remarkable Names.* Let me repeat: These are actual names found in bureaus of vital statistics, public health services, newspaper articles, and hospital, church, and school records: E. Pluribus Eubanks, Loch Ness Hontas, Golden Pancake, Halloween Buggage, Odious Champagne, and Memory Leake.
>
> Train says in *Even More Remarkable Names* that "what one might call the free-form nutty name — Oldmouse Waltz, Cashmere Tango Obedience, Eucalyptus Yoho — is the one indigenous American art form."
>
> We're lucky. No one in here has a name as colorful as any of those. But we all have at least two names — a personal and a family name. Today, I'll tell you, first, why personal names developed, and second, the legal status of names. Finally, I have something to tell each of you about the origin of your names.

Speeches about theories, particularly if they are controversial, sometimes use a pro-con division. A discussion of the merits and shortcomings of Felice Schwartz's "mommy track" theory of career advancement reflects a pro-con development.

Speeches About Conditions

Conditions are particular situations: living conditions in a third-world country; or social and political climates that give rise to movements such as witchcraft hysteria in Salem, Civil War in the United States, McCarthyism, the Women's Movement, labor movements, the Civil Rights Movement, and national independence movements.

The word *condition* can also refer to a state of fitness or health. Speeches about conditions can focus on a person's health and, indeed, medical topics are a popular source of student speeches. A speaker could choose as a specific purpose "to inform the audience about the symptoms, causes, and treatment of myasthenia gravis." Topical organization such as this is appropriate for many speeches about specific diseases or other health conditions. Another excellent topic for a speech to inform is *affluenza,* a word coined to denote chronic psychological disorders afflicting the wealthy. States of health also characterize the economy, individual communities, and specific institutions. Recession, depression, and full employment are terms economists use to describe the health of the economy. Speakers inform their listeners about conditions when they describe the state of the arts in their communities, assess the financial situation of most college students, or illustrate how catch limits have affected the whale population, for example.

Speeches About Issues

Speeches about issues deal with controversial ideas and policies. For example, some people today are investing in "viatical companies" that make large cash payments to people having terminal illnesses. The patients, many of them too ill to work, can thus keep their homes and afford medical care. In return, each cash recipient must name the company involved as sole beneficiary of his or her life insurance policies. People who invest in such viatical companies can receive returns of up to 25 percent each year.[6] Financial profit from the deaths of others is certainly a controversial issue and would make an interesting speech topic.

Other topics appropriate for informative speeches on issues include the use of polygraphs as a condition for employment; uniform sentencing of criminals; freedom of expression vs. freedom from pornography; regulation of big trucks on roads; and systematic instruction vs. child-oriented activities in preschools. Any issue being debated in your school, community, state, or nation can be a fruitful topic for your informative speech.

You may be thinking that controversial issues are better topics for persuasive speeches, but they can also be appropriate for speeches to inform. Just remember that an informative speech on a controversial topic must be researched and developed so that you present the issue objectively.

Two common organizational patterns for speeches about issues are the topical and pro-con divisions. If you use a topical pattern of organization for your speech about issues, it will be easier for you to maintain your objectivity. If you choose the pro-con pattern, you may run the risk of moving toward a persuasive speech. A pro-con strategy — presenting both sides of an issue — lets the listener decide which is stronger. If your informative speech on an issue is organized pro-con, guard against two pitfalls: lack of objectivity and lack of perspective.

Speakers predisposed toward one side of an issue sometimes have difficulty presenting both sides objectively.

> Carl presented a speech on the increasingly popular practice of adopting uniforms for public schools. He presented four good reasons for the practice: (1) uniforms are more economical for parents, (2) uniforms reduce student bickering and fighting over designer clothes, (3) uniforms increase student attentiveness in the classroom, and (4) uniforms identify various schools and promote school spirit. Carl's only argument against public school uniforms was that they limit students' freedom of expression. His speech was obviously out of balance. Though the assignment was an informative speech, Carl's pro-con approach was ultimately persuasive.

If, like Carl, you feel strongly committed to one side of an issue, save that topic for a persuasive speech.

A second pitfall that sometimes surfaces in the pro-con approach is lack of perspective.

Sometimes a speaker will characterize an issue as two-sided when, in reality, it is many-sided. For example, one of our students spoke on the issue of child care. He mentioned the state family leave laws that permit mothers of newborn infants to take paid leaves of absence from work and fathers to take unpaid leaves while their jobs are protected. The speaker characterized advocates of such bills as pro-family and opponents as pro-business. He failed to consider that some people oppose such laws because they feel the laws don't go far enough; many state laws exempt small companies with fewer than fifty employees. If you fail to recognize and acknowledge the many facets of an issue in this way, you lose perspective and polarize your topic.

In the preceding sections, we have discussed eight types of informative speeches. As you begin working on your own informative speech, remember to select a topic that will benefit your listeners and then communicate your information clearly and memorably. Use these eight subject categories to narrow and focus your topic. As you go through each category, use the self-, audience-, occasion-, and research-generated strategies we discussed in Chapter 6 on pages 108-116 to help you come up with many topics to consider for your informative speech.

As you review this list you will, no doubt, find several persuasive topics. Before excluding them, see if there are related topics suitable for an informative speech. For example, you may have some strong feelings about intercollegiate athletic programs and their role in colleges and universities. To argue their merits or to suggest that they be scaled back would make your speech persuasive rather than informative. However, you could change your focus to a more informative topic related to the issue of intercollegiate athletics. You could inform the audience of the history and intent of Proposition 48, the National Collegiate Athletic Association's statement of academic entrance requirements for college athletes. You could explain the reasons behind the breakup of the Southwest Conference, or trace the history of the athletic conference to which your school belongs.

As you go about selecting your topic, keep in mind this question: "How will the audience benefit from my topic?" Remember, your informative speech must bring new information or enhance the understanding of your audience. A speech detailing what employers look for in an employment résumé, for example, is clearly relevant to a class of students ready to enter the job market.

But, what about topics such as the golden age of vaudeville, the origins of superstitions, the history of aviation, the effect of music on livestock production, or the psychological aspects of aging? Maybe you think that these topics are not relevant to your audience. But part of the process of becoming an educated individual is learning more about the world around you. We are committed to this perspective and believe it is one you should encourage in your listeners. For example, in his speech on kites and competitive kite flying, our student Ken informed us about the use of kites in ancient religious worship. After a bountiful harvest, early tribes would tie a handful of the first wheat harvested to the tail of a kite and literally offer it up to the gods in thanks. After this historical background, Ken traced the evolution of kite designs. He showed examples of the large, colorful, aerodynamic kites he takes to the coast to fly on weekends. Speeches on such subjects that are interesting and fun to know always contribute to anyone's general education.

Once you have selected a topic that meets criteria discussed in Chapter 6, ask yourself the following three questions: (1) What does the audience already know about my topic? (2) What does the audience need to know to understand the topic? (3) Can I present this information in a way that is easy for the audience to understand and remember in the time allotted? If you are satisfied with your answers to these questions, your

Speeches about	Use	If your purpose is to
People	Topical organization	Explain various aspects of the person's life
People	Chronological organization	Survey events in the person's life
Objects	Topical organization	Explain various uses for the object
Objects	Chronological organization	Explain how the object was created or made
Objects	Spatial organization	Describe various parts of the object
Places	Topical organization	Emphasize various aspects of the place
Places	Chronological organization	Chart the history of or developments in the place
Places	Spatial organization	Describe the elements or parts of the place
Events	Topical organization	Explain the significance of the events
Events	Chronological organization	Explain a sequence of actions or events
Events	Causal organization	Explain how one event produced or resulted from another
Processes	Topical organization	Explain aspects of the process
Processes	Chronological organization	Explain how something is done
Processes	Pro-Con organization	Explore the arguments for or against the procedure
Processes	Causal organization	Discuss the causes and effects of the process
Concepts	Topical organization	Discuss aspects, definitions, or applications of the concept
Conditions	Topical organization	Explain aspects of the condition
Conditions	Chronological organization	Trace the stages or phases of the condition
Conditions	Causal organization	Show the causes and effects of the condition
Issues	Topical organization	Discuss aspects of the issue's significance
Issues	Chronological organization	Show how the issue evolved over time
Issues	Pro-Con organization	Present opposing viewpoints on the issue

Figure 14.1 *Organizing informative speeches*

next step is to begin developing the most effective strategy for conveying that information. Use Figure 14.1 as you select an appropriate organizational pattern.

■ GUIDELINES FOR SPEAKING TO INFORM

In the remainder of this chapter, we suggest ten guidelines for the informative speech. Use them as a checklist during your speech preparation and you will deliver a better informative speech than you would have otherwise.

Stress Your Informative Purpose.   The primary objective of your informative speech is to inform. It is important for you to be clear about this, especially if your topic is controversial or related to other topics that are controversial. For example, if you are discussing U.S. immigration policy, political correctness, or the role of women in religion, you must realize that some in your audience may already have some pretty strong feelings about your topic. Stress that your goal is to give additional information, not to try to change anyone's beliefs.

Be Specific.   At times we have had students tell us they will deliver a brief informative speech on "sports." This topic is far too broad and reflects little or no planning. Many of us know a little about a lot of subjects. An informative speech gives you the perfect opportunity to fill in the gaps by telling your audience a lot about a little. Narrow your topic. To help you do that, we have suggested in this chapter that you focus on specific people, objects, places, events, processes, concepts, conditions, and issues. Your "sports" topic could be narrowed to sports commentators; the history of astroturf; Forest Hills, former home of the U.S. Open Tennis Championships; competitive team sports and male bonding; and so on. The more specific you are about your topic, your purpose, and the materials you use to support your speech, the more time you will save during your research. Your specific focus will also make your speech easier for the audience to remember.

Be Clear.   If you choose your topic carefully and explain it thoroughly, your message should be clear. Do not choose a topic that is too complex. If your speech topic is Boolean polynomials or the biochemistry of bovine growth hormone, you run the risk of being too technical for most audiences. You would never be able to give your audience the background knowledge necessary to understand your presentation in the limited time you have. At the same time, be careful about using jargon. Impressing the audience with your vocabulary is counterproductive if they cannot understand your message. The purpose of informative speaking is not to impress the audience with complex data but to communicate information clearly.

Be Accurate.   Information that is inaccurate does not inform; it misinforms and has two negative consequences. First, inaccuracies can hurt your credibility as a speaker. If listeners recognize misstatements, they may begin to question the speaker's credibility: "If the speaker's wrong about that, could there be other inaccuracies in the speech?" Accurate statements help you develop a positive image or protect one you have established earlier.

Second, inaccurate information can do potential harm to listeners. Such harm can be mental or physical. For example, you give an informative speech on the life-threatening reactions some people have to sulfites, a common ingredient in certain food preservatives. Your audience leaves the class worried about their health and the damage they may have suffered. You neglected to mention that these reactions are rare. Your misinformation has harmed your audience. In another example, you give a speech on how to apply and check a tourniquet, but discuss outdated methods. If people in your audience later try your method, they could do serious physical damage. As you can see, if audience members are unaware of factual errors, they may form beliefs that are not valid or make decisions that are not wise.

Not only should your information be accurate, but you must accurately cite any sources you have used to develop your speech. Some speakers assume that because they do not take a controversial stand in an informative speech, they need not cite sources. An informative topic may require fewer sources than you would use to establish your side of a debatable point. Demonstrating the truth of your ideas and information is nevertheless important. Also, as we mentioned in Chapter 2, you must cite the sources for any quotations you use.

Limit Your Ideas and Supporting Materials.   Perhaps the most common mistake speakers make in developing the content of their speeches is including too much information. Do not make the mistake of thinking that the more information you put into a speech, the more informative it is. As we have mentioned previously, listeners cannot process all, or even most, of what you present. If you overload your audience with too much information, they will stop listening. Remember the adage that less is more. To spend more time explaining and developing a few ideas will probably result in greater retention of these ideas by your listeners than the "speed and spread" approach.

Be Relevant.   As you research your topic, you will no doubt discover information that is interesting but not central to your thesis. Because it is so interesting, you may be tempted to include it. Don't. If it is not relevant, leave it out.

> One student, Larry, delivered an intriguing informative speech on the Jains, a tribe of monks in India whose daily life is shaped by reverence for all living things. As you might guess, the Jains are vegetarians. But they don't eat vegetables that develop underground because harvesting them may kill insects in the soil. Larry had done a good deal of research on this fascinating topic, including his own travels in India. His firsthand knowledge was both a blessing and a curse. Listening to a speaker who had visited the Jains' monasteries certainly made the topic immediate and compelling. But because he knew so much about the country, Larry included a lot of information about India that was interesting but irrelevant to his main point. His speech became much too long.

To avoid this problem and to keep yourself on track, write out your central thesis and refer to it periodically. When you digress from your topic, you waste valuable preparation time, distort the focus of your speech, and confuse your audience.

Be Objective.   One of the most important criteria for an informative speech is objectivity. If you take a stand, you become a persuader. Informative speakers are committed to presenting a balanced view. People representing political parties, charitable organizations, business associations, and special interest groups are understandably committed to the objectives and policies of their groups. Your research should take into account all perspectives. If, as you develop and practice your speech, you find yourself becoming a proponent of a particular viewpoint, you may need to step back and assess whether your orientation has shifted from information to persuasion. If you do not think you can make your speech objective, save the topic for a persuasive speech.

In Chapter 11, "Wording Your Speech," we discussed the use of language. Nothing betrays the image of objectivity that is essential in an informative speech as quickly as the inappropriate use of language. For example, in an informative speech on the pros and cons of juvenile curfew laws, one of our students used language that telegraphed his personal opinion on the issue. Even when explaining the arguments for such laws, he described them as "silly," "costly," and "unenforceable." In an informative speech, your language should be descriptive rather than evaluative or judgmental.

Use Appropriate Organization.   As we stated earlier, there is no one best organizational pattern for informative speeches. You choose the pattern that is most appropriate to your topic and specific purpose. However, some patterns are inappropriate for an informative speech. While a pro-con approach is appropriate, a pro-con-assessment strategy moves the speech into persuasion. Problem-solution, need-plan, and motivated sequence patterns, to be discussed in Chapter 16, are also traditionally used for persuasive, not informative, speeches. Again, Figure 14.1 offers suggestions for selecting an appropriate organizational pattern. If you have any doubt that your organization is informative rather than persuasive, check with your instructor.

Use Appropriate Forms of Support.   As with persuasive speeches, speeches to inform require appropriate supporting materials such as those we discussed in Chapter 8. These materials should come from sources that are authoritative and free from bias. If you discuss a controversial issue, you must represent each side fairly. For example, if your specific purpose is to inform your audience on the effects of bilingual education, you must research and present information from both its proponents and its critics.

Use Effective Delivery.   Some speakers have a misconception that delivery is more important for a persuasive speech than for an informative speech. Regardless of the type of speech, show your involvement in your speech through your physical and vocal delivery. The suggestions we offered in Chapter 12, "Delivering Your Speech," are appropriate for the speaker who informs as well as the speaker who persuades. Your voice and body should reinforce your interest in and enthusiasm for your topic. Your delivery should also reinforce your objectivity. If you find your gestures, body tension, or voice conveying an emotional urgency, you have likely slipped into persuasion.

		KEY POINTS
1. Stress your informative purpose.	**6.** Be relevant.	**Guidelines for Informative Speaking**
2. Be specific.	**7.** Be objective.	
3. Be clear.	**8.** Use appropriate organization.	
4. Be accurate.	**9.** Use appropriate forms of support.	
5. Limit your ideas and supporting materials.	**10.** Use effective delivery.	

We hope that after reading this chapter you know the principles and characteristics of informative speaking, that you understand how they contribute to effective speaking, and that you will be able to apply them as you prepare your speeches. If you have that information and can use it, the chapter has been informative and you have been a careful reader.

SUMMARY

As part of your work in this class, you will present at least one *speech to inform*. An infor-

mative speech assignment provides you with the opportunity to be the sender rather than the receiver of information; it requires you to research a subject of your choice, synthesize data from various sources, and pass it on to your listeners. Your goals as an informative speaker are to expand listeners' knowledge, assist their understanding, or help them apply the information you communicate.

Classifying informative speeches by subject gives you an idea of the range of possible topics and the patterns of organization each subject typically uses. Speeches about *people* are often arranged chronologically, but may explore subtopics, such as aspects of the subject's life. Speeches about *objects* use spatial organization if your purpose is to describe various parts of the object, chronological organization if your purpose is to explain how the object was created, and topical organization if your purpose is to explain how the object is used. Speeches about *places* use chronological organization if your purpose is to explain the history or stages of development of the place, topical organization if you want to emphasize various aspects of the place, and spatial organization if your purpose is to describe the parts of the place. Speeches about *events* also use any of the following three methods of organization: Chronological organization to explain a sequence of events, topical organization to explain the significance of events, and causal organization to show how one event produced or led to another.

Speeches about *processes* can use chronological organization to tell listeners how to do something or how something is done, pro-con organization to explore the arguments for and against the process, or causal organization to discuss what caused or causes some process and the effects that result. Speeches about *concepts* typically use topical organization as the speaker discusses various aspects, definitions, or applications of the concept.

Speeches about *conditions* may use top-ical organization to discuss various aspects of the condition, chronological organization to trace the stages or phases of a condition, or causal organization to show the causes of the condition and the effects that the condition has. Finally, speeches about controversial *issues* may use a pro-con organization if your purpose is to explore opposing viewpoints on the issue, topical organization if your purpose is to discuss the significance of the issue, or chronological organization if your purpose is to discuss how the issue has evolved.

As you begin to prepare an informative speech on a subject from one of these categories, ask yourself three questions: (1) How much does the audience already know about this topic? (2) What does the audience need to know in order to understand this topic? (3) Can I present this information in the allotted time so that the audience will understand and remember it? When you answer these questions, you can be sure that your topic is sufficiently narrow and appropriate to your listeners.

Finally, we offer ten guidelines to help you develop and deliver an effective informative speech. (1) Begin with an overall picture; let your audience know that your purpose is to inform. (2) Be specific; narrow the topic you have chosen. (3) Be clear; remember that your audience probably knows much less about this topic than you do. (4) Be accurate; misinformation can harm your listeners. (5) Limit the ideas and supporting material that you try to include. Covering a few ideas in depth is usually more informative than discussing many ideas superficially. (6) Be relevant; do not be sidetracked by interesting but irrelevant information. (7) Be objective in your approach to the topic and the language you use. (8) Use the pattern of organization best suited to achieving your specific purpose. (9) Use appropriate forms of support. (10) Use lively, effective speech delivery.

EXERCISES

1. Using techniques of brainstorming and research, generate a list of two informative speech topics for each of the following categories: people, objects, places, events, processes, concepts, conditions, and issues. Place an asterisk (*) by the five topics you think are most appropriate for a speech in this class.

2. Using the list you generated in Exercise 1, select one topic from each of four categories and write a specific purpose statement for each. Think about how you could develop each specific purpose and then discuss what organizational pattern you think would be most appropriate.

3. Select an informative speech from *Vital Speeches of the Day* or some other published source. Analyze the speech to see if it adheres to the guidelines discussed in this chapter. If it does, show specifically how it fulfills the goals of each of these guidelines. If it does not, list the guidelines violated and give examples of where this occurs in the speech. Suggest how the speaker could revise the speech to meet the guidelines.

4. Using the speech you selected in Exercise 3, identify and write down the specific purpose of the speech. Does it meet the characteristics of a speech to inform? Why or why not? What method of organization is used in the speech? Do you think this is the best pattern to achieve the speech's specific purpose? Why or why not?

5. Analyze a lecture by one of your instructors to see if it adheres to the guidelines listed in this chapter. Which guidelines for informative speeches do you think also apply to class lectures? Which do not apply? If the instructor violated any guidelines you think apply to lecturing, how might the instructor remedy this?

NOTES

1. Diane Ravitch and Chester E. Finn, Jr. *What Do Our 17-Year-Olds Know? A Report on the First National Assessment of History and Literature.* (New York: Harper, 1987).

2. David A. Kaplan, "Dumber Than We Thought," *Newsweek* 20 Sept. 1993: 44.

3. Richard Saul Wurman, *Information Anxiety* (New York: Doubleday, 1989), cited in Stacey Okun, "Info Overload" *Self* October 1989: 164.

4. Bob Richmond, "Time Not on Side of Information Age" *San Antonio Light* 7 July 1990: B1.

5. William J. Banach, "Are You Too Busy to Think?" *Vital Speeches of the Day* 15 March 1991: 351.

6. Mark Miller, "Taking on 'Death Futures,'" *Newsweek* 21 March 1994: 54.

The humblest individual exerts some influence, either for good or evil, upon others.
~Henry Ward Beecher

The Strategy of Persuasion

Chapter *15*

*M*edia specialist Tony Schwartz, producer of political commercials for presidential and other political candidates, combined the words *manipulation* and *participation* to create a new word — *partipulation*. He argues that voters are not simply manipulated by campaign and advertising strategists. Voters do, after all, have the option of rejecting the messages politicians present them. So Schwartz contends, "You have to participate in your own manipulation."[1]

Persuasion is similar to Schwartz's concept of partipulation. The persuasive speaker tries to move the audience to his or her side of an issue. But, as we discussed in Chapter 2, you, the critical listener, have a right and an ethical responsibility to choose whether you are persuaded. Speakers should view listeners as active participants in the communication process. As a speaker, your goal should be to establish a common perspective and tap values your listeners share, not to manipulate, cajole, or trick your audience. Charles Larson echoes this speaker-listener orientation:

> The focus of persuasion is not on the source, the message, or the receiver. It is on *all* of them equally. They all *cooperate* to make a persuasive process. The idea of **co-creation** means that what is inside the receiver is just as important as the source's intent or the content of the message. In one sense, *all* persuasion is **self-persuasion** — we are rarely persuaded unless we *participate* in the process.[2]

In this chapter and in Chapter 16, we examine the three elements Larson describes — source, message, and receiver — that interact to co-create persuasion. Persuasion and persuasive speaking are complex activities, so we have divided our discussion into two separate chapters. In this chapter we introduce you first to the *strategy* of persuasion. Why is persuasive speaking important? How does the persuasive process work? What are some principles and strategies you can use as you prepare your message? The answers to these questions provide a blueprint for your speech. In the next chapter, we introduce you to the *structure* of persuasion. You will use your blueprint as you build your persuasive speech. You will study how to organize and test the arguments of your speech. You will then discover how to integrate those arguments into a clear and convincing message.

▬▬ THE IMPORTANCE OF PERSUASION

It is impossible to isolate yourself from persuasive messages, either as a receiver or as a sender. Each day, we are bombarded by appeals from political, business, education, and religious leaders, among others, who try to enlist our support, sell us products or services, and change our behaviors. Persuasive speaking is both inescapable and consequential. While we can all cite examples of messages that are intentionally misleading and patently unethical, we can also list persuasive messages that benefit us as senders and receivers.

In this public speaking course, you will probably be asked to deliver a persuasive mes-

*Highly visible public figures bring to speaking situations strong initial credibility, which may be favorable,
neutral, or unfavorable.*
(SOURCE: © Earl Dotter/Impact Visuals

sage to your classmates, and that will challenge and benefit you in several ways. First, it
will require you to select an issue you think is important and to communicate your concern to your audience. Voicing your beliefs will demand that you confront their logic and
support; in other words, you must test your ideas for their validity. That process, in turn,
will require that you gather supporting materials and draw valid inferences from them
as you develop your arguments. Approached seriously and researched energetically, a persuasive speech assignment can develop both your critical thinking and speech-making
skills. Finally, you may also use it as an opportunity to improve your school or community. Change can occur when people speak and audiences are moved. You can be an instrument of constructive social and political change.

As a listener, you also benefit by participating in the persuasive process. A speaker
can make you aware of problems around you and show how you can help solve them.
You hear other points of view and, consequently, may better understand why others have
beliefs different from yours. A speech that challenges your beliefs often forces you to reeval-
uate your position. Your "partipulation" can correct erroneous beliefs or confirm valid
beliefs you hold. Regardless, participating as a listener also heightens your critical thinking and improves your ability to explain and defend your beliefs. Finally, as a listener you
have an opportunity to judge how others use persuasive speaking techniques, thus
enabling you to improve your own persuasive speaking.

▰ A DEFINITION OF PERSUASION

persuasion: the process of influencing another person's values, beliefs, attitudes, or behaviors.

Persuasion is the *process by which a communicator influences the values, beliefs, attitudes, or behaviors of another*. Key to understanding persuasion is the concept of influence. Too often, we equate persuasion with power, but as you will learn, persuasion does not necessarily mean power. Power implies authority or control over another. For example, employers wanting you to be on time will state that policy and then issue reprimands, withhold promotions, and even terminate your employment to ensure that you obey the policy. They do not need to persuade you. Likewise, in this class, you probably speak on the days assigned because failing to do so would hurt your grade. In each of these instances, your behavior is shaped, at least in part, by the power residing in the other person's position.

Persuasion, however, is more accurately equated with influence than with power. As a speaker you try to influence the audience to adopt your position. You probably have little power over your listeners, and they have the freedom to reject your intended message. Suppose, for example, that your speech instructor wants your class to attend a lecture given on campus by author Tom Wolfe. You are not required to attend, and there is no penalty or reward. To influence you, however, your instructor emphasizes the importance of this opportunity by telling you about Wolfe's background. To make certain that you know who Wolfe is, your instructor lists some of Wolfe's best-known books: *The Bonfire of the Vanities, The Right Stuff,* and *The Kandy-Kolored Tangerine-Flake Streamline Baby.* Your instructor outlines the relevance of Wolfe's topic to work you are doing in English, journalism, or sociology classes, and also mentions Wolfe's reputation as a lively, entertaining speaker, quoting some of Wolfe's controversial views of modern novels.

In each of these cases, your instructor is using influence rather than power to persuade. The concept of persuasion as influence means that you can bring about change whether or not you are the more powerful party in a relationship. You can also see that compared to power, influence requires more effort, creativity, and sensitivity, but in the long run is probably more effective. If persuasion is our attempt to influence others, let's look more closely at the types of influence we can achieve.

▰ TYPES OF INFLUENCE

Our definition of persuasion suggests three types of influence. You can change, instill, or intensify your listeners' values, beliefs, attitudes, and behaviors. Your goal is to move your listeners closer to your position. It may help you to think of this process as a continuum:

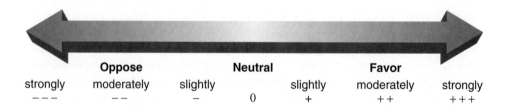

	Oppose		**Neutral**		**Favor**	
strongly	moderately	slightly		slightly	moderately	strongly
− − −	− −	−	0	+	+ +	+ + +

Remember, when you speak to persuade, you are speaking to listeners who may oppose, be indifferent to, or support your position. What strategy will you adopt to reach them? The information you gather and the assumptions you make about your audience before your speech determine the strategy you use as you develop your remarks.

Many students preparing persuasive speeches make the mistake of thinking that they must change their audiences' opinions from "oppose" to "favor," or vice versa. Take the example of Chris, who argued in his persuasive speech that the National Collegiate Athletic Association should adopt a playoff system to determine each year's college football champion. After his speech, only one classmate who opposed a playoff system said that Chris had persuaded her to support the proposal. Chris thought he had failed to persuade. Further class discussion, however, proved him wrong. A few listeners said they had changed their position from strong opposition to mild opposition. In addition, several who already supported the playoff system said that Chris's arguments had strengthened their opinion. And several listeners who were neutral before the speech found that Chris persuaded them to agree with him. As you can see, even though Chris persuaded only one audience member to move from "oppose" to "favor," his speech was quite successful. Persuasion occurs any time you move a listener's opinion in the direction you advocate, even if that movement is slight.

The most dramatic response you can request of your listeners is that they *change* a value, belief, attitude, or behavior. The response you seek is dramatic because you attempt to change opposition to support, or support to opposition. For example, if you know the audience supports asbestos removal programs and you urge them to oppose such programs, you are asking them to change an attitude. If your audience opposes putting rating labels on music albums, tapes, and CDs, you could argue in favor of such a policy. If you discover that the majority of listeners eat foods laden with cholesterol, you could give a persuasive speech encouraging them to alter their diets. In each of these cases, you would be trying to change your audience's values, beliefs, attitudes, or behaviors.

Second, you can attempt to *instill* a value, an attitude, a belief, or a behavior. You instill when you address a particular problem about which your listeners are unaware or undecided. If you persuade your audience that a problem exists, you have instilled a belief.

Yolanda discussed how language and culture affect access to medical care. She quoted from one source that for non-English-speaking hospital patients "language differences may cause treatment to take almost 25 to 50 percent longer than treatment for English-speaking patients."[3] She pointed out that different cultures respond to medical treatment in different ways. She supported this point with specific examples. Near the end of her speech, Yolanda argued that hospital staffs needed to include "culture brokers" — medical interpreters who understand not only the language but also the culture of non-English-speaking patients. After the speech, several listeners said they had not been aware of the problem and were now concerned about it. Yolanda had been successful in moving those individuals from a neutral to a supportive position. In short, she had instilled an attitude.

Finally, you may try to *intensify* values, beliefs, attitudes, or behaviors. In this case you must know before your speech that audience members agree with your position or behave as you will advocate. Your goal is to strengthen your listeners' positions and actions. For example, your audience may already believe that recycling is desirable and may even do it occasionally. If your persuasive speech causes your listeners to recycle more frequently, you have intensified their behavior. Your persuasive speech may even encourage them to persuade family and friends to adopt similar behavior. When you change believers into advocates and advocates into activists, you have intensified their attitudes and behavior.

◼ THE PYRAMID OF PERSUASION

You cannot know *how* to change your audience until you know *what* you want to change. As our definition of persuasion implies, you can target one of several changes in those listening to your persuasive speech. You can seek to influence their values, beliefs, attitudes, behaviors, or a combination of these. Recall that we discussed these four concepts in Chapter 5 and illustrated them as a pyramid (see Figure 5.2, p. 94). In that discussion, we suggested that our behavior is typically shaped by our attitudes, which are based on our beliefs, which are validated by our values. Figure 15.1, the Pyramid of Persuasion, reproduces that model. This figure emphasizes that persuasive speaking is an audience-centered activity. To be a successful persuader, you must connect with your audience. Organizing values, beliefs, attitudes, and behaviors into a pyramid will help you visualize your speaker-listener connection as you work on your persuasive speech.

This pyramid can help you formulate the specific purpose of your speech by identifying what you seek to change in your audience. Do you want to influence what they believe, how they feel, or how they act? More specifically, do you want to influence their values, beliefs, attitudes, or behaviors? Perhaps you want to affect more than one or all of them. For example, if you convince an audience that a new convention center would help revive the economy of your city (belief), they may consequently favor its construction (attitude) and vote for the necessary bond issue to pay for it (behavior).

As the Pyramid of Persuasion suggests, our values and beliefs interact to affect our

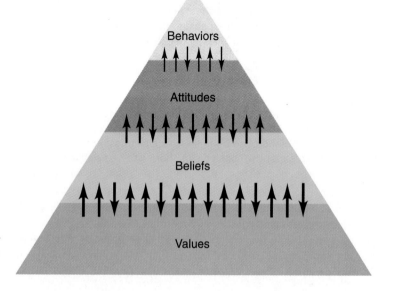

Figure 15.1   *The Pyramid of Persuasion*

attitudes; attitudes, in turn, affect our behavior. The upward arrows in the model reflect this traditional view of how we produce change. A speaker trying to persuade you not to smoke could argue in the following way: You shouldn't smoke because it is a bad habit. It is a bad habit because it increases your chances of getting cancer. Getting cancer is bad because it imperils your health, and you should value your health. Notice that the speaker uses values the listener is presumed to possess in order to justify the behavior sought. The pyramid helps you visualize the process of persuasion and develop your arguments accordingly. As you prepare your persuasive speech, use this pyramid to help you develop your strategy.

When you develop your persuasive strategy, begin by clarifying why you feel strongly about an issue. Providing reasons for your feelings moves you to consider the first and second levels of the pyramid — in other words, your values and beliefs. The example of Tony, whose persuasive speech called for a boycott of a department store, illustrates how you can use the pyramid for your persuasive speech.

Tony was bothered when his friend Mike told him about the hiring and promotion policies at the department store where Mike worked. Men and single women were given priority over married women whose husbands were employed. When a newspaper investigated and reported the charge, Tony decided to make this issue the topic of his persuasive speech. Using the pyramid structure, Tony sorted out his feelings and planned his persuasive strategy. He first asked himself, "Why do I think this topic is important to discuss?" His answer was that the store's policies were unfair. Knowing this, he worked through the various levels of the pyramid as follows:

Statement of values: I value equality and fairness.
Statement of belief: The local department store has discriminated against married women in its hiring and promotion decisions and policies.
Statement of attitude: No one should be denied employment on account of gender or marital status. I disapprove of the store's employment practices.
Statement of behavior sought: Therefore, I will not shop at this store, and I will urge others to join in the boycott.

Once he identified the values and beliefs underlying his and his listeners' attitudes and behaviors, Tony was able to generate the materials he needed to construct his persuasive appeal. Tony reminded his audience of their respect for the values of equality and fairness. He then quoted from a newspaper article to document that the local department store had indeed discriminated against two married women. Arguing that an injustice had been committed, Tony declared that everyone should be incensed by the store's employment practices and he urged a boycott.

The examples we have shown so far suggest that our beliefs affect our attitudes and our attitudes affect our behavior. The Pyramid in Figure 15.1 shows this clearly. But persuasion and influence do not move in only one direction — up. If you turn back to page 55 in Chapter 3, you will remember the discussion of self-perception. Just as beliefs and attitudes influence behavior, so too can behavior influence beliefs and attitudes. As the arrows in the pyramid suggest, influence moves up and down. Our behavior may filter down and affect our attitudes. This principle is practiced in a variety of contexts, as illustrated in the following examples.

Business executives assume that dressing the part of a "company person" will help create a company attitude. Parents assume that teaching children to share with others will develop a respect for others. At behavior modification clinics, clients sometimes speak publicly about their addiction. The clinic staff believes that this public behavior will bolster the speaker's attitudes and beliefs. In each of these instances, the persuader targets a change in behavior and assumes that a change or reinforcement in beliefs and attitudes will follow. The philosophy behind this assumption is simple: People are often uncomfortable when what they believe and what they do are inconsistent. One way to resolve that discrepancy is to modify their beliefs.

Are you wondering how these examples relate to you as a public speaker? Certainly, you do not want to force your audience into a public declaration and demonstration of support at the conclusion of each persuasive speech. You can, however, use the basic principle to your advantage. Take a close look at the following example.

> Beverly worked as a volunteer for a community literacy project and decided to use this experience as the basis for her persuasive speech. She realized that many people consider illiterate adults to be either stupid or lazy. Beverly decided that the best way to get them to change their belief would be to concentrate on convincing them to volunteer a few hours to work at the adult literacy center or in a tutorial program. From her own experience, Beverly knew that the volunteers would see how hard these adults worked to improve themselves. She believed that through this volunteer work, her classmates might also begin to understand the social, economic, and language barriers that keep some of these adults from becoming literate in English. By securing a behavior (getting listeners to work with an adult literacy program), she would give her classmates a firsthand experience that, she hoped, would change their beliefs and attitudes in a more permanent way than any speech alone could accomplish.

You can also use behavior to effect change by pointing out an existing behavior that is inconsistent with an existing belief or attitude. Note how Mike used this strategy in his persuasive speech.

> Two weeks before his persuasive speech, Mike distributed a short questionnaire to his classmates regarding their beliefs and attitudes about a state lottery. Mike supported a state lottery, but found that almost half of his audience opposed it, believing that gambling is morally wrong. In his speech he pointed out that bingo and the office sports pool were technically gambling and, like buying lottery tickets, done on a voluntary basis. Mike discovered some audience members' commitment to the behavior (gambling) was stronger than their commitment to their attitude (gambling is wrong). They adjusted their attitude to accommodate their behavior, and ended up thinking, "Some forms of gambling are worse than others." While these audience members might still oppose a state lottery on other grounds, Mike successfully weakened the argument that it was immoral. Other audience members had beliefs that were apparently stronger than their behavior. At the end of Mike's speech they still opposed the lottery and said they would quit the forms of betting he had pointed out.

As you see from these examples, your persuasive speech will target your audience's thoughts and actions. It's true that we sometimes act without fully considering the consequences of our actions; we also sometimes think about taking certain actions without ever acting. For this reason, your persuasive speech may aim to change your listeners' thoughts, actions, or both. Your goal determines the type of persuasive speech you will be giving, so let's consider your options in more detail.

TYPES OF PERSUASIVE SPEECHES

Persuasive speeches are generally classified according to their objectives. An effective persuasive speech may change what people believe, what people do, or how people feel. Persuasive speeches, then, may be divided into speeches to convince, to actuate, or to inspire, and our discussion in this chapter centers on these three divisions. Understanding these divisions can help you determine your primary objective as you work on your speech, but keep in mind that persuasive speeches often include two or more objectives. For example, if your purpose is to get your audience to boycott fur products, you must first convince them of the rightness of your cause. We usually act or become inspired after we are convinced.

Speeches to Convince

In a **speech to convince,** your objective is to affect your listeners' beliefs or attitudes. Each of the following specific purpose statements expresses a belief the speaker wants the audience to accept:

> To convince the audience that exit polls harm the balloting process.
> To convince the audience that air travel is safer than ground travel.
> To convince the audience that there is a constitutional right to privacy.
> To convince the audience that Franklin Roosevelt was a better president than his cousin Theodore Roosevelt.
> To convince the audience that Robert E. Lee was a better general than Ulysses S. Grant.

speech to convince: a persuasive speech designed to influence listeners' beliefs or attitudes.

The speaker's purpose in each of these speeches is to establish belief. While a speech to convince does not require listeners to act, action may be a natural outgrowth of their belief. So be aware that you may need an action step in your speech. For example, if you convince your audience that exit polling harms democracy but you suggest no remedy for the problem, you may leave your audience frustrated. In this case, you can suggest a simple action step, such as urging your listeners to express their views to their elected representatives. When a speech includes this step, it becomes a speech to actuate.

Speeches to Actuate

A **speech to actuate** may establish beliefs, but it always calls for the audience to act. The specific purpose statements listed here illustrate calls for action:

> To move, or actuate, the audience to donate nonperishable food to a local food bank.
> To move the audience to investigate charities before making cash donations.
> To move the audience to spay or neuter pet cats and dogs.

speech to actuate: a persuasive speech designed to influence listeners' behaviors.

To move the audience to begin a low-impact aerobic workout program.

To move the audience to vote for a limitation on the term of service of city council members.

Speeches to Inspire

A third type of persuasive speech is the **speech to inspire.** The speech to inspire attempts to change how listeners feel. Examples include commencement addresses, commemorative speeches, eulogies, and pep talks. Some specific purposes of speeches to inspire are:

To inspire the audience to respect those who volunteer their time to help others.

To inspire the audience to honor the journalistic integrity of Edward R. Murrow.

To inspire the audience to appreciate those who made their education possible.

To inspire audience members to give their best efforts to all college courses they take.

The purposes of inspiration are usually noble and uplifting. These speeches typically have neither the detailed supporting material nor the complex arguments characteristic of speeches to convince or actuate. Adlai Stevenson's eulogy of Eleanor Roosevelt in Chapter 17 (see pages 377-79) and Elie Wiesel's speech in Appendix C are examples of speeches to inspire.

Thus far, we have seen the importance of audience involvement in the important process of persuasion. We have provided a definition of persuasion and discussed the various goals that persuasive speakers can have. In the following section we will discuss nine important principles that apply to all persuasive speeches.

Effective persuasive speakers influence what listeners believe, how they act, and / or how they feel.
(Source: © Kuninori Takahashi/Impact Visuals)

Throughout this text, we have emphasized that any speech is shaped by the speaker, topic, audience, and occasion. Each of these variables affects the finished product. After all, no two people will give the same speech on the same topic to the same audience. Therefore, no person can give you a simple formula to make your persuasive speech effective. Your strategy for each speech must be based on your unique situation and on your own creativity. Nevertheless, we can give you some principles, or guidelines, to study as you prepare your persuasive speech.

1. Persuasion is more likely if goals are limited rather than global.	**KEY POINTS**
2. Persuasion is more permanent if achieved incrementally.	**Principles of Persuasion**
3. Persuasion is more likely if the audience lacks information on the topic.	
4. Persuasion is related to how important the audience considers the topic.	
5. Persuasion is more likely if the audience is self-motivated in the direction of the message.	
6. Persuasion is more likely if the speaker's message is consistent with listeners' values, beliefs, attitudes, and behaviors.	
7. Persuasion is more likely if arguments are placed appropriately.	
8. Persuasion is more likely if the source is credible.	
9. Persuasion is more likely if the speaker establishes common ground with the audience.	

Persuasion is More Likely If Goals Are Limited Rather Than Global. A common mistake many beginning speakers make is to seek dramatic change in the values, beliefs, attitudes, and behaviors of their listeners. In our experience, it is the rare speaker who can accomplish this, particularly if he or she seeks change on highly emotional and controversial issues such as abortion, gun control, capital punishment, religion, or politics. Keep in mind that the more firmly your audience is anchored to a position, the less likely you are to change their attitudes. It is unrealistic for you to expect dramatic change in a person's beliefs and values in a one-shot, five- to ten-minute speech. Instant conversions occur, but they are rare. Rather than try to convince your audience to support (or oppose) the death penalty, try convincing them of a smaller aspect of the topic; for example, that capital punishment deters crime (or does not). Once a listener accepts that belief, you or another speaker can build on it and focus on a successive objective: support for (or opposition to) the death penalty.

Which specific purpose statement in the following pairs is the more limited and reasonable goal?

Specific purpose: To persuade the audience to oppose the use of all animals in laboratory tests, *or*

Specific purpose: To persuade the audience to oppose the use of animals in laboratory tests of cosmetics and cleansers.

Specific purpose: To persuade the audience that violence on television promotes
aggression in viewers, *or*

Specific purpose: To persuade the audience that violence in television programs aimed
at children promotes aggression in children.

Specific purpose: To persuade the audience that actively involving students in classroom learning is desirable, *or*

Specific purpose: To persuade the audience that team learning is a cost-effective way
to promote student learning.

In each case, the second statement is the more limited and potentially more persuasive.
To be successful as a persuasive speaker, you must view persuasion as a process of moving a listener incrementally through a range of positions. Your speech may be only one
part of this process. Select a realistic goal and channel your efforts toward achieving it.

Persuasion Is More Permanent If Achieved Incrementally.   This second principle builds on the first one. To be effective and long-lasting, persuasion should occur
incrementally, or one step at a time. This principle becomes more important if your audience is likely to hear counterarguments to your argument. In any speech, you speak for
a fixed amount of time. The greater the number of points you must prove, the less time
you have to support and explain each. Because you must move through several steps, your
limited time may force you to abbreviate your support of some of these steps. When your
listeners hear another speaker attack one of those steps later, they may lack sufficient
evidence to counter those attacks; hence, what you accomplished may be only temporary. Your goal should be to "immunize" your listeners to possible counterarguments.
The stronger your arguments, the greater the likelihood that you will bring about endur-
ing change in the opinions of your audience. If you know your audience has been
exposed to counterarguments, you may need to address those arguments before introducing your own.

Persuasion Is More Likely If the Audience Lacks Information on the Topic.
In the absence of information, a single fact can be compelling. The more information
your listeners possess about an issue, the less likely you are to alter their perception. Sandra used this principle in a speech designed to persuade her audience that many medical tests give false or inaccurate results. She cited statistics from the American College
of Obstetricians and Gynecologists that the Pap smear fails to detect cervical cancer as
much as 40 percent of the time. She went on to say that "according to a report of the
National Cholesterol Education Program, almost 50 percent of cholesterol screenings
are wrong by 5 percent or more from their correct values."[4] Sandra gave her audience
information that was new and surprising, and it had great persuasive impact. This principle, of course, has significant ethical implications. Ethical speakers will not exploit their
listeners' lack of knowledge to advance positions they know are not logically supported.

Persuasion Is Related to How Important the Audience Considers the Topic.

Ken, Andrea, and Brad gave their persuasive speeches on the same day. Ken's
purpose was to persuade the audience to support the school's newly formed
lacrosse team. He urged his listeners to show their support by attending the next
home game. Andrea's topic concerned the increasing number of homeless adults

and children in the city. She told the class about Project Hope, sponsored by the Student Government Association, and asked everyone to donate either a can of food or a dollar at designated collection centers in campus dining halls or in the Student Center. Finally, Brad advocated legalization of marijuana, citing the drug's medical and economic potential.

Which speaker do you think had the most difficult challenge? In answering this question you must consider the audience. A significant factor is how important the audience considers the topic.

The importance of a topic can increase the likelihood of persuasion. Audience members in the above example probably agreed with both Ken and Andrea, and both may have been successful persuaders. Listeners who viewed combatting hunger as a more important goal than supporting the lacrosse team were probably more persuaded by Andrea and may have contributed to Project Hope.

Just as the importance of a topic can work for you as a persuasive speaker, it can also work against you and decrease the likelihood of persuasion. It is surely easier, for example, for someone to persuade you to change brands of toothpaste than to change your religion. The reason is simple: Your religion is more important to you. Brad probably had a tougher time persuading his listeners than did either Ken or Andrea. Legalizing marijuana probably ran counter to some deeply held audience opinions, and the intensity of those beliefs and values may have made them more resistant to Brad's persuasive appeals. The importance of an issue will vary according to each audience member, and you need to take this into account as you prepare your persuasive appeal.

Persuasion Is More Likely If the Audience Is Self-Motivated in the Direction of the Message. People change their values, beliefs, attitudes, and behaviors because they are motivated to do so. To be an effective persuader, you must discover what motivates your listeners. This requires an understanding of their needs and desires. How can you do this? You can enhance your persuasive appeal by following three steps. First, identify as many of the needs and desires of your listeners as possible. Second, review your list and select those that your speech satisfies. Third, as you prepare your speech, explain how the action you advocate fulfills audience needs. If you discover that your speech does not fulfill the needs or desires of your listeners, then you have probably failed to connect with these listeners. They may receive your speech with interest, but such listeners will probably not act on your message. What you intended as a persuasive speech may in fact be received as informative.

Persuasion Is More Likely If the Speaker's Message Is Consistent with Listeners' Values, Beliefs, Attitudes, and Behaviors. We have discussed the importance of consistency elsewhere in this text, but we think it important enough to mention here. People want to establish consistency in their lives. We expect coherence between our beliefs and actions, for example. In fact, we will call someone a hypocrite who professes one set of values but acts according to another. Your ability to persuade is thus enhanced if you request an action that is consistent with your audience's values.

Use this principle of consistency in constructing your persuasive appeal. For example, we have had students who persuaded their classroom audience to oppose the use of animals in nonmedical product testing. They first identified the beliefs that would cause a person to challenge such tests — for example, product testing harms animals and is unnecessary. Next they showed their audience that they share these beliefs. Once they accomplished that, the speakers then asked their listeners to act in accordance with their beliefs and boycott companies that continue to test cosmetics on animals, since continuing to buy such products would be inconsistent with their beliefs.

Persuasion Is More Likely If Arguments Are Placed Appropriately.   Once you have determined the key arguments in your speech, you must decide their order. To do that, you must know which of your arguments is the strongest. Assume for a moment that your persuasive speech argues that the public defender system needs to be reformed. Assume, too, that you use a problem-solution organization. Your argument supporting the first point in your speech could be:

> I. The public defender system is stacked against the defendant.
>   A. Public defenders have too heavy caseloads.
>   B. Public defenders have too little experience.
>   C. Public defenders have inadequate investigative staffs.

One of these three arguments will probably be stronger than the other two. You may have more evidence on one; you may have more recent evidence on it; or you may feel that one argument will be more compelling than the other two for your particular audience. Assume that you decide point B is your strongest. Where should you place it?

Two theories of argument placement are the primacy and recency theories. *Primacy* theorists recommend that you put your strongest argument first in the body of your speech to establish a strong first impression. Because you are most likely to win over your listeners with your strongest argument, this theory suggests that you should win your listeners to your side as early as possible. Primacy theorists would tell you to move your strongest argument to the position of point A.

Recency theorists, on the other hand, believe that you should present your strongest argument last, thus leaving your listeners with your best argument. They would have you move your strongest argument to the point C position. How do you as a persuasive speaker resolve this conflict?

Though the primacy and recency theorists argue whether the first or last position is stronger, they generally agree that the middle position is the weakest. Therefore, do not place your strongest argument in the middle position. When you sandwich a strong argument between weaker ones, you reduce its impact.

Persuasion Is More Likely If the Source Is Credible.   We are persuaded by those whom we respect and trust. We often defer to their opinions because we have neither the time nor the expertise to investigate and evaluate the issue under discussion. We cannot, for example, directly observe the relationship between capital punishment and the deterrence of crime, so we trust the opinions of those who have researched that relationship. We choose to see a movie because critics we respect praise the film. Trusted experts in a field are credible sources for us.

How do you use this principle as you prepare your persuasive speech? As you research your topic, you will, no doubt, find a variety of sources making similar statements. How do you decide which sources to include in your speech? Your decision should be based, of course, on the qualifications of the source, but consider also how your audience will view the source. For example, whom would your audience probably view as the most credible source discussing the rights of defendants: a college law professor, a court judge, a defense attorney, a police officer, or a public opinion poll? The answer may vary according to the specific audience. For example, a college law professor may have the highest credibility with college students. Make sure you select sources appropriate to your audience.

Persuasion Is More Likely If the Speaker Establishes Common Ground with the Audience. Which source advising you, "Take Carolyn DeLecour for public speaking; she's a great teacher," would you find more persuasive: a friend who is also a college student or a counselor at your school? If you are typical, your answer is, "my friend," particularly if that friend has already taken a public speaking class with Professor DeLecour. The counselor may have taken DeLecour's public speaking class, may know DeLecour personally, or may have heard many complimentary remarks about DeLecour from her former students. But the counselor may also just be trying to fill a class that other students are avoiding.

As this example shows, you are probably more easily persuaded by people similar to you than by those who are different. Your friends, for example, are credible sources not because they possess special expertise but because they share your values and interests. We all reason that individuals having backgrounds like ours will view situations and problems as we would. Furthermore, we believe that people who share our beliefs will investigate an issue and arrive at a judgment in the same manner we would if we had the time and the opportunity.

One way to increase your persuasion, then, is to identify with your listeners. Sonja, a weekend news anchor for a local television station, was asked to speak to a college television production class on employment opportunities in television. Notice how Sonja used the strategy of identification in her introduction as she focused on experiences she shared with her listeners.

> Seven years ago a timid freshman girl sat in a college classroom much like this. Just like you, she was taking a TV production class. And like some of you, I suspect, she dreamed of being in front of a camera someday, sitting at an anchor desk, reporting the news to thousands of families who would let her come into their homes through the magic of television.
>
> There was little reason to predict that this girl would achieve her dreams. In many ways she was rather ordinary. She didn't come from a wealthy family. She didn't have any connections that would get her a job in broadcasting. She was a B student who worked part-time in the university food service to help pay for her education. But she had a goal and was determined to attain it. And then one day, it happened. An instructor announced that a local TV station had an opening for a student intern. The instructor said the internship would involve long hours, menial work, and no pay. Hardly the opportunity of a lifetime! Nevertheless, after class, she approached the instructor, uncertain of what she was getting into. With her instructor's help, she applied for and received the internship. It is because of that decision that I am now the weekend anchor of the city's largest television station.

The rest of Sonja's speech focused on the importance of student internships in learning about the reality of the broadcast media and making contacts for future references and employment. Her opening comments made Sonja a more believable speaker by bridging the gap between her and her listeners. Sonja's suggestions had more impact on her audience because she had established common ground with them.

As this final principle demonstrates, who you are may be as persuasive as what you say. Even before you complete your research or organize and practice your speech, you may have one powerful, persuasive instrument already working for you: your reputation with your listeners. In the final section of this chapter, we discuss the persuasive potential of speaker credibility and the speaker's emotional appeals.

PERSUASIVE SPEAKING STRATEGIES

We can find evidence as far back as the era of Ancient Greece of people giving advice on how to be an effective persuasive speaker. Aristotle, for example, devoted much space in his classic work *The Rhetoric* to the subject. Aristotle discussed three modes of persuasion speakers have at their disposal: *ethos, logos,* and *pathos.*[5] These three modes remain an important foundation today for our understanding of persuasive speaking. What do these terms mean and how can they help you as you prepare a persuasive speech?

ethos: speaker credibility.
logos: logical appeal.
pathos: emotional appeal.

Ethos, or speaker credibility, derives from the character and reputation of the speaker. *Logos,* or logical appeal, relies on the form and substance of an argument. *Pathos,* or emotional appeal, taps the values and feelings of the audience. In Chapter 16, we will discuss *logos* in greater detail. We will introduce you to the elements of an argument, describe five types of arguments you can use in your persuasive speaking, and define several categories of faulty reasoning you should avoid. In the remainder of this chapter, we discuss the two other modes of persuasion — *ethos* and *pathos* — and offer several suggestions to assist you in building these into your persuasive speech.

Establishing Speaker Credibility

credibility: the degree to which listeners believe a speaker.
initial credibility or **antecedent ethos:** a speaker's image or reputation before speaking to a particular audience.

As a speaker, your first available source of persuasion is your own credibility, or *ethos.* **Credibility** is simply your reputation, and it helps determine how your listeners evaluate what you say. The higher your perceived credibility, the more likely the audience is to believe you.

Speaker credibility is fluid, varying according to your listeners. You possess only the credibility your listeners grant you. If you pepper your speaking with humor, for example, some listeners may see you as lively and interesting while others may think you frivolous. You probably have as many different images as you have audience members.

Credibility also varies according to time. Your credibility can be divided chronologically into the time before, during, and after your speech. These chronological divisions are sometimes referred to as initial, derived, and terminal credibility.[6] Your image or reputation prior to speaking comprises your **initial credibility,** sometimes called **antecedent ethos.** The more the audience knows about you, the firmer your image.

But what if your listeners do not know you personally? Even in this case, you still bring varying images to the speaking occasion. For example, if you are a spokesperson for an organization, you may assume the image of that organization in the minds of your audience. What if someone asked you to describe the kind of person who belongs to the Democratic Party, the Republican Party, the Sierra Club, or the National Rifle Association? An image probably comes to your mind for each group. If a representative from one of those associations were to speak to you, you would make certain assumptions about the individual based on what you know about that organization. Just as you do with strangers, you form impressions of your classmates based on what they say in class, how they dress, whether they arrive at class on time, their age and appearance, and any organization to which they belong. They have also formed impressions of you, of course. Such images constitute your initial credibility.

Derived credibility is the image the audience develops of you as you speak. The moment you enter the presence of your listeners, you provide stimuli from which the audience can evaluate you. As you begin your speech, the number of stimuli multiplies quickly. If you begin your speech with an offensive joke, listeners' images of you will become more negative. However, when you appeal to your listeners' values and present reasoned arguments to advance your position, you enhance your image. The credibility you derive during your presentation is a function of many factors. Your information, of course, helps your audience judge your credibility. Your audience will also judge your nonverbal behaviors (see Chapter 12), such as gestures, posture, eye contact, and appearance, to name a few. If you convey confidence, authority, and a genuine concern for your listeners, you will enhance your credibility.

derived credibility: the image listeners develop of a speaker as he or she speaks.

Terminal credibility is the image the audience has of you after your speech. Even this credibility is subject to change. The listener may be caught up in the excitement and emotion of your speech and end up with an elevated opinion of you. As time passes, that evaluation may moderate. As you can see, the process of generating and maintaining credibility is ongoing. In this class, for example, your credibility at the conclusion of one speech will naturally shape your initial credibility for your next speech.

terminal credibility: the image listeners develop of a speaker by the end of a speech and for a period of time after it.

Studies demonstrate that a speaker having high credibility can more successfully persuade than a speaker having low credibility. Clearly, you need to pay careful attention to your credibility at each stage in order to deliver a successful persuasive speech. How do you enhance your image? Communication theorists agree that speakers who appear competent, trustworthy, and dynamic are viewed as credible speakers.[7] If your audience believes you possess competence, trustworthiness, and dynamism, you can be effective in persuading them.

Competence. In this class you are among peers, and so your audience probably considers you a fellow student rather than an expert on your chosen topic. How can you get them to see you as knowledgeable and worthy of their trust? Your task is to establish an image of **competence** on your subject. Four strategies will help you do that.

competence: listeners' views of a speaker's qualifications to speak on a particular topic.

---

1. Know your subject.
2. Document your ideas.
3. Cite your sources.
4. Acknowledge personal involvement.

KEY POINTS

Guidelines for Enhancing Your Image of Competence

First, the obvious: *Know your subject.* From which of these people would you be more likely to buy a new video disc player: a salesperson who can answer all your questions about the product, or someone who doesn't know the answers and doesn't care to find out? The answer is obvious, isn't it? In a persuasive speaking situation, you as speaker are a salesperson and your audience members are consumers. To speak ethically, you must be well informed about your subject. You will discover that the more you read and listen, the easier it is to construct a message that is both credible and compelling.

Not only should you know your specific topic, but you should also understand how it interacts with related topics. Just as the salesperson must know the video disc player and how it will operate with other equipment you own, you should comprehend both the content and the context of your persuasive message. Persuading your classmates to begin recycling low-density plastics (LPDs) does you little good if your area has no processing plant for LDPs and thus recyclers will not accept them. In addition, you will feel foolish if an audience member asks after your speech, "Did you know that no recycling center will accept those plastics?" This is where your research helps you by enhancing your expertise on your subject. A well-researched speech increases persuasion by contributing to your image as a well-informed individual. In a public speaking course such as this, the image building you do is cumulative. Thorough, quality research not only enhances your credibility on the immediate topic, but also generates positive initial credibility for your next appearance before the same group.

Second, you can bolster your image of competence if you *document your ideas*. Unsupported ideas are mere assertions. Though your listeners don't expect you to be an expert on your topic, they need assurance that what you say is corroborated by facts or by experts. Providing documentation supports your statements and increases your believability.

A third strategy for enhancing your credibility is to *cite your sources*. Simply presenting the data upon which your conclusions are based is insufficient. Remember, your audience is not going to have the opportunity to read your bibliography. You need to tell your listeners the sources of your information. Citing sources enhances the credibility of your ideas by demonstrating that experts support your position. Of course, it also requires that your sources be unbiased and of good quality. We remember one student who cited *Hustler* magazine as the source for his contention that soft-core pornography does not exploit women, and thereby destroyed his credibility.

Fourth, *acknowledge any personal involvement* or experience with your subject. Listeners will probably assume that you have an edge in understanding color blindness if you let them know you are color-blind. They will probably make the same positive assumption if you are diabetic and speaking on diabetes, or if you are a child of an alcoholic and are speaking on codependency. If you have worked with terminally ill patients and are speaking on a related topic, mentioning your experience will add authority to your ideas.

trustworthiness:
listeners' views of a speaker's honesty.

Trustworthiness.   A second criterion of speaker credibility is **trustworthiness,** and it should tell us two things about you. First, we should trust you as an individual: You are honest in what you say. Second, we should trust you with your topic: You are unbiased in what you say. A speaker can demonstrate trustworthiness in two simple, practical ways.

1. *Establish common ground with your audience.* If listeners know that you understand their values, experiences, and aspirations, they will be more receptive to your arguments. When you let them know you identify with those values, experiences, and aspirations, you increase your persuasiveness.

2. *Demonstrate your objectivity in approaching the topic.* The information and sources you include in your speech should demonstrate thorough, unbiased research. One student gave his speech on cigarette smoking, arguing that its harmful effects were greatly exaggerated. In presenting his arguments, he relied on studies sponsored by the tobacco industry. Few in the audience were persuaded by his evidence. He undermined his image of trustworthiness because he limited his research to sources the audience considered biased on the topic, sources that had a financial interest in supporting one side of the issue.

Dynamism.   A third element of credibility is **dynamism.** Competence and trustworthiness are obviously legitimate criteria used to determine speaker credibility, but you may wonder why we include personal dynamism on this list. Dynamism is more closely associated with delivery than with content. We enjoy listening to speakers who are energetic, vigorous, exciting, inspiring, spirited, and stimulating. But should speakers whose delivery is static, timid, and unexciting be considered less credible than their more exuberant counterparts? Perhaps not, and the ethical listener will focus more on the content than on the form of the message. Yet you should know that studies continue to document dynamism as an element of speaker credibility, and it would be wise for you to develop this attribute.

dynamism: a speaker's confidence, energy, and enthusiasm for communicating.

Dynamism contributes to persuasion because it conveys both confidence and concern. You show confidence largely through your speech delivery. If you appear tentative or unsure of yourself, the audience may doubt your conviction. To the extent that you can strengthen your verbal, vocal, and physical delivery, you can enhance your image of confidence and, hence, your credibility. No one expects you to give a professional-level performance. Remember that mastering public speaking is a process that involves study and practice. If you take yourself and your speech seriously, you will do fine.

Dynamism also demonstrates a concern for the audience and a desire to communicate with them. If your delivery seems flippant, distracted, or detached from the audience, your listeners will assume that you are not concerned about the topic or about them. On the other hand, conveying enthusiasm for your topic and your listeners communicates a strong positive message.

As a speaker, then, present a well-researched and documented message and communicate it in an honest and unbiased manner. Your verbal, vocal, and physical delivery should show you to be a fluent, forceful, and friendly individual who takes seriously the issues you address. If listeners perceive you to be competent, trustworthy, and dynamic, you will have high source credibility and, hence, be an effective persuader.

Enhancing Emotional Appeals

As we have indicated earlier, *pathos* is the appeal to emotions. Among the emotions speakers can arouse are your anger, envy, fear, hate, jealousy, joy, love, or pride. When speakers use these feelings to try to get you to believe something or act in a particular way, they are using emotional appeals.

Many of the feelings listed above seem negative — anger, fear, hate, and jealousy, for example. Consequently, you may consider emotional appeals as unacceptable or inferior types of proof. Perhaps you have even heard someone say, "Don't be so emotional; use your head!" It is certainly possible to be emotional and illogical, but keep in mind that it is also possible to be both emotional and logical. Is it wrong, for example, to be angered by child abuse, to hate racism, or to fear chemical warfare? We don't think so. The strongest arguments combine reason with passion. *Logos* and *pathos* should not conflict but complement each other.

In his persuasive speech Chris examined problems caused by inadequate vaccination. He presented data gathered by the Centers for Disease Control showing that measles, rubella, tetanus, mumps, influenza, and pneumonia cause much unnecessary suffering. After these discussions, Chris concluded:

All told, every year diseases that we can prevent kill an estimated 70,000 people, take over 20 billion dollars worth of lost productivity and so-called free medical benefits from our pockets as taxpayers, and cause pain and suffering to hundreds of thousands of others.[8]

In this speech Chris' specific purpose was to advocate a nationwide vaccination campaign to save lives, reduce suffering, and conserve tax dollars. Did Chris construct a logical argument? Yes. He used statistics from a reliable source and explained how they supported his position. Did Chris construct an emotional argument? Again, yes. He appealed to his listeners' fear of death and their compassion toward others. *Logos* and *pathos* coalesced to form a compelling argument.

As you can see, when properly constructed, emotional appeals make your listeners active participants in the development of your message. By tapping their feelings, you involve them psychologically and physiologically. The following four guidelines will help you develop and enhance the *pathos* of your persuasive speech.

KEY POINTS

Guidelines for Enhancing Emotional Appeals

1. Tap audience values.
2. Use vivid examples.
3. Use emotive language.
4. Use effective delivery.

The first, and probably most important, guideline for developing emotional appeals is to *tap audience values.* As we have mentioned repeatedly, you must conduct careful audience analysis before you can deliver an effective speech. Demonstrate in your speech how your audience's values support your position. In Chapter 5, "Analyzing Your Audience," we discussed Maslow's hierarchy and how you can relate your topic to audience needs (see pages 89-91). Try some of the strategies discussed in that section. The more attached listeners are to the values a speaker promotes, the more emotional is the appeal. Part of your responsibility as a speaker is to make that connection evident to your listeners.

A second strategy for enhancing emotional appeals is to *use vivid, emotionally toned examples.* The example may not be sufficient to prove your point, but it should illustrate the concept and generate a strong audience feeling. Kellie used this strategy in her speech against marital rape exemptions in state laws. She told of a woman she had counseled:

> … Bill began to take his frustrations out on Jane, by beating her violently and demanding sex on call. One time, Jane refused his demands; Bill threw her to the bed with a gun to her head and tied her up. When she began to scream and fight, he wrapped the phone cord around and around her neck to keep her quiet; she almost couldn't breathe. While she lay there, helpless, with the gun on the nightstand, he repeatedly raped and sodomized her. When he was finished he just left her there. Sometime later, she got herself loose. She had bruises on her wrists, ankles, throat, inner thighs, breasts, and vaginal areas.[9]

Who can respond to Jane's situation without feeling compassion or anger?

Visual and audio aids can also enhance a speaker's *pathos*.

333

The Strategy of Persuasion

Duncan selected as the specific purpose of his speech to persuade the audience to become members of Amnesty International. He had joined the organization because he felt that as an individual, he could do little to help end torture and executions of prisoners of conscience throughout the world. As part of a concerted worldwide effort, however, he saw the opportunity to further social and political justice. His speech included ample testimony of persecution coupled with statistical estimates of the extent of the problem. Duncan wanted to infuse his speech with convincing emotional appeals to support the data. After presenting the facts, he paused and spoke these words to his listeners: "In the last four minutes you've heard about the anguish, the pain, the suffering, and the persecution experienced by thousands of people, simply because they want to be free and follow their consciences. I want you not only to *hear* of their plight, but also to *see* it." Duncan pushed the remote control button of a slide projector and proceeded to show five slides of people brutalized by their own governments. He did not speak, but simply showed each slide for ten seconds. After the last slide, he spoke again: "They say a picture is worth a thousand words. Well, these pictures speak volumes about man's inhumanity to man. But these pictures should also speak to *our consciences.* Can we stand back, detached, and do nothing, knowing what fate befalls these individuals?" Duncan then told the audience how they could become involved in Amnesty International and begin to make a difference. Duncan's speech had a powerful effect because he touched his audience's emotions with vivid examples.

Duncan also employed *pathos* by using a third technique: he *used emotive language,* such as "the anguish, the pain, the suffering, and the persecution…." In Chapter 11, "Wording Your Speech," we discussed the power of words. Nowhere can words be more powerful than when they work to generate emotional appeals. Take the example of Theresa, who argued in 1990 for derecognition of fraternities and sororities, citing as one reason the harms of hazing. Notice in the following passage how Theresa first presents statistics to document the problem, and then uses emotive language to intensify her argument.

According to the November 1988 issue of the *Washington Monthly,* in the past ten years alone, hazing incidents have killed about fifty college students and injured innumerable others. They've been beaten, branded, burned, buried, stabbed, shot, drowned, frozen, and poisoned. In fact, electric cattle prods, two-handled paddles, Jew baiting, gay bashing, alcohol poisoning, group grope encounters, and blackface slave auctions have all made national headlines as a result of what are politely called "fraternity mishaps."[10]

Beaten, branded, burned, buried, stabbed, shot, drowned, frozen, and *poisoned* are all strong, emotion-producing words. Whether you agree with her argument or not, you were probably moved by Theresa's language.

As a final method, you should *use effective delivery* to enhance emotional appeals. As we discussed in Chapter 12, "Delivering Your Speech," when a speaker's verbal and nonverbal messages conflict, we tend to trust the nonverbal message. For that reason, speakers who show little physical and vocal involvement with their speeches usually come across as uninterested or even insincere. When you display emotion yourself, you can sometimes generate audience emotion.

Before leaving the subject of *pathos*, a few parting comments are in order. Emotional appeals are powerful persuasive tools. They can stir passions, intensify beliefs, and impel actions. Speakers have an ethical responsibility to use emotional appeals wisely. Emotional appeals are never in order if the speaker disregards the logical basis of the speech. Emotion and logic are best used in concert with each other.

It is important to remember that these three modes of persuasion — *ethos, logos*, and *pathos* — all work to enhance your persuasive appeal. The best persuasive speeches combine all three. Effective persuaders are credible, present logically constructed and supported arguments, and tap the values of their listeners.

Summary

Persuasion is a dynamic activity requiring the participation of a speaker, a message, and at least one listener. Politicians, educators, business people, and religious leaders flood us with persuasive appeals daily. In order to benefit from sound persuasion, and avoid the pitfalls of flawed or unethical persuasion, speakers and listeners must understand what persuasion involves.

Persuasion is the process of influencing another person's values, beliefs, attitudes, or behaviors. *Influencing* can mean changing attitudes or actions, instilling new beliefs, or simply intensifying people's feelings about their existing beliefs or behaviors. The Pyramid of Persuasion helps you determine the specific purpose of your speech and generate arguments you can use to achieve that purpose. A persuasive speech aimed at changing beliefs and attitudes, but not requesting any overt behavior of listeners, is called a *speech to convince*. A *speech to actuate* seeks to change behaviors. A *speech to inspire* encourages positive changes in the way listeners feel about their beliefs or actions.

Whether you target values, beliefs, attitudes, behaviors, or a combination of these, your job as an effective persuader will be easier if you keep in mind nine principles of persuasion. First, if you seek modest and limited, rather than dramatic, changes in audience attitudes and behaviors, you will be more likely to persuade. Second, persuasion is more lasting if achieved step by step, or incrementally. Third, an audience is more easily persuaded on topics they do not know well. Fourth, persuasion depends upon how important the audience considers the topic. Fifth, persuasion is obviously easier when the audience is already self-motivated in the direction of the message. Sixth, an audience is more easily persuaded if they sense some inconsistency in their values, beliefs, attitudes, and behaviors. Seventh, persuasion is more likely if the speaker's arguments are appropriately placed within the speech. Eighth, persuasion is more likely if the audience considers the speaker's sources credible. Ninth, and finally, persuasion is more likely if the speaker establishes common ground with the audience.

Three modes of persuasion, discussed at least as early as the time of Aristotle, are *ethos, logos*, and *pathos*. *Ethos*, the first source of persuasion available to speakers, is their credibility or believability. *Logos* is a logical appeal based on the form and substance of the message. It appeals to the listener's intellect and reasoning. *Pathos*, or emotional appeal, relies on the audience's feelings for its persuasive impact.

Some speakers have *initial credibility* or *antecedent ethos* with a particular audience, based on the listeners' prior knowledge of the speaker. An unknown speaker may take on the credibility of the organization he or she represents. All speakers have *derived credibility*, developed from the ideas they present in their speech and their speech delivery, and *terminal credibility*, based on the audience's evaluation of speaker and message after the speech.

Competence, trustworthiness, and *dynamism* are three components of a speaker's credibility. To build images of competence, speakers should know their speech subjects, document their ideas, cite their sources, and mention any special experience they have with their topics. To demonstrate trust-worthiness, speakers should establish common ground with their audiences and show evidence of thorough, unbiased research. Because listeners associate dynamism with the energy, vigor, and friendliness of a speaker's delivery, developing a dynamic image requires showing confidence about speaking and concern for the well-being of the audience.

Pathos, or emotional appeal, is the final persuasive strategy discussed in this chapter. To develop powerful emotional appeals, a speaker should tap audience values; use vivid, emotionally toned examples; use emotive language; and display emotion in the physical and vocal delivery of the speech. *Pathos* should complement rather than replace the logical structure of a speech.

*E*XERCISES

1. Select three print or broadcast advertisements for the same kind of product (soft drinks, insurance, automobiles, and so on). Discuss the persuasive appeals of each ad. Which one do you think is the most effective? Why? Could any of these strategies of persuasion be incorporated in a speech? Provide some examples.
2. Select a topic and write a specific purpose statement that seeks dramatic change in the behavior or attitude of your audience. Divide the change you seek into several incremental steps. Discuss what you would need to prove to achieve each step. Could any of these steps be the basis for a speech by itself?
3. Listen to a speaker on C-SPAN, *The MacNeil/Lehrer News Hour, Nightline,* a news interview show, or some other broadcast. Keep a chronology of the speaker's initial, derived, and terminal credibility. What changes occurred in your impression of the speaker? What accounted for those changes? What might the speaker have done to improve his or her credibility?

*N*OTES

1. "The 30-Second President," narr. Bill Moyers, *A Walk Through the 20th Century,* exec. ed. Bill Moyers, PBS, 1984.

2. Charles U. Larson, *Persuasion: Reception and Responsibility,* 6th ed. (Belmont, CA: Wadsworth, 1992) 11.

3. Jill L. Sherer, "Crossing Cultures: Hospitals Begin Breaking Down Barriers to Care," *Medical Staff Leader* July 1993: 3.

4. Linda J. Heller, "How Accurate Are Medical Tests?" *Parade* 3 Feb. 1991: 4.

5. *The Rhetoric of Aristotle,* trans. Lane Cooper (New York: Appleton, 1960) 8.

6. James C. McCroskey, *An Introduction to Rhetorical Communication,* 2nd ed. (Englewood Cliffs, NJ: Prentice, 1972) 63-64.

7. In his book *An Introduction to Rhetorical Communication,* p. 65, James McCroskey credits D.K. Berlo and J.B. Lemmert with labeling these three dimensions of credibility in "A Factor Analytic Study of the Dimensions of Source Credibility," a paper presented at the 1961 convention of the Speech Association of America, New York.

8. Chris Thomas, "Better Safe Than Sorry," *Winning Orations, 1989* (Mankato, MN: Interstate Oratorical Association, 1989) 61.

9. Kellie Rider, "Happily Ever After?" *Winning Orations, 1990* (Mankato, MN: Interstate Oratorical Association, 1990) 95.

10. Theresa McGuinness, "Greeks in Crisis," *Winning Orations, 1990* (Mankato, MN: Interstate Oratorical Association, 1990) 73-74.

Good argument, like good architecture, reveals its structural elements so that what is being said and how it is being supported lie open to the consideration of all.
~Perry Weddle

The Structure of Persuasion

Chapter *16*

"There are about 650,000 lawyers in the United States — one for each 365 people — and their number is increasing at a rate seven times faster than our population. If that rate continues until the year 2074, everyone in the United States will be a lawyer."
V. H. KRULAK[1]

"In the space of one hundred and seventy-six years the Lower Mississippi has shortened itself two hundred and forty-two miles. That is an average of a trifle over one mile and a third per year. Therefore, any calm person, who is not blind or idiotic, can see that ... just a million years ago next November, the Lower Mississippi River was upwards of one million three hundred thousand miles long."
MARK TWAIN[2]

"More than at any time in history, mankind faces a crossroads. One path leads to despair and utter hopelessness, the other to total extinction. Let us pray we have the wisdom to choose correctly."
WOODY ALLEN[3]

o those arguments seem unconvincing to you? Do they strike you as more humorous than persuasive? If so, you have probably detected some flaws in them and would not be persuaded by speakers who said them. In order to be an effective and ethical speaker, you must be able to construct sound arguments and organize them in a convincing fashion. Speakers who knowingly use faulty reasoning act unethically. Understanding how to reason also benefits you as a listener. In order to make rational decisions, you must be able to analyze and assess what you hear.

The ability to structure sound arguments and detect flawed reasoning is an important skill for the public speaker. Thomas Gilovich, associate professor of psychology at Cornell University, explains:

> Thinking straight about the world is a precious and difficult process that must be carefully nurtured. By attempting to turn our critical intelligence off and on at will, we risk losing it altogether, and thus jeopardize our ability to see the world clearly. Furthermore, by failing to fully develop our critical faculties, we become susceptible to the arguments and exhortations of those with other than benign intentions. In the words of Stephen Jay Gould, "When people learn no tools of judgment and merely follow their hopes, the seeds of political manipulation are sown." As individuals and as society, we should be less accepting of superstition and sloppy thinking, and should strive to develop those "habits of mind" that promote a more accurate view of the world.[4]

In the previous chapter we discussed the *strategy* of persuasion. You learned what persuasion is and also some principles and strategies you can use to develop a convincing message. In this chapter we discuss the *structure* of persuasion. We will show you how to construct an argument and how to detect faulty arguments. In addition, you will study characteristics and types of persuasive propositions and special organizational patterns you can use in your persuasive speeches.

"A speech has two parts. Necessarily, you state your case, and you prove it."
ARISTOTLE[5]

Aristotle's description of the effective persuasive speech sounds simple, doesn't it? Before you can prove your case, however, you must understand the structure of arguments and how those arguments are organized in your speech. In the previous chapter, we referred to this type of persuasive appeal as *logos*. Let's see how all this works.

Steps of an Argument

Suppose you make the following statement: "I am more confident about public speaking now than I was at the beginning of this course." If someone asked you to justify your statement, you could respond in this way:

> Well, I experience fewer symptoms of nervousness. I seem to worry less about facing an audience. The night before my speech, I sleep better than I used to. I establish eye contact with my audience now rather than avoiding looking directly at them, as I did in my first speech. I no longer nervously shift my weight from foot to foot, and I've stopped playing with my high school class ring and have started gesturing.

Your statement and response together constitute an argument. You have made a claim ("I am more confident about public speaking now") and then supported it with evidence, in this case, examples from personal observation. Aristotle would be pleased!

At its simplest level, an argument includes three steps:

1. You make a claim.
2. You offer evidence.
3. You show how the evidence proves the claim.[6]

The *claim* is the conclusion of your argument. It is a statement you want your listeners to accept. Some examples of claims are:

Crime in our nation is rampant.
Textbook prices are too high.
Alcoholism is a disease.
The most important thing you can learn in college is how to learn.
Pornography is not a constitutionally protected form of free expression.
Visual aids make ideas easier to remember.
Cleanliness is next to godliness.
The certainty of punishment is a greater deterrent to crime than the severity of punishment.
Pizza is the ultimate health food.

evidence: supporting material a speaker uses to prove a point.

The validity of any claim depends on the evidence supporting it. **Evidence** is the supporting material you use to prove a point. As an advocate, you have an obligation to support your position with valid arguments. In other words, you must offer your listeners reasons to accept your conclusion.

When Rich heard President Clinton propose a national immunization program for all American children, he decided to research that topic for his persuasive speech. Rich became convinced that such a program was needed, and he used the following supporting materials to make the first point in his speech:

> Early this year [1993] President Clinton called for universal vaccination of all American children. Some of you may have been surprised when you heard about this. After all, aren't most American children already immunized against childhood diseases? The sad fact is that the answer is no. Millions of American children are *not* fully immunized.
>
> Donna Shalala, Secretary of Health and Human Services, gives us the bad news. Writing in the April 14, 1993, issue of the *Journal of the American Medical Association,* she says, "Today, between 37% and 56% of the 7.8 million 2-year-olds in America — about 4 million children — are not fully immunized." Did you catch that figure? Four million children! And the *New York Times* in February of this year points out that the percentage goes as high as 90 percent in some inner-city neighborhoods. Our record is so poor that we actually trail many developing nations in Latin America and Africa in vaccination rates for kids under two years old.
>
> As frightening as they are, you may forget the percentages I just gave you — and even how we compare with some developing countries. But Secretary Shalala and I want you to remember one statistic: Four million American children are not fully immunized! Four million!

In his speech, Rich followed the three steps in constructing and presenting an argument. First, he stated his claim (millions of American children are not fully immunized). Second, he offered evidence to support the point, from Secretary Shalala and the *New York Times*. Finally, he focused his listeners' attention on the key statistic that proved his point.

Types of Argument

Speakers can justify their claims by using any of five types of argument. You may offer proof by arguing from example, analogy, cause, deduction, or authority. The type of argument you select will depend on your topic, the available evidence, and your listeners. You may combine several types of argument in a single persuasive speech. In fact, the best speeches usually do combine types of argument. Let's look in more detail at these five basic types of argument available to you as a persuasive speaker.

argument by example or **inductive argument:** says that what is true of a few instances is true generally.

Argument by Example.   **Argument by example** is an inductive form of proof. **Inductive argument** uses a few instances to assert a broader claim. For example, if you have struggled through calculus and analytic geometry, you may conclude that math is a difficult subject for you. You arrive at this conclusion by generalizing from the few specific math classes you have taken.

We form many of our opinions through proofs provided from argument by example. We read of several murders in Chicago and assume that the city is plagued with violence. We hear a few friends complain of electrical problems with a particular make of car and decide not to buy that model. A speaker relates several examples of corruption in city hall, and we conclude that political corruption is widespread. Those are all examples of inductive reasoning.

Notice how James used a few instances to establish a broader claim in his speech on cosmetic plastic surgery:

> The number of Americans undergoing aesthetic plastic surgery has increased dramatically. According to the American Society of Plastic and Reconstructive Surgery, in just seven years, there have been increases of 215 percent in the number of "tummy tucks," 40 percent in eyelid surgeries, and 34 percent in nose jobs.[7]

While there are many other types of elective plastic surgery, James based his conclusion that elective aesthetic plastic surgery is increasing on the three procedures he mentions.

Perhaps as you read the preceding arguments, you questioned the validity of some of them. How can you test whether the examples used to support an argument are sound? The validity of argument by example hinges on the quality of the examples a speaker chooses. Ask yourself the following four questions to test the validity of argument by example. Keep in mind that argument by example is valid only if you can answer yes to each of four tests of argument.

---

1. Are the examples true?
2. Are the examples relevant?
3. Are the examples sufficient?
4. Are the examples representative?

KEY POINTS

Tests of Argument by Example

---

1. Are the examples true? The first test of argument by example is to determine if the examples are true. In Chapter 8, we noted that hypothetical or imaginary examples can clarify a point, but they do not prove it. Only when true examples are presented should you proceed to the next question.

2. Are the examples relevant? Suppose a speaker presented evidence that three murders were committed during the past weekend in a major city and concluded, "So you can see that it is not safe to walk the streets of this city." Do these examples relate to the claim? If these three homicides resulted from domestic violence, they would not relate to street crime and, thus, would not prove a threat to the city's visitors. The examples, in this case, are not relevant.

3. Are the examples sufficient? Three murders in one weekend is statistically significant for a small town such as London Mills, Illinois, but, even though tragic, that number is actually below the average number for several of our larger cities. In general, the greater the population for which you generalize, the more examples you need.

4. Are the examples representative? The examples you use as evidence should be typical, not exceptions. Was this weekend typical, or was the number of murders abnormally high?

argument by analogy:
says that what is true in
one case is or will be true
in another.

Argument by Analogy.   An analogy is a comparison. **Argument by analogy** links two objects or concepts and asserts that what is true of one will be true of the other. Arguing that computerized phone registration would work at your college because it works at State U is an example of reasoning by analogy.

Argument by analogy is appropriate when the program you advocate or oppose has been tried elsewhere. Some states have lotteries, no-fault insurance, and the line-item veto; others do not. Some school systems allow corporal punishment, offer magnet programs, and require a passing grade for participation in extracurricular activities; others do not. A speech defending or disputing one of these programs could demonstrate success or failure elsewhere to establish its position.

William Donald Schaefer, governor of Maryland, used argument by analogy to urge an expanded federal role in providing child-care services:

> Today's parents do all they can to keep their children safe. They scrutinize the toys they play with, the food they eat and clothes they wear. Because our world is so complicated, however, with thousands of children's products available to families, parents can't monitor everything. As a result, we the people, through the federal government, act to ensure the health and safety of children. Children's toys, food, and clothing are all tested. The federal government requires special caps on prescription drug bottles to prevent children from taking potentially harmful medication.
>
> These practices are accepted by our society as necessary for the protection of children, because we recognize that our kids are often too young or inexperienced to know what is harmful to them. If it is good policy to regulate what children play with, eat, and wear, is it not also prudent that we ensure safety in the places where they learn and grow while their parents are at work?[8]

The preceding example illustrates the persuasive appeal of argument by analogy. You introduce a situation that is familiar to the audience and explain why we respond to it as we do. You then assert that your idea or proposal is analogous and, therefore, deserves a similar response. The key to this pattern of argument is the similarity between the two entities. In testing the validity of your argument by analogy, you need to answer this question: "Are the two entities sufficiently similar to justify my conclusion that what is true of one will be true of the other?" If not, your reasoning is faulty. This question can best be answered by dividing it into two questions.

KEY POINTS

Tests of Argument by Analogy

1. Are the similarities between the two cases relevant?
2. Are any of the differences between the two cases relevant?

1. Are the similarities between the two cases relevant? If you decide to argue by analogy for a computerized phone registration system, you may find many similarities between your college and State U. However, the fact that both schools have similar library facilities and the same mascot is irrelevant to registration. Equivalent student enrollments, advising procedures, and periods for registration are highly relevant and can be forceful evidence as you build your case.

2. Are any of the differences between the two cases relevant? If so, how do those differences affect your claim? If you discover that, unlike State, your college has neither an integrated computer network nor the technical staff to program it, these differences are relevant to your topic and will undermine the validity of your claim.

345

The Structure of Persuasion

Argument by Cause.   **Argument by cause** connects two elements or events and claims that one is produced by the other. Causal reasoning takes two forms — reasoning from effect to cause and from cause to effect. The difference between the two is their chronological order. An *effect to cause argument* begins at a point of time (when the effects are evident) and moves back in time (to when the cause occurred). When you feel ill and go to the doctor, the doctor will usually identify the symptoms (the effects) of the problem and then diagnose the cause. The doctor is problem solving by reasoning from effect to cause.

argument by cause: says that one action or condition caused or will cause another.

In contrast, *cause to effect argument* begins at a point of time (when the cause occurred) and moves forward (to when the effects occurred or will occur). Doctors reason from cause to effect when they tell their patients who smoke that this habit may result in emphysema or lung cancer. Casey urged his listeners to support significantly higher taxes on cigarettes. He argued from effect to cause as he analyzed Canada's decline in smoking.

This year [1993], the Canadian government released a report that was good news for the health of Canadians. Cigarette consumption declined almost 25 percent from 1985 to 1991.

Effect

What caused this dramatic decrease? According to the July 13, 1993, *Globe and Mail,* since 1980 the Canadian government has raised tobacco taxes by more than 550 percent, and the provinces by more than 500 percent. The report concluded, "An increase in the level of tax does lead to a reduction in tax-paid tobacco consumption." David Sweanor, senior legal counsel for the Non-Smokers Rights Association, is more dramatic: "Federal policy has been a massive success. It represents one of the biggest single advances we've had in terms of public health, and it's been done through fiscal levers rather than new medical spending."

Cause

Casey focused on an effect — a decline in cigarette consumption — and then moved back to a cause — an increase in cigarette taxes. When he subsequently argued that the United States should follow Canada's lead, he was using argument by analogy.

The following example demonstrates cause to effect argument. D. Stanley Eitzen, sociology professor at Colorado State University, used a cause to effect pattern in a speech on problem students:

Young people see some 12,000 acts of televised violence a year. A study by the University of Pennsylvania's Annenberg School of Communication revealed that children watching Saturday morning cartoons in 1988 saw an average of 26.4 violent acts each hour (up from 18.6 per hour in 1980).

Cause

Two of the conclusions by the authors of this study were that: (1) Children see a mean and dangerous world in these cartoons where people are not to be trusted and disputes are legitimately settled by violence; and (2) children who see so much violence become desensitized to it.

Effect

The powerful and consistent messages from television are reinforced in the movies children watch, as well as the toys that are made for them, and the computerized games such as Nintendo that so many find addicting.

Cause

Given these strong cultural messages that pervade society, is it any wonder that violence is widespread among the youth of this generation?[9]

Effect

When you argue by cause, test your reasoning to make certain it is sound. In order to do this, ask yourself the following three questions.

KEY POINTS

Tests of Argument by Cause

1. Does a causal relationship exist?
2. Could the presumed cause produce the effect?
3. Could the effect result from other causes?

---

1. Does a causal relationship exist? In order for an argument from cause to effect or effect to cause to be valid, a causal relationship must exist between the two elements. As we will discuss later in this chapter, just because one event precedes another does not mean that the first caused the second. One student we mentioned earlier argued that the scholastic decline of American education began with, and was caused by, the Supreme Court's decision outlawing mandatory school prayer. We doubt the connection.

2. Could the presumed cause produce the effect? During the highly inflationary times of the late 1970s, one of our students gave a speech in which she argued that various price hikes had contributed to the high inflation rate. She provided three examples of price increases: The cost of postage stamps had increased 87.5 percent, chewing gum 100 percent, and downtown parking meter fees 150 percent. While she was able to document the dramatic percentage increase in the prices of each of these products, her examples had more interest than impact. Her examples did not convince her audience or her instructor that these increases by themselves could produce a significant influence on the inflation rate.

3. Could the effect result from other causes? A number of causes can converge to produce one effect. A student who argues that next year's increased tuition and fees are a result of the college president's fiscal mismanagement may have a point. But a number of other factors may have made the tuition increase necessary: state revenue shortfalls, decreased enrollment, cutbacks in federal aid, major spending on campus building projects, and so on. Speakers strengthen their arguments when they are able to prove the following: that the alleged cause contributed substantively to producing the effect, and that without the cause the effect would not have occurred or the problem would have been much less severe.

Argument by Deduction.   Ben began his speech on time management with the following statement:

> All of us are taking courses that require us to be in class and to study outside class. In addition, many of us are members of social, academic, religious, or career-oriented clubs and organizations. Some of us work. All of us like to party! Crowded into our school and work schedules are our responsibilities to friends and family members. In short, we're busy!
>
> College is a hectic time in our lives. Sometimes it seems that we're trying to cram thirty-four hours of activity into a twenty-four-hour day. In order to survive this schedule and beat the stress, college students need to develop effective time-management skills. You are no exception! If you listen to my speech today, you will learn how to set realistic goals, meet them, and still have time to socialize with friends and get a good night's sleep. Sound impossible? Just listen closely for the next eight minutes.

Ben used two types of arguments in his introduction. He opened by arguing from example, providing several instances to make his case that college life is busy. He then used deductive reasoning to make the speech relevant to each member of the audience. A **deductive argument** moves from a general category to a specific instance. In this sense, deductive arguments are the reverse of argument by example. To see why that's true, consider the structure of a deductive argument.

Deductive arguments consist of a pattern of three statements: a major premise, a minor premise, and a conclusion. This pattern of deductive argument is called a **syllogism.** The **major premise** is a claim about a general group of people, events, or conditions. Ben's major premise was this: "College students need to develop effective time-management skills." The **minor premise** places a person, event, or condition into a general class. Ben's minor premise could be phrased like this: "You are a college student." The **conclusion** argues that what is true of the general class is true of the specific instance or individual. Ben concluded that each college student in his audience needed to develop effective time-management skills.

Use the following steps to check the structure and flow of your deductive argument:

1. State your major premise.
2. Say "because" and then state your minor premise.
3. State your conclusion.

The resulting two sentences should flow together easily and make sense. This strategy tests the interconnectedness of the parts of your deductive argument. Ben could have tested the clarity of his argument by saying the following: "College students need to develop effective time-management skills. *Because* you are a college student, you need to develop effective time-management skills." Notice that if the two premises are true and relate to each other, the conclusion must also be true.

Major premises sometimes embody principles that shape our beliefs and guide our actions. A speaker who makes the following statement is using deductive reasoning: "Judge Shady committed an ethical violation when she accepted a campaign contribution from the defendant in a case scheduled for her court." A diagram of this argument is as follows:

Major premise: It is unethical for judges to accept campaign contributions from individuals involved in cases in their courts.
Minor premise: Judge I.M. Shady accepted a contribution from the defendant in a case scheduled for her court.
Conclusion: Judge Shady is guilty of unethical judicial conduct.

In order for deductive arguments to be valid, they must meet certain tests. Whether you are listening to others' arguments or evaluating arguments in your own speech, keep in mind three questions.

deductive argument: says that what is true generally is or will be true in a specific instance.

syllogism: the pattern of a deductive argument, consisting of a major premise, a minor premise, and a conclusion.

major premise: a claim about a general group of people, events, or conditions.

minor premise: a statement placing a person, an event, or a condition into a general class.

conclusion: the deductive argument that what is true of the general class is true of the specific instance.

1. Do the premises relate to each other? **2.** Is the major premise true? **3.** Is the minor premise true?	**KEY POINTS** **Tests of Argument by Deduction**

1. Do the premises relate to each other? "All men are created equal. Equal is an artificial sweetener. Therefore, all men are artificial sweeteners." This statement doesn't make much sense, does it? The first sentence uses the word *equal* to mean "equivalent." The second uses *Equal* as a product name for a sugar substitute. In order for an argument to be valid, the premises must relate to each other. In this case they clearly do not.

Let's construct another example. Suppose John prepares a speech trying to persuade his classmates to apply for a new academic scholarship named after his father, James Burke. In his speech, John makes the following statement:

> Any student enrolled in State U who is a U.S. citizen can apply for the Burke Scholarship. That includes everyone in this class. Just think, next year you could have your entire tuition and fees paid, and you can spend your money for something you've been wanting but were unable to afford. Maybe even that new CD player!

Before John convinces his classmates to apply for the scholarship, he first tells them that they are eligible. His argument may be depicted as follows:

Major premise: Any State U student who is a U.S. citizen can apply for the Burke Scholarship.

Minor premise: Every student in this class is a State U student who is a citizen of the United States.

Conclusion: Therefore, every student in this class can apply for the Burke Scholarship.

The terms in the minor premise fall within the scope of the major premise. Both premises relate to each other, and the conclusion seems logical.

2. Is the major premise true? Before John's classmates head to the financial aid office to begin filling out a scholarship application form, they should ask the question, "Is the major premise of the argument true?" Suppose two prerequisites for application are full-time student status and good academic standing. The statement "any State U student who is a U.S. citizen can apply for the Burke Scholarship" is then false. Part-time and probationary students cannot apply. The conclusion of the argument ("Every student in this class can apply for the Burke Scholarship") would therefore not necessarily be true. You must be able to prove your major premises before you draw conclusions.

3. Is the minor premise true? A false minor premise is just as damaging to an argument as a false major premise. Let's suppose that John's major premise is true, and that any State U student who is a U.S. citizen can apply for the Burke Scholarship. What if his class includes some foreign students? His minor premise ("Every student in this class is a State U student who is a citizen of the United States") is then false. Those students are not eligible for the scholarship, and John's conclusion is false. Arguing a position entails ethical considerations. You must know your facts and reason logically from them.

Argument by Authority. **Argument by authority** differs from the four other forms of argument we have discussed. To see how it is different, consider the following example from Lynn's speech:

argument by authority: uses testimony from an expert source to prove a speaker's claim.

> I believe that every student should be allowed to vote for Outstanding Professor on Campus, rather than having the award determined by a select committee of

the faculty. And I'm not alone in my opinion. Last year's recipient of the award, Dr. Linda Carter, agrees. The President of the Faculty Senate spoke out in favor of this proposal at last week's forum, and the Student Government Association passed a resolution supporting it.

Argument from authority uses testimony from an expert source to prove a speaker's claim; its validity depends on the credibility the authority has for the audience. In this example, Lynn did not offer arguments based on example, analogy, cause, or deduction to explain the validity of her position. Instead, she asserted that two distinguished professors and the SGA agreed with her. She asked her audience to believe her position based on the credentials of the authority figures who endorsed her claim. Her rationale was that her sources had access to sufficient information and had the expertise to interpret it accurately; thus, we should trust their conclusions.

Let's look at a second example of argument by authority. In testifying against a child-care services bill, Gary Bauer of the Family Research Council of America attacked the "perception that most preschool children in America today are primarily cared for by a non-family member," an argument he claimed "is patently untrue." To support his contention, he offered the following information:

According to the most recent survey of child care arrangements by the Census Bureau, 54 percent of the nearly 18 million children under the age of five are primarily cared for by a mother who stays home with her children. In addition, 7 percent have "tag-team parents" who work different shifts and share child-rearing responsibilities. And 4 percent have "double-time mothers" who care for their child while they babysit other children or earn income in some other way.

Thus the primary child-care arrangement for 65 percent of all preschool children is care by one or both parents. When the 11 percent primarily cared for by a grandmother or other relatives are added in, a whopping three-fourths of all children under the age of five are primarily cared for by one or more family members.[10]

The persuasiveness of Bauer's argument depends on the audience's perception of the credibility of the Census Bureau survey and of Bauer's reliability to report data accurately.

An argument based on authority is only as valid as the source's credibility. To test your argument, ask and answer two questions: (1) Is the source an expert? (2) Is the source unbiased? Our discussion of these questions, as well as other tests of supporting materials, in Chapter 8, "Supporting Your Speech," will help you select the best authority for your claim.

In this section, we have identified and discussed five types of argument. You will want to select as many of these forms as are appropriate to your topic and audience. We have also illustrated how to test these arguments so that they work to make your speech more believable.

Testing the arguments you use and hear others use is crucial to effective, ethical speaking and listening. When you analyze the arguments you use, you strengthen them and can save yourself the embarrassment of being caught using illogical or invalid proof. It is just as important to check the validity of persuasive arguments you hear, however. By doing this, you avoid being duped into misguided thoughts and actions.

In spite of these tests, persuasive speakers sometimes incorporate certain errors of proof into their speeches. These errors are so widely used that they have been named and studied. In the following section, we take a look at some of these mirages of persuasion — arguments that appear, but only appear, to say something authoritative. We want you to be able to identify these errors so you can avoid them.

Fallacies of Argument

"He who will not reason is a bigot; he who cannot is a fool; and he who dares not is a slave."
WILLIAM DRUMMOND

fallacy: a flaw in the logic of an argument.

A **fallacy** is "any defect in reasoning which destroys its validity."[11] Remember two of the arguments we presented at the beginning of this chapter — one about lawyers and the other about the Mississippi River? The first rests on the unproven and highly unlikely assumption that the number of lawyers will continue to increase at a rate seven times faster than the population. In the second example, Mark Twain assumes that what has occurred in the past 176-year history of the Mississippi River can be projected farther back in time. These examples are humorous because of their obvious distortion of figures. Unfortunately, not all distortions of logic we hear are so obvious, nor are they always used for humorous effect. In fact, fallacies are often persuasive and dangerous for the same reason: Because they resemble valid reasoning, we often accept them as legitimate. They can produce bad decisions leading to harmful consequences.

We want to stress that fallacies are flawed patterns of reasoning that you will want to avoid as both speaker and listener. As you construct your persuasive speech, make sure that the arguments you encounter in your research are valid. Then, use your research to develop sound arguments to support the ideas in your speech. As a listener, you have an ethical responsibility to evaluate critically the ideas other persuasive speakers present to you. Be alert for those arguments based on sound reasoning and for those based on flawed reasoning. Consider the valid arguments and reject fallacious ones. How can you tell the difference?

Fallacies come in many different varieties. In fact, *The New York Public Library Desk Reference* notes that "there are now over 125 separate fallacies, most with their own impressive-sounding names, many of them in Latin."[12] For our purposes, we will discuss eight of the most common fallacies. Some you will readily recognize while others may be new to you.

hasty generalization: a fallacy that makes claims from insufficient or unrepresentative examples.

Hasty Generalization. People who jump to conclusions commit the fallacy of **hasty generalization.** When speakers make claims based upon insufficient or unrepresentative instances, their reasoning is usually flawed. For example, a speaker names three members of Congress accused of ethical violations and concludes that Congress is a corrupt institution. A senator notes that gasoline prices are increasing and warns of impending spiraling inflation. An advertisement shows a dentist recommending a particular brand of toothbrush, and the consumer assumes that it carries the endorsement of dentists in general. A student concludes that a public speaking course will not be helpful based on a hectic first class meeting. People who rely too much on first impressions, who do not read widely, or who spend little time researching are prime candidates for reasoning from hasty generalization. They often develop beliefs and opinions that later prove erroneous. Just as dangerous, such people will often reason from hasty generalization in the speeches they deliver.

Post Hoc Ergo Propter Hoc. This fallacy uses the Latin title and literally means "after this, therefore because of this." A chronological fallacy, ***post hoc*** (as it is usually called) assumes that because one event preceded another, the first caused the second. Perhaps you have heard a friend comment, "I should have known it would rain; I just washed my car!" Your friend is probably making a joke based on the *post hoc* fallacy. People exhibit *post hoc* reasoning when they expect something good to happen if they carry a lucky charm while gambling in a Las Vegas casino, wear a lucky shirt to a football game, or cross their fingers as a teacher returns a graded exam. *Forbes* magazine reports this truly bizarre example of false causation:

> The friendly number crunchers at Minneapolis' IDS Financial Services Inc. have crunched the data on all past Super Bowl games and correlated their findings with the broad stock market averages. Their conclusion: If the National Conference football team wins the Super Bowl, the market, as measured by the Standard & Poor's 500 Index, will be up for the year. Conversely, if the American Conference team wins, the market will be down.
>
> Here's the evidence. So far there have been 22 Super Bowls.... National teams have won 15 times. Each time that happened the market was up for the year. American teams, on the other hand, have won 7 times, and all but twice … the market was down for the year. As barometers go, 20 for 22 is not bad.[13]

These examples may seem absurd, with obvious defects in reasoning. Yet, other examples of confusing coincidence with causation are more subtle and potentially more damaging. For example, a person rejects medical treatment, relying instead on an unresearched cure because someone else tried it and subsequently got well. An individual refuses to exercise and diet, citing the example of his Uncle Bert who "drank like a fish, smoked like a chimney, ate anything he wanted, never worked a day in his life, and lived to be 93!" An incumbent mayor takes credit for every city improvement that occurred since she took office; her opponent blames her for everything bad that happened during this time. An event may have more than one cause. It is also preceded by occurrences having no effect on it whatsoever. As a result, determining the relationship between two events or conditions is often difficult. But you must examine that relation if you are to avoid the *post hoc ergo propter hoc* fallacy.

Slippery Slope. Envision yourself at the top of a hill on a wintry day. You take one step, slip on a patch of ice, lose your footing, and begin sliding down the hill. You try to regain your balance, but you continue your slide, stopping only when you reach the bottom of the hill. This visual image depicts the slippery slope fallacy. **Slippery slope** is a fallacy of causation that asserts that one action inevitably sets in motion a chain of events or indicates a trend. This defect in reasoning is exemplified in the following two arguments:

> If you amend the Constitution to prohibit flag burning, you open the door to other amendments to our Bill of Rights. Ultimately, you destroy the freedoms upon which our nation is based.
>
> If we begin to control the sale of guns by restricting the purchase of handguns, where will it end? Will shotguns be next? And then hunting rifles? Soon the right to bear arms will disappear from the Constitution, and sportsmen and -women will be denied one of their basic freedoms.

post hoc: a chronological fallacy that says that a prior event caused a subsequent event.

slippery slope: a fallacy of causation that says that one action inevitably sets a chain of events in motion.

These speakers' arguments imply that a single act will set in motion a series of events that no one will be able to stop, but that is not necessarily the case. Just because legislators support one constitutional amendment or one law doesn't necessarily mean that they must support subsequent reforms. Most of the time, a slide down the slope is preventable. Each journey involves a series of decisions, and it is possible to retain or regain your footing.

red herring: a fallacy that introduces irrelevant issues to deflect attention from the subject under discussion.

Red Herring.   The name of the **red herring** fallacy apparently originated with the English fox hunt. When the hunt was over, the hunt master would drag a red herring — a type of fish that is smoked and salted — across the path of the hounds. The pungent scent would divert the dogs from their pursuit of the fox, and they could then be rounded up. This diversionary tactic was also supposedly used by escaping criminals to throw dogs off their trails.

How does the red herring fallacy work in a speech? Bruce Waller provides a vivid example and analysis of this defect in reasoning using the issue of gun control:

> If the debate is over whether handguns should be banned, it is relevant to consider how many people have been killed in handgun accidents. But suppose someone asserts, "Everybody talks about handgun accidents! But think of how many people are killed each year in auto accidents! Why don't we ban automobiles?" You must hold your breath and cover your nose and stay on the trail, for a red herring has just been dragged across the argument. The danger of auto accidents is certainly serious, and perhaps on another occasion we should discuss how to reduce that danger — but that has nothing to do with the question of banning handguns. Whether there are other unacceptable dangers in society is not the issue; the question is instead whether handguns pose an unacceptable risk. Perhaps they do, perhaps they do not, but no progress will be made on that issue if the arguers are distracted by irrelevant reasons.[14]

In essence, then, a speaker guilty of the red herring fallacy introduces an irrelevant issue to deflect attention from the subject under discussion. Thomas Kean, then governor of New Jersey, used this red herring in his keynote address at the 1988 Republican National Convention:

> A great deal about the Dukakis campaign can be summed up by one incident.
>   You see this flag of red, white, and blue? It symbolizes the "Land of the Free" and the "Home of the Brave." Well, their [the Democrats'] media consultants in Atlanta [site of the Democratic National Convention] said they didn't think the colors looked good on television. So they changed red to pink, blue to azure, and the white to eggshell. Well, I don't know about you, but I believe Americans, Democrat and Republican alike, have no use for pastel patriotism.[15]

The alliterative phrase "pastel patriotism" evokes a negative image and is certainly memorable, but color selection has nothing to do with a person's patriotism. This red herring, like all others, diverts discussion from germane issues to irrelevant concerns. When you present a persuasive speech, you are an advocate for the position you present. As such, you have an ethical responsibility to defend your arguments. Answer criticisms of your argument with evidence and logic; don't deflect criticism by diverting your audience to another track.

Appeal to Tradition.   This fallacy is grounded in a respect for traditional ways of doing things. On the surface, respect for tradition seems reasonable. But the fallacy commonly called **appeal to tradition** defends the status quo and opposes change by arguing that old ways are always superior to new ways. Its most common form of expression — "We've always done it that way" — is merely descriptive. It discourages discussion and reevaluation of our traditions.

As important as many traditions are to us, they should not be used to thwart needed change. Our nation's founders created a glorious document that gave us many of the freedoms we enjoy. Yet that document also precluded non-European Americans and women from full participation in our society. The fight to secure the right to vote for all citizens challenged that tradition, and we all agree that this change is for the better. Keep in mind that the old ways are not always the best ways.

appeal to tradition: a fallacy that opposes change by arguing that old ways are always superior to new ways.

False Dilemma.

"Our major obligation is not to mistake slogans for solutions." **EDWARD R. MURROW**

When forced to choose between alternatives, you face a dilemma. Dilemmas can be actual or false. In an actual dilemma, the alternatives you face are real; there is no room for compromise. For example, suppose you are asked to choose between going to a movie with friends and going to the library to research your upcoming speech. If the library and theatre hours coincide, your dilemma is real and you must forfeit either entertainment or study.

A **false dilemma** exists when you have more than the two options presented. For example, if there is a late showing of the movie, perhaps you can convince your friends to meet you at the theatre after you finish your research. In this instance, the dilemma is false because you do not have to choose between studying and seeing the movie; you can do both. Woody Allen's quotation at the beginning of this chapter is an example of a false dilemma. Certainly, humans face alternatives other than utter hopelessness and total extinction.

false dilemma: a fallacy that confronts listeners with two choices when, in reality, more options exist.

The fallacy of false dilemma, sometimes called the either-or fallacy, presents the listener with two choices when, in reality, there are more. Characterized by a "bumper sticker" mentality, the dilemma usually polarizes issues into two mutually exclusive categories, such as "America — love it or leave it!" and "When guns are outlawed, only outlaws will have guns!" Neither of those slogans allows for middle-ground positions. As cartoonist Charles Schulz has noted with wry understatement, "There's a difference between a philosophy and a bumper sticker."

Listeners should be especially attentive to all "either-or" and "if-then" statements they hear. These grammatical constructions lend themselves to the fallacy of false dilemma, as in the following examples:

A person is either a Republican or a Democrat. Because I know Carolyn isn't a Republican, she must be a Democrat.

The issue is very simple: Either you support the Constitution on which this nation was founded, or you're not a patriotic American.

That's the policy of this company. Either you're with us or against us.

I don't support a cutback in defense spending. I don't want to see a weakening of America's strength.

Each of these examples presents the listener with only two choices. However, they disregard other legitimate options: Carolyn may be a Libertarian, a Socialist, a member of some other political party, or an independent. We can exhibit patriotism and company loyalty and still question the laws and policies of nations and companies. Eliminating unnecessary defense spending does not necessarily weaken the country. Using that money for other important projects — like major road and bridge repair — may actually make America stronger.

Bandwagon.   In the 1800s and early 1900s, political candidates held parades to meet the people. A band rode on a wagon leading the parade through a town. As the wagon passed, local leaders would jump on the bandwagon to show their support. The number of people on board was considered a barometer of the candidate's popularity and political strength.

bandwagon: a fallacy that determines truth, goodness, or wisdom by popular opinion.

The **bandwagon** fallacy in reasoning is based on the assumption that popular opinion is an accurate measure of truth and wisdom. The Latin name for this appeal to popular opinion is *argumentum ad populum*. Frequently referred to as the "everybody's doing it" fallacy, bandwagon arguments commonly use phrases such as "everyone knows" or "most people agree." Door-to-door salespeople or intrusive phone solicitors who tell you that all your friends and neighbors are purchasing their encyclopedia or portrait package use the bandwagon appeal. They base their sales pitch on the product's popularity, not on its merits.

Speakers who defend the rightness of their positions by pointing to polls showing popular support similarly exploit the bandwagon fallacy. While agreement regarding a belief or action may be reassuring, it is no guarantee of accuracy or truth. "Truth is not always democratic."[16] History is cluttered with popularly held misconceptions. Remember, most people once believed that the world was flat; that the sun revolved around Earth; and that leeching, or bleeding, patients was state-of-the-art medical treatment. You decide the validity of an argument by its form and substance, not merely by how many people agree on it.

Ad Hominem.

"If you can't answer a man's argument, all is not lost; you can still call him vile names."

ELBERT HUBBARD

ad hominem: a fallacy that urges listeners to reject an idea because of the allegedly poor character of the person voicing it; name calling.

Ad hominem, literally meaning "to the man," arguments ask listeners to reject an idea because of the poor character of the person voicing it. Political speeches, especially those delivered at national conventions, are peppered with *ad hominem* arguments. These statements often evoke applause, cheers, and laughter, but they provide little insight into issues. When Texas state treasurer Ann Richards delivered the keynote address at the 1988 Democratic National Convention, she said of George Bush, "And now that he's after a job that he can't get appointed to, he's like Columbus discovering America — he's found child care, he's found education. Poor George, he can't help it — he was born with a silver foot in his mouth."[17]

In its most obvious form, this fallacy is name calling. For some people, simply knowing that a speaker is liberal, conservative, feminist, or fundamentalist is sufficient to close their minds. They disregard the merits of an idea because of the person giving the message. But, as we stated in Chapter 2, an ethical listener has a responsibility to give all ideas a fair hearing.

To be an effective and ethical persuader, you must know how to construct valid arguments and avoid defective ones such as those we have just discussed. Once you have mastered this ability, you can use your arguments to achieve the overall goal of your speech.

In the remainder of this chapter, we will show you how to develop a persuasive proposition and how you can effectively organize your arguments.

■ SELECTING PROPOSITIONS FOR PERSUASIVE SPEECHES

In Chapter 6, "Selecting Your Speech Topic," we explained that your first steps in constructing a speech are to select your topic, focus or narrow it, determine your general purpose, formulate your specific purpose, and construct a thesis statement. In persuasive speaking, you can add one additional step: state your proposition. Let's make sure that we understand the difference between a proposition and a thesis statement.

For example, if you speak on the topic of improving education, you may narrow this broad subject and select as your specific purpose to persuade the audience that teacher salaries should be increased. Your basic position — "teacher salaries should be increased" — can be thought of as a proposition. A **proposition** is a declarative sentence expressing a judgment you want the audience to accept. Notice that this proposition *expresses a judgment* that *is debatable* and that *requires proof.* We will discuss these three characteristics of propositions in the next section.

Your thesis statement, in contrast, lists the reasons you offer to prove your proposition. In the preceding example, your thesis statement could be this: Higher teacher salaries would recruit better teachers, retain better teachers, and improve student learning. The following example also demonstrates the difference between a proposition and a thesis statement:

> **Proposition:** The new campus classroom building should be named Richter Hall.
> **Specific Purpose:** To persuade the audience that the new classroom building should be named for Louise Richter.
> **Thesis Statement:** The new classroom building should be named for Louise Richter, an outstanding teacher, advisor, and friend.
> **Key Ideas:**   I. The name of the new classroom building should honor an outstanding educator.
>   II. Louise Richter deserves this recognition.
>   A. She was an outstanding teacher.
>   B. She was an outstanding advisor to student organizations.
>   C. She was a cherished friend.

Notice again that this proposition expresses a judgment, while the thesis statement includes the reasons the speaker will offer to prove the proposition.

proposition: a declarative sentence expressing a judgment a speaker wants listeners to accept.

Characteristics of Propositions

If you formulate a well-worded proposition early in preparing your persuasive speech, you will be sure of your persuasive goal and can keep it firmly in mind. Your proposition also helps you to focus your persuasive speech and test the relevance of supporting ideas as you develop them. Devising your proposition can be relatively easy. As we suggested before, propositions are marked by three characteristics.

KEY POINTS

Requirements of Propositions

1. Propositions express a judgment.
2. Propositions are debatable.
3. Propositions require proof.

Propositions Express a Judgment.   A proposition for a persuasive speech states the position you will defend. Consequently, it should be worded as a declarative sentence expressing your position. If you advocate statehood for Puerto Rico, you could word your proposition like this: The United States should grant Puerto Rico statehood. This simple declarative sentence clearly states your position on the issue.

Sometimes, however, you may be interested in a topic but lack enough information to have developed a position on it. In this case, you may first want to phrase a question to guide your research. Once you answer the question, you can then develop your proposition.

> Mark was a criminal justice student interested in the issue of the death penalty. He had read an article discussing the pros and cons of capital punishment for juveniles convicted of capital crimes, but he had not developed his own position on the issue. To guide his research, Mark worded the following question: Is the death penalty for juveniles cruel and unusual punishment? He researched the topic, reading articles by scholars and jurists on both sides of the issue. He made a list of arguments for and against capital punishment for juveniles. Although Mark supported capital punishment for adult offenders, his research convinced him to oppose it for juveniles. The proposition he subsequently decided to defend was "The death penalty for juveniles is cruel and unusual punishment." By phrasing his position statement, writing it out, and keeping it in front of him as he continued researching and assembling his arguments, Mark was able to keep his speech focused on arguments against capital punishment for juveniles.

Propositions Are Debatable.   Propositions are appropriate for persuasive speeches only if they are debatable. In other words, the judgment must include some degree of controversy. The proposition "The earth revolves around the sun" is not a good proposition for a persuasive speech because you are unlikely to find any qualified authority today opposing that statement. We now accept it as fact. Once we accept a proposition as fact, it ceases to be an appropriate topic for persuasive speeches. However, in the sixteenth century, when Copernicus's heliocentric theory opposed governmental and religious teaching as well as popular opinion, the topic was debatable. It was then a proposition appropriate for persuasive speaking.

Another example of a proposition that probably is not debatable is "Jack Ruby killed Lee Harvey Oswald." Millions of people watched the shooting live on television or saw it rebroadcast. The filmed account of the shooting convinced most people to accept the statement as fact. On the other hand, the proposition "Lee Harvey Oswald killed John F. Kennedy" is debatable and has been the subject of much discussion. Despite the findings of the Warren Commission Report, several theories of the assassination remain.

Propositions Require Proof.   Finally, propositions require proof. A proposition is an assertion, and assertions are statements that have not yet been proven. Your objective as a persuasive speaker is to offer compelling reasons for listeners to accept your proposition. As we discussed earlier in this chapter, you may support your proposition with arguments from example, analogy, cause, deduction, or authority.

Types of Propositions

Propositions for persuasive speeches are of three types: fact, value, and policy. The type of organization and support materials you will use depends on the type of proposition you defend.

Propositions of Fact. A **proposition of fact** focuses on belief. You ask the audience to affirm the truth or falsity of a statement. The following are examples of propositions of fact:

> Electric automobiles are commercially feasible.
> Conversion to a cashless society would reduce sales of illegal drugs.
> Irradiated food is harmful to your health.
> Heredity is not a significant risk factor for cancer.
> Gun control laws violate the second amendment of the U.S. Constitution.
> An aspirin a day can reduce the risk of heart disease.

proposition of fact:
an assertion about the truth or falsity of a statement.

Delegates debate propositions of policy when they consider proposals brought before an assembly.
(Source: © Owen Frank/Stock, Boston)

Jennifer's speech on random drug testing was a speech on a proposition of fact. Jennifer defended this proposition: Random drug testing on the job decreases workplace drug use. Her specific purpose and key ideas were as follows:

Specific Purpose: To convince the audience that random drug testing (RDT) decreases workplace drug use.

Key Ideas: **I.** RDT deters casual drug use.
               II. RDT helps decrease drug addiction.
                   A. Users are identified.
                   B. Users are encouraged to seek therapy.

proposition of value: an assertion about the relative worth of an idea or action.

Propositions of Value.   A **proposition of value** requires a judgment on the worth of an idea or action. You ask the audience to determine the "goodness" or "badness" of something, as in this proposition: "Corporal punishment in schools is wrong." Remember Mark's speech defending the proposition "The death penalty for juveniles is cruel and unusual punishment"? That too was a proposition of value. Propositions of value can also ask you to compare two items and determine which is better, as in Sir William Blackstone's statement, "It is better that ten guilty persons escape than one innocent suffer." Other propositions of value include:

Censorship is a greater evil than pornography.

Minority rule is morally indefensible.

Active euthanasia is immoral.

The no pass-no play rule for high school students undermines more important educational goals.

Retribution is a more important goal of criminal justice than rehabilitation.

Subliminal advertising is unethical.

A citizen's right to privacy is more important than the government's right to gather information.

Direct legislation (initiative and referendum) is good for democracy.

Civil disobedience is justifiable in a democracy.

Educational tracking of students by ability perpetuates social and racial inequality.

Suppose you decided to persuade your audience that free agency is bad for professional sports. You could develop your speech on this value proposition as follows:

Specific Purpose: To persuade the audience that free agency is hurting professional sports.

Key Ideas: **I.** It destroys the competitive balance of teams.
               II. It undermines the financial solvency of teams.
              III. It creates bad role models for kids.

Another example of a speech on a proposition of value is Cary's speech on "infotainment," the media's blending of news and entertainment:

Specific Purpose: To persuade the audience that "infotainment" harms the public's right to know.

Key Ideas: **I.** News reenactments mislead the public.
               II. Docudramas misinform the public.

proposition of policy: a statement requesting support for a course of action.

Propositions of Policy.   A **proposition of policy** advocates a course of action. You ask the audience to endorse a policy or to commit themselves to some action. These statements usually include the word *should*. Here are some examples of policy propositions:

> College athletes should be paid.
> There should be greater restrictions on the types of art funded by the National Endowment for the Arts.
> There should be a ban on advertising of all tobacco products.
> The National Park Service should allow forest fires that pose no threat to lives or property to burn themselves out.
> Workers striking against the federal government should face immediate loss of jobs.
> The Uniform Anatomical Gift Act should be amended to permit organ transplantation from anencephalic infants.

In her speech, Lisa argued the benefits of a multicultural college experience. She advocated that all students should be required to take ethnic studies courses. Organizing her speech topically, Lisa presented three reasons to support her proposal.

> ***Specific Purpose:*** To persuade the audience that ethnic studies (ES) courses should be required for all students.
> ***Key Ideas:*** **I.** ES courses promote cultural awareness.
> **II.** ES courses reduce ethnic and racial conflict.
> **III.** ES courses improve social skills.

ORGANIZING PERSUASIVE SPEECHES

In Chapter 9, "Organizing Your Speech," we introduced you to six ways to divide your speech into key ideas: topical, chronological, spatial, causal, pro-con, and gimmick divisions. As we mentioned, these patterns can be used for both informative and persuasive speeches. In fact, the examples we used in our foregoing discussion of propositions of fact, value, and policy all follow topical patterns. However, you have at your disposal four additional organizational patterns that are unique to persuasive speeches.

Refutational Strategy

refute: to dispute; to counter one argument with another.

refutational strategy: a pattern of organizing persuasive speeches by (1) stating the position you are refuting, (2) stating your position, (3) supporting your position, and (4) showing how your position undermines the opposing argument.

As we have noted, persuasive propositions must be debatable — a spark of controversy must be involved in discussing the issue. There is always another side, perhaps several sides, in addition to the one presented by the speaker. You may even select a topic because you read or hear a statement with which you disagree. Your purpose, then, is to **refute,** or disprove, that statement. For each argument you refute, you may want to use the following four-step **refutational strategy:**

1. State the position you are refuting.
2. State your position.
3. Support your position.
4. Show how your position undermines the opposing argument.

Joel became interested in the topic of irradiated food (food treated with gamma rays) when a classmate warned the class of the dangers of eating foods processed this way. After researching the topic, Joel decided that irradiation was a safe and beneficial process. He presented the following argument in his speech. Notice how he used each of the four steps of refutation.

States position to be refuted

One argument opponents make against irradiated foods is that they harm consumer health. Some have even claimed that these foods become radioactive and can cause death.

States speaker's position

Well, before you're taken in by these claims, let's replace the fear with facts. Rather than harming consumer health, irradiation actually protects it.

Supports speaker's position

In a 1992 issue of *Public Health Reports,* James Mason, Assistant Secretary of Health, writes: "More than 40 years of research involving literally hundreds of studies plainly demonstrate that foods processed with radiation using the permitted sources do not become radioactive...." Comparing irradiation with pasteurization, Dr. Mason says: "Not only does the technology extend the shelf life of produce by inhibiting ripening or sprouting, it kills or renders noninfective many harmful food-borne organisms...."

In the October-December 1992 issue of *Food Review,* three USDA [U. S. Department of Agriculture] economists point out how irradiation can be extremely helpful for poultry products. Salmonella is just one disease commonly associated with poultry, and of the 2 million cases each year, between 1,000 and 2,000 result in death. The U. S. Economic Research Service estimates that if just 15 percent of chickens were irradiated, approximately $100 million could be saved in reduced medical costs and lost productivity.

Shows how speaker's position undermines opposing argument

As consumers, we must be guided by facts, not fears. The experts, forty years of research, and statistics clearly demonstrate that irradiated food does not harm your health — it protects it!

Notice the marginal comments that show how Joel used each of the four steps of refutation. The refutational strategy may be used in speeches on propositions of fact, value, or policy. The remaining three organizational patterns we discuss are appropriate only for propositions of policy.

Problem-Solution Division

problem-solution division: a rigid organizational pattern that establishes a compelling problem and offers one or more convincing solutions.

The **problem-solution division** is a simple, rigid, organizational approach for a persuasive speech. In this approach the major divisions of your speech and their order are predetermined: You first establish a compelling problem and then present a convincing solution. Because you advocate a plan of action, this method is by nature persuasive.

A speaker discussing rape prevention could divide the problem area into physical and psychological effects of rape. The solution phase could include a six-step plan to prevent rape. Speeches that call for a law or some action often use a problem-solution format, as in the next example:

Specific Purpose: To persuade the audience to support reform of our national park system.

Key Ideas: **I.**   Our national parks are threatened.

  A.   Political influence is a threat.

The force of persuasion can mobilize people, focus world attention, and reform governments. (SOURCE: AP/Wide World Photos)

 B. Environmental pollution is a threat.
 C. Inadequate staffing is a threat.
II. Our national parks can be saved.
 A. The National Park Service should have greater independence.
 B. Environmental laws should be stricter.
 C. Funding should be increased.

Need-Plan Division

The **need-plan division** is a variation of the problem-solution division. This fourfold approach (1) establishes a need or deficiency in the present system, (2) presents a proposal to meet the need, (3) demonstrates how the proposal satisfies the need, and (4) suggests a plan for implementing the proposal.

Business executives and managers often intuitively employ the need-plan organizational strategy. For example, a company president informs the board of directors of the problem of being located in a town not having an airport. Documenting a loss of sales due to unnecessary driving time, the president proposes relocating company headquarters to a city having a major airport. This would permit the company to cover more territory without expanding its sales force. Finally, the president distributes to the board a detailed plan of action for selecting the appropriate city for relocation.

need-plan division: a variation of problem-solution organization that (1) establishes a need or deficiency, (2) offers a proposal to meet the need, (3) shows how the plan satisfies the need, and (4) suggests a plan for implementing the proposal.

Salespeople also use the need-plan strategy. They demonstrate or create a need, supply the product or service to meet that need, demonstrate or describe how well it will work, and often even arrange an easy payment plan to help guarantee your purchase. This fundamental sales approach is prevalent for one simple reason: It works! You can use this strategy when you want to prompt an audience to action.

Suppose the specific purpose of your speech is to persuade your audience that employers should provide health promotion programs for their employees. Using the need-plan pattern, you could make four arguments. First, employee illness results in absenteeism, lost productivity, and increased health care costs. Second, employers should establish on-site health and fitness centers for their employees. Third, when health promotion programs have been tried, they have reduced absenteeism, increased productivity, and capped health care costs. As your final step, you could suggest an implementation strategy to include exercise and conditioning programs, alcohol- and drug-awareness education, stress-management workshops, anti-smoking clinics, and health status testing and evaluation.

Monroe's Motivated Sequence

Monroe's motivated sequence: a persuasive pattern composed of (1) getting the audience's attention, (2) establishing a need, (3) offering a proposal to satisfy the need, (4) inviting listeners to visualize the results, and (5) requesting action.

In the 1930s, Alan Monroe developed one of the most popular patterns for organizing persuasive speeches and called it "the motivated sequence."[18] This pattern is particularly appropriate when you discuss a well-known or easily established problem. Monroe drew from the conclusions of educator and philosopher John Dewey that persuasion is best accomplished if a speaker moves a listener sequentially through a series of steps.[19] **Monroe's motivated sequence,** then, includes the following five steps, or stages: attention, need, satisfaction, visualization, and action.

Monroe argued that speakers must first command the *attention* of their listeners. Suppose your geographic area is experiencing a summer drought. You could begin your speech with a description of the landscape as you approached your campus a year ago, describing in detail the green grass, the verdant foliage, and the colorful, fragrant flowers. You then contrast the landscape of a year ago with its look now: bland, brown, and blossomless. With these contrasting visual images, you try to capture the attention and interest of your audience.

A speaker's second objective is to establish a *need*. This step is similar to the problem and need steps in the problem-solution and need-plan patterns of organizing a speech. For example, your speech on the drought situation could illustrate how an inadequate water supply hurts not only the beauty of the landscape but also agricultural production, certain industrial processes, and, ultimately, the economy of the entire region.

When you dramatize a problem, you create an urgency to redress it. In the *satisfaction* step of the motivated sequence, you propose a way to solve, or at least minimize, the problem. You may suggest voluntary or mandatory conservation as a short-term solution to the water shortage crisis in your area. As a longer-range solution, you may ask your audience to consider the merits of planting grasses, shrubs, and other plants requiring less water. You may advocate that the city adopt and enforce stricter regulations of water use by businesses, or that it develop alternative water sources.

However, Monroe argued that simply proposing a solution is seldom sufficient to bring about change. Through *visualization,* Monroe's fourth step, a speaker seeks to intensify an audience's desire to adopt and implement the proposed solution. You could direct the audience to look out the window at their campus and then ask if that is the scenery they want. More often, though, you create word pictures for the audience to visualize. With-

Hon. Mike Espy
United States Representative, Mississippi

From the House floor debate of February 6, 1990 on H.R. 2190, the National Voter Registration Act.

Attention: Appeals to common values

During the recess I had the privilege of visiting Eastern Europe. I had the privilege of witnessing first hand the people's historic movement for democracy, for the right to elect governments of their own choosing. I was proud to know that our country is the world's democratic model, that people everywhere are looking to the United States to point the way forward toward truly representative government.

Need: Introduces problem of poor voter participation and voter disenfranchisement

And yet, as I watched democracy struggling to be born in Eastern Europe, I was reminded that too many citizens in our country still do not take part in our own electoral process. I was reminded that our country has the worst voter participation rate of the world's major democracies. I was reminded that our own democratic process can and should be improved. That is why I urge my colleagues to support H.R. 2190.

The right to vote is the hallmark of our democracy. However, as we all know, in the beginning of our country's history that precious right to vote was preserved only for those white men who owned enough property to qualify. Blacks were themselves property. Since then, after years of struggle, the right to vote and participate in our democracy has been extended to everyone. But that struggle is not yet over.

Satisfaction: Introduces proposed solution

Today, many voter registration procedures around the country still effectively disenfranchise those who do not have the means to travel to a registrar. The National Voter Registration Act would effectively eliminate this problem by allowing voter registration by mail in every State where it is currently not allowed.

Visualization: Continues visualization of problem but points to improvement with enactment of proposed legislation

I represent a very poor, very rural district. I know that many citizens, particularly those who are elderly and without their own transportation, have a difficult time getting a ride to a registrar's office, which could be 10 or 20 minutes away. I have participated in many voter registration drives where the main expenditure is on gas money to take people to register. But many people are still being left behind.

This problem is so great in Mississippi that the Senate Elections Committee of the State legislature just last week approved a bill to allow mail-in voter registration. I am proud that Mississippi is moving in this direction.

I am also excited about provisions in this bill which would allow citizens to register when they apply for driver's licenses, and when they conduct business at government agencies, and public places such as schools and libraries. H.R. 2190 also ends the practice of purging voters because they choose not to vote in certain elections.

Action: Argues against impediments to action. Uses examples from common history to urge action today.

I realize that some colleagues are concerned about the proper role of the Federal Government in the registration process. However, I believe that procedures for registering and voting in all Federal elections should be the same, whether a citizen in Maine, Michigan, or Mississippi. On many issues States have the right to go their separate ways. But voting rights should not be one of them.

Lastly, several arguments have been advanced about the probable costs of implementing this legislation. It is true that we must be mindful of the costs to taxpayers of every piece of legislation we enact. However, I believe it is a mistake to oppose this legislation because of its cost in dollars. I don't believe the dollar amounts are prohibitive.

The right to register and vote has been paid for by countless Americans with their lives so that the blessings of liberty would be shared by all Americans.

They died so that America could point the way to genuine democracy for the peoples of the world. We must continue to point the way today.

Source: Mike Espy, *Congressional Digest* April 1990: 124, 126.

out adequate water, you could argue, crops will die, family farms will be foreclosed upon, industries will not relocate to the area, and the quality of life for everyone in the area will be depressed. In contrast, you could refer to the landscape of a year ago, the image you depicted as you began your speech. The future can be colored in green, red, yellow, and blue, and it can represent growth and vitality.

Figure 16.1 *Example of motivated sequence*

The final step of the motivated sequence is the *action* you request of your listeners. It is not enough to know that something must be done; the audience must know what you want them to do, and your request must be within their power to act. Do you want them to join you in voluntary conservation by watering their lawns in the evening when less water will evaporate, or by washing their cars less frequently? Are you asking them to sign petitions pressuring the city council to adopt mandatory conservation measures when the water table sinks to a designated level? Conclude your speech with a strong appeal for specific, reasonable action.

The speech in Figure 16.1 was delivered by Mike Espy to his colleagues in the U.S. House of Representatives during debate on the National Voter Registration Act. That legislation, and a similar version now passed, is designed to make voter registration more convenient. Espy's speech, delivered before he became Secretary of Agriculture, illustrates the natural, logical order that Monroe's organizational pattern advocates.

SUMMARY

Persuasion is the art of affecting other people's values, beliefs, attitudes, or behaviors. The logical impact of a persuasive speech springs from a speaker's *evidence* and reasoning. To be an effective persuader, you must know how to structure a valid argument, how to detect flaws in reasoning, how to word propositions, and how to select the best general organizational pattern for your persuasive message. The three steps of structuring an argument are (1) to make a claim you want the audience to accept, (2) to supply evidence supporting that claim, and (3) to explain how the evidence proves the claim. The validity of any claim ultimately depends on the quality of the evidence supporting it.

To give listeners a reason to accept a persuasive claim, speakers may use any of five types of arguments. First, *argument by example* uses specific instances to support a general claim. In order for an argument by example to be valid, the speaker must use examples that are true, relevant to the claim, sufficient in number, and representative.

Second, *argument by analogy* links two concepts, conditions, or experiences and claims that what is true of one will be true of the other. The validity of argument by analogy depends upon the quality of the comparison a speaker develops. To test that analogy, ask two questions: (1) Are the similarities between the cases relevant? and (2) Are any differences between the two cases relevant?

Argument by cause, the third type of argument, links two concepts, conditions, or experiences and claims that one causes the other. A speaker arguing by cause can move listeners' attention forward from cause to effect, or can trace effects back to their causes. To test the validity of the cause-effect relationship, speakers and listeners should consider three questions: (1) Does a causal relationship exist? (2) Could the presumed cause produce the effect? and (3) Could the effect result from other causes?

A fourth type of argument, *deductive argument*, employs a pattern called a *syllogism*, consisting of three parts. The major premise is a claim about a general group of people, events, or conditions. The minor premise places a person, event, or condition into that general class. And the conclusion argues that what is true of the general class is also true of the specific instance. In order for an argument by deduction to be valid, both the major and minor premises must be true and they must be related.

Finally, *argument by authority* uses testimony from an expert source to prove a speaker's claim. The validity of this type of argument depends upon the credibility the authority has with the audience. To be credible, the source should be competent and unbiased.

Both speakers and listeners must watch out for logical flaws or *fallacies* in persuasive arguments. Fallacious arguments are particularly dangerous because they may resemble sound reasoning as we read or listen to them. Unfortunately, eight fallacies of argument are common. The fallacy of *hasty generalization* involves making claims on the basis of insufficient or unrepresentative examples. *Post hoc ergo propter hoc* falsely argues that because event A preceded event B, A caused B. It confuses chronology with causation. The *slippery slope* fallacy asserts that one event inevitably unleashes a series of events. The *red herring* fallacy introduces irrelevant issues to deflect attention from the true question under discussion. The fallacy called *appeal to tradition* asserts that old ways of doing things are correct or best, simply because they are traditional. A *false dilemma* argues that we must choose between two alternatives, when in reality we may have a range of options. The *bandwagon* fallacy argues that we should behave or think a particular way because most people do. Finally, the *ad hominem* fallacy urges listeners to reject an idea because of the politics, religion, or lifestyle of the person voicing the idea.

All persuasive speeches advocate *propo-sitions*, position statements the speaker wants listeners to accept. Persuasive propositions must be stated as a declarative sentence expressing a judgment, must be debatable, and require proof in order to be accepted. The three types of persuasive propositions are propositions of fact, propositions of value, and propositions of policy. *Propositions of fact* ask the audience to accept the truth or falsity of a statement. *Propositions of value* ask the audience to determine the relative worth of an idea or action. *Propositions of policy* ask the audience to support a course of action.

Speakers sometimes select a particular persuasive topic because they hear or read an argument they wish to oppose. The act of countering one argument with another is called refutation. To *refute* an argument, follow this four-step *refutational strategy.* First, state the position you are refuting. Second, state your own position. Third, support your position with evidence. And fourth, show how your position undermines the argument you oppose.

Three other popular methods of organizing persuasive speeches are problem-solution, need-plan, and the motivated sequence patterns. A simple, rigid, organizational plan, *problem-solution division* establishes a compelling problem and presents one or more workable solutions to meet that problem. *Need-plan division* is a four-step variation of problem-solution organization. Using need-plan organization, a speaker (1) establishes a need, (2) suggests a proposal to meet that need, (3) shows how the plan meets the need, and (4) offers a plan for implementing the proposal. A final persuasive speech pattern, *Monroe's motivated sequence,* is a formal, five-step pattern for moving listeners to belief or action. It consists of (1) getting the attention of your listeners, (2) clarifying the need, (3) showing how to satisfy that need, (4) visualizing the solution, and (5) requesting action.

1. Select a persuasive speech in Appendix C and determine the speaker's key ideas. Analyze the structure of each major argument: (a) Identify the claim, (b) identify the supporting material, and (c) identify the speaker's explanation of how the support proves the claim. Are any of those steps missing? If so, what is the impact on the argument? Could any of the three steps be strengthened? If so, how?

2. You have been asked to visit your former high school to speak with a group of college-bound students. The school's counselor has asked you to speak on the topic "College Years Are the Best Years of Your Life!" Construct three arguments that support this position. Give an example of how you could use in your speech each of the types of argument: example, analogy, cause, deduction, and authority.

3. Using argument by analogy, construct a short speech on one or more of the following topics. What similarities between the two entities make your analysis credible? What differences undermine the believability of the statement?
   a. Being in college is like being in a demolition derby.
   b. Life is like an athletic contest.
   c. Studying for an exam is like tying your shoe.
   d. Marriage is like gardening.
   e. A job interview is like an audition for a role in a film.

4. Determine whether each of the following statements is a proposition of fact, value, or policy.
   a. The university should build a new library.
   b. A new library would cost the university seven million dollars.
   c. It is more important to build a new library than to expand our athletic facilities.
   d. Sex education encourages sexual activity among schoolchildren.
   e. The FDA should reduce required testing for experimental drugs to fight life-threatening illnesses.
   f. Workers in high-stress jobs should be subject to random periodic drug testing.
   g. *Citizen Kane* is the best American film ever made.
   h. It is more important for a country to do good than to feel good.
   i. If the proposed tuition increase is adopted, the university may lose up to five hundred students.
   j. U.S. schools should adopt a 12-month schedule.

5. Identify the major premise, minor premise, and conclusion in each of the following groups of statements:
   a. *Inquiring Minds* should be aired on the Trashy Cable Network.
      Inquiring Minds is a fluffy news show.
      All fluffy news shows should be aired on the Trashy Cable Network.
   b. A high grade point average is important to Charlotte.
      Today's college students value high grade point averages.
      Charlotte is a college student.
   c. A lot of the dance music of the 1990s sounds like disco music of the 1970s.
      A lot of the dance music of the 1990s is awful.
      The disco music of the 1970s was awful.

6. Locate examples of each of the fallacies discussed in this chapter. Examine adver-

tisements in newspapers, in magazines, on radio, and on television. Read editorials, letters to the editor, and transcripts of speeches.

367

The Structure of Persuasion

NOTES

1. V.H. Krulak, *Orange County Register,* qtd. in "On the Record," *National Review* 24 November 1989: 8.

2. Mark Twain, *Life on the Mississippi* (New York: Harper, 1917) 156.

3. Woody Allen, "My Speech to the Graduates," *Side Effects* (New York: Random, 1980) 57.

4. Thomas Gilovich, *How We Know What Isn't So* (New York: Free, 1991) 6.

5. Aristotle, *The Rhetoric of Aristotle,* trans. Lane Cooper (New York: Appleton, 1932) 220.

6. For a more elaborate discussion of the structure of an argument, see Stephen Toulmin, *The Uses of Argument* (New York: Cambridge UP, 1974).

7. Statistics are taken from Jonathan Carey, "Scar Wars," *The Spectator* 26 May 1990: 7.

8. William Schaefer, *The Congressional Digest* February 1990: 48, 50.

9. D. Stanley Eitzen, "Problem Students: The Socio-Cultural Roots," *Vital Speeches of the Day* 15 May 1990: 479.

10. Gary Bauer, *The Congressional Digest* February 1990: 59.

11. John M. Ericson and James J. Murphy with Raymond Bud Zeuschner, *The Debater's Guide,* rev. ed. (Carbondale: Southern Illinois UP, 1987) 139.

12. *The New York Public Library Desk Reference,* 2nd ed. (New York: Stonesong-Simon, 1993) 273.

13. "Bulls, Bears and Bowls," *Forbes* 6 February 1989: 172.

14. Bruce N. Waller, *Critical Thinking: Consider the Verdict* (Englewood Cliffs, NJ: Prentice, 1988) 30

15. Thomas H. Kean, "Keynote Address," *Vital Speeches of the Day* 15 October 1988: 7.

16. W. Ward Fearnside and William B. Holther. *Fallacy — The Counterfeit of Argument* (Englewood Cliffs, NJ: Prentice, 1959) 92.

17. Ann Richards, "Keynote Address," *Vital Speeches of the Day* 15 August 1988: 648.

18. Bruce E. Gronbeck, Kathleen German, Douglas Ehninger, and Alan H. Monroe, *Principles of Speech Communication,* 11th brief ed. (Glenview, IL: HarperCollins, 1992) 263-74. See also: Alan H. Monroe, *Principles and Types of Speech* (Chicago: Scott, 1935).

19. See our discussion of Dewey's Steps to Reflective Thinking in Chapter 18, pp. 400-02.

*I*n September 1993, Hillary Rodham Clinton testified before Congress, fielding tough questions about the Clinton administration's proposals for health care reform. Friends and foes alike praised her "gift for mastering the head-breaking details of a hard subject and then translating them into understandable English."[1]

At Ryan White's funeral in 1990, singer Elton John spoke briefly but movingly about Ryan's struggle against AIDS before playing and singing a special version of "Skyline Pigeon."

On a hot afternoon in Cooperstown, New York, in 1993, Reggie Jackson became the 216th person inducted into the Baseball Hall of Fame. Standing in front of 10,000 baseball fans — among them his 90-year-old father, a veteran of the Negro Baseball League — Jackson acknowledged the honor with a half-hour speech "filled with emotions, with memories, with personal moments."[2]

In April 1993, Elie Wiesel, 1986 winner of the Nobel Prize for Peace, spoke at ceremonies to dedicate the United States Holocaust Memorial Museum in Washington, D.C. He described a Jewish woman from the Carpathian mountains who was confused when she read about the Warsaw Ghetto uprising. "Treblinka, Ponar, Belzec, Chelmno, Birkenau; she had never heard of these places. One year later, together with her entire family, she was in a cattle-car traveling to the black-hole of history named Auschwitz." Many in the audience were quietly weeping as Wiesel revealed at the end of his speech, "She was my mother."[3]

Though none of us has the celebrity or visibility of the individuals mentioned in these examples, you can count on being called upon to deliver a speech on some special occasion: an oral report in a world history class, a speech introducing a guest speaker at a club meeting, a speech accepting an award from a civic group, or a eulogy at the funeral of a relative or friend. In addition to these "ordinary" special occasions, remember some of the truly special occasions we mentioned in Chapter 1: speaking to accept a Heisman Trophy, a Tony or Academy Award, or to present important research findings to a national convention and to the media.

To speak your best on any of these special occasions, you must consider the customs and audience expectations in each case. In this chapter, we will discuss nine special occasions or special circumstances for public speeches: the speech of introduction, the speech of presentation, the acceptance speech, the speech of tribute, the oral report, the speech to entertain, the impromptu speech, the question-answer period, and the videotaped speech. You will learn guidelines for each of these types of speeches and read examples of many of them. This information can serve you well beyond the classroom and prepare you for any occasion when you are requested, invited, or expected to speak.

■ THE SPEECH OF INTRODUCTION

speech of introduction: a speech introducing a featured speaker to an audience.

One of the most common types of special-occasion speeches is the **speech of introduction.** Some people use that phrase to indicate speeches by people introducing themselves to an audience. As we use the phrase in this chapter, however, we mean a speech introducing a featured speaker. The following guidelines will help you prepare such a speech of introduction.

1. Focus on the featured speaker.
2. Be brief.
3. Establish the speaker's credibility.
4. Create realistic expectations.
5. Set the tone for the speech.

The first guideline to remember is to *keep the focus on the person being introduced.* The audience has not gathered to hear you, so don't upstage the featured speaker. Keep your remarks short, simple, and sincere.

In order to achieve the first guideline, you will want to follow the second: *Be brief.* If you can, request and get a copy of the speaker's résumé. This will give you a body of information to select from when preparing your introductory remarks. The key word in that last sentence is *select.* Too often we have heard speeches of introduction begin with a sentence such as "Our speaker tonight was born in Sioux City, Iowa,...." Your listeners will tune out quickly if your introduction is a lengthy chronology of events in a person's life. A speech of introduction is not a dramatic reading of a résumé. Highlight information the audience does not know.

A third guideline is to *establish the speaker's credibility on the topic.* You do this by presenting the speaker's credentials. As you prepare your speech of introduction, ask and answer questions such as these: What makes the speaker qualified to speak on the subject? What education and experiences make the speaker's insights worthy of our belief?

Fourth, remember to *create realistic expectations.* Prepare the audience to listen intelligently to the remarks that will follow.

When Lashelle introduced the director of financial aid to her sorority, she included the statement, "I asked Mr. Palmerton to speak with us this afternoon because he's the person in charge of all scholarships. He will tell us how we all can receive financial assistance for next year." Lashelle's overstatement compelled Mr. Palmerton to begin his remarks by noting that the deadlines for most of next year's scholarships had already passed, and that not all in the audience would qualify for the limited number of scholarships still available. His comments embarrassed Lashelle, disappointed several in the audience, and made the speaker feel that he could not live up to audience expectations.

Genuine praise is commendable, just be careful not to oversell the speaker. Can you imagine walking to the microphone after the following introduction: "Our speaker tonight is one of the great speakers in this country. I heard her last year, and she had us laughing until our sides hurt. She will keep you spellbound from her first word to her last. Get ready for the best speech you've heard in your entire life!"

Finally, you should phrase your remarks to *establish a tone consistent with the speaker's presentation.* Would you give a humorous introduction for a speaker whose topic is "The Grieving Process: What to Do When a Loved One Dies"? Of course not. On the other hand, if the evening is designed for merriment, your introduction should help set that mood.

Communication professors should certainly know how to introduce a featured speaker. In the following example, Professor Don Ochs of the University of Iowa did an exemplary job of introducing his longtime colleague, Professor Samuel L. Becker. Becker was the keynote speaker at the Central States Communication Association convention in Chicago on April 12, 1991. You'll see that Ochs uses some communication jargon because he is speaking to a group of communication professionals. Notice, though, how Ochs's brief, cordial remarks focus on Becker, establishing his credibility and setting the tone for Becker's informative and inspirational speech:

> Thirty years ago I walked out of an Iowa City store onto the main street and noticed Sam Becker walking about twenty feet ahead of me. His youngest daughter was alongside Sam but she was terribly upset about something; crying, and obviously hurt about something. Sam put his arm around his daughter and, in the space of two blocks, said something that comforted and fixed the problem. She was smiling when they parted company.
>
> I share this snapshot of Sam with you because, for me, it captures Sam's approach to life, higher education, scholarship, and our profession.
>
> Sam Becker has figuratively put his arm around difficulties and problems for his entire career. He's made all of us as teachers and scholars better persons and better professionals with his intellect, his vision, his energy, and his instinctive willingness to help.
>
> As a rhetorician I would much prefer to introduce Sam with figures and tropes, with synechdoche, litotes, and hyperbole. But Sam is a social scientist, so I will be quantitative instead.
>
> How much has Sam helped us? Sam has taught at four universities; written six books; been active in eight professional associations; authored ten monographs; served on twelve editorial boards; worked on evaluation teams for thirty-two colleges and universities; served on thirty-six university committees; lectured at fifty colleges and universities; directed fifty-five PhDs; and authored 105 articles. Without doubt, he has helped and assisted and supported all of us. Our speaker today, Sam Becker.[4]

THE SPEECH OF PRESENTATION

speech of presentation: a speech conferring an award, a prize, or some other recognition on an individual or group.

The **speech of presentation** confers an award, a prize, or some other form of special recognition on an individual or a group. Such speeches are typically made on special occasions: after banquets or parties; as parts of business meetings or sessions of a convention; or at awards ceremonies such as the Tony Awards, the Academy Awards, or the Grammy Awards, during which many people will be recognized.

We will restrict our discussion of the speech of presentation to prepared statements commenting on and presenting an award to an individual or group. Thus, remarks made by a presenter about an actor honored with the American Film Institute's Lifetime Achievement Award would qualify as a speech of presentation; opening the envelope and reading the winner of the Grammy Award for Song of the Year is really an announcement rather than a prepared speech. When you give a speech of presentation, let the nature and importance of the award being presented, as well as the occasion on which it is being presented, shape your remarks. The following guidelines will help you plan this special-occasion speech.

1. State the purpose of the award or recognition.
2. State the recipient's qualifications.
3. Adapt your speech's organization to audience knowledge.
4. Compliment finalists for the award.

First, as a presenter, you should *state the purpose of the award or recognition*. If the audience is unfamiliar with the award — if it is a new or special award — or if they know nothing about the organization making the award, you will probably want to begin by briefly explaining the nature of the award or the rationale for presenting it. This is especially important if you as the speaker represent the organization making the award. In contrast, an award having a long history probably needs little if any explanation.

A second guideline is to *focus your speech on the achievements for which the award is being made;* don't attempt a detailed biography of the recipient. Because you are merely highlighting the honoree's accomplishments, the speech of presentation will be brief, rarely more than five minutes long and frequently much shorter.

Third, *organize a speech of presentation primarily according to whether your listeners know the name of the recipient in advance*. If they do not know the name of the individual you are honoring, capitalize on their curiosity. If you begin by announcing the name of the recipient and then explaining why that person was selected, the bulk of your speech will be anticlimactic. Instead, let ambiguity about who will receive the honor propel the speech and maintain the audience's attention. Begin by making general comments that could refer to several or many people; as the speech progresses, let your comments get more specific. If the person receiving your award is from a group containing both men and women, use gender-neutral descriptions ("this person" or "our honoree") rather than using "he" or "she." In this way, you keep your audience guessing and allow them the pleasure of solving a puzzle. If the audience knows in advance the name of the person being recognized, your strategy changes. In this case, begin the speech with specifics and end with more general statements that summarize the reasons for the presentation.

Finally, if a group of individuals has been nominated and you are announcing the winner with your speech of presentation, briefly *compliment the entire group of people who have been nominated for the award*.

The following speech was delivered at an annual convention of the Texas Speech Communication Association (TSCA) to honor a person giving lengthy and outstanding service to that organization. Notice how the speaker focuses on the reasons for the award and the honoree's qualifications. In addition, the speaker's organization carefully creates suspense for this surprise award.

The key word in "TSCA Outstanding Service Award" is "service." We who have been privileged to serve this association as officers soon learn that what we accomplish is not primarily a function of our own talents and hard work, but a function of the expertise and efforts of many individuals like you — individuals who understand what is important in making the Texas Speech Communication Association a vibrant and vital organization....

Important to TSCA is networking. Through letters, phone calls, and testifying, this year's recipient helped make our voice heard in her local community and in Austin....

Important to TSCA is service on the Executive Committee. As editor of the *TSCA Newsletter,* this year's recipient gave life to this instrument of communication, establishing the professional format it continues today.

Important to TSCA are the many programs which comprise our convention. Many of you have attended and learned from programs and workshops this year's recipient has conducted.

A Piper Professor and a Danforth Scholar, she was honored by her institution this year as the first recipient of the Dr. and Mrs. Z.T. Scott Fellowship for Excellence in Teaching. This award recognizes excellence in teaching, advising, and support for student organizations.

I have long believed that an important criterion for professional service is that an individual is not offended by doing the menial. This year's recipient is not offended by doing the menial and is capable of accomplishing the significant. She is professional, gracious, amiable, and hard-working.

I suspect that there is only one person in this room who will be surprised at this year's choice for the Outstanding Service Award — and that person is the recipient herself, for she will feel that she was just fulfilling her professional obligations. We know better. She represents the best of our association, the best of our discipline, and the best of our profession.

At the beginning of my remarks I said that this introduction is a personal privilege, for the individual we honor today is perhaps the most significant colleague in my professional life. It is with pleasure that I present to you this year's recipient of the TSCA Outstanding Service Award: Frances Swinny.[5]

◼︎ THE ACCEPTANCE SPEECH

acceptance speech: a speech responding to a speech of presentation by acknowledging an award, a tribute, or recognition.

At some point in your life, you may be commended publicly for service you have given to a cause or an organization. You may be presented a farewell or retirement gift from your friends or coworkers. You may receive an award for winning a sporting event, an essay contest, or a speech contest. Although these are different occasions, they have at least one thing in common — each requires a response. To accept a gift or an award without expressing appreciation is socially unacceptable. An **acceptance speech,** then, is a response to a speech of presentation. When a recipient acknowledges the award or tribute, he or she provides closure to the process. A gracious acceptance speech usually includes four steps.

KEY POINTS	
Guidelines for the Acceptance Speech	**1.** Thank those who bestowed the award. **2.** Compliment the competition. **3.** Thank those who helped you attain the award. **4.** Accept the award graciously.

First, *thank the person or organization bestowing the award.* You may wish to name not only the group sponsoring the award but also the person who made the speech of presentation. In addition, you may want to commend what the award represents. Your respect for the award and its donor authenticates your statement of appreciation.

Second, if you are accepting a competitively selected award, and especially if your competitors are in the audience, acknowledge their qualifications and compliment them. This step need not be lengthy; you can *compliment your peers* as a group rather than individually.

Third, *thank those who helped you achieve the honor.* Seldom do we achieve things by ourselves. Whether you are an accomplished pianist, vocalist, artist, athlete, or writer, you have usually had someone — parents, teachers, or coaches — who invested time, money, and expertise to help you achieve your best.

Finally, *accept your award graciously.* An acceptance speech is no time to be cocky or clever. Of well-known acceptance speeches, one of the most gracious and inspirational was delivered by Steven Spielberg on March 30, 1987, at the fifty-ninth Academy Awards ceremony. He was receiving the Irving G. Thalberg Memorial Award for his screenwriting accomplishments during 1986. Notice how Spielberg accomplishes each of the steps we have elaborated. He thanks the members of the Academy of Motion Picture Arts and Sciences and the audience. He shows his respect for the recognition by commenting on its history and by naming and complimenting some previous recipients of the Thalberg Award. He thanks those who helped him attain the award by mentioning people who influenced him, and he accepts the award in a particularly gracious and humble manner. His opening remark refers to Sally Field's impromptu remarks when she was named Best Actress for *Places in the Heart.* Field had gushed, "You like me! You really like me!" Spielberg's acceptance speech was as follows:

I'm resisting like crazy to use Sally Field's line from two years ago. Thank you very much. Following in the footsteps of some of my heroes, Cecil B. De Mille, and George Stevens, Alfred Hitchcock, William Wyler, Ingmar Bergman, and Robert Wise, this award is truly a great honor for me.

The Thalberg Award was first given fifty years ago in 1937, which was the year of *In Old Chicago, Captains Courageous, Dead End, The Life of Emile Zola, Lost Horizon, Stage Door,* and *A Star is Born* — all having been nominated for Best Picture that year. I'm told Irving Thalberg worshiped writers. And that's where it all begins. That we are first and foremost storytellers. And without, as he called it, "the photoplay," everybody is simply improvising. He also knew that a script is more than just a blueprint. That the whole idea of movie magic is that interweave of powerful image, and dialogue, and performance, and music that can never be separated. And when it's working right, can never be duplicated or even forgotten.

I've grown up — most of my life has been spent in the dark watching movies. Movies have been the literature of my life. The literature of Irving Thalberg's generation was books and plays. They read the great words of great minds. And I think in our romance with technology, and our excitement at exploring all the possibilities of film and video, I think we've partially lost something that we now have to reclaim. I think it's time to renew our romance with the word. I'm as culpable as anyone in having exulted the image … at the expense of the word. But only a generation of readers will spawn a generation of writers.

The five films nominated for Best Picture this year *[Children of a Lesser God, Hannah and Her Sisters, The Mission, Platoon,* and *A Room With a View]* are as much the writer's film as the director's. And it's good news that each of these films has found its audience. Because this audience, who we all work for, deserves everything that we have to give them. They deserve that fifth draft, that tenth take, that one extra cut, and those several dollars over budget. And Irving Thalberg knew that. He would have been proud to have been associated with any of these films, as I am proud to have my name on this award in his honor. Because it reminds me of really how much growth as an artist I have ahead of me, in order to be worthy of standing in the company of those who have received this before me. So my deepest thanks to the board of governors of the Academy, and the audience out there in the dark. Thank you very much.[6]

THE SPEECH OF TRIBUTE

Mr. Crenshaw is retiring after thirty years as a seventh-grade science teacher. At his retirement banquet, three former students tell the audience the important role he played in their lives.

Bonnie Taylor has been promoted to vice-president of sales and will move to the corporate headquarters in Atlanta. On her last day at work her employees throw her a farewell party. Rosa speaks for the employees, commenting on Bonnie's many contributions to the company and her co-workers.

A noted civil rights leader stands on the spot where thirty years earlier a group of 137 disenfranchised African Americans began a forty-mile march to the state capitol to demand full voting rights. He tells the crowd of the faith and forbearance of those who made those first steps toward justice.

speech of tribute: a speech honoring a person, group, or event.

Each of these is an example of a **speech of tribute.** This type of ceremonial speech honors a person, a group, or an event, and it can be one of the most moving forms of public address. Vivid and memorable examples include Ronald Reagan's tribute to the crew of the *Challenger* after the shuttle's explosion in 1986, Edward Kennedy's eulogy of his sister-in-law Jaqueline Kennedy Onassis in 1994, and Abraham Lincoln's "Gettysburg Address."

eulogy: a speech of tribute praising a person who has recently died.

A special form of the speech of tribute is the **eulogy,** a speech of praise usually given for those who have recently died. Peggy Noonan, speechwriter for presidents Ronald Reagan and George Bush, captures the power of eulogies:

They are the most moving kind of speech because they attempt to pluck meaning from the fog, and on short order, when the emotions are still ragged and raw and susceptible to leaps. It is a challenge to look at a life and organize our thoughts about it and try to explain to ourselves what it meant, and the most moving part is the element of implicit celebration. Most people aren't appreciated enough, and the bravest things we do in our lives are usually known only to ourselves. No one throws ticker tape on the man who chose to be faithful to his wife, on the lawyer who didn't take the drug money, or the daughter who held her tongue again and again. All this anonymous heroism. A eulogy gives us a chance to celebrate it.[7]

Five guidelines will help you write a eulogy or any other speech of tribute.

KEY POINTS

Guidelines for the Speech of Tribute

1. Establish noble themes.
2. Provide vivid examples.
3. Express audience feelings.
4. Create a memorable image.
5. Be genuine.

First, *establish noble themes.* As you begin developing the eulogy ask, "Why is this person worthy of my respect and praise?" Answer this question by developing themes you want the audience to remember. Remember to focus on the positive. A speech of tribute celebrates what is good about a person; it is not an occasion for a warts and all biography. You must be careful, however, not to exaggerate a person's accomplishments. To do so may undermine your speech by making it seem insincere or unbelievable.

Second, *develop the themes of your speech with vivid examples.* Anecdotes, stories, and personal testimony are excellent ways of making your speech more vivid, humane, and memorable.

Third, *express the feelings of the audience assembled* or those whom you represent. The audience needs to be a part of the occasion for any speech of tribute. If you are honoring a former teacher, you may speak for yourself, but you can also speak for your class or even all students who studied under Mr. Crenshaw. If the honoree is present, he or she should feel that the tribute expresses more than one person's view.

Your use of noble themes, vivid examples, and audience feelings should combine to *create a memorable image of the person being honored.* Your speech not only honors someone, it also helps audience members focus on that person's importance to them.

Finally, *be genuine.* If you are asked to deliver a speech of tribute about someone you do not know, you may want to decline respectfully. The personal bond and interaction you develop in getting to know someone well is essential for a speech of tribute. Also, the person being honored may find the tribute more meaningful if it comes from a person he or she knows well.

One of the most eloquent and moving speeches of tribute in modern American history was Adlai Stevenson's eulogy of former first lady Eleanor Roosevelt. Roosevelt died on November 7, 1962, and was buried three days later. Ten days after her death, an estimated 10,000 people gathered for a memorial service at New York City's Cathedral of St. John the Divine. The occasion called for a formal and substantial eulogy. Notice how Stevenson applied the guidelines we have discussed previously in the following excerpts from that speech.

One week ago this afternoon, in the Rose Garden at Hyde Park, Eleanor Roosevelt came home for the last time. Her journeys are over. The remembrance now begins.

In gathering here to honor her, we engage in a self-serving act. It is we who are trying, by this ceremony of tribute, to deny the fact that we have lost her, and, at least, to prolong the farewell, and — possibly — to say some of the things we dared not say in her presence, because she would have turned aside such testimonial with impatience and gently asked us to get on with some of the more serious business of the meeting.

A grief perhaps not equaled since the death of her husband seventeen years ago is the world's best tribute to one of the great figures of our age — a woman whose lucid and luminous faith testified always for sanity in an insane time and for hope in a time of obscure hope — a woman who spoke for the good toward which man aspires in a world which has seen too much of the evil of which man is capable....

We dare not try to tabulate the lives she salvaged, the battles — known and unrecorded — she fought, the afflicted she comforted, the hovels she brightened, the faces and places, near and far, that were given some new radiance, some sound of music, by her endeavors. What other single human being has touched and transformed the existence of so many others? What better measure is there of the impact of anyone's life? ...

Adlai Stevenson celebrated the life of the former first lady and comforted the nation in his eulogy of Eleanor Roosevelt.
(Source: UPI/Bettmann)

Many of the admonitions she bequeathed us are neither new thoughts nor novel concepts. Her ideas were, in many respects, old-fashioned — as old as the Sermon on the Mount, as the reminder that it is more blessed to give than to receive. In the words of St. Francis that she loved so well: "For it is in the giving that we receive." …

And now one can almost hear Mrs. Roosevelt saying that the speaker has already talked too long. So we must say farewell. We are always saying farewell in this world — always standing at the edge of loss attempting to retrieve some memory, some human meaning, from the silence — something which was precious and is gone....

> We pray that she has found peace, and a glimpse of sunset. But today we weep for ourselves. We are lonelier; someone has gone from one's life — who was like the certainty of refuge; and someone has gone from the world — who was like a certainty of honor.[8]

■ THE ORAL REPORT

You will encounter oral reports throughout your academic life. They will probably play an integral part in your professional life as well. You may be asked to synthesize the critical reactions to the plays of Tennessee Williams for an English class; to provide your history class with an account of the firebombing of Dresden, Germany, during World War II; or to present to your boss and coworkers the results of your two-month study of new software options for the office. Your material and your manner of presentation may affect what others learn and what actions they take, as well as your academic and career success.

The **oral report** differs from the other types of public speeches you have presented in this class in four important ways. First, your topic for an oral report is usually assigned by a teacher in a class or by a supervisor in a business or professional setting. You may not have even been involved in the process of generating topics for the reports. Second, oral reports are typically longer than speeches, often lasting up to half an hour or more. In the academic environment, however, class size and limited class time may force reports to be shorter. Under these conditions, the problem of covering a lot of information in a short period of time is even more significant. Third, reports are usually informational, compressing a lot of ideas and data. Often this information is important for classroom or business discussions that will follow. Finally, unlike the public speaker's typical audience, the audience for an oral report may be taking notes during the presentation. As a result, members of the audience may feel free to interrupt a speaker, asking questions or commenting on items they find interesting.

oral report: a substantial speech on an assigned or a selected topic delivered to an academic or a business audience.

Individuals assigning reports often have a particular format in mind, and you will want to use your audience analysis skills and adapt your presentation accordingly. Nevertheless, the following five suggestions should help make your oral report more effective.

KEY POINTS

Guidelines for the Oral Report

1. Organize your ideas clearly.
2. Synthesize your supporting materials.
3. Document your information.
4. Use visual support when possible.
5. Be creative.

First, *organize your ideas clearly.* Clear organization, important for any speech, is critical for the oral report. You will be presenting a great deal of information, and you don't want your listeners to get lost among the specifics. Remember the **"4 S's"** (see pages 181-84) and use them!

Second, *synthesize your supporting materials.* A key objective of an oral report is to help the audience make sense of all available ideas and information. To do this, you must integrate and unify the data you have collected, editing and organizing so that your main ideas are clear and impressive. Synthesis does not mean that you inject your point of view throughout the presentation. If your point of view is requested, give it at the end. In class assignments, for example, an instructor may ask you to offer your evaluation near the end of your report. In business and professional settings, a question-answer period often follows the oral presentation, and you may be asked for your perspective then.

A third guideline to follow as you prepare your oral report is to *document your ideas and cite your sources.* Because others may use the information you present, they need some assurance of its quality. Cite your sources carefully. You may even distribute a handout so that your audience can refer to it later; include your sources of information in that material.

Fourth, *support your ideas with visual aids* when appropriate. As we mentioned earlier, you will present much information, and aids can highlight significant points and trends. You may want to refer to handout materials, or to charts, graphs, and diagrams displayed on posterboard or overhead projections. Other students may be responsible for remembering material you cover in your class report and may use your handout as a study guide. In a business or professional setting, your company may consider adopting a new policy or implementing a plan of action you recommend. Decision makers may base their decision, in part, on information you present, and they may want to refer to it later.

Finally, although an oral report places heavy emphasis on research, organization, analysis, and synthesis, *don't forget your own creativity.* Certainly, an oral report does not need the same level of creativity as, for example, a speech to entertain. Nevertheless, do not disregard it in this type of presentation. You have already learned that what you say is only part of a speech. How you say it is also important. Like any other good speech, an oral report should get the audience's attention immediately, highlight key ideas memorably, and conclude vividly. All this requires your ingenuity and inspiration. That spark of creativity may help your audience better understand and remember your message. It may set your report apart from others and give you a more attentive and receptive audience.

■ THE SPEECH TO ENTERTAIN

As we discussed early in this text, the three main purposes of speaking are to inform, to persuade, and to entertain. Although many informative and persuasive speeches contain elements of humor, the speech designed specifically to entertain is a special case because it is often difficult to do well.

speech to entertain:
a speech used to make a point through the creative, organized use of the speaker's humor.

The **speech to entertain** seeks to make a point through the creative, organized use of the speaker's humor. The distinguishing characteristic of a speech to entertain is the entertainment value of its supporting materials. It is usually delivered on an occasion when people are in a light mood: after a banquet, as part of an awards ceremony, and on other festive occasions.

A *speech to entertain* is different from *speaking to entertain.* In their opening monologues, Jay Leno and David Letterman are both speaking to entertain. Their purpose is to relax the audience, establish some interaction with them, and set the mood for the rest of the show. Their remarks are not organized around a central theme, something essential to a speech to entertain. If you combine the following five guidelines with what you already know about developing a public speech, you will discover that a speech to entertain is not only challenging but also fun to present.

		KEY POINTS
1. Make a point.	**4.** Use appropriate humor.	
2. Be creative.	**5.** Use spirited delivery.	**Guidelines for the**
3. Be organized.		**Speech to Entertain**

The first requirement for a speech to entertain is that it *makes a point*, or communicates a thesis, no less than does the most carefully crafted informative or persuasive speech. Frequently, the person delivering a speech to entertain is trying to make the audience aware of conditions, experiences, or habits that they take for granted. Here are examples of topics on which we have heard students present successful speeches to entertain:

The imprecision and incorrectness of language, especially that used in some advertisements.

Many doctors' failure to speak language that their patients can understand and many patients' failure to ask their doctors the right questions.

Our interest in or curiosity about tabloid news stories.

"Momilies," familiar homilies or sayings that mommies (and daddies) tell their children.

The routine, expensive date and introducing some creative, less expensive dating options.

In some of these speeches, the speaker had stated the main point fairly bluntly by the end of the speech: Take a careful look at the language used to sell you things; you owe it to your health to ask questions of your doctor; you do not have to spend a fortune to have an interesting time on a date. In other speeches, speakers simply implied their thesis: Think about what you say to correct or otherwise manipulate your children. Each of these speeches did make a point, however.

Second, a *speech to entertain is creative*. To be creative you must make sure that your speech to entertain is your product, and not simply a replay of a Rosie O'Donnell or a Jerry Seinfeld monologue. A replay like this is not creative, no matter how great a job you think you do delivering the other person's lines. Moreover, if you copy Rosie's or Jerry's words and don't credit them, you are plagiarizing. Your speech to entertain should be original and creative. It should give your audience a glimpse of your unique view of the world.

Third, a *speech to entertain is organized*. It must have an introduction, body, and conclusion just as informative and persuasive speeches do. In other words, the speech to entertain must convey a sense of moving toward some logical point and achieving closure after adequately developing that point. Failure to organize your materials will cause you to ramble, embarrassing both you and your audience. You will feel, quite literally, like the novice comic caught without a finish, a sure-fire joke that makes a good exit line. The audience will sense that you are struggling and will have trouble relaxing and enjoying your humor.

To illustrate how you can organize materials that seem random, consider the experience of Steve, who selected as the topic of his speech to entertain "What This Graduating Senior Will Remember About His College Days."

Steve began by thinking of some humorous incidents he had experienced during his four years in college: mistaking a graduate teaching assistant for another student the first day of class and telling him all the bad things he had heard about the course; saying to an instructor, "I missed class last Tuesday. Did you say anything important?"; and having roommates soak his mattress with lime Jell-O, which they then let congeal. He continued brainstorming, thinking of other examples. Gradually, he recognized a possible pattern of organization. Rather than randomly recounting these various embarrassing incidents as a stand-up comic might, Steve organized them around three key ideas: (1) classroom catastrophes, (2) dormitory disasters, and (3) social setbacks. This organizational pattern focused Steve's speech, and he concluded by making the following point:

"College is a special time in our lives, a sort of interlude between being a child living at home and being an adult living in the Real World. College is a place where we learn, live, and laugh with others. Three of us in this class will walk across a stage next month and leave college behind. We will take with us memories of happy days. Most of you, however, still have time to create your own memories. Make the most of these precious days. But remember, keep an eye on your roommates — especially if they've just returned from Kroger's with a bagful of lime Jell-O!"

Steve's humor was relevant to his college audience, and to *use appropriate humor* is the fourth guideline for a speech to entertain. The speech to entertain is difficult to do well for a simple reason: Most people associate entertainment with lots of laughter and feel that if the audience is not laughing a good deal, they are not responding favorably to the speech. But stop to consider for a moment the range of things that entertain you, from the outrageous antics of the comedian Gallagher to the muttered ramblings of Steven Wright. Your humor should be adapted to your topic, your audience, the occasion, and your own personal style. Four suggestions should guide your use of humor.

1. Be Relevant. Good humor is relevant to your general purpose and makes the main ideas of your speech memorable. Humor not related to the point you are making should still be relevant to your general purpose: to entertain. Michael's speech to entertain discussed the ways we label products and people. One of his points was that the product warnings printed on packaging tell us about various companies' views of their customers. His examples at this point in the speech were relevant to that main idea and added humor to his speech by helping him show the absurdity of many product labels.

For example, the first thing I saw on the box my toaster came in was a warning. Warning — do not submerge in water, especially when the plug is connected to an electrical outlet. Now just at a practical level, I'm pretty sure that almost anyone should be able to figure out that the chances of getting your pop tart to turn brown at the bottom of a Jacuzzi are pretty slim to begin with. But as far as this whole electrocution thing is concerned, I'm not entirely sure how much damage 500 volts could do to these people. I mean let's face it, if you're going to plug in your toaster just so you can take it into the shower with you, a little shock there may not be such a bad idea.[9]

2. Be Tasteful. Important to any speech, audience analysis is vital for a speech to entertain. Taste is subjective. What delights some listeners may offend others. Do the best job you can in analyzing your audience, but when in doubt, err on the side of caution. Remember, humor that is off-color is off-limits.

3. Be Tactful. Avoid humor that generates laughter at the expense of others. There may be times when good natured ribbing is appropriate, but humor intended to belittle or demean a person or group is unethical and unacceptable.

4. Be Positive. The tone for most occasions featuring speeches to entertain should be festive. People have come together to relax and enjoy each other's company. Dark, negative humor is usually inappropriate as it casts a somber tone on the situation.

Finally, *a speech to entertain benefits from spirited delivery.* We have often heard good speeches to entertain and looked forward to reading transcripts of them later. We were usually disappointed. The personality, timing, and interaction with the audience that made the speech lively and unforgettable could not be captured on paper. We have also read manuscripts of speeches to entertain that promised to be dynamic when presented, only to see them diminished by a monotonous, colorless, and lifeless delivery.

■ THE IMPROMPTU SPEECH

You are sitting at a staff meeting listening to your coworkers argue about office assignments in the company's new building. Your boss suddenly turns to ask how you would solve the problem. Or you are standing in the back of a crowded orientation session when, to your surprise, your supervisor introduces you and says, "Come up here and say a few words to these folks." Or you receive an award you didn't know you were being considered for. As people begin to applaud and whistle, you start walking to the front of the room to accept an attractive plaque. These are but three situations in which you would deliver an impromptu speech.

The **impromptu speech,** one with limited or no advanced preparation, can be intimidating. You have not had time to think about the ideas you want to communicate. You begin speaking without knowing the exact words you will use. You have not practiced delivering your speech. Don't panic! All is not lost. By now you have a pretty good understanding of how to organize, support, and deliver a speech. You have practiced these skills in prepared classroom speeches. All this practice will help you in your impromptu speech. With experience comes confidence. You already know what it feels like to stand before an audience. "But this is different," you might be saying right about now. "In those cases I had time to prepare." Well, if you follow these four guidelines, you should be ready for almost any impromptu speech that comes along.

impromptu speech: a speech delivered with little or no advanced preparation.

383
Speaking on Special
Occasions

1. Speak on a topic you know well.
2. Make the most of the preparation time you have.
3. Focus on a single or a few key points.
4. Be brief.

KEY POINTS

Guidelines for the Impromptu Speech

The skills you develop in business and social conversation are useful preparation for delivering an impromptu public speech.
(SOURCE: © Jim Pickerell)

First, if you have a choice, *speak on a topic you know well.* The more you know about your topic, the better you will be able to select relevant ideas, organize them, and explain them as you speak. You will also be more comfortable talking about a subject you know, and your confidence will show in your delivery.

Even though your preparation time is limited or nonexistent, *make the most of the time you have.* Don't waste "walking time" from your seat to the front of the room worrying. Instead, ask yourself, "What do I want the audience to remember when I sit down? What two or three points will help them remember this?"

Third, *focus on a single or a few key points.* This may be easier if you think a bit like the character Charlie Fox in David Mamet's play *Speed-the-Plow.* A movie producer, Charlie's test of a screenplay is whether he can condense it to one sentence so that *TV Guide* can print a blurb about it. As silly as it may seem, this strategy could help you focus on the few ideas you want to get across to your listeners. If you have been asked to explain why you support building a new library instead of renovating the existing facility, think of the two or three most important reasons underlying your position. And remember to use the **4 S's** as you present those reasons to your audience.

Finally, *be brief.* One public speaking axiom is, "Stand up! Speak up! Shut up!" Although this can be carried to an extreme, it is probably good advice for the impromptu speaker. An impromptu speech is not the occasion for a long, rambling discourse. Say what you need to say, and then be seated.

One of us gave an impromptu speech to his public speaking students the second day of class. He had assigned an ungraded speech of self-introduction for that day, and he wanted students to think of the assignment as an important practice opportunity. As he walked to class, he considered how he could set a proper tone and relax his students. He remembered hearing that baseball spring training was just thirty days away. A baseball fan, he decided to illustrate his point with an analogy between baseball and the class. Three aspects of baseball spring training were similar to what he expected in his class. By the time he walked into the class, he was ready to deliver the following impromptu speech:

In less than a month, major league baseball players will pack their bags and head to Florida and Arizona for spring training. As part of their training, they do three things. They receive instruction from their coaches. They work on fundamental skills. And they play exhibition games in which they practice putting it all together. Spring training is important because it helps baseball players prepare for the regular season, when games really count.

I want you to think of the first weeks of this class as your spring training in public speaking. You will learn from your coach — that's me — public speaking strategies and techniques. You will work on fundamental skills such as supporting, organizing, and delivering your speech. And you will give ungraded, practice speeches to your classmates. If you take this spring training seriously, you'll be ready when it's your turn to walk to the front of the room, look at your audience, and begin giving your first graded speech.

Later he reflected on the speech. He had included the nonspecific word *things* at the end of his second sentence where a more specific word would have served better. The last sentence seemed OK, but maybe something with a baseball image would have been more catchy. What about coming to the plate and hitting a home run? Despite these weaknesses, he was satisfied with his impromptu remarks. Judging from the reactions of the class and their comments, he had succeeded in relaxing them before they gave their first speech to the class. If the instructor uses the strategy in subsequent semesters, he will reflect on his first attempt, polish his language, and improve his speech.

Notice how the instructor used the guidelines listed previously for the impromptu speech. He selected two topics he knew well: public speaking and baseball. He was comfortable talking about both topics. Had he chosen to compare public speaking preparation with thermonuclear physics, a topic on which he had little knowledge, he would have been in trouble — and so would his audience! He collected his thoughts and outlined the body of the speech in his mind as he walked to class. He focused on a single idea: The ungraded speaking assignments in this class give you an opportunity to prepare for future speeches. He established this position by developing three simple points. The speech was brief and to the point, just eleven sentences. And after the speech was over, he evaluated it in order to do a better job next time.

Impromptu speaking is spontaneous; it requires you to think on your feet. The more you study and practice public speaking principles and skills, the more confident you will be when someone taps you on the shoulder and says, "You're on!"

THE QUESTION-ANSWER PERIOD

TV reporter, asking question of Washington Redskins' quarterback before Super Bowl XXII, 1988: *"Doug, how long have you been a black quarterback?"*
Doug Williams: *"I've been a quarterback since I was a kid. I've been black my whole life."*[10]

Preparing for a public speech involves a lot of uncertainty. Even the most thorough audience analysis can never tell you everything you'd like to know about your listeners. You have to make a lot of educated guesses and take it from there. Sometimes you are unsure whether you have accurately assessed what your listeners need to hear.

**question-answer
period:** a time set aside
at the end of a speech for
audience questions of the
speaker.

Having the opportunity to field questions from the audience following your speech or oral report reduces this uncertainty. Rather than dreading the **question-answer period,** you should welcome it. First, it offers you an excellent opportunity to adapt to your audience. You know what your listeners want to hear because they ask the questions. Second, it gives you an opportunity to interact directly with your audience. This usually results in a more natural, lively delivery and makes for better speaker-listener rapport.

A third reason to welcome questions is that almost any question asked can help you. If questions are friendly, that is a high compliment: The audience is genuinely interested in you and your topic. If questions stem from audience confusion about your presentation, you have an opportunity to clarify. If someone asks you a combative and contentious question, you've just been given a second chance to win this person over to your point of view. Without the Q-A period you would not have had this opportunity. If time permits, then, seize the opportunity to answer your listeners' questions.

Before tackling the Q-A period, study the guidelines in the box. You will find them helpful when you stand in front of an audience and ask, "Are there any questions?"

KEY POINTS	**1.** Restate or clarify the question.
Guidelines to Answering Questions	**2.** Compliment the question.
	3. Answer the question.
	4. Check the response with the questioner.

The first step, *restating or clarifying the question,* is important for three reasons. First, repetition makes sure that the entire audience has heard the question. At times, your audience will be small enough that you can be reasonably sure that everyone has heard the question asked. Or if your audience is very large, the person asking the question may have stepped to a microphone located in the audience. As a rule, though, if you have any doubt that everyone in the audience has heard the question, repeat it. Second, repeating the question allows the questioner the opportunity to correct you if you misstate it, saving you the embarrassment of beginning to answer a different question. Third, if the question seems confusing to you or somehow misses the point, you should rephrase the question to make it clearer, more focused, and more relevant. Never answer a question you don't understand.

A second step in answering a question is to *compliment the question,* if deserved. We have all heard speakers say, "I'm glad you asked that." Of course, you cannot repeat that same remark after each question. But without seeming insincere you can say, "That's a good (or perceptive or interesting) question," or "I was hoping someone would ask that." If you know the questioner, you could even joke, "Can't put anything past you, Bernie."

You may face hostile questions, and they certainly pose special challenges for a speaker. Remember, though, that a hostile question is not necessarily a bad question. Hostile questions can be quite legitimate. Sincerely complimenting a hostile question or questioner can defuse a tense situation and focus attention on issues rather than on personal antagonism.

You are now ready for the third step: *answering the question.* Of course, the content and the form of your answers depend on the specific questions; nevertheless, the following suggestions may be helpful.

1. **Know Your Topic Thoroughly.** Your success during the Q-A period will depend, in large part, on your research and preparation for your speech. You should always know more than you included in your speech. Most of the time, poor answers reflect poor preparation.

2. **Be as Brief as Possible.** Obviously, some questions require longer, more thoughtful answers than others. The question, "How much did you say it will cost to complete Phase II of the new library?" can be answered simply, "Two and a half million dollars." The question, "What will that $2.5 million provide?" will require a much longer answer. There are two reasons for making your answers as succinct as possible. First, short answers are easier to remember than lengthy ones. Second, the shorter each answer, the greater the number of questions you can field.

3. **Be Methodical When Giving Lengthy Answers.** When you need to give a detailed answer, use the "frame it, state it, and explain it" approach. Suppose you were asked the question, "How will the $2.5 million budgeted for Phase II of the new library be spent?" You could answer as follows:

> In order to answer that question, we need to look at three categories of costs: construction, furniture and equipment, and instructional materials.
>
> Mike Phillips, the director of buildings and grounds, estimates cost breakdowns as follows: $1.7 million for construction, $300,000 for furniture and equipment, and $500,000 for instructional materials.
>
> Unlike many institutions, we're fortunate that we can provide a sizable amount of money — half a million dollars — in addition to our regular annual budget of $200,000 for instructional resources. This is a one-time infusion of money. You should also know, however, what these figures do not include. Not included are personnel costs, energy costs, and costs for purchases of materials and equipment beyond the first year.

4. **If You Don't Know an Answer, Admit It.** Making up an answer is potentially damaging. Fabricated answers can not only undermine your credibility, but the audience may also act on incorrect information you have provided. Besides, it's unethical. There is nothing wrong with saying, "I don't know," or, "I don't know, but I'll check on it and let you know." If you give the second response, make sure you follow up promptly.

5. **Be Careful About What You Say Publicly.** Remember that in a public gathering, there is no such thing as an off the record statement. Don't say, "It's not official and I would not want it reported yet, but we expect that the vice-president will be our commencement speaker." You will probably read the following headline in the next issue of your school paper: "Vice-President Possible Commencement Speaker." If the press is present, what you say may indeed be reported. As a rule, never say anything that would embarrass you or slander others if it were to appear in the next morning's paper.

The final step in answering a question is to *check the response with the questioner*. Did you answer the question to his or her satisfaction? Is there a follow-up question? Remember two drawbacks to this approach, however. If each person is allowed a question and a follow-up, you will be able to answer fewer people's questions. Second, if questioners are argumentative, asking them if you answered the question to their satisfaction gives them an opportunity to keep the floor and turn the Q-A period into a debate.

In Chapter 1, we introduced you to the components of the communication process: speaker, message, listener, channel, feedback, environment, and noise. Channel, you remember, refers to the way the message is sent. Messages may be written or spoken. If spoken, they may be delivered in person or transmitted electronically. Videotape is one popular electronic medium. Even though you still see and hear the speaker, videotape introduces a new dynamic to the public speech, and that dynamic affects how audience members receive the message.

videotaped speech: a speech taped during practice for the speaker's review or during actual delivery for viewing by another audience.

The **videotaped speech** is increasingly common, for both practice and presentation. If you have access to a camcorder, you may want to use it as you practice your speeches for this class. If you are nervous about your speech and self-conscious practicing in front of another person, just set up a camera, turn it on, walk to the front of the room, and deliver your speech. This rehearsal strategy gives you the advantage of a live critic, one who knows you well and wants to help you become a better speaker. That critic is you! You can watch yourself on the videotape and note what you do well and what still needs work. After viewing yourself, you may even ask some friends to look at the tape with you and offer their comments and suggestions. If you use the videotape strategy, keep a copy of your final practice tape for each of your speeches in this class. After you have a few examples, review them. You will probably be surprised to see how much you have improved since your first effort.

Videotaping actual presentations is also increasingly common. Speeches given to community groups or before governmental bodies are often taped for possible broadcast on local news. Corporations use videotaped presentations in their employee training programs. Your instructor may have played tapes of great speeches for you, or speeches other students gave when they took a public speaking class. These examples may have been particularly helpful, because videotape re-creates the event better than a lifeless manuscript does. In this section, we discuss videotaping an entire speech for playback, and we offer three guidelines to help you meet this challenge.

KEY POINTS

Guidelines for the Videotaped Speech

1. Adapt your delivery to your audience(s).
2. Adapt your delivery to your microphone.
3. Adapt your delivery to your camera shots.

Your first consideration in preparing for a videotaped or filmed speech is your *audience.* Are you speaking primarily to the immediate group assembled or to those who will view the videotape later? Which is your primary audience and which your secondary? Or are both equally important? Unlike traditional speaking situations requiring analysis of one audience, the videotaped speech often requires you to analyze several audiences. If these audiences differ in significant ways, the task of constructing your speech is more difficult.

The audience you expect to view your videotape should also guide the way you respond to the camera. If you are videotaping your speech for your own analysis, you want the camera to see what any audience member in the camera's location would see. In that case, don't look directly into the camera during your entire speech. Make eye contact with all parts of your audience as you practice, treating the camera as just another audience member. If you are speaking only to an external audience, as the president does when speaking to the public from a desk in the Oval Office, you will want to make eye contact only with the camera, treating it as your only listener. As a rule, if audience members viewing a videotape see another audience in the speaker's presence, they will expect the speaker to be interacting with those people. If audience members watching a videotape believe themselves to be the speaker's only audience, they will expect to receive the full measure of the speaker's eye contact.

A second concern is the *microphone* you will use. A lapel microphone clips to your shirt, blouse, tie, dress, or jacket. It moves with you. A fixed, or stationary, microphone is often fastened to the lectern or held in place by a microphone stand. You may or may not be given a choice of microphones. What are the advantages and drawbacks of each?

A *lapel microphone* allows you freedom of movement. You can walk and keep the same voice level. Some media experts believe that, because it is attached near the chest cavity, it adds resonance to your voice, making your vocal delivery richer. This mike is also unobtrusive, as it is not easily seen by you or your audience. Speakers who experience "mike fright" usually prefer the lapel to the fixed microphone because it is out of their sight. However, if you use a lapel mike that has a cord, you will need to watch your movement, being careful not to become entangled in the cord. You will also want to select your clothing carefully. If your jacket and shirt or blouse rustle as you move, the mike will pick up distracting noise.

Even a *fixed microphone* attached to the lectern sometimes picks up distracting nois-

A college television studio gives students valuable experience working with this mass medium and adapting to the camera. (SOURCE: © Frank Siteman)

es, such as nervous tapping of fingers on the lectern or shuffling of paper as you move your speaking notes. In order to do your best job as a speaker, you need to be aware of all that the audience hears. A disadvantage of the fixed microphone is that it restricts movement. As you walk away from the mike, your volume may fade. Most fixed microphones today, however, are multidirectional, or able to pick up sound from many directions. You do not need to stand rigidly twelve inches away from the fixed mike, speaking without turning your head from side to side. You may (and should) move your head as you make eye contact with various sections of your audience. Avoid looking at the mike and becoming preoccupied with its presence.

A third factor you should consider when planning and practicing your speech is the *camera*. Where is it positioned? What is its angle of vision? Will it record close-up or long shots? What the camera sees should help determine your delivery. If the camera takes only head shots, your facial expressions become more important and gesturing less so. Glancing down at your notes will be more noticeable. In a full body shot, you will be able to gesture and move about more freely. If the camera sees you from chest up, you will want to ensure that your gestures are high enough to convey your dynamism visibly. Someone videotaping your speech rehearsal or actual presentation may use the camera's zoom lens to get a variety of shots. If possible, find out this person's plans before you speak.

Here are some other tips to make your videotaped presentation more effective:

1. Avoid wearing predominantly white or black clothing. Pastel clothing is usually preferred.
2. Avoid wearing finely striped clothing, or other busy patterns.
3. Avoid wearing large or excessive jewelry.
4. Keep make-up simple and natural. Shiny facial and head areas should be treated with powdered make-up. Men who have "5 o'clock shadows" should shave or use corrective make-up before they speak.
5. Don't blow into or tap on a microphone.
6. Don't make exaggerated movements in front of the camera.
7. Exercise caution in using overhead projectors, slides, or other types of visual aids that require lights to be turned off. The camera may not be able to videotape these projections efficiently.

In summary, try to determine what the viewing audience will see. If possible, find out how your speech will be taped beforehand so that you can practice accordingly. If this is not possible, be prepared to adapt during the event. Arrive early and talk to the camera operator; you may even want to suggest how you would like the speech recorded. Let the camera operator know if and when you will use a visual aid so that he or she can zoom in on the chart or graph at the appropriate time. If your primary audience is the tape viewing audience and if you are given a choice, request many close-up shots. Remember, your eyes and face are the most expressive parts of your body. Emphasizing those aspects of your physical delivery can make the speaker-viewer relationship more personal.

As with any speech, practice is the key to effective delivery. Videotaping adds another dynamic to that delivery. You must be concerned not only with how your body and voice carry your message, but also with how the medium of transmission affects the message your listeners receive.

The *speech of introduction* presents a featured speaker to an audience. If you are called on to introduce another speaker, your speech should not compete with the one you are introducing. Be brief, focus your remarks on the featured speaker, establish that person's credibility, create positive but realistic audience expectations, and match the tone of the featured speech.

The *speech of presentation* confers an award, prize, or special recognition on an individual or group. Such a speech should state the purpose of the award or recognition, particularly if it is new or unfamiliar to the audience. The speaker should state the recipient's qualifications to reveal why the person deserves the award. If the audience does not know the name of the recipient in advance, the speech of presentation should create suspense, revealing the recipient's name only late in the speech. If the person being honored has been selected from nominees known to the audience, the speech of presentation should compliment those other individuals.

The *acceptance speech* is an honoree's response to a speech of presentation. Social custom dictates that you thank at least briefly any group presenting you an award, prize, or other recognition. When accepting an award, you should thank the people bestowing the award, compliment your competitors if you know them, and thank those who helped you attain the award. Your acceptance speech gives you a chance to say thanks humbly and sincerely.

The *speech of tribute* honors an individual, a group, or a significant event. A *eulogy*, spoken to honor a person who has recently died, is one of the most familiar speeches of tribute. In delivering a speech of tribute, you should establish noble or lofty themes built upon vivid examples from the subject's life. As a speaker, you should attempt to express the collective feelings of the audience. You should create a memorable image of the subject, and you should be genuine.

The *oral report* is a special type of public speech because the speaker is as likely to be assigned the topic as to have chosen it. Oral reports are usually longer than public speeches and they are usually informative. Because they cover a lot of material, oral reports should be well organized, should synthesize relevant supporting material before evaluating it, should be well documented, should use visual supports when appropriate, and should be creative.

The *speech to entertain* seeks to make a point through the creative, organized use of the speaker's humor. Usually delivered on a light, festive occasion, your speech to entertain should make a point, be creative, be well organized, use appropriate humor, and be delivered in a spirited manner. The humor you use in a speech to entertain should be relevant to your point, tasteful, tactful, and positive.

An *impromptu speech* is one delivered with little or no advance preparation. You speak impromptu whenever someone asks you a question or calls on you to speak with only a moment's notice. Under these circumstances, speak on a subject you know well, if possible, and use your limited preparation time in a positive way. Ask, "What do I want the audience to remember from what I say?" Then focus your remarks to achieve that goal. The impromptu speech should focus on only a few key points and should be brief. To improve your impromptu speaking, reflect on each speech to see how you could have improved its content, organization, and delivery.

The *question-answer period* after your speech gives you the opportunity to adapt your material to the specific needs or wishes of the audience because listeners will ask you what they want to know. Answering questions from audience members will be easier if you follow four steps. First, restate or clarify the question. Second, compliment the question or the questioner. Third, answer the question. Finally, check your response with the person who asked the question.

The *videotaped speech* is becoming increasingly common, both for practice and for actual presentation of the speech. Videotaping requires speakers to adapt their delivery to their various audiences, to the microphone, and to the camera. The presence of a video camera will influence your eye contact, movement, gestures, and other elements of your vocal and physical delivery.

EXERCISES

1. Pair up with another member of the class. Discuss each other's speech topic and relevant personal background. Following the guidelines discussed in this chapter, prepare a speech introducing your partner on the day of his or her speech. Your partner will introduce you when you speak.
2. Prepare and deliver a speech of tribute for someone you admire who is known to the class. This person may be a campus, local, national, or international figure.
3. Pair up with someone and discuss what each of you do well. Create an award that one of you will receive. One of you will give a speech of presentation and the other a speech of acceptance.
4. View a speech that was constructed for both public and mass communication. Examples include speeches at political conventions, inaugural addresses, State of the Union addresses, and State of the State addresses by governors. Analyze the speech in light of the different audiences. Did one audience seem more important to the speaker than the other? If so, what led you to this conclusion? Do you think the speaker adapted well to each audience? If so, what strategies and techniques did the speaker use well? If not, what could the speaker have done better?
5. Listen to a formal speech of introduction. The speech may be one you see on television, as in a C-SPAN broadcast of a National Press Club address. Or you may attend a campus or community meeting during which a speaker is introduced. Using the guidelines in this chapter, critique the speech of introduction. What did the introducer do well? What could he or she have done better? Did the introducer prepare the audience to listen intelligently to the speech that followed?

NOTES

1. Meg Greenfield, "Did She Take the Hill?" *Newsweek* 11 October 1993: 72.
2. Ira Berkow, "For Mr. Cooperstown, It's Still a One-Man Show," *The New York Times* 2 August 1993, late ed.: C1.
3. Diana Jean Schemo, "Holocaust Museum

Hailed as Sacred Debt to Dead," *The New York Times* 23 April 1993, natl. ed.: A1, 24.

4. Don Ochs, "Introduction of Samuel L. Becker, Central States Communication Association Convention, April 12, 1991," *The CSCA News* (Spring 1991): 2.

5. George L. Grice, "Remarks at the First General Session, Texas Speech Communication Association Convention, October 4, 1986," *TSCA Newsletter* (January 1987): 12.

6. Steven Spielberg, "Irving G. Thalberg Memorial Award Acceptance Speech," 59th Academy Awards, Los Angeles, 30 March 1987. © Copyright Academy of Motion Picture Arts and Sciences. Used with permission.

7. Peggy Noonan, *What I Saw at the Revolution* (New York: Random, 1990) 253.

8. Adlai Stevenson, "Eulogy on Eleanor Roosevelt," *Representative American Speeches: 1962-1963*, ed. Lester Thonssen (New York: Wilson, 1963) 179-183.

9. Michael McDonough, "Untitled Speech," *1990 Championship Debates and Speeches* (Annandale, VA: Speech Communication Association, 1990) 86.

10. Barry Wilner, "Thanks for the Memories," *Inside Sports* February 1991: 66.

THE IMPORTANCE OF SMALL GROUPS

*T*ake out a sheet of paper and start listing all the small groups to which you belong. Think of committees, subcommittees, boards, and councils on which you serve. Include your network of close friends. Add your family to the list. What about athletic teams, honor societies, fraternities or sororities, the chess club, the debating society, the arts council, study groups, and other groups? After a few minutes of this brainstorming, you will probably be surprised at the length of your list. In light of that discovery, you probably won't be surprised that one survey estimated that "35 to 60 percent of the average manager's day is taken up by meetings."[1] In fact, groups are so prevalent in our society that it is estimated that there are more groups in America than there are people.[2]

Not only are groups plentiful, they are also influential. They shape our society and our behavior. Government, businesses, educational institutions, and other organizations depend on groups to gather information, assess data, and propose courses of action. Our families and our close friends give us counsel and support in times of need. We do so much planning, problem solving, and recreating in small groups that we can all relate to the humorist's remark that "there are no great people, only great committees."

Because groups significantly influence our lives, it is essential that groups communicate effectively. Unfortunately, small group communication seems not to be a skill most of us master easily. For example, a communication professor and a consultant notes that "poor meeting preparation, ad hoc scheduling, and lack of participant training in meeting management are causing many companies to lose the *equivalent of thirty man-days and 240 man-hours a year for every person who participates in business conferences.*"[3] Clearly, poor group communication can be costly. But why study group work as an adjunct to public speaking? The answer is twofold: (1) Groups of people often make public presentations, and (2) the quality of those presentations depends on how well group members have functioned together.

For most of your work in your public speaking class, you have operated alone. *You* selected your speech topics. *You* researched as much as you wanted and at your own convenience. *You* organized your speeches as you thought best and practiced them as much as you thought necessary. As we suggested in Chapter 2, you were the author, artist, and director of your own success or failure.

As part of a group solving a problem and preparing a presentation, your work is more complex. The group's final presentation will allow you to apply everything you have learned about researching, organizing, and delivering a speech. Just as important, however, group processes will test your ability to work productively and congenially with other people. You will do that much more easily if you understand the subjects covered in this chapter: what constitutes a group, the types of groups, principles of group decision making, the responsibilities of group leaders and members, and the most frequently used formats for group presentations.

SMALL GROUPS DEFINED

small group: a collection of three or more people influencing and interacting with one another in pursuit of a common goal.

A **small group** is a collection of three or more individuals who interact with and influence each other in pursuit of a common goal. This definition includes four important concepts: individuals, interaction, influence, and goal.

The number of *individuals* in a group may vary. At a minimum, there must be three. Two people are not a group but rather an interpersonal unit, sometimes called a dyad. The addition of a third person adds a new dynamic, a new perspective. Paul Nelson describes the new relationship in the following way:

> Something happens to communication when it involves more than two people: It becomes much more complex. For example, imagine two people, A and B, having a conversation. There is only *one* possible conversation, A-B. Add one more person, C, however: Now there are *four* possible interactions, A-B, A-C, B-C, and A-B-C. Add another person, D, and there are *eleven* possible interactions. And so on.[4]

Although we can all agree that three is the minimum number for a small group, we do not always agree on the maximum number. Even communication experts disagree, with some using seven as a workable maximum and others stretching the range to twenty. What characterizes a small group is not a specific number of participants but the *type* of communication they undertake. A group that is too large cannot maintain meaningful interaction among members and may have to be divided into smaller working groups.

A group's size, then, affects a second characteristic of a small group: *interaction*. A small group offers each participant an opportunity to interact with all other members of the group. A group cannot function if its participants fail to interact, and it functions ineffectively when a few members dominate. Generally, the larger the group, the fewer opportunities for any one member to participate and the greater the likelihood that a few members will dominate the flow of communication, making certain that meaningful interaction does not take place.

A third characteristic of small groups is *influence*. Members of a group interact in order to influence others. As journalist Walter Lippman observed, "When all think alike, no one thinks very much." Groups function best when members express differences of opinions openly and try to persuade others with data and arguments.

Finally, a group has a purpose. As we noted in Chapter 1, a group is more than simply a collection of individuals who interact; it exists for a reason. Members interact and influence each other over a period of time in order to achieve a *goal*. The group process fails when members are unsure of their goal or when they fail to resolve conflicting perceptions of that goal.

■■■ TYPES OF GROUPS

People form groups for two reasons: because they enjoy interacting with each other or because they need to accomplish a task. Therefore, we can classify groups into two general types: social-oriented and task-oriented. A **social-oriented group** is one whose main goal is social. Group members may not have a major task in mind but rather be concerned mainly with relationships, enjoying time spent with other members of the group. A **task-oriented group** is more formal. Members interact having a specific goal in mind. For example, you and a few classmates may form a study group to review for examinations and to be an audience for each other as you practice your speeches.

The objectives of social- and task-oriented groups often intermingle. Say you and your friends decide to go to a movie. Clearly, this is a social occasion, but you still must accomplish certain tasks: What movie does the group want to see? When is the best time

social-oriented group: a small group that exists primarily because its members enjoy interacting with one another.

task-oriented group: a small group that exists primarily to accomplish some goal.

for everyone to see it? Will you carpool or will everyone meet at the theatre? Do you want to get a bite to eat before or after the movie? You have probably, at times, been frustrated when your social group was unable to make some of these "easy" task decisions.

While social-oriented groups may have task objectives, the converse is also true. You form a study group to accomplish certain tasks, but as you get to know the others in the group you discover that you enjoy their company. As social objectives emerge, the group meets more frequently and functions more effectively. If social purposes predominate, however, you may find that your group sacrifices studying for socializing. Even though most groups have both social and task objectives, one purpose usually takes precedence according to the situation. That purpose determines the structure of your group and the nature of the communication among its members.

In this chapter, we will focus on task-oriented groups, sometimes called working groups. These include study groups, problem-solving groups, and action groups. The objective of a **study group** is to learn about a topic. It gathers, processes, and evaluates information. When you and your classmates work together to prepare for an exam, you are a study group. A **problem-solving group** decides on courses of action. This type of group explores a problem, suggesting solutions to remedy it. The objective of an **action group** is, as its name implies, to act. It has the power to implement proposals. These categories may overlap. In fact, you may be a member of a group that studies a situation, devises a solution, *and* implements it.

As you go through this chapter, you will find that participating in task groups and delivering public speeches are similar in several ways. Both usually involve research, analysis of information and ideas, and the presentation of that information to others. In small groups your presentation may be to other group members, although sometimes a group will present its findings to an external body. Yet despite these similarities, there are notable differences between public speaking and group communication. The effective communicator will seek to master both sets of skills.

GROUP DISCUSSION AND DECISION MAKING

One of the most important reasons we form groups is to make decisions. We may seek a friend's guidance because we believe that two heads are better than one. The philosophy behind this decision is the foundation of group decision making. You may have heard the expression that in communication "the whole is greater than the sum of its parts." This is particularly true in group communication. What this means is that, if a group of five functions effectively, its product will be qualitatively or quantitatively superior to the total product of five people working individually. But a group is able to work most effectively when members follow certain principles of group decision making. We discuss these five principles next.

study group: a task-oriented group devoted to researching and learning about a topic.
problem-solving group: a task-oriented group devoted to deciding on courses of action to correct a problem.
action group: a task-oriented group devoted to implementing proposals for action.

KEY POINTS

Principles of Group Decision Making

1. Group decision making is a shared responsibility.
2. Group decision making requires a clear understanding of goals.
3. Group decision making benefits from a clear but flexible agenda.
4. Group decision making is enhanced by open communication.
5. Group decision making requires adequate information.

Group Decision Making Is a Shared Responsibility.   It is true that the group leader plays a special role in the group. As a matter of fact, we include separate sections in this chapter about the responsibilities of the group leader as well as of members. The presence of a group leader does not necessarily establish a leader-follower, or even an active-passive, association. In fact, this relationship is usually better represented as a partnership. Group decision making requires the active participation of all members performing mutually reinforcing responsibilities.

Group Decision Making Requires a Clear Understanding of Goals.   As we have stated earlier, every group has a goal. Sometimes that goal is predetermined. Your instructor may, for example, divide your class into small groups, assigning each group to generate a list of twenty-five topics suitable for a speech to inform. In your career, you may be part of a small group having the task of studying specific job-related problems and proposing workable solutions. In both of these instances, the group has a clear statement of its objective. In other situations, the goal of your group may be less clear. If that is the case, you will have to clarify, specify, or even determine your goals.

Group Decision Making Benefits From a Clear but Flexible Agenda.   Every group needs a plan of action. Because a group's process affects its product, it is vital that members spend sufficient time generating an action plan. The leader can facilitate this process by suggesting procedures that the group may adopt, modify, or reject. The best plan, or agenda, however, is one not dictated by the leader but rather developed by both the leader and the members of the group. Remember, the leader and the group members form a partnership.

   A group's agenda should be both specific and flexible. Group participants must know what is expected of them and how they will go about accomplishing the task at hand. Raising $1,000 for charity could be accomplished by dividing the membership into five teams, each having the responsibility for generating $200. These teams would need to communicate and coordinate to avoid unnecessary overlap as they decided on their fund-raising projects. Groups also need to be flexible as they pursue their goals. Unexpected obstacles may require revising the agenda. The group needs a backup plan, for example, if its car wash is canceled because of rain.

Group Decision Making is Enhanced by Open Communication.   If all members of a group think alike, there is no need for the group. One person can simply make the decision. Diversity is what gives a group breadth of perspective. Both the group leader and individual members should protect and encourage the expression of minority views.

   What a group wants to avoid is the problem of groupthink, a term coined by Irving Janis. **Groupthink** occurs when group members come to care more about conforming and not making waves than they do about exercising the critical evaluation necessary to weed out bad ideas.[5] Groupthink reduces open communication and adversely affects the quality of decision making. In order to be effective, a group must encourage each member to exercise his or her independent judgment.

groupthink: excessive agreement among group members who value conformity more than critical evaluation.

Group Decision Making Requires Adequate Information.   Access to information that is sufficient and relevant is extremely important. A group suffers if its information is based on the research of only one or two of its members. To avoid this problem, a group should follow a few simple steps. First, the leader should provide essential information to the group as a starting point. Second, each member of the group should contribute critical knowledge to the group. Third, the group should divide the gathering of information in a way that is efficient and yet provides some overlap. Later in this chapter, we provide some suggestions for gathering information. Now that we understand the principles of group decision making, let's take a look at how the group makes decisions.

The Process of Group Decision Making

In his celebrated book *How We Think*, published in 1910, John Dewey argued that decision making should be a logical, orderly process.[6] His "Steps to Reflective Thinking" have provided one of the most useful, and we think one of the best, approaches to problem solving. Authors and theorists differ in their adaptations of the reflective thinking model, organizing it around five, six, or seven steps. We prefer a seven-step approach.

If you are a member of a problem-solving discussion group or a task-oriented group and you have not been assigned a topic, the group will need to select a topic and word it. A good discussion topic is current, is controversial, and has a body of data and opinion from which to construct and refute positions. Once you select a topic meeting these criteria, you must word the topic according to the following guidelines.

First, it should be worded as a question the group will seek to answer. "The campus parking problem" fails to meet this criterion and, consequently, does not direct participants in the discussion toward a goal. A better wording is evident in the examples presented in the second criterion.

Second, the question should be open rather than closed. Open wording might include "What can be done to alleviate the parking problem on campus?" or "How should this college solve the campus parking problem?" These questions are open because they do not direct the group to one particular solution. They invite a variety of solutions and can generate lively and productive discussion. The question "Should the campus build a multistory parking facility to solve the campus parking problem?" is an example of a closed question, because it focuses attention on only one solution. This yes-or-no question limits discussion of alternative proposals. Because it forces individuals to choose sides, a closed question is probably more appropriate for a debate than for a discussion format.

After members have agreed upon a topic question, the group should begin answering it in a logical, methodical manner. The following seven-step process, based on Dewey's model, will aid your group. It is important that you go through these steps chronologically and not jump ahead in your discussion. Solutions are best discussed and evaluated only after a problem is thoroughly defined and analyzed.

KEY POINTS

The Steps to Problem Solving

1. Define the problem.
2. Analyze the problem.
3. Determine the criteria for the optimal solution.
4. Propose solutions.
5. Evaluate proposed solutions.
6. Select a solution.
7. Suggest strategies for implementing the solution.

Define the Problem. Before you can solve a problem, you must first define it. By defining the key terms of the question, group members decide how they will focus the topic, thus enabling them to keep on track and to avoid extraneous discussion. Suppose your college asks you to be part of a student advisory committee to address the issue, "What can be done to alleviate the parking problem on campus?" In order to answer the question, members must agree on what constitutes "the parking problem." Are there too few parking spaces? If there are sufficient spaces, are they not geographically located to serve the campus best? Is there congestion only during certain times of the day or week? Is the problem how the spaces are designated—for example, is there adequate parking for faculty but not for students? Is the problem not the number of spaces but the condition of the parking lots? How your group defines the problem determines, to a large extent, how you will solve it. If there is not a problem with the condition of the lots or the number of spaces for faculty, you can safely delete these considerations from your discussion agenda.

Analyze the Problem. In analyzing any problem, a group looks at both its symptoms and causes. We gauge the severity of a problem by examining its *symptoms*. For example, the group needs to know not only the approximate number of students unable to find parking spaces, but also why that is detrimental. Students may be late for class or may avoid going to the library because of parking congestion; accidents may occur as cars crowd into small spaces; the college may spark resentment from students who pay to attend but have no place to park; students may transfer to another school having more convenient access; students walking to dimly lit and distant parking spaces after an evening class may worry about physical attacks. These symptoms point to the magnitude of the problem. Certainly, some symptoms are more serious than others, and group members must identify those needing immediate action.

However, the group is still not ready to propose remedies. The group must now consider the *causes* of the problem. By examining how a difficulty developed, a group may find its solution. The parking problem may stem from a variety of causes, including increased enrollment, parking spaces converted to other uses, lack of funds to build new parking lots, too many classes scheduled at certain times, inadequate use of distant parking lots, and some student parking spaces earmarked for faculty and administrators.

Determine the Criteria for the Optimal Solution. Decision-making criteria are the standards we use to judge the merits of proposed solutions. It is wise to state these criteria before discussing solutions. Why select an action plan only to discover later that sufficient funding is unavailable? The group studying campus parking worked to avoid this pitfall. Some of the criteria they considered were as follows:

Criteria	Explanation
Economics	The proposal should be cost-effective.
Aesthetics	The proposal should not spoil the beauty of the campus.
Legality	The proposal cannot force residents and businesses adjacent to campus to sell their land to the college.
Growth	The proposal should account for future increases in enrollment.
Security	Students should be safe as they go to and from parking lots.

The group could also have considered ranking parking privileges according to student seniority or giving students parking status equal to faculty.

Propose Solutions. Only after completing the first three steps is the group ready to propose solutions. This is essentially a brainstorming step with emphasis on the quantity, not quality, of suggestions. At this stage, the group should not worry about evaluating any suggested solutions, no matter how farfetched they may seem. This group's brainstorming list included the following:

> Building a multistory parking lot in the center of campus.
> Constructing parking lots near the edge of campus.
> Reclaiming some faculty spaces for student use.
> Lighting and patrolling lots in the evening.
> Initiating bus service between apartment complexes and the campus.
> Encouraging students to carpool or to ride bicycles to campus.

Evaluate Proposed Solutions.   Now the group is ready to evaluate each of the proposed solutions. Each possibility is judged using the criteria listed in the third step. Next, the group considers the advantages of the proposed solution. Finally, they assess its disadvantages. The centrally located, high-rise parking garage may not be cost-efficient, and may intrude on the beauty of the campus, but may use valuable land efficiently and limit the extent of late-night walking.

Select a Solution.   After evaluating each proposed solution, you and your fellow group members should have a pretty good idea of those solutions to exclude from consideration and those to retain. You will then weigh the merits and deficiencies of each. Your final solution may be a combination of several of the proposed remedies. For example, the group working on the campus parking problem could issue a final report advocating a three-phase solution: short-range, middle-range, and long-range goals. A short-term approach may involve converting a little-used athletic practice field to a parking facility, creating more bicycle parking areas, and encouraging carpooling. A middle-range solution could involve creating a bus system between student apartment houses and the campus, or trying to get the city transit system to incorporate new routes. The proposal for the long-term could involve building a well-lit multistory parking facility, not in the middle of campus, but near the athletic complex, to be used during the week for general student parking and on weekends for athletic and entertainment events.

Suggest Strategies for Implementing the Solution.   Once the small group has worked out a solution, members would normally submit their recommendations to another body for approval, action, and implementation. Sometimes, however, decision makers should not only select feasible and effective solutions but also show how they can be implemented. How would the small group incorporate suggestions for implementing its solution? Members would probably recommend coordinating their plan with the long-range master plan for the college. Other administrators would have to be included. The group would probably also suggest a timetable detailing short-term and long-term projects, and might also identify possible funding sources.

In summary, the reflective thinking model enables a group to define a problem, analyze it, determine the criteria for a good solution, propose solutions, evaluate solutions, select a solution, and suggest ways to implement it. Decisions made by following this process are generally better, and group members are more satisfied with their work. Not only can this model benefit groups in business, government, education, and other organizations, it can also improve your individual decision making.

As we argued earlier, the leader-member relationship is not an active-passive partnership. In order to enhance the quality of the group's product, all members must participate actively. At this stage, you may be asking yourself, "What do group participants do?" If you reflect on our example of the group tackling the campus parking problem, you can see how those group members handled their responsibilities. Productive group members undertake six key responsibilities.

		KEY POINTS
1. Inform the group.	5. Advocate personal beliefs.	
2. Evaluate ideas and proposals.	6. Support other group members.	**Responsibilities of Group Members**
3. Question other participants.		
4. Challenge unfounded conclusions.		

Inform the Group.

"Just the facts, ma'am."   SGT. JOE FRIDAY, *DRAGNET*

Group members should enlarge the information base upon which decisions are made and action taken. As we have said elsewhere, a decision is only as good as the information upon which it is based. If the group does not know all the causes of a problem, for example, its proposed solution may not solve it. The greater the number of possible solutions a group considers, the greater its chance of selecting the best one.

You enlarge the group's information base in two ways. First, you contribute what you already know about the issue being discussed. Hearsay information is worth mentioning at this stage, as long as you acknowledge that it is something you have heard but cannot prove. Another member may be able to confirm or refute it, or it can be put on the agenda for further research. Dispelling popular misconceptions so that they do not contaminate the decision-making process is important.

Second, group members contribute to a group's understanding of a topic by gathering additional relevant information. Ideas surfacing during a group meeting may help shape the agenda for the next meeting. You may hear ideas that you want to explore further. You may need to check out facts before the group can clarify the dimensions of a problem or adopt a particular plan of action. The research and thought you give to a topic before a meeting will make the meeting itself more efficient and productive.

Evaluate Ideas and Proposals.   To be effective, a discussion should cover a range of positions on the issue being considered. Each idea should be discussed thoroughly and analyzed critically. A decision based on incorrect information or faulty reasoning may be ineffective or even counterproductive. Thus, all group members are obligated to evaluate the contributions of others and to submit their own positions for evaluation. This is sometimes difficult for us to do. Yet participants should not be defensive about their ideas, but instead open to constructive criticism.

Question Other Participants. Effective discussants not only give but also seek information and opinions. Knowing how and when to ask an appropriate question is an important skill for group members. The ability to ask effective questions requires active listening, sensitivity to the feelings of others, and a desire to learn. Group members should seek clarification of ideas they do not understand and encourage others to explain, defend, and extend their ideas.

Challenge Unfounded Conclusions.
"Freedom rings where opinions clash."
ADLAI STEVENSON

Too often, we accept what we hear at face value, or we may remain silent even though we disagree with what we hear. Discussion benefits when facts, opinions, and proposals are challenged. A significant part of this process is separating good ideas from bad. Ideas that have merit withstand rigorous testing, so group members should challenge the assumptions underlying others' opinions.

Advocate Personal Beliefs. Group members should not only provide information to help make decisions but should also use that data to develop positions on the issues being discussed. Discussants should be willing to state and defend their opinions. Although evaluating, questioning, and challenging are important skills, beware of the member who seems to tear down the contributions of others without offering alternative points of view. This person rarely helps the group.

Support Other Group Members. A group is a collection of individuals having different personalities. Some may be less assertive than others and may have fragile egos. Reluctant to express their ideas because they fear criticism, they may cause the group to lose important information and to rush into a decision. They may even foster the groupthink we discussed earlier. The climate of the group should encourage openness and acceptance. It is the job of both the leader and the group members to create and reinforce a climate of openness and acceptance.

The Responsibilities of Group Leaders

When individuals complain about the lack of cohesiveness and productivity of their group, much of their criticism is often directed toward the group's leader. Just as effective lead-

KEY POINTS

Responsibilities of Group Leaders

1. Plan the agenda.
2. Orient the group.
3. Establish an information base.
4. Involve all members in the discussion.
5. Encourage openness and critical evaluation.
6. Secure clarification of ideas and positions.
7. Keep the group on target.
8. Introduce new ideas and topics.
9. Summarize the discussion.
10. Manage conflict.

ership depends on effective membership, so does effective membership depend on effective leadership. Leaders have certain responsibilities that, if fulfilled, will help the group meet its goal.

Plan the Agenda.   A group leader has the primary responsibility for planning an agenda. This does not mean dictating the agenda; rather, the leader offers suggestions and solicits group input into the process.

Orient the Group.   How a meeting begins is extremely important in setting expectations that affect group climate and productivity. A leader may want to begin a meeting with some brief opening remarks to orient the group to its mission and the process it will follow. In analyzing business meetings, Roger Mosvick and Robert Nelson conclude, "The chairperson's orientation speech is the single most important act of the business meeting." They describe this speech as follows:

> It is a systematically prepared, fully rehearsed, sit-down speech of not less than three minutes nor more than five minutes (most problems require at least three minutes of orientation; anything over five minutes sets up a pattern of dominance and control by the chairperson).[7]

For some groups that you lead, it will not always be appropriate or even desirable to begin a meeting with a structured speech. Still, leaders should try to accomplish several objectives early in the group's important first meeting. They should (1) stress the importance of the task, (2) secure agreement on the process the group will follow, (3) encourage interaction among members, and (4) set an expectation of high productivity.

Establish an Information Base.   Leaders may wish to introduce background information to the group in an opening statement, or forward some relevant articles with background information to members before the first meeting. This sometimes makes the initial meeting more productive by establishing a starting point for discussion. Leaders should encourage input from all members, however, as the primary means of ensuring sufficient information for making decisions.

Involve All Members in the Discussion.   A leader must make certain that participation among group members is balanced. A person who speaks too much is as much a problem as one who speaks too little. In either case, the potential base of information and opinion is narrowed. Remember our position that all members share the responsibility of group leadership. If someone is not contributing to the discussion, any member of the group can ask the silent person for his or her opinion.

Encourage Openness and Critical Evaluation.   After the group has shared information and ideas, the leader must guide the group in evaluating them. The leader may do this by directing probing questions to specific individuals or to the group as a whole. To achieve and maintain a climate of free and honest communication, the group leader must be sensitive to the nonverbal communication of participants, encouraging them to verbalize both their reluctance and their excitement about the ideas other members are expressing. At the same time, the sensitive leader will keep criticism focused on ideas rather than on personalities.

Secure Clarification of Ideas and Positions.   Effective leaders are good at getting members of the discussion to make their positions and ideas clearer and more specific. They do this in two ways. First, the leader may encourage a member to continue talking by asking a series of probing follow-up questions ("So what would happen if …?"). Even the use of prods ("Uh-huh." "Okay?") can force discussants to think through and verbalize their ideas and positions. Second, the leader may close a particular line of discussion by paraphrasing the ideas of a speaker ("So what you're saying is that …"). This strategy confirms the leader's understanding, repeats the idea for the benefit of other group members, and invites their reaction.

Keep the Group on Target.   Effective leaders keep their sights on the group's task while realizing the importance of group social roles. There is nothing wrong with group members becoming friendly and socializing. This added dimension can strengthen your group. However, when social functions begin to impede work on the task, the group leader must "round up the strays" and redirect the entire group to its next goal.

Introduce New Ideas and Topics.   We've already mentioned that it is important for leaders to prepare for the first group meeting, either by researching and preparing an orientation speech or by circulating background materials to group members. In addition, the leader should be the most willing researcher among the group. If discussion stalls because the group lacks focus or motivation, the leader must be willing and able to initiate new topics for research and talk. If a lapse in the group's progress signals that research and discussion have been exhausted, the leader must recognize this situation and be willing to move on to the next phase of group work.

Summarize the Discussion.   A leader should provide the group periodic reviews of what has been decided and what remains to be decided. These summaries keep members focused on the group's task. Leaders may begin a group meeting with an *initial summary*, a brief synopsis of what the group decided previously. They may offer *internal summaries* during the discussion to keep the group on target. At the conclusion of the group task, leaders should provide a *final summary*, reviewing what the group accomplished.

Manage Conflict.   Conflict is not only inevitable in group discussion, it is essential. When ideas collide, participants must rethink and defend their positions. This process engenders further exploration of facts and opinions and enhances the likelihood of a quality outcome. It is important, then, that a group not discourage conflict but manage it.

While conflict of ideas contributes to group effectiveness, interpersonal antagonism may undermine it. When conflict becomes personal, it ceases to be productive. Such conflict disrupts the group. Some members may stop expressing their opinions for fear of attack. If the climate becomes too uncomfortable, members may withdraw from the group. Thus, it is essential that when conflict surfaces, the group responds appropriately. At some point, it may become evident that conflict cannot be solved by the group or in the presence of group members. In this event, the leader may have to meet with the disruptive member one-on-one and discuss the problem.

When a group, following the seven steps of problem solving, is composed of members and a leader fulfilling the various roles we have just outlined, it should produce results quickly. At times, the problem solving will benefit the group alone and no external report is needed. Often, however, the group will be requested or will want to present its findings to a larger group: company workers, company stockholders, or just an interested public audience, for example. In such cases, the group must continue to work together to plan its presentation.

In the following sections of this chapter, we discuss two popular formats for group presentations and provide a systematic checklist to help you develop a first-rate presentation.

Formats for the Presentation

There are several different formats for a group presentation, two of which are the public discussion and the symposium.

The Public Discussion.   In a **public discussion,** a group sits, usually in a semicircle, in front of the audience. Members are aware of an audience but usually address others in the group. The audience, in effect, eavesdrops on the group's conversation. If your public speaking class includes group presentations, your small group may be asked to use this format to present your report to the class.

    The problem-solving classroom discussion usually requires extensive preparation. The group has researched the topic, planned the discussion, and possibly practiced the presentation. Members have a general idea of the content and organization of their own and other participants' remarks, although the presentation is not memorized or scripted. The presentation is intended to inform and persuade the audience on the issue being discussed. Sometimes a question-answer period follows.

The Symposium.   A **symposium** is a series of speeches on a single topic presented to an audience. It differs from a public discussion in at least two ways. First, there is no interaction among the speakers during the presentation, unless a discussion period

public discussion: a small group exchanging ideas and opinions on a single topic in the presence of an audience.

symposium: a series of public speeches on a single topic, possibly followed by group discussion or a question-answer period.

In a public discussion, a group of experts discusses a specified topic in front of an audience, who may then ask questions.
(SOURCE: © Bob Daemmrich/ Uniphoto

follows. Each speaker has a designated amount of time to present his or her remarks. Second, speakers address members of the audience directly. Sometimes speakers are seated at a table; often they use a lectern. In most public symposiums, the speakers have not met beforehand to discuss what they will say. If you are assigned to a group for a presentation in this class, you will likely want to meet several times, following some of the guidelines we discuss in the following section.

Preparing a Group Presentation

A group presentation offers you a variety of learning experiences. You can enhance your research, organization, oral communication, and group interaction skills. This assignment, therefore, is a significant learning opportunity. In addition, your group presentation can be a positive learning experience for your classmates.

    Although there is no one correct way to prepare for a group presentation, the following suggestions will help you work more efficiently and produce a more effective product. This symbol (☞) denotes those steps requiring group interaction; the other steps can be done individually.

KEY POINTS

**Steps in Preparing a
Group Presentation**

  ☞ **1.** Brainstorm about the topic.
     2. Do some exploratory research.
  ☞ **3.** Discuss and divide the topic into areas of responsibility.
     4. Research your specific topic area.
     5. Draft an outline of your content area.
  ☞ **6.** Discuss how all the information interrelates.
  ☞ **7.** Finalize the group presentation format.
  ☞ **8.** Plan the introduction and conclusion of the presentation.
     9. Prepare and practice your speech.
  ☞ **10.** Rehearse and revise the presentation.

☞Brainstorm About the Topic.   If you've read the previous chapters, our first suggestion for preparing a group presentation shouldn't surprise you. Through brainstorming, you will discover knowledge that group members already possess, and you will uncover numerous ideas for further research. In addition to providing content, brainstorming also serves a relationship function. By giving all members an opportunity to participate, brainstorming affords you a glimpse of your peers' personalities and their approaches to group interaction. You get to know them, and they get to know you. Maintaining an atmosphere of openness and respect during this first meeting gets the group off to a good start. Once you have generated a list of areas concerning your group's topic, you are ready for the second step.

Do Some Exploratory Research.   Through brainstorming, you discover areas that need further investigation. The second phase of your group process is individual research. While there may be some merit in each person's selecting a different topic to research, research roles should not be too rigid. Rather than limit yourself by topic, you may wish to divide your research by resource. One member may look at popular news magazines, another at government documents, while a third may interview a professor who is knowledgeable on the topic, and so forth. It is important that you not restrict your discovery to the list of topics you have generated. Exploratory research is also a form of brainstorming. As you look in indexes and read articles you find, you will uncover more topics. Each member of the group should try to find a few good sources that are diverse in scope.

☛Discuss and Divide the Topic into Areas of Responsibility. After exploratory research, your group should reconvene to discuss what each member found. Which expectations were confirmed by your research? Which were not? What topics did you find that you had not anticipated? Your objective at this stage of the group process is to decide on the key areas you wish to investigate. Each person should probably be given primary responsibility for researching a particular area. That person becomes the content expert in that area. While this approach makes research more efficient, it has a drawback. If one person serves as a specialist, the group gambles that he or she will research thoroughly and be objective in reporting findings. If either assumption is not valid, the quantity of information can be insufficient and its quality contaminated. An alternative approach is to assign more than one person to a specific area.

Research Your Specific Topic Area. Using strategies we have discussed in Chapter 7, research your topic area. Your focus should be on the quality of the sources you discover, not on quantity. While your primary goal should be to gather information on your topic, you should also note information related to your colleagues' topics. As you consult indexes, jot down on a card sources that may be helpful to another member in the group. Group members who support each other in this way make the process more efficient and, hence, more enjoyable. This usually results in a better product.

Draft an Outline of Your Content Area. After you have concluded your initial research but before you meet again with your group, construct an outline of the ideas and information you've found. This step is important for two reasons. It forces you to make sense of all the information you have collected, and it will expedite the next step when you will share your information with the rest of the members of your group.

☛Discuss How All the Information Interrelates. You are now ready to meet again with the other members of your group. Members should briefly summarize what they have discovered through their research. After all have shared their ideas, the group should decide which ideas are most important and how these ideas relate to each other. There should be a natural development of the topic that can be divided among the members of the group.

☛Finalize the Group Presentation Format. The speaking order should already be determined. There are, nevertheless, certain procedural details that the group must decide. Will the first speaker introduce all presenters, or will each person introduce the next speaker? Where will the participants sit when they are not speaking, facing the audience or in the front row? The more details you decide beforehand, the fewer distractions you will have on the day you speak.

☛Plan the Introduction and Conclusion of the Presentation. A presentation should appear to be that of a group and not that of four or five individuals. Consequently, you must work on introducing and concluding the group's comments, and you must incorporate smooth transitions from one speaker's topic to the next. An introduction should state the topic, define important terms, and establish the importance of the subject. A conclusion should summarize what has been presented and end with a strong final statement.

Prepare and Practice Your Speech.   By this time in the course, you know the requirements of an excellent speech and have had the opportunity to deliver a few. Most of our earlier suggestions also apply to your speech in your group's presentation. Some differences are worth noting, however. For example, as part of a group presentation, you will need to refer to members' speeches and perhaps even use some of their supporting materials. The group presentation may also impose physical requirements you haven't encountered as a classroom speaker, such as using a microphone, speaking to those seated around you in addition to making direct contact with the audience, or speaking from a seated position.

☛**Rehearse and Revise the Presentation.**   Independent practice of your individual speech is important, but that is only one part of rehearsal. The group should practice its entire presentation. Group rehearsal will not only make participants more confident about their individual presentations, but will also give the group a feeling of cohesion.

S UMMARY

Whether they are part of our business, social, or personal lives, numerous formal and informal groups are important to us because they solve problems, get things done, and provide us with emotional support. A *small group* is a collection of three or more people influencing and interacting with one another in pursuit of a common goal.

Groups usually fulfill both *social-oriented* and *task-oriented* needs for their participants, though one of these types of needs will predominate depending upon the situation. Three types of task-oriented groups include the *study group*, which learns about a topic; the *problem-solving group*, which decides on courses of action; and the *action group*, which implements proposals. This chapter focused on the ways groups function and the tasks they accomplish: gathering, analyzing, and spreading information; and formulating, advocating, and implementing courses of action.

Group decisions are usually superior to decisions individuals make by themselves. To ensure valid decisions, groups must abide by five principles. First, group decision making is a shared responsibility and requires active participation of all members. Second, group members must share a goal that is specific and realistic. Third, groups make decisions best under a clear but flexible schedule or agenda. Fourth, groups can avoid *groupthink* and make the best decisions when members are free to express opinions openly. Fifth, group decision making requires and benefits from the research and information shared by all participants.

Problem-solving groups can speed their progress and simplify their task by following a seven-step modification of John Dewey's steps to reflective thinking. First, define the problem. Second, analyze the symptoms and the causes of the problem. Third, determine the criteria that an optimal solution to the problem must satisfy. Fourth, propose various solutions to the problem. Fifth, evaluate each possible solution against the established criteria. Sixth, decide on the best solution, and seventh, suggest ways of putting the solution into action. Following these steps in this order will streamline group problem-solving work.

Group participation involves six functions: sharing information, evaluating data and opinions, questioning other participants, challenging unfounded conclusions and opinions, advocating personal beliefs, and supporting other participants in the group. Responsibilities of group leaders include planning the group's agenda; orienting the group to the task at hand; providing background information on the problem to be discussed; involving all members in the group's discussion; encouraging a climate of open, honest critical evaluation; seeking clarification of members' ideas and positions; keeping the group focused on its task; introducing new ideas and topics for discussion; summarizing the discussion at various points; and managing interpersonal conflict. If group members and leaders perform these functions during the seven-step problem-solving process, they should reach a satisfactory conclusion, and may then be asked to present their findings in a public presentation.

The presentation may take the form of a *public discussion* before an audience. In this situation, participants speak to one another about aspects of the problem after researching, organizing, and practicing the presentation. Another popular form of group presentation is the *symposium*, a series of formal individual speeches on different aspects of a problem.

When given the opportunity to meet and plan a group presentation before delivering it, members should always do so. Both those experienced and inexperienced in preparing group presentations can benefit from a logical ten-step approach to developing them. First, brainstorm the topic with colleagues in the group. Second, do some individual exploratory research to gauge the scope of the topic. Third, discuss the topic with group members and divide areas of research responsibility by topic or source. Fourth, individually research your assigned area, noting sources in other group members' areas. Fifth, organize the data your research has yielded. Sixth, discuss with other group members how all the generated information interrelates. Seventh, determine the presentation format. Eighth, plan the introduction of group members and the material under discussion. Ninth, prepare and practice speeches individually. And tenth, rehearse and revise the entire group presentation.

EXERCISES

1. Select someone in a leadership position to interview. The person may be a business executive, an officer in an organization, a school principal, a college president, or any other leader. Construct and ask a series of questions designed to discover his or her views on characteristics of effective and ineffective leaders. Record the answers and be prepared to discuss them in class.

2. Using the topic areas listed below, select a specific problem area and word it in the form of a problem-solving discussion question.
   a. crime
   b. education
   c. international relations
   d. political campaigning
   e. public health

3. Choose four campus problems you think need to be addressed—for example, class registration. Word the topics as problem-solving questions. Analyze each topic asking the following questions:
   a. How important is the problem?
   b. What information do you need to analyze and solve the problem?
   c. Where would you find this information?
   d. What barriers keep the problem from being solved now?
   e. Which steps in the problem-solving process do you think will generate the most conflict? Why?

   Based on your answers to these questions, select the best topic for a problem-solving discussion. Justify your choice.

4. Think of a problem you are experiencing that you need to solve. Work through the seven steps of the reflective thinking model to arrive at a solution to the problem. Did the model help you arrive at a decision? If so, which steps were most helpful? If not, what are some limitations of the model?

5. Observe a meeting of a student, faculty, city, or some other decision-making group. What examples did you observe of good and bad group communication skills? Could the meeting have been conducted better? If so, how?

6. Discuss when it would be better for a group presentation to take the form of a public discussion. When would the symposium format be preferable?

NOTES

1. *Working Woman* July 1993: 39. The survey was conducted by Goodrich & Sherwood, a New York human-resources consulting firm.

2. Bobby R. Patton and Kim Giffin, *Decision-Making Group Interaction*, 2nd ed. (New York: Harper, 1978) 1.

3. Roger K. Mosvick and Robert B. Nelson, *We've Got to Start Meeting Like This!* (Glenview, IL: Scott, 1987) 4.

4. Paul E. Nelson, "Small-Group Communication," in Lilian O. Feinberg, *Applied Business Communication* (Sherman Oaks, CA: Alfred, 1982) 27.

5. Irving L. Janis, *Groupthink: Psychological Studies of Policy Decisions and Fiascoes*, 2nd ed. (Boston: Houghton, 1982) 9.

6. John Dewey, *How We Think* (Boston: Heath, 1910).

7. Mosvick 114.

Appendix A

Critiquing Speeches

lmost as important as the speeches you deliver in your public speaking course are the kinds of comments you can offer about the speeches others give. In this text, we have shown you how to prepare and deliver an effective speech. You should use this knowledge as you comment on the speeches you hear others deliver. Appropriate feedback is crucial to your development as a public speaker. What you learn from your instructor and classmates about distractions caused by language, voice, or body will help you polish your speaking skills. You, in turn, want to be an incisive and sensitive critic when you write or speak about others' speeches. This brief section aims to help you offer better critical comments.

For the purposes of this section, we define **criticism** as information (feedback) given to others in a way that enables them to use it for self-improvement.[1] Whether written or spoken, criticism, then, includes both positive comments that reinforce what a speaker did well and negative comments that point to potential improvements. If you say, "Your speech was well within the time limit at seven minutes and twelve seconds," you function as a speech critic as you spotlight a positive aspect of the speech. If you write or say, "I liked your speech a lot," you are also providing speech criticism. Notice, however, that while this last comment would no doubt make most speakers happy, it doesn't really teach them anything. In fact, finding out how long they spoke is probably more instructive for speakers than hearing simply, "I liked it." There is nothing wrong with saying to your classmates, "I enjoyed your speech," or, "I didn't care for this speech as much as your last one." Just don't stop there. Explain why.

All criticism contains three parts: *judgments, reasons,* and *norms.*[2] Figure A illustrates the relationships between these parts. The most familiar and superficial level of critical comments consists of **judgments.** We make them frequently about many different subjects: "I don't like Christie's restaurant," "I loved the movie *Sleepless in Seattle,*" "Dr. Hudson is an excellent teacher," or "I always enjoy your speeches."

Underlying those judgments, whether we voice them or not, are **reasons** of some sort: "I don't like Christie's restaurant because the seafood tastes mushy and the service is slow," "*Sleepless in Seattle* was a light romantic comedy with a wonderful soundtrack," "Dr. Hudson is an excellent teacher because her lectures make a course I dreaded live-

criticism: feedback offered for the purpose of improving a speaker's speech.

judgments: critics' opinions about the relative merits of a speech; the most common and superficial level of speech criticism.
reasons: statements that justify a critic's judgments.

413

norms: the values a critic believes necessary to make any speech good, effective, or desirable.

ly and interesting," or, "I always enjoy your speeches because you choose such unusual topics." Statements such as these specify reasons for the critics' judgments.

The statements in the preceding paragraph are instructive and useful because they help others infer your **norms,** the values you believe make something "good" or "effective" or "desirable." Such statements tell us that the individual critics value good seafood and prompt service in a restaurant, entertainment and music in movies, liveliness in class lectures, and unusual topics in public speeches. We may, of course, argue with the critics about whether these norms are actually valid. That is healthy and productive. The lesson for us as speech critics is to provide reasons for our judgments; only by doing so do we tell the speaker the basis of our reactions.

Here are some examples of helpful comments made by students about their classmates' speeches:

> Karen, your concern for children certainly shows in this speech on rating day care centers. Your personal examples really helped make the speech interesting.

> Adele, I liked your speech about the constellations a lot. The introduction was very interesting and piqued my curiosity. Your organization was clear, and you had excellent transitions from one area to the next. You used a good speaking style in easy to understand language and you defined unfamiliar terms. You also seemed really interested in what you were talking about and that made me interested, even though I thought you spoke rather quickly in places.

> Michael, your speech was interesting, but you need to slow down. I thought you also seemed to be distracted because you were looking out the windows or over toward the door occasionally.

> John, your speech on how to improve study habits was the best I heard. It was appropriate and beneficial to everyone in the class. Your language was simple and coherent. You explained just what we needed to know in the time you had.

> Lettie, one problem I saw was your use of visual aids. Once you have finished with the visual aid, you should put it away rather than leave it where the audience

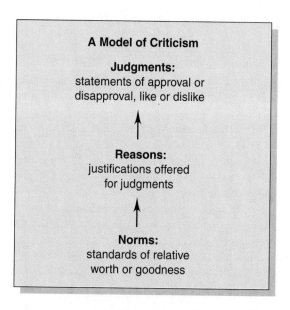

A Model of Criticism

Judgments:
statements of approval or
disapproval, like or dislike

↑

Reasons:
justifications offered
for judgments

↑

Norms:
standards of relative
worth or goodness

Figure A *Model of criticism*

can see it. That way, the audience will focus their attention on you rather than on the object.

One value of receiving written or oral comments from classmates about your speeches is that repetition of a criticism will reinforce it. If your instructor or an individual classmate tells you that you need to speak louder, you may discount the advice as one person's opinion. If twelve people in the class write or say that they had trouble hearing you, however, the criticism gains impact and you will likely give it more attention.

A second value of receiving criticism from many people is that different people value different aspects of a speech. Some people put a premium on delivery, others on speech content, and still others on organization. Individual classmates may notice different aspects of your speech simply because of where they sit in the classroom. With such a variety of perspectives and values, it would be a shame if all their criticism were reduced to "Good job!" or "I liked it." To provide the best criticism you can, just remember to specify the reasons for your judgments; ask yourself why a speech has the effect it does on you, and then try to communicate those reasons to the speaker.

We should also make a final note about the spirit in which you give speech criticism in this class. Your instructor may invite you to make oral or written comments about the speeches you hear others give. If your comments are written, they may be signed or unsigned. But whether your comments are written or oral, and whether your written critiques identify you or retain your anonymity, you should never make criticisms that are designed to belittle or hurt the speaker. Target the speech, not the speaker. Focus on specific behaviors rather than the person exhibiting those behaviors. You will probably never hear a speech so fine that the speaker could not make some improvement; and you will never hear a speech so inept or ill-prepared that it does not have some redeeming value. *Listen evaluatively* and then *respond empathetically*, putting yourself in the speaker's place, and you should make truly helpful comments about your classmates' speeches.

To help you become a better critic for your classmates, we offer nine suggestions you can use as you evaluate their speeches. One of our students, Susan, delivered an informative speech on three major tenets of the Amish faith. The text of that speech is included in Appendix C, pages 435-37. We asked other students to critique Susan's speech, and we have used their comments to illustrate our suggestions.

---

1. Begin with a positive statement.
2. Be specific.
3. Be honest but tactful.
4. Personalize your comments.
5. Reinforce the positive.
6. Problem solve the negative.
7. Organize your comments.
8. Provide the speaker with a plan of action.
9. End positively.

KEY POINTS

Guidelines for Critiquing Speeches

Begin with a Positive Statement.   Do you remember being told, "If you can't say something nice, don't say anything at all"? Well, that's good advice to follow when you critique your classmates' speeches. Public speaking is a personal experience. You stand in front of an audience expressing *your* thoughts in *your* words with *your* voice and *your* body. When you affirm the positive, you establish a healthy climate for constructive criticism. Demonstrate to speakers that what they said or how they said it was worthy. Fortunately, you can always find something helpful to say if you think about it. Be positive — and be sincere!

Three of our students began their critiques of Susan's speech with the opening statements below.

> I found your speech on the Amish to be very interesting; their beliefs are fascinating. They seem very simple but very committed to their group — what a unique way of living.

> It was great that you brought back and displayed certain items from your trip to the Amish settlement. As a result, you were able to *show* something about the Amish lifestyle and not just *speak* of it.

> I have lived near the Amish in Pennsylvania. Your speech explained the reasons for their behavior. You clearly explained why they do what they do.

Notice that in addition to complimenting the speaker, the third critic also demonstrates her involvement in the topic.

Be Specific.　Suppose instead of this list of nine suggestions for offering criticism, we simply said, "When you critique your classmates' speeches, be as helpful as possible so that they can improve their speaking." Although that is good advice, it's not very helpful, is it? By being more specific and detailing nine guidelines, we hope to provide you a handle on how you can improve your critiquing skills. Similarly, you will help your classmates if you provide them with specific suggestions for improvement.

In order for speakers to become more proficient, they need to know *what* to improve and *how* to improve. One of our students told Susan: "I liked the way you presented the speech as a whole." That statement provides a nice pat on the back, but it doesn't give Susan much direction. It certainly doesn't reflect what the listener had in mind. Is this a comment on Susan's vocal and physical delivery? Or does the verb *presented* include content and organization as well? The qualifying phrase "as a whole" seems to suggest that the listener noticed small problems that were minimized by the generally positive effect of Susan's speech. What were those problems, and what could Susan have done to minimize them? Remember, provide reasons for your judgments. In the two statements below, the listeners' comments are specific.

> I was really impressed with the fact that you did not use your note cards while you delivered the introduction or the conclusion. That suggests that you were confident and well prepared.

> Susan, you used good transitional phrases or words to move from subtopic to subtopic within each main point. An example of this was when you said, "Not only do the Amish have simple ways of dressing, but they also provide very simple toys for their children."

Be Honest But Tactful.

"Do not remove a fly from your friend's forehead with a hatchet."　CHINESE PROVERB

Providing suggestions for improvement tests your interpersonal skills. At times you may be reluctant to offer criticism because you think it may offend the speaker. If you are not honest, however, the speaker may not know that the topic was dull, the content superficial, and the delivery uninspiring. Still, you must respect your classmates' feelings. The statement "Your speech was dull, superficial, and uninspiring" may be honest, but it is hardly tactful. It may provoke resistance to your suggestions or damage the speaker's self-esteem.

One of our students thought Susan's speech content and organization were excellent but her delivery was to be mechanical and lifeless. The student could have said, "Your delivery lacked excitement." Instead, she wrote: "The only problem I saw with your speech was a lack of enthusiasm. Maybe the speech was too rehearsed. It just sounded kind of like a newscast. I think it needed some humor to break the monotony of your voice."

Personalize Your Comments.   The more interest and involvement your critique conveys, the more likely the speaker is to believe in and act on your advice. You can personalize your comments in three ways. First, use the speaker's name occasionally, as in: "Susan, your hand gestures would be more effective if you used them less. I found myself being distracted by them."

A second way of reducing a speaker's defensiveness and establishing speaker-critic rapport is by using "I-statements" in place of "you-statements." Tell how the speech affected you. Instead of saying, "Your organization was weak," say, "I had trouble following your key ideas," and then give some examples of places where you got lost. Following is an example of what one of our students could have said and what she actually did say in her critique of Susan's speech:

She could have said: "You lost my attention during the first part of your speech because you spoke so fast that I couldn't keep up with you."

Instead, she said: "I had difficulty following your words at first because your rate seemed fast to me. After you settled down into the speech, though, I could listen with more attention."

A third way of personalizing your comments is by stating how you have benefited from hearing the speech. The following statements from two student critiques let Susan know that her speech was interesting and helpful.

I found myself interested and saying, "Hmm," all through your speech. It especially caught my attention when you showed the toys, the quilt, and the art work. And putting the visual aids down after explaining them helped in keeping me interested in the next area.

Your topic was new and exciting information, which made the speech easy to listen to. I have always been curious about why the Amish live differently. Now I know why.

Reinforce the Positive.   Sometimes we want so much to help someone improve that we focus on what the speaker did wrong and forget to mention what the speaker did well. As you enumerate how speakers can improve, don't forget the things they did well and should continue doing. One student was impressed with Susan's language and vocal delivery. She made the following comment:

Susan, your delivery was excellent. You used your voice to emotionally color your message. I really felt as if I was living in the pictures that your descriptions created.

Problem Solve the Negative.   If you are serious about wanting to improve your speaking, you will want to know the weaknesses of your speech. Only then can you improve. As a critic, you have a responsibility to help your classmates become better speakers. Don't be afraid to let them know what went wrong with a speech.

As a general rule, though, you should not criticize behaviors that the speaker cannot correct. On the day she spoke, Susan was suffering an allergic reaction to molds and pollen in the air. As a result of antihistamines she was taking, her throat was dry. Even if this had detracted significantly from her message, it would have been inappropriate for a student to comment, "I had trouble listening to what you said because your mouth seemed dry. Avoid that in your next speech." Such a request may well be beyond the speaker's control. On the other hand, it would be useful to suggest that Susan take a drink of water immediately before speaking, and several of our students did offer that advice.

You will help speakers improve their speaking if you follow two steps in your criticism. First, point out a specific problem, and, second, suggest ways to correct it. Remember the title of this section is not "List the Negatives" but "Problem Solve the Negative." You want to propose ways to overcome problems.

One student was impressed with Susan's visual aids, but offered her the following advice about one of them:

> You said that the Amish don't like to have their pictures taken, and yet you used a picture of an Amish man as a visual aid. Next time, if you'd explain how or where you got the picture, it wouldn't leave picky people like me wondering during the rest of your speech how you got that picture.

Notice how another student offered a solution to a problem with one aspect of Susan's appearance.

> I liked your dress, but it tends to blend into the curtain behind you. Try wearing a lighter color dress next time, if at all possible.

Organize Your Comments.   A critique, just like a speech, is easier to follow if it is well organized. You can select from several options to frame your comments, and you should select the one that is most appropriate to you, the speaker, and the speech.

For example, you can organize your comments topically into the categories of speech *content, organization,* and *delivery.* A second option is chronological; you can discuss the speech's *introduction, body,* and *conclusion.* A third option is to divide your comments into speaking *strengths* and *weaknesses* (remember, give positive comments first). You could even combine these options. You could discuss the speaker's introduction, body, and conclusion, and within each of these categories discuss first the strengths and second the weaknesses.

Provide the Speaker with a Plan of Action.   When you give your comments, include a plan of action for the speaker. What should the speaker concentrate on when presenting the next speech? One student focused Susan's attention on her next speaking experience by suggesting the following action plan:

> Susan, your overall speech and style of presentation were very good. However, I detected two minor things that could be improved upon. First, except when you

were moving toward or away from a visual aid, you remained in one place. I believe that taking a few steps when you begin a subtopic would emphasize your transitions and enhance your message. Second, take more time to demonstrate and talk about the boy's toy that you showed us. You said, "It has marbles and fun moving parts," but I didn't really get a chance to see how it operates. Your organization, your vocal emphasis and inflection, your eye contact, and your knowledge of the topic were all terrific. You're an effective speaker, and if you use these suggestions for your next speech, you will be even more effective.

End Positively.   Conclude your critique on a positive note. Speakers should be reminded that both you and they benefited from this experience. One of the highest compliments you can give a speaker is that you learned something from the speech. Two of our students concluded their critiques of Susan's speech as follows:

Great job, Susan! You were very specific and enthusiastic about your subject, and your visual aids reinforced what was already thorough.

Susan, you did an outstanding job. Your speech was well organized and very informative. You showed some signs of nervousness, but more practice will alleviate most of them. Whenever and wherever you will be speaking next, I'd like to be there.

We began this textbook by talking about the contract that we believe always binds public speakers and their audiences. Speech criticism is further recognition of the commitment between speaker and listener. The ultimate aim of speech criticism is not just to improve a speaker's skills, or just to make a particular speech more enjoyable or instructive for an audience. Speech criticism should amplify and clarify the terms of the contract that any individual speaker will enter with all of his or her future audiences.

Keep that goal in mind as you react to the criticisms your classmates speak or write about your work. Some of us are just generally thin-skinned, easily hurt by anything that seems to be a negative criticism, and at times all of us can become defensive. But don't be too quick to dismiss the feedback others give you about your speeches. *Remember that your goal as you move from one speech to the next in a public speaking classroom is not consistency but improvement.* So rather than defending what you said or did in your speech, listen carefully and *act* upon those suggestions for improvement that you receive most frequently. If you have doubts about the validity of suggestions your classmates are making, discuss the matter with your instructor. You will make your most accelerated improvement if you graciously accept the compliments of your peers and your instructor, and then work quickly to eliminate problems that they bring to your attention.

Author Isaac Bashevis Singer once said, "The wastepaper basket is the writer's best friend." Yet self-criticism is difficult for both writers and speakers. You master public speaking faster and easier if you can rely on helpful criticism from your classmates as well as from your instructor. To be helpful, criticism must be balanced between positive and negative aspects of the speech, but should begin and end with positive comments. Critics should reinforce positive aspects of the speech and problem solve the negative. In addition, criticism should be specific, honest but tactful, personalized, organized, and should provide the speaker with a plan of action for future speeches. Our years of teaching experience have convinced us that following these guidelines will pay big dividends as you give and receive constructive, beneficial speech criticism.

NOTES

1. This definition is adapted from Hendrie Weisinger and Norman M. Lobsenz, *Nobody's Perfect: How to Give Criticism and Get Results* (New York: Warner, 1981) 9-10.

2. This model of criticism is adapted from Beverly Whitaker Long, "Evaluating Performed Literature," *Studies in Interpretation*, vol. 2, eds. Esther M. Doyle and Virginia Hastings Floyd (Amsterdam: Rodopi, 1977) 267-81. See also her earlier article: Beverly Whitaker, "Critical Reasons and Literature in Performance," *The Speech Teacher* 18 (November 1969): 191-93. Long attributes this three-part model of criticism to Arnold Isenberg, "Critical Communication," *The Philosophical Review* (July 1949): 330-44.

Appendix B

A Speaker's Journal

ne way to improve your own public speaking is to observe and analyze the speaking of others. What techniques of support, organization, and delivery do they use? What seems to work for them? What doesn't? How can you learn from their successes and mistakes? All these questions can help you improve as a speaker.

But there are other questions you might find instructive, if only you had the chance to ask: What are some of the decisions behind the speech? How did *this* speaker go about selecting *this* topic and developing it in *this* way? Published speeches rarely provide these insights. In addition, they are often edited from a manuscript, so that speakers appear never to have stumbled, lost their place, forgotten a transition, or been distracted by a loud noise or an audience member wandering into the room late.

The following Speaker's Journal is a record of what one student learned as she applied all she knew about developing and delivering a speech. Her journal is designed to let you see beyond the transcript of her delivered speech; you will "hear" her talk about some of the decisions she made before she walked into a classroom, looked at her audience, and began speaking.

Sandra Gomila, then an undergraduate student, delivered her persuasive speech "Volunteerism: Just Do It!" to a class at Radford University in Virginia during the summer of 1991. Her speech was delivered extemporaneously, and the following manuscript is an unedited transcript taken from her videotaped speech.

Following the speech, we asked Sandy to discuss how she selected her topic, developed her ideas, and rehearsed her speech.

VOLUNTEERISM: JUST DO IT!

SANDRA GOMILA, *Radford University*

A man was going down from Jerusalem to Jericho when he fell into the hands of robbers. They beat him, stripped him, and left him for dead. Two men passed right by, but a Samaritan came to where the man was and had compassion for him. He bandaged his wounds, took him to an inn, and took care of him.

The Biblical parable of the Good Samaritan provides one of the earliest examples and one of the best illustrations of the act of volunteerism. A volunteer is simply someone who sees a need and fills it. Volunteerism is something that many of us admire, yet few of us imitate. With this in mind, involvement in volunteerism deserves a closer look.

After all, how many of us would think it would be a waste of our time to go and buy groceries for an elderly woman who is confined to her home? Or how many of us would agree that it's worthless to help someone learn how to read? Probably not many of us would agree with those statements. The obstacle in volunteering lies not in our agreement, but in the movement from agreement to action.

Today, I'll be discussing volunteerism by addressing three questions you may have about volunteering. One, does society still need volunteers? Two, why should I get involved now? And three, how do I get involved?

Well, does society still need volunteers? Many people equate volunteerism with the social activism of the 1960s — seeing each as an idea and an era whose time has passed. But according to Kathy Hillard, who is a University of Illinois student and active volunteer, "Back then it was all talk. But this is action. College students are taken out of their homes to really do something."

We can see that volunteers are used in our society today, but does this mean that they are still necessary? Are they still needed? Well, national estimates for the homeless in the United States range from 250,000 all the way up to 735,000, with approximately one-half of all homeless adults never having finished high school. In the state of Virginia, almost 12 percent of the population lives below the poverty line. And according to the *Statistical Abstract of the United States, 1990,* 14 percent of all persons living right here in the city of Radford live below the poverty line. In addition to statistics regarding lack of education and housing, in 1987 approximately 7,000 alcohol and drug abuse treatment clinics were surveyed, and at that time the number of clients in treatment was nearly 600,000. In addition to all these statistics, we see a plethora of organizations in the United States devoted solely and singularly to volunteer work. These range from APO, the service fraternity right here on campus, to the Woman's Resource Center in the city of Radford, all the way up to national organizations such as COOL (the Campus Outreach Opportunity League), and organizations such as the United Way.

But rather than seeing all of these statistics and all of these organizations as overwhelming, we should see them as opportunities for us to discover our own interests and become personally involved, creating a niche for ourselves in volunteerism based on our own interests. Mr. [Wayne] Meisel, who is the coordinator of COOL, a national organization that attempts to match students with their interests, has this to say: "It's the joy of service! Self-interest is a win-win deal. This whole movement is about complementary needs."

I can personally attest to the benefits of volunteering in an area you feel strongly about. For the past six years, the cause I have been involved in is teenage drug abuse and drug addiction and its prevention. Had I not chosen to volunteer in an area I felt strongly about, I'm sure I would not have continued my volunteer work, nor would I have seen it as beneficial to myself. And I'm sure that the people I was working with would have really suffered because it wouldn't have been an issue that I cared about. So when we ask ourselves the question, "Does society still need volunteers?" I think we can see that the answer is clearly, *"Yes!"*

Which brings us to our second question: "Why should I volunteer now?" Many of us plan on volunteering our time but later on in life — once we've gotten settled down. But we have just settled down into this community for the next four years. And if you ever change your major, you have possibly settled down for the next five or even six years! So the time to volunteer is *now*. And thus the question becomes: "Is volunteering worth my time?" That's a perfectly legitimate question. College is certainly a busy time. There's homework, socializing, part-time jobs to think about — all these things are making demands of our time. The bottom line is: What's in it for me? Well, let's look at some of the benefits of volunteering.

One benefit is an enhanced résumé. One of the main reasons that we come to college is to enhance our employability, so that when we get out into the workforce we are attractive to prospective employers. Well, volunteer work enhances your employability. Says Carol Carter, author of the book *Majoring in the Rest of Your Life,* "If you've been active in volunteer work, your future employer will realize that you care about people and the community. Employers want to hire people who will be role models for others. Good citizenship is good business." Employers are clearly looking for well-rounded individuals. A résumé containing volunteer work is the résumé of an individual that is headed for success.

A second benefit of volunteerism is the acquisition of life skills. We have not come to college just to learn about what's in our textbooks and fill ourselves with head knowledge. We've come to learn about how to deal with everyday life and the problems it presents. Life skills enhanced by volunteer work include communication skills, relationship skills, and problem-solving skills. By choosing to volunteer in an area that is related to your major, you learn about your field of study both in and out of the classroom. For example, if you are an accounting major, perhaps you want to volunteer your time by filling out tax forms for the elderly. At Tulane University in Louisiana, prelaw students help to prepare clemency arguments for the release of elderly prison inmates. So you can see that it's quite easy to just look at yourself; see what is your major, what are your interests; and match them up with an organization. Says Jeff Segall, a college student involved with volunteer work, "Instead of just going out for beer to take your mind off your studies, it's important to contribute something to your community." We can clearly see that when we do volunteer work, we not only benefit others, but we benefit ourselves.

A third way that volunteerism is personally beneficial is in our own development, our own personal growth. Plato said that the unexamined life is not worth living. Volunteer work is a way of examining our lives. By helping others, we increase our understanding of ourselves. We all carry with us fears and prejudices that are unfounded, that have never been tested by daily experience. Volunteer work is a way of confronting them. Do you believe that all poor people are lazy? Perhaps you're afraid of homeless people. Well, by volunteering in these environments, this helps us to test our beliefs and strengthen our viewpoints with the benefit of firsthand experience.

Other benefits in the area of personal growth include broadening our horizons. When we do volunteer work, we interact with sections of society that we may otherwise know nothing about. In doing this, we learn more about others and we increase our own self-awareness. An added benefit of this in the area of personal growth is enhanced self-esteem, because we can take pride in the work that we do. An example of this would be George Montague, a Wharton student, who uses his skills and his time to help a Sioux Indian reservation that at this time has an 80 percent unemployment rate. Montague's using his skills in farming and agriculture to help bring this reservation closer to self-sufficiency. Says Montague of his experience: "I'll be fulfilled when the fields yield enough crops for them to make a profit."

In answer to question two, "Why should I become involved now?", we've seen that involvement in volunteer work is personally beneficial to us in a variety of ways, ranging from future employability to the development of our life skills and our own personal growth. We can see that society clearly has a desperate need for volunteers, and I believe that this alone should justify our time. And the benefits we've just discussed further justify our involvement.

Which brings us to the third and final question: "How do I get involved?" By matching particular issues with our own interests, we bring a focus and clarity to volunteer work. For example, if you are an education major, don't wait until you are student teaching. Start now! Volunteer with adults or children who need to learn how to read. Maybe you'd like to be outdoors or you're a physical education major. Well, then you can volunteer your time, quite enjoyably, by working with the Special Olympics, or working as a Big Brother, Big Sister, volunteering at a day camp. I would challenge each one of you to discover your own interests and match them to an agency. To aid in this, at the end of my speech I will give you a handout with the names, numbers, and contact people of agencies in our area that are in need of volunteers, as well as a brief description of the work involved. As you can see, the process of becoming involved is a relatively simple one — almost as easy as a phone call. And with that, I would ask each and every one of you to call three numbers on this list and to commit yourself to one organization for a period of just two weeks.

We have seen today that society definitely still has needs, and is in need of volunteers that are willing to give their time and their enthusiasm to the great needs in our society. We have explored some of the ways that volunteerism is personally beneficial, ranging from enhanced employability to the acquisition of life skills to our own development and personal growth. And we can now take the steps necessary to become involved in our community.

In trying to think of a way to wrap up the speech and help you to remember the key points discussed here today, I was reminded of a well-known athletics company whose slogan seems quite appropriate here: "Just Do It!" If we look at the letters of NIKE, we can easily remember the points discussed here today. Question one: Does society still need volunteers? [Visual aid: *N*eeds are everywhere.] Today we've seen that needs are everywhere. Question two: Why should I become involved now? [Visual aid: *I*nvolvement benefits me.] One reason might be because involvement benefits me in three ways: the development of our résumé and enhanced employability, development of our life skills, and our own personal growth.

In response to the third question, "How do I become involved?", this is where the *K* comes in — with knowledge of issues and interests. [Visual aid: *K*nowledge of interests & issues.] Know yourself, know your own interests, and have a working knowledge of the agencies and issues in your area.

Well, this covers the three points discussed here today, and so you may be wondering, "What's she going to use that *E* for?" Well, at the beginning of the speech, I discussed the idea that very few people have a problem with volunteerism. Most of us agree that it is a good thing. The problem lies in moving from that agreement into action. And that's where the *E* comes in. The *E* is eliminate excuses. [Visual aid: *E*liminate *E*xcuses.] Be a modern-day Good Samaritan. If you're afraid to do it yourself or you don't think you'll stay involved, go out in pairs and become involved in community service.

Just eliminate the excuses, become a modern-day Good Samaritan, see what needs to be done, and JUST DO IT!

425

A Speaker's Journal

REFERENCES

Carter, Carol. *Majoring in the Rest of Your Life*. New York: Noonday, 1990.

"Homeless, Report #14364," *American Statistics Index, 1989*. Washington, D.C.: Congressional Information Service, 1989, Supp. 5: 14.

Lee, Felicia R. "Students Reach Out to Help the Poor." *New York Times* 11 March 1909. 31.

Rice, Faye. "Volunteer Work: Better than Beer." *Fortune* 16 July 1990: 78-81.

Theus, Kathryn T. "Campus-Based Community Service." *Change* September/October 1988: 27-38.

United States. Dept. of Commerce. "Alcoholism and Drug Abuse Treatment Facilities and Clients," *Statistical Abstract of the United States: National Data Book*. Washington, D.C.: GPO, 1990.

—. —. Dept. of Commerce. "Persons Below Poverty Level," *Statistical Abstract of the United States: National Data Book*. Washington, D.C.: GPO, 1990.

Virginia Statistical Abstract. Charlottesville: UVA Center for Public Service, 1989.

INTERVIEW WITH SANDRA GOMILA

1. HOW DID YOU GO ABOUT SELECTING YOUR TOPIC?

When I first got the assignment, I was trying to decide between two topics: (1) the problems with the 911 emergency phone system, and (2) innumeracy, or math illiteracy. I had heard a television report about some problems with 911, and that interested and concerned me. A friend mentioned math illiteracy as a possible topic choice and gave me a copy of a book he had on the subject. I went to the library and looked first for books on these subjects, but found few recent and relevant sources. So I moved to periodicals. With the help of *InfoTrac* and other computer indexes, I soon found some references for newspaper and magazine articles. I located about five or six articles on each subject, brought them home, and read them.

In trying to decide on my topic, I asked other people for their opinions: "Do you think this would make a good persuasive speech?" "Do you see an argument here?" Then one day somebody suggested that I speak on volunteerism — persuading people to volunteer their time. I thought, "Well, that sounds like an interesting topic." I went back to the library and got some more stuff, this time on volunteerism, and I really liked what I saw.

At that point, I still could have chosen any of the three topics: 911, innumeracy, or volunteerism. I continued to work with each of these ideas, weighing the pros and cons of each. When you have a deadline to meet — you know, you have a time and a date to give your speech — it's very important that at some point you pick a topic and run with it. So after I looked at the pros and cons of each topic, I decided to go with volunteerism. The main reason was that it interested me the most, personally. As I said in my speech,

I am a volunteer and I've found this experience very rewarding. To develop a speech about something you're interested in makes a huge difference.

2. HOW DID YOU DETERMINE THE KEY IDEAS YOU WOULD COVER IN YOUR SPEECH?

Once I decided to do volunteerism, I had to figure out where to go from there. I bantered around, asking a couple of friends: "If you heard a speech about why we should volunteer, what would you *expect* to see in it? What would you *like* to see in it?" I thought about the topic and bounced some ideas off my roommates. I got this general idea that my main objective would be to talk about why we should volunteer based on the *needs*, the *benefits*, and the *process*.

3. WHAT OBSTACLES DID YOU SEE FOR THE TOPIC OF VOLUN-TEERISM?

Well, it's not a tremendously controversial topic. Few people would say, "Volunteering is not worth my time," or "I don't agree with volunteering." So that was one of the obstacles I had to confront: to develop a speech in light of the fact that it did not appear to be a controversial topic. Persuasive speeches usually should have an element of controversy. I had to try to zero in on what the controversy would be.

As I thought about the topic, I decided that the challenge was to get people to volunteer. People say they believe in volunteerism, yet many fail to participate. I really wanted to get the audience to take the next step: *to volunteer*. So as I was reading the articles and talking with some friends, I decided to make my speech different by not focusing so much on the *needs* of volunteering. That's what I'd expect to hear in a typical volunteerism speech (there are this many homeless, this many drug addicts; we have all these needs; get out there and help!). I decided instead to focus on the personal benefits of volunteering. I wanted to get the audience to see volunteerism as a way to enlarge or apply their own interests. You know, "If I know I'm going to live in the city, maybe I ought to get out and volunteer in issues I'll be confronted with in the city." Or, "If I'm an accounting major, I want to volunteer my time to help someone who's not skilled in accounting and that helps me practice my major at the same time." So I was very interested in pursuing this angle of the benefits of volunteerism.

As you can see from the text of the speech, that was my main focus: a brief description of why society still needs volunteers, then a *huge* section on why we should get involved now during college, and then, finally, ending with the process. In my speech I asked three questions: (1) Does society still need volunteers? (2) Why should I volunteer now? and (3) How do I get involved?

4. WHAT STRATEGIES DID YOU USE IN YOUR SPEECH TO HELP THE AUDIENCE REMEMBER AND REINFORCE YOUR MESSAGE?

I decided to include a handout in my speech because, like I said before, the main obstacle is moving listeners from agreement to action. I was trying to focus on how easy it is to become involved. I wanted to make it easy for my audience, so that once they walked away from the speech they would have something tangible to refer to. I also used the *N-I-K-E* gimmick as my conclusion. Maybe when those who heard my speech see a Nike ad on television, they will think of my speech.

When I learned that the speech was going to be videotaped, that brought in some other problems and concerns to deal with. I decided to have a visual aid and do my summary as a gimmick using the letters of Nike. I really wanted the audience to be stimulated in hearing and seeing it. And so once I found out I was going to be videotaped, I chose to have a yellow posterboard with black letters. Otherwise, I probably would have chosen black letters on white posterboard. But since I knew it was being videotaped, and you want to stay away from black on white, I chose yellow posterboard.

If I were doing this speech without being videotaped, I probably would have chosen a much darker dress since I tend to wear darker colors anyway. But because I was being videotaped, I knew that pastels would be a good choice. So that's why I chose what I wore. But I think it's important when we speak to be dressed on a level that's consistent with the seriousness of our topic. I don't think it would be appropriate, at least for me, to come in and give a speech sloppily dressed. Your appearance does make a statement.

One thing that added a lot to my nervousness once I got there was being miked. If I had had the chance to practice with the microphone, with all the wires tripping me up, I would have been much more at ease when I gave the speech.

6. HOW DID YOU PREPARE YOUR VISUAL AID?

I really took time with my visual aid. I chose the colors very carefully. I went out and bought stencil letters that I could rub onto the posterboard. And I chose very carefully the height of the beginning letters and each letter after that. I sat down with a ruler and penciled out how the letters would look best and how they would come across most clearly to the audience. It took a long time, but if you want a visual aid that will really reinforce what you're saying, then it's worth doing well. A visual aid should look professional.

7. HOW DID YOU PRACTICE YOUR SPEECH?

One thing that was especially beneficial before giving this speech was practicing in the room beforehand. I went to the classroom the evening before the speech, set up my visual aid, went through the speech, went through how I was going to move in the room, which was especially important because the speech was being videotaped. The next day when I had a microphone on me and a cord running down to the floor, I realized how important that practice was in getting used to just moving around the room.

So I went into the classroom the night before, got comfortable with where the audience was going to be sitting, and I think most important, I got comfortable with my visual aid. I bought two posterboards so that I could cover up the first with the second. I cut the top posterboard into four strips and paperclipped them over my visual aid. That way, I could uncover one letter at a time: *N,* then *I,* then *K,* then *E.* And so I practiced that, because otherwise I would have been really nervous.

It was also important for me to see how my visual aid was going to fit on the easel. Would it need to be taped? Would the ends curl around the back? How am I going to deal with that? It helped my level of nervousness tremendously to get those things out of the way the day before the speech instead of the morning of the speech.

8. WHAT ARE SOME OF THE TECHNIQUES YOU USED TO RELATE YOUR SPEECH TO THIS PARTICULAR AUDIENCE?

I thought it was really important to localize the topic, and that's one reason I wanted to use a handout. There are statistics in the speech from the state of Virginia, and even from the city of Radford itself. I used them to localize my speech. Instead of just saying, "There are X million homeless people in America," I could say, "X percent of people living right here in our city live below the poverty line," and bring it home. And I thought that was important.

9. HOW DID YOU FEEL ABOUT THE DELIVERY OF YOUR SPEECH?

I guess this was the first time I've given a speech just with notecards. It was difficult for me to get out from behind that lectern with my notes in one hand and still try to use my body and my other hand in my speech. I think I could have used fewer notecards, if I had condensed my notes to include just my key ideas and the quotations and statistics I needed. Using 4-by-6-inch instead of the 3-by-5 cards would probably also have helped.

I was very concerned about my delivery looking artificial instead of natural. It's important to practice, but I don't think we should practice ourselves to death. We should be confident that we know our topic. And if we do know our topic and how it's organized, I think we'll do all right — even if we get lost or trip over something. I know it was a big help for me to sit down and say:

> Okay, I start off with the story of the Good Samaritan and I talk about how that's a great example [of volunteerism]. I talk about how people admire volunteerism, but not many people do it. I move into my statement of topic, my rhetorical questions, and my preview step. And that's my introduction.

In just doing that, I've reasoned out how I've organized my speech, so that when I get up and give it, it's clear in my head.

In the actual delivery of the speech, there were a couple of times when I lost my place or stumbled over some words. But I just kept right on going. That's really important — to realize that it's very difficult to give a speech without any mistakes in it. In a public speaking class, I don't think professors are looking for perfection. I think they're looking for a well-rounded speech — good in content, good in organization, good in delivery, but not perfect. It's OK to make mistakes. After I got through the speech, I still felt good about it, even though there had been a couple of blunders here and there.

There was one point in the speech where I say that according to the *Statistical Abstract of the United States,* 14 percent of people living here in Radford live below the poverty line. When I was putting my sources together to turn in after the speech, I discovered that the 14 percent figure actually came from the *Virginia Statistical Abstract.* Even though that didn't change the point I was making, I felt bad that I hadn't quoted the correct source. I could have avoided this mistake if I had taken a little more time when I was researching. After photocopying my articles, I should have divided them, stapled each article, and written the source on the top page of each article.

10. WHAT TECHNIQUES DID YOU USE TO HELP YOU COPE WITH YOUR NERVOUSNESS?

I don't think that when we speak we should expect *not* to be nervous. It's only natural to be nervous. In fact, I get more frightened if I'm *not* nervous a little bit before I speak. If you're serious about your topic and really want to communicate it to your audience, you're probably going to be a little nervous. That's natural.

Practice, of course, is one way of reducing nervousness. As I said earlier, rehearsing in the room where I was going to speak and practicing using my visual aid helped make me more confident.

Another thing that helps me in giving a speech is seeing how the audience is reacting to me: their body language, their eye contact. And I can't analyze those things unless I'm looking at them. So for me, in doing any kind of audience analysis [during the speech], eye contact is critical. From their body language, eye contact, and facial expression, I found that most people seemed to be responding to the speech. There's one point in the speech where I tell a joke, and to see people smile and chuckle, you say, "OK, they must be with me."

Appendix C

Sample Speeches

"A STITCH IN TIME"

EMLYN KATHRYN CARLEY, *San Antonio College, San Antonio*

Lyn Carley delivered the following speech in a public speaking class at San Antonio College during the fall of 1990. Members of her class seemed particularly impressed with Lyn's visual aids, and we are grateful to Judy Martin for her permission to reprint them here. In the marginal annotations, we have indicated the major strengths of Lyn's speech, as well as some improvements she might make.

Lyn begins with a rhetorical question. Her topic is apparent by the time she finishes her second sentence. The surprising prices she mentions here certainly give the audience a reason to listen.

This section of the introduction builds the importance of Lyn's subject further.

Her third paragraph clearly previews the ideas she will develop in the body of her speech.

Here Lyn begins to apply the **4 S's** to her first point. She signposts ("One") and states her idea (quilts are historical records). She quickly introduces a source to support the idea.

1 How would you like to go to bed tonight with a dear old friend and find you've woken up with a millionaire? Well, the quilt your great-grandmother made, the one you toss over your bed on those cold winter nights, the quilt you carelessly throw into the washing machine, probably won't be worth a million dollars, but it could be worth a small fortune. Some antique quilts have been valued between $35,000 and $50,000 — and some have sold for more than $150,000!

2 Quilts were treasured in their own day for their beauty, utility, and craftmanship. Today they are perhaps even more highly regarded as documents of our American heritage. They tell us a lot about ourselves, and many of them are just beautiful to look at. But if you're absolutely unsentimental and don't have trouble eventually parting with them, quilts can also be solid investments.

3 So first, I would like to tell you how quilts are viewed as historical records. Second, I will describe quilting as an art form. Third, I will discuss a quilt's investment value. And finally, I will describe and show you a personal history quilt I've put together for a member of this class.

4 One of the most interesting ways of looking at antique quilts is as historical records. "Quilts are among the few tangible objects that reflect the role women played in the building of America," says Patricia Wilens, editor of the Better Homes and Gardens book, *America's Heritage Quilts.* She notes, "Pilgrim women brought to the New World [the] skills and styles of their European homeland." They also brought memories of those homelands. They created quilt patterns that they called "Windmill Blades" and "Dresden Plate," for example. Wilens says that as quiltmakers designed individual blocks for their patch-

work quilts, they frequently chose names to commemorate important people or events. Early pioneer women traveling across America named their quilt blocks "Kansas Troubles," "Road to California," "Oklahoma Wonder," or "Rocky Mountain Chain." As their families settled down, the women made quilts out of blocks with names like "Barn Raising" and "Straight Furrow." Blocks with names like "Hands-all-Around" and "Swing-in-the-Center" remind us how important the country dance was to them. With fabric scarce during the Civil War, the "Log Cabin" block, made of thin strips of material, became popular. As you can see, the names early Americans gave their quilt patterns tell us something about their lives.

5 In addition to telling us about individual lives, certain styles of quilting also identify particular historical periods. Today, if you find a "crazy quilt" made of odd shaped scraps of velvet, satin, silk, and ribbons, it may have been made in the Victorian era, from 1870 to 1900. If it's in good shape, that's probably because it was made to be thrown over a sofa or chair. It was decorative rather than useful. If you find a quilt made of bright, solid colors on a dark background, it could have been made by Amish women whose families settled in Pennsylvania or Kansas. Because their austere religious beliefs prohibited them from using printed fabrics, the Amish put together strong, solid colors that look very contemporary to us.

6 In the 1920s, quilts reflected the new "modern woman," and Wilens says that the widespread publication of quilt patterns for the first time greatly popularized quiltmaking. The Depression marked another change; quilters again were quilting out of necessity, like their colonial predecessors. Two sentences in a little booklet entitled *Quilts: Heirlooms of Tomorrow,* summarize quilts as historical records: "Today we treasure as part of our American culture the innumerable variety of patchwork patterns that have recorded gallant lives, the growth of our nation, and the symbols of a new society. Thousands of people take pride in preserving and further enriching this heritage by making quilts of beauty that generations to come will prize."

7 Quilting took a back seat during World War II and through the '50s and '60s. In fact, according to Beth Sherman, in an article in the February 1989 *Harper's Bazaar,* it wasn't until New York's Whitney Museum of American Art exhibited sixty pieced quilts in 1971 that people began to look at quilting as something more than a useful craft. And that second way of appreciating quilts is as a fine art.

8 *Aunt Martha's Favorite Quilts Magazine* notes, "For a 'Prize Winning' quilt, design is most important. The selection and combination of materials and colors, the skill of the needle worker, and artistic quilting all go to make the quilt a thing of beauty."

9 The most important step in achieving a beautiful quilt is the fabric selection. Cotton is the most popular fabric and the most durable of textiles. Cotton's color retention is exceptional as well. I have worked with denim and silk in the past and always return to cotton. Any fabric store will have a large selection of colors and prints to choose from. It takes practice to get the right combinations, but once you get the hang of it, you are on your way. I mentioned Amish quilts earlier, and Amish quilters were experts at combining colors. What they lost in the detail of printed fabric that was forbidden to them they made up for in color. The neon colors of Amish quilts remind many people of the pop art of the 1960s.

10 You may be curious as to the actual construction of a quilt. Maggie Malone, author of *500 Full-size Patchwork Patterns,* says, "Quilt patterns consist largely of geometric pieces; it is the different sizes of those pieces and their arrangements that give patchwork its tremendous variety." A quilt top is either pieced together from blocks or is a solid fabric with

These brief, vivid examples show that the names of quilt blocks tell a history and evoke images of pioneer life. "As you can see" begins a very brief summary of the point Lyn has made so far.

"In addition" begins a complementary transition. Lyn defines "crazy quilt" and reminds her listeners of the dates of the Victorian era. She uses "if you find" to introduce two brief hypothetical examples.

This quotation serves as an effective summary of Lyn's first point.

The information from *Harper's* serves as Lyn's transition to her next point. In the final sentence, Lyn signposts and states her second point.

Lyn gives no author for this source, nor did she for the booklet she quoted earlier.

Lyn mentions her own experience as a quilter at this point. If her topic had been controversial, she would have needed to build her credibility earlier in the speech.

other materials sewn, or appliquéd, to it. Shirley Thompson, who has a special interest in throws and crib quilts, writes in her book *Think Small,* "Quilts consist of three layers: top, batting, and backing. Quilting stitches hold the three layers together while adding ornamental surface interest to the quilt." The stitch count on a finely crafted quilt should be eight to twelve stitches per inch, and no area larger than the palm of your hand should be left unquilted. You will often see an obvious mistake somewhere in the pattern of an old quilt. Members of strict religious orders often made these mistakes on purpose as a sign of humility, a recognition that only God is perfect.

11 If you have absolutely no appreciation of craftsmanship and no eye for color and design, you may still be interested in quilts because of those dollar figures I mentioned at the beginning of my speech. Yes, a third way of looking at quilts is as investments. In their book *Quilts, Coverlets, Rugs, & Samplers,* Dr. Robert Bishop, director of New York's Museum of American Folk Art, and his coauthors tell the story of one quilt. They relate, "In the fall of 1980, an important collection of American textiles was sold at auction in New Hampshire." One particular quilt, signed by its maker and dated 1837, fetched only $85.00 at that time. However, the buyer then sold it to a museum curator in New York City for $650. "Today," they note, "it is one of the most prized examples of Americana in the museum's permanent collection and is valued at $6,500. This is not an isolated incident."

12 An article in *Business Week,* March 6, 1989, tells of the investment potential of unique quilts. For example, a "1930 quilt depicting interracial scenes, such as a black doctor caring for a white patient, sold for a few dollars in the 1960s. Despite the quilt's ordinary workmanship, a collector purchased it last year for more than $50,000."

13 Sherman says in her *Harper's Bazaar* article that today, "Quilts generally cost between $500 and $2,000, but in urban areas they may sell for $25,000 or more. The record for a quilt sold at auction was set [in 1987] at Sotheby's when a dealer paid $176,000 for a Baltimore album quilt," made around 1840. As you can see by these examples, these bed covers can be anything but ordinary. But even seemingly ordinary early twentieth-century quilts seem to be appreciating at about 10 percent a year, according to the *Business Week* article. A trip to an antique dealer's shop, a quilt shop, or to an organization such as the Greater San Antonio Quilt Guild might give your great-grandmother's quilt a new value, and even a new lease on life. If it's an heirloom, its value will increase steadily throughout the years.

14 But you don't have to be made out of money to get yourself a quilt today. With some skill and patience, you can make a special type of quilt, the personal history quilt. That's the final topic I'll briefly discuss today.

15 Quilters seem to take special joy in selecting blocks not only for their aesthetic qualities, but also for the blocks' names. Your quilt can tell a story. It can be a personal history or family sampler quilt. A quilter simply selects blocks with names that have special meaning for the person who is to receive the quilt.

16 I interviewed classmate Norma Falkner and asked her a few questions about herself. We came up with blocks representative of the special people, places, things, and times that are important to her. These are the blocks I selected for Norma's quilt and why they are significant in her life:

Night Owl — Norma rarely gets to bed before midnight.
Emerald Isle — The emerald is her birthstone.

Sister's Choice — Norma has two sisters.

Collector's Block — Antique collecting is a hobby of hers.

Texas Two-Step — She is a native Texan.

Mother's Day — This must be better than Christmas! Not only was Norma born and married on this day, but she's also the mother of a little boy.

Puppy Dog Tails — She is a pet lover.

Chocolate Lover — Need I say more?

Vagabond — Norma enjoys traveling and plans to see a lot of the world.

Baby Boomer — Without giving away her age, I'll just say that Norma qualifies.

Baby's Breath — For her two-year-old son.

Mexican Star — This final block proudly reflects Norma's heritage.

At this point, Lyn introduced a large visual aid composed of enlarged color copies of quilt blocks. As she mentioned the 12 blocks in Norma's quilt, Lyn pointed to each.

17 A quilt made up of those blocks and using fabrics I chose would be as unique as Norma herself. I could also make a personal history quilt for a group of people — a fam-

Night Owl

Emerald Isle

Sister's Choice

Collector's Block

Texas Two-Step

Mother's Day

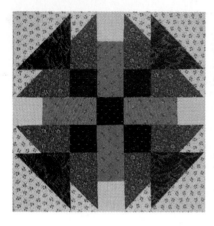

Puppy Dog Tails

Chocolate Lover

Vagabond

Baby Boomer

Baby's Breath

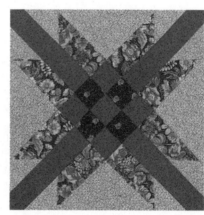

Mexican Star

Lyn shows excellent audience adaptation by mentioning other members of her classroom audience and their interests. Each of these people had spoken on the subject Lyn indicates.

Here Lyn acknowledges the source of the quilt blocks she used in her visual aid.

Lyn summarizes her points in reverse order.

ily or a group of friends. From speeches I've heard given in class this semester, I could create a class quilt. Let's start with the block "Classmates." How about "Carnival Ride" for Dianne Bloom's love of the roller coaster? Housebuilder Darin Turner would be well represented with a block entitled "Carpenter's Wheel." "Acrobats" might be the best block to describe our exercise guru John Caballero. To represent Sonja Heldt's expertise in photography, I'd choose a block named "Photo Album." My own block would be "Quilter's Dream." And to date our quilt, how about "Yellow Ribbons," signifying the safe return of our Desert Shield participants? Judy Martin, who was for eight years senior editor of *Quilter's Newsletter Magazine,* lists numerous quilt block patterns in her *Ultimate Book of Quilt Block Patterns,* my source for the blocks I've used in Norma's quilt. You can see the endless possibilities available to quilters today. You need only a subject and a little imagination to create a historical record, treasured for years to come.

18 Today, I've shown you a personal history quilt fashioned after classmate Norma Falkner's life. I've demonstrated how a quilt can be a valuable investment. I've described quilting as an art form and told you a little about the historical significance of quilts.

Personal history quilts are an excellent way to preserve family histories, as they would be handed down from generation to generation. As Dr. Bishop points out, "A quilt is often made as a document of love. It's a record of being in a certain place at a certain time. It's craftsmanship. It's emotional. It's art."

Delivered from memory and with appropriate pauses, Lyn's final quotation brings her speech to a solid psychological conclusion.

"THE AMISH: SEEKING TO LOSE THE SELF"

SUSAN CHONTOS, *San Antonio College, San Antonio*

*Susan was impressed with an Amish settlement she visited during her summer vacation. This personal interest is evident in her informative speech. Notice how meticulously Susan applies the **4 S's** to each of her main points.*

1 Our society is one that caters to the individual. We have seminars on how to be assertive, books on how to better your self-image, and countless articles on how to take control of your life. It seems that everyone today is in a great rush to find themselves. There is, however, a small group of people in our country who are seeking rather to lose themselves. They are the Amish.

2 The Amish were a small group of persecuted immigrants who came to this country 250 years ago seeking religious freedoms. They quietly settled along the northeastern coast of the United States, primarily in Pennsylvania. Last summer, I visited this Pennsylvania settlement and toured an Amish home. So, this morning, I would like to briefly examine the three major tenets of the Amish faith. They are based on Biblical scriptures. They are separation from the world, simplicity in the world, and a strong dedication to their group.

3 The first major tenet of the Amish faith is a desire to be separate from this world. 2 Corinthians 6: 17 states, "Therefore come out from them and be ye separate, says the Lord." You can see how the Amish separate themselves from society in many ways. First, they are an endogamous people. That is, they marry within their group. Marriage to non-Amish outsiders is strictly forbidden. Also, they separate themselves in that they speak a Germanic dialect among themselves, and this further distances them from their non-Amish neighbors. In addition, the Amish are separate from what would be considered the public life of most Americans. They don't seek public office. They don't participate in local sports teams or any other community organizations. Most recently, the Amish have separated themselves from our public school system. The Amish believe in attending school only from elementary up through the eighth grade, which they feel is adequate time to learn the basic skills necessary to succeed in Amish culture. In the 1950s, however, states began requiring attendance up through high school. The Amish parents and children protested this, and were fined and even imprisoned. According to the *Encyclopedia of World Cultures,* this controversy was finally resolved in 1972, when the Supreme Court unanimously ruled in favor of the Amish separating themselves on the basis of their religious beliefs.

4 This Amish desire to remain separate from our world — to be *in* our world but not *of* our world — has required them to strike many compromises with the rise of modern technology around them. Don Kraybill, in his book *The Puzzles of Amish Life,* describes some of these compromises. For example, the primary mode of transportation for the Amish is the horse and buggy. Today, however, they are permitted to ride in automobiles, although they can't own one. Similarly, they may use a telephone, but they can't

have one in their home. In addition, they may use modern farm equipment, but only if it's pulled by their plow horses. Certainly, it is becoming more and more difficult for the Amish to separate themselves from our modern world and its conveniences.

5 The second major tenet of the Amish faith is the desire to be simple, or plain. 1 Peter 3:3-4 states, "Your beauty should not come from outward adornment, such as braided hair or the wearing of gold jewelry or fine clothes. Rather, it should be that of your inner self." Therefore, the Amish don't seek any material possessions at all. Rather, they strive to be plain and simple. Nicknamed "the plain people," nowhere is this plainness more evident than in their dress. In their dress, the Amish don't allow anything that represents style: no buttons, belts, bright colors, or pockets. Instead, they use hooks and ties and straight pins to fasten their clothes. As you can see in this picture [visual aid], the Amish men are restricted to wearing only black and white. They must always have a wide-brimmed hat to cover their head, and you can tell that this man is married since he has a beard but no moustache. The Amish women are allowed a little more variation in their clothing, and they can wear different combinations of dark solids — dark purples or blues or browns. The Amish women must also wear bonnets to cover their hair, and they must never cut or curl their hair.

6 Not only do the Amish have simple ways of dressing, but they also provide very simple toys for their children to play with. I have here an example of a wooden bear toy [visual aid]. This toy is very popular among Amish boys, since it has fun marbles and moving parts. The Amish girls, however, as you might expect, like to play with dolls. And here is a traditional Amish doll [visual aid]. There are two things I'd like for you to notice about this doll. First, her simple dress. Notice again the dark colors and the ties and hooks instead of buttons. The second thing I'd like for you to notice is that she doesn't have a face. The Amish don't believe in putting the human face on any object, or even having their pictures taken. They feel that this represents a graven image and is a sign of personal pride.

7 There are two exceptions to this rule of simplicity for the Amish people, and these are the only two things that they may wear, or hang, or display in their homes. The first exception to the rule of being a simple people is their quilts [visual aid]. Notice again the dark colors and the simple patterns. John Ruth, in his book *A Quiet and Peaceable Life*, states that quilts began as a way for frugal housewives to use leftover scraps of cloth. Now quilts have grown into a beautiful expression of the artistry and creativity of the Amish women. A second exception to this rule of being a simple people is what's known as *Fraktur* art. And this dates back to the Middle Ages and is characterized by calligraphy writing and bright colors, with hearts or birds or flowers. What the Amish will do is they will write scripture verses in this *Fraktur* style and they will hang these plaques in their homes to remind them to be humble. We can see how this inner desire of the Amish to be a simple people is reflected outwardly in such tangibles as their dress and in their toys.

8 The third and final tenet of the Amish faith is a strong commitment to the group. 1 John 3:16 states, "This is how we know what love is. Jesus Christ laid down his life for us, and we ought to lay down our lives for our brothers." John Hostetler, in his book *Amish Society*, describes some of the ways the Amish care for and are committed to their brothers. Perhaps the most vivid example of this is what would be known as the barn-raising day. If any of you have seen the movie *Witness*, you will recall the barn-raising scene, where the entire community of twenty to thirty families came together to join forces and build a barn. Barn-raising day is a very common occurrence among Amish communities, and they use it to provide new barns, either for newlyweds who are just starting out,

or for families whose original barns have been destroyed by fire or rains. And this barn is actually a gift from the entire community to that family, since all of the builders of the barn share in the cost of the materials.

9 A second way we can see how the Amish are dedicated to their group is in times of hardship. For example, if there is a birth in the family or a death in the family, the neighbors of that family will come together and they will cook for the family, care for their children, tend for their crops, and do everything necessary until that family is able to emotionally and physically recuperate.

10 Lastly, we can see how the Amish are dedicated to their group in the way they care for their elderly. The Amish elderly are treated with the greatest respect, and they hold all of the authority and leadership positions in the community. Instead of sending their elderly to nursing homes, they build additions onto their farmhouses, where the elderly grandparents can live comfortably and have their needs provided for. Certainly, this strong dedication to the group has its benefits. John Ruth, in *A Quiet and Peaceable Life*, describes one of these benefits as "a powerful deliverance: to sense the blending of your thoughts and prayers with those who would give their lives for you."

11 This morning we have briefly reviewed the three major tenets of the Amish faith. That is separation from this world, simplicity in the world, and strong dedication to their group. Clearly, the Amish have chosen a different path in life than have most of us: One that is not so fancy, not so modern, not so fast-paced, and, perhaps, one that is not so bad after all.

"THE DOUBLE INDIGNITY — MEDICAL CONFIDENTIALITY"[1]

RYAN SISKOW, *University of Northern Iowa*

Ryan Siskow used a problem-solution approach to the issue of confidentiality of medical records. His speech won second place at the 1991 Interstate Oratorical Association contest.

1 Last August Edward Mulligan set up his picket in front of the Community General Hospital in Syracuse, New York. He wasn't demanding higher wages or even protesting some experimental drug. Rather, he was simply asking the hospital to give him something it had denied him for nearly three years: a copy of his medical records. You see, when Mulligan discovered that both his employer and his insurance company had been accessing his medical records, he naturally wanted to know what they were looking at. So, he also requested a copy, but he was denied. He then filed a lawsuit in the belief that legal action would help him obtain those documents. But because the state of New York, along with countless other states, does not require hospitals and doctors to release medical information to their patients, the case was thrown out of court.

2 While Edward Mulligan's case is seemingly unusual, his problem is not. In dozens of states, patients are denied the critical, personal details of their own medical records. Yet insurance companies, government agencies, and others have relatively easy access to those same documents — usually without the patient's knowledge. It's what *New York Times* writer Esther Schrader calls "the double indignity: You can't see your medical records, but everybody else can." And as United States Representative Ron Wyden argued in testimony before the Subcommittee on Civil and Constitutional Rights, "For any American with an established medical history, the potential damage from breaches in medical confidence is enormous."

3 In the effort to examine this threat to our medical confidentiality, we'll first look at how that confidence may be breached; we'll then look at how those threats make each of us vulnerable; and finally, we'll consider some solutions that may put an end to such intrusions.

4 Like most Americans, you probably assumed your medical records were confidential. But as Stuart Wesbury, president of the American College of Health Care Executives points out, "More and more people are demanding access to your medical records." And the orderly outflow of such information has gone virtually unchecked.

5 Ironically, you may be the one who unknowingly starts this flow of information. If you have health or life insurance, you've probably signed a standard waiver authorizing the insurance company to gather information about your medical history. That, unfortunately, is where the runaway medical record takes off. As *U. S. News and World Report* of June 5, 1990, explains, insurance companies, employers, and government agencies now pay nearly 70 percent of all medical bills in this country. They want to know where their money's going, so they scrutinize the records that doctors and hospitals keep on all of us.

6 A doctor's office can turn an insurer's request for information into a breach of confidence sometimes simply out of expediency. As San Francisco personal injury lawyer Bennett Cohen explains, "If an insurer wants records to see if someone has an asthma condition and that patient also saw the same doctor for an HIV test five years ago, the insurer gets that information, too."

7 In practice, your records may not even go directly from the doctor or hospital to the company requesting the information. Many insurers use reporting agencies to collect such information. As *Newsweek* of June 12, 1990, points out, one databank that is especially questionable is the Medical Information Bureau (MIB), which represents nearly 800 North American insurance companies and stores medical data on some 13 million Americans. As *U. S. News and World Report* of October 31, 1989, tells us, if you have ever filled out an application for health or life insurance, you're probably on file with the MIB and your medical records are an open commodity.

8 Here's how the system works, according to the *Washington Monthly.* When you sign that standard waiver, you authorize the company to gather information about you. While most policy holders are aware of this rather routine authorization, few people realize that through the MIB and other reporting agencies, medical information about them is available to other insurance companies, employers, and others across the country. You see, the information is then fed to a nationwide databank. Later, the bureau relays the information to virtually any other company that wants it. What's more alarming is that reporting agencies don't check those records for accuracy.

9 It's a situation Anne Stern knows all too well. After surgery, Stern's records, complete with an inaccurate transcription from one record to another, were circulated through the MIB. Shortly thereafter, Stern's medical benefits were suddenly cancelled and for nearly three years she had difficulty locating a doctor willing to treat her. To complicate matters, when she requested a copy of her medical records, she was denied access. Only after months of litigation were Stern's records released, the inaccurate transcription discovered, and eventually corrected.

10 Stern's case also raises an even more ominous question: How can government agencies, insurers, and others have easier access to our medical records than we do ourselves? The answer, unfortunately, is rather simple. Currently, 36 states have no law guar-

anteeing patients access to the records doctors and hospitals keep on them. As Robert Ellis Smith, publisher of the *Privacy Journal* explains, "The lack of control over what insurance companies and others do with medical information is the single biggest weakness in medical privacy law today."

11 Having examined the threats to our medical confidentiality, we can now explore the ramifications of such intrusions. For some it may simply mean a lack of privacy, yet for others it may mean lost educational and employment opportunities, even inappropriate health care.

12 *Scholastic Update* of January 12, 1990, tells us how substitute teacher Alan Rodway's decision to take an HIV test before marriage cost him his job. The University of Southern California Hospital illegally told the Los Angeles School District that Rodway had AIDS — when in fact he had tested negative for the HIV virus. Jerome Beigler, former chairperson of the American Psychiatric Association's Committee on Confidentiality, explains that cases such as Rodway's are becoming more and more prevalent. He points to an alarming trend of demoting, sometimes even firing, employees after it was discovered they had undergone psychiatric, drug abuse, or other forms of "controversial" treatment. The source of such information was company-run insurance plans that were paying the medical bills.

13 Even as students the risk is substantial. *Current* magazine of January, 1990, explains how after undergoing psychoanalysis as part of his field research for his psychology degree, medical student Scott Dillon was incorrectly [diagnosed] with manic-depression. He subsequently was denied admission to eight graduate schools, and failed to receive the timely treatment he needed for what turned out to be a genuine physical ailment — a degenerative disease of the spine. As a result, he was left half-crippled. It was only later that Dillon discovered that his college medical records, complete with the incorrect diagnosis, had been sent along with his official transcripts to all the graduate schools to which he had applied and to all the medical centers at which he sought treatment.

14 With an understanding of the threats to our medical confidentiality and the often devastating consequences, we can now consider steps that must be taken to rectify this problem. Perhaps the best news for our medical information is a model bill drafted by the National Conference of Commissioners on Uniform State Laws. The proposed law would guarantee patients' access to their own records and would require anyone other than doctors or hospitals to get written patient permission before obtaining those records. Montana is the only state to adopt the law so far, but your elected officials will be prompted to take action only when you express your concern.

15 On a more personal level, if you want to have any say about what's in your records and who has access to them, ask your physician for a copy of your records and make sure the information is accurate and complete. If you do have problems getting your records, contact your state's Attorney General's Office and the local chapter of the National Consumer Research Interest Group. Both offices can provide legal counsel and sometimes legal services to help you obtain your records.

16 Finally, you can practice a little preventive medicine on your insurance policy. When you sign that standard waiver, you can decrease your vulnerability by specifying certain dates and specific information that relate directly to your insurance coverage. That way the company doesn't have perpetual permission to take anything it wants, any time it wants. Several companies that offer this option include the Principal Financial Group,

The Allied Company, and Century Companies of America. Do keep in mind, however, that some insurance companies may ask you to take your business elsewhere. But for the cost of privacy, the move may be well worth it.

17 By examining the threats to our medical confidentiality, how those threats make each of us vulnerable, and solutions to counter such intrusions, perhaps we can avoid the double indignity suffered by an increasing number of Americans. After all, if your medical records aren't private, what is?

"AMERICA'S SLEEP DEFICIT"[2]

Andy Wood, *St. Petersburg Junior College, Florida*

Andy Wood's speech called for Americans to wake up to the problem of sleep deprivation. His topic was well chosen for a student audience preparing to enter, or already part of, the business and professional workforce.

1 America faces a dangerous and expensive deficit. This deficit started growing when Thomas Edison invented the light bulb so we would be more productive at night. It gained momentum when America became the world's first 24-hour service economy. And today, this deficit shows no sign of shrinking. America is paying the price for a sleep deficit. We're not just talking about long-distance truckers and midnight TV repairmen. This deficit affects everyone in a society in which mothers and fathers work, stores never close, and corporations race to keep up with events many time zones away. Yet in an age when alertness is essential, we are getting more and more tired. *Time,* December 17, 1990, reports that the typical adult needs about eight hours of sleep every night to function effectively. By that standard, millions of us are chronically sleep deprived.

2 To better understand the scope of this problem, we must first explore why America suffers from sleep deprivation. Then, we can examine the costs of our nation's sleeplessness. And finally, propose realistic solutions involving national, corporate, and personal steps we must take in order to eliminate this expensive sleep deficit.

3 Most of us consider ourselves experts on sleep. Yet many of us end up feeling like walking zombies during the day — and few know why. One of the main reasons for this feeling of sleeplessness is most of us are constantly out of synch with our own body clocks. The *Chicago Tribune,* January 14, 1990, reports that scientists are studying this by focusing research on a tiny cluster of neurons located behind the eyes. They believe that this set of brain cells forms a light-sensitive neurological clock that regulates our sleep-awake patterns. They also note that this clock runs on a 25-hour cycle. In *Health Magazine,* March, 1990, the director of the Mayo Clinic Sleep Center, Dr. Peter Hauri, says that this difference between our daily rhythms and our bodily rhythms is one of the main reasons for our constantly feeling tired. The *Washington Times,* March 26, 1990, takes this a step further by reporting that approximately 100 million of us routinely shortchange our sleeping time either by working at night or simply not sleeping enough hours. The fact is: We are constantly racing our own body clocks. And we are constantly losing.

4 Yet, catching up is difficult because few of us are concerned about getting enough sleep. When I asked Cornell University sleep researcher Dr. Scott Campbell to elaborate, he told me that 1 in 10 Americans have a serious sleep problem, but of those people, fewer than five percent even seek treatment. In *Health Magazine,* March, 1990, sleep researcher Dr. Charles Pollak says, "Sleeplessness is one of the least recognized sources

of disability in our society…. It doesn't make it difficult to walk, see, or hear. But people who don't get enough sleep can't think and they can't make appropriate judgments."

5 Perhaps the most disturbing cause of our nation's sleep deficit is the fact that American society is obsessed with staying awake. In *Working Woman*, September 1, 1990, the director of the Sleep Disorders Center at the Medical College of Pennsylvania, June Fry, says, "The feeling is that if you can't work all night and still do the job well, then you're not motivated…. People think that sleep isn't macho."

6 Well, sleep may not be macho, but sleeplessness does carry a heavy price — a price that can be broken down into three main areas: increased personal risk, accidents on the job, and lost productivity.

7 The most obvious cost of our nation's sleep deprivation is in your ability to drive safely. When I interviewed Cesar Reategui of the Department of Transportation, he explained that 200,000 traffic accidents each year are sleep related and that 20 percent of us have fallen asleep at the wheel at least once. *The New England Journal of Medicine*, May 3, 1990, explains some of the other personal costs of sleeplessness. The report concludes that not getting enough sleep increases your risk of heart disease, gastrointestinal illness, and a host of sleep disorders ranging from mild snoring to life-threatening insomnia.

8 Sleep deprivation also causes danger on the job. And, ironically, hospitals are the worst offenders. Around the country, interns work 120-hour work weeks, 36 hours at a stretch. This is a prescription for disaster. *Time* magazine, December 17, 1990, reports that one sleepy resident accidently ordered the wrong medication for a diabetic patient who ended up [going] into a coma. Airline pilots also face sleep deprivation in their constant crossing of time zones. In the *Time* magazine article, one pilot says, "There have been times I've been so sleepy, I was nodding off as we were getting into takeoff position." This is not rare. The *Washington Times*, March 26, 1990, reports that the *Exxon Valdez* oil spill, the Union Carbide disaster in India, and the Three Mile Island near-meltdown all have one thing in common: The accidents occurred after midnight when the operators were the most drowsy.

9 Our sleep deficit also poses a long-term menace to our nation's productivity. According to Cornell University sleep researcher Dr. Scott Campbell, sleep-related accidents and disorders cost our economy 70 billion dollars a year. He says, "People who are sleep deprived lose much of their capacity to work productively." For them, and our nation, this creates a serious problem.

10 Well, serious problems require realistic solutions. And although we can't turn back the clock on our 24-hour society, we can discuss realistic ways of attacking our sleep deficit.

11 The first step is on the national level. The federal government and the medical community must work together to increase funding for sleep research. In *USA Today*, January 9, 1991, Harvard sleep researcher Dr. Bob McCarley says, "There's not a single tenured spot for sleep research in the country…. There are no federally funded centers." To address this problem, the Department of Health should organize the various sleep centers around the country around a national policy. Government funding would help eliminate overlapping research and increase the study of sleep-related problems on the national level. As well, sleep education should be a larger part of medical school curriculums. This is essential because today's doctors have received little more than one hour of classroom instruction about sleep disorders.

12 The next step requires two changes on the corporate level: limits on work hours and better lighting in workplaces. *Time* magazine, December 17, 1990, reports that some

airlines now let pilots take scheduled naps on long-haul flights while a co-pilot commands the aircraft. And while many hospitals around the country require interns to work over a hundred hours a week, New York State has placed caps on the time that interns and residents can stand duty. Now they max out at 90 hours a week, 24 hours a shift. Other companies that employ shiftworkers are finding that brighter workplaces increase productivity. *The New England Journal of Medicine,* May 3, 1990, reports exposure to bright light during the early morning hours helps workers adjust their body clocks to their work schedules. It can be as simple as installing a higher watt light bulb or turning up the contrast on your computer screen.

13 On the personal level, while many of us aren't pilots, or doctors, or even shiftworkers, we all need to help attack the sleep deficit. The first step is simple: Get eight hours of sleep a night. Yet, sleep researchers say we should do more. According to *The New York Times,* January 14, 1990, they believe that a brief afternoon nap supplies essential energy to active people because our bodily rhythms tend to wind down in the mid-afternoon. In *The New York Times* article, the director of the Stanford University Sleep Disorders Clinic, Dr. William Dement, says, "It seems nature definitely intended that adults should nap in the middle of the day, perhaps to get out of the midday sun." Dr. Dement says that taking time to take a nap will help you work smarter and feel better. It might even help you stay awake through long speeches on sleep.

14 In the past few minutes, we've explored America's sleep deficit: its foundation, its costs, and its cure. Taking this information to heart is important because as the workplace becomes more technologically sophisticated, the price of sleep-related accidents grows. We must change our attitudes about sleep.

15 Certainly, this involves costs. The government must readjust funding to solve a problem that isn't front page news. And we must spend more time doing what seems to be the least productive thing in our lives: sleeping. But the benefits of eliminating this sleep deficit are clear: increased productivity for our nation, increased safety in our workplaces, and increased health in our personal lives. Now, more than ever, it's time to wake up America! You need more sleep!

"WORKPLACE OF THE 90'S: HI-TECH SWEATSHOP?"[3]

TERRI NIMMONS, *Towson State University, Maryland*

Discussing the uses and abuses of computerized monitoring technology in the workplace, Terri Nimmons raised some significant ethical questions in her speech and proposed a three-fold plan of action.

1 Last month, in my position as a customer service representative for a large telecommunications company, I received 862 calls from customers (but I should have taken 900), my average "talk time" on those calls was 394 seconds (though it should have been only 300 seconds), and I was "idle" 6.7 percent of the time. I know this because like millions of workers in a variety of professions, my actions on the job are continuously tracked by computerized monitoring systems.

2 Over the last decade, use of monitoring or surveillance technology in the workplace has increasingly been used to track individual activities ranging from number of keystrokes entered by a data processor to recording what calls are made to or from a college professor's office.

3 In the next few minutes, I'm going to outline, first, the uses of computerized mon-

itoring systems; second, the abuses of those systems; and finally, I will demonstrate the need for national legislation regulating computerized monitoring in the workplace, and simple personal action steps we must take.

4 An understanding of why legislative and personal actions are necessary requires an overview of the widespread applications of this technology. Computerized monitoring has become a pervasive, intrusive, and often invisible presence in the workplace. According to the Office of Technology Assessment, six million American workers were being monitored daily in the performance of their jobs in 1986, and that figure jumped to more than eight million by 1990. A study published in the 1989 *National Productivity Review* found monitoring systems in 98 percent of the clerical and customer service divisions of such industries as banking, insurance, airline reservations, telemarketing, and telecommunications.

5 Three general categories of information are usually collected by monitoring systems. A July, 1991, study reported in the *Journal of Business Ethics* identified those categories: (1) job performance characteristics, such as number of keystrokes entered, (2) job behaviors, like amount of time between calls, and (3) service performance, in which an employer actually listens in on employee phone calls.

6 "Sophisticated" systems can allow a manager to read another's electronic mail, or send subliminal messages through a PC, instructing an employee to "work faster, work faster." One software company stated in *Fortune* magazine, November, 1991, that two of its most popular programs, called Peek and Spy, are in place in many Fortune 500 companies to monitor and control PC users without their knowledge.

7 Managers defend and promote the use of monitoring technology, claiming that computers provide objective measures of performance and increase productivity. With regard to performance evaluation, the data provided is certainly objective; however, quantifiable measures — length of a call as measured in seconds, number of calls taken — are not indicative of quality of performance. Further, research does not support management's contentions of increased productivity from use of surveillance technology. Studies reported over the last five years in *National Productivity Review, Sloan Management Review, Journal of Business Ethics,* and *Employee Relations Labor Journal,* among others, have failed to prove that even the most well-managed systems increase productivity.

8 Despite this lack of evidence, use of monitoring systems is escalating rapidly. The Gartner Group, a data analysis firm interviewed in *Fortune* in November, estimates that sales of computerized spying equipment topped $175 million last year. That figure is projected over the next five years to soar to more than a quarter of a billion dollars.

9 With the increasing popularity of monitoring technology there have, unfortunately, come abuses to both workers and customers. Evidence indicates that computerized monitoring can be detrimental to employees. A 1990 study conducted at the University of Wisconsin, as cited in the *Wall Street Journal,* September 24, 1991, found significantly higher rates of stress-related illness among monitored workers than among those who were not monitored. When surveyed, employees of AT&T, TWA, Bell Canada, and Federal Express identified monitoring or surveillance as the chief source of stress in the workplace.

10 As a person who works in a monitored environment, I can attest to the stress of feeling tied to a PC; seemingly, my every action is covertly observed and recorded by unseen eyes. It is no wonder that the term "electronic sweatshop" is used to describe such conditions, where information and customers are processed in an assembly line fashion.

11 But the stressful working conditions are not the only problem created by moni-

toring technology. The customers of the businesses employing such devices can also experience negative ramifications. What happens when the needs of customers conflict with the desire of workers to meet productivity standards set by computers? This question was answered in part by a disturbing circumstance at Bell Canada in the late 1980s. As described in the *Wall Street Journal,* September 24, 1991, a sophisticated monitoring system was installed to record information about everyone from managers to operators. The monitoring system continuously collected [information] about the operators as they worked: Length of calls, number of calls taken, and number of seconds between calls were tracked. Operators felt so pressured by the computerized presence of the monitoring system that when they were having trouble finding a number, they began giving incorrect information in order to get the customer off the phone so they could receive the next call. Certainly, that is not customer service and it is not productive. Bell Canada was forced to change its practices.

12 Federal Express, a company internationally known for exemplary service to its customers, also abandoned individual monitoring of workers in response to service representatives' complaints of stress and deterioration of customer satisfaction ratings. In *Fortune,* November, 1991, Gordon F. MacPherson, founder of Incoming Calls Management Institute, labeled computerized quota-setting as "anathema" to quality customer service environments. In a personal interview I conducted with Mr. MacPherson on April 13, he stated that mismanagement of technology in the workplace shifts employee focus from quality to quantity. What emerges is a picture of an environment where the emphasis is on managing the technology as it spies on people doing their jobs, rather than promoting quality service to customers and providing a fair workplace.

13 Since evidence does not support a correlation between computerized monitoring and greater productivity, but is detrimental to workers and impedes quality service, I contend that national legislation and individual action are required to ensure ethical use of such technology.

14 The May, 1989, issue of *Management Review* documents unsuccessful efforts to pass state legislation regulating monitoring in New York, New Hampshire, New Jersey, and California. However, the power of corporations to quash legislative efforts at the state level was demonstrated in an exercise of corporate blackmail by C&P Telephone against the West Virginia legislature. The incident, as detailed in the previously cited *Management Review*, was as follows: West Virginia passed a "beep" bill which required that if an employer was monitoring or eavesdropping on a phone call, a tone must sound to alert the employee. In response, C&P dropped monitoring — and customer satisfaction ratings remained high. Yet the corporation was determined to use technology to monitor and control its workforce and threatened to cancel plans to build a large manufacturing plant in West Virginia unless the bill was overturned. The state, suffering from high unemployment and wanting to protect jobs, had no choice [but] to repeal the law. Such tactics demand a response on individual and national levels.

15 Our role in stemming the tide of monitoring technology is three-fold: As voters, as employees, and as consumers we must act. We do have recourse. First, as voters, we must support national legislation such as a bill recently drafted by Senator Paul Simon of Illinois. The Senator's proposal, which is backed by labor groups such as Communications Workers of America and 9-to-5, has two simple tenets: (1) An employee must be notified if a call is being tracked or monitored, and (2) workers may not be measured solely by performance data collected by computerized systems. Secondly, as employees, we must ask the questions: What technology is being used in my workplace to record my

activities? What data is being collected about me and how is it being used? Finally, as consumers, we must make businesses accountable for the level of service for which we pay. When you call your bank, or credit card company, and you have that feeling of being processed rather than served, voice your complaint to a supervisor. Jot a note on your bill when you make a payment. Insist that customer service be tailored to your needs as a consumer — not dictated by productivity standards set by a computer.

16 If we do not purposefully exercise our rights as voters, employees, and consumers, we will increasingly work under the watchful, unblinking eyes of surveillance technology. By not acting, we perpetuate a world where an employer may legally eavesdrop on our phone calls to businesses, clients, and friends. And when you call your phone company, you may just speak to me; and, of course, my employer may secretly be on that call with us. While you're expressing your concern, question, or complaint, and as we approach 300 seconds of conversation, I'll be thinking about how to get off the line so the next call can come in — and the next — and the next — and the next call. Because, frankly, a customer is just one of a thousand "widgets" to be processed at your phone company's electronic sweatshop.

"THE SHAME OF HUNGER"[4]

Elie Wiesel

A survivor of the concentration camps at Auschwitz and Buchenwald, Elie Wiesel has won a congressional medal and the 1986 Nobel Prize for Peace. He delivered the following speech at Brown University on April 5, 1990, at the presentation of the Alan Feinstein Awards for the Prevention and Reduction of World Hunger. Wiesel, whose parents and sister died in the Holocaust, spoke passionately on this topic. Notice the various figures and structures of speech he employs.

1 I have been obsessed with the idea of hunger for years and years because I have seen what hunger can do to human beings. It is the easiest way for a tormenter to dehumanize another human being. When I think of hunger, I see images: emaciated bodies, swollen bellies, long bony arms pleading for mercy, motionless skeletons. How can one look at these images without losing sleep?

2 And eyes, my God, eyes. Eyes that pierce your consciousness and tear your heart. How can one run away from those eyes? The eyes of a mother who carries her dead child in her arms, not knowing where to go, or where to stop. At one moment you think that she would keep on going, going, going — to the end of the world. Except she wouldn't go very far, for the end of the world, for her, is there. Or the eyes of the old grandfather, who probably wonders where creation had gone wrong, and whether it was all worthwhile to create a family, to have faith in the future, to transmit misery from generation to generation, whether it was worth it to wager on humankind.

3 And then the eyes of all eyes, the eyes of children, so dark, so immense, so deep, so focused and yet at the same time, so wide and so vague. What do they see? What do hungry children's eyes see? Death? Nothingness? God? And what if their eyes are the eyes of our judges?

4 Hunger and death, death and starvation, starvation and shame. Poor men and women who yesterday were proud members of their tribes, bearers of ancient culture and lore, and who are now wandering among corpses. What is so horrifying in hunger is that it makes the individual death an anonymous death. In times of hunger, the individual death

has lost its uniqueness. Scores of hungry people die daily, and those who mourn for them will die the next day, and the others will have no strength left to mourn.

5 Hunger in ancient times represented the ultimate malediction to society. Rich and poor, young and old, kings and servants, lived in fear of drought. They joined the priests in prayer for rain. Rain meant harvest, harvest meant food, food meant life, just as lack of food meant death. It still does.

6 Hunger and humiliation. A hungry person experiences an overwhelming feeling of shame. All desires, all aspirations, all dreams lose their lofty qualities and relate to food alone. I may testify to something I have witnessed, in certain places at certain times, those people who were reduced by hunger, diminished by hunger, they did not think about theology, nor did they think about God or philosophy or literature. They thought of a piece of bread. A piece of bread was, to them, God, because a piece of bread then filled one's universe. Diminished by hunger, man's spirit is diminished as well. His fantasy wanders in quest of bread. His prayer rises toward a bowl of milk.

7 Thus the shame.

8 In Hebrew, the word *hunger* is linked to shame. The prophet Ezekiel speaks about "Kherpat raav," the shame of hunger. Of all the diseases, of all the natural diseases and catastrophes, the only one that is linked to shame in Scripture is hunger — the shame of hunger. Shame is associated neither with sickness nor even with death, only with hunger. For man can live with pain, but no man ought to endure hunger.

9 Hunger means torture, the worst kind of torture. The hungry person is tortured by more than one sadist alone. He or she is tortured, every minute, by all men, by all women. And by all the elements surrounding him or her. The wind. The sun. The stars. By the rustling of trees and the silence of night. The minutes that pass so slowly, so slowly. Can you imagine time, can you imagine time, when you are hungry?

10 And to condone hunger means to accept torture, someone else's torture.

11 Hunger is isolating; it may not and cannot be experienced vicariously. He who never felt hunger can never know its real effects, both tangible and intangible. Hunger defies imagination; it even defies memory. Hunger is felt only in the present.

12 There is a story about the great French-Jewish composer Daniel Halevy who met a poor poet: "Is it true," he asked, "that you endured hunger in your youth?" "Yes," said the poet. "I envy you," said the composer, "I never felt hunger."

13 And Gaston Bachelard, the famous philosopher, voiced his view on the matter, saying, "My prayer to heaven is not, 'Oh God, give us our daily bread,' but give us our daily hunger."

14 I don't find these anecdotes funny. These anecdotes were told about and by people who were not hungry. There is no romanticism in hunger, there is no beauty in hunger, no creativity in hunger. There is no aspiration in hunger. Only shame. And solitude. Hunger creates its own prison walls; it is impossible to demolish them, to avoid them, to ignore them.

15 Thus, if hunger inspires anything at all, it is, and must be, only the war against hunger.

16 Hunger is not a matter of choice. Of course, you may say, but what about the hunger striker? Haven't they chosen to deprive themselves of nourishment, aren't they hungry? Yes, but not the same way. First, they suffer alone, those around them do not. Second, they are given the possibility to stop any time they so choose, any time they win, any time their cause is attained. No so [with] the people in Africa. Not so [with] the people in Asia. Their hunger is irrevocable. And last, hunger strikers confer a meaning, a

purpose, upon their ordeal. No so [with] the victims in Ethiopia or Sudan. Their hunger is senseless. And implacable.

17 The worst stage in hunger is to see its reflection in one's brother, one's father, one's child. Hunger renders powerless those who suffer its consequences. Can you imagine a mother unable, helpless, to alleviate her child's agony? There is the abyss in shame. There, suffering and hunger and shame multiply.

18 In times of hunger, family relations break down. The father is impotent, his authority gone, the mother is desperate, and the children, the children, under the weight of accumulated suffering and hunger, grow older and older, and soon, they will be older than their grandparents.

19 But then, on the other hand, perhaps of all of the woes that threaten and plague the human condition, hunger alone can be curtailed, attenuated, appeased, and ultimately vanquished, not by destiny, nor by the heavens, but by human beings. We cannot fight earthquakes, but we can fight hunger. Hence our responsibility for its victims. *Responsibility* is the key word. Our tradition emphasizes the question, rather than the answer. For there is a "quest" in question, but there is "response" in responsibility. And this responsibility is what makes us human, or the lack of it, inhuman.

20 Hunger differs from other cataclysms such as floods in that it can be prevented or stopped so easily. One gesture of generosity, one act of humanity, may put an end to it, at least for one person. A piece of bread, a bowl of rice or soup makes a difference. And I wonder, what would happen, just imagine, what would happen, if every nation, every industrialized or non-industrialized nation, would simply decide to sell one aircraft, and for the money, feed the hungry. Why shouldn't they? Why shouldn't the next economic summit, which includes the wealthiest, most powerful, the richest nations in the world, why shouldn't they decide that since there are so many aircrafts, why shouldn't they say, "Let's sell just one, just one, to take care of the shame and the hunger and the suffering of millions of people."

21 So the prophet's expression, "the shame of hunger," must be understood differently. When we speak of our responsibility for the hungry, we must go to the next step and say that the expression "shame of hunger" does not apply to the hungry. It applies to those who refuse to help the hungry. Shame on those who could feed the hungry, but are too busy to do so.

22 Millions of human beings constantly are threatened in Africa and Asia, and even in our own country, the homeless and the hungry. Many are going to die of starvation, and it will be our fault. For we could save them, and if we do not, we had better have a good reason why we don't.

23 If we could airlift food and sustenance and toothpaste to Berlin in 1948, surely we could do as much for all the countries, Ethiopia and Sudan and Mozambique and Bangladesh, in the year 1990. Nations capable of sending and retrieving vehicles in space must be able to save human lives on earth.

24 Let our country, and then other countries, see in hunger an emergency that must be dealt with right now. Others, our allies, will follow. Private relief often has been mobilized in the past: Jews and Christians, Moslems and Buddhists have responded to dramatic appeals from the African desert. One of my most rewarding moments was when I went to the Cambodian border 10 years ago and saw there the misery, the weakness, the despair, the resignation, of the victims.

25 But I also saw the extraordinary international community motivated by global solidarity to help them. And who were they? They represented humankind at its best:

There were Jews and Christians and Moslems and Buddhists from all over the world. And if ever I felt proud of the human condition, it was then. It is possible to help, but private help is insufficient. Government-organized help is required; only governments can really help solve this tragedy that has cosmic repercussions.

26 We must save the victims of hunger simply because they can be saved. We look therefore at the horror-filled pictures, when we dare to look, day after day. And I cannot help but remember those who had surrounded us elsewhere, years and years ago. Oh, I do not wish to make comparisons. I never do. But I do have the right to invoke the past, not as a point of analogy, but as a term of reference. I refuse to draw analogies with the Jewish tragedy during the era of darkness; I still believe and will always believe that no event ought to be compared to that event. But I do believe that human tragedies, all human tragedies, are and must be related to it. In other words, it is because one people has been singled out for extinction that others were marked for slavery. It is because entire communities were wiped out then that others were condemned to die later in other parts of the planet. All events are intertwined.

27 And it is because we have known hunger that we must eliminate hunger. It is because we have been subjected to shame that we must now oppose shame. It is because we have witnessed humanity at its worst that we must now appeal to humanity at its best.

"I HAVE A DREAM"[5]

Martin Luther King, Jr.

Speaking from the steps of the Lincoln Memorial on August 28, 1963, Martin Luther King, Jr., delivered the keynote address of the March on Washington, D. C., for Civil Rights. As you read his "I Have a Dream" speech, study the power of its language and see if you agree with many scholars that this is the greatest American speech of the twentieth century.

1 I am happy to join with you today in what will go down in history as the greatest demonstration for freedom in the history of our nation.

2 Five score years ago, a great American, in whose symbolic shadow we stand today, signed the Emancipation Proclamation. This momentous decree came as a great beacon light of hope to millions of Negro slaves, who had been seared in the flames of withering injustice. It came as a joyous daybreak to end the long night of their captivity.

3 But one hundred years later, the Negro still is not free. One hundred years later, the life of the Negro is still sadly crippled by the manacles of segregation and the chains of discrimination. One hundred years later, the Negro lives on a lonely island of poverty in the midst of a vast ocean of material prosperity. One hundred years later, the Negro is still languished in the corners of American society and finds himself an exile in his own land.

4 And so we've come here today to dramatize a shameful condition. In a sense we've come to our nation's Capitol to cash a check. When the architects of our republic wrote the magnificent words of the Constitution and the Declaration of Independence, they were signing a promissory note to which every American was to fall heir. This note was a promise that all men — yes, black men as well as white men — would be guaranteed the unalienable rights of life, liberty, and the pursuit of happiness.

5 It is obvious today that America has defaulted on this promissory note insofar as her citizens of color are concerned. Instead of honoring this sacred obligation, Ameri-

ca has given the Negro people a bad check — a check which has come back marked "insufficient funds."

6 But we refuse to believe that the bank of justice is bankrupt. We refuse to believe that there are insufficient funds in the great vaults of opportunity of this nation. And so we've come to cash this check — a check that will give us upon demand the riches of freedom and the security of justice.

7 We have also come to this hallowed spot to remind America of the fierce urgency of now. This is no time to engage in the luxury of cooling off or to take the tranquillizing drug of gradualism. Now is the time to make real the promises of democracy. Now is the time to rise from the dark and desolate valley of segregation to the sunlit path of racial justice. Now is the time to lift our nation from the quicksands of racial injustice to the solid rock of brotherhood. Now is the time to make justice a reality for all of God's children.

8 It would be fatal for the nation to overlook the urgency of the moment. This sweltering summer of the Negro's legitimate discontent will not pass until there is an invigorating autumn of freedom and equality. Nineteen sixty-three is not an end, but a beginning. Those who hope that the Negro needed to blow off steam and will now be content will have a rude awakening if the nation returns to business as usual. There will be neither rest nor tranquility in America until the Negro is granted his citizenship rights. The whirlwinds of revolt will continue to shake the foundations of our nation until the bright day of justice emerges.

9 But there is something that I must say to my people, who stand on the warm threshold which leads into the palace of justice. In the process of gaining our rightful place, we must not be guilty of wrongful deeds. Let us not seek to justify our thirst for freedom by drinking from the cup of bitterness and hatred.

10 We must forever conduct our struggle on the high plane of dignity and discipline. We must not allow our creative protest to degenerate into physical violence. Again and again we must rise to the majestic heights of meeting physical force with soul force.

11 The marvelous new militancy which has engulfed the Negro community must not lead us to a distrust of all white people. For many of our white brothers, as evidenced by their presence here today, have come to realize that their destiny is tied up with our destiny. They have come to realize that their freedom is inextricably bound to our freedom. We cannot walk alone.

12 As we walk, we must make the pledge that we shall always march ahead. We cannot turn back. There are those who are asking the devotees of civil rights, "When will you be satisfied?" We can never be satisfied as long as the Negro is the victim of the unspeakable horrors of police brutality. We can never be satisfied as long as our bodies, heavy with the fatigue of travel, cannot gain lodging in the motels of the highways and the hotels of the cities. We cannot be satisfied as long as a Negro in Mississippi cannot vote and a Negro in New York believes he has nothing for which to vote. No, no, we are not satisfied, and we will not be satisfied until justice rolls down like waters, and righteousness like a mighty stream.

13 I am not unmindful that some of you have come here out of great trials and tribulations. Some of you have come fresh from narrow jail cells. Some of you have come from areas where your quest for freedom left you battered by the storms of persecution and staggered by the winds of police brutality. You have been the veterans of creative suffering. Continue to work with the faith that unearned suffering is redemptive.

14 Go back to Mississippi, go back to Alabama, go back to South Carolina, go back

to Georgia, go back to Louisiana, go back to the slums and ghettos of our Northern cities, knowing that somehow this situation can and will be changed. Let us not wallow in the valley of despair.

15 I say to you today, my friends, so even though we face the difficulties of today and tomorrow, I still have a dream. It is a dream deeply rooted in the American dream.

16 I have a dream that one day this nation will rise up and live out the true meaning of its creed, "We hold these truths to be self-evident, that all men are created equal."

17 I have a dream that one day on the red hills of Georgia the sons of former slaves and the sons of former slaveowners will be able to sit down together at the table of brotherhood.

18 I have a dream that one day even the state of Mississippi, a state sweltering with the heat of injustice, sweltering with the heat of oppression, will be transformed into an oasis of freedom and justice.

19 I have a dream that my four little children will one day live in a nation where they will not be judged by the color of their skin but by the content of their character. I have a dream today.

20 I have a dream that one day, down in Alabama, with its vicious racists, with its governor having his lips dripping with the words of interposition and nullification, one day right there in Alabama little black boys and black girls will be able to join hands with the little white boys and white girls as sisters and brothers. I have a dream today.

21 I have a dream that one day every valley shall be exalted, every hill and mountain shall be made low, the rough places will be made plain and the crooked places will be made straight, and the glory of the Lord shall be revealed, and all flesh shall see it together.

22 This is our hope. This is the faith that I go back to the South with. With this faith we will be able to hew out of the mountain of despair a stone of hope. With this faith we will be able to transform the jangling discords of our nation into a beautiful symphony of brotherhood. With this faith we will be able to work together, to pray together, to struggle together, to go to jail together, to stand up for freedom together, knowing that we will be free one day.

23 This will be the day — this will be the day when all of God's children will be able to sing with new meaning, "My country 'tis of thee, sweet land of liberty, of thee I sing. Land where my fathers died, land of the pilgrim's pride, from every mountain side, let freedom ring." And if America is to be a great nation, this must become true.

24 So let freedom ring from the prodigious hilltops of New Hampshire. Let freedom ring from the mighty mountains of New York. Let freedom ring from the heightening Alleghenies of Pennsylvania!

25 Let freedom ring from the snowcapped Rockies of Colorado! Let freedom ring from the curvaceous slopes of California!

26 But not only that. Let freedom ring from Stone Mountain of Georgia!

27 Let freedom ring from Lookout Mountain of Tennessee!

28 Let freedom ring from every hill and molehill of Mississippi. From every mountainside, let freedom ring.

29 And when this happens, when we allow freedom to ring — when we let it ring from every village and every hamlet, from every state and every city — we will be able to speed up that day when all of God's children, black men and white men, Jews and Gentiles, Protestants and Catholics, will be able to join hands and sing in the words of the old Negro spiritual, "Free at last! Free at last! Thank God Almighty, we are free at last!"

"RESPECT"

Tamara L. Burk, *College of William and Mary*

Professor Tamara L. Burk now teaches in the Department of Theatre and Speech and in the Women's Studies Program at the College of William and Mary in Williamsburg, Virginia. The senior class voted to have Burk as faculty baccalaureate speaker on the evening of May 15, 1993 — a clear measure of their respect for her. We feel that her obvious respect for her students makes her speech a fitting postscript to Mastering Public Speaking. *We asked Professor Burk to assess how the occasion and her audience influenced her speech preparation, and to explain how she marked her manuscript for delivery. Her analysis and speech follow.*

The Baccalaureate Ceremony is a tradition held in front of the Christopher Wren Building (the oldest academic building still in use in the U. S.) on the evening before graduation. The mood of the occasion is festive and celebratory, but is equally marked by a sentimental and reflective tone. Graduating students and their families gather, and students wear their academic regalia and hold lit candles. The baccalaureate ceremony is a time for graduates and their families to reflect upon their accomplishments and their futures. Approximately 2,000 people attended this particular occasion.

I designed the beginning of the speech to help me establish an emotional link to the audience. I used humor to get their attention, and then made it clear to whom I was speaking by directing my thoughts to the students. In doing so, I sent the message that they were the reason for this occasion — that I was speaking "up" to them, not "down" to them. I also focused on them by remarking on their appearance. Then I developed my credibility by referring to my classes. Finally, I tried to bring them all together to the same point of reference by recognizing both the diversity of their backgrounds and experiences, and the commonalities in their achievements.

In the body of the speech, I tried to establish a rhythm that would carry the emotion of the occasion, like a song or a poem. I arranged my speaking notes with open lines and used punctuation to indicate where I should pause between ideas. At the same time, I tried to set up each segment so that it led logically to the next, maintaining the momentum of the speech. To keep the attention of the audience, I alternated between humor and seriousness, used repetitive structures, and emphasized empowering words (which I underlined in my notes).

I signaled my closing by repeating a series of lines from earlier in the speech. This strategy was meant to bring the audience together and to make them think back on the ideas I had expressed. After summarizing those ideas in a few carefully worded phrases, I returned to a somber and reflective mood for my closing. To establish a final link between the college and the students, I put myself in their shoes. I was fortunate to find a closing quotation that related not only to their experiences and mine, but also to the nature of the occasion.

1 Thank you.

2 At the beginning of a ceremonial speech like this, the speaker often goes through a brief attendance list, recognizing all of the important people present, usually in some hierarchical fashion:

3 I'm sure you've <u>all</u> heard it: *"Mr. President, distinguished colleagues, members of the press."*

4 I guess to <u>start</u>, I'd just like to say that having been invited here by the students, my thoughts and words tonight, are for <u>them</u>.

5 What a <u>beautiful</u> sight this is!

6 You look like stars.

7 You are stars in a way.

8 Because just like stars, you're shining with a light that will travel through time and space for years to come.

9 And <u>that's</u> what we've come here to celebrate. <u>That's</u> what we've come here to recognize and to symbolize, with these candles.

10 I've spent a lot of time the last couple of weeks thinking about what I could share with you that would be truly inspiring.

11 Part of my problem is that I think my students that are here have heard all my <u>truly</u> inspirational material.

12 On top of that, it's difficult for me to decide exactly who it is I'm talking to, because I know many of you in very different ways.

13 As a member of the Theatre & Speech faculty, I know you from my Public Speaking classes.

14 Now that puts me in an interesting situation, because I'm sure that those of you who have <u>been</u> in my classes are evaluating me as I speak — and I <u>know</u> that you're the world's harshest speech critics, because I trained you myself.

15 I also had the opportunity to teach in the Women's Studies Program this year. And while those of you who I know through <u>that</u> program probably don't care about the <u>structure</u> of my talk tonight, or whether or not my <u>inflection</u> is effective, I'm sure that I'm fully expected to have some type of political theme or agenda.

16 And then there are those of you whom I have never had in my classes, some whom I may never have <u>met</u>.

17 Students with different majors

18 Different interests

19 Different lifestyles

20 But there is <u>one</u> thing that you all have in common that I can talk about.

21 And that's, tomorrow.

22 Tomorrow you will each receive something <u>magnificent</u>! Something that will in all likelihood affect the rest of your lives.

23 But it <u>won't</u> be your degree… Oh — you'll get the degree <u>too</u> of course. That'll be like a piece of paper with a bunch of Latin on it, wrapped in a ribbon or something.

24 But what's <u>really</u> important is something else that you'll get. Something much more intangible. Something that you'll all have in <u>common</u>, but something that may be very <u>different</u> for each one of you.

25 Because the <u>form</u> that this magnificent thing <u>takes</u> will depend on <u>you</u>. It'll depend on your goals and expectations, and on the directions you'll take in the years to come.

26 I'm not even sure that it has a real name, but for lack of a better word, tonight I'll call it, respect.

27 Respect from your professors

28 From your families

29 Respect from people you haven't even met yet (including for many of you, your future employers, which is of course, a very important component of the reason that you're here).

30 But most of all, tomorrow you'll find that you've been given respect from your peers, and from within yourselves.

31 And if there's <u>one</u> thing that I want to do <u>tonight</u>, it's to heighten that sense of respect for yourselves.

32 Because whether you hang that degree on your wall, or just stick it in a drawer; — whether you <u>use</u> the skills you <u>learned</u> here, or try something entirely new, you're going to leave here with something that the College of William and Mary <u>didn't</u> give you.

33 And <u>that's</u> the sense of personal accomplishment, that you're going to feel tomorrow, and for some time into the future.

34 <u>That's</u> a gift that you gave your<u>selves</u>, when you came here four <u>years</u> ago (or, maybe it was five years ago, maybe six years ago; it doesn't really make any difference).

35 It's the gift that <u>you</u> give to yourself when you set a goal, and work to achieve it. Whether it's climbing a mountain, or finishing a race, or creating something beautiful.

36 So here you are:

37 looking down from the mountain,

38 standing at the finish line,

39 and you have <u>indeed</u> created something beautiful.

40 And you should be very <u>proud</u> of that, and <u>enjoy</u> that sense of accomplishment, and the <u>respect</u> that comes with it.

41 So tomorrow, it's time to celebrate.

42 Un<u>for</u>tunately, reaching such a big goal also means one other thing:

43 It's time to set <u>another</u> goal.

44 And <u>that's</u> scary. Probably even more scary than when you first got here and set your sights for today.

45 Believe me, I know how scary it is — <u>my</u> commencement speaker at the University of Maine was Stephen King.

46 I think that <u>part</u> of the reason that it's so scary is because of how <u>great</u> you feel right now — because of this <u>gift</u> you've given yourself, this sense of accomplishment, this respect.

47 Because somewhere down inside, you know that this feeling is not a permanent fixture. And you may wake up in a few weeks and feel like it's already gone.

48 But the <u>good</u> news is, that educational accomplishments are <u>more</u> than just trophies or certificates that sit on the shelf or hang on the wall, because: Education, is Power.

49 The power to choose.

50 The power to define.

51 The power to continue the process that you've been going through, to <u>maintain</u> that respect that you're feeling, from others and from within yourselves.

52 The power to open new avenues of accomplishment, <u>including</u> new opportunities to learn.

53 You see, whether or not you go on to graduate school, or law school, or med school, your education doesn't have to stop here. In fact, by stopping here, you could be depriving yourself of some <u>wonderful</u> things, <u>including</u> the things that you're feeling now.

54 Edith Hamilton, a brilliant 20th century American scholar and educator, said, "It has always seemed strange to me that in our endless discussions about education, so little stress is ever laid on the <u>pleasure</u> of becoming an educated person, the enormous <u>interest</u> it adds to life. To be able to be caught <u>up</u> in the world of thought — <u>that</u> is to be educated."

55 Last weekend I judged a state-wide oratorical competition for the Optimists International Club (and let me tell you these are happy people).

56 The competitors were between the ages of 12 and 16, and each spoke on the theme "I can make a difference."

57 They talked about solving world hunger, and recycling, and saving the rainforests, and a number of other very commendable topics, but what <u>I</u> found very interesting is

that without the benefit of hearing each other's speeches, almost <u>every one</u> of them talked about the importance of education in their lives.

58 And as they talked, they used words like *goals* and *accomplishments* and *respect*. And I think that without even knowing it, they came to the conclusion that the most important thing that they could do to make a difference is to get an education, so that when the opportunity presented itself, they would be <u>ready</u> to make a difference.

59 They would have the <u>power</u> to make a difference.

60 I thought that the Baccalaureate Ceremony during William and Mary's Tercentenary should have at least <u>one</u> obligatory quote by Thomas Jefferson, so here it is:

61 "I do not believe that the human condition will ever advance to such a state of perfection as to eliminate pain or vice in the world, yet I believe it is susceptible of much improvement, and that the diffusion of <u>knowledge</u> among the people is to be the instrument by which that improvement will be effected."

62 In many ways, I believe that <u>my</u> mission as an educator is to show students how to look at the world in ways they might not have otherwise. And I've found <u>that</u> to be one of the most rewarding aspects of my job.

63 Because of the nature of my classes, I often mediate arguments and debates among my students about controversial subjects involving human and civil rights, religion, race, culture, and philosophy.

64 And what I've found is that regardless of where students end up <u>standing</u> on these issues, they consistently discover <u>one</u> thing: that there are <u>always</u> more <u>gray</u> areas in the world than they originally thought.

65 And while they develop a sharper picture of where they <u>stand</u> on an issue, they often simultaneously come to see that their view isn't necessarily the <u>only</u> one that's defendable.

66 Now, I have to admit, that at times this process is very painful, as I'm <u>sure</u> that many of the lessons <u>you've</u> learned in <u>your</u> time here have been as well.

67 But <u>every now and then</u> I have a special conversation with a student, or I receive a letter or a note or a teaching evaluation thanking me for the positive impact I've had (<u>sometimes</u> without even realizing it).

68 And <u>that's</u> where I feel the power of <u>my</u> education. And <u>that's</u> how I maintain my sense of <u>accomplishment</u>, my self-respect. And that's why I <u>continue</u> my education, because we <u>all</u> have room left for growth and development. We <u>all</u> have things to learn from each other. We all have <u>gray</u> areas to explore.

69 <u>All of us</u> have the power to create positive change — in our own lives and in the lives of others. <u>But your education</u> amplifies that power <u>exponentially</u>.

70 <u>Some</u> will tell you that power can be used to <u>control</u> or even <u>demand</u> respect. But they're wrong. It can only be used to <u>exchange</u> respect.

71 Some educators believe that to gain the respect of their students, they need to act in a strict professional manner and exercise control over their classes at all times.

72 But if <u>I</u> do that, then I won't be able to <u>learn</u> from my students. You see, I believe very firmly that it's <u>impossible</u> to teach effectively without learning, and that education is about <u>exchanging</u>, not just transferring.

73 And I can't think of <u>any</u> way that you could have shown more respect for my ability and my passion for teaching, than by giving me the honor of being able to speak to you tonight.

74 So, once again, here you are:

75 gazing down from the mountain,

76 standing at the finish line,

77 and looking beautiful.

78 According to the standards of this college, you're ready for the next challenge, the next goal, because you are "educated."

79 My hope for you is that in leaving here and setting your new goals, you find some way to use the power of your education to <u>maintain</u> the process of learning that you've started. And that, along the way, you'll be alert when opportunities for exchange present themselves.

80 Continue to cultivate your mind, your voice and your spirit. And celebrate your achievements, because it's <u>not</u> the awards or the degrees or the promotions that you're going to remember, it's the celebrations.

81 On a final personal note, I'd like to say that although I've spoken tonight about some of the rewards of being an educator, this is a sadder profession than you might think. I remember a day when a very special mentor of <u>mine</u> [Dr. Kristin M. Langellier] told me that working in education was very painful for her, because she knew every year that all the people in her classes whom she came to care for would eventually leave.

82 As I stand here tonight, I feel those words more than ever.

83 So many of you have made a difference for me.

84 So many of you, have been a part of <u>my</u> learning process.

85 British novelist Jane Porter wrote that being an educator is like lighting other people's candles from your own lamp; for a brief moment, when the flames are together, they burn brighter.

86 <u>Please, hold those candles high.</u>

87 Thank you.

NOTES

1. Ryan Siskow, "The Double Indignity — Medical Confidentiality," *Winning Orations, 1991* (Mankato, MN: Interstate Oratorical Association, 1991) 32-34. Coached by Bruce Wickelgren.

2. Andy Wood, "America's Sleep Deficit," *Winning Orations, 1991* (Mankato, MN: Interstate Oratorical Association, 1991) 23-26. Coached by Bonnie Clark.

3. Terri Nimmons, "Workplace of the 90's: Hi-Tech Sweatshop?" *Winning Orations, 1992* (Mankato, MN: Interstate Oratorical Association, 1992) 51-54. Coached by Brenda Logue.

4. Elie Wiesel, "The Shame of Hunger," *Representative American Speeches: 1990-1991*, ed. Owen Peterson (New York: Wilson, 1991) 70-74.

5. Martin Luther King, Jr. , "I Have a Dream," August 28, 1963, Washington, D.C. Reprinted by permission of Joan Daves Agency. Copyright 1963 by Martin Luther King, Jr.

Credits

Name Index

Subject Index

*Boldface page numbers indicate marginal glossary entries.

459

movement, **262**-63
   posture, **261**
qualities of effective, 251-52
of speech to entertain, 383
time of, 99
vocal, elements of, 252-58
   articulation, **256**-57
   inflection, **255**-56
   pause, **254**
   pitch, **255**-56
   pronunciation, **257**-58
   rate, **252**-53
   voice quality or timbre, **256**
   volume, **254**-55
Democratic National Convention (1984), 248
Democratic society, benefits of public
   speaking to, 4-5
Demographics, audience, **83**-88
Denotation, **226**
Derived credibility, **329**
Devotion to topic, excessive, 110-11
Diagrams, **275**
Dictionaries, 138-39
Differences in argument by analogy,
   relevance of, 344-45
Direct questions, **187**-88
Discussion
   group. *See* Group discussion and decision
     making
   public, **407**
Disposition, audience, **93**-96
Distortion, message, 62-63
Distractions
   factual, **69**
   focusing on message despite, 70-71
   physical, **68**
   physiological, **68**
   practice to overcome, 55-56
   psychological, **68**
   semantic, **69**
Diversity, cultural, 85-86, 72, 250
Documentation
   of ideas, 330
   for oral report, 380
Dress for Success (Molloy), 259
Dyad, 8, 397
Dyadic communication, 8-9
Dynamism, 192, **331**
   visual aids for, 273

Economic status of audience, 87-88
Educational level of audience, 86-87
Effect to cause argument, 345-46
Either-or fallacy, 353
Electronic media, research using, 145
Emotional appeals, enhancing, 331-34
Emotive language, 224, 332-33
Encoding, **12**
Encyclopedia of Associations, 145

Encyclopedias, 139
Energizing the audience, 192
Entertain, speeches to, **120, 380**-83
Environment, **14**
   physical, 98-99
Esteem needs, 90
Ethics, 29-44
   definition of, **30**-31
   ethical listening, 36-39
   ethical speaking, 32-36
   plagiarism and, **39**-43
   principles of, 31-32
Ethnicity of audience, 85-86
Ethos, **328,** 334
   establishing speaker, 328-31
Etymology, definition by, **160**-61
Eulogy, 237, 322, **376**-79
Evaluation
   analyzing audience's, 100
   critical listening, 67
   ethical listening and obligation of, 38
   group leader's responsibility to encourage
     critical, 405
   group members' responsibility in, 403
   of information gathered in research, 148
   of message by audience, 100
   of proposed solutions to problems, 402
   of speech by speaker, 22-23
Events, informative speech about, 300-02,
   306
"Everybody's doing it" fallacy, 354
Evidence, 341-**42**
Example(s), **158**-59, 170
   argument by, **342**-43
   definition by, **161**
   in speech of tribute, 376-79
   types of, 158-59
   vivid, emotionally toned, 332
Expanded Academic Index, 135
Expectations, introducing speaker and
   creating realistic, 371
Experience
   credibility and acknowledging one's, 330
   learning from, 56-57
Extemporaneous speech, **266**-67
Extended examples, 158
Eye contact, **261**-62, 267, 287, 389

Facial expression, **261**
Fact, propositions of, **357**-58
Facts on File Yearbook, 140
Factual distractions, **69**
Factual information, presentation of, 34-35
Fallacies of argument, **350**-55
False dilemma, fallacy of, **353**-54
Familiar language, clarity and use of, 230-31
Favorable audience, 94-96
Fear of public speaking, 48-49. *See also*
   Nervousness.

Federal government, publications by, 136
Feedback, **13**-14
   in interpersonal communication, 8-9
   in intrapersonal communication, 8
   from listener, 74
   in mass communication, 10
   about nonverbal behavior, 249-50
   in public communication, 10
   See also Criticism
"Fight or flight" syndrome, 49
Figurative comparison and contrast, **164**,
   170
Figures of speech, using, 238-39
Files, personal, 130
Films, **283**-84
Filmstrips, **282**-83
Final statement, 19, 196-98
Final summary, 19, **196**
Finding Facts Fast (Todd), 148
First impressions, 258-59
First speech, 15-23
Fixed microphone, 389-90
Focus
   in impromptu speech, 384
   of speech of introduction, 371
   of speech of presentation, 373
Formal outline, **213**-15
Formats for group presentations, 407-08
4 S strategy of developing key ideas, 19, 181-
   84
Frame of reference, understanding, 71-72

Gallup Poll Monthly, The, 88
Galvanic skin response, 49
Gender of audience, 84-85
Generalization, hasty, fallacy of, **350**
General purpose, 118-20, **120**
Genuineness of speech of tribute, 377
Gestures, **263**-64
   variations in meanings of, 263-64
   visual aids and, 273
Gettysburg Address, 80
Gimmick division, **180**-81, 426
Goals
   of persuasion, limiting, 323
   of small groups, 396-97
Government documents, research using, 136
Graphics, **275**-81
Graphics, computer-generated, 281-82
Graphs, 276-79
Group(s)
   social-oriented, **397**-98
   task-oriented, **397**-98
   See also Small groups
Group communication, **9**-10
Group discussion and decision making,
   398-402
   principles of, 398-400
   process of, 400-02

responsibilities of leaders, 404-06
responsibilities of members, 403-04
Group membership of audience, 88
Group presentation, 407-10
Groupthink, **399**, 404
Gustatory images, **236**

Habits, 249
Handouts, **284**, 288, 426
Hasty generalization, fallacy of, **350**
Hearing, listening vs., **64**-65
Hierarchy of needs, 89-91
Honesty in speech critique, 416-17
How We Think (Dewey), 400
Humor, use of
appropriate, 382-83
to get audience's attention, 190-92
Hypothetical examples, **159**

Ideas
coordinate, **204**-06
documentation of, 330
group leader's introduction of new, 406
in informative speech, limiting, 17, 308
language and communication of, 223-24
listening for main, 71
preconceived, 110
relevance of supporting, testing, 205
subordinate, **205**-06
for topic, generating, 107-16
audience-generated topics, **111**-112
occasion-generated topics, **112**-114
research-generated topics, **114**-116
self-generated topics, **108**-111
See also Key ideas
Image
clothing choice and, 259-60
of person honored in speech, creating, 376-79
Images, sensory, 234-36
Imagination, stimulating audience's, 189
Importance of topic, persuasion and, 324-25
Impromptu speaking, **264**, **383**-85
Incremental persuasion, permanence of, 324
Indexes
to government documents, 136
to magazines and journals, 132-35
to newspapers, 135-36
of periodicals, 132-35
research-generated topics and, 114
Inductive argument, **342**-43
Inflection, **255**-56
Influence, 316-21
levels of, 91-94
in pyramid of persuasion, 318-21
in small groups, 396-97
types of, 316-18
See also Persuasion

Information
on audience, gathering, 93
group decision making and adequate, 399-400, 408-09
persuasion and audience's lack of, 324
See also Research
Informational literature from organizations, 145
Information base
group leader's establishment of, 405
group members' responsibility to contribute to, 403
Information overload, 294
Informative speech (speech to inform), **119**, 293-311, **295**
characteristics of, 294-96
guidelines for, 306-09
organization of, 296-306, 308-09
types of,
about concepts, 303
about conditions, 303-04
about events, 300-02
about issues, 304-05
about objects, 298-99
about people, 296-98
about places, 299-300
about processes, 302
InfoTrac, 135
Initial credibility, **328**-29
Initial summary, group leader's, 406
Inspire, speech to, **322**
Instilling value, attitude, belief or behavior, influence and, 316-18
Intensification of values, beliefs, attitudes or behaviors, 316-18
Intentional plagiarism, 40-41
Intentions, ethical speaking and clarity of, 35
Interaction, small group, 396-97
Interactive model of communication, 12-15
Interest of audience, analyzing, 99
speech title and, 122-23
Internal summary, group leader's, 406
Interpersonal communication, 7-9, **8**
Interpreter, **5**-7
Interpreting, 66
Interview
gathering audience information using, 93
research based on, 141-44
conducting, 144
following up on, 144
preparing for, 142-44
Intrapersonal communication, 7-**8**
Introduction
of group presentation, 409-10
organizing, 18, 186-95
establishing importance of topic, 18, 194
getting audience's attention, 18, 187-93

previewing key ideas, 18, **194**-95
stating topic, 18, 193-94
speech of, **370**-72
Investigative reports, 145
Issues, informative speeches about, 304-05, 306

Jargon, 109-10, 134, **231**
Journal, speaker's, 421-29
Journals, research using, 132-35
Judgment(s)
in criticism, **413**-14
proposition expressing, 355-56
withholding, 72-73

Key ideas
connecting, 184-86
determining, 18-19, 203-18, 426
development of, 181-84
dividing body of speech into, 177-81
previewing, **194**-95
Key word or phrase outline, **206**
Kinesthetic images, **236**
Kinetic images, **236**
Knowing Where to Look: The Ultimate Guide to Research (Horowitz), 132
Knowledge
personal, assessing, 16-17, 108-11, 129-30
reasons for seeking, 295

Language, 221-45
active, 233-34
common errors of, 227-29
emotive, 224, 332-33
functions of, 223-26
jargon, 109-10, 134, **231**
objectivity and, 308
opaque, 224
principles of effective use of, 20, 227-41
appropriateness, 239-41
clarity, 20, 229-31
correctness, 20, 227-29
vividness, 20, 231-39
transparent, 226
as weapon, 222-23, 227
Language abuse, 227-29
Lapel microphone, 389
Leaders, group, 404-06
Learned skill, listening as, 64
Library cataloguing systems, 137-38
Library research, 131-41
Linear model of communication, 12
Line graph, **276**-77
Listen, desire to, 70
Listener analysis. *See* Audience analysis.
Listening, **64**
active, 64
critical, 38

462

Structures of speech, using, 236-38
Study group, **398**
Style manuals, 147-48
Subject, knowing one's, 53-54, 329-30, 387
Subordinate ideas, **205**-06
Substitution, articulation error of, 256-57
Sufficiency, testing inductive argument for, 343
Summary
  by group leaders, 406
  of key ideas, **196**
  as listening skill, 74
Support among group members, 404
Supporting materials, 153-73
  appropriate, 309
  for informative speech, limiting, 17, 308
  purposes of, 154-57
  in speaking outlines, 215-16
  tests of, 167-71
    expert, 168
    freedom from bias, 168-69
    quotation in context, 167-68
    relevance of, 169
    specificity of, 169
    sufficiency of, 169-71
    timeliness of, 171
  types of, 157-67
    comparison and contrast, **163**-64
    definition, **159**-62
    examples, **158**-59
    narration, **162**-63
    statistics, **165**-66
    testimony, **166**-67
Syllogism, **347**
Symbol, **5**-7
Symposium, **407**-08
Synesthesia, **236**
Synonym, definition by, **160**
Synthesis of ideas in oral report, 380

Tact
  in critique, using, 416-17
  in speech to entertain, 383
Tactile images, **235**
Task-oriented group, **397**-98
Taste in speech to entertain, 383
Technical language, 109-10, 134
Television, information from, 145
Terminal credibility, **329**
Testimony, **166**-67
Thermal image, **235**-36
Thesis in speech to entertain, 120, 381
Thesis statement, **121**
  wording, 121-22
Thinking skills, critical, 23-24, 315
Third-person narrative, **163**

Timbre, 256
Time of delivery, 99
Title, developing, 122-24
Tone, **240**
  of speech of introduction, 371
  of speech to entertain, 383
Topic(s)
  believing in one's, 54
  clothing choice and, 259
  establishing importance of, 18, 194
  ethical speaking and choice of, 33-36
  focusing, 118
  generating ideas for, 107-16
    audience-generated topics, **111**-112
    occasion-generated topics, **112**-114
    research-generated topics, **114**-116
    self-generated topics, **108**-111
  group leader's introduction of new, 406
  importance to audience, persuasion and, 324-25
  purpose of speech, 118-21
    determining general, **119-20**
    formulating specific, **120**-21
  selecting, 117
  stating, 18, 193-94
  thesis statement, **121**-22
  title, developing, 122-24
  See also Informative speech (speech to inform); Research
Topical division, **177**-78
Tradition, fallacy of appeal to, 352-**53**
Transitions, **184**-86
  causal, **185**
  chronological, **185**-86
  complementary, **185**
  contrasting, **185**
Transparencies, **283**
Transparent language, 226
Transportation of visual aids, 287
Transposition, articulation error of, 256-57
Triangle of meaning, 5-7
Tribute, speech of, **376**-79
Trustworthiness, **330**
Truth, testing inductive argument for, 343

Undecided audience, 94
Understanding
  analyzing audience's, 100
  seeking knowledge for, 295-96
  stimuli, 66-67
Unfavorable audience, 94-96
Unintentional plagiarism, 41-42

Value(s), **91**-93
  instilling, 316-18
  intensification of, 316-18

propositions of, **358**
  in pyramid of persuasion, 318-21
  tapping audience, 332
Verbal cues, 13
Videotaped speech, **388**-90
Videotapes, **283**-84
  research using, 145
Visual aids, 271-89
  to enhance emotional appeals, 333
  importance of using, 272-73
  for oral report, 380
  to show relationships among statistics, 165-66
  in speeches about places, 300
  strategies for using, 285-88
    before speech, 285-87
    during speech, 287-88
  types of, 274-85
    audio aids, **284**-85
    computer-generated graphics, 281-82
    graphics, **275**-81
    handouts, **284**
    objects, **274**
    projections, **282**-84
Visual brainstorming, **115**-16, 118, 209-10
Visual examples, 161
Visual images, **235**
Visualization in motivated sequence, 362-63
Vividness
  of language, 20, 231-39
  supporting materials for, 155-56
Vocal cues, 14, 252-58
Vocal delivery, elements of, 252-58
  articulation, **256**-57
  inflection, **255**-56
  pause, **254**
  pitch, **255**-56
  pronunciation, **257**-58
  rate, **252**-53
  voice quality or timbre, **256**
  volume, **254**-55
Voice, active, 233
Voice quality, **256**
Volume, 22, **254**-55
Voluntary audience, **93**-96

Wall Street Journal Index, The, 136
Weaknesses and strengths, knowing one's, 51
Witnesses, selective perceptions of, 66
Wording. *See* Language
Working groups, 398
Working outline, **209**-13
Writing, differences between speaking and, 21, 176-77, 240

Yearbooks, 140